D1592184

Speculation and Financial Markets
Volume I

The International Library of Critical Writings in Economics

Series Editor: Mark Blaug

Professor Emeritus, University of London, UK
Professor Emeritus, University of Buckingham, UK
Visiting Professor, University of Amsterdam, The Netherlands
Visiting Professor, Erasmus University of Rotterdam, The Netherlands

This series is an essential reference source for students, researchers and lecturers in economics. It presents by theme a selection of the most important articles across the entire spectrum of economics. Each volume has been prepared by a leading specialist who has written an authoritative introduction to the literature included.

A full list of published and future titles in this series is printed at the end of this volume.

Wherever possible, the articles in these volumes have been reproduced as originally published using facsimile reproduction, inclusive of footnotes and pagination to facilitate ease of reference.

For a list of all Edward Elgar published titles visit our site on the World Wide Web at
http://www.e-elgar.co.uk

Speculation and Financial Markets Volume I

Edited by

Liam A. Gallagher

Lecturer in Economics
University College Cork, Ireland

and

Mark P. Taylor

Professor of Economics and Finance
University of Warwick, UK

THE INTERNATIONAL LIBRARY OF CRITICAL WRITINGS IN ECONOMICS

An Elgar Reference Collection
Cheltenham, UK • Northampton, MA, USA

Published by
Edward Elgar Publishing Limited
Glensanda House
Montpellier Parade
Cheltenham
Glos GL50 1UA
UK

Edward Elgar Publishing, Inc.
136 West Street
Suite 202
Northampton
Massachusetts 01060
USA

A catalogue record for this book is available from the British Library.

ISBN 1 84064 406 0 (2 volume set)

Printed and bound in Great Britain by MPG Books Ltd, Bodmin, Cornwall

Contents

Acknowledgements

The editors and publishers wish to thank the authors and the following publishers who have kindly given permission for the use of copyright material.

American Economic Association for articles: Robert J. Shiller (1981), 'Do Stock Prices Move Too Much to be Justified by Subsequent Changes in Dividends?', *American Economic Review*, **71** (3), June, 421–36; Behzad T. Diba and Herschel I. Grossman (1988), 'Explosive Rational Bubbles in Stock Prices?', *American Economic Review*, **78** (3), June, 520–30; Stephen F. LeRoy (1989), 'Efficient Capital Markets and Martingales', *Journal of Economic Literature*, **XXVII** (4), December, 1583–1621; Andrei Shleifer and Lawrence H. Summers (1990), 'The Noise Trader Approach to Finance', *Journal of Economic Perspectives*, **4** (2), Spring, 19–31; Kenneth A. Froot and Maurice Obstfeld (1991), 'Intrinsic Bubbles: The Case of Stock Prices', *American Economic Review*, **81** (5), December, 1189–214.

Blackwell Publishers Ltd for articles: Eugene F. Fama (1970), 'Efficient Capital Markets: A Review of Theory and Empirical Work', *Journal of Finance*, **25** (2), May, 383–417; Werner F.M. De Bondt and Richard Thaler (1985), 'Does the Stock Market Overreact?', *Journal of Finance*, **XL** (3), July, 793–805; Fischer Black (1986), 'Noise', *Journal of Finance*, **XLI** (3), July, 529–43; Kenneth D. West (1988), 'Bubbles, Fads and Stock Price Volatility Tests: A Partial Evaluation', *Journal of Finance*, **XLIII** (3), July, 639–56; M. Hashem Pesaran and Allan Timmermann (1995), 'Predictability of Stock Returns: Robustness and Economic Significance', *Journal of Finance*, **L** (4), September, 1201–28; Andrei Shleifer and Robert W. Vishny (1997), 'The Limits of Arbitrage', *Journal of Finance*, **LII** (1), March, 35–55.

Brookings Institution Press for article: Robert J. Shiller (1984), 'Stock Prices and Social Dynamics', *Brookings Papers on Economic Activity*, **2**, 457–98.

Econometric Society for articles: Alfred Cowles 3rd and Herbert E. Jones (1937), 'Some A Posteriori Probabilities in Stock Market Action', *Econometrica*, **5** (3), July, 280–94; Stephen F. LeRoy and Richard D. Porter (1981), 'The Present-value Relation: Tests Based on Implied Variance Bounds', *Econometrica*, **49** (3), May, 555–74.

Elsevier Science for articles: James M. Poterba and Lawrence H. Summers (1988), 'Mean Reversion in Stock Prices: Evidence and Implications', *Journal of Financial Economics*, **22** (1), October, 27–59; Eugene F. Fama (1998), 'Market Efficiency, Long-term Returns, and Behavioral Finance', *Journal of Financial Economics*, **49** (3), September, 283–306.

MIT Press Journals for article: Kenneth D. West (1987), 'A Specification Test for Speculative Bubbles', *Quarterly Journal of Economics*, **CII** (3), August, 553–80.

University of Chicago Press for articles: Eugene F. Fama (1965), 'The Behavior of Stockmarket Prices', *Journal of Business*, **38** (1), January, 34–105; Eugene F. Fama and Kenneth R. French (1988), 'Permanent and Temporary Components of Stock Prices', *Journal of Political Economy*, **96** (2), April, 246–73; J. Bradford De Long, Andrei Shleifer, Lawrence H. Summers and Robert J. Waldmann (1990), 'Noise Trader Risk in Financial Markets', *Journal of Political Economy*, **98** (4), August, 703–38.

Every effort has been made to trace all the copyright holders but if any have been inadvertently overlooked the publishers will be pleased to make the necessary arrangement at the first opportunity.

In addition the publishers wish to thank the Library of the London School of Economics and Political Science, the Marshall Library of Economics, Cambridge University, B & N Microfilm, London and the Library of Indiana University at Bloomington, USA for their assistance in obtaining these articles.

Introduction

Liam A. Gallagher and Mark P. Taylor

Overview

In these two volumes of critical writings we have gathered together some of the most important contributions in the area of speculation and financial markets.

The first of the two volumes covers the theoretical and empirical evidence surrounding financial market efficiency. It guides the reader through the change that has occurred in the understanding of financial price behavior.

The price behavior of financial assets has traditionally been characterized in the academic literature by the Efficient Market Hypothesis (EMH). The interpretation of the EMH has changed considerably over the past three decades. At its core, however, is the view that asset prices are determined by the equilibrium of rational traders supplying and demanding funds in a competitive market, with no riskless arbitrage positions available. Assuming that traders have the same information set and assimilate information rapidly in adjusting their trading position, prices will always be in equilibrium and only new information should cause changes in asset prices. Thus, asset returns are unforecastable and follow a random walk.

The early interpretation of the EMH, in particular that financial asset price movements are best represented as a random walk – the random walk hypothesis (RWH) – was widely accepted in the 1970s as it proved very difficult empirically to beat the random walk model (Eugene Fama, 1970). Although researchers found it difficult to reject the RWH, a large volume of related evidence (in particular, persistent anomalies, excess volatility and predictability in financial markets) questioned the appropriateness of the RWH definition of market efficiency. These findings resulted in a re-evaluation of the RWH as a best description of the EMH. Stock (and other asset) prices contain a slowly mean-reverting component. That is, stock prices move way from their fundamental value in a highly persistent way that reflects a random walk process and slowly revert towards their fundamental value in time.

Rejection of the RWH has resulted in an alternative approach to modeling stock price behavior. A common element of this new approach is the rejection of the homogeneous traders assumption in favor of the assumption of two types of traders – smart money (rational traders) and noise (irrational traders). Noise introduces risk into the arbitrage condition, thus arbitrageurs do not always bring stock prices back to their fundamental value. The seminal work in modelling stock price behavior in this context is attributed to Bradford De Long, Andrei Shleifer, Lawrence Summers and Robert Waldmann (1990).

The increasing role that institutional investors play in financial markets introduces an additional form of complexity into modelling asset price behavior. Traders that are in the market as intermediaries act on behalf of non-participating investors and thus introduce a principal-agent problem (Shleifer and Summers, 1990). More recently, the arbitrage model of DeLong,

Shleifer, Summers and Waldmann (1990) has been modified by Shleifer and Robert Vishny (1997) in which arbitrage activity is viewed in an agency context.

In contrast to the noise trader approaches, an alternative explanation of the rejection of the RWH is that, even if traders are perfectly rational, asset prices contain a bubble element that causes prices to deviate from their fundamental value. Since market efficiency involves a joint hypothesis, empirical evidence in favor of either the bubble or noise trader approaches is inconclusive.

In the second volume of critical writings, we have gathered together some of the most important contributions concerning puzzles in finance and consider three financial markets – the bond market, the foreign exchange market and the derivatives market.

The single financial puzzle that has attracted the greatest attention by financial economists is the equity premium puzzle. Over the last century the average annual return on US equity is around 10 per cent whereas US government bonds yield an average annual return of less than 4 per cent. This difference is persistent over time and cannot be explained by the different level of risk associated with the two types of assets. One theoretical approach that has proven successful in resolving the puzzle is to describe consumer behavior as 'habit formation' (see, George Constantinides, 1990; and John Campbell and John Cochrane, 1999).

Other finance puzzles that have been explored in the literature are the stock return-inflation puzzle, the new issue puzzle and the home bias puzzle. Attention is also drawn to the latter puzzle in the context of emerging equity markets.

The second volume also explores the theory and evidence relating to the pricing of bonds, exchange rates and derivative financial instruments.

1. Efficient Markets

The driving force behind much of the financial markets' literature has centered on the ability to predict price behavior. To economists this comes as no surprise as the rewards from such ability would seem vast, if not infinite. The predictability of stock returns is probably the most well-researched topic in the empirical literature on financial economics, dating back at least to Alfred Cowles and Herbert Jones in 1937. In their study, Cowles and Jones provided a basic test of the random walk hypothesis (RWH) in answering the question 'if the stock market rises for 1 hour, day, week, month, or year, is there a probability of one-half that it will decline in the succeeding comparable unit of time?' In a comparison of historical stock return sequences (sequential returns are of the same sign) and reversals (sequential returns are of the differing signs), Cowles and Jones could not reject the hypothesis that stock prices move in a random fashion.[1]

The subsequent abundance of evidence in favor of purely random security prices (as indicated by the RWH), at the time, implied no role for fundamentals – the present discounted value of future cash flow – and, thus, security prices were seen as unpredictable. The random walk argument is not a new one, as it can be traced back to 1900. In an empirical study of French government bonds, a French mathematician, Louis Bachelier, found that bond prices were consistent with the random walk model. Fama (1965) presents an extensive exposition of the random walk model in the modeling of stock price behavior.

The absence of an economic equilibrium framework in the random walk model did not sit easy with economists. It is only in the last three decades that a common link between the random walk model and an economic model of asset prices has formally been outlined. This relationship is based on the argument that rates of return are a 'fair game' (security prices are a martingale) – that is, in a competitive market that is peopled by rational traders (informationally efficient market), price changes are random and unforecastable if they are properly anticipated. Stephen LeRoy (1989) presents a comprehensive account of martingales and market efficiency. The efficient capital markets (as indicated by the fair game model) is completely consistent with the fundamentalist model (as indicated by the standard present value model of security prices – security prices equal the expected present value of future dividends).

In replacing the random walk model with the less restricted fair game (or martingale) model, a formal definition of the efficient market hypothesis (EMH) can be derived. It was Fama's influential paper in 1970 that coined 'capital market efficient' in terms of the market being efficient if security prices 'fully reflect' all available information. Fama identifies three testable hypotheses of capital market efficiency based on the specification of the information set; that is, defining somewhat more exactly what is meant by the term 'fully reflect'.

Capital markets are said to be *weak form efficient* if the information set is just historical prices. Capital markets are *semi-strong form efficient* if the information set is expanded to include all publicly available (for example, announcements of annual earnings, stock splits and so on) information. Finally, capital markets are considered to be *strong form efficient* if the information set is further broadened to include insider information. A test of capital market efficiency, under these alternative definitions, is that no trading rule based on the information set can systematically be profitable.

Fama's survey reports consistent evidence of positive dependence (serial correlations) in day-to-day price changes and returns on common stocks. However, the dependence is of a form that inclusive of transaction costs is not large enough to profitably exploit in a trading rule. Thus, this positive dependence does not seem of sufficient importance to warrant rejection of the fair game efficient markets model.

Similarly, semi-strong form tests, in which prices are assumed to fully reflect all obviously publicly available information, have also supported the efficient market hypothesis. At the time, testing of strong form efficiency was limited to investigating corporate insiders and specialists. Fama reports that there is no evidence that deviations from the strong form of the efficient markets model permeate down any further through the investment community. Thus, Fama concludes that for the purpose of most investors the efficient markets model seems a good first (and second) approximation to reality. The evidence at the time in support of the efficient markets model was extensive and (somewhat uniquely in economics) contradictory evidence was sparse.

2. Market Inefficiency and Stock Price Predictability

The fair game (or martinagle) model of asset prices, where agents have rational expectations and a symmetric information set, asserts that real stock prices equal the present value of rationally expected (or optimally forecasted) future real dividends discounted by a constant real discount rate.[2] An implication of this representation implies a specific relationship between the volatility of asset prices and that of dividends (in the form of a variance inequality). Working independently, Robert Shiller (1981) and LeRoy and Richard Porter (1981) presented similar results of tests of these volatility relations (variance-bounds inequality and orthogonality tests) and their implications for market efficiency.

Stock prices appear to be more volatile than is consistent with the efficient capital markets model. Shiller finds that stock prices appear to be five to thirteen times too volatile than projected by the present value model. However, as a caveat, these tests are actually tests of a joint hypothesis: the present value model, the assumption of constant expected returns and rational expectations.

The strong findings of LeRoy–Porter and Shiller reopened the efficient market debate. What followed was a multitude of second-generation variance bounds tests that, in particular, addressed econometric problems identified with LeRoy–Porter and Shiller tests. However, the same qualitative finding of excess volatility remained – rejecting the EMH.

Two related testing methodologies to the variance-bounds inequality tests are the test of autoregression on multi-period returns (the regression-based test) and the variance-ratio test. The regression-based approach considers the pattern of the return's autocorrelation function over increasing investment horizons. The influential work of Eugene Fama and Kenneth French (1988) report a U-shaped pattern of the autocorrelation function – one that is consistent with mean reversion in stock prices.

The variance-ratio test compares the relative variability of returns over different horizons. This is a test of whether the ratio of return variance for a q-period investment horizon ($q > 0$) to the one-period return variance is equal to q, as would be the case if prices followed a random walk. Similar to Fama and French (1988) findings, James Poterba and Summers (1988) also reject the random walk in favor of the presence of a mean-reverting component for intermediate (3 to 5 years) investment horizons.

Fama and French (1988) report that between 25 and 45 per cent of the movement in stock prices (for a 3 to 5 year investment horizon) can be explained by price movements of the previous (3 to 5 year investment horizon) period. Thus, about 40 per cent of the variation of 3 to 5 year US stock returns appears to be predictable from past returns. Poterba and Summers (1988) also find that stock returns contain large predictable components of similar magnitude.[3]

In subsequent years there has been an extensive literature on the predictability of stock returns. In one of the more recent studies, Hashem Pesaran and Allan Timmermann (1995) find that returns are predictable and about 60 per cent of the variability in annual US excess returns can be explained by a relatively small number of independent variables.

3. Noise Traders, Investor Sentiment and Behavioral Finance

The rejection of the present value model of stock prices on US data (LeRoy and Porter, 1981; Shiller, 1981; and others) increased the interest into exploring the reasons as to why short-horizon returns are unforecastable (short-horizon asset prices behave like a random walk process) and there exists a wide discrepancy between asset prices and their fundamental values (as measured by the present value model). To reconcile these two features Shiller (1984) considered the role of 'ordinary' investor (also known in Fischer Black (1986) as 'noise trader') behavior. Shiller provides evidence that these investors, to a large extent, trade on sentiment that is not associated with market fundamentals but with fads or fashion.

Employing a simple model with asset prices represented as the sum of a random walk and a mean-reverting (a simple autoregressive) process, Shiller is able to predict near-zero autocorrelations for short-horizon returns (consistent with the RWH/EMH) and negative autocorrelation for longer-horizon (several years) returns (consistent with the mean-reverting and excess volatility findings). Thus, asset prices contain a slowly mean-reverting component. That is, asset prices move away from their fundamental value for periods of time in a persistent manner and in time slowly revert to their fundamental value. The fact that asset prices deviate from fundamentals in a highly persistent way reflects a random walk process.

Since fads are inherently unpredictable and since noise traders overreact to fundamental news (see, for example, Werner De Bondt and Richard Thaler, 1985), the aggregate demand of noise traders may itself not be entirely unlike a random walk. As a result, their demand is relatively unpredictable. Thus, the limited number of risk-averse smart money (arbitrageurs) will only be willing to take limited positions when they perceive valuation errors, and therefore, errors will not be eliminated unless they are widely noticed. In doing so, smart money may not be preventing noise traders from causing major swings in the market and, moreover, may be part of the source of volatility in the market. Therefore, although stock prices may reflect their fundamentals in the long run, they may deviate substantially from their fundamentals for long periods of time. This feature of asset price behavior is captured by De Long, Shleifer, Summers and Waldmann, in their 1990 paper on noise trader risk and later by Shleifer and Summers (1990) among others.

While excess volatility and the rejection of the variance-bounds tests may be taken as evidence against the EMH, an alternative view would be that the instantaneous arbitrage assumed in the simple present value model is too restrictive. In recent arbitrage models developed by, *inter alios*, De Long, Shleifer, Summers and Waldmann (1990), arbitrage is generally less than perfect because arbitrageurs face either fundamental or noise trader risk.

In particular, given that the actions of noise traders may lead to greater fundamental mispricing of an asset, perceived deviations of asset prices from their fundamental values represent risky arbitrage opportunities (Shleifer and Summers, 1990). Thus, small deviations from fundamentals may not be arbitraged because the perceived gains may not be enough to outweigh this risk. Given a distribution of degrees of risk aversion across smart traders, arbitrage will increase as the degree of fundamental mispricing increases, so that arbitrage is stabilizing and becomes more stabilizing in extreme circumstances.

This approach may be contrasted with the more recent 'limits of arbitrage' hypothesis, suggested by Shleifer and Vishny (1997), in which arbitrage activity is viewed in an agency context. In the Shleifer–Vishny model, arbitrageurs (the agents) have access to funds mainly from outside investors (the principals), who will generally gauge the ability of arbitrageurs – and hence decide on the amount of funds to allocate to them – based on their past performance. Since the track record of smart arbitrageurs is likely to be poorest when prices have deviated far from their fundamental values, the implication of the limits of arbitrage hypothesis is that arbitrage is likely to be least effective in returning prices to fundamental values when investor sentiment has driven them far away. That is, '[w]hen arbitrage requires capital, arbitrageurs can become most constrained when they have the best opportunities, i.e., when the mispricing they have bet against gets even worse' (Shleifer and Vishny, 1997: 37). In contrast, the risky arbitrage models are without agency problems and arbitrageurs are more aggressive when prices move further from fundamental values. However, both approaches predict similar patterns of asset price movement and similar to that predicted by Shiller (1984).

Shleifer and Summers (1990) provide an accessible summary of the fundamental and noise trader risks facing arbitrageurs and the role of investor sentiment in driving stock prices away from fundamentals.

Shiller's (1984) influential paper introduced a new approach in the exploration of asset price behavior. The notion that investor sentiment is a key element in understanding asset price movement led to a number of papers addressing micro-structure issues in markets. In particular, there has been a large growth of papers in behavioral finance – a subset of financial economics that looked at 'irrational behavior' (later reinterpreted by Black as 'noise behavior') as an alternative to the EMH. One significant challenge to the EMH has come from the literature on long-term return anomalies. One of the first papers to explore this *long-term* return anomaly was DeBondt and Thaler in 1985. Since then, an enormous volume of literature has been written about financial market anomalies. DeBondt and Thaler (1985) found that winners and losers over a 3-year horizon tend to reverse their performance in the subsequent 3-year period. An implication of this finding is in forming their expectations; investors tend to give too much weight to past performance and too little to the fact that performance tends to be mean-reverting. More recent evidence, summarized by Fama (1998), suggests that such anomalies are chance results and also tend to disappear with improvements in technique.

4. Bubbles

In contrast to the behavioral finance and noise trader approaches, an alternative explanation of the deviation of actual asset prices from their fundamental values – as indicated by the rejection of the EMH – is that asset prices equal not only their fundamental value (discounted present value) but also a 'bubble term'.[4] Even if traders are perfectly rational, asset prices can deviate from their fundamental value if actual asset prices contain a bubble element.

The idea that prices contain self-fulfilling bubbles (or 'sunspots') is not a new one and is documented back to the infamous Dutch Tulipmania bubble of 1634–37. A popular specification of a rational bubble is one that allows for the bubble to burst in any period with a constant probability. If it does not burst it grows at a positive constant rate and the bubble becomes an increasing proportion of the actual price. Investors are willing to pay a price over the fundamental value (that is, pay for the bubble) as long as the bubble element yields them the required rate of return next period and is expected to persist. Bubbles can only exist where there is no upper limit on the asset price. The lower limit (zero price) of asset prices implies that bubbles can never be negative (otherwise prices inclusive of a bubble will end at a zero price). Therefore, bubbles can only have a zero expectation if it is zero in the future with probability one. If a bubble is ever zero it cannot restart.

Two general classifications of rational bubbles: (i) those that are exogenous to fundamentals such as dividends (see, Kenneth West, 1987; Behzad Diba and Herschel Grossman, 1988); and (ii) those that are intrinsic (endogenous) on fundamentals (see, Kenneth Froot and Maurice Obstfeld, 1991). A comprehensive account of the theory and evidence of bubbles is provided by West (1988).

West (1987) tests for the presence of a rational bubble using Shiller's (1981) US stock price data. He rejects the null of no bubbles. The results are robust to alternative dividend-generating processes, but however are not robust to time-varying discount rates. Employing unit root and cointegration tests, Diba and Grossman (1988) reject the presence of bubbles. This, along with other tests, has come under criticism by a number of more recent studies. In particular, the estimates of the discount rate used in testing for bubbles, as well as unit root and cointegration tests, are not robust when bubbles periodically collapse.

Froot and Obstfeld (1991) test for the presence of intrinsic bubbles where asset prices contain a rational bubble that depends (in a non-linear deterministic way) exclusively on aggregate dividends. The intrinsic bubble specification is consistent with the overreaction of asset price movement to dividend news (see DeBondt and Thaler, 1985). A positive (negative) dividend news will increase (decrease) asset prices since the fundamental value has increased (decreased), but the asset price will additionally increase (decrease) because of the increase (decrease) in the intrinsic bubble element – an overreaction to the dividend news. If aggregate dividends remain constant, so too does the intrinsic bubble. Froot and Obstfeld (1991) find that US stock prices overreact to dividends and that unit root and cointegration tests tend to reject the fundamentals model in favor of the presence of an intrinsic bubble. As in the case of the exogenous rational bubbles (for example, Diba and Grossman, 1988), there are a number of econometric issues that have been identified recently. In particular, the power and size of test for stationarity in the presence of a bubble are problematic and thus weaken the interpretation of these results.

Because the market efficiency hypothesis involves a complex joint hypothesis, evidence of a bubble could also be consistent with other hypotheses, for example the presence of slowly mean-reverting fads (Shiller, 1988) or a time-varying required rate of return. Thus, evidence for or against rational bubbles is inconclusive.

5. Puzzles in Finance

Of the many puzzles that exist in the finance literature, the one that has attracted most interest in recent times is the equity premium puzzle coined by Rajnish Mehra and Edward Prescott (1985). The puzzle refers to the puzzlingly high historical average returns of stocks relative to bonds. Over the last century the average annual return on equity is around 10 per cent whereas bonds yield a return of less than 4 per cent. This equity premium is thought to be attributable to the higher risk associated with equities; however, it is too large to be explained by standard economic models. It is thus not clear why such a (risk-adjusted) premium exists and, moreover, why in light of the evidence it continues to persist.

Mehra and Prescott (1985) present the equity premium puzzle in the context of a present-value investor intertemporal optimizing model. In this setting they are able to determine the amount of risk aversion that would justify the equity premium. Their findings suggest that the coefficient of relative risk aversion is somewhere between 30 and 40. Given that most empirical estimates of risk aversion are in the neighborhood of 1.0–2.0, estimates into the 30s are much too high to be reasonable. An implication of high risk aversion is that individuals will want to smooth consumption over time by borrowing now (against future wealth), thus pushing up real interest rates. With average real interest rates less than 1 per cent over the last century, the equity premium puzzle may not be thought of as why equity returns are so high but rather why were interest rates so low.

A number of authors have considered empirical explanations of the equity premium puzzle by seeking alternative data sets, for example adjusting for new issues, survivorship bias, small-cap markets, period of study and so on. Interestingly, introducing the feature that stock returns exhibit mean reversion implies that for long-horizon investors, the risk of holding equity is reduced and therefore the equity premium is larger.[5]

Theoretical approaches have proven more successful in resolving the puzzle. One class of models modify the utility function;[6] for example Constantinides (1990) describes consumer behavior as 'habit formation'. He finds that this has the effect of making an investor more sensitive to short-term reductions in consumption and, thus, increases the short-run risk aversion, but lowers long-run risk aversion. A similar result is found by Campbell and Cochrane (1999). In their paper, they model individual behavior as an *external* habit formation of the form of 'catching up with the Joneses'. In their model, individuals fear stocks primarily because they do badly in recessions unrelated to the risks of long-run average consumption growth. These theoretical models provide the beginning of thoughts as to why there is, and will be, a large equity premium. Whether this is the answer to the puzzle is not yet clear.

The stock return-inflation puzzle is based on the traditional view that common stocks are a good hedge against inflation. The puzzle is that this relationship is not empirically supported for postwar data for the USA and for other countries. A significant negative correlation between inflation and real stock returns and between inflation and nominal stock returns is always found. Thus, real stock returns are not independent of inflation. This contradicts the classic Fisher model, in which nominal asset returns move one-for-one with the rate of inflation so that real returns are determined by real factors independent of the inflation rate.

In a pioneering paper, Fama (1981) sought to explain the stock return-inflation puzzle by hypothesizing that the negative correlation is induced by negative correlations between inflation and real activity together with a positive relationship between stock returns and real activity. While the latter of these correlations is intuitive, Fama (1981) argues that inflation may negatively covary with real activity, effectively to clear the money market. In effect, Fama is assuming a quantity theory of money framework. While many economists might wish to debate the applicability of such a framework in the short run, its long-run applicability would probably achieve greater consensus. Fama's proxy hypothesis suggests that the apparent anomalous relationship between stock returns and inflation is simply proxying the positive relationship one would expect between stock prices and fundamentals.

Along the lines of Fama (1981), David Marshall (1992) models the relationship between stock returns, inflation, real activity and monetary growth in a general equilibrium framework and finds supporting evidence for the Fama's proxy hypothesis as an explanation of the stock return-inflation puzzle. Common stocks do not offer a hedge against that portion of inflation caused by fluctuations in real economic activity but are a good hedge over the long run against purely monetary inflation. It is the interdependence of economic variables that provides the explanation of the negative stock return-inflation relationship (Marshall, 1992).

Two other puzzles that have attracted substantial attention are the new issue puzzle and the home bias puzzle. The performance of new issues or initial public offerings (IPOs) significantly underperform relative to nonissuing firms for five years after the offering date. Tim Loughran and Jay Ritter (1995) find that the average annual return during the five years after issue is only 5 per cent for firms conducting IPOs compared to the 12 per cent for their (nonissuing) matching firms. This underperformance effect of 7 per cent per year is significant. The underperformance cannot be explained by risk or other fundamental factors, for example, book-to-market effects, nor is it proxying for long-term return reversals.[7] Loughran and Ritter (1995) suggest one potential explanation in that firms take advantage of transitory windows of opportunity by issuing equity when, on average, they are substantially overvalued. As with the other puzzles in finances there are many alternative competing explanations.

The explanations of the equity premium puzzle put forward by Constantinides (1990) and Campbell and Cochrane (1999) suggest that investors are creatures of habit. The home-bias puzzle provides anecdotal evidence of this behavior. In spite of the fact that the benefits from international diversification have been recognized for decades, most investors hold nearly all of their wealth in domestic assets. French and Poterba (1991) report that around 90 per cent of the world's five largest stock markets are in domestic ownership. Employing a simple model of expected utility shows that current portfolio patterns imply that investors expect returns in their domestic equity market to be up to 500 basis points (that is, 5 percentage points) higher than returns in foreign markets. French and Poterba (1991) explain this home-bias puzzle in terms of investor choices, rather than institutional constraints. Investors' perception of risk in equity markets may not be based solely on the historical variance of returns and, thus, investors may *ex ante* measure risk with an additional component for foreign investments because they know less about foreign markets, institutions and firms.

Until recently the home-bias puzzle and more generally stock price behavior concentrated on the investigation of developed markets. The emergence of, and recent growth in, new equity markets in Europe, Latin America, Asia, the Mideast and Africa prompted Geert Bekaert and Campbell Harvey (1997) to investigate the opportunities for investors in these markets. They found that these markets exhibit high expected returns as well as high volatility. Returns in emerging markets relative to developed markets are found to be more likely to be influenced by local information rather than global information. Incorporating emerging market equities in world portfolios significantly reduces unconditional risk.

The fact that emerging markets' expected returns are influenced by local information is consistent with the possibility that some of the emerging markets countries are segmented from world capital markets. Low correlations between emerging markets and developed countries' equity markets are found. One would expect that as markets become more liberal through the relaxation of regulatory constraints and information becomes more accessible, the degree of integration may increase through time. Thus, global information will play an increasing influence in price movement in emerging markets. Bekaert and Harvey (1997) find that capital market liberalizations increases the correlation between local market returns and the world market but does not drive up local market volatility.

6. Bond Markets and the Term Structure of Interest Rates

The study of interest rate behavior has a long and important tradition for economists. On the macroeconomic side short-term interest rates are the link with monetary policy. As in the case of equity markets, bond (and other fixed income assets) markets are of interest to financial institutions and investors. Furthermore, in that they can be used to test for various behavioral hypotheses about market efficiency and agent behavior.

As in the case of stocks, under the EMH, bond prices are given as the discounted present value of future cash flows. Furthermore, market efficiency issues, discussed in the previous sections, are also applicable to the bond market. The crucial difference between the two is the fact that bonds are contracts which (ignoring default risk) specify a 'known fixed' future cash flow in the form of coupon payments. There are a number of theories of the determination of one-period bond yields of different maturities, also known as the term structure of interest.[8]

In its simplest (or 'pure') form, the expectations hypothesis states that forward rates implied by the term structure are an unbiased predictor of expected future spot rates.[9] In a more general form the expectations hypothesis allows the forward rates to contain a constant premium. Other classifications of the expectations hypothesis (for example, liquidity preference and preferred habitat) suggest that the premium is not constant but a function of, for example, the term to maturity (as in the case of the liquidity preference hypothesis). In their seminal works, John Cox, Jonathan Ingersoll and Stephen Ross (1981, 1985) examine the traditional expectations theories of the term structure of interest rates in a general equilibrium setting and also develop testable hypotheses. As a result a large empirical literature has emerged. Almost all studies statistically reject the 'pure' expectations theory of the term structure.

Fama (1984) finds that (expected) premiums are time varying and are captured in forward rates. Thus, forward rates contain variation in expected returns on multi-period US Treasury bills. Furthermore, forward rates for bills that are adjusted for variation in premiums can reliably predict interest rate changes over a few (up to five) months, but the predictive power decreases rapidly with the horizon.

Studies that have considered the forecastability of rates at a long horizon have suggested that the expectations hypothesis does not hold at the short end of the maturity spectrum but there is evidence that it holds at the long end. Fama and Robert Bliss (1987) suggest that the predictive power of the term structure for changes in short rates improves the longer the forecast horizon. Campbell and Shiller (1991) using zero-coupon bond yields on postwar US government securities also support this argument.

7. Foreign Exchange Market Efficiency

The foreign exchange market is among the most active of all speculative financial markets and its importance is highlighted by the volume of trading activity relative to trade in goods and services. In comparison to the pricing of other assets (for example, stocks and bonds), the pricing of exchange rates is of particular importance since the exchange rate simultaneously affects the prices of all foreign assets, goods, services and factors of production. The issue of whether exchange rates reflect their fundamental value is an issue of market efficiency similar to any traded asset. Froot and Thaler (1990) provide an accessible account of foreign exchange market efficiency and Mark Taylor (1995) presents a comprehensive account of the economics of exchange rates.

If the risk-neutral EMH holds, then the expected foreign exchange gain from holding one currency rather than another (the expected exchange rate change) must be just offset by the opportunity cost of holding funds in this currency rather than the other (the interest rate differential). This is the cornerstone parity condition for testing foreign exchange market efficiency. The uncovered interest parity condition implies that the interest differential is, assuming rational expectations, an unbiased estimate of the future spot exchange rate change.

Early tests involved simple tests for a random walk in the spot rate and later tests involved basic linear regression analyses of uncovered interest parity. These tests tended to reject the simple market efficient hypothesis (Froot and Thaler, 1990). The use of more sophisticated techniques and estimators has generated increasingly strong evidence against the simple market efficiency hypothesis for exchange rates.

Strong rejection of the EMH may be due to the risk aversion of market participants – the uncovered interest parity condition might be distorted by a (variable) risk premium – or due to a departure from the pure rational expectations hypothesis, or both. To avoid this joint hypothesis problem, Froot and Jeffrey Frankel (1989) have employed survey data on exchange rate expectations to conduct tests of each component of the joint hypothesis. The evidence suggests that both risk aversion and departures from rational expectations are responsible for rejection of the simple EMH. The forward premium is found to be a biased predictor of subsequent changes in the spot rate, and this bias is due to systematic expectational errors and very little is due to the variations in the risk premium. The failure of the EMH could be interpreted that the market is populated by 'irrational' (or noise) traders that make systematic forecast errors. It could also be due to the fact that agents take time to learn or, alternatively, there may be a 'Peso problem'.

Irrational behavior by foreign exchange traders has been investigated by Frankel and Froot (1990), Taylor and Helen Allen (1992) and others. These studies suggest that foreign exchange traders do not base their (short-horizon) predictions on economic theory – the fundamentals – but on the identification of supposedly recurring patterns in graphs of exchange rate movements – that is, 'technical' or 'chart' analysts. Taylor and Allen (1992) reveal that extremely high proportions of traders employ technical or chartist analysis, especially when forecasting over shorter horizons. Some chartists were able to outperform a range of alternative forecasting procedures.

Frankel and Froot (1990) show that the volume of trade and market volatility is related to the heterogeneity of exchange rate expectations, as reflected in dispersion in survey expectations. Evidence of a dispersion of expectations across market participants runs counter to traditional exchange rate analyses which assume rational expectations and hence homogeneous expectations across market participants. In contrast, most microstructure analyses of exchange rates place heterogeneity at center stage. However, the literature on microstructure analyses is still in its infancy and is potentially to prove promising in explaining short-term movements in exchange rates.

8. Derivatives and Efficiency

One of the great successes of modern financial economics is the pricing of derivative securities, especially the pricing of options (see Merton Miller (1986) for a discussion of the growth in financial derivatives). Derivative securities are assets whose values depend on other securities. For example, a call option on an asset gives the owner the right to purchase a unit of that asset at a set (exercise) price. The value of the option depends on the price of the underlying asset, the exercise price, the time remaining to expiration of the option, the expected price volatility of the underlying asset, the short-term risk-free rate, and any anticipated cash payments on the underlying asset over the life of the option.

Theoretical pricing of derivatives is based on the assumption of market efficiency and the no-arbitrage condition. The most famous financial pricing model is the option pricing models of Black and Myron Scholes (1973) and Robert Merton (1973). Black–Scholes and Merton show that, if asset price volatility is known, for a given riskless debt, options prices on this underlying asset are completely determined and any deviation is random and unpredictable. This pricing formula has been used to price hundreds of different types of derivative securities and the creation of ever more complex financial instruments. The resulting vast volume of related academic research has been an important stimulus in establishing financial engineering as an area of research in financial economics.

An alternative to the Black–Scholes and Merton derivation of the option pricing formula in continuous time is provided by Cox, Ross and Mark Rubinstein (1979) who present a more simple derivation of option pricing in a binomial setting.

Similar to options and other derivatives, the main role of futures contracts is to spread and hence reduce risk. In his classic paper, Holbrook Working (1953) presents the theory that two individuals with different probability assessments regarding the future value of an asset can both increase their utility *ex ante* by entering into a futures contract. Futures are standardized forward contracts – in which two agents agree on the details of a transaction for delivery at a specific future date – that are continuously traded in a market operated by a clearing house. Futures markets provide greater transparency and liquidity than forward markets. Cox, Ingersoll and Ross (1981) provide a comprehensive account of the differences between forward prices and futures prices.

Futures prices based on the assumption of market efficiency and the no-arbitrage condition are such that the rate of return on the futures contracts equal the rate of return in the cash market of the underlying asset less the net cost of carry (that is, the difference between the risk-free rate and the dividend yield on the underlying asset in the cash market). Working (1953) shows that, in an efficient market, futures prices are the best predictor of spot prices at the expiration of the futures contract. If futures prices move out of line with expectations about fundamentals, arbitrage activity will restore equilibrium conditions in both the futures and the cash markets. However, Pradeep Yadav and Peter Pope (1990) argue that arbitrage opportunities do exist for stock index futures. This is evident from the substantial and sustained discrepancies (in excess of any transaction costs) between cash and futures indexes in the UK. Similar evidence is also reported by other researchers for US stock index futures. Notably, the extent and frequency of systematic mispricing violations have considerably decreased and the tendency for mispricing reversals has substantially increased after market deregulation.

Notes

1. The random walk hypothesis is reflected by the current price of a security 'fully reflects' available information, such that successive price changes (or more usually, successive one-period returns) are independent and identically distributed (iid). For a discussion of this see Fama (1965).

2. We ignore here the definitions of capital market efficiency that rely on asymmetric information.
3. Since the publication of Fama and French (1988) and Poterba and Summers (1988), recent studies on mean reversion in stock prices have questioned the underlying econometric methods employed. The significance of the mean-reverting component is not certain because of the small non-overlapping sample size, the distribution property of the tests and the sensitivity to the prewar period. However, more recent multivariate studies are not subject to similar criticism and report a significant mean-reverting component of the order of 50 to 60 per cent.
4. Economists consider the bubble explanation of speculative events only after one has exhausted all reasonable economic explanations.
5. Evidence that returns on fixed income assets exhibit mean aversion implies that for long-horizon investors the risk of holding fixed income assets is increased. This further suggests that for long-horizon investors the equity premium is an even bigger puzzle.
6. For the most part this involves a relaxation of Mehra and Prescott's (1985) assumption that utility is time separable.
7. There is substantial evidence that firms set the offer price at a discount (due to, for example, winners' curse problems) resulting in short-term underpricing and, therefore, short-term overperformance. Coupled with the long-term underperformance, this suggests that the price behavior of new issues (and also for seasoned equity offering) play a role in the mean reversion behavior of aggregate stock prices.
8. We assume that zero-coupon bond prices are observed or can be estimated from coupon bonds.
9. In empirical work, realized rates are used instead of expected rates.

Part I
Efficient Markets

[1]

SOME A POSTERIORI PROBABILITIES IN STOCK MARKET ACTION

By ALFRED COWLES 3RD AND HERBERT E. JONES

IN 1933, one of the authors[1] published an analysis of the results secured by 45 representative financial agencies in forecasting the prices of common stocks. This study, embracing the period of $4\frac{1}{2}$ years from January, 1928 to June, 1932, and including several thousand individual forecasts, showed that these were unsuccessful more often than successful and that, indeed, better results in the aggregate would probably have been secured by investors through following purely random investment programs. This result naturally suggested the question: Is stock price action random in nature or, if not, to what extent is it possible statistically to define the nature of its structure? Herewith is presented at least a partial answer to this question on the basis of evidence adduced from internal elements in the stock price series themselves.

Among the different viewpoints from which this problem may be approached are those which consider (1) the element of inertia, and (2) harmonic analysis for the purpose of disclosing evidence as to regular periodicity.

With respect to the latter, Professor Harold T. Davis[2] has presented evidence of periodicity in stock prices by means of Schuster's periodogram analysis, and has attempted tests of the significance of these periods by R. A. Fisher's technique. By this method, however, only *average* periods can be found and even then their significance can not be accurately determined because of uncertainty as to the independence of observations. Variable periodicity can be taken into account by a number of techniques, such as Frisch's changing harmonics,[3] or by using varying moving averages,[4] but there seems to be no way to determine the probabilities of significance in connection with any of these methods. For this reason in the following analysis a method more susceptible of interpretation in terms of probability has been used.

Carl Snyder,[5] in referring to measurements of the industrial growth

[1] Alfred Cowles 3rd, "Can Stock Market Forecasters Forecast?", ECONOMETRICA, Vol. 1, 1933, pp. 309–324.

[2] In a paper presented before the Econometric Society in St. Louis, January, 1936. See abstract in ECONOMETRICA, Vol. 4, 1936, pp. 189–190.

[3] Ragnar Frisch, "Changing Harmonics and Other General Types of Components in Empirical Series," *Skandinavisk Aktuarietidskrift*, 1928, pp. 220–236.

[4] Gerhard Tintner, *Prices In the Trade Cycle*, Vienna, 1935, p. 23.

[5] "Concepts of Momentum and Inertia," presented at the Atlantic City meeting of the Econometric Society, December, 1932, and published in *Stabilization of Employment*, Charles F. Roos, editor, 1933, p. 77.

of the United States since 1830, says, "The picture that these measures give is that of an amazingly even rate of growth not merely from generation to generation but actually of *each separate decennium* throughout the last century. As if there was at work a kind of momentum or inertia that sweeps on in spite of all obstacles."

The term "inertia," as employed by Mr. Snyder, may be said to be macroscopic, whereas its use in the present study is microscopic. He was concerned with the trend over a period of 100 years or more and concluded that all deviations from that trend were nothing more than inconsequential "jiggles." The present analysis, on the other hand, is concerned primarily with evidence as to inertia in movements of a few hours, days, weeks, months, or years, which Mr. Snyder, with his longer-range viewpoint, would designate as mere "jiggles."

Evidence of inertia may be disclosed in the following manner. In a penny-tossing series there is a probability of one-half that tails will follow heads and vice versa. If the stock market rises for 1 hour, day, week, month, or year, is there a probability of one-half that it will decline in the succeeding comparable unit of time? In an attempt to answer this question sequences and reversals were counted, a sequence occurring when a rise follows a rise, or a decline a decline, and a reversal occurring when a decline follows a rise, or a rise a decline.

A study of the ratio of sequences to reversals will disclose structure as defined above, if it exists within the series, and the significance of this structure can be defined by ordinary statistical methods. For instance, the probability can be determined that any ratio occurred by chance from a random population.[6] Also, the consistency of these ratios can be investigated and from their frequency distributions one can determine the probabilities of success in forecasting a rise or decline in stock prices. Samples, of adequate length where available, were ex-

[6] L. Besson, "On the Comparison of Meteorological Data with Results of Chance," translated and abridged by E. W. Woolard, *Monthly Weather Review*, Vol. 48, 1920, pp. 89–94, pointed out that in a *random series*, the ratio of sequences to reversals will be 0.5, that is, there will be twice as many reversals as sequences. It should be noted that, in the present analysis, the data employed are not *random*, but rather *cumulated random series*, that is series in which the first differences, rather than the actual observations, are random. In a truly random series the auto-correlation drops to zero when the series is lagged against itself by so much as one observation. In a cumulated random series this is not the case. For example, in the stock price series under consideration, even when the first differences have been rearranged in a random manner, an auto-correlation with a lag of one observation will yield a very high coefficient. This correlation coefficient will be a function of the length of the series and is approximately equal to $1-\log n/(n-1)$. In such a series, with the first differences random, the ratio of sequences to reversals will be, if n is large, 1.0 instead of 0.5 as observed in the case of a series in which the observations themselves are random.

amined, the intervals between observations being successively 20 minutes, 1 hour, 1 day, 1, 2, and 3 weeks, 1, 2, 3, · · · , 11 months, and 1, 2, 3, · · · , 10 years. The results of this investigation are presented in Table 1 and are shown graphically in Figure 1.

It was found that, for every series with intervals between observations of from 20 minutes up to and including 3 years, the sequences outnumbered the reversals. For example, in the case of the monthly series

TABLE 1

RATIO OF SEQUENCES TO REVERSALS IN STOCK PRICE INDEXES

UNIT	INDEX	PERIOD	NUMBER OF OBSERVATIONS	RATIO OF SEQUENCES TO REVERSALS	PROBABILITY OF OCCURANCE BY CHANCE	UNIT	INDEX	PERIOD	NUMBER OF OBSERVATIONS	RATIO OF SEQUENCES TO. REVERSALS	PROBABILITY OF OCCURANCE BY CHANCE
20 MINUTES	HARRIS UPHAM	1935-1936	2800	1.44	<.000001	8 MONTHS	INDEX OF RAILROAD STOCK PRICES	1835-1935	156	148	.01640
1 HOUR	DOW JONES HOURLY AVGS	1933-1934	800	1.29	.00040	9 MONTHS	INDEX OF RAILROAD STOCK PRICES	1835-1935	138	1.57	.01016
1 DAY	DOW JONES HOURLY AVGS.	1931-1935	1200	118	.00094	10 MONTHS	INDEX OF RAILROAD STOCK PRICES	1835-1935	124	1.49	.03000
1 WEEK	STANDARD STATISTICS	1918-1935	938	1.24	.00386	11 MONTHS	INDEX OF RAILROAD STOCK PRICES	1835-1935	113	127	.21870
2 WEEKS	DOW JONES	1897-1935	976	1.02	.80258	1 YEAR	INDEX OF RAILROAD STOCK PRICES	1835-1935	100	1.17	.42952
3 WEEKS	DOW JONES	1897-1935	652	1.08	.30772	2 YEARS	INDEX OF RAILROAD STOCK PRICES	1835-1935	50	1.63	.08726
1 MONTH	INDEX OF RAILROAD STOCK PRICES	1835-1935	1200	1.66	<.000001	3 YEARS	INDEX OF RAILROAD STOCK PRICES	1835-1934	33	1.46	.28914
2 MONTHS	INDEX OF RAILROAD STOCK PRICES	1835-1935	600	1.50	<.000001	4 YEARS	INDEX OF RAILROAD STOCK PRICES	1835-1935	25	0.85	.68180
3 MONTHS	INDEX OF RAILROAD STOCK PRICES	1835-1935	400	129	.01242	5 YEARS	INDEX OF RAILROAD STOCK PRICES	1835-1935	20	1.00	1.00000
4 MONTHS	INDEX OF RAILROAD STOCK PRICES	1835-1935	300	1.18	.16452	6 YEARS	INDEX OF RAILROAD STOCK PRICES	1835-1931	16	0.67	.44130
5 MONTHS	INDEX OF RAILROAD STOCK PRICES	1835-1935	249	1.52	.00120	7 YEARS	INDEX OF RAILROAD STOCK PRICES	1835-1933	14	0.71	.56192
6 MONTHS	INDEX OF RAILROAD STOCK PRICES	1835-1935	208	1.40	.01778	8 YEARS	INDEX OF RAILROAD STOCK PRICES	1835-1931	12	0.22	.03486
7 MONTHS	INDEX OF RAILROAD STOCK PRICES	1835-1935	178	1.38	.03486	10 YEARS	INDEX OF RAILROAD STOCK PRICES	1835-1935	10	0.60	.74140

The Index of Railroad Stock Prices is composed of several series which were assembled and put together by the Cleveland Trust Company. Canal stock prices were used for the period 1831 through 1833. From 1834 through 1879 the index is based on three Harvard series. The one from 1834 through 1852 includes eight stocks, and that from 1853 through 1865 includes 18. The data are from *The Review of Economic Statistics* for August, 1928. The index from 1866 through 1879 includes 10 stocks, and the data are from *The Review of Economic Statistics* for 1919. The index from 1880 through 1896 includes 10 stocks, and from 1897 to date it includes 15. These two latter indexes were compiled by the Cleveland Trust Company. All the earlier indexes were adjusted to form a continuous series terminating with the final index of 15 stocks.

from 1835 to 1935, a total of 1200 observations, there were 748 sequences and 450 reversals. That is, the probability appeared to be .625 that, if the market had risen in any given month, it would rise in the succeeding month, or, if it had fallen, that it would continue to decline for another month. The standard deviation[7] for such a long series

[7] In a random penny-tossing series the probability of a sequence or reversal is

constructed by random penny tossing would be 17.3; therefore the deviation of 149 from the expected value 599 is in excess of eight times the standard deviation. The probability of obtaining such a result in a penny-tossing series is infinitesimal. If the unit of time be increased to 6 months, we find that there are 120 sequences to 86 reversals or what appears to be a .583 probability that a sequence will occur in any successive pair of periods. The probability in this case is

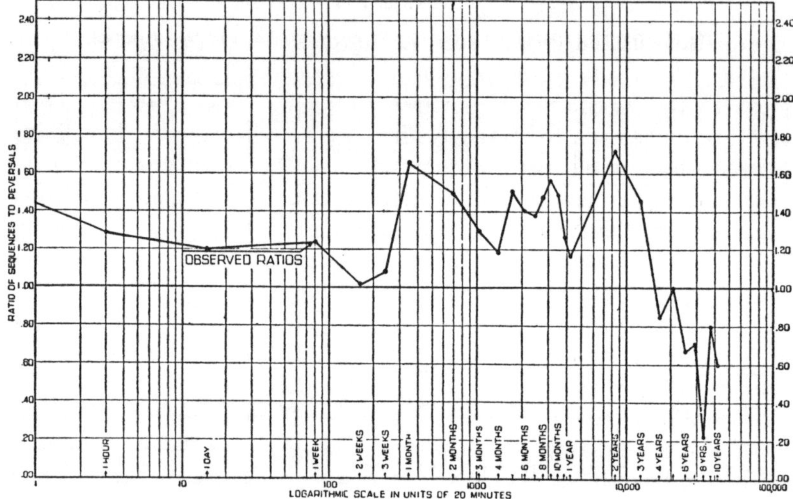

FIGURE 1.—Ratio of sequences to reversals in direction of stock price indexes for various time intervals.

.01778 that such a ratio of sequences to reversals might occur in a random series such as that of penny tossing previously referred to.

For annual series, the probability for chance occurrence, on the same basis as before, is .42952. In fact, the probabilities are inconclusive for all series using units of over 6 months, although this may be due to the limitations of the data. There seems to be a good chance that with more data it might be possible to demonstrate the existence of struc-

½ and the standard deviation is $\sqrt{npq}$ or $\sqrt{n}/2$ where n is the number of observations and p and q are respectively the probabilities of success and failure. Sequences or reversals are determined from the first differences of the original price series. The total number of sequences and reversals is one less than the number of first differences. The standard deviation of the number of sequences, therefore, will be $\sqrt{n-2}/2$ where n is the number of observations of the original price series. The actual deviation will be $S-(n-2)/2$ where S is the observed number of sequences and the ratio $[S-(n-2)/2]/[(n-2)^{\frac{1}{2}}/2]$ is the observed deviation in terms of the standard deviation. The probability of as large a deviation occurring by chance can be found in the ordinary table of the normal probability function.

ture for all units of time up to and including 3 years. It is difficult, however, to explain the very small excess of sequences over reversals for series using intervals of 2 weeks and 3 weeks in view of the fact that for the slightly shorter unit of 1 week we have significant indication of structure and also for series using intervals of 1 month. In fact, as will be shown later, the series represented by units of 1 month proves to be the most significant from a practical point of view.

The above analysis was based upon a study of the stock market as a whole. It may now be of interest for us to examine the evidence with regard to industrial groups such as motors, oils, steels, and so forth. To this end the indexes of common stock prices of 61 industrial groups, prepared by the Standard Statistics Company, were analyzed. Their monthly deviations from the median were noted, the median being used because more groups are normally below, than above, the arithmetic means, in view of the fact that extremely large gains are larger in percentage than extremely large declines. Sequences and reversals were counted for the purpose of determining whether there was a tendency for such groups to persist in exceeding, or falling below, the median. In other words, if the oil stocks, as a group, were in the 30 of the 61 industrial groups which advanced more than the median group in January, what is the probability that the oils will also be found in the strongest 30 groups in February? For the 16 months from January, 1934 to April, 1935, when the general market movement was approximately horizontal, in 917 observations there were 570 sequences and 345 reversals. That is, if the oil stocks were among the strongest 30 groups in January the probabilities would appear to be .623 that they would also be found among the strongest 30 groups in February. The application of the theory of probability to interpret the significance of this result is hampered, as in many other analyses of economic time series, by uncertainty as to what is the number of independent observations in the sample. The action of the oils, for example, may be correlated with that of the motors or some other group, so that when one is stronger than the median, the other also tends to be stronger. Modern statistical technique appears to offer no ready solution for this problem of the independence of observations, and we must, therefore, content ourselves with obtaining unusually favorable probabilities.

In the period, May, 1935 to February, 1936, a rising market of 551 observations, there were 379 sequences and 170 reversals, indicating an apparent probability of .690 in favor of a sequence. Here, however, another factor has intruded itself. The stocks of certain industries can be shown to be more cyclical in nature than those of other industries. For instance, in severe depressions the building of new houses is almost completely stopped, and yet people under such conditions go on eating almost as much food as in periods of prosperity. These tendencies are reflected by wider fluctuations in the earnings of producers of building materials than in the case of purveyors of food, and also by wider cyclical fluctuations in the stocks of the former corporations than of the latter. This tendency results, in the case of a rising market, in the building-stock prices being persistently stronger than the average, and the food stocks persistently weaker. A count of sequences and reversals under such conditions measures, therefore, to some extent, the differences in cyclical behavior among the various groups rather than the tendency toward inertia which is measured in the case of a period where the market as a whole is moving horizontally. Since there are not many periods of great length in which the market as a whole has moved horizontally, we are limited in the data available for this particular analysis. Considering only the data for the horizontal 16 months from January, 1934 to April, 1935, the excess of sequences over reversals is 7.5 times the standard error for a random series. Even assuming that half of the observations are not independent, there is still the exceedingly small probability of .00168 of occurrence in a random series.

The action of individual stocks was also investigated. Instead of the oils as a group, it was considered, for example, whether the Standard Oil Company of New Jersey, if it were stronger than the median of all stocks in January, would more likely than not be stronger in February. Taking 190 representative stocks for the years 1934 and 1935 and the first three months of 1936, and using the same technique as that employed in the case of the industrial groups, a total of 4659 observations, there was found, when the market moved horizontally, from January, 1934 to May, 1935, a ratio of sequences to reversals of 1.07 to 1 which is 9 times the standard error. In the last 12 months, a rising period, the ratio of sequences to reversals was 1.29 to 1. It follows from the previous discussion of cyclical behavior that the difference between the two periods is to be expected and that the evidence of the second period must be brought in question.

Taking 1 year as the unit of measurement for the period from 1920 to 1935, the tendency is very pronounced for stocks which have exceeded the median in one year to exceed it also in the year following. In 1837 observations were 1200 sequences and 635 reversals. The excess of sequences was about 13 times the standard error for a random series constructed on the basis of equal probabilities. During the period under consideration the market as a whole manifested 8 sequences and 7 reversals. The evidence therefore seems to indicate that, when 1 year is the unit of time, individual stocks will persist in doing better, or worse, than the median of all stocks.

This evidence of structure in stock prices suggests alluring possibilities in the way of forecasting. In fact, many professional speculators, including in particular exponents of the so-called "Dow Theory" widely publicized by popular financial journals, have adopted systems based in the main on the principle that it is advantageous to swim with the tide. The practicability of such forecasts, however, will depend,

TABLE 2

ABSOLUTE PERCENTAGE CHANGES IN STOCK PRICE INDEXES

UNIT	INDEX	PERIOD	NUMBER OF OBSERVATIONS	AVERAGE ABSOLUTE CHANGE IN PERCENT	STANDARD DEVIATION OF AVERAGE	UNIT	INDEX	PERIOD	NUMBER OF OBSERVATIONS	AVERAGE ABSOLUTE CHANGE IN PERCENT	STANDARD DEVIATION OF AVERAGE
20 MINUTES	HARRIS-UPHAM	JULY-9-1936 JULY-17-1936	111	0.12	.01	9 MONTHS	INDEX OF RAILROAD STOCK PRICES	JUNE 1859 JUNE 1934	100	12.73	1.29
1 HOUR	DOW JONES HOURLY AVGS.	SEPT-12-1935 OCT-8-1935	102	0.32	.03	10 MONTHS	INDEX OF RAILROAD STOCK PRICES	JAN 1851 APRIL 1934	100	13.00	1.31
2 HOURS	DOW JONES HOURLY AVGS.	AUG-1-1935 OCT-6-1935	103	0.47	.04	11 MONTHS	INDEX OF RAILROAD STOCK PRICES	DEC 1842 JULY 1934	100	13.99	1.25
1 DAY	DOW JONES	AUG-27-1934 DEC-31-1934	102	0.73	.07	1 YEAR	INDEX OF RAILROAD STOCK PRICES	JAN 1831 JAN 1934	103	14.70	1.43
1 WEEK	DOW JONES	JAN-6-1913 DEC-31-1934	1128	2.56	.21	2 YEARS	INDEX OF RAILROAD STOCK PRICES	JAN 1831 JAN 1933	51	22.58	2.78
1 MONTH	DOW JONES	JAN-1-1897 DEC-31-1934	451	3.70	.46	3 YEARS	INDEX OF RAILROAD STOCK PRICES	JAN 1831 JAN 1933	34	28.03	4.81
2 MONTHS	DOW JONES	APRIL-1-1918 DEC-1-1934	100	5.02	.91	4 YEARS	INDEX OF RAILROAD STOCK PRICES	JAN 1831 JAN 1932	25	30.59	4.77
3 MONTHS	INDEX OF RAILROAD STOCK PRICES	JAN 1835 DEC 1934	400	8.92	.79	5 YEARS	INDEX OF RAILROAD STOCK PRICES	JAN 1831 JAN 1931	20	33.95	5.71
4 MONTHS	DOW JONES	DEC 1900 DEC 1934	100	10.79	.99	6 YEARS	INDEX OF RAILROAD STOCK PRICES	JAN 1831 JAN 1933	17	38.59	8.90
5 MONTHS	INDEX OF RAILROAD STOCK PRICES	JAN 1893 SEPT 1934	100	8.62	.82	7 YEARS	INDEX OF RAILROAD STOCK PRICES	JAN 1831 JAN 1929	14	33.54	9.62
6 MONTHS	INDEX OF RAILROAD STOCK PRICES	DEC 1884 DEC 1934	100	10.04	1.20	8 YEARS	INDEX OF RAILROAD STOCK PRICES	JAN 1831 JAN 1927	12	32.38	9.15
7 MONTHS	INDEX OF RAILROAD STOCK PRICES	JUNE 1876 OCT 1934	100	11.81	1.30	9 YEARS	INDEX OF RAILROAD STOCK PRICES	JAN 1831 JAN 1930	11	45.98	13.64
8 MONTHS	INDEX OF RAILROAD STOCK PRICES	APRIL 1868 DEC 1934	100	11.30	1.13	10 YEARS	INDEX OF RAILROAD STOCK PRICES	JAN 1831 JAN 1931	10	51.64	10.90

not only on the ratio of sequences to reversals, but also on the brokerage costs and the average change in stock prices during the unit of time selected. The brokerage costs, of course, are known. To determine the average percentage change in the stock prices for various units of time an extensive study was made. The difference between the index at the beginning of one unit and the beginning of the next, given in percentage of the former value, was computed. The results are shown in Table 2. These averages are absolute values, that is, the directions of the moves were not considered. The values, plotted on a time scale, are shown in Figure 2. The increase is very regular, approximating a smooth exponential curve as shown in the diagram.

With these data it is possible to compute the net gain which would have resulted from an application of this type of forecasting to the stock market averages.

Let

$I(t)$ = Expected annual net profit, in per cent,
$R(t)$ = Ratio of sequences to reversals for time interval t,
$C(t)$ = Average change per time interval t in per cent,
$Y(t)$ = Number of time intervals, t, in one year,
B = Brokerage cost for one complete trade, in per cent.

In the long run there will be an average of $R(t)$ sequences for each reversal, that is, a speculator will, on the average, be on the right side of the market for $R(t)$ units of time for each unit that he is on the wrong side, if his market position is changed only *after* the occurrence of each reversal. The average net time in the right direction between changes of position will then be $[R(t)-1]$ time units. The average move per unit of time is $C(t)$; therefore, the *gross* gain per position will then be $[R(t)-1]C(t)$. The *net* gain per position will be

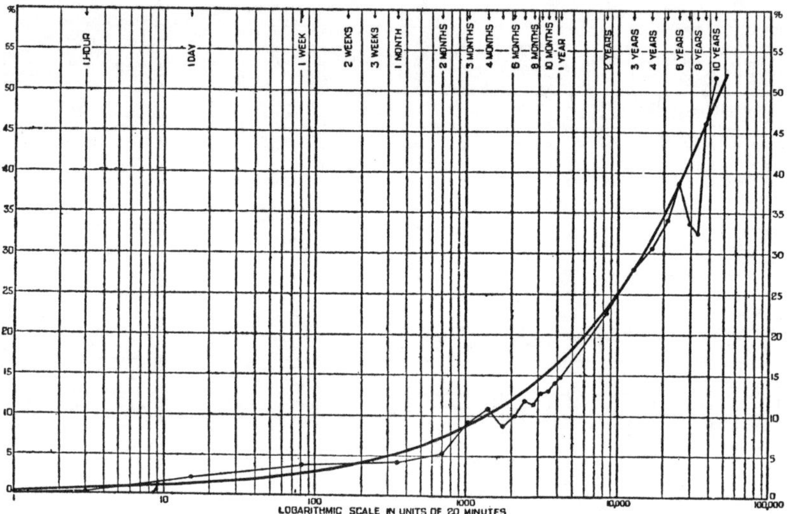

FIGURE 2.—Absolute percentage changes in stock price indexes.

$$[R(t) - 1]\cdot C(t) - B.$$

Since one will be in the market in the right direction $R(t)$ units of time and in the wrong direction 1 unit, the total time per position will be $[R(t)+1]$. The number of positions taken per year will be $Y(t)/[R(t)+1]$. The net annual gain, in per cent, will then be given by

$$I(t) = 100\left[\{[R(t) - 1]C(t) - B\}\frac{1}{100} + 1\right]^{Y(t)/[R(t)+1]} - 100.$$

When the values of $R(t)$ and $C(t)$ are substituted in this equation values of the expected annual net gain for various units of time and brokerage costs are obtained as shown in Table 3.

TABLE 3

Time Unit	Ratio of Sequences to Reversals $R(t)$	Average Percentage Changes $C(t)$	Expected Annual Net Profit — Brokerage Costs of: 1%	1½%	2%
1 day	1.18	0.73%	−67.4%	−83.0%	−91.1%
1 week	1.24	2.56	− 8.55	−18.6	−27.6
1 month	1.66	3.70	6.66	4.25	2.00
2 months	1.50	5.02	3.66	2.44	1.23
3 months	1.29	8.92	2.79	1.91	1.03

As might be expected, the daily and weekly units are too short. The probability of success is not sufficient to compensate for the fact that the changes per unit of time are small relative to brokerage costs. The average net gain *per trade* is largest for units of 2 months but, because with this unit so few trades are completed in a year, the annual net gain is less than when units of one month are used. It appears, indeed, that, for the period under consideration, one month is the optimum unit of time.

At this point a study was undertaken to determine whether it would be possible to select a group of stocks which would continue to be more volatile than the average and whether, if this could be done, the results of speculation, employing such a list, would be more successful than where average stocks were used. An investigation was made covering the period from 1900 to 1919. The number of stocks examined was 44 at the beginning of the period, increasing to 81 by 1918. The 10 per cent manifesting the greatest movement for 1 year, in the direction of the market, was chosen as the volatile group. It was found that such a group was about 1.7 times as volatile as the market for 6 months following its selection. The list of stocks making up the volatile group was adjusted at the end of each 6-month period.

The list of rapidly moving stocks, selected as described above, was then subjected to a comparison with the results secured employing average stocks for the period under consideration. The average stocks would have yielded an average annual net gain of 8.9 per cent while the volatile stocks would have shown an average net gain of but 5.4 per cent. Though the volatile group manifested an average move considerably more than that of the market, this was more than offset by the fact that its ratio of sequences to reversals was less favorable. The substitution of volatile for average stocks was therefore abandoned.

In the case of the stock market averages a study was undertaken to determine the degree of consistency in the data by considering distributions of the variables over finite periods of time. Figure 3 represents the frequency distributions of the ratios of sequences to reversals for units of 1 day, 1 week, 1 month, and 3 months. Periods of 12 and 24 units of time were considered in all cases except the last, where insufficient data made it necessary to consider periods of only 4 units. In the upper part of each diagram are the actual histograms, or frequency distributions. A better way to illustrate the probability of variations is by summation, or cumulative frequency distribution. The histograms, therefore, were smoothed, as shown by the solid continuous curve, and the cumulated curves computed from the smoothed distributions. The dotted curves represent the distributions that would be expected from series for which the probability of a sequence or reversal is $\frac{1}{2}$. They were computed from the formula

$$P(S) = \frac{{}_{n-2}C_S}{2^{n-2}},$$

where $P(S)$ is the probability of obtaining S sequences in a sample of n observations.[8]

For units of 1 day the periods of 12 units have a distribution very nearly random with a slight tendency towards a skewness to the right. This skewness is more pronounced in the diagram for periods of 24 units.

The cumulative frequency curves have a scale on the left giving the probabilities of a smaller ratio, and a scale on the right, the probabilities of a larger ratio. From the figure it will be seen that the probability of obtaining a ratio of sequences to reversals less than 1 is about .43. Or again, the probability of obtaining a ratio larger than 2 is about .20 in the case of periods of 12 days and about .09 for periods of 24 days. From such a diagram it is possible to determine the limiting ratio for any probability. For instance, the limits of a probability band of .50 can be determined by finding the ratios for which the probabilities are .75 and .25, respectively, of obtaining a larger ratio. In this case, for

[8] In n observations there are $(n-1)$ first differences. In this set of $(n-1)$ first differences there can be S sequences and $(n-2)-S$ reversals. The number of different orders in which $(n-2)$ things can be arranged in two sets, S and $(n-2)-S$, is $(n-2)!/S!(n-2-S)! = {}_{n-2}C_S$. But a sequence can occur when either a rise follows a rise or a decline follows a decline. The total number of samples containing S sequences, therefore, will be $2 \cdot {}_{n-2}C_S$. Since there are 2^{n-1} possible samples, the probability of obtaining S sequences will be given by the above equation.

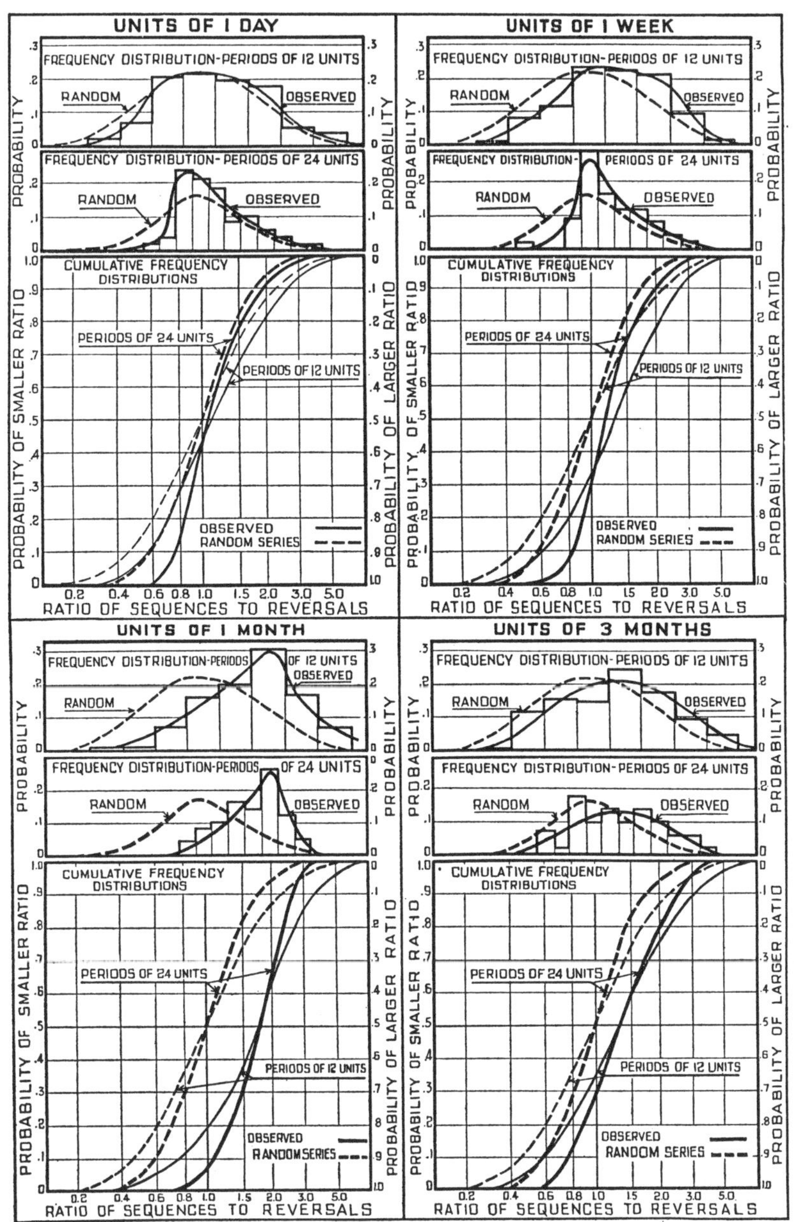

FIGURE 3.—Frequency distributions of ratio of sequences to reversals in direction of stock price indexes.

periods of 24 units, 0.9 is the lower limiting ratio and 1.4 the upper ratio. The median ratio is 1.1. Therefore, the ratio of sequences to reversals, for periods of 24 days, is 1.1; and 50 per cent of the time the ratios will lie between .9 and 1.4.

The distribution for units of 1 week shows a greater tendency towards structure than in the case of daily units. In this case the cumulative curve indicates that the probabilities are about 2 to 1 in favor of a ratio greater than unity. The tendency towards structure is even more

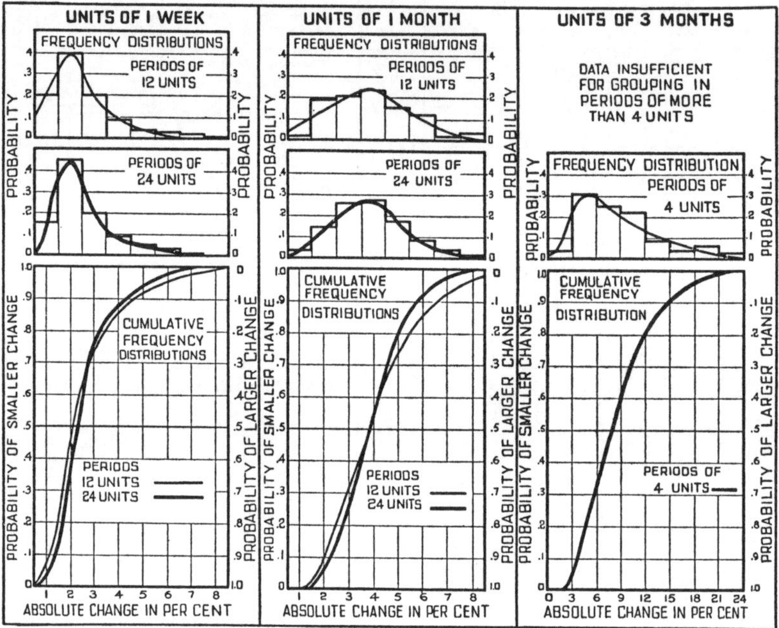

FIGURE 4.—Frequency distributions of absolute percentage changes in stock price indexes.

pronounced for units of 1 month where, for periods of 12 months, the chances are about 4 to 1 in favor of a ratio greater than unity. The cumulative curves are relatively steep, also, which indicates a high concentration around the average. This is especially true for the periods of 24 months. For units of 3 months the distributions are not nearly so favorable as in the previous case. They are flatter, indicating large variations, and the average ratio is much smaller.

Figure 4 shows the results of the same type of analysis applied to the data for the percentage changes. In this case only three units of time were investigated as the daily units already had proved to be impracti-

TABLE 4

COMPUTATION OF DISTRIBUTION OF $I(t) = 100\left[\{[R(t) - 1]C(t) - B\}\frac{1}{100} + 1\right]^{Y(t)/[R(t)+1]} - 100$

For Units of 1 Month, i.e., $Y(t) = 12$, and Brokerage $(B) = 1\%$
Roman type figures within table give values of $I(t)$
Italic type figures within table give probabilities of $I(t)$

Ratio of Sequences to Reversals—$R(t)$	Average Percentage Changes—$C(t)$: 1.5	2.5	3.5	4.5	5.5	6.5	7.5	8.5	Probability of $R(t)$
.50	−13.17 *.0015*	−16.65 *.0042*	−20.00 *.0054*	−23.23 *.0043*	−26.34 *.0025*	−29.35 *.0010*	−32.25 *.0006*	−35.04 *.0004*	*.020*
.71	− 9.65 *.0060*	−11.50 *.0166*	−13.32 *.0216*	−15.10 *.0174*	−16.85 *.0100*	−18.57 *.0040*	−20.26 *.0024*	−21.92 *.0016*	*.080*
1.00	− 5.85 *.0109*	− 5.85 *.0302*	− 5.85 *.0392*	− 5.85 *.0315*	− 5.85 *.0181*	− 5.85 *.0072*	− 5.85 *.0044*	− 5.85 *.0029*	*.145*
1.40	− 1.98 *.0172*	0 *.0478*	2.02 *.0621*	4.07 *.0499*	6.15 *.0288*	8.26 *.0115*	10.41 *.0069*	12.59 *.0046*	*.230*
2.00	2.02 *.0029*	6.14 *.0634*	10.38 *.0824*	14.75 *.0662*	19.25 *.0381*	23.88 *.0152*	28.65 *.0092*	33.55 *.0061*	*.305*
3.00	6.12 *.0112*	12.49 *.0312*	19.10 *.0405*	25.97 *.0326*	33.10 *.0188*	40.49 *.0075*	48.15 *.0045*	56.09 *.0030*	*.150*
5.00	10.25 *.0038*	18.81 *.0104*	27.69 *.0135*	36.89 *.0108*	46.41 *.0062*	56.25 *.0025*	66.41 *.0015*	76.89 *.0010*	*.050*
Probability of $C(t)$	*.075*	*.208*	*.270*	*.217*	*.125*	*.050*	*.030*	*.020*	

cable. For units of 3 months the data were insufficient for grouping in periods of more than 4 units. For units of 1 week and 1 month the difference between the periods of 12 units and 24 units is so slight as to be without statistical significance.

The next step was to combine these distributions in order to determine the distribution of the expected net gain. To do this mathematically gives rise to hopeless complications unless certain simplifying assumptions are made which themselves cast doubt on the value of the solutions. Therefore, it was necessary to compute the distributions by empirical means.

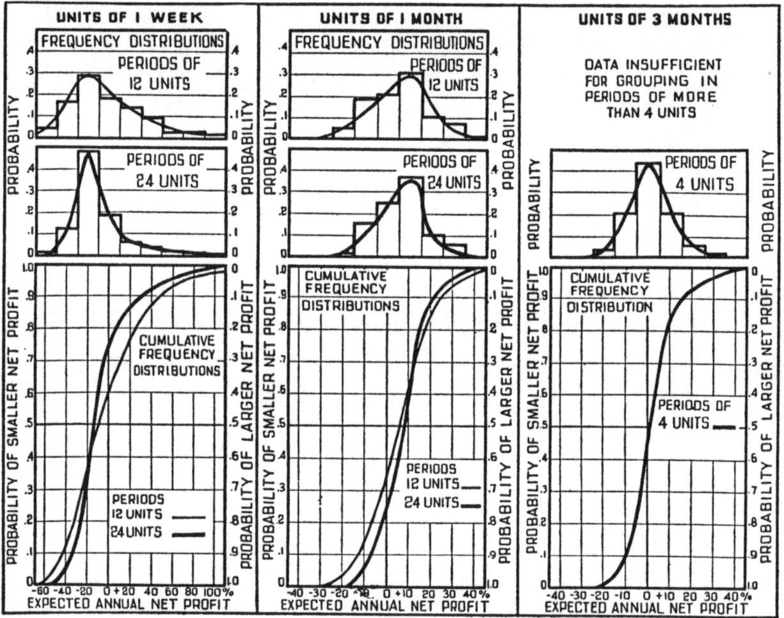

FIGURE 5.—Frequency distributions of expected annual net profits based on method of sequence probabilities. Brokerage computed at 1 per cent.

To determine these empirical distributions, values of $R(t)$ and $C(t)$ were taken which adequately covered their range of variation, and $I(t)$ was computed for all possible combinations of these values. The average brokerage charge was assumed to be 1 per cent per trade. To facilitate computation tables were employed of the type illustrated in Table 4.

The roman type figures in the body of the table give the values of $I(t)$ for the various values of $R(t)$ in the first column and $C(t)$ in the first row. The probabilities for each value of $R(t)$ and $C(t)$ are shown in the last column and the bottom row respectively. The probabilities for the various values of $I(t)$ are the products of the probabilities of $R(t)$ and $C(t)$ and are shown by the figures in italics in the table.[9] The values of $I(t)$ have been classified and the sum of the probabilities for each value of $I(t)$ in any class taken as the probability of that class. The results of this analysis are presented in Figure 5.

Here again are shown the histograms and cumulative frequency curves representing units of 1 week, 1 month, and 3 months. For units of 1 week the cumulative curves indicate an average annual loss of about 10 per cent, with but 1 chance in 3 of obtaining a net profit over any period of 24 weeks. The same is true to a lesser extent when we use units of 3 months. In this case we see there is about an even chance of a loss or gain. For units of 1 month, however, an average net gain of about 7 per cent is indicated. But, even here, no great consistency is evident. In fact the cumulative curve indicates that the chance of loss for any one year is about 1 in 3.

Furthermore the results should be interpreted with caution in view of the fact that various units of time, other than 1 month, were considered and rejected. In all, 26 such units, ranging from 20 minutes up to 10 years, were examined. The series represented by units of one month, therefore, was selected by hindsight as the most favorable one in 26 trials.

This type of forecasting could not be employed by speculators with any assurance of consistent or large profits. On the other hand, the significant excess of sequences over reversals for all units from 20 minutes up to 6 months, with the exception of units of 2 weeks and 3 weeks mentioned previously, represents conclusive evidence of structure in stock prices.

Alfred Cowles 3rd
Herbert E. Jones

Cowles Commission for
Research in Economics
Colorado Springs, Colorado

[9] The values of $R(t)$ and $C(t)$ for the periods studied are randomly distributed and a correlation analysis between $R(t)$ and $C(t)$ gave a coefficient of -0.2 with a standard error of 0.1. This coefficient is on the borderline of significance but is very small. Therefore, the probabilities of $I(t)$ may be computed in this manner without great error.

[2]

THE BEHAVIOR OF STOCK-MARKET PRICES*

EUGENE F. FAMA†

I. Introduction

For many years the following question has been a source of continuing controversy in both academic and business circles: To what extent can the past history of a common stock's price be used to make meaningful predictions concerning the future price of the stock? Answers to this question have been provided on the one hand by the various chartist theories and on the other hand by the theory of random walks.

Although there are many different chartist theories, they all make the same basic assumption. That is, they all assume that the past behavior of a security's price is rich in information concerning its future behavior. History repeats itself in that "patterns" of past price behavior will tend to recur in the future. Thus, if through careful analysis of price charts one develops an understanding of these "patterns," this can be used to predict the future behavior of prices and in this way increase expected gains.[1]

By contrast the theory of random walks says that the future path of the price level of a security is no more predictable than the path of a series of cumulated random numbers. In statistical terms the theory says that successive price changes are independent, identically distributed random variables. Most simply this implies that the series of price changes has no memory, that is, the past cannot be used to predict the future in any meaningful way.

The purpose of this paper will be to discuss first in more detail the theory underlying the random-walk model and then to test the model's empirical validity. The main conclusion will be that the data seem to present consistent and strong support for the model. This implies, of course, that chart reading, though perhaps an interesting pastime, is of no real value to the stock market investor. This is an extreme statement and the chart reader is certainly free to take exception. We suggest, however, that since the empirical evidence produced by this and other studies in support of the random-walk model is now so voluminous, the counterarguments of the chart reader will be completely lacking in force if they are not equally well supported by empirical work.

* This study has profited from the criticisms, suggestions, and technical assistance of many different people. In particular I wish to express my gratitude to Professors William Alberts, Lawrence Fisher, Robert Graves, James Lorie, Merton Miller, Harry Roberts, and Lester Telser, all of the Graduate School of Business, University of Chicago. I wish especially to thank Professors Miller and Roberts for providing not only continuous intellectual stimulation but also painstaking care in reading the various preliminary drafts.

Many of the ideas in this paper arose out of the work of Benoit Mandelbrot of the IBM Watson Research Center. I have profited not only from the written work of Dr. Mandelbrot but also from many invaluable discussion sessions.

Work on this paper was supported in part by funds from a grant by the Ford Foundation to the Graduate School of Business of the University of Chicago, and in part by funds granted to the Center for Research in Security Prices of the School by the National Science Foundation. Extensive computer time was provided by the 7094 Computation Center of the University of Chicago.

† Assistant professor of finance, Graduate School of Business, University of Chicago.

[1] The Dow Theory, of course, is the best known example of a chartist theory.

II. Theory of Random Walks in Stock Prices

The theory of random walks in stock prices actually involves two separate hypotheses: (1) successive price changes are independent, and (2) the price changes conform to some probability distribution. We shall now examine each of these hypotheses in detail.

A. INDEPENDENCE

1. MEANING OF INDEPENDENCE

In statistical terms independence means that the probability distribution for the price change during time period t is independent of the *sequence* of price changes during previous time periods. That is, knowledge of the *sequence* of price changes leading up to time period t is of no help in assessing the probability distribution for the price change during time period t.[2]

Now in fact we can probably never hope to find a time series that is characterized by *perfect* independence. Thus, strictly speaking, the random walk theory cannot be a completely accurate description of reality. For practical purposes, however, we may be willing to accept the independence assumption of the model as long as the dependence in the series of successive price changes is not above some "minimum acceptable" level.

What constitutes a "minimum acceptable" level of dependence depends, of course, on the particular problem that one is trying to solve. For example, someone who is doing statistical work in the stock market may wish to decide whether dependence in the series of *successive* price changes is sufficient to account for some particular property of the *distribution* of price changes. If the actual dependence in the series is not sufficient to account for the property in question, the statistician may be justified in accepting the independence hypothesis as an adequate description of reality.

By contrast the stock market trader has a much more practical criterion for judging what constitutes important dependence in successive price changes. For his purposes the random walk model is valid as long as knowledge of the past behavior of the series of price changes cannot be used to increase expected gains. More specifically, the independence assumption is an adequate description of reality as long as the actual degree of dependence in the series of price changes is not sufficient to allow the past history of the series to be used to predict the future in a way which makes expected profits greater than they would be under a naïve buy-and-hold model.

Dependence that is important from the trader's point of view need not be important from a statistical point of view, and conversely dependence which is important for statistical purposes need not be important for investment purposes. For example, we may know that on alternate days the price of a security always increases by ϵ and then decreases by ϵ. From a statistical point of view knowledge of this dependence would be important information since it tells us quite a bit about the shape of the distribution of price changes. For trading purposes, however, as long as ϵ is very small, this perfect, negative, statistical dependence is unimportant. Any profits the trader

[2] More precisely, independence means that

$$Pr(x_t = x \mid x_{t-1}, x_{t-2}, \ldots) = Pr(x_t = x) ,$$

where the term on the right of the equality sign is the unconditional probability that the price change during time t will take the value x, whereas the term on the left is the conditional probability that the price change will take the value x, conditional on the knowledge that previous price changes took the values x_{t-1}, x_{t-2}, etc.

may hope to make from it would be washed away in transactions costs.

In Section V of this paper we shall be concerned with testing independence from the point of view of both the statistician and the trader. At this point, however, the next logical step in the development of a theory of random walks in stock prices is to consider market situations and mechanisms that are consistent with independence in successive price changes. The procedure will be to consider first the simplest situations and then to successively introduce complications.

2. MARKET SITUATIONS CONSISTENT WITH INDEPENDENCE

Independence of successive price changes for a given security may simply reflect a price mechanism which is totally unrelated to real-world economic and political events. That is, stock prices may be just the accumulation of many bits of randomly generated noise, where by noise in this case we mean psychological and other factors peculiar to different individuals which determine the types of "bets" they are willing to place on different companies.

Even random walk theorists, however, would find such a view of the market unappealing. Although some people may be primarily motivated by whim, there are many individuals and institutions that seem to base their actions in the market on an evaluation (usually extremely painstaking) of economic and political circumstances. That is, there are many private investors and institutions who believe that individual securities have "intrinsic values" which depend on economic and political factors that affect individual companies.

The existence of intrinsic values for individual securities is not inconsistent with the random-walk hypothesis. In order to justify this statement, however, it will be necessary now to discuss more fully the process of price determination in an intrinsic-value–random-walk market.

Assume that at any point in time there exists, at least implicitly, an intrinsic value for each security. The intrinsic value of a given security depends on the earnings prospects of the company which in turn are related to economic and political factors some of which are peculiar to this company and some of which affect other companies as well.[3]

We stress, however, that actual market prices need not correspond to intrinsic values. In a world of uncertainty intrinsic values are not known exactly. Thus there can always be disagreement among individuals, and in this way actual prices and intrinsic values can differ. Henceforth uncertainty or disagreement concerning intrinsic values will come under the general heading of "noise" in the market.

In addition, intrinsic values can themselves change across time as a result of either new information or trend. New information may concern such things as the success of a current research and development project, a change in management, a tariff imposed on the industry's product by a foreign country, an increase in industrial production or any other *actual or anticipated* change in a factor which is likely to affect the company's prospects.

[3] We can think of intrinsic values in either of two ways. First, perhaps they just represent market conventions for evaluating the worth of a security by relating it to various factors which affect the earnings of a company. On the other hand, intrinsic values may actually represent equilibrium prices in the economist's sense, i.e., prices that evolve from some dynamic general equilibrium model. For our purposes it is irrelevant which point of view one takes.

On the other hand, an anticipated long-term trend in the intrinsic value of a given security can arise in the following way.[4] Suppose we have two unlevered companies which are identical in all respects except dividend policy. That is, both companies have the same current and anticipated investment opportunities, but they finance these opportunities in different ways. In particular, one company pays out all of its current earnings as dividends and finances new investment by issuing new common shares. The other company, however, finances new investment out of current earnings and pays dividends only when there is money left over. Since shares in the two companies are subject to the same degree of risk, we would expect their expected rates of returns to be the same. This will be the case, however, only if the shares of the company with the lower dividend payout have a higher expected rate of price increase than do the shares of the high-payout company. In this case the trend in the price level is just part of the expected return to equity. Such a trend is not inconsistent with the random-walk hypothesis.[5]

The simplest rationale for the independence assumption of the random walk model was proposed first, in a rather vague fashion, by Bachelier [6] and then much later but more explicitly by Osborne [42]. The argument runs as follows: If successive bits of new information arise independently across time, and if noise or uncertainty concerning intrinsic values does not tend to follow any consistent pattern, then successive price changes in a common stock will be independent.

As with many other simple models, however, the assumptions upon which the Bachelier-Osborne model is built are rather extreme. There is no strong reason to expect that each individual's estimates of intrinsic values will be independent of the estimates made by others (i.e., noise may be generated in a dependent fashion). For example, certain individuals or institutions may be opinion leaders in the market. That is, their actions may induce people to change their opinions concerning the prospects of a given company. In addition there is no strong reason to expect successive bits of new information to be generated independently across time. For example, good news may tend to be followed more often by good news than by bad news, and bad news may tend to be followed more often by bad news than by good news. Thus there may be dependence in either the noise generating process or in the process generating new information, and these may in turn lead to dependence in successive price changes.

Even in a situation where there are dependencies in either the information or the noise generating process, however, it is still possible that there are offsetting mechanisms in the market which tend to produce independence in price changes for individual common stocks. For example, let us assume that there are many sophisticated traders in the stock market and that sophistication can take two forms: (1) some traders may be much better at predicting the appearance of new information and estimating its effects on intrinsic values than others, while (2) some may be much better at doing statistical analyses of price behavior. Thus these two types of sophisticated traders can be roughly thought of as superior intrinsic-value analysts

[4] A trend in the price level, of course, corresponds to a non-zero mean in the distribution of price changes.

[5] A lengthy and rigorous justification for these statements is given by Miller and Modigliani [40].

and superior chart readers. We further assume that, although there are sometimes discrepancies between actual prices and intrinsic values, sophisticated traders in general feel that actual prices usually tend to move toward intrinsic values.

Suppose now that the noise generating process in the stock market is dependent. More specifically assume that when one person comes into the market who thinks the current price of a security is above or below its intrinsic value, he tends to attract other people of like feelings and he causes some others to change their opinions unjustifiably. In itself this type of dependence in the noise generating process would tend to produce "bubbles" in the price series, that is, periods of time during which the accumulation of the same type of noise causes the price level to run well above or below the intrinsic value.

If there are many sophisticated traders in the market, however, they may cause these "bubbles" to burst before they have a chance to really get under way. For example, if there are many sophisticated traders who are extremely good at estimating intrinsic values, they will be able to recognize situations where the price of a common stock is beginning to run up above its intrinsic value. Since they expect the price to move eventually back toward its intrinsic value, they have an incentive to sell this security or to sell it short. If there are enough of these sophisticated traders, they may tend to prevent these "bubbles" from ever occurring. Thus their actions will neutralize the dependence in the noise-generating process, and successive price changes will be independent.

In fact, of course, in a world of uncertainty even sophisticated traders cannot always estimate intrinsic values exactly. The effectiveness of their activities in erasing dependencies in the series of price changes can, however, be reinforced by another neutralizing mechanism. As long as there are important dependencies in the series of successive price changes, opportunities for trading profits are available to any astute chartist. For example, once they understand the nature of the dependencies in the series of successive price changes, sophisticated chartists will be able to identify statistically situations where the price is beginning to run up above the intrinsic value. Since they expect that the price will eventually move back toward its intrinsic value, they will sell. Even though they are vague about intrinsic values, as long as they have sufficient resources their actions will tend to erase dependencies and to make actual prices closer to intrinsic values.

Over time the intrinsic value of a common stock will change as a result of new information, that is, actual or anticipated changes in any variable that affects the prospects of the company. If there are dependencies in the process generating new information, this in itself will tend to create dependence in successive price changes of the security. If there are many sophisticated traders in the market, however, they should eventually learn that it is profitable for them to attempt to interpret both the price effects of current new information and of the future information implied by the dependence in the information generating process. In this way the actions of these traders will tend to make price changes independent.[6]

Moreover, successive price changes may be independent even if there is usually consistent vagueness or uncertainty

[6] In essence dependence in the information generating process is itself relevant information which the astute trader should consider.

surrounding new information. For example, if uncertainty concerning the importance of new information consistently causes the market to underestimate the effects of new information on intrinsic values, astute traders should eventually learn that it is profitable to take this into account when new information appears in the future. That is, by examining the history of prices subsequent to the influx of new information it will become clear that profits can be made simply by buying (or selling short if the information is pessimistic) after new information comes into the market since on the average actual prices do not initially move all the way to their new intrinsic values. If many traders attempt to capitalize on this opportunity, their activities will tend to erase any consistent lags in the adjustment of actual prices to changes in intrinsic values.

The above discussion implies, of course, that, if there are many astute traders in the market, on the average the full effects of new information on intrinsic values will be reflected nearly instantaneously in actual prices. In fact, however, because there is vagueness or uncertainty surrounding new information, "instantaneous adjustment" really has two implications. First, actual prices will initially overadjust to the new intrinsic values as often as they will underadjust. Second, the lag in the complete adjustment of actual prices to successive new intrinsic values will itself be an independent random variable, sometimes preceding the new information which is the basis of the change (i.e., when the information is anticipated by the market before it actually appears) and sometimes following. It is clear that in this case successive price changes in individual securities will be independent random variables.

In sum, this discussion is sufficient to show that the stock market *may* conform to the independence assumption of the random walk model even though the processes generating noise and new information are themselves dependent. We turn now to a brief discussion of some of the implications of independence.

3. IMPLICATIONS OF INDEPENDENCE

In the previous section we saw that one of the forces which helps to produce independence of successive price changes may be the existence of sophisticated traders, where sophistication may mean either (1) that the trader has a special talent in detecting dependencies in series of prices changes for individual securities, or (2) that the trader has a special talent for predicting the appearance of new information and evaluating its effects on intrinsic values. The first kind of trader corresponds to a superior chart reader, while the second corresponds to a superior intrinsic value analyst.

Now although the activities of the chart reader may help to produce independence of successive price changes, once independence is established chart reading is no longer a profitable activity. In a series of independent price changes, the past history of the series cannot be used to increase expected profits.

Such dogmatic statements cannot be applied to superior intrinsic-value analysis, however. In a dynamic economy there will always be new information which causes intrinsic values to change over time. As a result, people who can consistently predict the appearance of *new* information *and* evaluate its effects on intrinsic values will usually make larger profits than can people who do not have this talent. The fact that the activities of these superior analysts help to make successive price changes independent does *not* imply that their expected profits cannot be greater than those of the investor who follows some naïve buy-and-hold policy.

It must be emphasized, however, that the comparative advantage of the superior analyst over his less talented competitors lies in his ability to predict consistently the appearance of *new* information and evaluate its impact on intrinsic values. If there are enough superior analysts, their existence will be sufficient to insure that actual market prices are, on the basis of all *available* information, best estimates of intrinsic values. In this way, of course, the superior analysts make intrinsic value analysis a useless tool for both the average analyst and the average investor.

This discussion gives rise to three obvious question: (1) How many superior analysts are necessary to insure independence? (2) Who are the "superior" analysts? and (3) What is a rational investment policy for an average investor faced with a random-walk stock market?

It is impossible to give a firm answer to the first question, since the effectiveness of the superior analysts probably depends more on the extent of their resources than on their number. Perhaps a single, well-informed and well-endowed specialist in each security is sufficient.

It is, of course, also very difficult to identify *ex ante* those people that qualify as superior analysts. *Ex post*, however, there is a simple criterion. A superior analyst is one whose gains over many periods of time are *consistently* greater than those of the market. Consistently is the crucial word here, since for any given short period of time, even if there are no superior analysts, in a world of random walks some people will do much better than the market and some will do much worse.

Unfortunately, by this criterion this author does not qualify as a superior analyst. There is some consolation, however, since, as we shall see later, other more market-tested institutions do not seem to qualify either.

Finally, let us now briefly formulate a rational investment policy for the average investor in a situation where stock prices follow random walks and at every point in time actual prices represent good estimates of intrinsic values. In such a situation the primary concern of the average investor should be *portfolio analysis*. This is really three separate problems. First, the investor must decide what sort of tradeoff between risk and expected return he is willing to accept. Then he must attempt to classify securities according to riskiness, and finally he must also determine how securities from different risk classes combine to form portfolios with various combinations of risk and return.[7]

In essence in a random-walk market the *security analysis* problem of the average investor is greatly simplified. If actual prices at any point in time are good estimates of intrinsic values, he need not be concerned with whether individual securities are over- or under-priced. If he decides that his portfolio requires an additional security from a given risk class, he can choose that security randomly from within the class. On the average any security so chosen will have about the same effect on the expected return and riskiness of his portfolio.

B. THE DISTRIBUTION OF PRICE CHANGES

1. INTRODUCTION

The theory of random walks in stock prices is based on two hypotheses: (1) successive price changes in an indi-

[7] For a more complete formulation of the portfolio analysis problem see Markowitz [39].

vidual security are independent, and (2) the price changes conform to some probability distribution. Of the two hypotheses independence is the most important. Either successive price changes are independent (or at least for all practical purposes independent) or they are not; and if they are not, the theory is not valid. All the hypothesis concerning the distribution says, however, is that the price changes conform to *some* probability distribution. In the general theory of random walks the form or shape of the distribution need not be specified. Thus any distribution is consistent with the theory as long as it correctly characterizes the process generating the price changes.[8]

From the point of view of the investor, however, specification of the shape of the distribution of price changes is extremely helpful. In general, the form of the distribution is a major factor in determining the riskiness of investment in common stocks. For example, although two different possible distributions for the price changes may have the same mean or expected price change, the probability of very large changes may be much greater for one than for the other.

The form of the distribution of price changes is also important from an academic point of view since it provides descriptive information concerning the nature of the process generating price changes. For example, if very large price changes occur quite frequently, it may be safe to infer that the economic structure that is the source of the price changes is itself subject to frequent and sudden shifts over time. That is, if the distribution of price changes has a high degree of dispersion, it is probably safe to infer that, to a large extent, this is due to the variability in the process generating new information.

Finally, the form of the distribution of price changes is important information to anyone who wishes to do empirical work in this area. The power of a statistical tool is usually closely related to the type of data to which it is applied. In fact we shall see in subsequent sections that for some probability distributions important concepts like the mean and variance are not meaningful.

2. THE BACHELIER-OSBORNE MODEL

The first complete development of a theory of random walks in security prices is due to Bachelier [6], whose original work first appeared around the turn of the century. Unfortunately his work did not receive much attention from economists, and in fact his model was independently derived by Osborne [42] over fifty years later. The Bachelier-Osborne model begins by assuming that price changes from transaction to transaction in an individual security are independent, identically distributed random variables. It further assumes that transactions are fairly uniformly spread across time, and that the distribution of price changes from transaction to transaction has finite variance. If the number of transactions per day, week, or month is very large, then price changes across these differencing intervals will be sums of many independent variables. Under these conditions the central-limit theorem leads us to expect that the daily,

[8] Of course, the theory does imply that the parameters of the distribution should be stationary or fixed. As long as independence holds, however, stationarity can be interpreted loosely. For example, if independence holds in a strict fashion, then for the purposes of the investor the random walk model is a valid approximation to reality even though the parameters of the probability distribution of the price changes may be non-stationary.

For statistical purposes stationarity implies simply that the parameters of the distribution should be fixed at least for the time period covered by the data.

weekly, and monthly price changes will each have normal or Gaussian distributions. Moreover, the variances of the distributions will be proportional to the respective time intervals. For example, if σ^2 is the variance of the distribution of the daily changes, then the variance for the distribution of the weekly changes should be approximately $5\sigma^2$.

Although Osborne attempted to give an empirical justification for his theory, most of his data were cross-sectional and could not provide an adequate test. Moore and Kendall, however, have provided empirical evidence in support of the Gaussian hypothesis. Moore [41, pp. 116–23] graphed the weekly first differences of log price of eight NYSE common stocks on normal probability paper. Although the extreme sections of his graphs seem to have too many large price changes, Moore still felt the evidence was strong enough to support the hypothesis of approximate normality.

Similarly Kendall [26] observed that weekly price changes in British common stocks seem to be approximately normally distributed. Like Moore, however, he finds that most of the distributions of price changes are leptokurtic; that is, there are too many values near the mean and too many out in the extreme tails. In one of his series some of the extreme observations were so large that he felt compelled to drop them from his subsequent statistical tests.

3. MANDELBROT AND THE GENERALIZED CENTRAL-LIMIT THEOREM

The Gaussian hypothesis was not seriously questioned until recently when the work of Benoit Mandelbrot first began to appear.[9] Mandelbrot's main assertion is that, in the past, academic research has too readily neglected the implications of the leptokurtosis usually observed in empirical distributions of price changes.

The presence, in general, of leptokurtosis in the empirical distributions seems indisputable. In addition to the results of Kendall [26] and Moore [41] cited above, Alexander [1] has noted that Osborne's cross-sectional data do not really support the normality hypothesis; there are too many changes greater than $\pm$ 10 per cent. Cootner [10] has developed a whole theory in order to explain the long tails of the empirical distributions. Finally, Mandelbrot [37, Fig. 1] cites other examples to document empirical leptokurtosis.

The classic approach to this problem has been to assume that the extreme values are generated by a different mechanism than the majority of the observations. Consequently one tries a posteriori to find "causal" explanations for the large observations and thus to rationalize their exclusion from any tests carried out on the body of the data.[10] Unlike the statistician, however, the investor cannot ignore the possibility of large price changes before committing his funds, and once he has made his decision to invest, he must consider their effects on his wealth.

Mandelbrot feels that if the outliers are numerous, excluding them takes away much of the significance from any tests carried out on the remainder of the data. This exclusion process is all the more subject to criticism since probability distributions are available which accurately represent the large observations

[9] His main work in this area is [37]. References to his other works are found through this report and in the bibliography.

[10] When extreme values are excluded from the sample, the procedure is often called "trimming." Another technique which involves reducing the size of extreme observations rather than excluding them is called "Winsorization." For a discussion see J. W. Tukey [45].

as well as the main body of the data. The distributions referred to are members of a special class which Mandelbrot has labeled stable Paretian. The mathematical properties of these distributions are discussed in detail in the appendix to this paper. At this point we shall merely introduce some of their more important descriptive properties.

Parameters of stable Paretian distributions.—Stable Paretian distributions have four parameters: (1) a location parameter which we shall call δ, (2) a scale parameter henceforth called γ, (3) an index of skewness, β, and (4) a measure of the height of the extreme tail areas of the distribution which we shall call the characteristic exponent α.[11]

When the characteristic exponent α is greater than 1, the location parameter δ is the expectation or mean of the distribution. The scale parameter γ can be any positive real number, but β, the index of skewness, can only take values in the interval $-1 \leq \beta \leq 1$. When $\beta = 0$ the distribution is symmetric. When $\beta > 0$ the distribution is skewed right (i.e., has a long tail to the right), and the degree of right skewness is larger the larger the value of β. Similarly, when $\beta < 0$ the distribution is skewed left, and the degree of left skewness is larger the smaller the value of β.

The characteristic exponent α of a stable Paretian distribution determines the height of, or total probability contained in, the extreme tails of the distribution, and can take any value in the interval $0 < \alpha \leq 2$. When $\alpha = 2$, the relevant stable Paretian distribution is the normal or Gaussian distribution. When α is in the interval $0 < \alpha < 2$, the extreme tails of the stable Paretian distributions are higher than those of the normal distribution, and the total probability in the extreme tails is larger the smaller the value of α. The most important consequence of this is that the variance exists (i.e., is finite) only in the extreme case $\alpha = 2$. The mean, however, exists as long as $\alpha > 1$.[12]

Mandelbrot's hypothesis states that for distributions of price changes in speculative series, α is in the interval $1 < \alpha < 2$, so that the distributions have means but their variances are infinite. The Gaussian hypothesis, on the other hand, states that α is exactly equal to 2. Thus both hypotheses assume that the distribution is stable Paretian. The disagreement between them concerns the value of the characteristic exponent α.

Properties of stable Paretian distributions.—Two important properties of stable Paretian distributions are (1) stability or invariance under addition, and (2) the fact that these distributions are the only possible limiting distributions for sums of independent, identically distributed, random variables.

By definition, a stable Paretian distribution is any distribution that is stable or invariant under addition. That is, the distribution of sums of independent, identically distributed, stable Paretian variables is itself stable Paretian and, except for origin and scale, has the same form as the distribution of the individual summands. Most simply, stability means that the values of the parameters α and β remain constant under addition.[13]

The property of stability is responsible

[11] The derivation of most of the important properties of stable Paretian distributions is due to P. Levy [29]. A rigorous and compact mathematical treatment of the theory can be found in B. V. Gnedenko and A. N. Kolmogorov [17]. A more comprehensive mathematical treatment can be found in Mandelbrot [37].

[12] For a proof of these statements see Gnedenko and Kolmogorov [17], pp. 179–83.

[13] A more rigorous definition of stability is given in the appendix.

for much of the appeal of stable Paretian distributions as descriptions of empirical distributions of price changes. The price change of a stock for any time interval can be regarded as the sum of the changes from transaction to transaction during the interval. If transactions are fairly uniformly spread over time and if the changes between transactions are independent, identically distributed, stable Paretian variables, then daily, weekly, and monthly changes will follow stable Paretian distributions of exactly the same form, except for origin and scale. For example, if the distribution of daily changes is stable Paretian with location parameter δ and scale paremeter γ, the distribution of weekly (or five-day) changes will also be stable Paretian with location parameter 5δ and scale parameter 5γ. It would be very convenient if the form of the distribution of price changes were independent of the differencing interval for which the changes were computed.

It can be shown that stability or invariance under addition leads to a most important corollary property of stable Paretian distributions; they are the only possible limiting distributions for sums of independent, identically distributed, random variables.[14] It is well known that if such variables have finite variance, the limiting distribution for their sum will be the normal distribution. If the basic variables have infinite variance, however, and if their sums follow a limiting distribution, the limiting distribution must be stable Paretian with $0 < \alpha < 2$.

In light of this discussion we see that Mandelbrot's hypothesis can actually be viewed as a generalization of the central-limit theorem arguments of Bachelier and Osborne to the case where the underlying distributions of price changes from transaction to transaction are allowed to have infinite variances. In this sense, then, Mandelbrot's version of the theory of random walks can be regarded as a broadening rather than a contradiction of the earlier Bachelier-Osborne model.

Conclusion.—Mandelbrot's hypothesis that the distribution of price changes is stable Paretian with characteristic exponent $\alpha < 2$ has far reaching implications. For example, if the variances of distributions of price changes behave as if they are infinite, many common statistical tools which are based on the assumption of a finite variance either will not work or may give very misleading answers. Getting along without these familiar tools is not going to be easy, and before parting with them we must be sure that such a drastic step is really necessary. At the moment, the most impressive single piece of evidence is a direct test of the infinite variance hypothesis for the case of cotton prices. Mandelbrot [37, Fig. 2 and pp. 404–7] computed the sample second moments of the first differences of the logs of cotton prices for increasing sample sizes of from 1 to 1,300 observations. He found that the sample moment does not settle down to any limiting value but rather continues to vary in absolutely erratic fashion, precisely as would be expected under his hypothesis.[15]

As for the special but important case

[14] For a proof see Gnedenko and Kolmogorov [17], pp. 162–63.

[15] The second moment of a random variable x is just $E(x^2)$. The variance is just the second moment minus the square of the mean. Since the mean is assumed to be a constant, tests of the sample second moment are also tests of the sample variance.

In an earlier privately circulated version of [37] Mandelbrot tested his hypothesis on various other series of speculative prices. Although the results in general tended to support his hypothesis, they were neither as extensive nor as conclusive as the tests on cotton prices.

of common-stock prices, no published evidence for or against Mandelbrot's theory has yet been presented. One of our main goals here will be to attempt to test Mandelbrot's hypothesis for the case of stock prices.

C. THINGS TO COME

Except for the concluding section, the remainder of this paper will be concerned with reporting the results of extensive tests of the random walk model of stock price behavior. Sections III and IV will examine evidence on the shape of the distribution of price changes. Section III will be concerned with common statistical tools such as frequency distributions and normal probability graphs, while Section IV will develop more direct tests of Mandelbrot's hypothesis that the characteristic exponent α for these distributions is less than 2. Section V of the paper tests the independence assumption of the random-walk model. Finally, Section VI will contain a summary of previous results, and a discussion of the implications of these results from various points of view.

III. A First Look at the Empirical Distributions

A. INTRODUCTION

In this section a few simple techniques will be used to examine distributions of daily stock-price changes for individual securities. If Mandelbrot's hypothesis that the distributions are stable Paretian with characteristic exponents less than 2 is correct, the most important feature of the distributions should be the length of their tails. That is, the extreme tail areas should contain more relative frequency than would be expected if the distributions were normal. In this section no attempt will be made to decide whether the actual departures from normality are sufficient to reject the Gaussian hypothesis. The only goal will be to see if the departures are usually in the direction predicted by the Mandelbrot hypothesis.

B. THE DATA

The data that will be used throughout this paper consist of daily prices for each of the thirty stocks of the Dow-Jones Industrial Average.[16] The time periods vary from stock to stock but usually run from about the end of 1957 to September 26, 1962. The final date is the same for all stocks, but the initial date varies from January, 1956 to April, 1958. Thus there are thirty samples with about 1,200–1,700 observations per sample.

The actual tests are not performed on the daily prices themselves but on the first differences of their natural logarithms. The variable of interest is

$$u_{t+1} = \log_e p_{t+1} - \log_e p_t \,, \qquad (1)$$

where p_{t+1} is the price of the security at the end of day $t + 1$, and p_t is the price at the end of day t.

There are three main reasons for using changes in log price rather than simple price changes. First, the change in log price is the yield, with continuous compounding, from holding the security for that day.[17] Second, Moore [41, pp. 13–15] has shown that the variability of simple price changes for a given stock is an increasing function of the price level of the stock. His work indicates that taking

[16] The data were very generously supplied by Professor Harry B. Ernst of Tufts University.

[17] The proof of this statement goes as follows:

$$\frac{p_{t+1}}{p_t} = \exp\left(\log_e \frac{p_{t+1}}{p_t}\right).$$

$$p_{t+1} = p_t \exp\left(\log_e \frac{p_{t+1}}{p_t}\right)$$

$$= p_t \exp(\log_e p_{t+1} - \log_e p_t).$$

logarithms seems to neutralize most of this price level effect. Third, for changes less than ± 15 per cent the change in log price is very close to the percentage price change, and for many purposes it is convenient to look at the data in terms of percentage price changes.[18]

In working with daily changes in log price, two special situations must be noted. They are stock splits and ex-dividend days. Stock splits are handled as follows: if a stock splits two for one on day t, its actual closing price on day t is doubled, and the difference between the logarithm of this doubled price and the logarithm of the closing price for day $t - 1$ is the first difference for day t. The first difference for day $t + 1$ is the difference between the logarithm of the closing price on day $t + 1$ and the logarithm of the actual closing price on day t, the day of the split. These adjustments reflect the fact that the process of splitting a stock involves no change either in the asset value of the firm or in the wealth of the individual shareholder.

On ex-dividend days, however, other things equal, the value of an individual share should fall by about the amount of the dividend. To adjust for this the first difference between an ex-dividend day and the preceding day is computed as

$$u_{t+1} = \log_e (p_{t+1} + d) - \log_e p_t ,$$

where d is the dividend per share.[19]

One final note concerning the data is in order. The Dow-Jones Industrials are not a random sample of stocks from the New York Stock Exchange. The component companies are among the largest and most important in their fields. If the behavior of these blue-chips stocks differs consistently from that of other stocks in the market, the empirical results to be presented below will be strictly applicable only to the shares of large important companies.

One must admit, however, that the sample of stocks is conservative from the point of view of the Mandelbrot hypothesis, since blue chips are probably more stable than other securities. There is reason to expect that if such a sample conforms well to the Mandelbrot hypothesis, a random sample would fit even better.

C. FREQUENCY DISTRIBUTIONS

One very simple way of analyzing the distribution of changes in log price is to construct frequency distributions for the individual stocks. That is, for each stock the empirical proportions of price changes within given standard deviations of the mean change can be computed and compared with what would be expected if the distributions were exactly normal. This is done in Tables 1 and 2. In Table 1 the proportions of observations within 0.5, 1.0, 1.5, 2.0, 2.5, 3.0, 4.0, and 5.0 standard deviations of the mean change, as well as the proportion greater than 5 standard deviations from the mean, are computed for each stock. In the first line of the body of the table the proportions for the unit normal distribution are given.

Table 2 gives a comparison of the unit normal and the empirical distributions.

[18] Since, for our purposes, the variable of interest will *always* be the change in log price, the reader should note that henceforth when the words "price change" appear in the text, we are actually referring to the change in log price.

[19] I recognize that because of tax effects and other considerations, the value of a share may not be expected to fall by the full amount of the dividend. Because of uncertainty concerning what the correct adjustment should be, the price changes on ex-dividend days were discarded in an earlier version of the paper. Since the results reported in the earlier version differ very little from those to be presented below, it seems that adding back the full amount of the dividend produces no important distortions in the empirical results.

Each entry in this table was computed by taking the corresponding entry in Table 1 and subtracting from it the entry for the unit normal distribution in Table 1. For example, the entry in column (1) Table 2 for Allied Chemical was found by subtracting the entry in column (1) Table 1 for the unit normal, 0.3830, from the entry in column (1) Table 1 for Allied Chemical, 0.4595.

A positive number in Table 2 should be interpreted as an excess of relative frequency in the empirical distribution over what would be expected for the given interval if the distribution were normal. For example, the entry in column (1) opposite Allied Chemical implies that the empirical distribution contains about 7.6 per cent more of the total frequency within one-half standard deviation of the mean than would be expected if the distribution were normal. The number in column (9) implies that in the empirical distribution about 0.16 per cent more of the total frequency is greater than five standard deviations from the mean than would be expected under the normal or Gaussian hypothesis.

Similarly, a negative number in the table should be interpreted as a deficiency of relative frequency within the

TABLE 1

FREQUENCY DISTRIBUTIONS

Stocks	Intervals								
	0.5 S (1)	1.0 S (2)	1.5 S (3)	2.0 S (4)	2.5 S (5)	3.0 S (6)	4.0 S (7)	5.0 S (8)	>5.0 S (9)
Unit normal	0.3830	0.6826	0.8664	0.9545	0.9876	0.9973	0.999938	0.9999994	0.0000006
Allied Chemical	.4595	.7449	.8782	.9550	.9755	.9869	0.996729	0.9983647	.0016353
Alcoa	.4378	.7260	.8706	.9420	.9765	.9941	1.000000	1.0000000	.0000000
American Can	.4938	.7695	.8983	.9491	.9672	.9844	0.995078	0.9975390	.0024610
A.T.&T.	.5824	.8162	.9237	.9582	.9795	.9860	0.992617	0.9950779	.0049221
American Tobacco	.5394	.7818	.8893	.9462	.9704	.9844	0.994544	0.9968823	.0031177
Anaconda	.4300	.7075	.8785	.9522	.9757	.9933	0.999162	1.0000000	.0000000
Bethlehem Steel	.4792	.7350	.8850	.9483	.9750	.9875	0.996667	0.9991667	.0008333
Chrysler	.4350	.7264	.8794	.9486	.9781	.9905	0.997636	0.9994090	.0005910
Du Pont	.4336	.7257	.8825	.9469	.9775	.9936	0.997586	0.9991955	.0008045
Eastman Kodak	.4410	.7472	.8780	.9467	.9733	.9895	0.998384	0.9983845	.0016155
General Electric	.4631	.7460	.8771	.9427	.9775	.9870	0.997047	0.9994093	.0005907
General Foods	.4489	.7493	.8871	.9467	.9751	.9844	0.997869	0.9992898	.0007102
General Motors	.4716	.7455	.8859	.9571	.9792	.9910	0.995851	0.9979253	.0020741
Goodyear	.4638	.7487	.8898	.9509	.9854	.9914	0.996558	0.9982788	.0017212
International Harvester	.4408	.7450	.8967	.9475	.9750	.9875	0.996667	0.9991667	.0008338
International Nickel	.4722	.7635	.8833	.9413	.9686	.9871	0.995173	1.0000000	.0000000
International Paper	.4444	.7498	.8742	.9433	.9758	.9869	0.996545	1.0000000	.0000000
Johns Manville	.4365	.7377	.8730	.9485	.9809	.9909	0.997510	0.9991701	.0008299
Owens Illinois	.4778	.7389	.8909	.9466	.9717	.9838	0.997575	0.9991916	.0008084
Procter & Gamble	.5017	.7706	.8887	.9378	.9710	.9862	0.995853	0.9986178	.0013822
Sears	.5388	.7856	.9021	.9490	.9701	.9830	0.993528	0.9959547	.0040453
Standard Oil (Calif.)	.4584	.7348	.8724	.9439	.9764	.9917	0.997047	0.9994093	.0005907
Standard Oil (N.J.)	.5035	.7751	.8953	.9559	.9766	.9896	0.997405	0.9982699	.0017301
Swift & Co.	.4647	.7476	.8817	.9405	.9703	.9875	0.997234	1.0000000	.0000000
Texaco	.4599	.7282	.8697	.9517	.9750	.9879	0.998274	1.0000000	.0000000
Union Carbide	.4168	.7191	.8783	.9401	.9785	.9946	0.999106	1.0000000	.0000000
United Aircraft	.4583	.7483	.8858	.9500	.9808	.9908	0.997500	0.9991667	.0008333
U.S. Steel	.4125	.6933	.8758	.9508	.9817	.9933	0.999167	1.0000000	.0000000
Westinghouse	.4392	.7320	.8847	.9503	.9765	.9903	0.997928	0.9986188	.0013812
Woolworth	0.4969	0.7668	0.8844	0.9474	0.9737	0.9841	0.996540	0.9986159	0.0013841
Averages	0.4667	0.7469	0.8847	0.9478	0.9756	0.9886	0.996959	0.9988368	0.0011632

given interval. For example, the number in column (5) opposite Allied Chemical implies that about 1.21 per cent less total frequency is within 2.5 standard deviations of the mean than would be expected under the Gaussian hypothesis. This means there is about twice as much frequency beyond 2.5 standard deviations deviations than would be expected under the Gaussian hypothesis. In columns (4) through (8) the overwhelming preponderance of negative numbers indicates that there is a general deficiency of relative frequency within any interval 2 to 5 standard deviations from the mean and thus a general excess of relative fre-

TABLE 2

COMPARISON OF EMPIRICAL FREQUENCY DISTRIBUTIONS WITH UNIT NORMAL

STOCK	INTERVALS								
	0.5 S (1)	1.0 S (2)	1.5 S (3)	2.0S (4)	2.5 S (5)	3.0 S (6)	4.0 S (7)	5.0 S (8)	>5.0 S (9)
Allied Chemical	0.0765	0.0623	0.0118	0.0005	—0.0121	—0.0104	—0.003209	—0.0016347	0.0016347
Alcoa	.0548	.0434	.0042	— .0125	— .0111	— .0032	.000062	.0000006	— .0000006
American Can	.1108	.0669	.0319	— .0054	— .0204	— .0129	— .004860	— .0024604	.0024604
A.T.&T.	.1994	.1336	.0573	.0037	— .0081	— .0112	— .007321	— .0049215	.0049215
American Tobacco	.1564	.0992	.0229	— .0083	— .0172	— .0129	— .005394	— .0031171	.0031171
Anaconda	.0470	.0249	.0121	— .0023	— .0119	— .0040	— .000776	.0000006	— .0000006
Bethlehem Steel	.0962	.0524	.0186	— .0062	— .0126	— .0098	— .003271	— .0008327	.0008327
Chrysler	.0520	.0438	.0130	— .0059	— .0095	— .0068	— .002302	— .0005904	.0005904
Du Pont	.0506	.0431	.0161	— .0076	— .0101	— .0037	— .002351	— .0008039	.0008039
Eastman Kodak	.0580	.0646	.0116	— .0078	— .0142	— .0078	— .001553	— .0016149	.0016149
General Electric	.0801	.0634	.0107	— .0118	— .0100	— .0103	— .002891	— .0005901	.0005901
General Foods	.0659	.0667	.0207	— .0078	— .0125	— .0129	— .002069	— .0007096	.0007096
General Motors	.0886	.0629	.0195	.0026	— .0083	— .0063	— .004087	— .0020749	.0020741
Goodyear	.0808	.0661	.0234	— .0035	— .0022	— .0059	— .003380	— .0017206	.0017206
International Harvester	.0578	.0624	.0303	— .0070	— .0126	— .0098	— .003271	— .0008327	.0008327
International Nickel	.0892	.0809	.0169	— .0132	— .0190	— .0102	— .004765	.0000006	— .0000006
International Paper	.0614	.0672	.0078	— .0112	— .0118	— .0104	— .003393	.0000006	— .0000006
Johns Manville	.0535	.0551	.0066	— .0059	— .0067	— .0064	— .002428	— .0008293	.0008293
Owens Illinois	.0948	.0563	.0245	— .0078	— .0159	— .0135	— .002363	— .0008078	.0008078
Procter & Gamble	.1187	.0880	.0223	— .0167	— .0166	— .0111	— .004084	— .0013822	.0013822
Sears	.1558	.1030	.0537	— .0055	— .0175	— .0143	— .006411	— .0040447	.0040447
Standard Oil (Calif.)	.0754	.0522	.0060	— .0106	— .0112	— .0056	— .002891	— .0005901	.0005901
Standard Oil (N.J.)	.1204	.0925	.0289	.0014	— .0109	— .0077	— .002533	— .0017295	.0017295
Swift & Co.	.0817	.0650	.0153	— .0140	— .0173	— .0097	— .002704	.0000006	— .0000006
Texaco	.0769	.0456	.0033	— .0028	— .0126	— .0094	— .001664	.0000006	— .0000006
Union Carbide	.0338	.0365	.0119	— .0144	— .0091	— .0027	— .000832	.0000006	— .0000006
United Aircraft	.0753	.0657	.0194	— .0045	— .0068	— .0065	— .002438	— .0008327	.0008327
U.S. Steel	.0295	.0107	.0094	— .0037	— .0059	— .0040	— .000771	.0000006	— .0000006
Westinghouse	.0562	.0494	.0183	— .0042	— .0111	— .0070	— .002010	— .0013806	.0013806
Woolworth	0.1139	0.0842	0.0180	—0.0071	—0.0139	—0.0132	—0.003398	—0.0013835	0.0013835
Averages	0.0837	0.0636	0.0183	—0.0066	—0.0120	—0.0086	—0.002979	—0.0011632	—0.0011632

than would be expected if the distribution were normal.

The most striking feature of the tables is the presence of some degree of leptokurtosis for every stock. In every case the empirical distributions are more peaked in the center and have longer tails than the normal distribution. The pattern is best illustrated in Table 2. In columns (1), (2), and (3) all the numbers are positive, implying that in the empirical distributions there are more observations within 0.5, 1.0, and 1.5 standard quency beyond these points. In column (9) twenty-two out of thirty of the numbers are positive, pointing to a general excess of relative frequency greater than five standard deviations from the mean.

At first glance it may seem that the absolute size of the deviations from normality reported in Table 2 is not important. For example, the last line of the table tells us that the excess of relative frequency beyond five standard deviations from the mean is, on the average, about 0.12 per cent. This is misleading, however, since under the Gaussian hypothesis the total predicted relative frequency beyond five standard deviations is 0.00006 per cent. Thus the actual *excess* frequency is 2,000 times larger than the total expected frequency.

Figure 1 provides a better insight into the nature of the departures from normality in the empirical distributions. The dashed curve represents the unit normal density function, whereas the solid curve represents the general shape of the empirical distributions. A consistent departure from normality is the excess of observations within one-half standard deviation of the mean. On the average there is 8.4 per cent too much relative frequency in this interval. The curves of the empirical density functions are above the curve for the normal distribution. Before 1.0 standard deviation from the mean, however, the empirical curves cut down through the normal curve from above. Although there is a general excess of relative frequency within 1.0 standard deviation, in twenty-four out of thirty cases the excess is not as great as that within one-half standard deviation. Thus the empirical relative frequency between 0.5 and 1.0 standard deviations must be less than would be expected under the Gaussian hypothesis.

Somewhere between 1.5 and 2.0 standard deviations from the mean the empirical curves again cross through the normal curve, this time from below. This is indicated by the fact that in the empirical distributions there is a consistent deficiency of relative frequency within 2.0, 2.5, 3.0, 4.0, and 5.0 standard deviations, implying that there is too much relative frequency beyond these intervals. This is, of course, what is meant by long tails.

The results in Tables 1 and 2 can be cast into a different and perhaps more illuminating form. In sampling from a normal distribution the probability that an observation will be more than two standard deviations from the mean is 0.04550. In a sample of size N the expected number of observations more than two standard deviations from the mean is $N \times 0.04550$. Similarly, the expected numbers greater than three, four, and five standard deviations from the mean are, respectively, $N \times 0.0027$, $N \times 0.000063$, and $N \times 0.0000006$. Following this procedure Table 3 shows for each

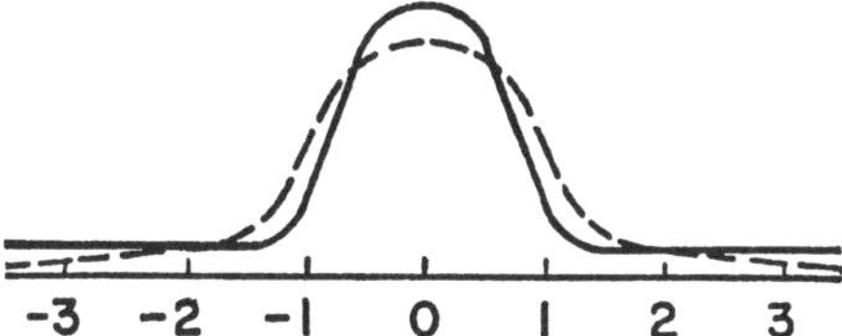

FIG. 1.—Comparison of empirical and unit normal probability distributions.

stock the expected and actual *numbers* of observations greater than 2, 3, 4, and 5 standard deviations from their means.

The results are consistent and impressive. Beyond three standard deviations there should only be, on the average, three to four observations per security. The actual numbers range from six to twenty-three. Even for the sample sizes under consideration the expected number of observations more than four standard deviations from the mean is only about 0.10 per security. In fact for all stocks but one there is at least one observation greater than four standard deviations from the mean, with one stock having as many as nine observations in this range.

In simpler terms, if the population of price changes is strictly normal, on the average for any given stock we would expect an observation greater than 4 standard deviations from the mean about once every fifty years. In fact observations this extreme are observed about four times in every five-year period. Similarly, under the Gaussian hypothesis for any given stock an observation more than five standard deviations from the mean should be observed about once every 7,000 years. In fact such observations seem to occur about once every three to four years.

These results can be put into the form of a significance test. Tippet [44] in 1925 calculated the distribution of the largest value in samples of size 3–1,000 from a normal population. In Table 4 his results for $N = 1{,}000$ have been used to find the approximate significance levels of the most extreme positive and negative first differences of log price for each stock. The significance levels are only approximate because the actual sample sizes are greater than 1,000. The effect of this is

TABLE 3

ANALYSIS OF EXTREME TAIL AREAS IN TERMS OF NUMBER OF OBSERVATIONS RATHER THAN RELATIVE FREQUENCIES

Stock	N*	Interval							
		>2 S		>3 S		>4 S		>5 S	
		Expected No.	Actual No.	Expected No.	Actual No.	Expected No.	Actual No.	Expected No.	Actual No.
Allied Chemical	1,223	55.5	55	3.3	16	0.08	4	0.0007	2
Alcoa	1,190	54.1	69	3.2	7	.07	0	.0007	0
American Can	1,219	55.5	62	3.3	19	.08	6	.0007	3
A.T.&T.	1,219	55.5	51	3.3	17	.08	9	.0007	6
American Tobacco	1,283	58.4	69	3.5	20	.08	7	.0008	4
Anaconda	1,193	54.3	57	3.2	8	.08	1	.0007	0
Bethlehem Steel	1,200	54.6	62	3.2	15	.08	4	.0007	1
Chrysler	1,692	77.0	87	4.6	16	.11	4	.0010	1
Du Pont	1,243	56.6	66	3.4	8	.08	3	.0007	1
Eastman Kodak	1,238	56.3	66	3.3	13	.08	2	.0007	2
General Electric	1,693	77.0	97	4.6	22	.11	5	.0010	1
General Foods	1,408	64.1	75	3.8	22	.09	3	.0008	1
General Motors	1,446	65.8	62	3.9	13	.09	6	.0009	3
Goodyear	1,162	52.9	57	3.1	10	.07	4	.0007	2
International Harvester	1,200	54.6	63	3.2	15	.08	4	.0007	1
International Nickel	1,243	56.5	73	3.4	16	.08	6	.0007	0
International Paper	1,447	65.8	82	3.9	19	.09	5	.0009	0
Johns Manville	1,205	54.8	62	3.2	11	.08	3	.0007	1
Owens Illinois	1,237	56.3	66	3.3	20	.08	3	.0007	1
Procter & Gamble	1,447	65.8	90	3.9	20	.09	6	.0009	2
Sears	1,236	56.2	63	3.3	21	.08	8	.0007	5
Standard Oil (Calif.)	1,693	77.0	95	4.6	14	.11	5	.0010	1
Standard Oil (N.J.)	1,156	52.5	51	3.1	12	.07	3	.0007	2
Swift & Co.	1,446	65.8	86	3.9	18	.09	4	.0009	0
Texaco	1,159	52.7	56	3.1	14	.07	2	.0007	0
Union Carbide	1,118	50.9	67	3.0	6	.07	1	.0007	0
United Aircraft	1,200	54.6	60	3.2	11	.08	3	.0007	1
U.S. Steel	1,200	54.6	59	3.2	8	.08	1	.0007	0
Westinghouse	1,448	65.9	72	3.9	14	.09	3	.0009	2
Woolworth	1,445	65.7	78	3.9	23	0.09	5	0.0009	2
Totals	....	1,787.4	2,058	105.8	448	2.51	120	0.0233	45

* Total sample size.

to overestimate the significance level, since in samples of 1,300 an extreme value greater than a given size is more probable than in samples of 1,000. In most cases, however, the error introduced in this way will affect at most the third decimal place and hence is negligible in the present context.

Columns (1) and (4) in Table 4 show the most extreme negative and positive changes in log price for each stock. Columns (2) and (5) show these values measured in units of standard deviations from their means. Columns (3) and (6) show the significance levels of the extreme values. The significance levels should be interpreted as follows: in samples of 1,000 observations from a normal population on the average in a proportion P of all samples, the most extreme value of a given tail would be smaller in absolute value than the extreme value actually observed.

As would be expected from previous discussions, the significance levels in Table 4 are very high, implying that the observed extreme values are much more extreme than would be predicted by the Gaussian hypothesis.

D. NORMAL PROBABILITY GRAPHS

Another sensitive tool for examining departures from normality is probability graphing. If u is a Gaussian random variable with mean μ and variance σ^2, the standardized variable

$$z = \frac{u - \mu}{\sigma} \qquad (2)$$

TABLE 4

SIGNIFICANCE TESTS FOR EXTREME VALUES

Stock	Smallest Value (1)	Standardized Variable (2)	P (3)	Largest Value (4)	Standardized Variable (5)	P (6)
Allied Chemical	−0.07178	− 5.012	0.99971	0.08377	5.820	0.99999
Alcoa	− .05314	− 3.381	0.71391	.06188	3.945	0.95304
American Can	− .06230	− 5.446	0.99997	.06752	5.853	0.99999
A.T.&T.	− .10376	−10.342	1.00000	.09890	9.724	1.00000
American Tobacco	− .08004	− 6.678	1.00000	.07238	5.949	0.99999
Anaconda	− .05733	− 3.851	0.93020	.06004	4.015	0.96882
Bethlehem Steel	− .07250	− 5.571	0.99999	.06195	4.748	0.99870
Chrysler	− .08049	− 4.660	0.99870	.10085	5.853	0.99999
Du Pont	− .05990	− 5.843	0.99999	.05148	4.950	0.99952
Eastman Kodak	− .04434	− 3.399	0.71391	.07788	5.832	0.99999
General Electric	− .06466	− 5.135	0.99983	.05647	4.456	0.99460
General Foods	− .04683	− 3.937	0.95304	.06246	5.065	0.99983
General Motors	− .09764	− 7.761	1.00000	.08292	6.547	1.00000
Goodyear	− .09459	− 5.919	0.99999	.17435	10.879	1.00000
International Harvester	− .08701	− 6.290	0.99999	.06870	4.880	0.99952
International Nickel	− .05917	− 4.917	0.99952	.05670	4.628	0.99789
International Paper	− .05072	− 4.219	0.98674	.05327	4.454	0.99460
Johns Manville	− .06868	− 4.386	0.99460	.11935	7.575	1.00000
Owens Illinois	− .06372	− 5.195	0.99990	.06062	4.881	0.99952
Procter & Gamble	− .06351	− 5.504	0.99998	.06560	5.559	0.99998
Sears	− .10728	− 9.338	1.00000	.06062	5.148	0.99983
Standard Oil (Calif.)	− .06333	− 4.793	0.99921	.06738	5.056	0.99983
Standard Oil (N.J.)	− .10318	− 9.275	1.00000	.10073	9.013	1.00000
Swift & Co.	− .06752	− 4.761	0.99921	.06283	4.418	0.99460
Texaco	− .05932	− 4.650	0.99789	.05476	4.193	0.98674
Union Carbide	− .04556	− 4.396	0.99460	.03943	3.783	0.93020
United Aircraft	− .15234	− 8.878	1.00000	.08490	4.939	0.99952
U.S. Steel	− .05386	− 3.968	0.96882	.05550	4.091	0.97955
Westinghouse	− .08037	− 5.415	0.99997	.08630	5.808	0.99999
Woolworth	−0.06744	− 5.890	0.99999	0.08961	7.743	1.00000

will be unit normal. Since z is just a linear transformation of u, the graph of z against u is just a straight line

The relationship between z and u can be used to detect departures from normality in the distribution of u. If u_i, $i = 1, \ldots, N$ are N sample values of the variable u arranged in ascending order, then a particular u_i is an estimate of the f fractile of the distribution of u, where the value of f is given by[20]

$$f = \frac{(3i-1)}{(3N+1)}. \qquad (3)$$

Now the exact value of z for the f fractile of the unit normal distribution need not be estimated from the sample data. It can be found easily either in any standard table or (much more rapidly) by computer. If u is a Gaussian random variable, then a graph of the *sample* values of u against the values of z derived from the *theoretical* unit normal cumulative distribution function (c.d.f.) should be a straight line. There may, of course, be some departures from linearity due to sampling error. If the departures from linearity are extreme, however, the Gaussian hypothesis for the distribution of u should be questioned.

The procedure described above is called normal probability graphing. A normal probability graph has been constructed for each of the stocks used in this report, with u equal, of course, to the daily first difference of log price. The graphs are found in Figure 2.

The scales of the graphs in Figure 2 are determined by the two most extreme values of u and z. The origin of each graph is the point (u_{min}, z_{min}), where u_{min} and z_{min} are the minimum values of u and z for the particular stock. The last point in the upper right-hand corner of each graph is (u_{max}, z_{max}). Thus if the Gaussian hypothesis is valid, the plot of z against u should for each security approximately trace a 45° straight line from the origin.[21]

Several comments concerning the graphs can be made immediately. First, probability graphing is just another way of examining an empirical frequency distribution, and there is a direct relationship between the frequency distributions examined earlier and the normal probability graphs. When the tails of empirical frequency distributions are longer than those of the normal distribution, the slopes in the extreme tail areas of the normal probability graphs should be lower than those in the central parts of the graphs, and this is in fact the case. That is, the graphs in general take the shape of an elongated S with the curvature at the top and bottom varying directly with the excess of relative frequency in the tails of the empirical distribution.

Second, this tendency for the extreme tails to show lower slopes than the main portions of the graphs will be accentuated by the fact that the central bells of the empirical frequency distributions are higher than those of a normal distribution. In this situation the central portions of the normal probability graphs should be steeper than would be the case

[20] This particular convention for estimating f is only one of many that are available. Other popular conventions are $i/(N+1)$, $(i-\frac{3}{8})/(N+\frac{1}{4})$, and $(i-\frac{1}{2})/N$. All four techniques give reasonable estimates of the fractiles, and with the large samples of this report, it makes very little difference which specific convention is chosen. For a discussion see E. J. Gumbel [20, p. 15] or Gunnar Blom [8, pp. 138–46].

[21] The reader should note that the origin of every graph is an actual sample point, even if it is not always visible in the graphs because it falls at the point of intersection of the two axes. It is probably of interest to note that the graphs in Figure 2 were produced by the cathode ray tube of the University of Chicago's I.B.M. 7094 computer.

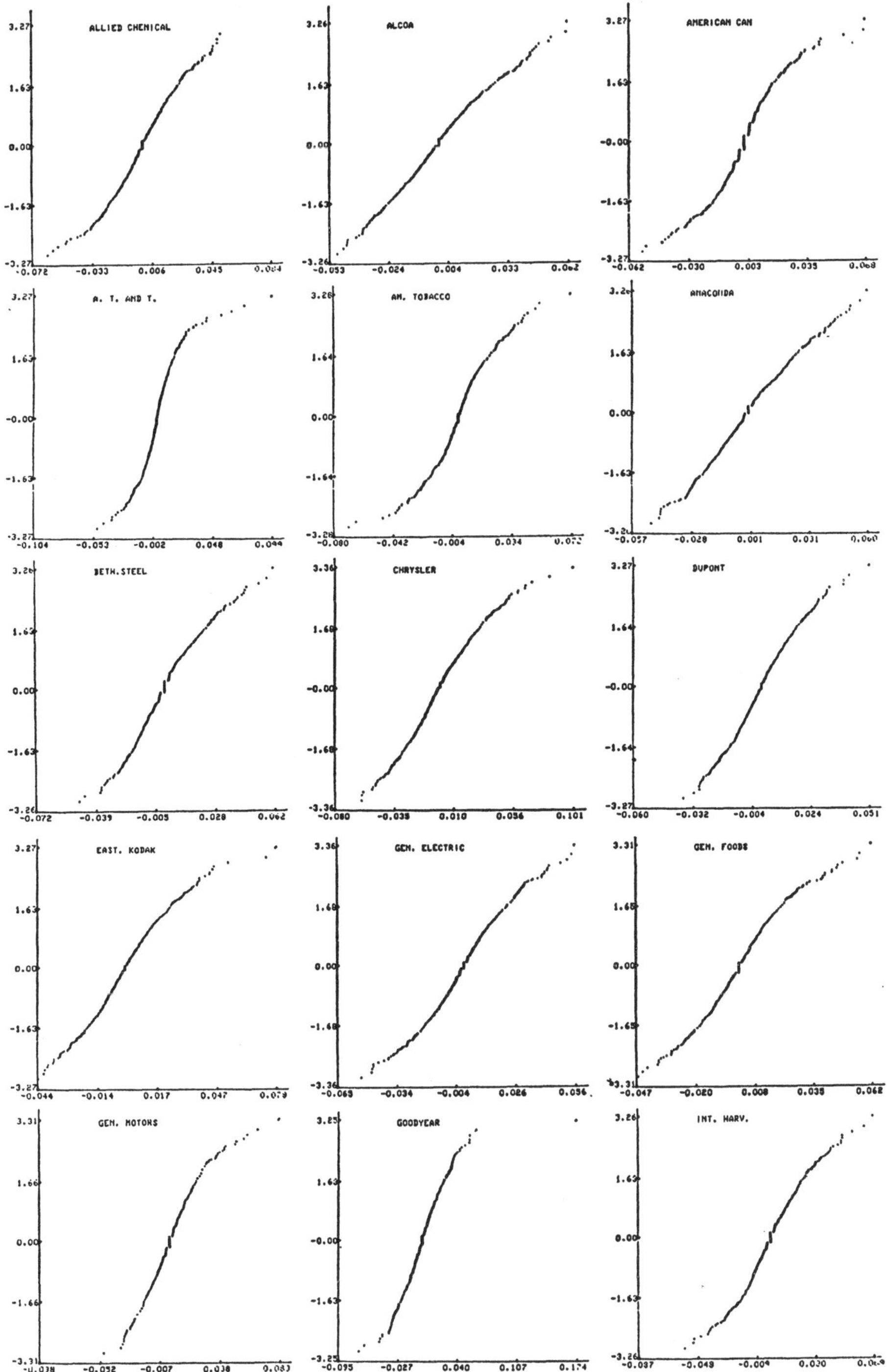

FIG. 2.—Normal probability graphs for daily changes in log price of each security. Horizontal axes of graphs show u, values of the daily changes in log price; vertical axes show z, values of the unit normal variable at different estimated fractile points.

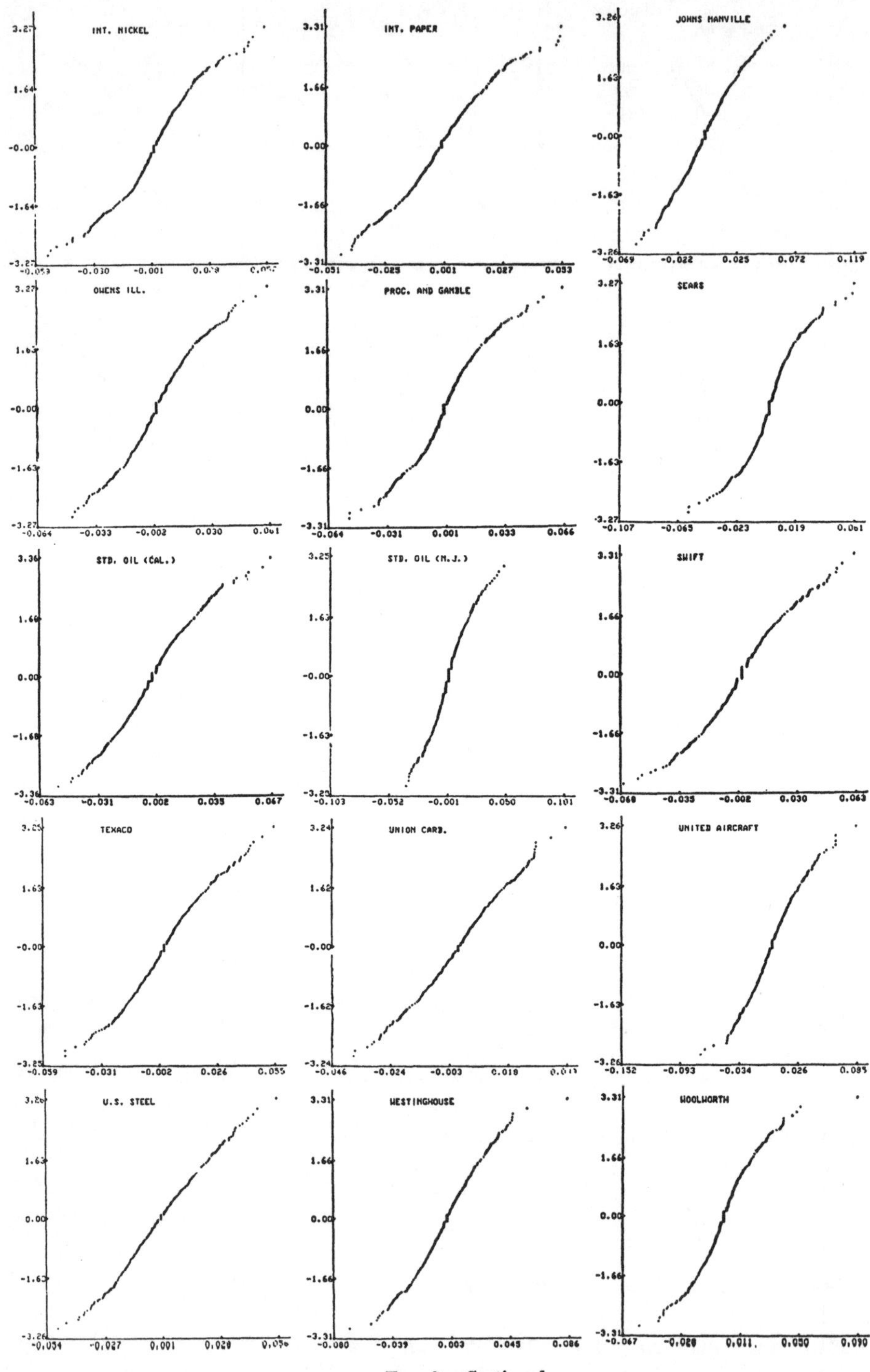

FIG. 2.—*Continued*

if the underlying distributions were strictly normal. This sort of departure from normality is evident in the graphs.

Finally, before the advent of the Mandelbrot hypothesis, some of our normal probability graphs would have been considered acceptable within a hypothesis of "approximate" normality. This is true, for example, for Anaconda and Alcoa. It is not true, however, for most of the graphs. The tail behavior of stocks such as American Telephone and Telegraph and Sears is clearly inconsistent with any simple normality hypothesis. The emphasis is on the word simple. The natural next step is to consider complications of the Gaussian model that could give rise to departures from normality of the type encountered.

E. TWO POSSIBLE ALTERNATIVE EXPLANATIONS OF DEPARTURES FROM NORMALITY

1. MIXTURE OF DISTRIBUTIONS

Perhaps the most popular approach to explaining long-tailed distributions has been to hypothesize that the distribution of price changes is actually a mixture of several normal distributions with possibly the same mean, but substantially different variances. There are, of course, many possible variants of this line of attack, and little can be done to test them unless the investigator is prepared to specify some details of the mechanism instead of merely talking vaguely of "contamination." One such plausible mechanism is the following suggested by Lawrence Fisher of the Graduate School of Business, University of Chicago.

It is possible that the relevant unit of time for the generation of information bearing on stock prices is the chronological day rather than the trading day. Political and economic news, after all, occurs continuously, and if it is assimilated continuously by investors, the variance of the distribution of price changes between two points in time would possibly be proportional to the actual number of days elapsed rather than to the number of trading days. Thus in our tests a mixture of distributions would be produced by the fact that changes in log price from Friday (close) to Monday (close) involve three chronological days while the changes during the week involve only one chronological day.

To test this hypothesis, eleven stocks were randomly chosen from the sample of thirty, and for each stock two arrays were set up. One array contained changes involving only one chronological day. These are, of course, the daily changes from Monday to Friday of each week. The other array contained changes involving more than one chronological day. These include Friday-to-Monday changes and changes across holidays

Table 5 gives a comparison of the total variances for each type of price change. Column (1) shows the variances for changes involving one chronological day. Column (2) contains the variances for weekend and holiday changes. Column (3) shows the ratio of column (2) to column (1). If the chronological day rather than the trading day were the relevant unit of time, then, according to the well-known law for the variance of sums of independent variables, the variance of the weekend and holiday changes should be a little less than three times the variance of the day-to-day changes within the week. It should be a little less than three because three days pass between Friday (close) and Monday (close), but holidays normally involve a lapse of only two days. Actually, however, it turns out that the weekend and holiday variance is not three times but only about 22 per cent greater than the within week variance—a rather small discrepancy.[22]

However, for the moment let us continue under the assumption that the weekend and holiday changes and the changes within the week come from different normal distributions. This implies that the normal probability graphs for the weekend and daily changes should each be straight lines, even though the combined distributions plot as elongated S's. In fact when the within-week and weekend changes were plotted separately, the graphs turned out to be of exactly the same form as the graph for the two distributions combined. The same departures from normality were present and the same elongated S shapes occurred.

As an example, Figure 3 shows three normal probability graphs for Procter and Gamble.[23] The first shows the graph of the first differences of log price for daily changes within the week. The second is the graph of Friday-to-Monday changes and of changes across holidays. The third is the combined graph for changes where the differencing interval is the trading day and chronological time is ignored.

The conclusion drawn from the above discussion is that it makes no substantial difference whether weekend and holiday changes are considered separately or together with the daily changes within the week. The nature of the tails of the distribution seems the same under each type of analysis.

TABLE 5

VARIANCE COMPARISON OF DAILY AND WEEKEND CHANGES

Stock	Daily Variance (1)	Weekend Variance (2)	Weekend Variance/ Daily Variance (3)
Alcoa	0.000247	0.000252	1.020
A.T.&T.	.000091	.000105	1.154
Anaconda	.000212	.000252	1.189
Chrysler	.000278	.000363	1.306
International Harvester	.000186	.000226	1.215
International Nickel	.000146	.000145	0.993
Procter & Gamble	.000125	.000178	1.424
Standard Oil (Calif.)	.000162	.000215	1.327
Standard Oil (N.J.)	.000114	.000153	1.342
Texaco	.000153	.000209	1.366
U.S. Steel	0.000176	0.000198	1.125

2. CHANGING PARAMETERS

Another popular explanation of long-tailed empirical distributions is non-stationarity. It may be that the distribution of price changes at any point in time is normal, but across time the parameters

[22] The relative unimportance of the weekend effect is also documented, in a different way, by Godfrey, Granger, and Morgenstern [18.]

[23] The reader will note that the normal probability graphs of Figure 3 (and also Figure 4) follow the more popular convention of showing the c.d.f. on the vertical axis rather than the standardized variable z. Since there is a one-to-one correspondence between values of z and points on the c.d.f., from a theoretical standpoint it is a matter of indifference as to which variable is shown on the vertical axis. From a practical standpoint, however, when the graphs are done by hand it is easier to use "probability paper" and the c.d.f. When the graphs are done by computer, it is easier to use the standardized variable z.

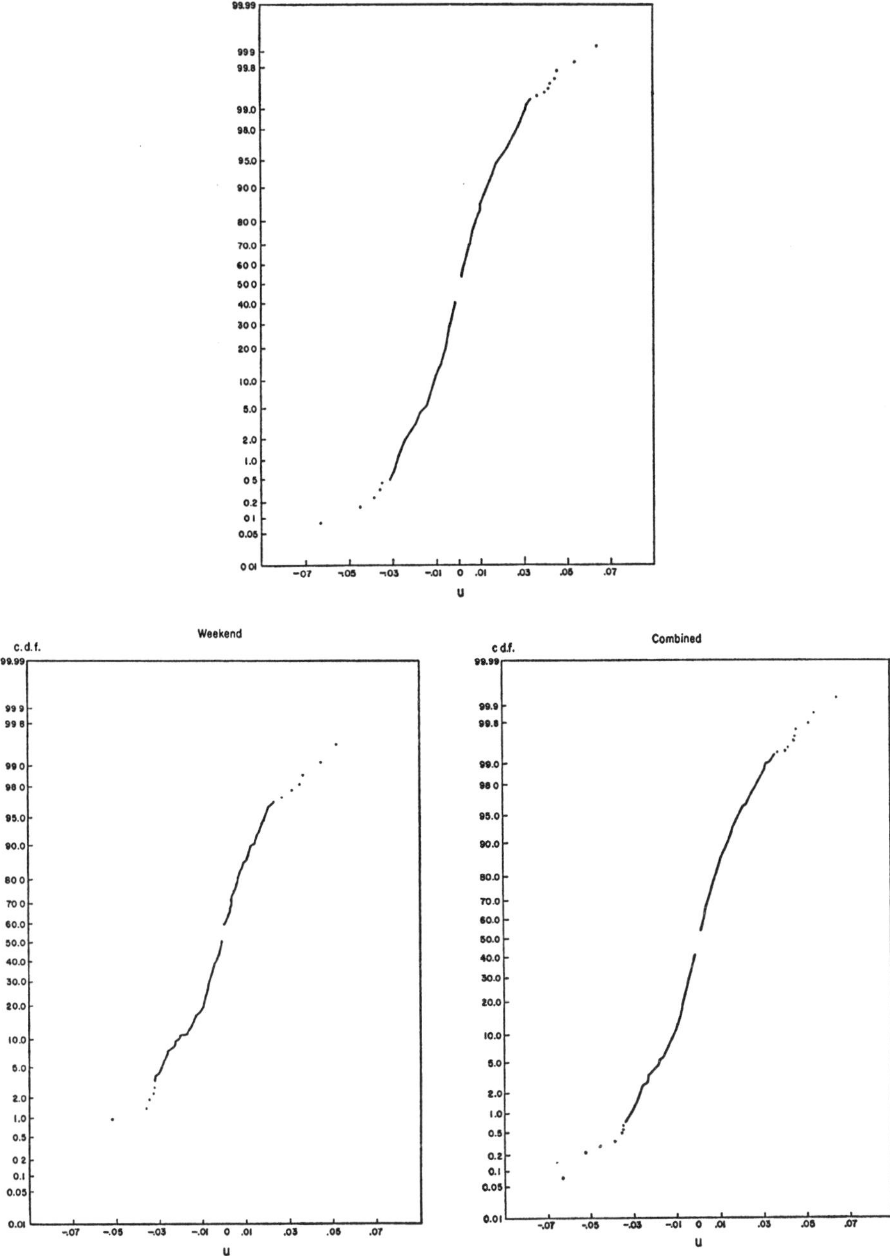

FIG. 3.—Daily, weekend, and combined normal probability graphs for Procter & Gamble. Horizontal axes show u, values of the daily changes in log price; vertical axes show fractiles of the c.d.f.

of the distribution change. A company may become more or less risky, and this may bring about a shift in the variance of the first differences. Similarly, the mean of the first differences can change across time as the company's prospects for future profits follow different paths. This paper will consider only changes in the mean.

If a shift in the mean change in log price of a daily series is to persist for any length of time, it must be small, unless the eventual change in price is to be astronomical. For example, a stock's price will double in less than four months if the mean of the daily changes in log price shifts from zero to 0.01. It is not that large changes in the mean are uninteresting. It is just that unless the eventual price change is to be phenomenal, a large change in the mean will not persist long enough to be identified. The basic problem is one of identification. "Trends" that do not last very long are numerous. It is usually difficult to explain these short "trends" plausibly whether the eventual price change is large or small. On the other hand, changes in the mean that persist are presumably identifiable by their very persistence. It is not particularly unreasonable to treat a period of, say, a year or more that shows a fairly steady trend differently from other periods.

In an effort to test the non-stationarity hypothesis, five stocks were chosen which seemed to show changes in trend that persisted for rather long periods of time during the period covered by this study.[24] "Trends" were "identified" simply by examining a graph of the stock's price during the sampling period. The procedure, though widely practiced, is of course completely arbitrary.

The results, however, are quite interesting. For each stock, normal probability graphs were constructed for each separate trend period. In all cases the results were the same; each of the subperiods of different apparent trend showed exactly the same type of tail behavior as the total sample of price changes for the stock for the entire sampling period.

As an example three normal probability graphs for American Telephone and Telegraph are presented in Figure 4. The first covers the time period November 25, 1957–December 11, 1961, when the mean of the distribution of first differences of log price was 0.00107. The second covers the period December 11, 1961–September 24, 1962, when the mean was —0.00061. The third is the graph of the total sample with over-all mean 0.000652. As was typical of all the stocks the graphs are extremely similar. The same type of elongated **S** appears in all three.

Thus it seems that the behavior of the distribution in the tails is independent of the mean. This is not really a very unusual result. A change in the mean, if it is to persist, must be rather small. In particular the shift is small relative to the largest values of a random variable from a long-tailed distribution.

It is true that we have only considered changes in the mean that persist for fairly long periods of time, and this is a possible shortcoming of the preceding tests. It is also true, however, that any distribution, no matter how wild, can be represented as a mixture of normals if one is willing to postulate many short-lived periods of non-stationarity. One of the main sources of appeal of Mandelbrot's model, however, is that it is capable of explaining both periods of turbu-

[24] The stocks chosen were American Can, American Telephone and Telegraph, American Tobacco, Procter and Gamble, and Sears.

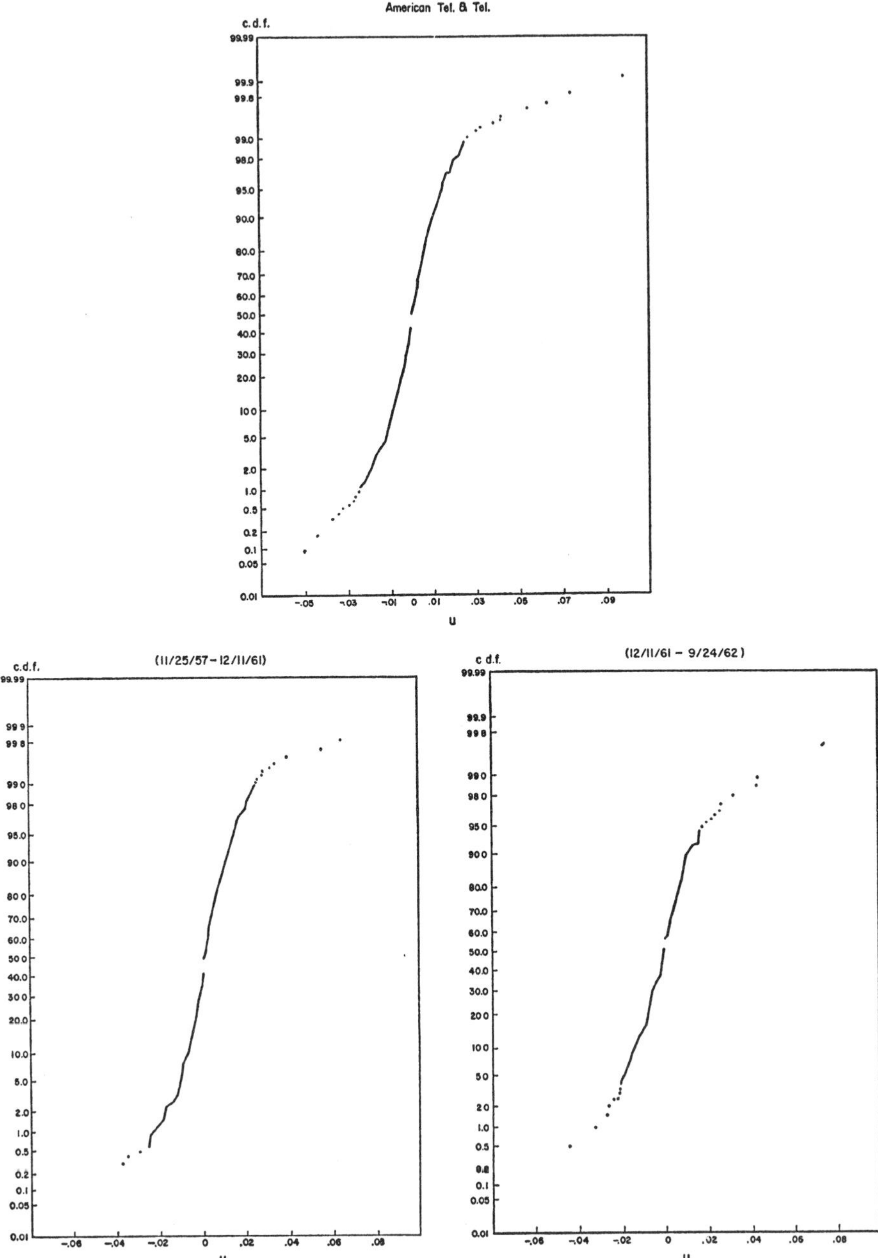

FIG. 4.—Normal probability graphs for American Telephone and Telegraph for different time periods. Horizontal axes of graphs show u, values of the daily changes in log price; vertical axes show fractiles of the c.d.f.

lence and periods of calm, without resorting to non-stationarity arguments.

F. CONCLUSION

The main result of this section is that the departures from normality in the distributions of the first differences of the logarithms of stock prices are in the direction predicted by the Mandelbrot hypothesis. Moreover, the two more complicated versions of the Gaussian model that were examined are incapable of explaining the departures. In the next section further tests will be used to decide whether the departures from normality are sufficient to warrant rejection of the Gaussian hypothesis.

IV. A Closer Look at the Empirical Distributions

The first step in this section will be to test whether the distributions of price changes have the crucial property of stability. If stability seems to hold, the problem will have been reduced to deciding whether the characteristic exponent α of the underlying stable Paretian process is less than 2, as assumed by the Mandelbrot hypothesis, or equal to 2 as assumed by the Gaussian hypothesis.

A. STABILITY

By definition, stable Paretian distributions are stable or invariant under addition. That is, except for origin and scale, sums of independent, identically distributed, stable Paretian variables have the same distribution as the individual summands. Hence, if successive daily changes in stock prices follow a stable Paretian distribution, changes across longer intervals such as a week or a month will follow stable Paretian distributions of exactly the same form.[25] Most simply this means that the characteristic exponent α of the weekly and monthly distributions will be the same as the characteristic exponent of the distribution of the daily changes.

Thus the most direct way to test stability would be to estimate α for various differencing intervals to see if the same value holds in each case. Unfortunately, this direct approach is not feasible. We shall see later that in order to make reasonable estimates of α very large samples are required. Though the samples of *daily* price changes used in this report will probably be sufficiently large, the sampling period covered is not long enough to make reliable estimates of α for differencing intervals longer than a single day.

The situation is not hopeless, however. We can develop an alternative, though cruder and more indirect, way of testing stability by making use of certain properties of the parameter α. The characteristic exponent α of a stable Paretian distribution determines the length or height of the extreme tails of the distribution. Thus, if α has the same value for different distributions, the behavior of the extreme tails of the distributions should be at least roughly similar.

A sensitive technique for examining the tails of distributions is normal probability graphing. As explained in Section III, the normal probability plot of ranked values of a Gaussian variable will be a straight line. Since the Gaussian distribution is stable, sums of Gaussian variables will also plot as a straight line on a normal probability graph. A stable Paretian distribution with $\alpha < 2$ has longer tails than a Gaussian distribution, however, and thus its normal probability graph will have the appearance of an elongated S, with the degree of curvature in the extreme tails larger the smaller the value of α. Sums of such variables

[25] Weekly and monthly changes in log price are, of course, just sums of daily changes.

should also plot as elongated S's with roughly the same degree of curvature as the graph of the individual summands.

Thus if successive daily changes in log price for a given security follow a stable Paretian distribution with characteristic exponent $\alpha < 2$, the normal probability graph for the changes should have the appearance of an elongated S. Since, by the property of stability, the value of α will be the same for distributions involving differencing intervals longer than a single day, the normal probability graphs for these longer differencing intervals should also have the appearance of elongated S's with about the same degree of curvature in the extreme tails as the graph for the daily changes.

A normal probability graph for the distribution of changes in log price across successive, non-overlapping periods of four trading days has been plotted for each stock. The graphs for four companies (American Tobacco, Eastman Kodak, International Nickel, and Woolworth) are shown in Figure 5. In each case the graph for the four-day changes in Figure 5 seems, except for scale, almost indistinguishable from the corresponding graph for the daily changes in Figure 2. On this basis we conclude that the assumption of stability seems to be justified. The problem in the remainder of Section IV will be to decide whether the underlying stable Paretian process has characteristic exponent less than 2, as proposed by the Mandelbrot hypothesis, or equal to 2, as proposed by the Gaussian hypothesis.

Unfortunately, however, estimation of α is not a simple problem. In most cases there are no known explicit density functions for the stable Paretian distributions, and thus there is virtually no sam-

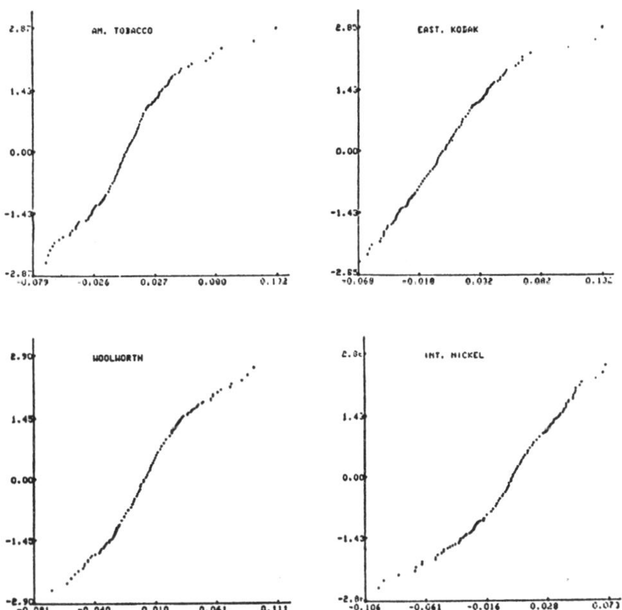

FIG. 5.—Normal probability graphs for price changes across four trading days. Horizontal axes show u, values of the changes in log price; vertical axes show z, the values of the unit normal variable at different estimated fractile points.

pling theory available. Because of this the best that can be done is to make as many different estimates of α as possible in an attempt to bracket the true value. In the remainder of Section IV three different techniques will be used to estimate α. First, each technique will be examined in detail, and then a comparison of the results will be made.

B. ESTIMATING α FROM DOUBLE-LOG AND PROBABILITY GRAPHS

If the distribution of the random variable u is stable Paretian with characteristic exponent $0 < \alpha < 2$, its tails follow an asymptotic form of the law of Pareto such that

$$\begin{aligned} Pr(u > \hat{u}) &\rightarrow (\hat{u}/U_1)^{-\alpha}, \ \hat{u} > 0\,, \quad \text{and} \\ Pr(u < \hat{u}) &\rightarrow (|\hat{u}|/U_2)^{-\alpha}, \ \hat{u} < 0\,, \end{aligned} \qquad (4)$$

where U_1 and U_2 are constants and the symbol $\rightarrow$ means that the ratio[26]

$$\frac{Pr(u > \hat{u})}{(u/U_1)^{-\alpha}} \rightarrow 1 \quad \text{as} \quad \hat{u} \rightarrow \infty\,.$$

Taking logarithms in expression (4) we have,

$$\log Pr(u > \hat{u}) \rightarrow -\alpha(\log \hat{u} - \log U_1)\,,$$

$$\text{and} \quad \log Pr(u < \hat{u}) \qquad (5)$$

$$\rightarrow -\alpha(\log |u| - \log U_2)\,.$$

Expression (5) implies that if $Pr(u > \hat{u})$ and $Pr(u < \hat{u})$ are plotted against $|\hat{u}|$ on double-log paper, the two curves should become asymptotically straight and have slope that approaches $-\alpha$ as $|\hat{u}|$ approaches infinity. Thus double-log graphing is one technique for estimating α. Unfortunately it is not very powerful if α is close to 2.[27] If the distribution is normal (i.e., $\alpha = 2$), $Pr(u > \hat{u})$ decreases faster than $|u|$ increases, and the slope of the graph of $\log Pr\ (u > \hat{u})$ against $\log |\hat{u}|$ will approach $-\infty$. Thus the law of Pareto does not hold even asymptotically for the normal distribution.

When α is less than 2 the law of Pareto will hold, but on the double-log graph the true asymptotic slope will only be observed within a tail area containing total probability $p_0(\alpha)$ that is smaller the larger the value of α. This is demonstrated in Figure 6[28] which shows plots of log

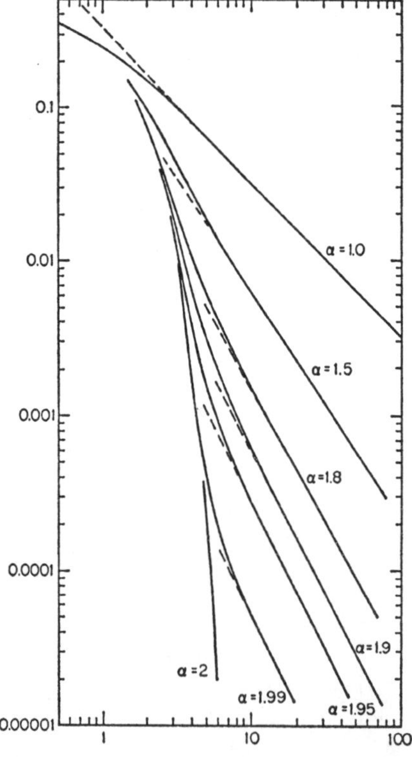

FIG. 6.—Double-log graphs for symmetric stable Paretian variables with different values of α. The various lines are double-log plots of the symmetric stable Paretian probability distributions with $\delta = 0$, $\gamma = 1$, $\beta = 0$ and various values of α. Horizontal axis shows $\log u$; vertical axis shows $\log Pr(u > u)$ $\log Pr(u < -u)$. Taken from Mandelbrot [37, p. 402].

[26] Thus we see that the name stable Paretian for these distributions arises from the property of stability and the asymptotically Paretian nature of the extreme tail areas.

[27] Cf. Mandelbrot [35].

[28] Taken from Mandelbrot [37], p. 402.

$Pr(u > \hat{u})$ against log $|\hat{u}|$ for values of α from one to two, and where the location, skewness, and scale parameters are given the values $\delta = 0$, $\beta = 0$, and $\gamma = 1$. When α is between 1.5 and 2, the absolute value of the slope in the middle of the double-log graph is greater than the true asymptotic slope, which is not reached until close to the bottom of the graph. For example, when $\alpha = 1.5$, the asymptotic slope is closely attained only when $Pr(u > \hat{u}) \leq 0.015$, so that $p_0(\alpha) = 0.015$; and when $\alpha = 1.8$, $p_0(\alpha) = 0.0011$.

If, on the average, the asymptotic slope can be observed only in a tail area containing total probability $p_0(\alpha)$, it will be necessary to have more than $N_0(\alpha) = 1/p_0(\alpha)$ observations before the slope of the graph will even *begin* to approach $-\alpha$. When α is close to 2, extremely large samples are necessary before the asymptotic slope becomes observable.

As an illustration Table 6 shows $p_0(\alpha)$ and $N_0(\alpha)$ for different values of α. The most important feature of the table is the rapid increase of $N_0(\alpha)$ with α. On the average, the double-log graph will *begin* to approach its asymptotic slope in samples of less than 100 only if α is 1.5 or less. If the true value of α is 1.80, usually the graph will only begin to approach its asymptotic slope for sample sizes greater than 909. For higher values of α the minimum sample sizes become almost unimaginable by most standards.

Moreover, the expected number of extreme values which will exhibit the true asymptotic slope is $Np_0(\alpha)$, where N is the size of the sample. If, for example, the true value of α is 1.8 and the sample contains 1,500 observations, on the average the asymptotic slope will be observable only for the largest one or two observations in each tail. Clearly, for large values of α double-log graphing puts much too much weight on the one or two largest observations to be a good estimation procedure. We shall see later that the values of α for the distributions of daily changes in log price of the stocks of the DJIA are definitely greater than 1.5. Thus for our data double-log graphing is not a good technique for estimating α.

The situation is not hopeless, however, the asymptotically Paretian nature of the extreme tails of stable Paretian distributions can be used, in combination with *probability* graphing, to estimate the characteristic exponent α. Looking back

TABLE 6

α	$p_0(\alpha)$	$N_0(\alpha)$
1.00	0.13000	8
1.50	.01500	67
1.80	.00110	909
1.90	.00050	2,000
1.95	.00030	3,333
1.99	.00006	16,667
2.00	0	. . . .

at Figure 6, we see that the theoretical double-log graph for the case $\alpha = 1.99$ breaks away from the double-log graph for $\alpha = 2$ at about the point where $Pr(u > \hat{u}) = 0.001$. Similarly, the double-log plot for $\alpha = 1.95$ breaks away from the double-log plot for $\alpha = 1.99$ at about the point where $Pr(u > \hat{u}) = 0.01$. From the point of view of the normal-probability graphs this means that, if α is between 1.99 and 2, we should begin to observe curvature in the graphs somewhere beyond the point where $Pr(u > \hat{u}) = 0.001$. Similarly, if the true value of α is between 1.95 and 1.99, we should observe that the normal-probability graph begins to show curvature somewhere between the point where $Pr(u > \hat{u}) = 0.01$ and the point where $Pr(u > \hat{u}) = 0.001$.

This relationship between the theoretical double-log graphs for different values of α and the normal-probability graphs provides a natural procedure for estimating α. Continuing the discussion of the previous paragraph, we see in Figure 6 that the double-log plot for $\alpha = 1.90$ breaks away from the plot for $\alpha = 1.95$ at about the point where $Pr(u > u) = 0.05$. Thus, if a particular normal-probability graph for some stock begins to show curvature somewhere between the points where $Pr(u > \hat{u}) = 0.05$ and $Pr(u > \hat{u}) = 0.01$, we would estimate that α is probably somewhere in the interval $1.90 \leq \alpha \leq 1.95$. Similarly, if the curvature in the normal-probability graphs begins to become evident somewhere between the points where $Pr(u > \hat{u}) = 0.10$ and $Pr(u > \hat{u}) = 0.05$, we shall say that α is probably somewhere in the interval $1.80 \leq \alpha \leq 1.90$. If none of the normal-probability graph is even vaguely straight, we shall say that α is probably somewhere in the interval $1.50 \leq \alpha \leq 1.80$.

Thus we have a technique for estimating α which combines properties of the normal-probability graphs with properties of the double-log graphs. The estimates produced by this procedure are found in column (1) of Table 9. Admittedly the procedure is completely subjective. In fact, the best we can do with it is to try to set *bounds* on the true value of α. The technique does not readily lend itself to point estimation. It is better than just the double-log graphs alone, however, since it takes into consideration more of the total tail area.

C. ESTIMATING α BY RANGE ANALYSIS

By definition, sums of independent, identically distributed, stable Paretian variables are stable Paretian with the same value of the characteristic exponent α as the distribution of the individual summands. The process of taking sums, however, does change the scale of the distribution. In fact it is shown in the appendix that the scale of the distribution of sums is $n^{1/\alpha}$ times the scale of the distribution of the individual summands, where n is the number of observations in each sum.

This property can be used as the basis of a procedure for estimating α. Define an interfractile range as the difference between the values of a random variable at two different fractiles of its distribution. The interfractile range, R_n, of the distribution of sums of n independent realizations of a stable Paretian variable as a function of the same interfractile range, R_1, of the distribution of the individual summands is given by

$$R_n = n^{1/\alpha} R_1 . \qquad (6)$$

Solving for α, we have

$$\alpha = \frac{\log n}{\log R_n - \log R_1} . \qquad (7)$$

By taking different summing intervals (i.e., different values of n), and different interfractile ranges, (7) can be used to get many different estimates of α from the same set of data.

Range analysis has one important drawback, however. If successive price changes *in the sample* are not independent, this procedure will produce "biased" estimates of α. If there is positive serial dependence in the first differences, we should expect that the interfractile range of the distribution of sums will be more than $n^{1/\alpha}$ times the fractile range of the distribution of the individual summands. On the other hand, if there is negative serial dependence in the first differences, we should expect that the interfractile range of the distribution of sums will be less than $n^{1/\alpha}$ times that of the individual summands. Since the range of the sums comes into the denominator of (7), these biases will work in the opposite direction in the estimation of the characteristic exponent α. Positive dependence will produce downward biased estimates of α, while the estimates will be upward biased in the case of negative dependence.[29]

We shall see in Section V, however, that there is, in fact, no evidence of important dependence in successive price changes, at least for the sampling period covered by our data. Thus it is probably safe to say that dependence will not have important effects on any estimates of α produced by the range analysis technique.

Range analysis has been used to compute fifteen different estimates of α for each stock. Summing intervals of four, nine, and sixteen days were used; and for each summing interval separate estimates of α were made on the basis of interquartile, intersextile, interdecile, 5 per cent, and 2 per cent ranges.[30] The procedure can be clarified by adding a superscript to the formula for α as follows:

$$\alpha = \log n/(\log R_n^i - \log R_1^i)\,, \tag{8}$$

$$n = 4, 9, 16, \quad \text{and} \quad i = 1, \ldots, 5\,,$$

[29] It must be emphasized that the "bias" depends on the serial dependence shown by the sample and not the true dependence in the population. For example, if there is positive dependence in the sample, the interfractile range of the sample sums will usually be more than $n^{1/\alpha}$ times the interfractile range of the individual summands, even if there is no serial dependence in the population. In this case the nature of the sample dependence allows us to pinpoint the direction of the *sampling error* of the estimate of α. On the other hand, when the sample dependence is indicative of true dependence in the population, the error in the estimate of α is a genuine *bias* rather than just sampling error. This distinction, however, is irrelevant for present purposes.

[30] The ranges are defined as follows:

Interquartile	= 0.75 fractile − 0.25 fractile;
Intersextile	= 0.83 fractile − 0.17 fractile;
Interdecile	= 0.90 fractile − 0.10 fractile;
5 per cent	= 0.95 fractile − 0.05 fractile;
2 per cent	= 0.98 fractile − 0.02 fractile.

where n refers to the summing interval and i refers to a particular fractile range. For each value of n there are five different values of i, the different fractile ranges.

Column (2) of Table 9 shows the average values of α computed for each stock by the range analysis technique. The number for a given stock is the average of the fifteen different values of α computed for the stock.

D. ESTIMATING α FROM THE SEQUENTIAL VARIANCE

Although the *population* variance of a stable Paretian process with characteristic exponent $\alpha < 2$ is infinite, the variance computed from any *sample* will always be finite. If the process is truly stable Paretian, however, as the sample size is increased, we should expect to see some upward growth or trend in the sample variance. In fact the appendix shows that, if u_t is an independent stable Paretian variable generated in time series, then the median of the distribution of the cumulative sample variance of u_t at time t_1, as a function of the sample variance at time t_0, is given by

$$S_1^2 = S_0^2\left(\frac{n_1}{n_0}\right)^{-1+2/\alpha}, \tag{9}$$

where n_1 is the number of observations in the sample at time t_1, n_0 is the number at time t_0, and S_1^2 and S_0^2 are the cumulative sample variances. Solving equation (9) for α we get,

$$\alpha = \frac{2(\log n_1 - \log n_0)}{2\log S_1 - 2\log S_0 + \log n_1 - \log n_0}\,. \tag{10}$$

It is easy to see that estimates of α from equation (10) will depend largely on the difference between the values of the sample variances at times t_0 and t_1. If S_1^2 is greater than S_0^2, then the estimate of α will be less than 2. If the sample variance has declined between t_0 and t_1, then the estimate of α will be more than 2.

Now equation (10) can be used to obtain many estimates of α for each stock. This is done by varying the starting point n_0 and the ending point n_1 of the interval of estimation. For this study starting points of from $n_0 = 200$ to $n_0 = 800$ observations by jumps of 100 observations were used. Similarly, for each value of n_0, α was computed for values of $n_1 = n_0 + 100$, $n_1 = n_0 + 200$, $n_1 = n_0 + 300, \ldots,$ and $n_1 = N$, where N is the total number of price changes for the given security. Thus, if the sample of price changes for a stock contains 1,300 observations, the sequential variance procedure of expression (10) would be used to compute fifty-six different estimates of α. For each stock the median of the different estimates of α produced by the sequential variance procedure was computed. These median values of α are shown in column (3) of Table 9.

We must emphasize, however, that, of the three procedures for estimating α used in this report, the sequential-variance technique is probably the weakest. Like probability graphing and range analysis, its theoretical sampling behavior is unknown, since explicit expressions for the density functions of stable Paretian distributions are unknown. In addition, however, the sequential-variance procedure depends on the properties of sequential estimates of a sample parameter. Sampling theory for sequential parameter estimates is not well developed even for cases where an explicit expression for the density function of the basic variable is known. Thus we may know that in general the sample sequential variance grows proportionately to $(n_1/n_0)^{-1+2/\alpha}$ but we do not know how large the sample must be before this growth tendency can be used to make meaningful estimates of α.

TABLE 7

ESTIMATES OF α FOR AMERICAN TOBACCO BY THE SEQUENTIAL-VARIANCE PROCEDURE

n_0	n_1										
	300	400	500	600	700	800	900	1,000	1,100	1,200	$N=$ 1,283
200	18.54	2.64	2.49	2.39	2.23	1.63	1.63	1.62	1.61	1.42	1.32
300		1.19	1.47	1.58	1.57	1.18	1.22	1.24	1.25	1.12	1.05
400			2.11	2.05	1.87	1.18	1.23	1.26	1.27	1.10	1.02
500				1.99	1.74	0.97	1.06	1.11	1.14	0.98	0.91
600					1.52	0.74	0.88	0.96	1.01	0.87	0.80
700						0.46	0.69	0.83	0.91	0.77	0.72
800							1.65	1.59	1.52	0.99	0.85

The problems in estimating α by the sequential variance procedure are illustrated in Table 7 which shows all the different estimates for American Tobacco. The estimates are quite erratic. They range from 0.46 to 18.54. Reading across any line in the table makes it clear that the estimates are highly sensitive to the ending point (n_1) of the interval of estimation. Reading down any column, one sees that they are also extremely sensitive to the starting point (n_0).

By way of contrast, Table 8 shows the different estimates of α for American Tobacco that were produced by the range analysis procedure. Unlike the sequential-variance estimates, the estimates in Table 8 are relatively stable. They range from 1.67 to 2.06. Moreover, the results for American Tobacco are quite representative. For each stock the estimates produced by the sequential-variance procedure show much greater dispersion than do the estimates produced by range analysis. It seems safe to conclude, therefore, that range analysis is a much more precise estimation procedure than sequential-variance analysis.

E. COMPARISON OF THE THREE PROCEDURES FOR ESTIMATING α

Table 9 shows the estimates of α given by the three procedures discussed above. Column (1) shows the estimates produced by the double-log–normal-probability graphing procedure. Because of the subjective nature of this technique,

TABLE 8

ESTIMATES OF α FOR AMERICAN TOBACCO BY RANGE-ANALYSIS PROCEDURE

Range	Summing Interval (Days)		
	Four	Nine	Sixteen
Interquartile	1.98	1.99	1.67
Intersextile	1.99	1.87	1.70
Interdecile	1.80	2.02	1.87
5 per cent	1.86	1.99	2.06
2 per cent	1.80	1.89	1.70

TABLE 9

COMPARISON OF ESTIMATES OF THE CHARACTERISTIC EXPONENT

Stock	Double-Log-Normal-Probability Graphs (1)	Range Analysis (2)	Sequential Variance (3)
Allied Chemical	1.99–2.00	1.94	1.40
Alcoa	1.95–1.99	1.80	2.05
American Can	1.85–1.90	2.10	1.71
A.T.&T.	1.50–1.80	1.77	1.07
American Tobacco	1.85–1.90	1.88	1.24
Anaconda	1.95–1.99	2.03	2.55
Bethlehem Steel	1.90–1.95	1.89	1.85
Chrysler	1.90–1.95	1.95	1.36
Du Pont	1.90–1.95	1.88	1.65
Eastman Kodak	1.90–1.95	1.92	1.76
General Electric	1.80–1.90	1.95	1.57
General Foods	1.85–1.90	1.87	1.86
General Motors	1.95–1.99	2.05	1.44
Goodyear	1.80–1.95	2.06	1.39
International Harvester	1.85–1.90	2.06	2.22
International Nickel	1.90–1.95	1.77	2.80
International Paper	1.90–1.95	1.87	1.95
Johns Manville	1.85–1.90	2.08	1.75
Owens Illinois	1.85–1.90	1.95	2.06
Procter & Gamble	1.80–1.90	1.84	1.70
Sears	1.85–1.90	1.75	1.66
Standard Oil (Calif.)	1.95–1.99	2.08	2.41
Standard Oil (N.J.)	1.90–1.95	2.02	2.09
Swift & Co.	1.85–1.90	1.99	1.87
Texaco	1.90–1.95	1.85	1.76
Union Carbide	1.80–1.90	1.75	1.56
United Aircraft	1.80–1.90	1.93	1.13
U.S. Steel	1.95–1.99	1.96	1.78
Westinghouse	1.95–1.99	2.10	1.35
Woolworth	1.80–1.99	1.93	1.02
Averages	1.87–1.94	1.93	1.73

the best that can be done is to estimate the interval within which the true value appears to fall. Column (2) shows the estimates of α based on range analysis, while column (3) shows the estimates based on the sequential variance procedure.

The reasons why different techniques for estimating α are used, as well as the shortcomings of each technique, are fully discussed in preceding sections. At this point we merely summarize the previous discussions.

First of all, since explicit expressions for the density functions of stable Paretian distributions are, except for certain very special cases, unknown sampling theory for the parameters of these distributions is practically non-existent. Since it is not possible to make firm statements about the sampling error of any given estimator, the only alternative is to use many different estimators of the same parameter in an attempt at least to bracket the true value.

In addition to the lack of sampling theory, each of the techniques for estimating α has additional shortcomings. For example, the procedure based on properties of the double-log and normal-probability graphs is entirely subjective. The range procedure, on the other hand, may be sensitive to whatever serial dependence is present in the sample data. Finally, the sequential-variance technique produces estimates which are erratic and highly dependent on the time interval chosen for the estimation.

It is not wholly implausible, however, that the errors and biases in the various estimators may, to a considerable extent, be offsetting. Each of the three procedures represents a radically different approach to the estimation problem. Therefore there is good reason to expect the results they produce to be independent. At the very least, the three different estimating procedures should allow us to decide whether α is strictly less than 2, as proposed by the Mandelbrot hypothesis, or equal to 2, as proposed by the Gaussian hypothesis.

Even a casual glance at Table 9 is sufficient to show that the estimates of α produced by the three different procedures are consistently less than 2. In combination with the results produced by the frequency distributions and the normal-probability graphs, this would seem to be conclusive evidence in favor of the Mandelbrot hypothesis.

F. CONCLUSION

In sum, the results of Sections III and IV seem to indicate that the daily changes in log price of stocks of large mature companies follow stable Paretian distributions with characteristic exponents close to 2, but nevertheless less than 2. In other words, the Mandelbrot hypothesis seems to fit the data better than the Gaussian hypothesis. In Section VI the implications of this conclusion will be examined from many points of view. In the next section we turn our attention to tests of the independence assumption of the random-walk model.

V. Tests for Dependence

In this section, three main approaches to testing for dependence will be followed. The first will be a straightforward application of the usual serial correlation model; the second will make use of a new approach to the theory of runs; while the third will involve Alexander's [1], [2] well-known filter technique.

Throughout this section we shall be interested in independence from two points of view, the statistician's and the investor's. From a statistical standpoint we are interested in determining whether the departures from normality in the distributions of price changes are due to patterns of dependence in successive changes. That is, we wish to determine whether dependence in successive price changes accounts for the long tails that have been observed in the empirical distributions. From the investor's point of view, on the other hand, we are interested in testing whether there are dependencies in the series that he can use to increase his expected profits.

A. SERIAL CORRELATION

1. THE MODEL

The serial correlation coefficient (r_τ) provides a measure of the relationship between the value of a random variable in time t and its value τ periods earlier. For example, for the variable u_t, defined as the change in log price of a given security from the end of day $t-1$ to the end of day t, the serial correlation coefficient for lag τ is

$$r_\tau = \frac{\text{covariance}(u_t, u_{t-\tau})}{\text{variance}(u_t)}. \quad (11)$$

If the distribution of u_t has finite variance, then in very large samples the standard error of r_τ will be given by

$$\sigma(r_\tau) = \sqrt{1/(N-\tau)}\,, \quad (12)$$

where N is the sample size (cf. Kendall [25]).

Previous sections have suggested, however, that the distribution of u_t is stable Paretian with characteristic exponent α less than 2. Thus the assumption of finite variance is probably not valid, and as a result equation (12) is not a precise measure of the standard error of r_τ, even for extremely large samples. Moreover, since the variance of u_t comes into the denominator of the expression for r_τ, it would seem questionable whether serial correlation analysis is an adequate tool for examining our data.

Wise [49] has shown, however, that as long as the characteristic exponent α of the underlying stable Paretian process is greater than 1, the statistic r_τ is a consistent and unbiased estimate of the true serial correlation in the population. That is, the sample estimate of r_τ is unbiased and converges in probability to its population value as the sample size approaches infinity.[31]

In order to shed some light on the convergence rate of r_τ when $\alpha < 2$, the serial correlation coefficient for lag $\tau = 1$ has been computed sequentially for each stock on the basis of randomized first differences. The purpose of randomization was to insure that the expectation of the serial coefficient would be zero. The procedure was first to reorder randomly the array of first differences for each stock and then to compute the cumulative sample serial correlation coefficient for samples of size $n = 5, 10, \ldots, N$. Thus, except for five additional observations, each sample contains the same values of u as the preceding one.

Although the estimator r_1 is consistent and unbiased, we should expect that, when $\alpha < 2$, the variability of the sample serial correlation coefficients will be greater than if the distribution of u_t had finite variance. The estimates, however, should converge to the true value, zero, as the sample size is increased. In order to judge the variability of the sample

[31] What Wise actually shows is that the least-squares estimate of b_τ in the regression equation,

$$u_t = a + b_\tau u_{t-\tau} + \xi_t\,,$$

is consistent and unbiased as long as the characteristic exponent α of the distribution of ξ_t is greater than 1. Since the least squares estimate of b_τ is identical to the estimate of r_τ, however, this is equivalent to proving that the estimate of r_τ is also consistent and unbiased.

coefficients two σ control limits were computed by means of the formula

$$r_1 \pm 2\,\sigma(r_1) = 0 \pm 2\sqrt{1/(n-1)}\,,$$
$$n = 5\,, 10, \ldots, N\,.$$

Although the results must be judged subjectively, the sample serial correlation coefficients for the randomized first differences appear to break through their control limits only slightly more often than would be the case if the underlying distribution of the first differences had finite variance. From the standpoint of consistency the most important feature of the sample coefficients is that for every stock the serial correlation coefficient is very close to the true value, zero, for samples with more than, say, three hundred observations. In addition, the sample coefficient stays close to zero thereafter.

For purposes of illustration graphs of the sequential randomized serial correlation coefficients for Goodyear and U.S. Steel are presented in Figure 7. The ordinates of the graphs show the values of the sequential serial correlation coefficents, while the abscissas show sequential sample size. The irregular lines on the graphs show the path of the coefficent while the smooth curves represent the two σ control limits. The striking feature of both graphs is the quickness with which the sample coefficient settles down to its true value, zero, and stays close to the true value thereafter. On the basis of this evidence we conclude that, for large samples and for the values of α observed for our stocks, the sample serial correlation coefficient seems to be an effective tool in testing for serial independence.

2. COEFFICIENTS FOR DAILY CHANGES

Using the data as they were actually generated in time, the sample serial correlation coefficient for daily changes in log price has been computed for each stock for lag τ of from 1 to 30 days. The results for $\tau = 1, 2, \ldots, 10$ are shown in Table 10. Essentially the sample coefficients in the table tell us whether any of the price changes for the last ten days are likely to be of much help in predicting tomorrow's change.

All the sample serial correlation coefficients in Table 10 are quite small in absolute value. The largest is only .123. Although eleven of the coefficients for lag $\tau = 1$ are more than twice their computed standard errors, this is not regarded as important in this case. The standard errors are computed according to equation (12); and, as we saw earlier, this formula underestimates the true variability of the coefficient when the underlying variable is stable Paretian with characteristic exponent $\alpha < 2$. In addition, for our large samples the standard error of the serial correlation coefficient is very small. In most cases a coefficient as small as .06 is more than twice its standard error. "Dependence" of such a small order of magnitude is, from a practical point of view, probably unimportant for both the statistician and the investor.

3. COEFFICIENTS FOR FOUR-, NINE-, AND SIXTEEN-DAY CHANGES

Although the sample serial correlation coefficients for the daily changes are all very small, it is possible that price changes across longer differencing intervals would show stronger evidence of dependence. To test this, serial correlation coefficients for lag $\tau = 1, 2, \ldots, 10$ were computed for each stock for non-overlapping differencing intervals of four, nine, and sixteen days. The results for $\tau = 1$ are shown in Table 11.[32]

[32] Of course, in taking longer differencing intervals the sample size is considerably reduced. The

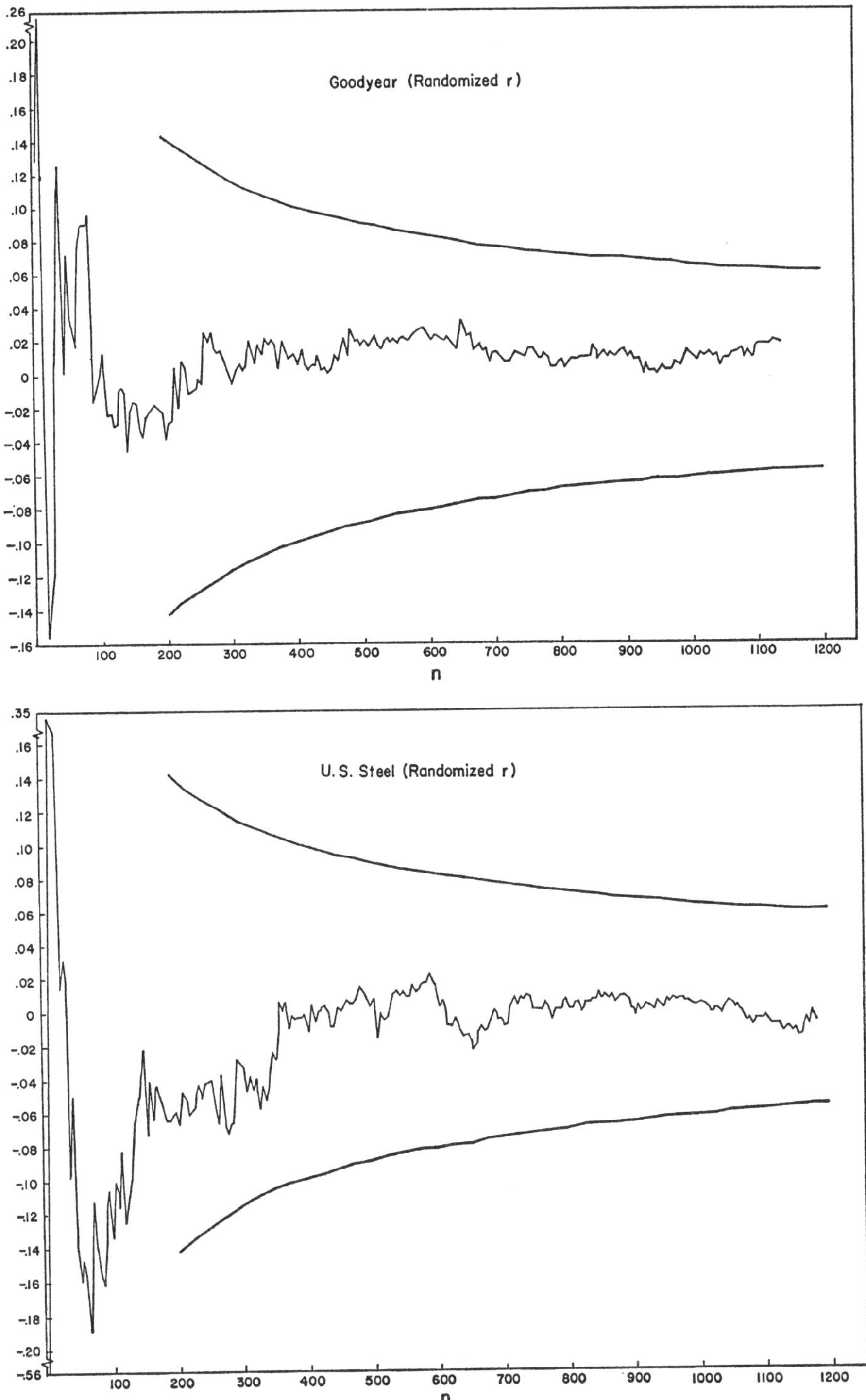

FIG. 7.—Randomized sequential serial correlation coefficients

Again, all the sample serial correlation coefficients are quite small. In general, the absolute size of the coefficients seems to increase with the differencing interval. This does not mean, however, that price changes over longer differencing intervals show more dependence, since we know that the variability of r is inversely related to the sample size. In fact the average size of the coefficients relative to their standard errors decreases with the differencing interval. This is demonstrated by the fact that for four-, nine-, and sixteen-day differencing intervals there are, respectively, five, two, and one coefficients greater than twice their standard errors in Table 11.

An interesting feature of Tables 10 and 11 is the pattern shown by the signs of the serial correlation coefficients for lag $\tau = 1$. In Table 10 twenty-three out of thirty of the first-order coefficients for the daily differences are positive, while twenty-one and twenty-four of the coefficients for the four- and nine-day differences are negative in Table 11. For

sample for the four-day changes is only one-fourth as large as the sample for the daily changes. Similarly, the samples for the nine- and sixteen-day changes are only one-ninth and one-sixteenth as large as the corresponding samples for the daily changes.

TABLE 10

DAILY SERIAL CORRELATION COEFFICIENTS FOR LAG $\tau = 1, 2, \ldots, 10$

Stock	Lag									
	1	2	3	4	5	6	7	8	9	10
Allied Chemical	.017	−.042	.007	−.001	.027	.004	−.017	−.026	−.017	−.007
Alcoa	.118*	.038	−.014	.022	−.022	.009	.017	.007	−.001	−.033
American Can	−.087*	−.024	.034	−.065*	−.017	−.006	.015	.025	−.047	−.040
A.T.&T.	−.039	−.097*	.000	.026	.005	−.005	.002	.027	−.014	.007
American Tobacco	.111*	−.109*	−.060*	−.065*	.007	−.010	.011	.046	.039	.041
Anaconda	.067*	−.061*	−.047	−.002	.000	−.038	.009	.016	−.014	−.056
Bethlemen Steel	.013	−.065*	.009	.021	−.053	−.098*	−.010	.004	−.002	−.021
Chrysler	.012	−.066*	−.016	−.007	−.015	.009	.037	.056*	−.044	.021
Du Pont	.013	−.033	.060*	.027	−.002	−.047	.020	.011	−.034	.001
Eastman Kodak	.025	.014	−.031	.005	−.022	.012	.007	.006	.008	.002
General Electric	.011	−.038	−.021	.031	−.001	.000	−.008	.014	−.002	.010
General Foods	.061*	−.003	.045	.002	−.015	−.052	−.006	−.014	−.024	−.017
General Motors	−.004	−.056*	−.037	−.008	−.038	−.006	.019	.006	−.016	.009
Goodyear	−.123*	.017	−.044	.043	−.002	−.003	.035	.014	−.015	.007
International Harvester	−.017	−.029	−.031	.037	−.052	−.021	−.001	.003	−.046	−.016
International Nickel	.096*	−.033	−.019	.020	.027	.059*	−.038	−.008	−.016	.034
International Paper	.046	−.011	−.058*	.053*	.049	−.003	−.025	−.019	−.003	−.021
Johns Manville	.006	−.038	−.027	−.023	−.029	−.080*	.040	.018	−.037	.029
Owens Illinois	−.021	−.084*	−.047	.068*	.086*	−.040	.011	−.040	.067*	−.043
Procter & Gamble	.099*	−.009	−.008	.009	−.015	.022	.012	−.012	−.022	−.021
Sears	.097*	.026	.028	.025	.005	−.054	−.006	−.010	−.008	−.009
Standard Oil (Calif.)	.025	−.030	−.051*	−.025	−.047	−.034	−.010	.072*	−.049*	−.035
Standard Oil (N.J.)	.008	−.116*	.016	.014	−.047	−.018	−.022	−.026	−.073*	.081*
Swift & Co.	−.004	−.015	−.010	.012	.057*	.012	−.043	.014	.012	.001
Texaco	.094*	−.049	−.024	−.018	−.017	−.009	.031	.032	−.013	.008
Union Carbide	.107*	−.012	.040	.046	−.036	−.034	.003	−.008	−.054	−.037
United Aircraft	.014	−.033	−.022	−.047	−.067*	−.053	.046	.037	.015	−.019
U.S. Steel	.040	−.074*	.014	.011	−.012	−.021	.041	.037	−.021	−.044
Westinghouse	−.027	−.022	−.036	−.003	.000	−.054*	−.020	.013	−.014	.008
Woolworth	.028	−.016	.015	.014	.007	−.039	−.013	.003	−.088*	−.008

* Coefficient is twice its computed standard error.

the sixteen-day differences the signs are about evenly split. Seventeen are positive and thirteen are negative.

The preponderance of positive signs in the coefficients for the daily changes is consistent with Kendall's [26] results for weekly changes in British industrial share prices. On the other hand, the results for the four- and nine-day differences are in agreement with those of Cootner [10] and Moore [41], both of whom found a preponderance of negative signs in the serial correlation coefficients of weekly changes in log price of stocks on the New York Stock Exchange.

Given that the absolute size of the serial correlation coefficients is always quite small, however, agreement in sign among the coefficients for the different securities is ***not necessarily*** evidence for consistent patterns of dependence. King [27] has shown that the price changes for different securities are related (although not all to the same extent) to the behavior of a "market" component common to all securities. For any given sampling period the serial correlation coefficient for a given security will be partly determined by the serial behavior of this market component and partly by the serial behavior of factors peculiar to that security and perhaps also to its industry.

TABLE 11

FIRST-ORDER SERIAL CORRELATION COEFFICIENTS FOR FOUR-, NINE-, AND SIXTEEN-DAY CHANGES

Stock	Differencing Interval (Days)		
	Four	Nine	Sixteen
Allied Chemical	.029	−.091	−.118
Alcoa	.095	−.112	−.044
American Can	−.124*	−.060	.031
A.T. & T.	−.010	−.009	−.003
American Tobacco	−.175*	.033	.007
Anaconda	−.068	−.125	.202
Bethlehem Steel	−.122	−.148	.112
Chrysler	.060	−.026	.040
Du Pont	.069	−.043	−.055
Eastman Kodak	−.006	−.053	−.023
General Electric	.020	−.004	.000
General Foods	−.005	−.140	−.098
General Motors	−.128*	.009	−.028
Goodyear	.001	−.037	.033
International Harvester	−.068	−.244*	.116
International Nickel	.038	.124	.041
International Paper	.060	−.004	−.010
Johns Manville	−.068	−.002	.002
Owens Illinois	−.006	.003	−.022
Procter & Gamble	−.006	.098	.076
Sears	−.070	−.113	.041
Standard Oil (Calif.)	−.143*	−.046	.040
Standard Oil (N.J.)	−.109	−.082	−.121
Swift & Co.	−.072	.118	−.197
Texaco	−.053	−.047	−.178
Union Carbide	.049	−.101	.124
United Aircraft	−.190*	−.192*	−.040
U.S. Steel	−.006	−.056	.236*
Westinghouse	−.097	−.137	.067
Woolworth	−.033	−.112	.040

* Coefficient is twice its computed standard error.

Since the market component is common to all securities, however, its behavior during the sampling period may tend to produce a common sign for the serial correlation coefficients of all the different securities. Thus, although both the market component and the factors peculiar to individual firms and industries may be characterized by serial independence, the *sample* behavior of the market component during any given time period may be expected to produce agreement among the signs of the sample serial correlation coefficients for different securities. The fact that this agreement in sign is caused by pure sampling error in a random component common to all securities is evidenced by the small absolute size of the sample coefficients. It is also evidenced by the fact that, although different studies have invariably found some sort of consistency in sign, the actual direction of the "dependence" varies from study to study.[33]

[33] The model, in somewhat oversimplified form, is as follows. The change in log price of stock j during day t is a linear function of the change in a market component, I_t, and a random error term, ξ_{tj}, which expresses the factors peculiar to the individual security. The form of the function is $u_{tj} = b_j I_t + \xi_{tj}$, where it is assumed that the I_t and ξ_{tj} are both serially independent and that ξ_{tj} is independent of current and past values of I_t. If we further assume, solely for simplicity, that $E(\xi_{tj}) = E(I_t) = 0$ for all t and j, we have

$$\begin{aligned}\text{cov}\,(u_{tj}, u_{t-\tau,\,j}) = E[b_j I_t + \xi_{tj})(b_j I_{t-\tau} \\ + \xi_{t-\tau,\,j})] = b_j^2 \,\text{cov}\,(I_t, I_{t-\tau}) \\ + b_j \,\text{cov}\,(I_t, \xi_{t-\tau,\,j}) \\ + b_j \,\text{cov}\,(I_{t-\tau}, \xi_{tj}) + \text{cov}\,(\xi_{tj}, \xi_{t-\tau,\,j})\,.\end{aligned}$$

Although the expected values of the covariances on the right of the equality are all zero, their sample values for any given time period will not usually be equal to zero. Since cov $(I_t, I_{t-\tau})$ will be the same for all j, it will tend to make the signs of cov $(u_{tj}, u_{t-\tau,\,j})$ the same for different j. Essentially we are saying that the serial correlation coefficients for different securities for given lag and time period are not independent of each other. Thus we should not be surprised when we find a preponderance of signs in one direction or the other.

In sum, the evidence produced by the serial-correlation model seems to indicate that dependence in successive price changes is either extremely slight or completely non-existent. This conclusion should be regarded as tentative, however, until further results, to be provided by the runs tests of the next section, are examined.

B. THE RUNS TESTS

1. INTRODUCTION

A run is defined as a sequence of price changes of the same sign. For example, a plus run of length i is a sequence of i consecutive positive price changes preceded and followed by either negative or zero changes. For stock prices there are three different possible types of price changes and thus three different types of runs.

The approach to runs-testing in this section will be somewhat novel. The differences between expected and actual numbers of runs will be analyzed in three different ways, first by totals, then by sign, and finally by length. First, for each stock the difference between the total actual number of runs, irrespective of sign, and the total expected number will be examined. Next, the total expected and actual numbers of plus, minus, and no-change runs will be studied. Finally, for runs of each sign the expected and actual numbers of runs of each length will be computed.

2. TOTAL ACTUAL AND EXPECTED NUMBER OF RUNS

If it is assumed that the sample proportions of positive, negative, and zero price changes are good estimates of the population proportions, then under the hypothesis of independence the total expected number of runs of all signs for a stock can be computed as

$$m=\left[N(N+1)-\sum_{i=1}^{3}n_i^2\right]\Big/N, \quad (13)$$

where N is the total number of price changes, and the n_i are the numbers of price changes of each sign. The standard error of m is

$$\sigma_m=\left(\frac{\sum_{i=1}^{3}n_i^2\left[\sum_{i=1}^{3}n_i^2+N(N+1)\right]-2N\sum_{i=1}^{3}n_i^3-N^3}{N^2(N-1)}\right)^{1/2}, \quad (14)$$

and for large N the sampling distribution of m is approximately normal.[34]

Table 12 shows the total expected and actual numbers of runs for each stock for

[34] Cf. Wallis and Roberts [48], pp. 569–72. It should be noted that the asymptotic properties of the sampling distribution of m do not depend on the assumption of finite variance for the distribution of price changes. We saw previously that this is not true for the sampling distribution of the serial correlation coefficient. In particular, except for the properties of consistency and unbiasedness, we

TABLE 12

TOTAL ACTUAL AND EXPECTED NUMBERS OF RUNS FOR ONE-, FOUR-, NINE-, AND SIXTEEN-DAY DIFFERENCING INTERVALS

STOCK	DAILY		FOUR-DAY		NINE-DAY		SIXTEEN-DAY	
	Actual	Expected	Actual	Expected	Actual	Expected	Actual	Expected
Allied Chemical	683	713.4	160	162.1	71	71.3	39	38.6
Alcoa	601	670.7	151	153.7	61	66.9	41	39.0
American Can	730	755.5	169	172.4	71	73.2	48	43.9
A.T.&T.	657	688.4	165	155.9	66	70.3	34	37.1
American Tobacco	700	747.4	178	172.5	69	72.9	41	40.6
Anaconda	635	680.1	166	160.4	68	66.0	36	37.8
Bethlehem Steel	709	719.7	163	159.3	80	71.8	41	42.2
Chrysler	927	932.1	223	221.6	100	96.9	54	53.5
Du Pont	672	694.7	160	161.9	78	71.8	43	39.4
Eastman Kodak	678	679.0	154	160.1	70	70.1	43	40.3
General Electric	918	956.3	225	224.7	101	96.9	51	51.8
General Foods	799	825.1	185	191.4	81	75.8	43	40.5
General Motors	832	868.3	202	205.2	83	85.8	44	46.8
Goodyear	681	672.0	151	157.6	60	65.2	36	36.3
International Harvester	720	713.2	159	164.2	84	72.6	40	37.8
International Nickel	704	712.6	163	164.0	68	70.5	34	37.6
International Paper	762	826.0	190	193.9	80	82.8	51	46.9
Johns Manville	685	699.1	173	160.0	64	69.4	39	40.4
Owens Illinois	713	743.3	171	168.6	69	73.3	36	39.2
Procter & Gamble	826	858.9	180	190.6	66	81.2	40	42.9
Sears	700	748.1	167	172.8	66	70.6	40	34.8
Standard Oil (Calif.)	972	979.0	237	228.4	97	98.6	59	54.3
Standard Oil (N.J.)	688	704.0	159	159.2	69	68.7	29	37.0
Swift & Co.	878	877.6	209	197.2	85	83.8	50	47.8
Texaco	600	654.2	143	155.2	57	63.4	29	35.6
Union Carbide	595	620.9	142	150.5	67	66.7	36	35.1
United Aircraft	661	699.3	172	161.4	77	68.2	45	39.5
U.S. Steel	651	662.0	162	158.3	65	70.3	37	41.2
Westinghouse	829	825.5	198	193.3	87	84.4	41	45.8
Woolworth	847	868.4	193	198.9	78	80.9	48	47.7
Averages	735.1	759.8	175.7	175.8	74.6	75.3	41.6	41.7

one-, four-, nine-, and sixteen-day price changes. For the daily changes the actual number of runs is less than the expected number in twenty-six out of thirty cases. This agrees with the results produced by the serial correlation coefficients. In Table 10, twenty-three out of thirty of the first-order serial correlation coefficients are positive. For the four- and nine-day differences, however, the results of the runs tests do not lend support to the results produced by the serial correlation coefficients. In Table 11 twenty-one and twenty-four of the serial correlation coefficients for four- and nine-day changes are negative. To be consistent with negative dependence, the actual numbers of runs in Table 12 should be greater than the expected numbers for these differencing intervals. In fact, for the four-day changes the actual number of runs is greater than the expected number for only thirteen of the thirty stocks, and for the nine-day changes the actual number is greater than the expected number in only twelve cases. For the sixteen-day differences there is no evidence for dependence of any form in either the serial correlation coefficients or the runs tests.

For most purposes, however, the absolute amount of dependence in the price changes is more important than whether the dependence is positive or negative. The amount of dependence implied by the runs tests can be depicted by the size of the differences between the total actual numbers of runs and the total expected numbers. In Table 13 these differences are standardized in two ways.

For large samples the distribution of the total number of runs is approximately normal with mean m and standard error σ_m as defined by equations (13) and (14). Thus the difference between the actual number of runs, R, and the expected number can be expressed by means of the usual standardized variable,

$$K = \frac{(R + \frac{1}{2}) - m}{\sigma_m}, \qquad (15)$$

where the $\frac{1}{2}$ in the numerator is a discontinuity adjustment. For large samples K will be approximately normal with mean 0 and variance 1. The columns labeled K in Table 13 show the standardized variable for the four differencing intervals. In addition, the columns labeled $(R - m)/m$ show the differences between the actual and expected numbers of runs as proportions of the expected numbers.

For the daily price changes the values of K show that for eight stocks the actual number of runs is more than two standard errors less than the expected number. Caution is required in drawing conclusions from this result, however. The expected number of runs increases about proportionately with the sample size, while its standard error increases proportionately with the square root of the sample size. Thus a constant but small *percentage* difference between the expected and actual number of runs will produce higher and higher values of the standardized variable as the sample size is increased. For example, for General Foods the actual number of runs is about 3 per cent less than the expected number for both the daily and the four-day changes. The standardized variable, however, goes from −1.46 for the daily changes to −0.66 for the four-day changes.

In general, the percentage differences between the actual and expected numbers of runs are quite small, and this is

know very little about the distribution of the serial correlation coefficient when the price changes follow a stable Paretian distribution with characteristic exponent $\alpha < 2$. From this standpoint at least, runs-testing is, for our purposes, a better way of testing independence than serial correlation analysis.

probably the more relevant measure of dependence.

3. ACTUAL AND EXPECTED NUMBERS OF RUNS OF EACH SIGN

If the signs of the price changes are generated by an independent Bernoulli process with probabilities $P(+)$, $P(-)$, and $P(0)$ for the three types of changes, for large samples the expected number of plus runs of length i in a sample of N changes[35] will be approximately

$$NP(+)^i[1 - P(+)]^2 \,. \tag{16}$$

The expected number of plus runs of all lengths will be

$$\sum_{i=1}^{\infty} NP(+)^i[1-P(+)]^2 = NP(+)[1-P(+)] \,. \tag{17}$$

Similarly the expected numbers of minus and no-change runs of all lengths will be

$$NP(-)[1 - P(-)] \quad \text{and} \quad NP(0)[1 - P(0)] \,. \tag{18}$$

For a given stock, the sum of the expected numbers of plus, minus, and no-change runs will be equal to the total expected number of runs of all signs, as defined in the previous section. Thus the

[35] Cf. Hald [21], pp. 342–53.

TABLE 13

RUNS ANALYSIS: STANDARDIZED VARIABLES AND PERCENTAGE DIFFERENCES

STOCK	DAILY		FOUR-DAY		NINE-DAY		SIXTEEN-DAY	
	K	$(R-m)/m$	K	$(R-m)/m$	K	$(R-m)/m$	K	$(R-m)/m$
Allied Chemical	−1.82	−0.043	−0.19	−0.013	0.04	−0.004	0.21	0.011
Alcoa	−4.23	− .104	− .26	− .018	−0.95	− .089	0.60	.052
American Can	−1.54	− .034	− .35	− .020	−0.30	− .030	1.16	.090
A.T.&T.	−1.88	− .046	1.14	.058	−0.71	− .060	−0.65	− .083
American Tobacco	−2.80	− .063	.70	.032	−0.63	− .054	0.22	.010
Anaconda	−2.75	− .066	.73	.035	0.44	.030	−0.30	− .047
Bethlehem Steel	−0.63	− .015	.50	.023	1.57	.114	−0.16	− .028
Chrysler	−0.24	− .006	.19	.006	0.54	.032	0.20	.010
Du Pont	−1.32	− .033	− .16	− .012	1.16	.086	0.93	.090
Eastman Kodak	−0.03	− .002	− .64	− .038	0.06	− .002	0.77	.066
General Electric	−1.94	− .040	.08	.001	0.68	.042	−0.06	− .015
General Foods	−1.46	− .032	− .66	− .033	0.99	.068	0.71	.061
General Motors	−2.02	− .042	− .30	− .016	−0.37	− .032	−0.50	− .061
Goodyear	0.59	.013	− .75	− .042	−0.83	− .080	0.05	− .008
International Harvester	0.45	.010	− .58	− .032	2.16	.156	0.67	.059
International Nickel	−0.49	− .012	− .06	− .006	−0.35	− .036	−0.75	− .096
International Paper	−3.53	− .077	− .38	− .020	−0.38	− .034	0.98	.087
Johns Manville	−0.83	− .020	1.62	.081	−0.89	− .078	−0.22	− .035
Owens Illinois	−1.81	− .041	.34	.014	−0.68	− .059	−0.65	− .082
Procter & Gamble	−1.82	− .038	−1.13	− .056	−2.51	− .188	−0.59	− .068
Sears	−2.94	− .064	− .66	− .034	−0.79	− .066	1.69	.149
Standard Oil (Calif.)	−0.33	− .007	.92	.038	−0.16	− .016	1.03	.086
Standard Oil (N.J.)	−0.98	− .023	.03	− .001	0.15	.005	−1.78	− .216
Swift & Co.	0.05	.000	1.34	.060	0.28	.015	0.58	.045
Texaco	−3.33	− .083	−1.43	− .078	−1.08	− .101	−1.51	− .186
Union Carbide	−1.60	− .042	− .99	− .056	0.16	.005	0.33	.024
United Aircraft	−2.32	− .055	1.33	.066	1.63	.128	1.42	.140
U.S. Steel	−0.63	− .017	.49	.023	−0.85	− .075	−0.90	− .102
Westinghouse	0.22	.004	.56	.024	0.51	.031	−0.92	− .105
Woolworth	−1.18	−0.025	−0.59	−0.030	−0.38	−0.035	0.17	0.006
Averages	−1.44	−0.033	0.03	−0.001	−0.05	−0.010	0.09	0.005

above expressions give the breakdown of the total expected number of runs into the expected numbers of runs of each sign.

For present purposes, however, it is not desirable to compute the breakdown by sign of the total *expected* number of runs. This would blur the results of this section, since we know that for some differencing intervals there are consistent discrepancies between the total actual numbers of runs of all signs and the total expected numbers. For example, for twenty-six out of thirty stocks the total expected number of runs of all signs for the daily differences is greater than the total actual number. If the total expected number of runs is used to compute the expected numbers of runs of each sign, the expected numbers by sign will tend to be greater than the actual numbers. And this will be the case even if the breakdown of the total actual number of runs into the actual number of runs of each sign is proportional to the expected breakdown.

This is the situation we want to avoid in this section. What we will examine here are discrepancies between the *expected* breakdown by sign of the total *actual* number of runs and the actual breakdown. To do this we must now define a method of computing the expected breakdown by sign of the total actual number of runs.

The probability of a plus run can be expressed as the ratio of the expected number of plus runs in a sample of size N to the total expected number of runs of all signs, or as

$$P(+\text{ run}) = NP(+)[1 - P)(+)]/m\,. \quad (19)$$

Similarly, the probabilities of minus and no-change runs can be expressed as

$$\begin{aligned} &P(-\text{ run}) \\ &\quad = NP(-)[1 - P(-)]/m\,, \quad \text{and} \end{aligned} \quad (20)$$

$$P(0\text{ run}) = NP(0)[1 - P(0)]/m\,. \quad (21)$$

The expected breakdown by sign of the total actual number of runs (R) is then given by

$$\begin{aligned} \bar{R}(+) &= R[P(+\text{ run})]\,, \\ \bar{R}(-) &= R[P(-\text{ run})]\,, \quad \text{and} \quad (22) \\ \bar{R}(0) &= R[P(0\text{ run})]\,, \end{aligned}$$

where $\bar{R}(+)$, $\bar{R}(-)$, and $\bar{R}(0)$ are the expected numbers of plus, minus, and no-change runs. These formulas have been used to compute the expected numbers of runs of each sign for each stock for differencing intervals of one, four, nine, and sixteen days. The actual numbers of runs and the differences between the actual and expected numbers have also been computed. The results for the daily changes are shown in Table 14. The results for the four-, nine-, and sixteen-day changes are similar, and so they are omitted.

The differences between the actual and expected numbers of runs are all very small. In addition there seem to be no important patterns in the signs of the differences. We conclude, therefore, that the actual breakdown of runs by sign conforms very closely to the breakdown that would be expected if the signs were generated by an independent Bernoulli process.

4. DISTRIBUTION OF RUNS BY LENGTH

In this section the expected and actual distributions of runs by length will be examined. As in the previous section, an effort will be made to separate the analysis from the results of runs tests discussed previously. To accomplish this, the discrepancies between the total actual and expected numbers of runs and those between the actual and expected numbers of runs of each sign will be taken as given. Emphasis will be placed on the *expected distributions* by length of the total *actual* number of runs of each sign.

As indicated earlier, the expected number of plus runs of length i in a sample of N price changes is $NP(+)^i[1 - P(+)]^2$, and the total expected number of plus runs is $NP(+)[1 - P(+)]$. Out of the total expected number of plus runs, the expected proportion of plus runs of length i is

$$NP(+)^i[1 - P(+)]^2/NP(+) \times [1 - P(+)] = P(+)^{i-1}[1 - P(+)]. \quad (23)$$

This proportion is equivalent to the conditional probability of a plus run of length i, given that a plus run has been observed. The sum of the conditional probabilities for plus runs of all lengths is one. The analogous conditional probabilities for minus and no-change runs are

$$P(-)^{i-1}[1 - P(-)] \quad \text{and} \quad P(0)^{i-1}[1 - P(0)]. \quad (24)$$

These probabilities can be used to compute the expected distributions by length of the total actual number of runs of each sign. The formulas for the expected numbers of plus, minus, and no-change runs of length i, $i = 1, \ldots, \infty$, are

$$\bar{R}_i(+) = R(+)\,P(+)^{i-1}[1 - P(+)],$$
$$\bar{R}_i(-) = R(-)\,P(-)^{i-1} \times [1 - P(-)], \quad (25)$$
$$\bar{R}_i(0) = R(0)\,P(0)^{i-1}[1 - P(0)],$$

TABLE 14

RUNS ANALYSIS BY SIGN (DAILY CHANGES)

Stock	Positive			Negative			No Change		
	Actual	Expected	Actual-Expected	Actual	Expected	Actual-Expected	Actual	Expected	Actual-Expected
Allied Chemical	286	290.1	− 4.1	294	290.7	3.3	103	102.2	0.8
Alcoa	265	264.4	0.6	262	266.5	− 4.5	74	70.1	3.9
American Can	289	290.2	− 1.2	285	284.6	0.4	156	155.2	0.8
A.T.&T.	290	291.2	− 1.2	285	285.3	− 0.3	82	80.5	1.5
American Tobacco	296	300.2	− 4.2	295	294.0	1.0	109	105.8	3.2
Anaconda	271	272.9	− 1.9	276	278.8	− 2.8	88	83.3	4.7
Bethlehem Steel	282	286.4	− 4.4	300	294.6	5.4	127	128.0	−1.0
Chrysler	417	414.9	2.1	421	421.1	− 0.1	89	91.0	−2.0
Du Pont	293	300.3	− 7.3	305	299.2	5.8	74	72.5	1.5
Eastman Kodak	306	308.6	− 2.6	312	308.7	3.3	60	60.7	−0.7
General Electric	404	404.5	− 0.5	401	404.7	− 3.7	113	108.8	4.2
General Foods	346	340.8	5.2	320	331.3	−11.3	133	126.9	6.1
General Motors	340	342.7	− 2.7	339	340.3	− 1.3	153	149.0	4.0
Goodyear	294	291.9	2.1	292	293.0	− 1.0	95	96.1	−1.1
International Harvester	303	300.1	2.9	301	298.8	2.2	116	121.1	−5.1
International Nickel	312	307.0	5.0	296	301.9	− 5.9	96	95.1	0.9
International Paper	322	330.2	− 8.2	338	333.2	4.8	102	98.6	3.4
Johns Manville	293	292.6	0.4	296	293.5	2.5	96	98.9	−2.9
Owens Illinois	297	293.7	3.3	295	291.2	3.8	121	128.1	−7.1
Procter & Gamble	343	346.4	− 3.4	342	340.3	1.7	141	139.3	1.7
Sears	291	289.3	1.7	265	271.3	− 6.3	144	139.4	4.6
Standard Oil (Calif.)	406	417.9	−11.9	427	416.6	10.4	139	137.5	1.5
Standard Oil (N.J.)	272	277.3	− 5.3	281	277.9	3.1	135	132.8	2.2
Swift & Co.	354	354.3	− 0.3	355	356.9	− 1.9	169	166.8	2.2
Texaco	266	265.6	0.4	258	263.6	− 5.6	76	70.8	5.2
Union Carbide	266	268.1	− 2.1	265	265.6	− 0.6	64	61.3	2.7
United Aircraft	281	280.4	0.6	282	282.2	− 0.2	98	98.4	−0.4
U.S. Steel	292	293.5	− 1.5	296	295.2	0.8	63	62.3	0.7
Westinghouse	359	361.3	− 2.3	364	362.1	1.9	106	105.6	0.4
Woolworth	349	348.7	0.3	350	345.9	4.1	148	152.4	−4.4

where $\bar{R}_i(+)$, $\bar{R}_i(-)$, and $\bar{R}_i(0)$ are the expected numbers of plus, minus, and no-change runs of length i, while $R(+)$, $R(-)$, and $R(0)$ are the total actual numbers of plus, minus, and no-change runs. Tables showing the expected and actual distributions of runs by length have been computed for each stock for differencing intervals of one, four, nine, and sixteen days. The tables for the daily changes of three randomly chosen securities are found together in Table 15. The tables show, for runs of each sign, the probability of a run of each length and the expected and actual numbers of runs of each length. The question answered by the tables is the following: Given the total actual number of runs of each sign, how would we *expect* the totals to be distributed among runs of different lengths and what is the actual distribution?

For all the stocks the expected and actual distributions of runs by length turn out to be extremely similar. Impressive is the fact that there are very few long runs, that is, runs of length longer than seven or eight. There seems to be no tendency for the number of long runs to be higher than expected under the hypothesis of independence.

5. SUMMARY

There is little evidence, either from the serial correlations or from the various runs tests, of any large degree of dependence in the daily, four-day, nine-day, and sixteen-day price changes. As far as these tests are concerned, it would seem that any dependence that exists in these series is not strong enough to be used either to increase the expected profits of the trader or to account for the departures from normality that have been observed in the empirical distribution of price changes. That is, as far as these tests are concerned, there is no evidence of important dependence from either an investment or a statistical point of view.

We must emphasize, however, that although serial correlations and runs tests are the common tools for testing dependence, there are situations in which they do not provide an adequate test of either practical or statistical dependence. For example, from a practical point of view the chartist would not regard either type of analysis as an *adequate* test of whether the past history of the series can be used to increase the investor's expected profits. The simple linear relationships that underlie the serial correlation model are much too unsophisticated to pick up the complicated "patterns" that the chartist sees in stock prices. Similarly, the runs tests are much too rigid in their approach to determining the duration of upward and downward movements in prices. In particular, a run is terminated whenever there is a change in sign in the sequence of price changes, regardless of the size of the price change that causes the change in sign. A chartist would like to have a more sophisticated method for identifying movements—a method which does not always predict the termination of the movement simply because the price level has temporarily changed direction. One such method, Alexander's filter technique, will be examined in the next section.

On the other hand, there are also possible shortcomings to the serial correlation and runs tests from a statistical point of view. For example, both of these models only test for dependence which is present all through the data. It is possible, however, that price changes are dependent only in special conditions. For example, although small changes may be independent, large changes may tend to be followed consistently by large changes of the same sign, or perhaps by large changes of the opposite sign. One version of this hypothesis will also be tested later.

C. ALEXANDER'S FILTER TECHNIQUE

The tests of independence discussed thus far can be classified as primarily statistical. That is, they involved computation of sample estimates of certain statistics and then comparison of the results with what would be expected under the assumption of independence of successive price changes. Since the sample estimates conformed closely to the values that would be expected by an independent model, we concluded that the independence assumption of the random-walk model was upheld by the data. From this we then *inferred* that there are probably no mechanical trading rules based solely on properties of past histories of price changes that can be used to make the expected profits of the trader greater than they would be under a simple buy-and-hold rule. We stress, however, that until now this is just an *inference;* the actual profitability of mechanical trading rules has not yet been directly tested. In this section one such trading rule, Alexander's filter technique [1], [2], will be discussed.

An x per cent filter is defined as follows. If the daily closing price of a particular security moves up at least x per cent, buy and hold the security until its price moves down at least x per cent from a subsequent high, at which time simultaneously sell and go short. The short position is maintained until the daily closing price rises at least x per cent above a subsequent low, at which time one should simultaneously cover and buy. Moves less than x per cent in either direction are ignored.

In his earlier article [1, Table 7] Alexander reported tests of the filter technique for filters ranging in size from 5 per cent to 50 per cent. The tests covered different time periods from 1897 to 1959 and involved closing "prices" for two *indexes,* the Dow-Jones Industrials from 1897 to 1929 and Standard and Poor's Industrials from 1929 to 1959. Alexander's results indicated that, in general, filters of all different sizes and for all the different time periods yield substantial profits—indeed, profits significantly greater than those earned by a simple buy-and-hold policy. This led him to conclude that the independence assumption of the random-walk model was not upheld by his data.

Mandelbrot [37], however, discovered a flaw in Alexander's computations which led to serious overstatement of the profitability of the filters. Alexander assumed that his hypothetical trader could always buy at a price exactly equal to the low plus x per cent and sell at a price exactly equal to the high minus x per cent. There is, of course, no assurance that such prices ever existed. In fact, since the filter rule is defined in terms of a trough plus *at least* x per cent or a peak minus *at least* x per cent, the purchase price will usually be something higher than the low plus x per cent, while the sale price will usually be below the high minus x per cent.

In a later paper [2, Table 1], however, Alexander derived a bias factor and used it to correct his earlier work. With the corrections for bias it turned out that the filters only rarely compared favorably with buy-and-hold, even though the higher broker's commissions incurred under the filter rule were ignored. It would seem, then, that at least for the purposes of the individual investor Alexander's filter results tend to support the independence assumption of the random walk model.

In the later paper [2, Tables 8, 9, 10,

TABLE 15—EXPECTED AND ACTUAL DISTRIBUTIONS OF RUNS BY LENGTH

LENGTH	PLUS RUNS			MINUS RUNS			NO-CHANGE RUNS		
	Probability	Expected No.	Actual No.	Probability	Expected No.	Actual No.	Probability	Expected No.	Actual No.
	American Tobacco								
1...........	0.52221	154.58	133	0.57521	169.69	164	0.90257	98.38	94
2...........	.24951	73.85	80	.24434	72.08	66	.08794	9.58	14
3...........	.11921	35.29	40	.10379	30.62	34	.00857	0.93	1
4...........	.05696	16.86	25	.04409	13.01	19	.00083	0.09	0
5...........	.02721	8.06	9	.01873	5.52	3	.00008	0.01	0
6...........	.01300	3.85	8	.00796	2.35	7	.00001	0.00	0
7...........	.00621	1.84	1	.00338	1.00	2	.00000	0.00	0
8...........	.00297	0.88	0	.00144	0.42	0	.00000	0.00	0
9...........	.00142	0.42	0	.00061	0.18	0	.00000	0.00	0
10...........	.00068	0.20	0	.00026	0.08	0	.00000	0.00	0
11...........	.00032	0.10	0	.00011	0.03	0	.00000	0.00	0
12...........	.00015	0.05	0	.00005	0.01	0	.00000	0.00	0
13...........	.00007	0.02	0	.00002	0.01	0	.00000	0.00	0
14...........	.00004	0.01	0	.00001	0.00	0	.00000	0.00	0
15...........	0.00003	0.01	0	0.00001	0.00	0	0.00000	0.00	0
Totals....	....	296.00	296	....	295.00	295	....	109.00	109
	Bethlehem Steel								
1...........	0.59000	166.38	159	0.53333	160.00	155	0.87667	111.34	107
2...........	.24190	68.22	73	.24889	74.67	79	.10812	13.73	19
3...........	.09918	27.97	29	.11615	34.84	37	.01334	1.69	1
4...........	.04066	11.47	11	.05420	16.26	16	.00164	0.21	0
5...........	.01667	4.70	6	.02529	7.59	9	.00020	0.03	0
6...........	.00684	1.93	2	.01180	3.54	2	.00003	0.00	0
7...........	.00280	0.79	2	.00551	1.65	1	.00000	0.00	0
8...........	.00115	0.32	0	.00257	0.77	1	.00000	0.00	0
9...........	.00047	0.13	0	.00120	0.36	0	.00000	0.00	0
10...........	.00019	0.05	0	.00056	0.17	0	.00000	0.00	0
11...........	.00008	0.02	0	.00026	0.08	0	.00000	0.00	0
12...........	.00003	0.01	0	.00012	0.04	0	.00000	0.00	0
13...........	.00001	0.00	0	.00006	0.02	0	.00000	0.00	0
14...........	.00001	0.00	0	.00003	0.01	0	.00000	0.00	0
15...........	0.00000	0.00	0	0.00002	0.01	0	0.00000	0.00	0
Totals....	....	282.00	282	....	300.00	300	....	127.00	127
	International Harvester								
1...........	0.55167	167.15	171	0.56083	168.81	168	0.88750	102.95	98
2...........	.24733	74.94	75	.24630	74.14	82	.09984	11.58	17
3...........	.11089	33.60	33	.10817	32.56	27	.01123	1.30	1
4...........	.04971	15.06	8	.04750	14.30	14	.00126	0.15	0
5...........	.02229	6.75	13	.02086	6.28	5	.00014	0.02	0
6...........	.00999	3.03	1	.00916	2.76	3	.00002	0.00	0
7...........	.00448	1.36	1	.00402	1.21	1	.00000	0.00	0
8...........	.00201	0.61	1	.00177	0.53	1	.00000	0.00	0
9...........	.00090	0.27	0	.00078	0.23	0	.00000	0.00	0
10...........	.00040	0.12	0	.00034	0.10	0	.00000	0.00	0
11...........	.00018	0.05	0	.00015	0.05	0	.00000	0.00	0
12...........	.00008	0.02	0	.00007	0.02	0	.00000	0.00	0
13...........	.00004	0.01	0	.00003	0.01	0	.00000	0.00	0
14...........	.00002	0.00	0	.00001	0.00	0	.00000	0.00	0
15...........	0.00001	0.00	0	0.00001	0.00	0	0.00000	0.00	0
Totals....	....	303.00	303	....	301.00	301	....	116.00	116

and 11], however, Alexander goes on to test various other mechanical trading techniques, one of which involved a simplified form of the Dow theory. It turns out that most of these other techniques provide better profits than his filter technique, and indeed better profits than buy-and-hold. This again led him to conclude that the independence assumption of the random-walk model had been overturned.

Unfortunately a serious error remains, even in Alexander's latest computations. The error arises from the fact that he neglects dividends in computing profits for all of his mechanical trading rules. This tends to overstate the profitability of these trading rules relative to buy-and-hold. The reasoning is as follows. Under the buy-and-hold method the total profit is the price change for the time period plus any dividends that have been paid. Thus dividends act simply to increase the profitability of holding stock. All of Alexander's more complicated trading rules, however, involve short sales. In a short sale the borrower of the securities is usually required to reimburse the lender for any dividends that are paid while the short position is outstanding. Thus taking dividends into consideration will always tend to reduce the profitability of a mechanical trading rule relative to buy-and-hold. In fact, since in Alexander's computations the more complicated techniques are not substantially better than buy-and-hold, we would suspect that in most cases proper adjustment for dividends would probably completely turn the tables in favor of the buy-and-hold method.

The above discussion would seem to raise grave doubts concerning the validity of Alexander's most recent empirical results and thus of the conclusions he draws from these results. Because of the complexities of the issues, however, these doubts cannot be completely or systematically resolved within the confines of this paper. In a study now in progress various mechanical trading rules will be tested on data for individual securities rather than price indices. We turn now to a discussion of some of the preliminary results of this study.

Alexander's filter technique has been applied to the price series for the individual securities of the Dow-Jones Industrial Average used throughout this report. Filters from 0.5 per cent to 50 per cent were used. All profits were computed on the basis of a trading block of 100 shares, taking proper account of dividends. That is, if an ex-dividend date occurs during some time period, the amount of the dividend is added to the net profits of a long position open during the period, or subtracted from the net profits of a short position. Profits were also computed gross and net of broker's commissions, where the commissions are the exact commissions on lots of 100 shares at the time of transaction. In addition, for purposes of comparison the profits before commissions from buying and holding were computed for each security.

The results are shown in Table 16. Columns (1) and (2) of the table show average profits per filter, gross and net of commissions. Column (3) shows profits from buy-and-hold. Although they must be regarded as very preliminary, the results are nevertheless impressive. We see in column (2) that, when commissions are taken into account, profits per filter are positive for only four securities. Thus, from the point of view of the average investor, the results produced by the filter technique do not seem to invalidate the independence assumption of the random-walk model. In practice the largest profits under the filter technique would seem to be those of the broker.

A comparison of columns (1) and (3) also yields negative conclusions with respect to the filter technique. Even excluding commissions, in only seven cases are the profits per filter greater than those of buy-and-hold. Thus it would seem that even for the floor trader, who of course avoids broker commissions, the filter technique cannot be used to make expected profits greater than those of buy-and-hold. It would seem, then, that from the trader's point of view the independence assumption of the random-walk model is an adequate description of reality.

Although in his later article [2] Alexander seems to accept the validity of the independence assumption for the purposes of the investor or the trader, he argues that, from the standpoint of the academician, a stronger test of independence is relevant. In particular, he argues

TABLE 16

SUMMARY OF FILTER PROFITABILITY IN RELATION TO NAÏVE BUY-AND-HOLD TECHNIQUE*

Stock	Profits per Filter†		
	Without Commissions (1)	With Commissions (2)	Buy-and-Hold (3)
Allied Chemical	648.37	−10,289.33	2,205.00
Alcoa	3,207.40	− 3,929.42	− 305.00
American Can	− 844.32	− 5,892.85	1,387.50
A.T.&T.	16,577.26	4,912.84	20,005.00
American Tobacco	8,342.61	− 1,467.71	7,205.00
Anaconda	− 28.26	− 7,145.82	862.50
Bethlehem Steel	− 837.94	− 6,566.80	652.50
Chrysler	− 954.68	−12,258.61	− 1,500.00
Du Pont	6,564.21	− 465.35	9,550.00
Eastman Kodak	6,584.95	− 5,926.10	11,860.50
General Electric	− 107.06	− 8,601.28	2,100.00
General Foods	11,370.33	2,266.89	11,420.00
General Motors	− 1,099.40	− 8,440.42	2,025.00
Goodyear	− 2,241.28	−17,323.20	2,920.70
International Harvester	− 735.95	− 7,444.92	3,045.00
International Nickel	5,231.25	− 3,509.97	5,892.50
International Paper	2,266.82	− 7,976.68	− 278.10
Johns Manville	− 1,090.22	− 8,368.44	1,462.50
Owens Illinois	727.27	− 5,960.05	3,437.50
Procter & Gamble	12,202.83	4,561.52	8,550.00
Sears	4,871.36	408.65	5,195.00
Standard Oil (Calif.)	− 3,639.79	−21,055.08	5,326.50
Standard Oil (N.J.)	− 1,416.48	− 6,208.68	1,380.00
Swift & Co.	− 923.07	− 8,161.76	552.50
Texaco	2,803.98	− 5,626.11	6,546.50
Union Carbide	3,564.02	− 1,612.83	1,592.50
United Aircraft	− 1,190.10	− 8,369.88	562.50
U.S. Steel	1,068.23	− 5,650.03	475.00
Westinghouse	− 338.85	−12,034.56	745.00
Woolworth	4,190.78	− 2,403.34	3,225.00

* All figures are computed on the basis of 100 shares. Column (1) is total profits minus total losses on all filters, divided by the number of different filters tried on the security. Column (2) is the same as column (1) except that total profits and losses are computed net of commissions. Column (3) is last price plus any dividends paid during the period, minus the initial price for the period.

† The different filters are from 0.5 per cent to 5 per cent by steps of 0.5 per cent; from 6 per cent to 10 per cent by steps of 1 per cent; from 12 per cent to 20 per cent by steps of 2 per cent; and then 25 per cent, 30 per cent, 40 per cent and 50 per cent.

that the academic researcher is not interested in whether the dependence in series of price changes can be used to increase expected profits. Rather, he is primarily concerned with determining whether the independence assumption is an *exact* description of reality. In essence he proposes that we treat independence as a extreme null hypothesis and test it accordingly.

At this time we will ignore important counterarguments as to whether a strict test of an extreme null hypothesis is likely to be meaningful, given that for practical purposes the hypothesis would seem to be a valid approximation to reality for *both* the statistician and the investor. We simply note that a signs test applied to the profit figures in column (1) of Table 16 would not reject the extreme null hypothesis of independence for any of the standard significance levels. Sixteen of the profit figures in column (1) are positive and fourteen are negative, which is not very far from the even split that would be expected under a pure random model without trends in the price levels. If we allowed for the long-term upward bias of the market, the results would conform even more closely to the predictions of the strict null hypothesis. Thus the results produced by the filter technique do not seem to overturn the independence assumption of the random-walk model, regardless of how strictly that assumption is interpreted.

Finally, we emphasize again that these results must be regarded as preliminary. Many more complicated analyses of the filter technique are yet to be completed. For example, although average profits per filter do not compare favorably with buy-and-hold, there may be particular filters which are consistently better than buy-and-hold for all securities. We prefer, however, to leave such issues to a later paper. For now suffice it to say that preliminary results seem to indicate that the filter technique does not overturn the independence assumption of the random-walk model.

D. DISTRIBUTION OF SUCCESSORS TO LARGE VALUES

Mandelbrot [37, pp. 418–19] has suggested that one plausible form of dependence that could partially account for the long tails of empirical distributions of price changes is the following: Large changes may tend to be followed by large changes, but of random sign, whereas small changes tend to be followed by small changes.[36] The economic rationale for this type of dependence hinges on the nature of the information process in a world of uncertainty. The hypothesis implicitly assumes that when important new information comes into the market, it cannot always be evaluated precisely. Sometimes the immediate price change caused by the new information will be too large, which will set in motion forces to produce a reaction. In other cases the immediate price change will not fully discount the information, and impetus will be created to move the price again in the same direction.

The statistical implication of this hypothesis is that the conditional probability that tomorrow's price change will be large, given that today's change has been large, is higher than the unconditional probability of a large change. To test this, empirical distributions of the immediate successors to large price changes have been computed for the daily differ-

[36] Although the existence of this type of price behavior could not be used by the investor to increase his expected profits, the behavior does fit into the statistical definition of dependence. That is, knowledge of today's price change does condition our prediction of the *size,* if not the *sign,* of tomorrow's change.

ences of ten stocks. Six of the stocks were chosen at random. They include Allied Chemical, American Can, Eastman Kodak, Johns Manville, Standard Oil of New Jersey, and U.S. Steel. The other four were chosen because they showed longer than average tails in the tests of Sections III and IV. A large daily price change was defined as a change in log price greater than 0.03 in absolute value.

The results of the computations are shown in Table 17. The table is arranged to facilitate a direct comparison between the frequency distributions of successors to large daily price changes and the frequency distributions of all price changes. It shows for each stock the number and relative frequency of observations in the distribution of successors within given ranges of the distribution of all price changes. For example, the number in column (1) opposite Allied Chemical indicates that there are twenty-seven observations in the distribution of successors to large values that fall within the intersextile range of the distribution of all price changes for Allied Chemical. The number in column (6) opposite Allied Chemical indicates that twenty-seven observations are 55.1 per cent of

TABLE 17

DISTRIBUTIONS OF SUCCESSORS TO LARGE VALUES*

Stock	Intersextile (1)	2 Per Cent (2)	1 Per Cent (3)	>1 Per Cent (4)	Total (5)
	Number				
Allied Chemical	27	46	48	1	49
American Can	13	26	27	5	32
A.T.&T.	4	12	14	2	16
Eastman Kodak	25	35	39	5	44
Goodyear	40	66	66	4	70
Johns Manville	38	62	63	3	66
Sears	14	25	28	3	31
Standard Oil (N.J.)	11	18	18	2	20
United Aircraft	49	78	84	4	88
U.S. Steel	14	27	31	5	36
	Frequency				
	(6)	(7)	(8)	(9)	
Expected frequency	0.6667	0.9600	0.9800	0.0200	
Allied Chemical	.5510	.9388	.9796	.0204	
American Can	.4063	.8125	.8438	.1562	
A.T.&T.	.2500	.7500	.8750	.1250	
Eastman Kodak	.5682	.7955	.8864	.1136	
Goodyear	.5714	.9429	.9429	.0571	
Johns Manville	.5758	.9394	.9545	.0455	
Sears	.4516	.8065	.9032	.0968	
Standard Oil (N.J.)	.5500	.9000	.9000	.1000	
United Aircraft	.5568	.8864	.9545	.0455	
U.S. Steel	0.3889	0.7500	0.8611	0.1389	

* Number and frequency of observations in the distributions of successors within given ranges of the distributions of all changes. The ranges are defined as follows: Intersextile = 0.83 fractile —0.17 fractile; 2 per cent = 0.98 fractile —0.02 fractile; 1 per cent = 0.99 fractile —0.01 fractile. The fractiles are the fractiles of the distributions of all price changes and not of the distributions of successors to large changes.

the total number of successors to large values, whereas the distribution of all price changes contains, by definition, 66.7 per cent of its observations within its intersextile range. Similarly, the number in column (9) opposite Goodyear indicates that in the distribution of successors 5.7 per cent of the observations fall outside of the 1 per cent range, whereas by definition only 2 per cent of the observations in the distribution of all changes are outside this range.

It is evident from Table 17 that the distributions of successors are flatter and have longer tails than the distributions of all price changes. This is best illustrated by the relative frequencies. In every case the distribution of successors has less relative frequency within each fractile range than the distribution of all changes, which implies that the distribution of successors has too much relative frequency outside these ranges.

These results can be presented graphically by means of simple scatter diagrams. This is done for American Telephone and Telegraph and Goodyear in Figure 8. The abscissas of the graphs show X_1, the value of the large price change. The ordinates show X_2, the price change on the day immediately following a large change. Though it is difficult to make strong statements from such graphs, as would be expected in light of Table 17, it does seem that the successors do not concentrate around the abscissas of the graphs as much as would be expected if their distributions were the same as the distributions of all changes. Even a casual glance at the graphs shows, however, that the signs of the successors do indeed seem to be random. Moreover, these statements hold for the graphs of the securities not included in Figure 8.

In sum, there is evidence that large changes tend to be followed by large changes, but of random sign. However, though there does seem to be more bunching of large values than would be predicted by a purely independent model, the tendency is not very strong. In Table 17 most of the successors to large observations do fall within the intersextile range even though more of the successors fall into the extreme tails than would be expected in a purely random model.

E. SUMMARY

None of the tests in this section give evidence of any important dependence in the first differences of the logs of stock prices. There is some evidence that large changes tend to be followed by large changes of either sign, but the dependence from this source does not seem to be too important. There is no evidence at all, however, that there is any dependence in the stock-price series that would be regarded as important for investment purposes. That is, the past history of the series cannot be used to increase the investor's expected profits.

It must be emphasized, however, that, while the observed departures from independence are extremely slight, this does not mean that they are unimportant for every conceivable purpose. For example, the fact that large changes tend to be followed by large changes may not be information which yields profits to chart readers; but it may be very important to the economist seeking to understand the process of price determination in the capital market. The importance of any observed dependence will always depend on the question to be answered.

VI. Conclusion

The purpose of this paper has been to test empirically the random-walk model of stock price behavior. The model makes

American Tel. & Tel.

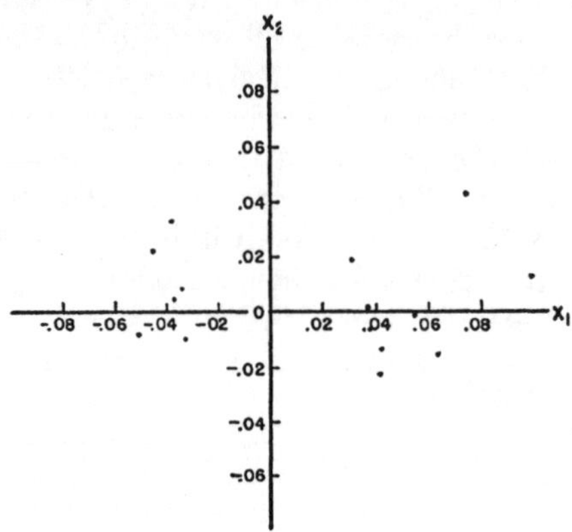

Goodyear

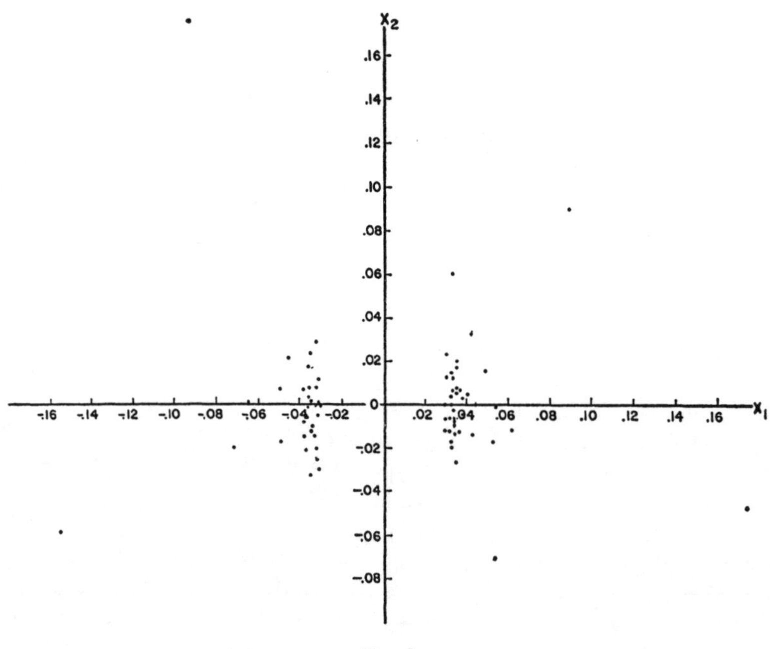

FIG. 8

two basic assumptions: (1) successive price changes are independent, and (2) the price changes conform to some probability distribution. We begin this section by summarizing the evidence concerning these assumptions. Then the implications of the results will be discussed from various points of view.

A. DISTRIBUTION OF PRICE CHANGES

In previous research on the distribution of price changes the emphasis has been on the general shape of the distribution, and the conclusion has been that the distribution is approximately Gaussian or normal. Recent findings of Benoit Mandelbrot, however, have raised serious doubts concerning the validity of the Gaussian hypothesis. In particular, the Mandelbrot hypothesis states that empirical distributions of price changes conform better to stable Paretian distributions with characteristic exponents less than 2 than to the normal distribution (which is also stable Paretian but with characteristic exponent exactly equal to 2). The conclusion of this paper is that Mandelbrot's hypothesis does seem to be supported by the data. This conclusion was reached only after extensive testing had been carried out. The results of this testing will now be summarized.

If the Mandelbrot hypothesis is correct, the empirical distributions of price changes should have longer tails than does the normal distribution. That is, the empirical distributions should contain more relative frequency in their extreme tails than would be expected under a simple Gaussian hypothesis. In Section III frequency distributions were computed for the daily changes in log price of each of the thirty stocks in the sample. The results were quite striking. The empirical distribution for *each* stock contained more relative frequency in its central bell than would be expected under a normality hypothesis. More important, however, in *every* case the extreme tails of the distributions contained more relative frequency than would be expected under the Gaussian hypothesis. As a further test of departures from normality, a normal probability graph for the price changes of each stock was also exhibited in Section III. As would be expected with long-tailed frequency distributions, the graphs generally assumed the shape of an elongated S.

In an effort to explain the departures from normality in the empirical frequency distributions, two simple complications of the Gaussian model were discussed and tested in Section III. One involved a variant of the mixture of distributions approach and suggested that perhaps weekend and holiday changes come from a normal distribution, but with a higher variance than the distribution of daily changes within the week. The empirical evidence, however, did not support this hypothesis. The second approach, a variant of the non-stationarity hypothesis, suggested that perhaps the leptokurtosis in the empirical frequency distributions is due to changes in the mean of the daily differences across time. The empirical tests demonstrated, however, that the extreme values in the frequency distributions are so large that reasonable shifts in the mean cannot adequately explain them.

Section IV was concerned with testing the property of stability and developing estimates of the characteristic exponent α of the underlying stable Paretian process. It was emphasized that rigorously established procedures for estimating the parameters of stable Paretian distributions are practically unknown because for most values of the characteristic exponent there are no known, explicit expressions for the density functions. As a result there is virtually no sampling theory available. It was concluded that at present the only way to get satisfactory estimates of the characteristic exponent is to use more than one estimating procedure. Thus three different techniques for estimating α were discussed, illustrated, and compared. The techniques involved double-log–normal-probability graphing, sequential computation of variance, and range analysis. In a very few cases α seemed to be so close to 2 that it was indistinguishable from 2 in the estimates. In the vast majority of cases, however, the estimated values were less than 2, with some dispersion about an average value close to 1.90. On the basis of these estimates of α and the results produced by the frequency distributions and normal probability graphs, it was concluded that the Mandelbrot hypothesis fits the data better than the Gaussian hypothesis.

B. INDEPENDENCE

Section V of this paper was concerned, with testing the validity of the independence assumption of the random-walk model on successive price changes for differencing intervals of one, four, nine, and sixteen days. The main techniques used were a serial correlation model, runs analysis, and Alexander's filter technique. For all tests and for all differencing intervals the amount of dependence in the data seemed to be either extremely slight or else non-existent. Finally, there was some evidence of bunching of large values in the daily differences, but the degree of bunching seemed to be only slightly greater than would be expected in a purely random model. On the basis of all these tests it was concluded that the independence assumption of the random-walk model seems to be an adequate description of reality.

C. IMPLICATIONS OF INDEPENDENCE

We saw in Section II that a situation where successive price changes are independent is *consistent with* the existence of an "efficient" market for securities, that is, a market where, given the available information, actual prices at every point in time represent very good estimates of intrinsic values. We also saw that two factors that could possibly contribute toward establishing independence are (1) the existence of many sophisticated chart readers actively competing with each other to take advantage of any dependencies in series of price changes, and (2) the existence of sophisticated analysts, where sophistication implies an ability both to *predict* better the occurrence of economic and political events which have a bearing on prices and to evaluate the eventual effects of such events on prices.

If his activities succeed in helping to establish independence of successive price changes, then the sophisticated chart reader has defeated his own purposes. When successive price changes are independent, there can be no chart-reading technique which makes the expected profits of the investor greater than they would be under a naïve buy-and-hold model. Such dogmatic statements do not apply to superior intrinsic value analysis, however. People who can consistently predict the occurrence of important events and evaluate their effects on prices will usually make larger profits than people who do not have this talent. The fact that the activities of these superior analysts help to make successive price changes independent does *not* imply that their expected profits cannot be greater than those of the investor who follows a buy-and-hold policy.

Of course, in practice, identifying people who qualify as superior analysts is not an easy task. The simple criterion put forth in Section II was the following: A superior analyst is one whose gains over many periods of time are ***consistently*** greater than those of the market. There are many institutions and individuals that claim to meet this criterion. In a separate paper their claims will be systematically tested. We present here some of the preliminary results for open-end mutual funds.[37]

In their appeals to the public, mutual funds usually make two basic claims: (1) because it pools the resources of many individuals, a fund can diversify much more effectively than the average small investor; and (2) because of its management's closeness to the market, the fund is better able to detect "good buys" in individual securities. In most cases the first claim is probably true. The second, however, implies that mutual funds provide returns higher than those earned by the market as a whole. It is this second claim that we now wish to test.

The return earned by the "market" during any time period can be measured in various ways. One possibility has been extensively explored by Fisher and Lorie [16] in a recent issue of this *Journal.* The basic assumption in all their computations is that at the beginning of each period studied the investor puts an equal amount of money in each common stock listed at that time on the New York Stock Exchange. Different rates of return for the period are then computed for different possible tax brackets of the investor, first under the assumption that all dividends are reinvested in the month paid and then under the assumption that dividends are not reinvested. All computations include the relevant brokers' commissions. Following the Lorie-Fisher procedure, a tax-exempt investor who initially entered the market at the end of 1950 and reinvested subsequent dividends in the securities paying them would have made a compound annual rate of return of 14.7 per cent upon disinvesting his entire portfolio at the end of 1960.

Similar computations have been carried out for thirty-nine open-end mutual funds. The funds studied have been chosen on the following basis: (1) the fund was operating during the entire period from the end of 1950 through the end of 1960; and (2) no more than 5 per cent of its total assets were invested in bonds at the end of 1960. It was assumed that the investor put $10,000 into each fund at the end of 1950, reinvested all subsequent dividend distributions, and then cashed in his portfolio at the end of 1960. It was also assumed, for simplicity, that the investor was tax exempt.

For our purposes, two different types of rates of return are of interest, gross and net of any loading charges. Most funds have a loading charge of about 8 per cent on new investment. That is, on a gross investment of $10,000 the investor receives only about $9,200 worth of the fund's shares. The remainng $800 is usually a straight salesman's commission and is not available to the fund's management for investment. From the investor's point of view the relevant rate of return on mutual funds to compare with the "market" rate is the return gross of loading charges, since the gross sum is the amount that the investor allocates to the funds. It is also interesting, however, to compute the yield on mutual funds net of any loading changes, since the net sum is the amount actually available to management. Thus the net return is the relevant measure of management's performance in relation to the market.

For the period 1950–60 our mutual-fund investments had a gross return of

[37] The preliminary results reported below were prepared as an assigned term paper by one of my students, Gerhard T. Roth. The data source for all the calculations was Wiesenberger [24].

14.1 per cent which is below the 14.7 per cent earned by the "market," as defined by Fisher and Lorie. The return, net of loading charges, on the mutual funds was 14.9 per cent, slightly but not significantly above the "market" return. Thus it seems that, at least for the period studied, mutual funds in general did not do any better than the market.

Although mutual funds taken together do no better than the market, in a world of uncertainty, during any given time period some funds will do better than the market and some will do worse. When a fund does better than the market during some time period, however, this is not necessarily evidence that the fund's management has knowledge superior to that of the average investor. A good showing during a particular period may merely be a chance result which is, in the long run, balanced by poor showings in other periods. It is only when a fund *consistently* does better than the market that there is any reason to feel that its higher than average returns may not be the work of lady luck.

In an effort to examine the consistency of the results obtained by different funds across time two separate tests were carried out. First, the compound rate of return, net of loading charges, was computed for each fund for the entire 1950–60 period. Second, the return for each fund for each year was computed according to the formula

$$r_{j,\,t+1}=\frac{p_{j,\,t+1}+d_{j,\,t+1}-p_{jt}}{p_{jt}},$$

$$t=1950,\ldots,1959$$

where P_{jt} is the price of a share in fund j at the end of year t, $p_{j,\,t+1}$ is the price at the end of year $t+1$, and $d_{j,\,t+1}$ are the dividends per share paid by the fund during year $t+1$. For each year the returns on the different funds were then ranked in ascending order, and a number from 1 to 39 was assigned to each.

The results are shown in Table 18. The order of the funds in the table is according to the return, net of loading charges, shown by the fund for the period 1950–60. This net return is shown in column (1). Columns (2)–(11) show the relative rankings of the year-by-year returns of each fund.

The most impressive feature of Table 18 is the *inconsistency* in the rankings of year-by-year returns for any given fund. For example, out of thirty-nine funds, *no* single fund consistently had returns high enough to place it among the top twenty funds for every year in the time period. On the other hand *no* single fund had returns low enough to place it among the bottom twenty of each year. Only two funds, Selected American and Equity, failed to have a return among the top ten for some year, and only three funds, Investment Corporation of America, Founders Mutual, and American Mutual, do not have a return among the bottom ten for some year. Thus funds in general seem to do no better than the market; in addition, individual funds do not seem to outperform consistently their competitors.[38] Our conclusion, then, must be that so far the sophisticated analyst has escaped detection.

D. IMPLICATIONS OF THE MANDELBROT HYPOTHESIS

The main conclusion of this paper with respect to the distribution of price changes is that a stable Paretian distribution with characteristic exponent α less than 2 seems to fit the data better

[38] These results seem to be in complete agreement with those of Ira Horowitz [22] and with the now famous "Study of Mutual Funds," prepared for the Securities and Exchange Commission by the Wharton School, University of Pennsylvania (87th Cong., 2d sess. [Washington, D.C.: Government Printing Office, 1962]).

than the normal distribution. This conclusion has implications from two points of view, economic and statistical, which we shall now discuss in turn.

1. ECONOMIC IMPLICATIONS

The important difference between a market dominated by a stable Paretian process with characteristic exponent $\alpha < 2$ and a market dominated by a Gaussian process is the following. In a Gaussian market, if the sum of a large number of price changes across some long time period turns out to be very large, chances are that each individual price change during the time period is negligible when compared to the total change. In a market that is stable Paretian with $\alpha < 2$,

TABLE 18

YEAR-BY-YEAR RANKING OF INDIVIDUAL FUND RETURNS

Fund	Return on Net	Year									
		1951	1952	1953	1954	1955	1956	1957	1958	1959	1960
	(1)	(2)	(3)	(4)	(5)	(6)	(7)	(8)	(9)	(10)	(11)
Keystone Lower Price..	18.7	29	1	38	5	3	8	35	1	1	36
T Rowe Price Growth..	18.7	1	33	2	8	14	15	2	25	7	4
Dreyfuss.............	18.4	37	37	14	3	7	11	3	2	3	7
Television Electronic...	18.4	21	4	9	2	33	20	16	2	4	20
National Investors Corp.	18.0	3	35	4	19	27	4	5	5	8	1
De Vegh Mutual Fund..	17.7	32	4	1	8	14	4	8	15	23	36
Growth Industries.....	17.0	7	34	14	17	9	9	20	5	6	11
Massachusetts Investors Growth............	16.9	5	36	31	11	9	1	23	4	9	4
Franklin Custodian.....	16.5	26	2	4	13	33	20	16	5	9	4
Investment Co. of America.................	16.0	21	15	14	11	17	15	23	15	15	15
Chemical Fund, Inc....	15.6	1	39	14	27	3	33	1	27	4	23
Founders Mutual......	15.6	21	13	25	8	2	20	16	11	13	28
Investment Trust of Boston................	15.6	6	3	25	3	14	26	31	20	29	20
American Mutual......	15.5	14	13	4	22	14	13	16	25	25	4
Keystone Growth......	15.3	29	15	25	1	1	1	39	11	18	38
Keystone High........	15.2	10	7	3	27	23	36	5	27	25	11
Aberdeen Fund........	15.1	32	23	9	25	9	7	10	27	7	30
Massachusetts Investors Trust...............	14.8	8	9	14	16	9	15	20	18	32	28
Texas Fund, Inc.......	14.6	3	15	9	32	23	26	5	27	37	7
Eaton & Howard Stock.	14.4	14	9	4	17	20	15	13	37	29	17
Guardian Mutual......	14.4	21	26	25	34	31	29	13	20	15	2
Scudder, Stevens, Clark.	14.3	14	23	14	19	27	15	29	9	15	30
Investors Stock Fund...	14.2	8	28	21	22	27	20	23	5	29	23
Fidelity Fund, Inc......	14.1	21	6	31	6	23	29	33	11	25	23
Fundamental Inv......	13.8	14	15	31	15	9	11	31	18	25	30
Century Shares........	13.5	14	28	35	25	3	20	23	31	34	2
Bullock Fund Ltd......	13.5	29	9	21	19	14	9	20	34	34	20
Financial Industries....	13.0	26	15	31	13	19	29	34	20	9	35
Group Common Stock..	13.0	38	8	25	27	27	33	8	20	34	17
Incorporated Investors.	12.9	14	13	37	6	3	13	37	11	18	39
Equity Fund..........	12.9	14	27	21	32	31	33	13	31	18	23
Selected American Shares.............	12.8	21	15	21	31	23	20	23	15	32	30
Dividend Shares.......	12.7	32	7	14	34	20	32	4	37	37	11
General Capital Corp...	12.4	10	28	9	38	35	39	23	34	13	23
Wisconsin Fund.......	12.3	32	26	4	37	35	38	10	34	18	7
International Resources.	12.3	10	37	39	22	35	1	37	39	1	11
Delaware Fund........	12.1	36	23	25	27	39	26	29	9	23	30
Hamilton Fund........	11.9	38	28	9	34	35	36	10	31	18	17
Colonial Energy.......	10.9	10	15	35	39	20	4	36	20	39	10

however, the size of the total will more than likely be the result of a few very large changes that took place during much shorter subperiods. In other words, whereas the path of the price level of a given security in a Gaussian market will be fairly continuous, in a stable Paretian market with $\alpha < 2$ it will usually be discontinuous. More simply, in a stable Paretian market with $\alpha < 2$, the price of a security will often tend to jump up or down by very large amounts during very short time periods.[39]

When combined with independence of successive price changes, the discontinuity of price levels in a stable Paretian market may provide important insights into the nature of the process that generates changes in intrinsic values across time. We saw earlier that independence of successive price changes is consistent with an "efficient" market, that is, a market where prices at every point in time represent best estimates of intrinsic values. This implies in turn that, when an intrinsic value changes, the actual price will adjust "instantaneously," where instantaneously means, among other things, that the actual price will initially overshoot the new intrinsic value as often as it will undershoot it.

In this light the combination of independence and a *Gaussian* distribution for the price changes would imply that intrinsic values do not very often change by large amounts. On the other hand, the combination of independence and a *stable Paretian* distribution with $\alpha < 2$ for the price changes would imply that intrinsic values often change by large amounts during very short periods of time—a situation quite consistent with a dynamic economy in a world of uncertainty.

[39] For a proof of these statements see Darling [13] or Anov and Bobnov [4].

The discontinuous nature of a stable Paretian market has some more practical implications, however. The fact that there are a large number of abrupt changes in a stable Paretian market means that such a market is inherently more risky than a Gaussian market. The variability of a given expected yield is higher in a stable Paretian market than it would be in a Gaussian market, and the probability of large losses is greater.

Moreover, in a stable Paretian market with $\alpha < 2$ speculators cannot usually protect themselves from large losses by means of such devices as "stop-loss" orders. If the price level is going to fall very much, the total decline will probably be accomplished very rapidly, so that it may be impossible to carry out many "stop-loss" orders at intermediate prices.

Finally, in some cases it may be possible a posteriori to find "causal explanations" for specific large price changes in terms of more basic economic variables. If the behavior of these more basic variables is itself largely unpredictable, however, the "causal explanation" will not be of much help in forecasting the appearance of large changes in the future. In addition it must be kept in mind that in the series we have been studying, there are very many large changes and the "explanations" are far from obvious. For example, the two largest changes in the Dow-Jones Industrial Average during the period covered by the data occurred on May 28 and May 29, 1962. Market analysts are still trying to find plausible "explanations" for these two days.

2. STATISTICAL IMPLICATIONS

The statistical implications of the Mandelbrot hypothesis follow mostly from the absence of a finite variance for stable Paretian distributions with characteristic exponents less than 2. In practical terms "infinite" variance means that the sample variance and standard deviation of a stable Paretian process with $\alpha < 2$ will show extremely erratic behavior even for very large samples. That is, for larger and larger sample sizes the variability of the sample variance and standard deviation will not tend to dampen nearly as much as would be expected with a Gaussian process. Because of their extremely erratic behavior, the sample variance and standard deviation are not meaningful measures of the variability inherent in a stable Paretian process with $\alpha < 2$.

This does not mean, however, that we are helpless in describing the dispersion of such a process. There are other measures of variability, such as interfractile ranges and the mean absolute deviation, which have both finite expectation and much less erratic sampling behavior than the variance and standard deviation.[40]

Figure 9 presents a striking demonstration of these statements. It shows the path of the sequential sample standard deviation and the sequential mean absolute deviation for four securities.[41] The upper set of points on each graph represents the path of the standard deviation, while the lower set represents the sample sequential mean absolute deviation. In every case the sequential mean absolute deviation shows less erratic behavior as the sample size is increased than does the sequential standard deviation. Even for very large samples the sequential standard deviation often shows very large discrete jumps, which are of course due to the occurrence of extremely large price changes in the data. As the sample size is increased, however, these same large price changes do not have nearly as strong an effect on the sequential mean absolute deviation. This would seem to be strong evidence that for distributions of price changes the mean absolute deviation is a much more reliable estimate of variability than the standard deviation.

In general, when dealing with stable Paretian distributions with characteristic exponents less than 2, the researcher should avoid the concept of variance both in his empirical work and in any economic models he may construct. For example, from an empirical point of view, when there is good reason to believe that the distribution of residuals has infinite variance, it is not very appealing to use a regression technique that has as its criterion the minimization of the sum of squared residuals from the regression line, since the expectation of that sum will be infinite.

This does not mean, however, that we are helpless when trying to estimate the parameters of a linear model if the variables of interest are subject to stable Paretian distributions with infinite variances. For example, an alternative technique, absolute-value regression, involves minimizing the sum of the absolute values of the residuals from the regression line. Since the expectation of the absolute value of the residual will be finite as long as the characteristic exponent α of the distribution of residuals is greater than 1, this minimization criterion is meaning-

[40] The mean absolute deviation is defined as

$$|D| = \sum_{i=1}^{N} \frac{|x_i - \bar{x}|}{N},$$

where x is the variable and N is the total sample size.

[41] Sequential computation of a parameter means that the *cumulative* sequential sample value of the parameter is recomputed at fixed intervals subsequent to the beginning of the sampling period. Each new computation of the parameter in the sequence contains the same values of the random variable as the computation immediately preceding it, plus any new values of the variable that have since been generated.

ful for a wide variety of stable Paretian processes.[42]

A good example of an economic model which uses the notion of variance in situations where there is good reason to believe that variances are infinite is the classic Markowitz [39] analysis of efficient portfolios. In Markowitz' terms, efficient portfolios are portfolios which have maximum expected return for given variance of expected return. If yields on securities follow distributions with infinite variances, however, the expected yield of a diversified portfolio will also follow a

[42] For a discussion of the technique of absolute value regression see Wagner [46], [47]. Wise [49] has shown that when the distribution of residuals has characteristic exponent $1 < \alpha < 2$, the usual least squares estimators of the parameters of a regression equation are consistent and unbiased. He has further shown, however, that when $\alpha < 2$, the least squares estimators are not the most efficient linear estimators, i.e., there are other techniques for which the sampling distributions of the regression parameters have lower dispersion than the sampling distributions of the least squares estimates. Of course it is also possible that some non-linear technique, such as absolute value regression, provides even more efficient estimates than the most efficient linear estimators.

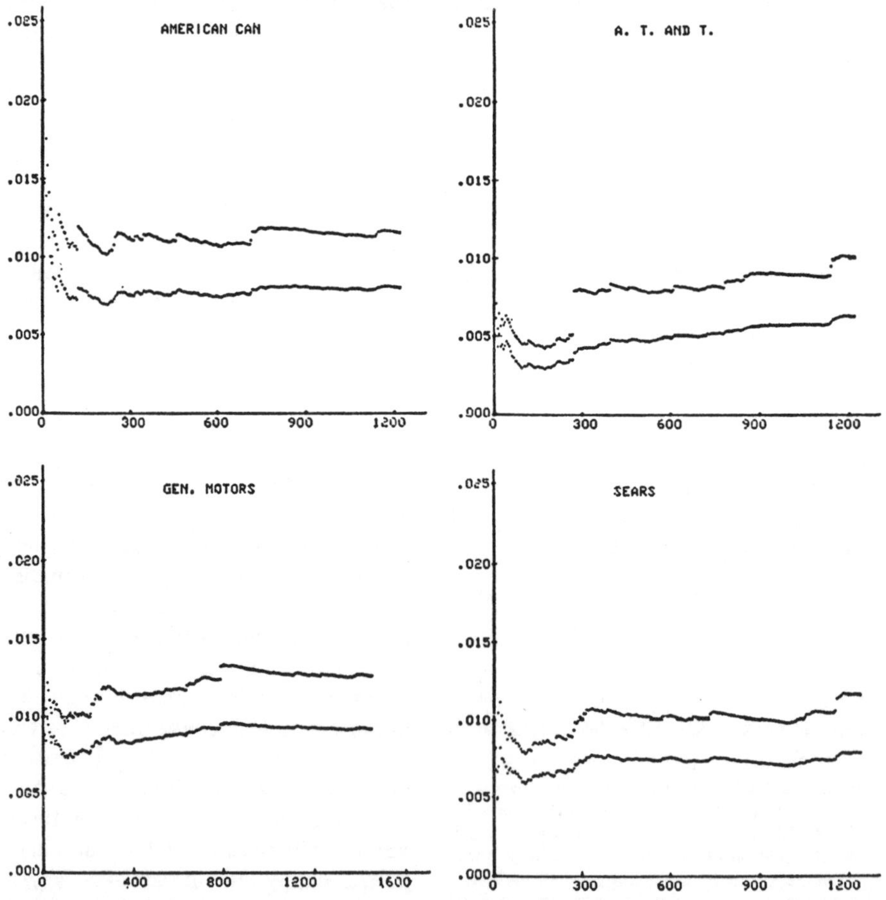

FIG. 9.—Sequential standard deviations and sequential mean absolute deviations. Horizontal axes show sequential sample sizes; vertical axes show parameter estimates.

distribution with an infinite variance. In this situation the mean-variance concept of an efficient portfolio loses its meaning.

This does *not* mean, however, that diversification is a meaningless concept in a stable Paretian market, or that it is impossible to develop a model for portfolio analysis. In a separate paper [15] this author has shown that, if concepts of variability other than the variance are used, it is possible to develop a model for portfolio analysis in a stable Paretian market. It is also possible to define the conditions under which increasing diversification has the effect of reducing the dispersion of the distribution of the return on the portfolio, even though the variance of that distribution may be infinite.

Finally, although the Gaussian or normal distribution does not seem to be an adequate representation of distributions of stock price changes, it is not necessarily the case that stable Paretian distributions with infinite variances provide the only alternative. It is possible that there are long-tailed distributions with finite variances that could also be used to describe the data.[43] We shall now argue, however, that one is forced to accept many of the conclusions discussed above, regardless of the position taken with respect to the finite-versus-infinite-variance argument.

For example, although one may feel that it is nonsense to talk about infinite variances when dealing with real-world variables, one is nevertheless forced to admit that for distributions of stock price changes the sampling behavior of the standard deviation is much more erratic than that of alternative dispersion parameters such as the mean absolute deviation. For this reason it may be better to use these alternative dispersion parameters in empirical work even though one may feel that in fact all variances are finite.

Similarly, the asymptotic properties of the parameters in a classical least-squares regression analysis are strongly dependent on the assumption of finite variance in the distribution of the residuals. Thus, if in some practical situation one feels that this distribution, though long-tailed, has finite variance, in principle one may feel justified in using the least-squares technique. If, however, one observes that the sampling behavior of the parameter estimates produced by the least-squares technique is much more erratic than that of some alternative technique, one may be forced to conclude that for reasons of efficiency the alternative technique is superior to least squares.

The same sort of argument can be applied to the portfolio-analysis problem. Although one may feel that in principle real-world distributions of returns must have finite variances, it is well known that the usual Markowitz-type efficient set analysis is highly sensitive to the estimates of the variances that are used. Thus, if it is difficult to develop good estimates of variances because of erratic sampling behavior induced by long-tailed distributions of returns, one may feel forced to use an alternative measure of dispersion in portfolio analyses.

Finally, from the point of view of the individual investor, the name that the researcher gives to the probability distribution of the return on a security is irrelevant, as is the argument concerning whether variances are finite or infinite. The investor's sole interest is in the *shape* of the distribution. That is, the only information he needs concerns the proba-

[43] It is important to note, however, that stable Paretian distributions with characteristic exponents less than 2 are the only long-tailed distributions that have the crucial property of stability or invariance under addition.

bility of gains and losses greater than given amounts. As long as two different hypotheses provide adequate descriptions of the relative frequencies, the investor is indifferent as to whether the researcher tells him that distributions of returns are stable Paretian with characteristic exponent $\alpha < 2$ or just long-tailed but with finite variances.

In essence, all of the above arguments merely say that, given the long-tailed empirical frequency distributions that have been observed, in most cases one's subsequent behavior in light of these results will be the same whether one leans toward the Mandelbrot hypothesis or toward some alternative hypothesis involving other long-tailed distributions. For most purposes the implications of the empirical work reported in this paper are independent of any conclusions concerning the name of the hypothesis which the data seem to support.

E. POSSIBLE DIRECTIONS FOR FUTURE RESEARCH

It seems safe to say that this paper has presented strong and voluminous evidence in favor of the random-walk hypothesis. In business and economic research, however, one can never claim to have established a hypothesis beyond question. There are always additional tests which would tend either to confirm the validity of the hypothesis or to contradict results previously obtained. In the final paragraphs of this paper we wish to suggest some possible directions which future research on the random-walk hypothesis could take.

1. ADDITIONAL POSSIBLE TESTS OF DEPENDENCE

There are two different approaches to testing for independence. First, one can carry out purely statistical tests. If these tend to support the assumption of independence, one may then infer that there are probably no mechanical trading rules based on patterns in the past history of price changes which will make the profits of the investor greater than they would be under a buy-and-hold policy. Second, one can proceed by directly testing different mechanical trading rules to see whether or not they do provide profits greater than buy-and-hold. The serial-correlation model and runs tests discussed in Section V are representative of the first approach, while Alexander's filter technique is representative of the second.

Academic research to date has tended to concentrate on the statistical approach. This is true, for example, of the extremely sophisticated work of Granger and Morgenstern [19], Moore [41], Kendall [26], and others. Aside from Alexander's work [1], [2], there has really been very little effort by academic people to test directly the various chartist theories that are popular in the financial world. Systematic validation or invalidation of these theories would represent a real contribution.

2. POSSIBLE RESEARCH ON THE DISTRIBUTION OF PRICE CHANGES

There are two possible courses which future research on the distribution of price changes could take. First, until now most research has been concerned with simply finding statistical distributions that seem to coincide with the empirical distributions of price changes. There has been relatively little effort spent in exploring the more basic processes that give rise to the empirical distributions. In essence, there is as yet no general model of price formation in the stock market which explains price levels and distributions of price changes in terms of the behavior of more basic economic variables. Developing and testing such a model would contribute greatly toward establishing sound theoretical foundations in this area.

Second, if distributions of price changes are truly stable Paretian with characteristic exponent $\alpha < 2$, then it behooves us to develop further the statistical theory of stable Paretian distributions. In particular, the theory would be much advanced by evidence concerning the sampling behavior of different estimators of the parameters of these distributions. Unfortunately, rigorous analytical sampling theory will be difficult to develop as long as explicit expressions for the density functions of these distributions are not known.

Using Monte Carlo techniques, however, it is possible to develop an approximate sampling theory, even though explicit expressions for the density functions remain unknown. In a study now under way the series-expansion approximation to stable Paretian density functions derived by Bergstrom [7] is being used to develop a stable Paretian random numbers generator. With such a random numbers generator it will be possible to examine the behavior of different estimators of the parameters of stable Paretian distributions in successive random samples and in this way to develop an approximate sampling theory. The same procedure can be used, of course, to develop sampling theory for many different types of statistical tools.

In sum, it has been demonstrated that first differences of stock prices seem to follow stable Paretian distributions with characteristic exponent $\alpha < 2$. An important step which remains to be taken is the development of a broad range of statistical tools for dealing with these distributions.

REFERENCES

1. ALEXANDER, S. S. "Price Movements in Speculative Markets: Trends or Random Walks," *Industrial Management Review*, II (May, 1961), 7–26.
2. ———. "Price Movements in Speculative Markets: Trends or Random Walks, No. 2" in PAUL H. COOTNER (ed.) [9], pp. 338–72.
3. ANDERSON, R. L. "The Distribution of the Serial Correlation Coefficient," *Annals of Mathematical Statistics*, XIII (1942), 1–13.
4. ANOW, D. Z., and BOBNOV, A. A. "The Extreme Members of Samples and Their Role in the Sum of Independent Variables," *Theory of Probability and Its Applications*, V (1960), 415–35.
5. BACHELIER, L. J. B. A. *Le Jeu, la chance, et le hasard*. Paris: E. Flammarion, 1914, chaps. xviii–xix.
6. ———. *Théorie de la speculation*. Paris: Gauthier-Villars, 1900. Reprinted in PAUL H. COOTNER (ed.) [9], pp. 17–78.
7. BERGSTROM, H. "On Some Expansions of Stable Distributions," *Arkiv for Matematik*, II (1952), 375-78.
8. BLOM, GUNNAR. *Statistical Estimates and Transformed Beta-Variables*. New York: John Wiley & Sons, 1958.
9. COOTNER, PAUL H. (ed.). *The Random Character of Stock Market Prices*. Cambridge: M.I.T. Press, 1964. This is an excellent compilation of past work on random walks in stock prices. In fact it contains most of the studies listed in these references.
10. ———. "Stock Prices: Random vs. Systematic Changes," *Industrial Management Review*, III (Spring, 1962), 25–45.
11. COWLES, A. "A Revision of Previous Conclusions Regarding Stock Price Behavior, *Econometrica*, XXVIII (October, 1960), 909–15.
12. COWLES, A., and JONES, H. E. "Some A Posteriori Probabilities in Stock Market Action, *Econometrica*, V (July, 1937), 280–94.
13. DARLING, DONALD. "The Influence of the Maximum Term in the Addition of Independent Variables," *Transactions of the American Mathematical Society*, LXXIII (1952), 95–107.
14. FAMA, EUGENE F. "Mandelbrot and the

Stable Paretian Hypothesis," *Journal of Business*, XXXVI (October, 1963), 420–29.

15. FAMA, EUGENE F. "Portfolio Analysis in a Stable Paretian Market," *Management Science* (January, 1965).
16. FISHER, L. and LORIE, J. H., "Rates of Return on Investments in Common Stocks," *Journal of Business*, XXXVII (January, 1964), 1–21.
17. GNEDENKO, B. V., and KOLMOGOROV, A. N. *Limit Distributions for Sums of Independent Random Variables*. Translated from Russian by K. L. CHUNG. Cambridge, Mass.: Addison-Wesley, 1954.
18. GODFREY, MICHAEL D., GRANGER, CLIVE W. J., and MORGENSTERN, OSKAR. "The Random Walk Hypothesis of Stock Market Behavior," *Kyklos*, XVII (1964), 1–30.
19. GRANGER, C. W. J., and MORGENSTERN, O. "Spectral Analysis of New York Stock Market Prices," *Kyklos*, XVI (1963), 1–27.
20. GUMBEL, E. J. *Statistical Theory of Extreme Values and Some Practical Applications*. Applied Mathematics Series, No. 33, (Washington, D.C.: National Bureau of Standards, February 12, 1954).
21. HALD, ANDERS. *Statistical Theory with Engineering Applications*. New York: John Wiley & Sons, 1952.
22. HOROWITZ, IRA. "The Varying (?) Quality of Investment Trust Management," *Journal of the American Statistical Association*, LVIII (December, 1963), 1011–32.
23. IBRAGIMOV, I. A., and TCHERNIN, K. E. "On the Unimodality of Stable Laws," *Theory of Probability and Its Applications*, IV (Moscow, 1959), 453–56.
24. *Investment Companies*. New York: Arthur Wiesenberger & Co., 1961.
25. KENDALL, M. G. *The Advanced Theory of Statistics*. London: C. Griffin & Co., 1948, p. 412.
26. ———. "The Analysis of Economic Time-Series," *Journal of the Royal Statistical Society* (Ser. A), XCVI (1953), 11–25.
27. KING, BENJAMIN F. "The Latent Statistical Structure of Security Price Changes," unpublished Ph.D. dissertation, Graduate School of Business, University of Chicago, 1964.
28. LARSON, ARNOLD B. "Measurement of a Random Process in Futures Prices," *Food Research Institute Studies*, I (November, 1960), 313–24.
29. LEVY, PAUL. *Calcul des probabilitiés*. Paris: Gauthier-Villars, 1925.
30. LINTNER, JOHN. "Distribution of Incomes of Corporations among Dividends, Retained Earnings and Taxes," *Papers and Proceedings of the American Economic Association*, XLVI (May, 1956), pp. 97–113.
31. MANDELBROT, BENOIT. "A Class of Long-tailed Probability Distributions and the Empirical Distribution of City Sizes," Research note, Thomas J. Watson Research Center, Yorktown Heights, N.Y., May 23, 1962.
32. ———. "New Methods in Statistical Economics," *Journal of Political Economy*, LXI (October, 1963), 421–40.
33. ———. "Paretian Distributions and Income Maximization," *Quarterly Journal of Economics*, LXXVI (February, 1962), 57–85.
34. ———. "The Pareto-Lévy Law and the Distribution of Income," *International Economic Review*, I (May, 1960), 79–106.
35. ———. "The Stable Paretian Income Distribution when the Apparent Exponent Is Near Two," *International Economic Review*, IV (January, 1963), 111–14.
36. ———. "Stable Paretian Random Functions and the Multiplicative Variation of Income," *Econometrica*, XXIX (October, 1961), 517–43.
37. ———. "The Variation of Certain Speculative Prices," *Journal of Business*, XXXVI (October, 1963), 394–419.
38. MANDELBROT, BENOIT, and ZARNFALLER, FREDERICK. "Five Place Tables of Certain Stable Distributions," Research note, Thomas J. Watson Research Center, Yorktown Heights, N. Y., December 31, 1959.
39. MARKOWITZ, HARRY. *Portfolio Selection: Efficient Diversification of Investments*. New York: John Wiley & Sons, 1959.
40. MILLER, MERTON H., and MODIGLIANI, FRANCO. "Dividend Policy, Growth, and the Valuation of Shares," *Journal of Business*, XXXIV (October, 1961), 411–33.
41. MOORE, ARNOLD. "A Statistical Analysis of Common-Stock Prices," unpublished Ph.D. dissertation, Graduate School of Business, University of Chicago, 1962.
42. OSBORNE, M. F. M. "Brownian Motion in the Stock Market," *Operations Research*, VII (March–April, 1959), 145–73.

43. ROBERTS, HARRY V. "Stock Market 'Patterns' and Financial Analysis: Methodological Suggestions," *Journal of Finance*, XIV (March, 1959), 1–10.
44. TIPPET, L. H. C. "On the Extreme Individuals and the Range of Samples Taken from a Normal Population," *Biometrika*, XVII (1925), 364–87.
45. TUKEY, J. W. "The Future of Data Analysis," *Annals of Mathematical Statistics*, XXXIII (1962), 14–21.
46. WAGNER, HARVEY M. "Linear Programming Techniques for Regression Analysis," *Journal of the American Statistical Association*, LIV (1959), 206–12.
47. ———. "Non-Linear Regression with Minimal Assumptions," *Journal of the American Statistical Association*, LVII (1962), 572–78.
48. WALLIS, W. A., and ROBERTS, H. V. *Statistics: A New Approach*. Glencoe Ill.: Free Press, 1956.
49. WISE, JOHN. "Linear Estimators for Linear Regression Systems Having Infinite Variances," paper presented at the Berkeley-Stanford Mathematical Economics Seminar, October, 1963.
50. WORKING, H. "A Random Difference Series for Use in the Analysis of Time Series," *Journal of the American Statistical Association*, XXIX (March, 1934), 11–24.

APPENDIX

STATISTICAL THEORY OF STABLE PARETIAN DISTRIBUTIONS

A. STABLE PARETIAN DISTRIBUTIONS: DEFINITION AND PARAMETERS

The stable Paretian family of distributions is defined by the logarithm of its characteristic function which has the general form

$$\begin{aligned}\log f(t) &= \log E(e^{iut}) \\ &= i\delta t - \gamma|t|^{\alpha}[1 + i\beta(t/|t|)w(t, \alpha)]\,,\end{aligned} \qquad (A1)$$

where u is the random variable, t is any real number, i is $\sqrt{-1}$, and

$$w(t, \alpha) = \begin{cases} \tan \dfrac{\pi\alpha}{2}, & \text{if} \quad \alpha \neq 1\,, \\ \dfrac{2}{\pi}\log|t|, & \text{if} \quad \alpha = 1\,. \end{cases} \qquad (A2)$$

Stable Paretian distributions have four parameters, α, β, δ, and γ. The parameter α is called the characteristic exponent of the distribution. It determines the height of, or total probability contained in, the extreme tails of the distribution and can take any value in the interval $0 < \alpha \leq 2$. When $\alpha = 2$, the relevant stable Paretian distribution is the normal distribution.[44] When α is in the interval $0 < \alpha < 2$, the extreme tails of the stable Paretian distributions are higher than those of the normal distribution, and the total probability in the extreme tails is larger the smaller the value of α. The most important consequence of this is that the variance exists (i.e., is finite) only in the limiting case $\alpha = 2$. The mean, however, exists as long as $\alpha > 1$.[45]

The parameter β is an index of skewness which can take any value in the interval $-1 \leq \beta \leq 1$. When $\beta = 0$, the distribution is symmetric. When $\beta > 0$, the distribution is skewed right (i.e., has a long tail to the right), and the degree of right skewness is larger the larger the value of β. Similarly when $\beta < 0$ the distribution is skewed left, and the degree of left skewness is larger the smaller the value of β.

The parameter δ is the location parameter of the stable Paretian distribution. When the characteristic exponent α is greater than 1, δ is the expected value or mean of the distribution. When $\alpha \leq 1$, however, the mean of the distribution is not defined. In this case δ will be some other parameter (e.g., the median when $\beta = 0$), which will describe the location of the distribution.

Finally, the parameter γ defines the scale of a stable Paretian distribution. For example, when $\alpha = 2$ (the normal distribution), γ is one-half the variance. When $\alpha < 2$, however, the variance of the stable Paretian distribution is infinite. In this case there will be a finite parameter γ which defines the scale of the distri-

[44] The logarithm of the characteristic function of a normal distribution is $\log f_i(t) = i\mu t - (\sigma^2/2)t^2$. This is the log characteristic function of a stable Paretian distribution with parameters $\alpha = 2$, $\delta = \mu$, and $\gamma = \sigma^2/2$. The parameters μ and σ^2 are, of course, the mean and variance of the normal distribution.

[45] For a proof of these statements see Gnedenko and Kolmogorov [17], pp. 179–83.

bution, but it will not be the variance. For example, when $\alpha = 1, \beta = 0$ (which is the Cauchy infinite. In this case there will be a finite parameter γ which defines the scale of the distribution), γ is the semi-interquartile range (i.e., one-half of the 0.75 fractile minus the 0.25 fractile).

B. KEY PROPERTIES OF STABLE PARETIAN DISTRIBUTIONS

The three most important properties of stable Paretian distributions are (1) the asymptotically Paretian nature of the extreme tail areas, (2) stability or invariance under addition, and (3) the fact that these distributions are the only possible limiting distributions for sums of independent, identically distributed, random variables.

1. *The law of Pareto.*—Lévy [29] has shown that the tails of stable Paretian distributions follow a weak or asymptotic form of the law of Pareto. That is,

$$Pr(u > \hat{u}) \rightarrow (\hat{u}/U_1)^{-\alpha} \text{ as } \hat{u} \rightarrow \infty , \quad \text{(A3)}$$

and

$$Pr(\hat{u} < \hat{u}) \rightarrow (|\hat{u}|/U_2)^{-\alpha} \quad \text{as} \quad \hat{u} \rightarrow -\infty , \quad \text{(A4)}$$

where u is the random variable, and the constants U_1 and U_2 are defined by[46]

$$\beta = \frac{U_1^\alpha - U_2^\alpha}{U_1^\alpha + U_2^\alpha} . \quad \text{(A5)}$$

From expressions (A3) and (A4) it is possible to define approximate densities for the extreme tail areas of stable Paretian distributions. If a new function $P(u)$ for the tail probabilities is defined by expressions (A3) and (A4), the density functions for the asymptotic portions of the tails are given by

$$\begin{aligned} p(u) &\approx -d\,P(u)/du \\ &\approx \alpha(U_1)^\alpha u^{-(\alpha+1)}, \quad u \rightarrow \infty , \end{aligned} \quad \text{(A6)}$$

$$p(u) \approx \alpha(U_2)^\alpha |u|^{-(\alpha+1)}, \quad u \rightarrow -\infty . \quad \text{(A7)}$$

Although it has been proven that stable Paretian distributions are unimodal,[47] closed expressions for the densities of the *central areas* of these distributions are known for only three cases, the Gaussian ($\alpha = 2$), the Cauchy ($\alpha = 1, \beta = 0$), and the well-known coin-tossing case ($\alpha = \frac{1}{2}, \beta = 1, \delta = 0$ and $\gamma = 1$). At this point this is probably the greatest weakness in the theory. Without density functions it is very difficult to develop sampling theory for the parameters of stable Paretian distributions. The importance of this limitation has been stressed throughout this paper.[48]

2. *Stability or invariance under addition.*—By definition, a stable Paretian distribution is any distribution that is stable or invariant under addition. That is, the distribution of sums of independent, identically distributed, stable Paretian variables is itself stable Paretian and has the same form as the distribution of the individual summands. The phrase "has the same form" is, of course, an imprecise verbal expression for a precise mathematical property. A more rigorous definition of stability is given by the logarithm of the characteristic function of sums of independent, identically distributed, stable Paretian variables. The expression for this function is

$$\begin{aligned} n \log f(t) &= i(n\delta)t \\ &- (n\gamma)|t|^\alpha\left[1 + i\beta\frac{t}{|t|}w(t, \alpha)\right], \end{aligned} \quad \text{(A8)}$$

where n is the number of variables in the sum and $\log f(t)$ is the logarithm of the characteristic function for the distribution of the individual summands. Expression (A8) is the same as (A1), the expression for $\log f(t)$, except that the parameters δ (location) and γ (scale) are multiplied by n. That is, except for origin and scale,

---

[46] The constants U_1 and U_2 can be regarded as scale parameters for the positive and negative tails of the distribution. The relative size of these two constants determines the value of β and thus the skewness of the distribution. If U_2 is large relative to U_1, the distribution is skewed left (i.e., $\beta < 0$), and skewed right when U_1 is large relative to U_2 (i.e., $\beta > 0$). When U_1 is zero the distribution has maximal left skewness. When U_2 is zero, the distribution has maximal right skewness. These two limiting cases correspond, of course, to values of β of -1 and 1. When $U_1 = U_2$, $\beta = 0$, and the distribution is symmetric.

[47] Ibraginov and Tchernin [23].

[48] It should be noted, however, that Bergstrom [7] has developed a series expansion to approximate the densities of stable Paretian distributions. The potential use of the series expansion in developing sampling theory for the parameters by means of Monte Carlo methods is discussed in Section VI of this paper.

the distribution of the sums is exactly the same as the distribution of the individual summands. More simply, stability means that the values of the parameters α and β remain constant under addition.

The definition of stability is always in terms of independent, identically distributed random variables. It will now be shown, however, that any linear weighted sum of independent, stable Paretian variables with the same characteristic exponent α will be stable Paretian with the same value of α. In particular, suppose we have n independent, stable Paretian variables, u_j, $j = 1, \ldots, n$. Assume further that the distributions of the various u_j have the same characteristic exponent α, but possibly different location, scale, and skewness parameters (δ_j, γ_j, and β_j, $j = 1, \ldots, n$). Let us now form a new variable, V, which is a weighted sum of the u_j with constant weights $p_j, j = 1, \ldots, n$. The log characteristic function of V will then be

$$\log F(t) = \sum_{j=1}^{n} \log f_j(p_j t)$$
$$= i\left(\sum_{j=1}^{n} p_j\delta_j\right)t - \left(\sum_{j=1}^{n} \gamma_j |p_j|^{\alpha}\right) \quad \text{(A9)}$$
$$\times |t|^{\alpha}\left[1 + i\bar{\beta}\frac{t}{|t|}w(t, \alpha)\right],$$

where

$$\bar{\beta} = \frac{\sum_{j=1}^{n} \gamma_j |p_j|^{\alpha}\beta_j}{\sum_{j=1}^{n} \gamma_j |p_j|^{\alpha}}, \quad \text{(A10)}$$

and $\log f_j(t)$ is the log characteristic function of u_j. Expression (A9) is the log characteristic function of a stable Paretian distribution with characteristic exponent α and with location, scale, and skewness parameters that are weighted sums of the location, scale, and skewness parameters of the distributions of the u_j.

3. *Limiting distributions.*—It can be shown that stability or invariance under addition leads to a most important corollary property of stable Paretian distributions; they are the only possible limiting distributions for sums of independent, identically distributed, random variables.[49] It is well known that if such variables have finite variance the limiting distribution for their sum will be the normal distribution. If the basic variables have infinite variance, however, and if their sums follow a limiting distribution, the limiting distribution must be stable Paretian with $0 < \alpha < 2$.

It has been proven independently by Gnedenko and Doeblin that, in order for the limiting distribution of sums to be stable Paretian with characteristic exponent $\alpha(0 < \alpha < 2)$, it is necessary and sufficient that[50]

$$\frac{F(-u)}{1-F(u)} \to \frac{C_1}{C_2} \quad \text{as} \quad u \to \infty, \quad \text{(A11)}$$

and for every constant $k > 0$,

$$\frac{1-F(u)+F(-u)}{1-F(ku)+F(-ku)} \to k^{\alpha} \quad \text{(A12)}$$
$$\text{as} \quad u \to \infty,$$

where F is the cumulative distribution function of the random variable u and C_1 and C_2 are constants. Expressions (A11) and (A12) will henceforth be called the conditions of Doeblin and Gnedenko.

It is clear that any variable that is asymptotically Paretian (regardless of whether it is also stable) will satisfy these conditions. For such a variable, as $u \to \infty$,

$$\frac{F(-u)}{1-F(u)} \to \left[\frac{(|-u|/U_2)}{(u/U_1)}\right]^{-\alpha} = \frac{U_2^{\alpha}}{U_1^{\alpha}},$$

and

$$\frac{1-F(u)+F(-u)}{1-F(ku)+F(-ku)}$$
$$\to \frac{(u/U_1)^{-\alpha} + (|-u|/U_2)^{-\alpha}}{(ku/U_1)^{-\alpha} + (|-ku|/U_2)^{-\alpha}} = k^{\alpha},$$

and the conditions of Doeblin and Gnedenko are satisfied.

To the best of my knowledge non-stable, asymptotically Paretian variables with exponent $\alpha < 2$ are the only known variables of infinite variance that satisfy conditions (A11) and (A12). Thus they are the only known non-stable variables whose sums approach stable Paretian limiting distributions with characteristic exponents less than 2.

[49] For a proof see Gnedenko and Kolmogorov [17], pp. 162–63.

[50] For a proof see Gnedenko and Kolmogorov [17], pp. 175–80.

C. PROPERTIES OF RANGES OF SUMS OF STABLE PARETIAN VARIABLES

By the definition of stability, sums of independent realizations of a stable Paretian variable are stable Paretian with the same value of the characteristic exponent α as the distribution of the individual summands. The process of taking sums does, of course, change the scale or unit of measurement of the distribution.

Let us now pose the problem of finding a constant by which to weight each variable in the sum so that the scale parameter of the distribution of sums is the same as that of the distribution of the individual summands. This amounts to finding a constant, a, such that

$$n\gamma|at|^{\alpha} = \gamma|t|^{\alpha}. \qquad \text{(A13)}$$

Solving this expression for a we get

$$a = n^{-1/\alpha}, \qquad \text{(A14)}$$

which implies that each of the summands must be divided by $n^{1/\alpha}$ if the scale, or unit of measurement, of the distribution of sums is to be the same as that of the distribution of the individual summands. The converse proposition, of course, is that the scale of the distribution of unweighted sums is $n^{1/\alpha}$ times the scale of the distribution of the individual summands. Thus, for example, the intersextile range of the distribution of sums of n independent realizations of a stable Paretian variable will be $n^{1/\alpha}$ times the intersextile range of the distribution of the individual summands. This property provides the basis of the range analysis approach to estimating α discussed in Section IV, C of this paper.[51]

D. PROPERTIES OF THE SEQUENTIAL VARIANCE OF A STABLE PARETIAN VARIABLE

Let u be a stable Paretian random variable with characteristic exponent $\alpha < 2$, and with location, scale, and skewness parameters δ, γ, and β. Define a new variable, $y = u - \delta$, whose distribution is exactly the same as that of u, except that the location parameter has been set equal to 0.

Suppose now that we are interested in the probability distribution of y^2. The positive tail of the distribution of y^2 is related to the tails of the distribution of y in the following way:

$$Pr(y^2 > \hat{y}) = Pr(y > \hat{y}^{1/2}) + Pr(y < -[\hat{y}^{1/2}]), \quad \hat{y} > 0. \qquad \text{(A15)}$$

But since the tails of the distribution of y follow an asymptotic form of the law of Pareto, for very large values of y this is just

$$Pr(y^2 > \hat{y}) \to (\hat{y}^{1/2}/U_1)^{-\alpha} + (\hat{y}^{1/2}/U_2)^{-\alpha}, \quad \hat{y} \to \infty. \qquad \text{(A16)}$$

Substituting $C_1 = U_1^{\alpha}$ and $C_2 = U_2^{\alpha}$ into expression (A16) and simplifying we get

$$Pr(y^2 > \hat{y}) \to (C_1 + C_2)\,\hat{y}^{-(\alpha/2)}, \qquad \text{(A17)}$$

which is a Paretian expression with exponent $\alpha' = \alpha/2$ and scale parameter $C'_1 = C_1 + C_2$.

The tail probabilities for the negative tail of the distribution of y^2 are, of course, all identically zero. This is equivalent to saying that the scale parameter, C'_2, in the Paretian expression for the negative tail of the distribution of y^2 is zero.

Let us now turn our attention to the distribution of sums of independent realizations of the variable y^2. Since y^2 is asymptotically Paretian, it satisfies the conditions of Doeblin and Gnedenko, and thus sums of y^2 will approach a stable Paretian distribution with characteristic exponent $\alpha' = \alpha/2$ and skewness

$$\beta' = \frac{C'_1 - C'_2}{C'_1 + C'_2} = 1. \qquad \text{(A18)}$$

We know from previous discussions that, if the scale of the distribution of sums is to be the same as that of the distribution of $\hat{y}^2$, the sums must be scaled by $n^{-1/\alpha'} = n^{-2/\alpha}$, where n is the number of summands. Thus the distributions of

$$y^2 \text{ and } n^{-2/\alpha}\sum_{i=1}^{n} y^2 \qquad \text{(A19)}$$

will be identical.

This discussion provides us with a way to analyze the distribution of the sample variance of the stable Paretian variable u. For values

[51] It is worth noting that although the scale of the distribution of sums expands with n at the rate $n^{1/\alpha}$, the scale parameter γ expands directly with n. Thus γ itself represents some more basic scale parameter raised to the power of α. For example, in the normal case ($\alpha = 2$) γ is related to the variance, but the variance is just the square of the standard deviation. The standard deviation, of course, is the more direct measure of the scale of the normal distribution.

of α less than 2, the population variance of the random variable u is infinite. The sample variance of n independent realizations of u is

$$S^2 = n^{-1} \sum_{i=1}^{n} y_i^2. \qquad \text{(A20)}$$

This can be multiplied by $n^{-2/\alpha + 2/\alpha} = 1$ with the result

$$S^2 = n^{-1+2/\alpha} \left(n^{-2/\alpha} \sum_{i=1}^{n} y_i^2 \right). \qquad \text{(A21)}$$

Now we know that the distribution of

$$n^{-2/\alpha} \sum_{i=1}^{n} y_i^2$$

is stable Paretian and independent of n. In particular, the median (or any other fractile) of this distribution has the same value for all n. This is not true, however, for the distribution of S^2. The median or any other fractile of the distribution of S^2 will grow in proportion to $n^{-1+2/\alpha}$. For example, if u_t is an independent, stable Paretian variable generated in time series, then the $.f$ fractile of the distribution of the cumulative sample variance of u_t at time t_1, as a function of the $.f$ fractile of the distribution of the sample variance at time t_0 is given by

$$S_1^2 = S_0^2 \left(\frac{n_1}{n_0} \right)^{-1+2/\alpha}, \qquad \text{(A22)}$$

where n_1 is the number of observations in the sample at time t_1, n_0 is the number at t, and S_1^2 and S_0^2 are the $.f$ fractiles of the distributions of the cumulative sample variances.

This result provides the basis for the sequential variance approach to estimating α discussed in Section IV, D of this paper.

[3]

SESSION TOPIC: STOCK MARKET PRICE BEHAVIOR

SESSION CHAIRMAN: BURTON G. MALKIEL

EFFICIENT CAPITAL MARKETS: A REVIEW OF THEORY AND EMPIRICAL WORK*

EUGENE F. FAMA**

I. INTRODUCTION

THE PRIMARY ROLE of the capital market is allocation of ownership of the economy's capital stock. In general terms, the ideal is a market in which prices provide accurate signals for resource allocation: that is, a market in which firms can make production-investment decisions, and investors can choose among the securities that represent ownership of firms' activities under the assumption that security prices at any time "fully reflect" all available information. A market in which prices always "fully reflect" available information is called "efficient."

This paper reviews the theoretical and empirical literature on the efficient markets model. After a discussion of the theory, empirical work concerned with the adjustment of security prices to three relevant information subsets is considered. First, *weak form* tests, in which the information set is just historical prices, are discussed. Then *semi-strong form* tests, in which the concern is whether prices efficiently adjust to other information that is obviously publicly available (e.g., announcements of annual earnings, stock splits, etc.) are considered. Finally, *strong form* tests concerned with whether given investors or groups have monopolistic access to any information relevant for price formation are reviewed.[1] We shall conclude that, with but a few exceptions, the efficient markets model stands up well.

Though we proceed from theory to empirical work, to keep the proper historical perspective we should note to a large extent the empirical work in this area preceded the development of the theory. The theory is presented first here in order to more easily judge which of the empirical results are most relevant from the viewpoint of the theory. The empirical work itself, however, will then be reviewed in more or less historical sequence.

Finally, the perceptive reader will surely recognize instances in this paper where relevant studies are not specifically discussed. In such cases my apologies should be taken for granted. The area is so bountiful that some such injustices are unavoidable. But the primary goal here will have been accomplished if a coherent picture of the main lines of the work on efficient markets is presented, along with an accurate picture of the current state of the arts.

* Research on this project was supported by a grant from the National Science Foundation. I am indebted to Arthur Laffer, Robert Aliber, Ray Ball, Michael Jensen, James Lorie, Merton Miller, Charles Nelson, Richard Roll, William Taylor, and Ross Watts for their helpful comments.

** University of Chicago—Joint Session with the Econometric Society.

1. The distinction between weak and strong form tests was first suggested by Harry Roberts.

II. The Theory of Efficient Markets

A. *Expected Return or "Fair Game" Models*

The definitional statement that in an efficient market prices "fully reflect" available information is so general that it has no empirically testable implications. To make the model testable, the process of price formation must be specified in more detail. In essence we must define somewhat more exactly what is meant by the term "fully reflect."

One possibility would be to posit that equilibrium prices (or expected returns) on securities are generated as in the "two parameter" Sharpe [40]-Lintner [24, 25] world. In general, however, the theoretical models and especially the empirical tests of capital market efficiency have not been this specific. Most of the available work is based only on the assumption that the conditions of market equilibrium can (somehow) be stated in terms of expected returns. In general terms, like the two parameter model such theories would posit that conditional on some relevant information set, the equilibrium expected return on a security is a function of its "risk." And different theories would differ primarily in how "risk" is defined.

All members of the class of such "expected return theories" can, however, be described notationally as follows:

$$E(\tilde{p}_{j,t+1}|\Phi_t) = [1 + E(\tilde{r}_{j,t+1}|\Phi_t)]p_{jt}, \qquad (1)$$

where E is the expected value operator; p_{jt} is the price of security j at time t; $p_{j,t+1}$ is its price at $t + 1$ (with reinvestment of any intermediate cash income from the security); $r_{j,t+1}$ is the one-period percentage return $(p_{j,t+1} - p_{jt})/p_{jt}$; Φ_t is a general symbol for whatever set of information is assumed to be "fully reflected" in the price at t; and the tildes indicate that $p_{j,t+1}$ and $r_{j,t+1}$ are random variables at t.

The value of the equilibrium expected return $E(\tilde{r}_{j,t+1}|\Phi_t)$ projected on the basis of the information Φ_t would be determined from the particular expected return theory at hand. The conditional expectation notation of (1) is meant to imply, however, that whatever expected return model is assumed to apply, the information in Φ_t is fully utilized in determining equilibrium expected returns. And this is the sense in which Φ_t is "fully reflected" in the formation of the price p_{jt}.

But we should note right off that, simple as it is, the assumption that the conditions of market equilibrium can be stated in terms of expected returns elevates the purely mathematical concept of expected value to a status not necessarily implied by the general notion of market efficiency. The expected value is just one of many possible summary measures of a distribution of returns, and market efficiency per se (i.e., the general notion that prices "fully reflect" available information) does not imbue it with any special importance. Thus, the results of tests based on this assumption depend to some extent on its validity as well as on the efficiency of the market. But some such assumption is the unavoidable price one must pay to give the theory of efficient markets empirical content.

The assumptions that the conditions of market equilibrium can be stated in terms of expected returns and that equilibrium expected returns are formed on the basis of (and thus "fully reflect") the information set Φ_t have a major empirical implication—they rule out the possibility of trading systems based only on information in Φ_t that have expected profits or returns in excess of equilibrium expected profits or returns. Thus let

$$x_{j,t+1} = p_{j,t+1} - E(p_{j,t+1}|\Phi_t). \tag{2}$$

Then

$$E(\tilde{x}_{j,t+1}|\Phi_t) = 0 \tag{3}$$

which, *by definition*, says that the sequence $\{x_{jt}\}$ is a "fair game" with respect to the information sequence $\{\phi_t\}$. Or, equivalently, let

$$z_{j,t+1} = r_{j,t+1} - E(\tilde{r}_{j,t+1}|\Phi_t), \tag{4}$$

then

$$E(\tilde{z}_{j,t+1}|\Phi_t) = 0, \tag{5}$$

so that the sequence $\{z_{jt}\}$ is also a "fair game" with respect to the information sequence $\{\Phi\}$.

In economic terms, $x_{j,t+1}$ is the excess market value of security j at time $t+1$: it is the difference between the observed price and the expected value of the price that was projected at t on the basis of the information Φ_t. And similarly, $z_{j,t+1}$ is the return at $t+1$ in excess of the equilibrium expected return projected at t. Let

$$\alpha(\Phi_t) = [\alpha_1(\Phi_t), \alpha_2(\Phi_t), \ldots, \alpha_n(\Phi_t)]$$

be any trading system based on Φ_t which tells the investor the amounts $\alpha_j(\Phi_t)$ of funds available at t that are to be invested in each of the n available securities. The total excess market value at $t+1$ that will be generated by such a system is

$$V_{t+1} = \sum_{j=1}^{n} \alpha_j(\Phi_t)\,[r_{j,t+1} - E(\tilde{r}_{j,t+1}|\Phi_t)],$$

which, from the "fair game" property of (5) has expectation,

$$E(\tilde{V}_{t+1}|\Phi_t) = \sum_{j=1}^{n} \alpha_j(\Phi_t) E(\tilde{z}_{j,t+1}|\Phi_t) = 0.$$

The expected return or "fair game" efficient markets model[2] has other important testable implications, but these are better saved for the later discussion of the empirical work. Now we turn to two special cases of the model, the submartingale and the random walk, that (as we shall see later) play an important role in the empirical literature.

2. Though we shall sometimes refer to the model summarized by (1) as the "fair game" model, keep in mind that the "fair game" properties of the model are *implications* of the assumptions that (i) the conditions of market equilibrium can be stated in terms of expected returns, and (ii) the information Φ_t is fully utilized by the market in forming equilibrium expected returns and thus current prices.

The role of "fair game" models in the theory of efficient markets was first recognized and studied rigorously by Mandelbrot [27] and Samuelson [38]. Their work will be discussed in more detail later.

B. *The Submartingale Model*

Suppose we assume in (1) that for all t and Φ_t

$$E(\tilde{p}_{j,t+1}|\Phi_t) \geqslant p_{jt}, \quad \text{or equivalently,} \quad E(\tilde{r}_{j,t+1}|\Phi_t) \geqslant 0. \tag{6}$$

This is a statement that the price sequence $\{p_{jt}\}$ for security j follows a submartingale with respect to the information sequence $\{\Phi_t\}$, which is to say nothing more than that the expected value of next period's price, as projected on the basis of the information Φ_t, is equal to or greater than the current price. If (6) holds as an equality (so that expected returns and price changes are zero), then the price sequence follows a martingale.

A submartingale in prices has one important empirical implication. Consider the set of "one security and cash" mechanical trading rules by which we mean systems that concentrate on individual securities and that define the conditions under which the investor would hold a given security, sell it short, or simply hold cash at any time t. Then the assumption of (6) that expected returns conditional on Φ_t are non-negative directly implies that such trading rules based only on the information in Φ_t cannot have greater expected profits than a policy of always buying-and-holding the security during the future period in question. Tests of such rules will be an important part of the empirical evidence on the efficient markets model.[3]

C. *The Random Walk Model*

In the early treatments of the efficient markets model, the statement that the current price of a security "fully reflects" available information was assumed to imply that successive price changes (or more usually, successive one-period returns) are independent. In addition, it was usually assumed that successive changes (or returns) are identically distributed. Together the two hypotheses constitute the random walk model. Formally, the model says

$$f(r_{j,t+1}|\Phi_t) = f(r_{j,t+1}), \tag{7}$$

which is the usual statement that the conditional and marginal probability distributions of an independent random variable are identical. In addition, the density function f must be the same for all t.[4]

3. Note that the expected profitability of "one security and cash" trading systems vis-à-vis buy-and-hold is not ruled out by the general expected return or "fair game" efficient markets model. The latter rules out systems with expected profits in excess of equilibrium expected returns, but since in principle it allows equilibrium expected returns to be negative, holding cash (which always has zero actual and thus expected return) may have higher expected return than holding some security.

And negative equilibrium expected returns for some securities are quite possible. For example, in the Sharpe [40]-Lintner [24, 25] model (which is in turn a natural extension of the portfolio models of Markowitz [30] and Tobin [43]) the equilibrium expected return on a security depends on the extent to which the dispersion in the security's return distribution is related to dispersion in the returns on all other securities. A security whose returns on average move opposite to the general market is particularly valuable in reducing dispersion of portfolio returns, and so its equilibrium expected return may well be negative.

4. The terminology is loose. Prices will only follow a random walk if price changes are independent, identically distributed; and even then we should say "random walk with drift" since expected price changes can be non-zero. If one-period returns are independent, identically distributed, prices will not follow a random walk since the distribution of price changes will depend

Expression (7) of course says much more than the general expected return model summarized by (1). For example, if we restrict (1) by assuming that the expected return on security j is constant over time, then we have

$$E(\tilde{r}_{j,t+1}|\Phi_t) = E(\tilde{r}_{j,t+1}). \tag{8}$$

This says that the mean of the distribution of $r_{j,t+1}$ is independent of the information available at t, Φ_t, whereas the random walk model of (7) in addition says that the entire distribution is independent of Φ_t.[5]

We argue later that it is best to regard the random walk model as an extension of the general expected return or "fair game" efficient markets model in the sense of making a more detailed statement about the economic environment. The "fair game" model just says that the conditions of market equilibrium can be stated in terms of expected returns, and thus it says little about the details of the stochastic process generating returns. A random walk arises within the context of such a model when the environment is (fortuitously) such that the evolution of investor tastes and the process generating new information combine to produce equilibria in which return distributions repeat themselves through time.

Thus it is not surprising that empirical tests of the "random walk" model that are in fact tests of "fair game" properties are more strongly in support of the model than tests of the additional (and, from the viewpoint of expected return market efficiency, superfluous) pure independence assumption. (But it is perhaps equally surprising that, as we shall soon see, the evidence against the independence of returns over time is as weak as it is.)

D. *Market Conditions Consistent with Efficiency*

Before turning to the empirical work, however, a few words about the market conditions that might help or hinder efficient adjustment of prices to information are in order. First, it is easy to determine *sufficient* conditions for capital market efficiency. For example, consider a market in which (i) there are no transactions costs in trading securities, (ii) all available information is costlessly available to all market participants, and (iii) all agree on the implications of current information for the current price and distributions of future prices of each security. In such a market, the current price of a security obviously "fully reflects" all available information.

But a frictionless market in which all information is freely available and investors agree on its implications is, of course, not descriptive of markets met in practice. Fortunately, these conditions are sufficient for market efficiency, but not necessary. For example, as long as transactors take account of all

---

on the price level. But though rigorous terminology is usually desirable, our loose use of terms should not cause confusion; and our usage follows that of the efficient markets literature.

Note also that in the random walk literature, the information set Φ_t in (7) is usually assumed to include only the past return history, $r_{j,t}, r_{j,t-1}, \ldots$

5. The random walk model does not say, however, that past information is of no value in *assessing* distributions of future returns. Indeed since return distributions are assumed to be stationary through time, past returns are the best source of such information. The random walk model does say, however, that the *sequence* (or the order) of the past returns is of no consequence in assessing distributions of future returns.

available information, even large transactions costs that inhibit the flow of transactions do not in themselves imply that when transactions do take place, prices will not "fully reflect" available information. Similarly (and speaking, as above, somewhat loosely), the market may be efficient if "sufficient numbers" of investors have ready access to available information. And disagreement among investors about the implications of given information does not in itself imply market inefficiency unless there are investors who can consistently make better evaluations of available information than are implicit in market prices.

But though transactions costs, information that is not freely available to all investors, and disagreement among investors about the implications of given information are not necessarily sources of market inefficiency, they are potential sources. And all three exist to some extent in real world markets. Measuring their effects on the process of price formation is, of course, the major goal of empirical work in this area.

III. The Evidence

All the empirical research on the theory of efficient markets has been concerned with whether prices "fully reflect" particular subsets of available information. Historically, the empirical work evolved more or less as follows. The initial studies were concerned with what we call *weak form* tests in which the information subset of interest is just past price (or return) histories. Most of the results here come from the random walk literature. When extensive tests seemed to support the efficiency hypothesis at this level, attention was turned to *semi-strong form* tests in which the concern is the speed of price adjustment to other obviously publicly available information (e.g., announcements of stock splits, annual reports, new security issues, etc.). Finally, *strong form* tests in which the concern is whether any investor or groups (e.g., managements of mutual funds) have monopolistic access to any information relevant for the formation of prices have recently appeared. We review the empirical research in more or less this historical sequence.

First, however, we should note that what we have called *the* efficient markets model in the discussions of earlier sections is the hypothesis that security prices at any point in time "fully reflect" *all* available information. Though we shall argue that the model stands up rather well to the data, it is obviously an extreme null hypothesis. And, like any other extreme null hyposthesis, we do not expect it to be literally true. The categorization of the tests into weak, semi-strong, and strong form will serve the useful purpose of allowing us to pinpoint the level of information at which the hypothesis breaks down. And we shall contend that there is no important evidence against the hypothesis in the weak and semi-strong form tests (i.e., prices seem to efficiently adjust to obviously publicly available information), and only limited evidence against the hypothesis in the strong form tests (i.e., monopolistic access to information about prices does not seem to be a prevalent phenomenon in the investment community).

A. *Weak Form Tests of the Efficient Markets Model*

1. Random Walks and Fair Games: A Little Historical Background

As noted earlier, all of the empirical work on efficient markets can be considered within the context of the general expected return or "fair game" model, and much of the evidence bears directly on the special submartingale expected return model of (6). Indeed, in the early literature, discussions of the efficient markets model were phrased in terms of the even more special random walk model, though we shall argue that most of the early authors were in fact concerned with more general versions of the "fair game" model.

Some of the confusion in the early random walk writings is understandable. Research on security prices did not begin with the development of a theory of price formation which was then subjected to empirical tests. Rather, the impetus for the development of a theory came from the accumulation of evidence in the middle 1950's and early 1960's that the behavior of common stock and other speculative prices could be well approximated by a random walk. Faced with the evidence, economists felt compelled to offer some rationalization. What resulted was a theory of efficient markets stated in terms of random walks, but usually implying some more general "fair game" model.

It was not until the work of Samuelson [38] and Mandelbrot [27] in 1965 and 1966 that the role of "fair game" expected return models in the theory of efficient markets and the relationships between these models and the theory of random walks were rigorously studied.[6] And these papers came somewhat after the major empirical work on random walks. In the earlier work, "theoretical" discussions, though usually intuitively appealing, were always lacking in rigor and often either vague or *ad hoc*. In short, until the Mandelbrot-Samuelson models appeared, there existed a large body of empirical results in search of a rigorous theory.

Thus, though his contributions were ignored for sixty years, the first statement and test of the random walk model was that of Bachelier [3] in 1900. But his "fundamental principle" for the behavior of prices was that speculation should be a "fair game"; in particular, the expected profits to the speculator should be zero. With the benefit of the modern theory of stochastic processes, we know now that the process implied by this fundamental principle is a martingale.

After Bachelier, research on the behavior of security prices lagged until the

6. Basing their analyses on futures contracts in commodity markets, Mandelbrot and Samuelson show that if the price of such a contract at time t is the expected value at t (given information Φ_t) of the spot price at the termination of the contract, then the futures price will follow a martingale with respect to the information sequence $\{\Phi_t\}$; that is, the expected price change from period to period will be zero, and the price changes will be a "fair game." If the equilibrium expected return is not assumed to be zero, our more general "fair game" model, summarized by (1), is obtained.

But though the Mandelbrot-Samuelson approach certainly illuminates the process of price formation in commodity markets, we have seen that "fair game" expected return models can be derived in much simpler fashion. In particular, (1) is just a formalization of the assumptions that the conditions of market equilibrium can be stated in terms of expected returns and that the information Φ_t is used in forming market prices at t.

coming of the computer. In 1953 Kendall [21] examined the behavior of weekly changes in nineteen indices of British industrial share prices and in spot prices for cotton (New York) and wheat (Chicago). After extensive analysis of serial correlations, he suggests, in quite graphic terms:

> The series looks like a wandering one, almost as if once a week the Demon of Chance drew a random number from a symetrical population of fixed dispersion and added it to the current price to determine the next week's price [21, p. 13].

Kendall's conclusion had in fact been suggested earlier by Working [47], though his suggestion lacked the force provided by Kendall's empirical results. And the implications of the conclusion for stock market research and financial analysis were later underlined by Roberts [36].

But the suggestion by Kendall, Working, and Roberts that series of speculative prices may be well described by random walks was based on observation. None of these authors attempted to provide much economic rationale for the hypothesis, and, indeed, Kendall felt that economists would generally reject it. Osborne [33] suggested market conditions, similar to those assumed by Bachelier, that would lead to a random walk. But in his model, independence of successive price changes derives from the assumption that the decisions of investors in an individual security are independent from transaction to transaction—which is little in the way of an economic model.

Whenever economists (prior to Mandelbrot and Samuelson) tried to provide economic justification for the random walk, their arguments usually implied a "fair game." For example, Alexander [8, p. 200] states:

> If one were to start out with the assumption that a stock or commodity speculation is a "fair game" with equal expectation of gain or loss or, more accurately, with an expectation of zero gain, one would be well on the way to picturing the behavior of speculative prices as a random walk.

There is an awareness here that the "fair game" assumption is not sufficient to lead to a random walk, but Alexander never expands on the comment. Similarly, Cootner [8, p. 232] states:

> If any substantial group of buyers thought prices were too low, their buying would force up the prices. The reverse would be true for sellers. Except for appreciation due to earnings retention, the conditional expectation of tomorrow's price, given today's price, is today's price.
>
> In such a world, the only price changes that would occur are those that result from new information. Since there is no reason to expect that information to be non-random in appearance, the period-to-period price changes of a stock should be random movements, statistically independent of one another.

Though somewhat imprecise, the last sentence of the first paragraph seems to point to a "fair game" model rather than a random walk.[7] In this light, the second paragraph can be viewed as an attempt to describe environmental conditions that would reduce a "fair game" to a random walk. But the specification imposed on the information generating process is insufficient for this purpose; one would, for example, also have to say something about investor

7. The appropriate conditioning statement would be "Given the sequence of historical prices."

tastes. Finally, lest I be accused of criticizing others too severely for ambiguity, lack of rigor and incorrect conclusions,

> By contrast, the stock market trader has a much more practical criterion for judging what constitutes important dependence in successive price changes. For his purposes the random walk model is valid as long as knowledge of the past behavior of the series of price changes cannot be used to increase expected gains. More specifically, the independence assumption is an adequate description of reality as long as the actual degree of dependence in the series of price changes is not sufficient to allow the past history of the series to be used to predict the future in a way which makes expected profits greater than they would be under a naive buy-and hold model [10, p 35].

We know now, of course, that this last condition hardly requires a random walk. It will in fact be met by the submartingale model of (6).

But one should not be too hard on the theoretical efforts of the early empirical random walk literature. The arguments were usually appealing; where they fell short was in awareness of developments in the theory of stochastic processes. Moreover, we shall now see that most of the empirical evidence in the random walk literature can easily be interpreted as tests of more general expected return or "fair game" models.[8]

2. Tests of Market Efficiency in the Random Walk Literature

As discussed earlier, "fair game" models imply the "impossibility" of various sorts of trading systems. Some of the random walk literature has been concerned with testing the profitability of such systems. More of the literature has, however, been concerned with tests of serial covariances of returns. We shall now show that, like a random walk, the serial covariances of a "fair game" are zero, so that these tests are also relevant for the expected return models.

If x_t is a "fair game," its unconditional expectation is zero and its serial covariance can be written in general form as:

$$E(\tilde{x}_{t+\tau}\tilde{x}_t) = \int_{x_t} x_t E(\tilde{x}_{t+\tau}|x_t) f(x_t) dx_t,$$

where f indicates a density function. But if x_t is a "fair game,"

$$E(\tilde{x}_{t+\tau}|x_t) = 0.^{9}$$

8. Our brief historical review is meant only to provide perspective, and it is, of course, somewhat incomplete. For example, we have ignored the important contributions to the early random walk literature in studies of warrants and other options by Sprenkle, Kruizenga, Boness, and others. Much of this early work on options is summarized in [8].

9. More generally, if the sequence $\{x_t\}$ is a fair game with respect to the information sequence $\{\Phi_t\}$, (i.e., $E(\tilde{x}_{t+1}|\Phi_t) = 0$ for all Φ_t); then x_t is a fair game with respect to any Φ'_t that is a subset of Φ_t (i.e., $E(\tilde{x}_{t+1}|\Phi'_t) = 0$ for all Φ'_t). To show this, let $\Phi_t = (\Phi'_t, \Phi''_t)$. Then, using Stieltjes integrals and the symbol F to denote cumulative distinction functions, the conditional expectation

$$E(\tilde{x}_{t+1}|\Phi'_t) = \int_{\Phi''_t}\int_{x_{t+1}} x_{t+1} dF(x_{t+1}, \Phi''_t|\Phi'_t) = \int_{\Phi''_t}\left[\int_{x_{t+1}} x_{t+1} dF(x_{t+1}|\Phi'_t, \Phi''_t)\right] dF(\Phi''_t|\Phi'_t).$$

From this it follows that for all lags, the serial covariances between lagged values of a "fair game" variable are zero. Thus, observations of a "fair game" variable are linearly independent.[10]

But the "fair game" model does not necessarily imply that the serial covariances of *one-period returns* are zero. In the weak form tests of this model the "fair game" variable is

$$z_{j,t} = r_{j,t} - E(\tilde{r}_{j,t}|r_{j,t-1}, r_{j,t-2}, \ldots). \quad \text{(Cf. fn. 9)} \tag{9}$$

But the covariance between, for example, r_{jt} and $r_{j,t+1}$ is

$$E([\tilde{r}_{j,t+1} - E(\tilde{r}_{j,t+1})]\,[\tilde{r}_{jt} - E(\tilde{r}_{jt})])$$
$$= \int_{r_{jt}} [r_{jt} - E(\tilde{r}_{jt})]\,[E(\tilde{r}_{j,t+1}|r_{jt}) - E(\tilde{r}_{j,t+1})]f(r_{jt})dr_{jt},$$

and (9) does not imply that $E(\tilde{r}_{j,t+1}|r_{jt}) = E(\tilde{r}_{j,t+1})$: In the "fair game" efficient markets model, the deviation of the return for $t + 1$ from its conditional expectation is a "fair game" variable, but the conditional expectation itself can depend on the return observed for t.[11]

In the random walk literature, this problem is not recognized, since it is assumed that the expected return (and indeed the entire distribution of returns) is stationary through time. In practice, this implies estimating serial covariances by taking cross products of deviations of observed returns from the overall sample mean return. It is somewhat fortuitous, then, that this procedure, which represents a rather gross approximation from the viewpoint of the general expected return efficient markets model, does not seem to greatly affect the results of the covariance tests, at least for common stocks.[12]

But the integral in brackets is just $E(\tilde{x}_{t+1}|\Phi_t)$ which by the "fair game" assumption is 0, so that

$$E(x_{t+1}|\Phi'_t) = 0 \text{ for all } \Phi'_t \subset \Phi_t.$$

10. But though zero serial covariances are consistent with a "fair game," they do not imply such a process. A "fair game" also rules out many types of non linear dependence. Thus using arguments similar to those above, it can be shown that if x is a "fair game," $E(\tilde{x}_t\tilde{x}_{t+1} \cdots \tilde{x}_{t+\tau}) = 0$ for all τ, which is not implied by $E(\tilde{x}_t\tilde{x}_{t+\tau}) = 0$ for all τ. For example, consider a three-period case where x must be either ± 1. Suppose the process is $x_{t+2} = \text{sign}\,(x_t x_{t+1})$, i.e.,

x_t	x_{t+1}	$\rightarrow$	x_{t+2}
+	+	→	+
+	−	→	−
−	+	→	−
−	−	→	+.

If probabilities are uniformly distributed across events,

$$E(\tilde{x}_{t+2}|x_{t+1}) = E(\tilde{x}_{t+2}|x_t) = E(\tilde{x}_{t+1}|x_t) = E(\tilde{x}_{t+2}) = E(\tilde{x}_{t+1}) = E(\tilde{x}_t) = 0,$$

so that all pairwise serial covariances are zero. But the process is not a "fair game," since $E(\tilde{x}_{t+2}|x_{t+1}, x_t) \neq 0$, and knowledge of (x_{t+1}, x_t) can be used as the basis of a simple "system" with positive expected profit.

11. For example, suppose the level of one-period returns follows a martingale so that

$$E(\tilde{r}_{j,t+1}|r_{jt}, r_{j,t-1} \ldots) = r_{jt}.$$

Then covariances between successive returns will be nonzero (though in this special case first differences of returns will be uncorrelated).

12. The reason is probably that for stocks, changes in equilibrium expected returns for the

TABLE 1 (from [10])
First-order Serial Correlation Coefficients for One-, Four-, Nine-, and Sixteen-Day Changes in Log_e Price

Stock	Differencing Interval (Days)			
	One	Four	Nine	Sixteen
Allied Chemical	.017	.029	−.091	−.118
Alcoa	.118*	.095	−.112	−.044
American Can	−.087*	−.124*	−.060	.031
A. T. & T.	−.039	−.010	−.009	−.003
American Tobacco	.111*	−.175*	.033	.007
Anaconda	.067*	−.068	−.125	.202
Bethlehem Steel	.013	−.122	−.148	.112
Chrysler	.012	.060	−.026	.040
Du Pont	.013	.069	−.043	−.055
Eastman Kodak	.025	−.006	−.053	−.023
General Electric	.011	.020	−.004	.000
General Foods	.061*	−.005	−.140	−.098
General Motors	−.004	−.128*	.009	−.028
Goodyear	−.123*	.001	−.037	.033
International Harvester	−.017	−.068	−.244*	.116
International Nickel	.096*	.038	.124	.041
International Paper	.046	.060	−.004	−.010
Johns Manville	.006	−.068	−.002	.002
Owens Illinois	−.021	−.006	.003	−.022
Procter & Gamble	.099*	−.006	.098	.076
Sears	.097*	−.070	−.113	.041
Standard Oil (Calif.)	.025	−.143*	−.046	.040
Standard Oil (N.J.)	.008	−.109	−.082	−.121
Swift & Co.	−.004	−.072	.118	−.197
Texaco	.094*	−.053	−.047	−.178
Union Carbide	.107*	.049	−.101	.124
United Aircraft	.014	−.190*	−.192*	−.040
U.S. Steel	.040	−.006	−.056	.236*
Westinghouse	−.027	−.097	−.137	.067
Woolworth	.028	−.033	−.112	.040

* Coefficient is twice its computed standard error.

For example, Table 1 (taken from [10]) shows the serial correlations between successive changes in the natural log of price for each of the thirty stocks of the Dow Jones Industrial Average, for time periods that vary slightly from stock to stock, but usually run from about the end of 1957 to September 26, 1962. The serial correlations of successive changes in $\log_e$ price are shown for differencing intervals of one, four, nine, and sixteen days.[13]

common differencing intervals of a day, a week, or a month, are trivial relative to other sources of variation in returns. Later, when we consider Roll's work [37], we shall see that this is not true for one week returns on U.S. Government Treasury Bills.

13. The use of changes in $\log_e$ price as the measure of return is common in the random walk literature. It can be justified in several ways. But for current purposes, it is sufficient to note that for price changes less than fifteen per cent, the change in $\log_e$ price is approximately the percentage price change or one-period return. And for differencing intervals shorter than one month, returns in excess of fifteen per cent are unusual. Thus [10] reports that for the data of Table 1, tests carried out on percentage or one-period returns yielded results essentially identical to the tests based on changes in $\log_e$ price.

The results in Table 1 are typical of those reported by others for tests based on serial covariances. (Cf. Kendall [21], Moore [31], Alexander [1], and the results of Granger and Morgenstern [17] and Godfrey, Granger and Morgenstern [16] obtained by means of spectral analysis.) Specifically, there is no evidence of substantial linear dependence between lagged price changes or returns. In absolute terms the measured serial correlations are always close to zero.

Looking hard, though, one can probably find evidence of statistically "significant" linear dependence in Table 1 (and again this is true of results reported by others). For the daily returns eleven of the serial correlations are more than twice their computed standard errors, and twenty-two out of thirty are positive. On the other hand, twenty-one and twenty-four of the coefficients for the four and nine day differences are negative. But with samples of the size underlying Table 1 (N = 1200-1700 observations per stock on a daily basis) statistically "significant" deviations from zero covariance are not necessarily a basis for rejecting the efficient markets model. For the results in Table 1, the standard errors of the serial correlations were approximated as $(1/(N\text{-}1))^{1/2}$, which for the daily data implies that a correlation as small as .06 is more than twice its standard error. But a coefficient this size implies that a linear relationship with the lagged price change can be used to explain about .36% of the variation in the current price change, which is probably insignificant from an economic viewpoint. In particular, it is unlikely that the small absolute levels of serial correlation that are always observed can be used as the basis of substantially profitable trading systems.[14]

It is, of course, difficult to judge what degree of serial correlation would imply the existence of trading rules with substantial expected profits. (And indeed we shall soon have to be a little more precise about what is implied by "substantial" profits.) Moreover, zero serial covariances are consistent with a "fair game" model, but as noted earlier (fn. 10), there are types of nonlinear dependence that imply the existence of profitable trading systems, and yet do not imply nonzero serial covariances. Thus, for many reasons it is desirable to directly test the profitability of various trading rules.

The first major evidence on trading rules was Alexander's [1, 2]. He tests a variety of systems, but the most thoroughly examined can be decribed as follows: If the price of a security moves up at least y%, buy and hold the security until its price moves down at least y% from a subsequent high, at which time simultaneously sell and go short. The short position is maintained until the price rises at least y% above a subsequent low, at which time one covers the short position and buys. Moves less than y% in either direction are

14. Given the evidence of Kendall [21], Mandelbrot [28], Fama [10] and others that large price changes occur much more frequently than would be expected if the generating process were Gaussian, the expression $(1/(N\text{-}1))^{1/2}$ understates the sampling dispersion of the serial correlation coefficient, and thus leads to an overstatement of significance levels. In addition, the fact that sample serial correlations are predominantly of one sign or the other is not in itself evidence of linear dependence. If, as the work of King [23] and Blume [7] indicates, there is a market factor whose behavior affects the returns on all securities, the sample behavior of this market factor may lead to a predominance of signs of one type in the serial correlations for individual securities, even though the population serial correlations for both the market factor and the returns on individual securities are zero. For a more extensive analysis of these issues see [10].

ignored. Such a system is called a y% filter. It is obviously a "one security and cash" trading rule, so that the results it produces are relevant for the submartingale expected return model of (6).

After extensive tests using daily data on price indices from 1897 to 1959 and filters from one to fifty per cent, and after correcting some incorrect presumptions in the initial results of [1] (see fn. 25), in his final paper on the subject, Alexander concludes:

> In fact, at this point I should advise any reader who is interested only in practical results, and who is not a floor trader and so must pay commissions, to turn to other sources on how to beat buy and hold. The rest of this article is devoted principally to a theoretical consideration of whether the observed results are consistent with a random walk hypothesis [8], p. 351).

Later in the paper Alexander concludes that there is some evidence in his results against the independence assumption of the random walk model. But market efficiency does not require a random walk, and from the viewpoint of the submartingale model of (6), the conclusion that the filters cannot beat buy-and-hold is support for the efficient markets hypothesis. Further support is provided by Fama and Blume [13] who compare the profitability of various filters to buy-and-hold for the individual stocks of the Dow-Jones Industrial Average. (The data are those underlying Table 1.)

But again, looking hard one can find evidence in the filter tests of both Alexander and Fama-Blume that is inconsistent with the submartingale efficient markets model, if that model is interpreted in a strict sense. In particular, the results for very small filters (1 per cent in Alexander's tests and .5, 1.0, and 1.5 per cent in the tests of Fama-Blume) indicate that it is possible to devise trading schemes based on very short-term (preferably intra-day but at most daily) price swings that will on average outperform buy-and-hold. The average profits on individual transactions from such schemes are miniscule, but they generate transactions so frequently that over longer periods and ignoring commissions they outperform buy-and-hold by a substantial margin. These results are evidence of persistence or positive dependence in very short-term price movements. And, interestingly, this is consistent with the evidence for slight positive linear dependence in successive daily price changes produced by the serial correlations.[15]

15. Though strictly speaking, such tests of pure independence are not directly relevant for expected return models, it is interesting that the conclusion that very short-term swings in prices persist slightly longer than would be expected under the martingale hypothesis is also supported by the results of non-parametric runs tests applied to the daily data of Table 1. (See [10], Tables 12-15.) For the daily price changes, the actual number of runs of price changes of the same sign is less than the expected number for 26 out of 30 stocks. Moreover, of the eight stocks for which the actual number of runs is more than two standard errors less than the expected number, five of the same stocks have positive daily, first order serial correlations in Table 1 that are more than twice their standard errors. But in both cases the statistical "significance" of the results is largely a reflection of the large sample sizes. Just as the serial correlations are small in absolute terms (the average is .026), the differences between the expected and actual number of runs on average are only three per cent of the total expected number.

On the other hand, it is also interesting that the runs tests do not support the suggestion of slight negative dependence in four and nine day changes that appeared in the serial correlations. In the runs tests such negative dependence would appear as a tendency for the actual number of runs to exceed the expected number. In fact, for the four and nine day price changes, for 17 and

But when one takes account of even the minimum trading costs that would be generated by small filters, their advantage over buy-and-hold disappears. For example, even a floor trader (i.e., a person who owns a seat) on the New York Stock Exchange must pay clearinghouse fees on his trades that amount to about .1 per cent per turnaround transaction (i.e., sales plus purchase). Fama-Blume show that because small filters produce such frequent trades, these minimum trading costs are sufficient to wipe out their advantage over buy-and-hold.

Thus the filter tests, like the serial correlations, produce empirically noticeable departures from the strict implications of the efficient markets model. But, in spite of any statistical significance they might have, from an economic viewpoint the departures are so small that it seems hardly justified to use them to declare the market inefficient.

3. Other Tests of Independence in the Random Walk Literature

It is probably best to regard the random walk model as a special case of the more general expected return model in the sense of making a more detailed specification of the economic environment. That is, the basic model of market equilibrium is the "fair game" expected return model, with a random walk arising when additional environmental conditions are such that distributions of one-period returns repeat themselves through time. From this viewpoint violations of the pure independence assumption of the random walk model are to be expected. But when judged relative to the benchmark provided by the random walk model, these violations can provide insights into the nature of the market environment.

For example, one departure from the pure independence assumption of the random walk model has been noted by Osborne [34], Fama ([10], Table 17 and Figure 8), and others. In particular, large daily price changes tend to be followed by large daily changes. The signs of the successor changes are apparently random, however, which indicates that the phenomenon represents a denial of the random walk model but not of the market efficiency hypothesis. Nevertheless, it is interesting to speculate why the phenomenon might arise. It may be that when important new information comes into the market it cannot always be immediately evaluated precisely. Thus, sometimes the initial price will overadjust to the information, and other times it will underadjust. But since the evidence indicates that the price changes on days following the initial large change are random in sign, the initial large change at least represents an unbiased adjustment to the ultimate price effects of the information, and this is sufficient for the expected return efficient markets model.

Niederhoffer and Osborne [32] document two departures from complete randomness in common stock price changes from transaction to transaction. First, their data indicate that reversals (pairs of consecutive price changes of opposite sign) are from two to three times as likely as continuations (pairs of consecutive price changes of the same sign). Second, a continuation is

18 of the 30 stocks in Table 1 the actual number of runs is less than the expected number. Indeed, runs tests in general show no consistent evidence of dependence for any differencing interval longer than a day, which seems especially pertinent in light of the comments in footnote 14.

slightly more frequent after a preceding continuation than after a reversal. That is, let (+|++) indicate the occurrence of a positive price change, given two preceding positive changes. Then the events (+|++) and (−|−−) are slightly more frequent than (+|+−) or (−|−+).[16]

Niederhoffer and Osborne offer explanations for these phenomena based on the market structure of the New York Stock Exchange (N.Y.S.E.). In particular, there are three major types of orders that an investor might place in a given stock: (a) buy limit (buy at a specified price or lower), (b) sell limit (sell at a specified price or higher), and (c) buy or sell at market (at the lowest selling or highest buying price of another investor). A book of unexecuted limit orders in a given stock is kept by the specialist in that stock on the floor of the exchange. Unexecuted sell limit orders are, of course, at higher prices than unexecuted buy limit orders. On both exchanges, the smallest non-zero price change allowed is ⅛ point.

Suppose now that there is more than one unexecuted sell limit order at the lowest price of any such order. A transaction at this price (initiated by an order to buy at market[17]) can only be followed either by a transaction at the same price (if the next market order is to buy) or by a transaction at a lower price (if the next market order is to sell). Consecutive price increases can usually only occur when consecutive market orders to buy exhaust the sell limit orders at a given price.[18] In short, the excessive tendency toward reversal for consecutive non-zero price changes could result from bunching of unexecuted buy and sell limit orders.

The tendency for the events (+|++) and (−|−−) to occur slightly more frequently than (+|+−) and (−|−+) requires a more involved explanation which we shall not attempt to reproduce in full here. In brief, Niederhoffer and Osborne contend that the higher frequency of (+|++) relative to (+|+−) arises from a tendency for limit orders "to be concentrated at integers (26, 43), halves (26½, 43½), quarters and odd eighths in descending order of preference."[19] The frequency of the event (+|++), which usually requires that sell limit orders be exhausted at at least two consecutively higher prices (the last of which is relatively more frequently at an odd eighth), more heavily reflects the absence of sell limit orders at odd eighths than the event (+|+−), which usually implies that sell limit orders at only one price have been exhausted and so more or less reflects the average bunching of limit orders at all eighths.

But though Niederhoffer and Osborne present convincing evidence of sta-

16. On a transaction to transaction basis, positive and negative price changes are about equally likely. Thus, under the assumption that price changes are random, any pair of non-zero changes should be as likely as any other, and likewise for triplets of consecutive non-zero changes.

17. A buy limit order for a price equal to or greater than the lowest available sell limit price is effectively an order to buy at market, and is treated as such by the broker.

18. The exception is when there is a gap of more than ⅛ between the highest unexecuted buy limit and the lowest unexecuted sell limit order, so that market orders (and new limit orders) can be crossed at intermediate prices.

19. Their empirical documentation for this claim is a few samples of specialists' books for selected days, plus the observation [34] that actual trading prices, at least for volatile high priced stocks, seem to be concentrated at integers, halves, quarters and odd eighths in descending order.

tistically significant departures from independence in price changes from transaction to transaction, and though their analysis of their findings presents interesting insights into the process of market making on the major exchanges, the types of dependence uncovered do not imply market inefficiency. The best documented source of dependence, the tendency toward excessive reversals in pairs of non-zero price changes, seems to be a direct result of the ability of investors to place limit orders as well as orders at market, and this negative dependence in itself does not imply the existence of profitable trading rules. Similarly, the apparent tendency for observed transactions (and, by implication, limit orders) to be concentrated at integers, halves, even eighths and odd eighths in descending order is an interesting fact about investor behavior, but in itself is not a basis on which to conclude that the market is inefficient.[20]

The Niederhoffer-Osborne analysis of market making does, however, point clearly to the existence of market inefficiency, but with respect to strong form tests of the efficient markets model. In particular, the list of unexecuted buy and sell limit orders in the specialist's book is important information about the likely future behavior of prices, and this information is only available to the specialist. When the specialist is asked for a quote, he gives the prices and can give the quantities of the highest buy limit and lowest sell limit orders on his book, but he is prevented by law from divulging the book's full contents. The interested reader can easily imagine situations where the structure of limit orders in the book could be used as the basis of a profitable trading rule.[21] But the record seems to speak for itself:

> It should not be assumed that these transactions undertaken by the specialist, and in which he is involved as buyer or seller in 24 per cent of all market volume, are necessarily a burden to him. Typically, the specialist sells above his last purchase on 83 per cent of all his sales, and buys below his last sale on 81 per cent of all his purchases ([32], p. 908).

Thus it seems that the specialist has monopoly power over an important block of information, and, not unexpectedly, uses his monopoly to turn a profit. And this, of course, is evidence of market inefficiency in the strong form sense. The important economic question, of course, is whether the market making

20. Niederhoffer and Osborne offer little to refute this conclusion. For example ([32], p. 914):

> Although the specific properties reported in this study have a significance from a statistical point of view, the reader may well ask whether or not they are helpful in a practical sense. Certain trading rules emerge as a result of our analysis. One is that limit and stop orders should be placed at odd eights, preferably at ⅞ for sell orders and at ⅛ for buy orders. Another is to buy when a stock advances through a barrier and to sell when it sinks through a barrier.

The first "trading rule" tells the investor to resist his innate inclination to place orders at integers, but rather to place sell orders ⅛ below an integer and buy orders ⅛ above. Successful execution of the orders is then more likely, since the congestion of orders that occur at integers is avoided. But the cost of this success is apparent. The second "trading rule" seems no more promising, if indeed it can even be translated into a concrete prescription for action.

21. See, for example, ([32], p. 908). But it is unlikely that anyone but the specialist could earn substantial profits from knowledge of the structure of unexecuted limit orders on the book. The specialist makes trading profits by engaging in many transactions, each of which has a small average profit; but for any other trader, including those with seats on the exchange, these profits would be eaten up by commissions to the specialist.

function of the specialist could be fulfilled more economically by some non-monopolistic mechanism.[22]

4. Distributional Evidence

At this date the weight of the empirical evidence is such that economists would generally agree that whatever dependence exists in series of historical returns cannot be used to make profitable predictions of the future. Indeed, for returns that cover periods of a day or longer, there is little in the evidence that would cause rejection of the stronger random walk model, at least as a good first approximation.

Rather, the last burning issue of the random walk literature has centered on the nature of the distribution of price changes (which, we should note immediately, is an important issue for the efficient markets hypothesis since the nature of the distribution affects both the types of statistical tools relevant for testing the hypothesis and the interpretation of any results obtained). A model implying normally distributed price changes was first proposed by Bachelier [3], who assumed that price changes from transaction to transaction are independent, identically distributed random variables with finite variances. If transactions are fairly uniformly spread across time, and if the number of transactions per day, week, or month is very large, then the Central Limit Theorem leads us to expect that these price changes will have normal or Gaussian distributions.

Osborne [33], Moore [31], and Kendall [21] all thought their empirical evidence supported the normality hypothesis, but all observed high tails (i.e., higher proportions of large observations) in their data distributions vis-à-vis what would be expected if the distributions were normal. Drawing on these findings and some empirical work of his own, Mandelbrot [28] then suggested that these departures from normality could be explained by a more general form of the Bachelier model. In particular, if one does not assume that distributions of price changes from transaction to transaction necessarily have finite variances, then the limiting distributions for price changes over longer differencing intervals could be any member of the stable class, which includes the normal as a special case. Non-normal stable distributions have higher tails than the normal, and so can account for this empirically observed feature of distributions of price changes. After extensive testing (involving the data from the stocks in Table 1), Fama [10] concludes that non-normal stable distributions are a better description of distributions of daily returns on common stocks than the normal. This conclusion is also supported by the empirical work of Blume [7] on common stocks, and it has been extended to U.S. Government Treasury Bills by Roll [37].

Economists have, however, been reluctant to accept these results,[23] primar-

22. With modern computers, it is hard to believe that a more competitive and economical system would not be feasible. It does not seem technologically impossible to replace the entire floor of the N.Y.S.E. with a computer, fed by many remote consoles, that kept all the books now kept by the specialists, that could easily make the entire book on any stock available to anybody (so that interested individuals could then compete to "make a market" in a stock) and that carried out transactions automatically.

23. Some have suggested that the long-tailed empirical distributions might result from processes

ily because of the wealth of statistical techniques available for dealing with normal variables and the relative paucity of such techniques for non-normal stable variables. But perhaps the biggest contribution of Mandelbrot's work has been to stimulate research on stable distributions and estimation procedures to be applied to stable variables. (See, for example, Wise [46], Fama and Roll [15], and Blattberg and Sargent [6], among others.) The advance of statistical sophistication (and the importance of examining distributional assumptions in testing the efficient markets model) is well illustrated in Roll [37], as compared, for example, with the early empirical work of Mandelbrot [28] and Fama [10].

5. "Fair Game" Models in the Treasury Bill Market

Roll's work is novel in other respects as well. Coming after the efficient markets models of Mandelbrot [27] and Samuelson [38], it is the first weak form empirical work that is consciously in the "fair game" rather than the random walk tradition.

More important, as we saw earlier, the "fair game" properties of the general expected return models apply to

$$z_{jt} = r_{jt} - E(\tilde{r}_{jt}|\Phi_{t-1}). \qquad (10)$$

For data on common stocks, tests of "fair game" (and random walk) properties seem to go well when the conditional expected return is estimated as the average return for the sample of data at hand. Apparently the variation in common stock returns about their expected values is so large relative to any changes in the expected values that the latter can safely be ignored. But, as Roll demonstrates, this result does not hold for Treasury Bills. Thus, to test the "fair game" model on Treasury Bills requires explicit economic theory for the evolution of expected returns through time.

Roll uses three existing theories of the term structure (the pure expectations hypothesis of Lutz [26] and two market segmentation hypotheses, one of which is the familiar "liquidity preference" hypothesis of Hicks [18] and Kessel [22]) for this purpose.[24] In his models r_{jt} is the rate observed from the term structure at period t for one week loans to commence at $t + j - 1$, and can be thought of as a "futures" rate. Thus $r_{j+1,\, t-1}$ is likewise the rate on

that are mixtures of normal distributions with different variances. Press [35], for example, suggests a Poisson mixture of normals in which the resulting distributions of price changes have long tails but finite variances. On the other hand, Mandelbrot and Taylor [29] show that other mixtures of normals can still lead to non-normal stable distributions of price changes for finite differencing intervals.

If, as Press' model would imply, distributions of price changes are long-tailed but have finite variances, then distributions of price changes over longer and longer differencing intervals should be progressively closer to the normal. No such convergence to normality was observed in [10] (though admittedly the techniques used were somewhat rough). Rather, except for origin and scale, the distributions for longer differencing intervals seem to have the same "high-tailed" characteristics as distributins for shorter differencing intervals, which is as would be expected if the distributions are non-normal stable.

24. As noted early in our discussions, all available tests of market efficiency are implicitly also tests of expected return models of market equilibrium. But Roll formulates explicitly the economic models underlying his estimates of expected returns, and emphasizes that he is simultaneously testing economic models of the term structure as well as market efficiency.

one week loans to commence at $t + j - 1$, but observed in this case at $t - 1$. Similarly, L_{jt} is the so-called "liquidity premium" in r_{jt}; that is

$$r_{jt} = E(\tilde{r}_{0,t+j-1}|\Phi_t) + L_{jt}.$$

In words, the one-week "futures" rate for period $t + j - 1$ observed from the term structure at t is the expectation at t of the "spot" rate for $t + j - 1$ plus a "liquidity premium" (which could, however, be positive or negative).

In all three theories of the term structure considered by Roll, the conditional expectation required in (10) is of the form

$$E(\tilde{r}_{j,t}|\Phi_{t-1}) = r_{j+1,t-1} + E(\tilde{L}_{jt}|\Phi_{t-1}) - L_{j+1,t-1}.$$

The three theories differ only in the values assigned to the "liquidity premiums." For example, in the "liquidity preference" hypothesis, investors must always be paid a positive premium for bearing interest rate uncertainty, so that the L_{jt} are always positive. By contrast, in the "pure expectations" hypothesis, all liquidity premiums are assumed to be zero, so that

$$E(\tilde{r}_{jt}|\Phi_{t-1}) = r_{j+1,t-1}.$$

After extensive testing, Roll concludes (i) that the two market segmentation hypotheses fit the data better than the pure expectations hypothesis, with perhaps a slight advantage for the "liquidity preference" hypothesis, and (ii) that as far as his tests are concerned, the market for Treasury Bills is effcient. Indeed, it is interesting that when the best fitting term structure model is used to estimate the conditional expected "futures" rate in (10), the resulting variable z_{jt} seems to be serially independent! It is also interesting that if he simply assumed that his data distributions were normal, Roll's results would not be so strongly in support of the efficient markets model. In this case taking account of the observed high tails of the data distributions substantially affected the interpretation of the results.[25]

6. Tests of a Multiple Security Expected Return Model

Though the weak form tests support the "fair game" efficient markets model, all of the evidence examined so far consists of what we might call "single security tests." That is, the price or return histories of individual securities are examined for evidence of dependence that might be used as the basis of a trading system for *that* security. We have not discussed tests of whether securities are "appropriately priced" vis-à-vis one another.

But to judge whether differences between average returns are "appropriate" an economic theory of equilibrium expected returns is required. At the moment, the only fully developed theory is that of Sharpe [40] and Lintner [24,

25. The importance of distributional assumptions is also illustrated in Alexander's work on trading rules. In his initial tests of filter systems [1], Alexander assumed that purchases could always be executed exactly (rather than at least) y% above lows and sales exactly y% below highs. Mandelbrot [28] pointed out, however, that though this assumption would do little harm with normally distributed price changes (since price series are then essentially continuous), with non-normal stable distributions it would introduce substantial positive bias into the filter profits (since with such distributions price series will show many discontinuities). In his later tests [2], Alexander does indeed find that taking account of the discontinuities (i.e., the presence of large price changes) in his data substantially lowers the profitability of the filters.

25] referred to earlier. In this model (which is a direct outgrowth of the mean-standard deviation portfolio models of investor equilibrium of Markowitz [30] and Tobin [43]), the expected return on security j from time t to t + 1 is

$$E(\tilde{r}_{j,t+1}|\Phi_t) = r_{f,t+1} + \left[\frac{E(\tilde{r}_{m,t+1}|\Phi_t) - r_{f,t+1}}{\sigma(\tilde{r}_{m,t+1}|\Phi_t)}\right]\frac{\text{cov}\,(\tilde{r}_{j,t+1}, \tilde{r}_{m,t+1}|\Phi_t)}{\sigma(\tilde{r}_{m,t+1}|\Phi_t)}, \tag{11}$$

where $r_{f,t+1}$ is the return from t to t + 1 on an asset that is riskless in money terms; $r_{m,t+1}$ is the return on the "market portfolio" m (a portfolio of all investment assets with each weighted in proportion to the total market value of all its outstanding units); $\sigma^2(\tilde{r}_{m,t+1}|\Phi_t)$ is the variance of the return on m; cov $(\tilde{r}_{j,t+1}, \tilde{r}_{m,t+1}|\Phi_t)$ is the covariance between the returns on j and m; and the appearance of Φ_t indicates that the various expected returns, variance and covariance, could in principle depend on Φ_t. Though Sharpe and Lintner derive (11) as a one-period model, the result is given a multiperiod justification and interpretation in [11]. The model has also been extended in (12) to the case where the one-period returns could have stable distributions with infinite variances.

In words, (11) says that the expected one-period return on a security is the one-period riskless rate of interest $r_{f,t+1}$ plus a "risk premium" that is proportional to $\text{cov}(\tilde{r}_{j,t+1}, \tilde{r}_{m,t+1}|\Phi_t)/\sigma(\tilde{r}_{m,t+1}|\Phi_t)$. In the Sharpe-Lintner model each investor holds some combination of the riskless asset and the market portfolio, so that, given a mean-standard deviation framework, the risk of an individual asset can be measured by its contribution to the standard deviation of the return on the market portfolio. This contribution is in fact cov $(\tilde{r}_{j,t+1}, \tilde{r}_{m,t+1}|\Phi_t)/\sigma(\tilde{r}_{m,t+1}|\Phi_t)$.[26] The factor

$$[E(\tilde{r}_{m,t+1}|\Phi_t) - r_{f,t+1}]/\sigma(\tilde{r}_{m,t+1}|\Phi_t),$$

which is the same for all securities, is then regarded as the market price of risk.

Published empirical tests of the Sharpe-Lintner model are not yet available, though much work is in progress. There is some published work, however, which, though not directed at the Sharpe-Lintner model, is at least consistent with some of its implications. The stated goal of this work has been to determine the extent to which the returns on a given security are related to the returns on other securities. It started (again) with Kendall's [21] finding that though common stock price changes do not seem to be serially correlated, there is a high degree of cross-correlation between the *simultaneous* returns of different securities. This line of attack was continued by King [23] who (using factor analysis of a sample of monthly returns on sixty N.Y.S.E. stocks for the period 1926-60) found that on average about 50% of the variance of an individual stock's returns could be accounted for by a "market factor" which affects the returns on all stocks, with "industry factors" accounting for at most an additional 10% of the variance.

26. That is,

$$\sum_j \text{cov}\,(\tilde{r}_{j,t+1}, \tilde{r}_{m,t+1}|\Phi_t)/\sigma(\tilde{r}_{m,t+1}|\Phi_t) = \sigma(\tilde{r}_{m,t+1}|\Phi_t).$$

For our purposes, however, the work of Fama, Fisher, Jensen, and Roll [14] (henceforth FFJR) and the more extensive work of Blume [7] on monthly return data is more relevant. They test the following "market model," originally suggested by Markowitz [30]:

$$\tilde{r}_{j,t+1} = \alpha_j + \beta_j \tilde{r}_{M,t+1} + \tilde{u}_{j,t+1} \qquad (12)$$

where $r_{j,t+1}$ is the rate of return on security j for month t, $r_{M,t+1}$ is the corresponding return on a market index M, α_j and β_j are parameters that can vary from security to security, and $u_{j,t+1}$ is a random disturbance. The tests of FFJR and subsequently those of Blume indicate that (12) is well specified as a linear regression model in that (i) the estimated parameters $\hat{\alpha}_j$ and $\hat{\beta}_j$ remain fairly constant over long periods of time (e.g., the entire post-World War II period in the case of Blume), (ii) $r_{M,t+1}$ and the estimated $\hat{u}_{j,t+1}$, are close to serially independent, and (iii) the $\hat{u}_{j,t+1}$ seem to be independent of $r_{M,t+1}$.

Thus the observed properties of the "market model" are consistent with the expected return efficient markets model, and, in addition, the "market model" tells us something about the process generating expected returns from security to security. In particular,

$$E(\tilde{r}_{j,t+1}) = \alpha_j + \beta_j E(\tilde{r}_{M,t+1}). \qquad (13)$$

The question now is to what extent (13) is consistent with the Sharpe-Lintner expected return model summarized by (11). Rearranging (11) we obtain

$$E(\tilde{r}_{j,t+1}|\Phi_t) = \alpha_j(\Phi_t) + \beta_j(\Phi_t)E(\tilde{r}_{m,t+1}|\Phi_t), \qquad (14)$$

where, noting that the riskless rate $r_{f,t+1}$ is itself part of the information set Φ_t, we have

$$\alpha_j(\Phi_t) = r_{f,t+1}[1 - \beta_j(\Phi_t)], \qquad (15)$$

and

$$\beta_j(\Phi_t) = \frac{\text{cov}\,(\tilde{r}_{j,t+1}, \tilde{r}_{m,t+1}|\Phi_t)}{\sigma^2(\tilde{r}_{m,t+1}|\Phi_t)}. \qquad (16)$$

With some simplifying assumptions, (14) can be reduced to (13). In particular, if the covariance and variance that determine $\beta_j(\Phi_t)$ in (16) are the same for all t and Φ_t, then $\beta_j(\Phi_t)$ in (16) corresponds to β_j in (12) and (13), and the least squares *estimate* of β_j in (12) is in fact just the ratio of the sample values of the covariance and variance in (16). If we also assume that $r_{f,t+1}$ is the same for all t, and that the behavior of the returns on the market portfolio m are closely approximated by the returns on some representative index M, we will have come a long way toward equating (13) and (11). Indeed, the only missing link is whether in the estimated parameters of (12)

$$\hat{\alpha}_j \cong r_f(1 - \hat{\beta}_j). \qquad (17)$$

Neither FFJR nor Blume attack this question directly, though some of Blume's evidence is at least promising. In particular, the magnitudes of the estimated $\hat{\alpha}_j$ are roughly consistent with (17) in the sense that the estimates are always close to zero (as they should be with monthly return data).[27]

In a sense, though, in establishing the apparent empirical validity of the "market model" of (12), both too much and too little have been shown *vis-à-vis* the Sharpe-Lintner expected return model of (11). We know that during the post-World War II period one-month interest rates on riskless assets (e.g., government bills with one month to maturity) have not been constant. Thus, if expected security returns were generated by a version of the "market model" that is fully consistent with the Sharpe-Lintner model, we would, according to (15), expect to observe some non-stationarity in the estimates of α_j. On a monthly basis, however, variation through time in one-period riskless interest rates is probably trivial relative to variation in other factors affecting monthly common stock returns, so that more powerful statistical methods would be necessary to study the effects of changes in the riskless rate.

In any case, since the work of FFJR and Blume on the "market model" was not concerned with relating this model to the Sharpe-Lintner model, we can only say that the results for the former are somewhat consistent with the implications of the latter. But the results for the "market model" are, after all, just a statistical description of the return generating process, and they are probably somewhat consistent with other models of equilibrium expected returns. Thus the only way to generate strong empirical conclusions about the Sharpe-Lintner model is to test it directly. On the other hand, any alternative model of equilibrium expected returns must be somewhat consistent with the "market model," given the evidence in its support.

B. *Tests of Martingale Models of the Semi-strong Form*

In general, semi-strong form tests of efficient markets models are concerned with whether current prices "fully reflect" all obviously publicly available information. Each individual test, however, is concerned with the adjustment of security prices to one kind of information generating event (e.g., stock splits, announcements of financial reports by firms, new security issues, etc.). Thus each test only brings supporting evidence for the model, with the idea that by accumulating such evidence the validity of the model will be "established."

In fact, however, though the available evidence is in support of the efficient markets model, it is limited to a few major types of information generating events. The initial major work is apparently the study of stock splits by Fama,

27. With least squares applied to monthly return data, the estimate of α_j in (12) is

$$\hat{\alpha}_j = \bar{r}_{j,t} - \hat{\beta}_j \bar{r}_{M,t},$$

where the bars indicate sample mean returns. But, in fact, Blume applies the market model to the wealth relatives $R_{jt} = 1 + r_{jt}$ and $R_{Mt} = 1 + r_{Mt}$. This yields precisely the same estimate of β_j as least squares applied to (12), but the intercept is now

$$\hat{\alpha}'_j = \bar{R}_{jt} - \hat{\beta}_j \bar{R}_{Mt} = 1 + \bar{r}_{jt} - \hat{\beta}_j(1 + \bar{r}_{Mt}) = 1 - \hat{\beta}_j + \hat{\alpha}_j.$$

Thus what Blume in fact finds is that for almost all securities, $\hat{\alpha}'_j + \hat{\beta}_j \cong 1$, which implies that $\hat{\alpha}_j$ is close to 0.

Fisher, Jensen, and Roll (FFJR) [14], and all the subsequent studies summarized here are adaptations and extensions of the techniques developed in FFJR. Thus, this paper will first be reviewed in some detail, and then the other studies will be considered.

1. Splits and the Adjustment of Stock Prices to New Information

Since the only apparent result of a stock split is to multiply the number of shares per shareholder without increasing claims to real assets, splits in themselves are not necessarily sources of new information. The presumption of FFJR is that splits may often be associated with the appearance of more fundamentally important information. The idea is to examine security returns around split dates to see first if there is any "unusual" behavior, and, if so, to what extent it can be accounted for by relationships between splits and other more fundamental variables.

The approach of FFJR to the problem relies heavily on the "market model" of (12). In this model if a stock split is associated with abnormal behavior, this would be reflected in the estimated regression residuals for the months surrounding the split. For a given split, define month O as the month in which the effective date of a split occurs, month 1 as the month immediately following the split month, month -1 as the month preceding, etc. Now define the average residual over all split securities for month m (where for each security m is measured relative to the split month) as

$$u_m = \sum_{j=1}^{N} \frac{\hat{u}_{jm}}{N},$$

where $\hat{u}_{jm}$ is the sample regression residual for security j in month m and N is the number of splits. Next, define the cumulative average residual U_m as

$$U_m = \sum_{k=-29}^{m} u_k.$$

The average residual u_m can be interpreted as the average deviation (in month m relative to split months) of the returns of split stocks from their normal relationships with the market. Similarly, U_m can be interpreted as the cumulative deviation (from month -29 to month m). Finally, define u_m^+, u_m^-, U_m^+, and U_m^- as the average and cumulative average residuals for splits followed by "increased" (+) and "decreased" (−) dividends. An "increase" is a case where the percentage change in dividends on the split share in the year after the split is greater than the percentage change for the N.Y.S.E. as a whole, while a "decrease" is a case of relative dividend decline.

The essence of the results of FFJR are then summarized in Figure 1, which shows the cumulative average residuals U_m U_m^+, and U_m^- for $-29 \leq m \leq 30$. The sample includes all 940 stock splits on the N.Y.S.E. from 1927-59, where the exchange was at least five new shares for four old, and where the security was listed for at least twelve months before and after the split.

For all three dividend categories the cumulative average residuals rise in the 29 months prior to the split, and in fact the average residuals (not shown here) are uniformly positive. This cannot be attributed to the splitting process, since in only about ten per cent of the cases is the time between the announcement and effective dates of a split greater than four months. Rather, it seems that firms tend to split their shares during "abnormally" good times—that is, during periods when the prices of their shares have increased more than would

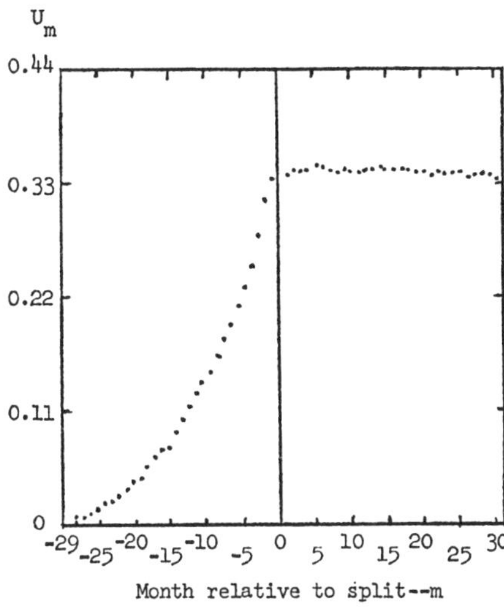

Figure 1a
Cumulative average residuals—all splits.

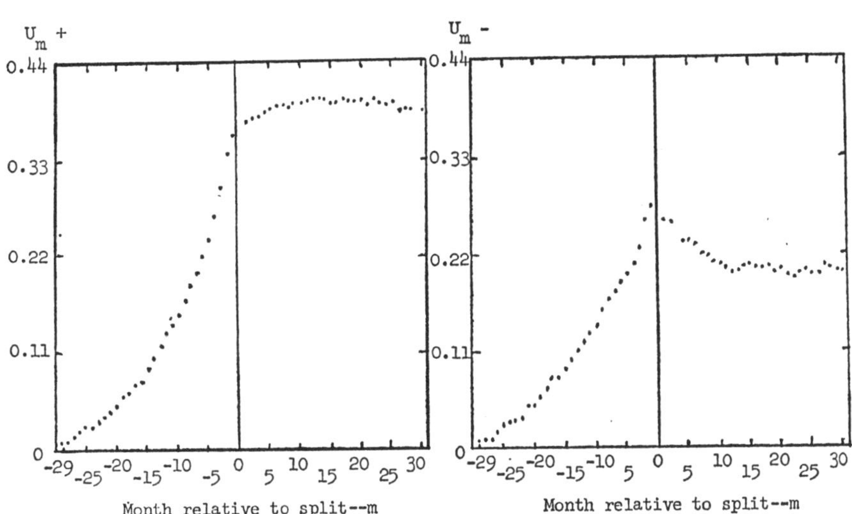

Figure 1b
Cumulative average residuals for dividend "increases."

Figure 1c
Cumulative average residuals for dividend "decreases."

be implied by their normal relationships with general market prices, which itself probably reflects a sharp improvement, relative to the market, in the earnings prospects of these firms sometime during the years immediately preceding a split.[28]

After the split month there is almost no further movement in U_m, the cumulative average residual for all splits. This is striking, since 71.5 per cent (672 out of 940) of all splits experienced greater percentage dividend increases in the year after the split than the average for all securities on the N.Y.S.E. In light of this, FFJR suggest that when a split is announced the market interprets this (and correctly so) as a signal that the company's directors are probably confident that future earnings will be sufficient to maintain dividend payments at a higher level. Thus the large price increases in the months immediately preceding a split may be due to an alteration in expectations concerning the future earning potential of the firm, rather than to any intrinsic effects of the split itself.

If this hypothesis is correct, return behavior subsequent to splits should be substantially different for the cases where the dividend increase materializes than for the cases where it does not. FFJR argue that in fact the differences are in the directions that would be predicted. The fact that the cumulative average residuals for the "increased" dividends (Figure 1b) drift upward but only slightly in the year *after* the split is consistent with the hypothesis that when the split is *declared*, there is a price adjustment in anticipation of future dividend increases. But the behavior of the residuals for stock splits associated with "decreased" dividends offers even stronger evidence for the split hypothesis. The cumulative average residuals for these stocks (Figure 1c) rise in the few months before the split, but then fall dramatically in the few months after the split when the anticipated dividend increase is not forthcoming. When a year has passed after the split, the cumulative average residual has fallen to about where it was five months prior to the split, which is about the earliest time reliable information about a split is likely to reach the market. Thus by the time it becomes clear that the anticipated dividend increase is not forthcoming, the apparent effects of the split seem to have been wiped away, and the stock's returns have reverted to their normal relationship with market returns.

Finally, and most important, although the behavior of post-split returns will be very different depending on whether or not dividend "increases" occur, and in spite of the fact that a large majority of split securities do experience dividend "increases," when all splits are examined together (Figure 1a), subsequent to the split there is no net movement up or down in the cumulative

28. It is important to note, however, that as FFJR indicate, the persistent upward drift of the cumulative average residuals in the months preceding the split is not a phenomenon that could be used to increase expected trading profits. The reason is that the behavior of the average residuals is not representative of the behavior of the residuals for individual securities. In months prior to the split, successive sample residuals for individual securities seem to be independent. But in most cases, there are a few months in which the residuals are abnormally large and positive. The months of large residuals differ from security to security, however, and these differences in timing explain why the signs of the average residuals are uniformly positive for many months preceding the split.

average residuals. Thus, apparently the market makes unbiased forecasts of the implications of a split for future dividends, and these forecasts are fully reflected in the prices of the security by the end of the split month. After considerably more data analysis than can be summarized here, FFJR conclude that their results lend considerable support to the conclusion that the stock market is efficient, at least with respect to its abiliy to adjust to the information implicit in a split.

2. Other Studies of Public Announcements

Variants of the method of residual analysis developed in [14] have been used by others to study the effects of different kinds of public announcements, and all of these also support the efficient markets hypothesis.

Thus using data on 261 major firms for the period 1946-66, Ball and Brown [4] apply the method to study the effects of annual earnings announcements. They use the residuals from a time series regression of the annual earnings of a firm on the average earnings of all their firms to classify the firm's earnings for a given year as having "increased" or "decreased" relative to the market. Residuals from regressions of monthly common stock returns on an index of returns (i.e., the market model of (12)) are then used to compute cumulative average return residuals separately for the earnings that "increased," and those that "decreased." The cumulative average return residuals rise throughout the year in advance of the announcement for the earnings "increased" category, and fall for the earnings "decreased" category.[29] Ball and Brown [4, p. 175] conclude that in fact no more than about ten to fifteen percent of the information in the annual earnings announcement has not been anticipated by the month of the announcement.

On the macro level, Waud [45] has used the method of residual analysis to examine the effects of announcements of discount rate changes by Federal Reserve Banks. In this case the residuals are essentially just the deviations of the daily returns on the Standard and Poor's 500 Index from the average daily return. He finds evidence of a statistically significant "announcement effect" on stock returns for the first trading day following an announcement, but the magnitude of the adjustment is small, never exceeding .5%. More interesting from the viewpoint of the efficient markets hypothesis is his conclusion that, if anything, the market anticipates the announcements (or information is somehow leaked in advance). This conclusion is based on the non-random patterns of the signs of average return residuals on the days immediately preceding the announcement.

Further evidence in support of the efficient markets hypothesis is provided in the work of Scholes [39] on large secondary offerings of common stock (ie., large underwritten sales of existing common stocks by individuals and institutions) and on new issues of stock. He finds that on average secondary issues are associated with a decline of between one and two per cent in the cumulative average residual returns for the corresponding common stocks. Since the magnitude of the price adjustment is unrelated to the size of the

29. But the comment of footnote 28 is again relevant here.

issue, Scholes concludes that the adjustment is not due to "selling pressure" (as is commonly believed), but rather results from negative information implicit in the fact that somebody is trying to sell a large block of a firm's stock. Moreover, he presents evidence that the value of the information in a secondary depends to some extent on the vendor; somewhat as would be expected, by far the largest negative cumulative average residuals occur where the vendor is the corporation itself or one of its officers, with investment companies a distant second. But the identity of the vendor is not generally known at the time of the secondary, and corporate insiders need only report their transactions in their own company's stock to the S.E.C. within six days after a sale. By this time the market on average has fully adjusted to the information in the secondary, as indicated by the fact that the average residuals behave randomly thereafter.

Note, however, that though this is evidence that prices adjust efficiently to public information, it is also evidence that corporate insiders at least sometimes have important information about their firm that is not yet publicly known. Thus Scholes' evidence for secondary distributions provides support for the efficient markets model in the semi-strong form sense, but also some strong-form evidence against the model.

Though his results here are only preliminary, Scholes also reports on an application of the method of residual analysis to a sample of 696 new issues of common stock during the period 1926-66. As in the FFJR study of splits, the cumulative average residuals rise in the months preceding the new security offering (suggesting that new issues tend to come after favorable recent events)[30] but behave randomly in the months following the offering (indicating that whatever information is contained in the new issue is on average fully reflected in the price of the month of the offering).

In short, the available semi-strong form evidence on the effect of various sorts of public announcements on common stock returns is all consistent with the efficient markets model. The strong point of the evidence, however, is its consistency rather than its quantity; in fact, few different types of public information have been examined, though those treated are among the obviously most important. Moreover, as we shall now see, the amount of semi-strong form evidence is voluminous compared to the strong form tests that are available.

C. *Strong Form Tests of the Efficient Markets Models*

The strong form tests of the efficient markets model are concerned with whether all available information is fully reflected in prices in the sense that no individual has higher expected trading profits than others because he has monopolistic access to some information. We would not, of course, expect this model to be an exact description of reality, and indeed, the preceding discussions have already indicated the existence of contradictory evidence. In particular, Niederhoffer and Osborne [32] have pointed out that specialists on the N.Y.S.E. apparently use their monopolistic access to information concern-

30. Footnote 28 is again relevant here.

ing unfilled limit orders to generate monopoly profits, and Scholes' evidence [39] indicates that officers of corporations sometimes have monopolistic access to information about their firms.

Since we already have enough evidence to determine that the model is not strictly valid, we can now turn to other interesting questions. Specifically, how far down through the investment community do deviations from the model permeate? Does it pay for the average investor (or the average economist) to expend resources searching out little known information? Are such activities even generally profitable for various groups of market "professionals"? More generally, who are the people in the investment community that have access to "special information"?

Though this is a fascinating problem, only one group has been studied in any depth—the managements of open end mutual funds. Several studies are available (e.g., Sharpe [41, 42] and Treynor [44]), but the most thorough are Jensen's [19, 20], and our comments will be limited to his work. We shall first present the theoretical model underlying his tests, and then go on to his empirical results.

1. Theoretical Framework

In studying the performance of mutual funds the major goals are to determine (a) whether in general fund managers seem to have access to special information which allows them to generate "abnormal" expected returns, and (b) whether some funds are better at uncovering such special information than others. Since the criterion will simply be the ability of funds to produce higher returns than some norm with no attempt to determine what is responsible for the high returns, the "special information" that leads to high performance could be either keener insight into the implications of publicly available information than is implicit in market prices or monopolistic access to specific information. Thus the tests of the performance of the mutual fund industry are not strictly strong form tests of the efficient markets model.

The major theoretical (and practical) problem in using the mutual fund industry to test the efficient markets model is developing a "norm" against which performance can be judged. The norm must represent the results of an investment policy based on the assumption that prices fully reflect all available information. And if one believes that investors are generally risk averse and so on average must be compensated for any risks undertaken, then one has the problem of finding appropriate definitions of risk and evaluating each fund relative to a norm with its chosen level of risk.

Jensen uses the Sharpe [40]-Lintner [24, 25] model of equilibrium expected returns discussed above to derive a norm consistent with these goals. From (14)-(16), in this model the expected return on an asset or portfolio j from t to t + 1 is

$$E(\tilde{r}_{j,t+1}|\Phi_t) = r_{f,t+1}\,[1 - \beta_j(\Phi_t)] + E(\tilde{r}_{m,t+1}|\Phi_t)\beta_j(\Phi_t), \tag{18}$$

where the various symbols are as defined in Section III. A. 6. But (18) is an *ex ante* relationship, and to evaluate performance an *ex post* norm is needed.

One way the latter can be obtained is to substitute the realized return on the market portfolio for the expected return in (18) with the result[31]

$$E(\tilde{r}_{j,t+1}|\Phi_t, r_{m,t+1}) = r_{f,t+1}[1 - \beta_j(\Phi_t)] + r_{m,t+1}\beta_j(\Phi_t). \tag{19}$$

Geometrically, (19) says that within the context of the Sharpe-Lintner model, the expected return on j (given information Φ_t and the return $r_{m,t+1}$ on the market portfolio) is a linear function of its risk

$$\beta_j(\Phi_t) = \text{cov}\,(\tilde{r}_{j,t+1}, \tilde{r}_{m,t+1}|\Phi_t)/\sigma^2(\tilde{r}_{m,t+1}|\Phi_t),$$

as indicated in Figure 2. Assuming that the value of $\beta_j(\Phi_t)$ is somehow known, or can be reliably estimated, if j is a mutual fund, its *ex post* performance from t to t + 1 might now be evaluated by plotting its combination of realized return $r_{j,t+1}$ and risk in Figure 2. If (as for the point a) the combination falls above the expected return line (or, as it is more commonly called, the "market line"), it has done better than would be expected given its level of risk, while if (as for the point b) it falls below the line it has done worse.

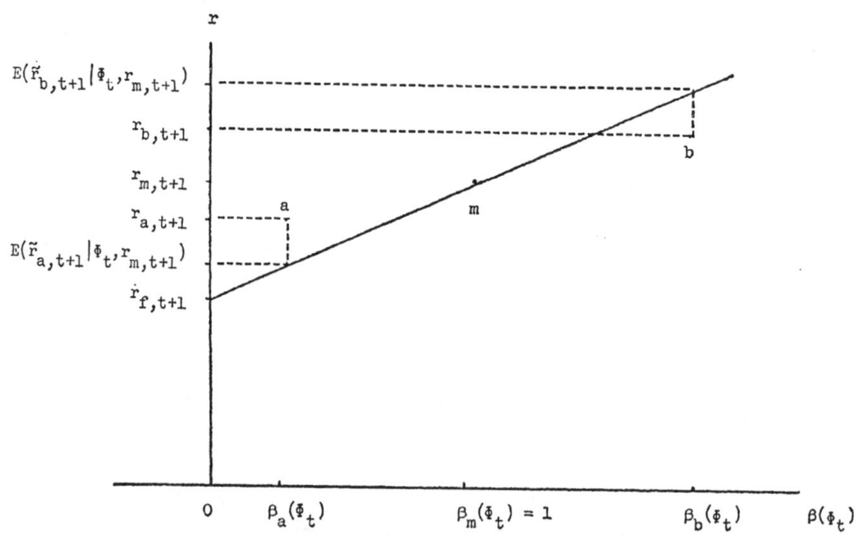

FIGURE 2
Performance Evaluation Graph

Alternatively, the market line shows the combinations of return and risk provided by portfolios that are simple mixtures of the riskless asset and the market portfolio m. The returns and risks for such portfolios (call them c) are

$$r_{c,t+1} = \alpha r_{f,t+1} + (1 - \alpha) r_{m,t+1}$$

$$\beta_c(\Phi_t) = \frac{\text{cov}\,(\tilde{r}_{c,t+1}, \tilde{r}_{m,t+1}|\Phi_t)}{\sigma^2(\tilde{r}_{m,t+1}|\Phi_t)} = \frac{\text{cov}\,((1-\alpha)\tilde{r}_{m,t+1}, \tilde{r}_{m,t+1}|\Phi_t)}{\sigma^2(\tilde{r}_{m,t+1}|\Phi_t)} = 1 - \alpha,$$

31. The assumption here is that the return $\tilde{r}_{j,t+1}$ is generated according to

$$\tilde{r}_{j,t+1} = r_{f,t+1}[1 - \beta_j(\Phi_t)] + r_{m,t+1}\beta_j(\Phi_t) + \tilde{u}_{j,t+1},$$

and

$$E(\tilde{u}_{j,t+1}|r_{m,t+1}) = 0 \text{ for all } r_{m,t+1}.$$

where α is the proportion of portfolio funds invested in the riskless asset. Thus, when $1 \geqslant \alpha \geqslant 0$ we obtain the combinations of return and risk along the market line from $r_{f,t+1}$ to m in Figure 2, while when $\alpha < 0$ (and under the assumption that investors can borrow at the same rate that they lend) we obtain the combinations of return and risk along the extension of the line through m. In this interpretation, the market line represents the results of a naive investment strategy, which the investor who thinks prices reflect all available information might follow. The performance of a mutual fund is then measured relative to this naive strategy.

2. Empirical Results

Jensen uses this risk-return framework to evaluate the performance of 115 mutual funds over the ten year period 1955-64. He argues at length for measuring return as the nominal ten year rate with continuous compounding (i.e., the natural log of the ratio of terminal wealth after ten years to initial wealth) and for using historical data on nominal one-year rates with continuous compounding to estimate risk. The Standard and Poor Index of 500 major common stocks is used as the proxy for the market portfolio.

The general question to be answered is whether mutual fund managements have any special insights or information which allows them to earn returns above the norm. But Jensen attacks the question on several levels. First, can the funds in general do well enough to compensate investors for loading charges, management fees, and other costs that might be avoided by simply choosing the combination of the riskless asset f and the market portfolio m with risk level comparable to that of the fund's actual portfolio? The answer seems to be an emphatic no. As far as net returns to investors are concerned, in 89 out of 115 cases, the fund's risk-return combination for the ten year period is below the market line for the period, and the average over all funds of the deviations of ten year returns from the market time is -14.6%. That is, on average the consumer's wealth after ten years of holding mutual funds is about fifteen per cent less than if he held the corresponding portfolios along the market line.

But the loading charge that an investor pays in buying into a fund is usually a pure salesman's commission that the fund itself never gets to invest. Thus one might ask whether, ignoring loading charges (i.e., assuming no such charges were paid by the investor), in general fund managements can earn returns sufficiently above the norm to cover all other expenses that are presumably more directly related to the management of the fund portfolios. Again, the answer seems to be no. Even when loading charges are ignored in computing returns, the risk-return combinations for 72 out of 115 funds are below the market line, and the average deviation of ten year returns from the market line is -8.9%.

Finally, as a somewhat stronger test of the efficient markets model, one would like to know if, ignoring all expenses, fund managements in general showed any ability to pick securities that outperformed the norm. Unfortunately, this question cannot be answered with precision for individual funds since, curiously, data on brokerage commissions are not published regularly.

But Jensen suggests the available evidence indicates that the answer to the question is again probably negative. Specifically, adding back all other published expenses of funds to their returns, the risk-return combinations for 58 out of 115 funds were below the market line, and the average deviation of ten year return from the line was −2.5%. But part of this result is due to the absence of a correction for brokerage commissions. Estimating these commissions from average portfolio turnover rates for all funds for the period 1953-58, and adding them back to returns for all funds increases the average deviation from the market line from −2.5% to .09%, which still is not indicative of the existence of special information among mutual fund managers.

But though mutual fund managers in general do not seem to have access to information not already fully reflected in prices, perhaps there are individual funds that consistently do better than the norm, and so provide at least some strong form evidence against the efficient markets model. If there are such funds, however, they escape Jensen's search. For example, for individual funds, returns above the norm in one subperiod do not seem to be associated with performance above the norm in other subperiods. And regardless of how returns are measured (i.e., net or gross of loading charges and other expenses), the number of funds with large positive deviations of returns from the market line of Figure 2 is less than the number that would be expected by chance with 115 funds under the assumption that fund managements have no special talents in predicting returns.[32]

Jensen argues that though his results apply to only one segment of the investment community, they are nevertheless striking evidence in favor of the efficient markets model:

> Although these results certainly do not imply that the strong form of the martingale hypothesis holds for all investors and for all time, they provide strong evidence in support of that hypothesis. One must realize that these analysts are extremely well endowed. Moreover, they operate in the securities markets every day and have wide-ranging contacts and associations in both the business and financial communities. Thus, the fact that they are apparently unable to forecast returns accurately enough to recover their research and transactions costs is a striking piece of evidence in favor of the strong form of the martingale hypothesis—at least as far as the extensive subset of information available to these analysts is concerned [20, p. 170].

IV. Summary and Conclusions

The preceding (rather lengthy) analysis can be summarized as follows. In general terms, the theory of efficient markets is concerned with whether prices at any point in time "fully reflect" available information. The theory only has empirical content, however, within the context of a more specific model of

32. On the other hand, there is some suggestion in Scholes' [39] work on secondary issues that mutual funds may occassionally have access to "special information." After corporate insiders, the next largest negative price changes occur when the secondary seller is an investment company (including mutual funds), though on average the price changes are much smaller (i.e., closer to 0) than when the seller is a corporate insider.

Moreover, Jensen's evidence itself, though not indicative of the existence of special information among mutual fund managers, is not sufficiently precise to conclude that such information never exists. This stronger conclusion would require exact data on unavoidable expenses (including brokerage commissions) of portfolio management incurred by funds.

market equilibrium, that is, a model that specifies the nature of market equilibrium when prices "fully reflect" available information. We have seen that all of the available empirical literature is implicitly or explicitly based on the assumption that the conditions of market equilibrium can be stated in terms of expected returns. This assumption is the basis of the expected return or "fair game" efficient markets models.

The empirical work itself can be divided into three categories depending on the nature of the information subset of interest. *Strong-form* tests are concerned with whether individual investors or groups have monopolistic access to any information relevant for price formation. One would not expect such an extreme model to be an exact description of the world, and it is probably best viewed as a benchmark against which the importance of deviations from market efficiency can be judged. In the less restrictive *semi-strong-form* tests the information subset of interest includes all obviously publicly available information, while in the *weak form* tests the information subset is just historical price or return sequences.

Weak form tests of the efficient market model are the most voluminous, and it seems fair to say that the results are strongly in support. Though statistically significant evidence for dependence in successive price changes or returns has been found, some of this is consistent with the "fair game" model and the rest does not appear to be sufficient to declare the market inefficient. Indeed, at least for price changes or returns covering a day or longer, there isn't much evidence against the "fair game" model's more ambitious offspring, the random walk.

Thus, there is consistent evidence of positive dependence in day-to-day price changes and returns on common stocks, and the dependence is of a form that can be used as the basis of marginally profitable trading rules. In Fama's data [10] the dependence shows up as serial correlations that are consistently positive but also consistently close to zero, and as a slight tendency for observed numbers of runs of positive and negative price changes to be less than the numbers that would be expected from a purely random process. More important, the dependence also shows up in the filter tests of Alexander [1, 2] and those of Fama and Blume [13] as a tendency for very small filters to produce profits in excess of buy-and-hold. But any systems (like the filters) that attempt to turn short-term dependence into trading profits of necessity generate so many transactions that their expected profits would be absorbed by even the minimum commissions (security handling fees) that floor traders on major exchanges must pay. Thus, using a less than completely strict interpretation of market efficiency, this positive dependence does not seem of sufficient importance to warrant rejection of the efficient markets model.

Evidence in contradiction of the "fair game" efficient markets model for price changes or returns covering periods longer than a single day is more difficult to find. Cootner [9], and Moore [31] report preponderantly negative (but again small) serial correlations in weekly common stock returns, and this result appears also in the four day returns analyzed by Fama [10]. But it does not appear in runs tests of [10], where, if anything, there is some slight indication of positive dependence, but actually not much evidence of any dependence at all. In any case, there is no indication that whatever dependence exists in weekly returns can be used as the basis of profitable trading rules.

Other existing evidence of dependence in returns provides interesting insights into the process of price formation in the stock market, but it is not relevant for testing the efficient markets model. For example, Fama [10] shows that large daily price changes tend to be folowed by large changes, but of unpredictable sign. This suggests that important information cannot be completely evaluated immediately, but that the initial first day's adjustment of prices to the information is unbiased, which is sufficient for the martingale model. More interesting and important, however, is the Niederhoffer-Osborne [32] finding of a tendency toward excessive reversals in common stock price changes from transaction to transaction. They explain this as a logical result of the mechanism whereby orders to buy and sell at market are matched against existing limit orders on the books of the specialist. Given the way this tendency toward excessive reversals arises, however, there seems to be no way it can be used as the basis of a profitable trading rule. As they rightly claim, their results are a strong refutation of the theory of random walks, at least as applied to price changes from transaction to transaction, but they do not constitute refutation of the economically more relevant "fair game" efficient markets model.

Semi-strong form tests, in which prices are assumed to fully reflect all obviously publicly available information, have also supported the efficient markets hypothesis. Thus Fama, Fisher, Jensen, and Roll [14] find that the information in stock splits concerning the firm's future dividend payments is on average fully reflected in the price of a split share at the time of the split. Ball and Brown [4] and Scholes [39] come to similar conclusions with respect to the information contained in (i) annual earning announcements by firms and (ii) new issues and large block secondary issues of common stock. Though only a few different types of information generating events are represented here, they are among the more important, and the results are probably indicative of what can be expected in future studies.

As noted earlier, the strong-form efficient markets model, in which prices are assumed to fully reflect all available information, is probably best viewed as a benchmark against which deviations from market efficiency (interpreted in its strictest sense) can be judged. Two such deviations have in fact been observed. First, Niederhoffer and Osborne [32] point out that specialists on major security exchanges have monopolistic access to information on unexecuted limit orders and they use this information to generate trading profits. This raises the question of whether the "market making" function of the specialist (if indeed this is a meaningful economic function) could not as effectively be carried out by some other mechanism that did not imply monopolistic access to information. Second, Scholes [39] finds that, not unexpectedly, corporate insiders often have monopolistic access to information about their firms.

At the moment, however, corporate insiders and specialists are the only two groups whose monopolistic access to information has been documented. There is no evidence that deviations from the strong form of the efficient markets model permeate down any further through the investment community. For the purposes of most investors the efficient markets model seems a good first (and second) approximation to reality.

In short, the evidence in support of the efficient markets model is extensive, and (somewhat uniquely in economics) contradictory evidence is sparse. Nevertheless, we certainly do not want to leave the impression that all issues are closed. The old saw, "much remains to be done," is relevant here as elsewhere. Indeed, as is often the case in successful scientific research, now that we know we've been in the past, we are able to pose and (hopefully) to answer an even more interesting set of questions for the future. In this case the most pressing field of future endeavor is the development and testing of models of market equilibrium under uncertainty. When the process generating equilibrium expected returns is better understood (and assuming that some expected return model turns out to be relevant), we will have a more substantial framework for more sophisticated intersecurity tests of market efficiency.

REFERENCES

1. Sidney S. Alexander. "Price Movements in Speculative Markets: Trends or Random Walks." *Industrial Management Review,* 2 (May 1961), 7-26. Also reprinted in [8], 199-218.
2. ———. "Price Movements in Speculative Markets: Trends or Random Walks. No. 2," in [8], 338-72.
3. Louis Bachelier. *Théorie de la Speculation* (Paris: Gauthier-Villars, 1900), and reprinted in English in [8], 17-78.
4. Ray Ball and Phillip Brown. "An Empirical Evaluation of Accounting Income Numbers." *Journal of Accounting Research,* 6 (Autumn, 1968), 159-78.
5. William Beaver. "The Information Content of Annual Earnings Announcements." *Empirical Research in Accounting: Selected Studies, 1968,* supplement to Vol. 7 of the *Journal of Accounting Research,* 67-92.
6. Robert Blattberg and Thomas Sargent. "Regression with Non-Gaussian Disturbances: Some Sampling Results," forthcoming in Econometrica.
7. Marshall Blume. "The Assessment of Portfolio Performance." Unpublished Ph.D. thesis, University of Chicago, 1968. A paper summarizing much of this work will appear in the April, 1970, Journal of Business.
8. Paul Cootner (ed.). *The Random Character of Stock Market Prices.* Cambridge: M.I.T., 1964.
9. ———. "Stock Prices: Random vs. Systematic Changes." *Industrial Management Review,* 3 (Spring 1962), 24-45. Also reprinted in [8], 231-52.
10. Eugene F. Fama. "The Behavior of Stock Market Prices." *Journal of Business,* 38 (January, 1965), 34-105.
11. ———. "Multiperiod Consumption-Investment Decisions." *American Economic Review,* (March, 1970).
12. ———. "Risk, Return and Equilibrium." Report No. 6831, University of Chicago, Center for Math. Studies in Business and Economics, June, 1968.
13. ——— and Marshall Blume. "Filter Rules and Stock Market Trading Profits." *Journal of Business,* 39 (Special Supplement, January, 1966), 226-41.
14. ———, Lawrence Fisher, Michael Jensen and Richard Roll. "The Adjustment of Stock Prices to New Information." *International Economic Review,* X (February, 1969), 1-21.
15. ——— and Richard Roll. "Some Properties of Symmetric Stable Distributions." *Journal of the American Statistical Association,* 63 (September, 1968), 817-36.
16. Michael D. Godfrey, C. W. J. Granger and O. Morgenstern. "The Random Walk Hypothesis of Stock Market Behavior." *Kyklos,* 17 (1964), 1-30.
17. C. W. J. Granger and O. Morgenstern. "Spectral Analysis of New York Stock Market Prices," *Kyklos,* 16 (1963), 1-27. Also reprinted in [8], 162-88.
18. John R. Hicks. *Value and Capital.* Oxford: The Clarendon Press, 1946.
19. Michael Jensen. "The Performance of Mutual Funds in the Period 1945-64," *Journal of Finance,* 23 (May, 1968), 389-416.

20. ——————. "Risk, the Pricing of Capital Assets, and the Evaluation of Investment Portfolios," *Journal of Business,* 42 (April, 1969), 167-247.
21. Maurice G. Kendall. "The Analysis of Economic Time-Series, Part I: Prices," *Journal of the Royal Statistical Society,* 96 (Part I, 1953), 11-25.
22. Ruben A. Kessel. "The Cyclical Behavior of the Term Structure of Interest Rates," National Bureau of Economic Research Occasional Paper No. 91. New York: Columbia University Press, 1965.
23. Benjamin F. King. "Market and Industry Factors in Stock Price Behavior," *Journal of Business,* 39 (Special Supplement January, 1966), 139-90.
24. John Lintner. "Security Prices, Risk, and Maximal Gains from Diversification," *Journal of Finance,* 20 (December, 1965), 587-615.
25. ——————. "The Valuation of Risk Assets and the Selection of Risky Investments in Stock Portfolios and Capital Budgets," *Review of Economics and Statistics,* 47 (February, 1965), 13-37.
26. Fredrich A. Lutz. "The Structure of Interest Rates," *Quarterly Journal of Economics,* 40 (1940-41).
27. Benoit Mandelbrot. "Forecasts of Future Prices, Unbiased Markets, and Martingale Models," *Journal of Business,* 39 (Special Supplement, January, 1966), 242-55.
28. ——————. "The Variation of Certain Speculative Prices." *Journal of Business,* 36 (October, 1963), 394-419.
29. —————— and Howard M. Taylor. "On the Distribution of Stock Price Differences." *Operations Research,* 15 (November-December, 1967), 1057-62.
30. Harry Markowitz. *Portfolio Selection:Efficient Diversification of Investment.* New York: John Wiley & Sons, 1959.
31. Arnold Moore. "A Statistical Analysis of Common Stock Prices. Unpublished Ph.D. thesis, Graduate School of Business, University of Chicago, 1962.
32. Victor Niederhoffer and M. F. M. Osborne. "Market Making and Reversal on the Stock Exchange." *Journal of the American Statistical Association,* 61 (December, 1966), 897-916.
33. M. F. M. Osborne. "Brownian Motion in the Stock Market," *Operations Research,* 7 (March-April, 1959), 145-73. Also reprinted in [8], 100-28.
34. ——————. "Periodic Structure in the Brownian Motion of Stock Prices." *Operations Research,* 10 (May-June, 1962), 345-79. Also reprinted in [8], 262-96.
35. S. James Press. "A compound Events Model for Security Prices." *Journal of Business,* 40 (July, 1968), 317-35.
36. Harry V. Roberts. "Stock Market 'Patterns' and Financial Analysis: Methodological Suggestions." *Journal of Finance,* 14 (March, 1959), 1-10.
37. Richard Roll. "The Efficient Market Model Applied to U.S. Treasury Bill Rates." Unpublished Ph.D. thesis, Graduate School of Business, University of Chicago, 1968.
38. Paul A. Samuelson. "Proof That Properly Anticipated Prices Fluctuate Randomly." *Industrial Management Review,* 6 (Spring, 1965), 41-9.
39. Myron Scholes. "A Test of the Competitive Hypothesis: The Market for New Issues and Secondary Offerings." Unpublished PH.D. thesis, Graduate School of Business, University of Chicago, 1969.
40. William F. Sharpe. "Capital Asset Prices: A Theory of Market Equilibrium under Conditions of Risk." *Journal of Finance,* 19 (September, 1964), 425-42.
41. ——————. "Mutual Fund Performance." *Journal of Business,* 39 (Special Supplement, January, 1966), 119-38.
42. ——————. "Risk Aversion in the Stock Market." *Journal of Finance,* 20 (September, 1965), 416-22.
43. James Tobin. "Liquidity Preference as Behavior Towards Risk," *Review of Economic Studies,* 25 (February, 1958), 65-85.
44. Jack L. Treynor. "How to Rate Management of Investment Funds." *Harvard Business Review,* 43 (January-February, 1965), 63-75.
45. Roger N. Waud. "Public Interpretation of Discount Rate Changes: Evidence on the 'Announcement Effect.'" forthcoming in *Econometrica.*
46. John Wise. "Linear Estimators for Linear Regression Systems Having Infinite Variances." Unpublished paper presented at the Berkeley-Stanford Mathematical Economics Seminar, October, 1963.
47. Holbrook Working. "A Random Difference Series for Use in the Analysis of Time Series." *Journal of the American Statistical Association,* 29 (March, 1934), 11-24.

[4]

Journal of Economic Literature
Vol. XXVII (December 1989), pp. 1583–1621

Efficient Capital Markets and Martingales

By STEPHEN F. LEROY
University of California, Santa Barbara, and Federal Reserve Bank of San Francisco

I have received helpful comments from Frank Diebold, Steven Durlauf, Christian Gilles, Pete Kyle, Stephen Ross, Kevin Salyer, Robert Shiller, and Christopher Sims. The paper benefited from exceptionally diligent and capable refereeing. I am indebted to Aarne Dimanlig, Judy Horowitz, and Barbara Bennett for research assistance and editing. This paper was written while I was a visiting scholar at the Federal Reserve Banks of Minneapolis and San Francisco. I am grateful to both institutions. Views expressed here are those of the author and are not necessarily those of the Federal Reserve System or its staff.

I. *Overview*

AT ITS MOST GENERAL LEVEL, the theory of efficient capital markets is just the theory of competitive equilibrium applied to asset markets. An important idea in the theory of competitive equilibrium is the Ricardian principle of comparative advantage: England exported cloth to Portugal and imported wine from Portugal not because England necessarily had an absolute advantage over Portugal in producing cloth, but because England produced cloth comparatively more cheaply than wine relative to Portugal.[1] The same idea applies in analyzing equilibrium in financial markets, except that comparative advantage is conferred by differences in information held by investors, rather than differences in productivity among producers. The analogue in financial markets of Ricardo's assertion that absolute advantage is irrelevant is the proposition that information that is universally available cannot provide the basis for profitable trading rules. Thus if it is generally known that a firm has favorable earnings prospects, the theory of efficient capital markets says that the price of the firm's stock will be bid to the point where no extranormal capital gain on the stock will occur when the high earnings actually materialize. Therefore knowledge that earnings will rise in the future does not imply that the stock should be bought now. It is only differences in information—information that is not "fully reflected" in

[1] Ricardo gracefully headed off a criticism of chauvinism by specifying that Portugal had an absolute advantage over England in producing both cloth and wine ([1817], 1960, p. 82), rather than England over Portugal.

prices—that confer comparative advantage, and that therefore can form the basis for profitable trading rules.

Most of the lessons of market efficiency are direct consequences of thinking about financial asset prices as determined by the conditions of equilibrium in competitive markets populated by rational agents. Some of these lessons are obvious. For example, the decision by a company to split its stock (i.e., issue two or three new shares in exchange for each old share) should have no effect on the rate of return on this stock. This proposition is a direct corollary of the fact that in any economic equilibrium the choice of numeraire is arbitrary. Other lessons of market efficiency, however, while apparently equally direct consequences of the nature of competitive equilibrium, go deeply against the grain of finance practitioners and financial journalists. For example, during the era of conglomerate formation in the 1960s and 1970s (which, of course, has since been succeeded by the current wave of leveraged buyouts accompanied by conglomerate breakups), firms routinely justified acquiring other firms in unrelated lines of business on the grounds that the acquisition served to diversify their activities, thereby reducing risks to stockholders. In an efficient market, this justification makes no sense at all. Firms have no comparative advantage over individuals in diversifying risk because individuals can diversify risk simply by buying the stock of several firms or the shares of a mutual fund that holds many firms' stocks. This example indicates that in finance, as everywhere else in economics, economists risk offending entrenched opinion to the extent that they insist on taking seriously even elementary conclusions drawn from equilibrium analysis.

When economists defend some statement as being a consequence of the fact (or assumption) that capital markets are efficient, they are signaling that at a minimum they want to think of asset prices as being determined by the interaction of rational agents—that is, as being determined as an economic equilibrium—and that they see the proposed statement as following from this fact. Frequently, however, the term *efficient capital markets* carries in addition the presumption that the amount of information which is publicly available, and which for this reason cannot be used to construct profitable trading rules, is large. In the limit, the doctrine of capital market efficiency contains the assertion that individuals do not in fact have different comparative advantages in information acquisition. In such a world there are no profitable trading rules. This extended meaning of capital market efficiency underlies statements such as the following: In an efficient capital market, agents should have no investment goals other than to diversify to the maximum extent possible so as to minimize idiosyncratic risk, and to hold the amount of risk appropriate to their risk tolerance.

The importance of the topic of capital market efficiency is evident. Investors have no choice but to base their investment decisions on information. In evaluating their information, investors must consider not only whether it is accurate, but also whether it is generally known—in practitioners' parlance, whether it has already been discounted in the market price. Because the value of information depends on the extent of its dispersion, investors' decisions about what information to acquire depend on whether they think capital markets are efficient; to the extent that markets are informationally efficient, acquisition of information is a waste of time.

Suppose that capital markets are efficient with respect to some information set Φ. Then by definition an individual investor who acquires information Φ

does not gain comparative advantage over his rivals, this information being already fully reflected in prices. The earliest empirical investigations of capital market efficiency tested this postulated failure of information to confer comparative advantage by constructing hypothetical trading rules based on particular information sets and testing their profitability under actual securities returns. Buying and selling stocks according to some prescribed formula based on Φ should not result in systematic success if capital markets are efficient with respect to Φ, but might do so otherwise.

Although it was insufficiently realized at first, these empirical tests of whether asset prices fully reflect available information also presume the validity of a particular equilibrium model specifying precisely how information is reflected in prices: the martingale model. Martingales will be defined and described below. The fact that the empirical literature on capital market efficiency is inextricably linked to the martingale model justifies our taking the martingale model as the unifying theme for this survey. It is true, however, that there exist branches of the literature on efficient capital markets that are unrelated to martingales but that nonetheless are important to a full understanding of market efficiency. These are sketched in the following two paragraphs. Coverage of these subliteratures in addition to the martingale literature would result in a survey that is disjointed and superficial. Accordingly, topics are emphasized and deleted here primarily according to how closely they are linked to the martingale model.

The principal omission that is justified on grounds of unrelatedness to the martingale topic is the large and important literature on rational expectations equilibria under asymmetric information. In the asymmetric information literature the focus is on how agents who are rational (and who have rational expectations) interact when it is common knowledge that they have different information. There is no question that mastery of the asymmetric information literature is indispensable to a deep understanding of capital market efficiency. However, this area, besides having no close connection with martingales, does not bear directly on the empirical work on market efficiency.

Another important literature that bears on capital market efficiency as defined above, but which is not discussed in this paper, is that on portfolio separation. Contrary to the implication in the first paragraph, it is not generally true that only differences in information give agents reason to trade securities. If futures markets are incomplete, changes in wealth and conditional distributions of future returns will in general interact with agents' risk aversion so as to induce them to trade even when there is no disagreement about the conditional distribution of returns. However, under certain restrictions on preferences and return distributions it can be shown that identically informed agents will hold identical, or virtually identical, portfolios. Under these restrictions it is true that all, or virtually all, differences in comparative advantage in holding securities can be traced to differential information. The theory of portfolio separation, which derives these restrictions on agents' optimal portfolios from assumptions about preferences and return distributions, is discussed in introductory graduate texts in finance (e.g., Jonathan Ingersoll, Jr. 1987; Chi-fu Huang and Robert Litzenberger 1988).

If the origin of the efficient capital markets literature is dated in the 1930s, as is reasonable, the martingale model appeared on the scene after the chronological midpoint of the literature (1965). Up to the mid-1960s, market efficiency was associated with the random walk model. The literature on the random walk model is reviewed in Section II. After this background material is presented, the martingale model is presented in Section III. It is shown there that, as just indicated, empirical tests of market efficiency are in fact tests of a joint hypothesis which includes the martingale specification. Further, it is shown that, despite being a descendant of the random walk model, the martingale is closely related to the fundamentalist model which had earlier been thought to be diametrically opposed to the random walk. In Section IV Eugene Fama's influential analyses of capital market efficiency are discussed.

Section V begins the presentation of empirical developments in the analysis of efficient capital markets over the past two decades. It was realized around 1975 that the martingale model implied that asset prices should be less volatile than they apparently are. An extended debate, not yet concluded, then began over whether the observed volatility of asset prices in fact exceeds that which capital market efficiency implies, or whether instead the apparent violations reflect nothing more than statistical problems in the (purported) demonstrations of excess volatility. A closely related literature, that on mean reversion in asset prices, is then reviewed. The discussion of the latter topic is abbreviated because the literature on mean reversion, being still at a very early stage in its development, has not yet arrived at any kind of consensus. Section VI turns to examination of alternatives to the martingale model. It is easy to show that relaxation of the strong restrictions on preferences and return distributions required for the martingale model could in principle reconcile observed asset price volatility with that implied by market efficiency. However, it turns out that empirically these generalizations of the martingale model do not succeed well. Continuing, the large finance literature on anomalies in asset pricing is reviewed in Section VII. Finally, conclusions are presented in Section VIII.

II. *The Prehistory of Efficient Capital Markets*

Early works that were directly related to securities analysis as it is now practiced were J. B. Williams' *The Theory of Investment Value* (1938) and Benjamin Graham and David Dodd's *Security Analysis* (1934), upon which a generation of financial analysts was educated. These put forth the idea that the "intrinsic" or "fundamental" value of any security equals the discounted cash flow which that security gives title to, and that actual prices fluctuate around fundamental values. Accordingly, analysts were instructed to recommend buying (selling) securities that are priced below (above) fundamental value so as to realize trading profits when the disparity is eliminated. Because calculating present values is analytically trivial—particularly so inasmuch as the theory gave little practical guidance as to what discount rate to use—"fundamental analysis" consisted in practice mostly of forming projections of future cash flow. This involved analyzing demand for the product, possible future development of substitutes, the probability of recession, changes in the regulatory environment; in short, all information relevant to future profitability.

The only problem with fundamental analysis was that it appeared not to work. Alfred Cowles (1933) demonstrated that the recommendations of major brokerage houses, presumably based at least partly on fundamental analysis, did not outperform the market. The implication was that investors who paid for these recommendations were wasting their money. Other clouds shortly began appearing on the horizon. In (1934) Holbrook Working argued that random walks—cumulated series of probabilistically independent shocks—characteristically developed patterns that look like those commonly ascribed by market analysts to stock prices. Was it possible that stock prices follow a random walk? In his (1960) paper, Working provided additional evidence in favor of purely random stock prices by showing that, if data generated by a random walk were averaged over time, spurious correlation between successive changes would result. Thus existence of such correlations did not necessarily constitute evidence against the random walk model.

The "random walk hypothesis"—forerunner of the efficient capital markets model—was inaugurated in earnest with a major statistical study by M. G. Kendall (1953) which examined seriously the proposition that stock prices follow a random walk. Kendall found that they do, as Working's results had suggested. Clive Granger and Oskar Morgenstern (1963) followed up Kendall's result with an econometric study using spectral analysis that supported the same conclusion. As it turned out, however, the results of Kendall and Granger and Morgenstern had been anticipated in a remarkable PhD dissertation written in 1900 by Louis Bachelier, a French mathematician. Bachelier conducted an empirical study of French government bonds, finding that their prices were consistent with a random walk model. Besides anticipating the empirical work that was to come more than a half a century later, Bachelier also developed many of the mathematical properties of Brownian motion (the continuous-time analogue of the random walk) which had been thought to have been first derived later in the physical sciences. In particular, Bachelier had anticipated many of the mathematical results developed in Albert Einstein's 1905 paper. Bachelier's study is excerpted in Paul Cootner's (1964) collection of papers on the random walk model.

At first the random walk model seemed flatly to contradict not only the received orthodoxy of fundamental analysis, but also the very idea of rational securities pricing.[2] If stock prices were patternless, was there any point to fundamental analysis? The random walk model seemed to imply that stock prices are exempt from the laws of supply and demand that determine other prices, and instead look more like the casino or musical chairs game that John Maynard Keynes (1936) chose as metaphors for the stock market. However, economists immediately realized that such a conclusion was premature. Harry Roberts (1959) pointed out that in the economist's idealized market of rational individuals one would expect exactly the instantaneous adjustment of prices to new information that the random walk model implies. A pattern of systematic slow adjustment to new information, on the other hand, would imply the existence of readily available and profitable trading opportunities that were not being exploited.

These considerations raised awkward questions for proponents of fundamental analysis: If fundamental analysis worked, why did not new entrants into the business of fundamental analysis, realizing this fact and planning to participate in the trading gains, compete these gains away? That is what happens in every other competitive industry in which profits exceed costs—why not in financial analysis? Alfred Cowles' (1933) results

[2] "Adam Smith" (1968) expressed the skepticism about the random walk model that was characteristic of market professionals, and also the sense that the random walk model is diametrically opposed to the fundamentalist model: "I suspect that even if the random walkers announced a perfect mathematic proof of randomness, I would go on believing that in the long run future earnings influence present value . . ." (pp. 157–58).

suggested that in fact this was exactly what did happen. Fundamentalists had no good answers to these questions.

However, the random walk model left as many questions unanswered as it resolved, and its ablest proponents, such as Roberts, fully realized this. It was embarrassing for economists to have to shelve the competitive theory of price—surely the jewel in their professional crown—when it came to analyzing stock market prices, instead making do with informal and qualitative remarks such as if stock prices did not follow a random walk there must exist unexploited profit opportunities. If stock prices had nothing to do with preferences and technology, what about the prices of the machines that firms use? What about the wheat the farmer produces and the baker uses, but which is also traded on organized exchanges just like stock? Where does Marshall's *Principles* stop and the random walk start? Plainly there must be more to be said.

There is another problem with the random walk model. Critics of the random walk model can turn the random walkers' own method of argument back on them: Huge sums of money are spent every year on an activity—securities analysis—which, if the random walk model is correct, is entirely unproductive. Random walkers, the critics observe, expect us to believe at once: (1) that unexploited patterns in securities prices cannot persist because for them to do so would imply that investors are irrationally passing up profit opportunities, but also (2) that investors are nonetheless irrationally wasting their money year after year employing useless securities analysts. If the argument that no behavior inconsistent with rationality and rational expectations can persist in equilibrium is employed it must be employed consistently, and this the random walkers were not doing. Thus the continuing existence of large incomes based on generating investment advice is as much a thorn in the side of the random walkers as the failure of this advice to generate extranormal trading returns is a thorn in the side of fundamentalists.

III. *Martingale Models*

Resolutions to the puzzles pointed out in the preceding section required situating the random walk model within the framework of economic equilibrium. Such an account was not forthcoming within the random walk literature. A quarter-century later, it is easy to see why: By requiring probabilistic independence between successive price increments, the random walk model is simply too restrictive to be generated within a reasonably broad class of optimizing models. However, a weaker restriction on asset prices that still captures the flavor of the random walk arguments—the martingale[3] model—turned out to be more tractable. Paul Samuelson's (1965) paper was the first to develop the link between capital market efficiency and martingales. The simplicity of Samuelson's argument led some (for example, Mark Rubinstein 1975) to dismiss the result as obvious. Perhaps it is, particularly with hindsight. However that may be, when the dust had cleared and the implications of Sameulson's argument were fully assimilated, the random walk model had been jettisoned and replaced with the martingale model. Most analysts now consider Samuelson's to be the most im-

[3] The word *martingale* refers in French to a betting system designed to make a sure franc. Ironically, this meaning is close to that for which the English language appropriated the French word *arbitrage*. The French word *martingale* refers to Martigues, a city in Provence. Inhabitants of Martigues were reputed to favor a betting strategy consisting of doubling the stakes after each loss so as to assure a favorable outcome with arbitrarily high probability.

I am indebted to Christian Gilles for supplying this background.

portant paper in the efficient capital markets literature because of its role in effecting this shift from the random walk to the martingale model. The martingale model does not resolve all the puzzles that accompany the random walk, but it does resolve many of them. Unlike the random walk, the martingale model does constitute a bona fide economic model of asset prices, in the sense that it can be linked with primitive assumptions on preferences and returns which, although restrictive, are not so restrictive as to trivialize the claim to economic justification.

A stochastic process x_t is a *martingale* with respect to a sequence of information sets Φ_t if x_t has the property

$$E(x_{t+1}|\Phi_t) = x_t \qquad (3.1)$$

and a stochastic process y_t is a *fair game* if it has the property

$$E(y_{t+1}|\Phi_t) = 0. \qquad (3.2)$$

Here (3.1) says that if x_t is a martingale, the best forecast of x_{t+1} that could be constructed based on current information Φ_t would just equal x_t (it is assumed that x_t is in Φ_t).[4] This is true for any possible value of the information Φ_t. Similarly, (3.2) says that if y_t is a fair game the corresponding forecast would be zero for any possible value of Φ_t. It is obvious that x_t is a martingale if and only if $x_{t+1} - x_t$ is a fair game.[5]

The martingale and fair game models are two names for the same characterization of equilibrium in financial markets; rates of return are a fair game if and only if a series closely related to prices—that is, prices plus cumulated dividends, discounted back to the present—is a martingale. To prove this, let r_t be the rate of return on stock (for example)[6] from $t - 1$ to t, and suppose that r_t, less a constant ρ, is a fair game. Using the definition of the rate of return as the sum of dividend yield plus capital gain, less one, it follows from the fair game assumption that stock price p_t is given by

$$p_t = (1 + \rho)^{-1}E(p_{t+1} + d_{t+1}|\Phi_t), \qquad (3.3)$$

where d is dividends. Equation (3.3) says that the stock price today equals the sum of the expected future price and dividends, discounted back to the present at rate ρ. When there is no ambiguity about the information set, as here, it is convenient to rewrite (3.3) more compactly as

$$p_t = (1 + \rho)^{-1}E_t(p_{t+1} + d_{t+1}). \qquad (3.4)$$

None of the variables defined so far is a martingale. The variable that is a martingale is the discounted value of a mutual fund that holds stock the price of which follows (3.4). The mutual fund is assumed to reinvest received dividends in further share purchases. To see that the discounted value of this mutual fund follows a martingale, let $v_t = (1 + \rho)^{-t}p_t h_t$ be the value of the mutual fund discounted back to date zero, where h_t is the number of shares of stock the mutual fund holds at t. The assumption that the mutual fund plows back its dividend income implies that h_{t+1} satisfies

$$p_{t+1}\, h_{t+1} = (p_{t+1} + d_{t+1})h_t. \qquad (3.5)$$

Now consider $E_t(v_{t+1})$. We have

[4] The exposition to follow comes with apologies to Donald McCloskey who, in instructing writers of economics to avoid "prefabricated and predictable" prose—boilerplate—wrote: "Explaining a model of efficient capital markets by writing for the thousandth time 'P_t given I_t, where I_t is all the information' does not advance understanding. If it didn't much help to make Eugene Fama's work clear when he first uttered it, why suppose it will enlighten someone now?" (McCloskey 1987, p. 24).

[5] Fair games are for this reason sometimes called *martingale differences*.

[6] Stock prices will be the principal source of examples throughout this paper. Justification for martingale models for other sorts of financial prices—for example, futures prices—is sometimes different (Danthine 1977; LeRoy 1982; Gilles and LeRoy 1986).

$$E_t(v_{t+1}) = E_t[(1+\rho)^{-(t+1)}p_{t+1}h_{t+1}]$$
$$= E_t[(1+\rho)^{-(t+1)}(p_{t+1} + d_{t+1})h_t]$$
$$= (1+\rho)^{-t}p_t h_t = v_t. \quad (3.6)$$

Here the second equality uses (3.5) and the third uses (3.4). Hence v_t is a martingale.

It is worth emphasizing that (3.4) implies that the price itself, without dividends added in, is not generally a martingale in the class of models just set out: If the dividend-price ratio changes over time because of fluctuations in current dividends relative to the variables that predict future dividends, as it generally will, the fair game model implies that the conditionally expected rate of capital gain must vary in an offsetting manner so as to maintain the nonrandomness of the conditionally expected rate of return. Such variation in expected capital gain conflicts with the martingale definition (3.1) (where p_t and p_{t+1} are substituted for x_t and x_{t+1}). Nevertheless, the practice in the efficient capital markets literature is to speak of stock prices as following a martingale; in such cases "price" should be understood to include reinvested dividends. We will follow this imprecise but convenient usage.

The most direct empirical tests of the martingale model attempt to determine whether some variable in agents' information set is a predictor of future returns. If so, the martingale model is violated. For example, if agents know past returns and are able to use these to predict future returns, returns cannot follow a fair game. Of course, this result points to a fundamental ambiguity in the simplest tests of the martingale model: Finding some variable that predicts future returns could mean either that the capital market is inefficient—that is, does not satisfy the martingale property—or that that variable is not in agents' information sets. However, some more sophisticated tests of the martingale model do not suffer from this ambiguity. For example, rejection of the variance-bounds inequality (discussed in Section V) implies rejection of the martingale model for any specification of agents' information sets.

The specification that a stochastic process x_t follows a random walk (coupled with the additional assumption that the increments have zero mean) is more restrictive than the requirement that x_t follows a martingale. The martingale rules out any dependence of the conditional expectation of $x_{t+1} - x_t$ on the information available at t, whereas the random walk rules out this and also dependence involving the higher conditional moments of x_{t+1}. The importance of the distinction between the martingale and the random walk is evident: Securities prices are known to go through protracted quiet periods and equally protracted turbulent periods. Formally, one might represent this behavior using a model in which successive conditional variances of stock prices (but not their successive levels) are positively autocorrelated. Such a specification is consistent with a martingale, but not with the more restrictive random walk.

Samuelson (1965) proved a result—more precisely, pointed out the relevance of a well-known result from probability theory, the rule of iterated expectations—which put the theory of efficient capital markets on a firm footing for the first time. Similar results were presented by Benoit Mandelbrot (1966) at about the same time. Samuelson cast his original statement in terms of futures prices. However, continuity of exposition is best maintained here if his result is restated in terms of stock prices; in fact, Samuelson (1973) himself provided such a restatement. Samuelson's result was that the fair game model (3.4) implies that stock prices equal the expected present value of future dividends:

$$p_t = \sum_{i=1}^{\infty} (1 + \rho)^{-i} E_t(d_{t+i}). \quad (3.7)$$

To derive (3.7), replace t by $t + 1$ in (3.4) and use the resulting equation to substitute out p_{t+1} in (3.4) as written. There results

$$p_t = (1 + \rho)^{-1} E_t[(1 + \rho)^{-1} E_{t+1}(p_{t+2} + d_{t+2}) + d_{t+1}]. \quad (3.8)$$

If it is assumed that agents never forget the past, so that Φ_{t+1} is more informative than Φ_t, the rule of iterated expectations guarantees that $E_t[E_{t+1}(p_{t+2})]$ equals $E_t(p_{t+2})$, and similarly for dividends. Therefore (3.8) becomes

$$p_t = (1 + \rho)^{-1} E_t(d_{t+1}) + (1 + \rho)^{-2} E_t(p_{t+2} + d_{t+2}). \quad (3.9)$$

Proceeding similarly n times and assuming that $(1 + \rho)^{-n} E_t(p_{t+n})$ converges to zero so as to rule out speculative bubbles,[7] (3.7) results. Also, the reverse implication obtains: The expected present-value model (3.7) implies that rates of return are a fair game.

Samuelson's result implies that the appearance noted in Section II of diametric opposition between the fundamentalist model and the efficient capital markets model of asset prices—with the former (latter) apparently implying that asset prices are completely systematic (unsystematic)—is entirely illusory. In fact, Samuelson's result implies that if fundamentalists are correct in viewing stock prices as equal to discounted expected cash flows, then it follows that future returns are unpredictable, just as the martingale model postulates. The fundamentalists, in focusing on the predictable part of asset prices, are asserting that the glass is half full, while the martingale model contends that the glass is half empty. As the analogy implies, there is no contradiction even though the focus is different.

To be sure, in arguing for the similarity between the fundamentalists' model and the martingale model we have implicitly redefined the fundamentalist theory of asset valuation in a subtle but critically important way. Instead of assuming that price fluctuates around fundamental value (discounted expected cash flow), Samuelson assumed (or proved, depending on which direction of implication is being considered) that price actually equals fundamental value. The importance of this change is evident: If price always equals fundamental value, then no profit can be earned by trading on a discrepancy between the two, contrary to the fundamentalists' assertion. This observation implies that it would be no more correct to regard the fundamentalist model as originally formulated as identical to the martingale model than it would be to view the two as diametrically opposed. Contrary to both of these, it is best to regard the martingale model as an extreme version of the fundamentalists' model: If we start with the fundamentalists' model and modify it by assuming that a large majority of traders are conducting fundamental analysis, are arriving at the same estimates of fundamental value, and are trading appropriately, then price will be bid to equality with fundamental value and trading profits will disappear.

Under what assumptions regarding preferences is the martingale model satisfied? Samuelson pointed out that it would be satisfied if agents have common and constant time preference, have common probabilities, and are risk-neutral. If these conditions are satisfied, investors will always prefer to hold whichever asset generates the highest expected return, completely ignoring differences in risk. If all assets are to be held willingly, as must be the case in equilibrium, all must

[7] See Gilles (forthcoming) or Gilles and LeRoy (1988b) for a statement of conditions under which this convergence is guaranteed.

therefore earn the same expected rate of return, equal to the real interest rate. The interest rate, being equal to the constant discount factor, is itself constant over time. Therefore returns follow the fair game model (3.2), or, equivalently, prices plus reinvested dividends follow a martingale.

Risk neutrality implies the martingale (3.1), but not the more restrictive random walk. If agents do not care what the higher moments of their return distributions are, as risk neutrality implies, they will do nothing to bid away serial dependence in the higher conditional moments of returns. Therefore risk neutrality is consistent with nonzero serial correlation in conditional variances: The fact that future conditional variances are partly forecastable is irrelevant because risk neutrality implies that no one cares about these variances. Following Samuelson's paper, analysts realized that the theoretical underpinnings for efficient-markets models in fact point toward the martingale rather than the random walk. Once aware of the distinction between random walks and martingales, they also realized that most (but not all; see the following section) of the empirical tests for randomness were in fact tests of the weaker martingale model or, for example, the still weaker specification that rates of return are uncorrelated.

IV. *Fama's Definitions and Evidence*

The dividing line between the "prehistory" of efficient capital markets, associated with the random walk model, and the modern literature is Fama's (1970) survey. This influential paper brought the term *efficient capital markets* into general use and is widely interpreted as associating market efficiency with the martingale model, although it will be seen that this interpretation reflects a misreading of the paper.

Fama's paper, like the literature it surveyed, was devoted almost exclusively to empirical work. However, some preliminary theoretical discussion was also included, and Fama's (1970) definition of capital market efficiency became the industry standard, reproduced in innumerable subsequent papers, until it was supplanted by his equally influential (1976a) definition. In Fama's (1970) usage, a capital market is efficient if all the information in some information set Φ is "fully reflected" in securities prices. Fama, crediting Harry Roberts with the original statement, then distinguished three versions of the efficient markets model depending on the specification of the information set Φ. Capital markets are "weak-form efficient" if Φ comprises just historical prices. Weak-form efficiency implies that no trading rule based on historical prices alone can succeed on average. Capital markets are "semistrong-form efficient" if Φ is broadened to include all information that is publicly available. Finally, capital markets are "strong-form efficient" if Φ is broadened still further to include even insider information.

In light of the discussion in the preceding section of the martingale model, it would seem natural to identify market efficiency with the specification that returns follow a fair game, with (1) weak-form, (2) semistrong-form, and (3) strong-form efficiency obtaining depending on whether the information set includes (1) past prices and returns alone, (2) all public information, or (3) private as well as public information. An attractive feature of this specification is that, from a mathematical property of conditional expectations, strong-form efficiency implies semistrong-form efficiency, which in turn implies weak-form efficiency, just as Fama's choice of terminology suggests.

However, Fama explicitly rejected this specification. Instead, he identified market efficiency with the assumption that y_t is a fair game:

$$E(y_{t+1} | \Phi_t) = 0, \qquad (4.1)$$

where y_{t+1} is defined to equal the price of some security at $t + 1$ less its conditional expectation:

$$y_{t+1} = p_{t+1} - E(p_{t+1} | \Phi_t). \qquad (4.2)$$

Fama correctly observed that the fair game model so defined

> does not necessarily imply that the serial covariances of *one-period returns* are zero. . . . In the 'fair game efficient markets model [as defined by (4.1) and (4.2)], the deviation of the return for $t + 1$ from its conditional expectation is a 'fair game' variable, but the conditional expectation itself can depend on the return observed for t. (p. 392)

Here Fama is explicitly rejecting the identification of capital market efficiency with the requirement that rates of return themselves be a fair game variable—if they were, the serial covariances of one-period returns would in fact necessarily equal zero (because past returns are assumed to be in agents' information sets under all three forms of market efficiency). In Fama's definition, however, it is only the deviation of price from its conditional expectation that is a fair game.

The problem with Fama's characterization of market efficiency is that (4.1) follows tautologously from the definition (4.2) of y_{t+1}—just take expectations conditional on Φ_t, on both sides of (4.2). Therefore the characterization of y_{t+1} as defined in (4.2) as a fair game variable does not restrict the stochastic process for price in any way. On Fama's definition, any capital market is efficient, and no empirical evidence can possibly bear on the question of market efficiency. The passage quoted in the preceding paragraph was not an isolated slip. In his theoretical discussion Fama observed that most empirical tests of market efficiency are based on the assumption that "the conditions of market equilibrium can (somehow) be stated in terms of expected returns . . . , described notationally as follows:

$$E(p_{t+1} | \Phi_t) = [1 + E(r_{t+1} | \Phi_t)]p_t\text{''} \qquad (4.3)$$

(p. 384). Again we have a tautology: (4.3) is obtained by applying a conditional expectations operator to the identity defining the rate of return as equal to the price relative p_{t+1}/p_t (less one). The tautologous nature of Fama's characterization of capital market efficiency was pointed out in LeRoy's (1976) comment; in his (1976b) reply, however, Fama rejected the argument, explicitly denying the existence of any tautologous elements in his definition.

In a subsequent section continuing his gloss on what it would mean for prices to "fully reflect" available information, Fama proposed the *submartingale* model

$$E(p_{t+1} | \Phi_t) \geq p_t, \qquad (4.4)$$

so that (neglecting dividends) conditionally expected rates of return are nonnegative. This submartingale characterization of market efficiency is, of course, not tautologous. Fama asserted that if stock prices follow a submartingale, then no trading rule based on Φ can outperform buy-and-hold. No support was given for this claim, and it is easy to produce examples of economies in which the prices of all primitive securities follow submartingales but in which there exist trading rules that outperform buy-and-hold in terms of expected return. In any case, the capital asset pricing model (CAPM) implies that equilibrium asset returns will not necessarily follow a submartingale: A stock that covaries negatively and sufficiently strongly with the market might well be priced to yield a negative expected return. Despite the negative expected return, risk-averse investors would be willing to include the stock in question in their portfolios because its negative correlation with the market implies that it helps to insure the returns on the other stocks held, thereby reducing overall risk.

The ambiguity in Fama's theoretical discussion of capital market efficiency carried over to his interpretation of the empirical evidence. Fama generally interpreted the near-zero autocorrelations of successive stock price changes as favoring market efficiency, suggesting that he in fact identified efficiency with the characterization of returns as a fair game, contray to his formal statement. Evidence that mechanical trading rules do not outperform buy-and-hold (Sidney Alexander 1961, 1964; Fama and Blume 1966) was similarly interpreted as favoring weak-form efficiency, providing further support for this reading. However, Fama's interpretation of Victor Niederhoffer and M. F. M. Osborne's (1966) evidence on runs—successive price changes of the same sign—is difficult to square with the fair game interpretation. Niederhoffer and Osborne found that reversals (pairs of successive price changes of opposite sign) occurred two to three times as frequently as continuations. Such systematic patterns are inconsistent with the fair game model. Despite this, Fama concluded and emphasized that such patterns, even though statistically significant, do not imply market inefficiency (p. 398).[8] Fama apparently based this conclusion on the fact that a plausible explanation for the predominance of reversals over continuations, reflecting the way limit orders are executed on the organized stock exchanges, can be constructed (see Niederhoffer and Osborne).

[8] Strictly, Niederhoffer and Osborne's evidence contradicts the more restrictive random walk, not the martingale. However, this distinction does not appear to be what Fama had in mind in denying that Niederhoffer and Osborne's evidence was inconsistent with market efficiency.

Generally, the implication of Fama's discussion of Niederhoffer and Osborne seems to be that markets are to be interpreted as efficient either if price changes are serially independent or if they are serially dependent but a convincing economic explanation can be found for the dependence. This is very different from the fair game interpretation of market efficiency, according to which departures from the fair game per se are identified with inefficiency.

Also arguing against Fama's identification of market efficiency with the martingale model is the fact that several of the studies he interpreted as bearing on market effciency use the CAPM to remove the risk-premium component of asset returns (Michael Jensen 1968, 1969, for example). In the CAPM (strictly, in the intertemporal extension of the CAPM discussed in Section VII), prices do not generally follow a martingale.

Fama acknowledged the existence of some evidence against efficiency, particularly against the implausibly restrictive strong-form version, which requires that the information set with respect to which the market is efficient include even inside information. For example, Niederhoffer and Osborne documented the fact that market makers on organized exchanges have no difficulty converting their monopolistic knowledge of supply and demand functions for stock, as embodied in limit orders, into extranormal trading gains. This example is somewhat isolated, however; Fama reported that, surprisingly, the evidence against even strong-form efficiency is sparse. Mutual fund managers, who presumably have access to expert securities analysis, are apparently unable to acquire portfolios that systematically outperform the market (Jensen 1968, 1969). With regard to semi-strong-form efficiency, Fama et al. (1969) demonstrated that the information contained in stock splits is accurately reflected in stock prices at the time of the split, implying that stock splits cannot be used to construct profitable trading rules (unless, of course, one can find out about forthcoming splits before they become public knowledge).

In sum, Fama (1970) concluded that the evidence strongly but not unanimously supported market efficiency.

Fama proposed a different definition of capital market efficiency in his (1976a) finance text. A capital market is efficient if (1) it does not neglect any information relevant to the determination of securities prices, and (2) it (acts as if it) has rational expectations. The assumption of rational expectations means that investors use their information to make those inferences about future events that are justified by objective correlations between the information variables and the future events, and only those inferences. In other words, rational expectations models treat the agents being modeled as knowing the structure of the model and the values of its parameters. Putting these ideas together, Fama defined capital markets as efficient if the market uses all relevant information to determine securities prices, and uses the information correctly. Fama emphasized that efficiency can be tested only jointly with some particular model of market equilibrium, the nature of which depends on endowments and preferences, but which is not implied by market efficiency. Although his (1976a) definition has a major drawback, it is a great improvement over the (1970) definition. Most important, by clearly and unambiguously defining capital market efficiency in a way that is logically independent of particular market models, Fama resolved many of the ambiguities in his (1970) treatment of market efficiency. The drawback lies in his anthropomorphic characterization of "the market": One can speak unambiguously of "the market's" information only if all agents have the same information, in which case informational efficiency is satisfied trivially.

The term *efficient capital markets* is seen to have several possible meanings, even if one ignores definitions proposed in the asymmetric information literature (Sanford Grossman 1978; Grossman and Joseph Stiglitz 1976, 1980; James Jordan 1983), as we do here. Nonetheless, the practice in the empirical finance literature is to speak of *tests of market efficiency* as if this phrase had unambiguous meaning. For the most part, in the empirical literature market efficiency is in practice equated with rational expectations plus the martingale model, and we will follow this convention.

V. *Empirical Evidence: Variance Bounds and Mean Reversion*

Fama's (1970) survey marked a high point for capital market efficiency; most of the evidence accumulated in the nearly 20 years since then has been contradictory rather than supportive. In this section the discussion will concentrate on the variance-bounds violations and the literature on mean reversion that grew out of it. These topics are chosen because they are directly related to martingales. Also, other types of evidence, such as the calendar-based "anomalies" explored in the finance literature, have recently been surveyed elsewhere. This other evidence will be acknowledged very briefly in Section VII.

Beginning in the mid-1970s, analysts came to realize that the same models which imply that returns should be unforecastable also imply that asset prices should have volatility which is, in a precise sense, low relative to the volatility of dividends. Results of tests of these volatility implications of market efficiency were circulated in 1975 in the paper by LeRoy and Richard Porter (published

1981). Robert Shiller, working independently, reported the results of tests of similar volatility relations in his (1979) and (1981b) papers. In both cases the outcome was the same: Asset prices appear to be more volatile than is consistent with the efficient-markets model. In setting out the "variance-bounds" theorems (as LeRoy and Porter called them) here, I present the version that we developed rather than Shiller's version because, as will be seen shortly, much of the subsequent original (as opposed to critical) work on the variance-bounds theorems turned out to be more closely related to our paper than to Shiller's.

To begin, note that the fair game assumption (3.4) plus the definition of the rate of return imply that p_t can be written as

$$p_t = (1+\rho)^{-1}(d_{t+1} + p_{t+1}) - (1+\rho)^{-1}e_{t+1}, \quad (5.1)$$

where e_{t+1} is the unexpected component of the one-period return on stock:

$$e_{t+i} \equiv p_{t+i} + d_{t+i} - E_{t+i-1}(p_{t+i} + d_{t+i}) \quad (5.2)$$

(it is assumed throughout that all variables have finite means and variances). Now replace t by $t+i$ in (5.1) and multiply both sides by $(1+\rho)^{-i}$:

$$(1+\rho)^{-i}p_{t+i} = (1+\rho)^{-(i+1)}(d_{t+i+1} + p_{t+i+1}) - (1+\rho)^{-(i+1)}e_{t+i+1}. \quad (5.3)$$

Summing (5.3) over i from zero to infinity and assuming convergence, there results

$$p_t^* = p_t + x_t, \quad (5.4)$$

where

$$p_t^* = \sum_{i=1}^{\infty} (1+\rho)^{-i}d_{t+i} \quad \text{and } x_t = \sum_{i=1}^{\infty} (1+\rho)^{-i}e_{t+i}. \quad (5.5)$$

Here p_t^* is the price of stock that would obtain if future realizations of dividends were perfectly forecastable. Following Shiller, I call p_t^* the "ex post rational" stock price. The difference between ex post rational and actual price, x_t, is seen to equal the discounted sum of the unexpected component of future returns.

Taking conditional expectations, (5.4) yields

$$p_t = E(p_t^* \mid \Phi_t), \quad (5.6)$$

so that p_t is a forecast of p_t^* given agents' information Φ_t. Given (5.6), (5.4) says that p_t^* can be expressed as the sum of a forecast (p_t) and a forecast error (x_t). Optimal forecasting implies that forecasts and forecast errors are uncorrelated. Uncorrelatedness in turn implies that

$$V(p_t^*) = V(p_t) + V(x_t). \quad (5.7)$$

Because variances—specifically, $V(x_t)$—are always nonnegative, $V(p_t^*)$ is an upper bound for $V(p_t)$.

The implied variance inequality,

$$V(p_t) \leq V(p_t^*), \quad (5.8)$$

is attractive because the upper bound depends only on the dividends model and the discount factor, but not on agents' information sets. Thus, econometric problems aside, rejection of (5.8) unambiguously implies rejection of the martingale model for any specification of agents' information sets. It will be recalled that, in contrast, under conventional tests rejection could mean either that markets are inefficient or that whatever variable allows prediction of future returns is not in agents' information sets.

The variance of the (unobservable) forecast error x_t turns out to be proportional to the variance of the (observable) unexpected component of returns, where the factor of proportionality depends on the discount factor alone. To prove this, begin with the second equation of (5.5), which says that the forecast error x_t is a discounted sum of the unexpected components of future returns. Taking variances and evaluating an infinite sum,

$V(x_t)$ is seen to be related to $V(e_t)$ according to

$$V(x_t) = \frac{V(e_t)}{2\rho + \rho^2}, \qquad (5.9)$$

assuming that $V(e_t)$ is constant.[9] This equation will prove useful later.

As LeRoy and Porter observed, equation (5.7) may be shown to imply that the more information agents have, the greater will be the variance of price and the lower will be the variance of discounted returns. To see the first implication, consider some information set H_t which is less informative than agents' actual information set Φ_t. Define $\hat{p}_t$ to be the price of stock that would obtain under the information set H_t:

$$\hat{p}_t = E(p_t^* | H_t). \qquad (5.10)$$

Here $\hat{p}_t$, like p_t^*, is a fictional stock price series that would obtain if investors had different information than they actually do. In a sense, $\hat{p}_t$ and p_t^* are on opposite sides of p_t: The former is the price that would prevail if agents had less information than they do, while the latter would prevail if they had perfect information. Because of this, one would expect that the relation of $\hat{p}_t$ to p_t would be qualitatively similar (in some sense) to the relation of p_t to p_t^*. Specifically, one might guess that, just as $V(p_t^*)$ is an upper bound for $V(p_t)$, it might also be true that $V(p_t)$ is an upper bound for $V(\hat{p}_t)$, or, equivalently, that $V(\hat{p}_t)$ is a lower bound for $V(p_t)$. This guess turns out to be correct. The rule of iterated expectations[10] implies that

$$\hat{p}_t = E[E(p_t^* | \Phi_t) | H_t] \qquad (5.11)$$

or

$$\hat{p}_t = E(p_t | H_t), \qquad (5.12)$$

using (5.6). Repeating the reasoning presented in the derivation of (5.8) from (5.6), but substituting $\hat{p}_t$ for p_t, H_t for Φ_t, p_t *for* p_t^*, and z_t for x_t, where $z_t = p_t - \hat{p}_t$, it follows from the fact that $V(z_t) \geq 0$ that

$$V(\hat{p}_t) \leq V(p_t). \qquad (5.13)$$

Proving the second implication—that the more information agents have, the lower will be the variance of discounted returns—amounts to showing that returns are more volatile under information H_t than under Φ_t. This demonstration is direct. Defining $\hat{x}_t$ as $p_t^* - \hat{p}_t$ and observing that (5.7) continues to hold with $\hat{p}_t$ and $\hat{x}_t$ replacing p_t and x_t, it follows from (5.13) that

$$V(\hat{x}_t) \geq V(x_t) \qquad (5.14)$$

which, in light of (5.9), implies

$$V(\hat{e}_t) \geq V(e_t), \qquad (5.15)$$

where $\hat{e}_t$ is the forecast error for returns under the information set H_t.

This completes the statement of LeRoy and Porter's theoretical results. It is useful to summarize what has been proven. Two basic facts about the martingale model are that the variance of stock price and the variance of returns (multiplied by a constant) add up to the variance of ex post rational price (5.7 and 5.9), and that the variance of the ex post rational price does not depend on how much information agents have. These facts imply that hypothetical variations in agents' information induce a negative relation between the variance of price and the variance of returns: That is, the more information agents have, the higher is the variance of price and the lower is the variance of returns. Thus if agents

[9] Derivation of (5.9) makes use of the fact that because the e_t are serially uncorrelated, the variance of the sum of the $(1 + \rho)^{-i}e_{t+i}$ terms equals the sum of the variances (the covariance terms drop out). Also used is the fact that the variance of a constant times a random variable equals the constant squared times the variance of the random variable.

[10] Formally, the rule of iterated expectations is used in exactly the same way here as in passing from (3.8) to (3.9) in the derivation of the present-value relation. Its use may be easier to understand intuitively there than here.

have very little information, stock prices are usually not much different from the discounted sum of unconditional expected dividends, a constant. Therefore stock prices have low volatility. In this case realizations of actual dividends come as near-complete surprises, inducing high volatility in actual returns. However, if agents have a great deal of information about future dividends, stock prices have almost as much volatility as discounted actual dividends, the two being highly correlated. In this case significant surprises occur very seldom, implying that returns will usually be nearly equal to their unconditional expectation.

Given that the volatilities of price and returns depend monotonically on how much information agents have, it follows that if we can place bounds on agents' information, these will induce bounds on the variances of price and returns. The obvious choice for the upper bound on agents' information is perfect information, implying that $V(p_t^*)$ is an upper bound for $V(p_t)$ and, unhelpfully, that zero is a lower bound for $V(e_t)$. Given Fama's definition of weak-form efficiency, the obvious choice of a lower bound on agents' information is that agents know past returns, but nothing else. It follows that $V(\hat{p}_t)$ is a lower bound for $V(p_t)$, and $V(\hat{e}_t)$ is an upper bound for $V(e_t)$. Of the four variance bounds, two are interesting empirically: $V(p_t^*)$ as an upper bound for $V(p_t)$, and $V(\hat{e}_t)$ as an upper bound for $V(e_t)$.

LeRoy and Porter reported the results of two types of tests: bounds tests and orthogonality tests. The null hypothesis in a bounds test is satisfied if the variance of price (or returns) is less than its theoretical upper bound. An orthogonality test, on the other hand, is a test of the implications for variances of the equality restrictions on parameters implied by the orthogonality of forecasts and forecast errors. The null hypothesis of a bounds test is thus an inequality restriction on parameters, whereas the null hypothesis of an orthogonality test is an equality restriction. We constructed both tests using the estimated parameters of a bivariate autoregression model for prices and dividends (i.e., two regressions in which price and dividends, respectively, were regressed on their own and the other's lagged values). This model, together with the estimated discount factor, implies an estimate of the upper bound $V(p_t^*)$. The bounds test compared the estimate of $V(p_t)$ implied by the bivariate model with the estimated upper bound. The inequality (5.8) was reversed empirically, contradicting the martingale model. Shiller (1981a) reported rejection of a similar inequality.

LeRoy and Porter's orthogonality test was conducted by constructing an estimate of each term of (5.7) from the estimated bivariate model for price and dividends: Instead of using only the information that $V(x_t)$ is nonnegative, as in the bounds test, the orthogonality test used the fact that $V(x_t)$ is related to the variance of one-period returns according to (5.9). The test then consists of evaluating the null hypothesis

$$H_0\colon V(p_t) = V(p_t^*) - \frac{V(e_t)}{2\rho + \rho^2} \quad (5.16)$$

against the alternative

$$H_1\colon V(p_t) > V(p_t^*) - \frac{V(e_t)}{2\rho + \rho^2}. \quad (5.17)$$

Again the martingale model was rejected, although the confidence interval for the null hypothesis turned out to be extremely large.

A major difference between Shiller's and LeRoy and Porter's interpretations of the variance-bounds violations was that Shiller saw them as constituting evidence against efficiency and in favor of the existence of elements of irrationality in securities pricing, whereas LeRoy and Porter characterized the violations merely as an anomaly requiring explanation (LeRoy 1984). At first it appeared that LeRoy and Porter's reluctance to draw any but the weakest conclusions from the variance-bounds violations was better justified than Shiller's willingness to base strong conclusions on the finding of excess volatility: Shortly after publication of the original studies it became clear that at least some of the variance-bounds tests were subject to severe econometric problems. Focusing on Shiller's tests, Marjorie Flavin (1983) demonstrated that small-sample problems led to bias against acceptance of efficiency. She did this by showing that the estimated variances of both p^* and p were biased downward, with the bias in the former estimate exceeding that in the latter. The reason for the downward bias in estimating the variances of p^* and p is that the sample means of both p^* and p must be estimated, and the usual fixup (reduce degrees of freedom by one) gives an inadequate correction for the induced downward bias in the sample variance to the extent that the underlying series is autocorrelated. Because p^* is more highly autocorrelated than p, the downward bias is greater in estimating the variance of p^* than of p, which is why the net effect is to bias the test toward rejection.[11] Allan Kleidon (1986a) focused on the econometric consequences of violation of a stationarity assumption. He showed that, if dividends have unit roots, problems similar to Flavin's could persist even in arbitrarily large samples.[12]

Flavin and Kleidon's papers gave proponents of market efficiency reason to hope that the apparent evidence of excess volatility was entirely a consequence of flawed econometric procedures. However, the next round of variance-bounds papers made it evident that the variance-bounds violations were here to stay, and that Shiller's willingness to draw far-reaching conclusions based on these violations (and other evidence) may in fact have been justified. Shiller (1988), responding to Kleidon (1986), contended that under realistic parameter values the bias which Kleidon had pointed out was insufficient to explain the magnitude of the violations (in turn, Kleidon, 1988a, took issue with Shiller's criticism).[13] More important, a new round of "second-generation" variance-bounds tests, allegedly free of the biases that had been pointed out in Shiller's original tests, led to the same conclusion of excess volatility. These are surveyed by Gilles and LeRoy (1988a) and West (1988b). N. Gregory Mankiw, David Romer, and Matthew Shapiro (1985), following Porter's suggestion to Flavin (see Footnote 11), tested the variance-bounds inequality using second moments around zero

[11] Incidentally, Flavin noted a potential remedy (suggested to her by Porter; see Flavin 1983, p. 950) for this problem: estimate variances around zero rather than around the sample mean. It is easy to verify that, under the null hypothesis, the noncentral variances of p^* and p obey the same inequality as the variances around their common mean.

[12] Other papers making similar points as Flavin and Kleidon in different ways were Kleidon (1986b) and Marsh and Merton (1986). For brief summaries of these papers see LeRoy (1984) or Kenneth West (1988b); for a fairly detailed exposition and evaluation of these papers see Gilles and LeRoy (1988a).

[13] Also, Gilles and LeRoy (1988a) showed that the criticisms leveled at Shiller by Kleidon and Flavin do not extend to LeRoy and Porter. Because LeRoy and Porter used a different trend correction than Shiller did, Kleidon's demonstration that Shiller's tests are invalid if the underlying data are nonstationary does not apply to LeRoy and Porter (however, see LeRoy and William Parke 1988). With regard to Flavin's criticism, Gilles and LeRoy showed that in addition to Flavin's bias toward rejection of efficiency, there exists another bias which skews the test toward acceptance. It is not known which bias is stronger. In establishing that LeRoy and Porter's test has a bias of indeterminate sign, however, we have said no more than would in any case follow immediately from the fact that the variance of ex post rational price is a nonlinear function of the underlying parameters.

rather than around the sample means so as to avoid the bias Flavin had pointed out. The particular form of their test was ingenious. Suppose that p_t^0 is any "naive" forecast of p_t^*—that is, any function of investors' information, however inaccurate as a forecast of p_t^*. Subtracting and adding p_t, we have the identity

$$p_t^* - p_t^0 \equiv (p_t^* - p_t) + (p_t - p_t^0). \quad (5.18)$$

If p_t is an optimal estimator of p_t^*, the difference between the two will be uncorrelated with investors' information variables, and therefore also with $p_t - p_t^0$. Accordingly, we have

$$E(p_t^* - p_t^0)^2 = E(p_t^* - p_t)^2 + E(p_t - p_t^0)^2, \quad (5.19)$$

implying in turn

$$E(p_t^* - p_t^0)^2 \geq E(p_t^* - p_t)^2 \quad (5.20)$$

and

$$E(p_t^* - p_t^0)^2 \geq E(p_t - p_t^0)^2. \quad (5.21)$$

Mankiw, Romer, and Shapiro constructed the sample counterparts of the population parameters in (5.20) and (5.21) and checked the associated inequalities empirically. They found that both were reversed, implying excess volatility of p_t. They characterized this exercise as an unbiased test of the variance-bounds inequality, although they proved only that the expectation of the sample statistic has the same positive sign as the corresponding population parameter, not that it necessarily has the same magnitude. Further discussion of Mankiw, Romer, and Shapiro is found in Gilles and LeRoy (1988a).[14]

Finally, John Campbell and Shiller (1988a) reported a variety of tests, including what are effectively variance-bounds tests, of a class of models that include the martingale. Campbell and Shiller's paper shows much greater similarity to LeRoy and Porter's (1981) paper than to Shiller's earlier papers.[15] Unlike Shiller's earlier papers, Campbell and Shiller's is an orthogonality test rather than a bounds test. Also like LeRoy and Porter, Campbell and Shiller tested the martingale model by constructing a bivariate time-series model for stock prices and dividends and determining whether the restrictions on the coefficients of the model implied by the martingale model are satisfied. Specifically, Campbell and Shiller noted that if current stock price is used to construct forecasts of dividends, and if these forecast dividends are discounted back to the present, the result should equal current price. This equality between constructed and actual price implies testable restrictions on the parameters of the bivariate process for dividends and stock price. Campbell and Shiller found that these restrictions are not satis-

[14] West's (1988a) variance-bounds test is essentially the same as the upper-bound test on return variances (5.15), which LeRoy and Porter derived but did not conduct. However, there are minor differences. West defined the inequality on the variances of innovations in p_t and $\hat{p}_t$ rather than on the forecast errors as in (5.15), which turned out greatly to complicate the derivation of the bound. West's innovations version, unlike LeRoy and Porter's, does not hold for all information sets H_t and I_t obeying $I_t \supset H_t$ (for example, West noted in a footnote that if H_t contains no information at all, the innovations in p_t^* will be zero identically, implying that the purported upper bound will be zero). For practical purposes this limitation is inconsequential, however, because if H_t contains at least past returns, as is always assumed in efficiency tests, then innovations in p_t^* do in fact coincide with returns, implying that West's upper-bound test on innovations coincides with LeRoy and Porter's upper-bound test on returns.

West, like LeRoy and Porter, Shiller, and Mankiw, Romer, and Shapiro, found empirically that the volatility of returns exceeds its theoretical upper bound, indicating rejection of the martingale model.

[15] However, Campbell and Shiller's tests were superior to LeRoy and Porter's for several reasons. Most important, by postulating an underlying log-linear process and then linearizing, they eliminated the need for trend correction, therefore avoiding any error introduced by faulty trend removal (see Gilles and LeRoy 1988a for exposition of LeRoy and Porter's trend removal algorithm; LeRoy and Parke 1988 showed that this algorithm induces a downward trend in the supposedly trend-adjusted data).

fied, actual prices having about twice the standard deviation of the constructed price series.

The second-generation variance-bounds tests, like the first-generation tests, found excess volatility.[16] This outcome conflicted with the early work reviewed by Fama (1970): How can it be that, if stock price volatility is excessive, successive daily or weekly stock returns are uncorrelated? This discrepancy posed a major analytical problem. Several explanations resting on sophisticated econometric arguments were proposed before it was recognized that there is a simple answer. The central point, inadequately recognized at first, is that the variance-bounds inequalities are implications of return orthogonality conditions just as conventional efficiency tests are. To see this, write (5.4) and (5.5) as

$$\begin{aligned} p_t^* &= p_t + x_t \\ &= p_t + \sum_{i=1}^{\infty} (1+\rho)^{-i} e_{t+i}, \end{aligned} \qquad (5.22)$$

so that the restriction on which the variance-bounds theorems are based—orthogonality of p_t and x_t—says that a particular weighted average of past returns (which is all that p_t is) must be uncorrelated with a different weighted average of future returns. Excess volatility means that, empirically, these weighted averages of returns are negatively correlated—otherwise $V(p_t)$ could not exceed $V(p_t^*)$. The crucial difference between conventional efficiency tests and variance-bounds tests is this: The former tests the orthogonality of returns over short intervals (for example, successive daily or weekly returns), whereas the variance-bounds theorems test the orthogonality of a smooth average of past returns over a period of years and a similar smooth average of future returns.

The obvious way to evaluate this explanation for the differing results of variance-bounds tests and the conventional return autocorrelation tests is to estimate directly the correlation between average returns over the interval from $t - T$ to t—call this $r_{t-T,t}$—with $r_{t,t+T}$ for various values of T. Fama and Kenneth French (1988a) conducted exactly this exercise. They found a U-shaped pattern: For T of one year the correlation was essentially zero. For T on the order of three to five years about 35 percent of the variation of $r_{t,t+T}$ is explained by $r_{t-T,t}$, with the correlation being negative as expected. For T of ten years the correlation reverts to approximately zero. Fama and French's finding that five-year returns have a large forecastable component is exactly what the variance-bounds violations would lead one to expect. The simplicity of Fama and French's test and its outcome provide independent corroboration of the econometric soundness of the variance-bounds tests.

The question becomes: What sort of model would generate the U-shaped pattern in the return autocorrelations that Fama and French reported? Shiller (1981a, 1984) and Lawrence Summers (1986) proposed that instead of modeling stock price (with dividends added in) as a martingale, analysts should consider assuming that price comprises a random walk plus a fad variable, where the latter is modeled as a slowly mean-reverting stationary series. This specification, simple as it is, generates exactly the forecastability pattern required. That returns over short intervals are approximately uncorrelated is a basic, but not adequately known, fact about (a wide class

[16] LeRoy and Parke's (1988) paper is an exception. Our purpose was to construct a bounds test of the inequality (5.8) that is valid if dividends follow a geometric random walk. We found that the variance of stock prices is lower than the theoretical upper bound, conforming to the variance-bounds inequality. However, LeRoy and Parke concluded that this evidence in favor of the martingale model is extremely weak. This is so because bounds tests inherently have lower power than orthogonality tests.

of) stochastic processes (Christopher Sims 1984). Intuitively, the reason the return from $t - T$ to t is for small T approximately uncorrelated with the return from t to $t + T$ is that the contribution of the drift term to the variation of price is proportional to T^2, whereas the contribution of the dispersion term is proportional to T (recall from econometrics the analogous fact that mean square error is the sum of variance plus bias squared). For small T the dispersion dominates the drift, implying that the return autocorrelations for (almost) any stationary stochastic process look like those of a fair game (zero). Similarly, return autocorrelations over long horizons approach zero because the random walk term dominates the mean-reverting component of price. In between, however, a negative correlation is to be expected. This occurs because for intermediate values of T high returns from $t - T$ to t imply a positive value (on average) for the fad variable at t. Mean reversion implies that the fad will probably have diminished by $t + T$, implying an abnormally low return from t to $t + T$. The extent of the induced negative correlation between $r_{t-T,t}$ and $r_{t,t+T}$ depends on how quickly fads die out and on the respective error variances.

The preceding discussion exaggerated the similarity between the variance-bounds and return autocorrelation tests. The problem lies with the assertion following equation (5.22) that current price is a weighted average of past returns, so that variance-bounds tests (which are based on the orthogonality of price and future returns) and return autocorrelation tests (which are based on the orthogonality of past and future returns) are essentially equivalent. In fact, price is a nonlinear function of past returns; even if the function relating current price to past returns is linearized, the weights depend on dividends, which are random and correlated with returns. It is not yet known whether this qualification to the assertion above that variance-bounds and return autocorrelation tests are essentially similar is important empirically.

A third type of test, which can be interpreted as a hybrid of variance-bounds and return autocorrelation tests, determines directly whether price, or some variable closely related to price such as the dividends-price ratio, predicts future returns. These tests usually lead to strong rejection of the martingale model (Fama and French 1988b; Campbell and Shiller 1988a, 1988b).

The variance-bounds, return autocorrelation, and price-return orthogonality tests constitute three ways to test the martingale model. A fourth way to test for mean reversion is to use variance ratios (John Cochrane 1988).[17] The variance ratio is defined as the variance of k-period returns divided by the variance of one-period returns, and also by k. Under a random walk the variance ratio should equal unity for any value of k. However, James Poterba and Summers (1988) showed that the variance ratios declined with k, indicating the presence of a mean-reverting component.

The presence of a mean-reverting component in stock prices implies substantial forecastability of intermediate-term returns, and therefore also (by the variance-bounds theorem) substantial differences between price and "fundamentals," meaning by the latter the (rational) expectation of ex post rational price. Thus there is no inconsistency between essentially unforecastable short-term returns and wide discrepancies

[17] The material under discussion was anticipated by Holbrook Working. In his (1949) paper, Working proposed that statistical series be modeled as the sum of a random walk and a stationary series, and explicitly proposed the use of variance ratios to determine the relative importance of each component.

I am indebted to Frank Diebold for this reference. See also Diebold (1988).

between price and fundamental value. This result is best seen as documenting a pronounced bias in our psychological metric—even though there is no question that complete unpredictability of short-term returns implies exact equality between price and fundamental value (speculative bubbles aside), the result here is that a "surprisingly small" degree of forecastability of short-term returns is consistent with a "surprisingly large" discrepancy between price and fundamental value (Shiller 1984; Summers 1986).

Shiller's suggestion that asset prices be modeled as the sum of a random walk and a mean-reverting process is seen to give a parsimonious model that predicts (1) near-zero autocorrelations for daily and weekly returns as reported in the early efficient markets literature, (2) negative autocorrelations for returns over holding periods of several years, and (3) variance-bounds violations. Unfortunately for this tidy story, however, several recent studies have raised questions about the validity of the purported facts for which the mean-reversion model gives a unified explanation. Andrew Lo and A. Craig MacKinlay (1988) found that weekly and monthly stock returns had positive autocorrelation coefficients on the order of 30 percent, contradicting both the finding of approximately zero autocorrelation reported in the early efficient markets literature and the prediction of approximately zero autocorrelation from the mean-reversion model. Moreover, several studies have questioned Fama and French's conclusion that returns are significantly negatively autocorrelated over three- to five-year holding periods. Myung Jig Kim, Charles Nelson, and Richard Startz (1988), for example, found evidence of mean reversion only in data sets that include the 1930s—for the post–World War II period they found no evidence of negative return autocorrelation. This finding, together with the fact that the most recent studies continue to conclude that the variance-bounds inequalities are violated empirically, raises further questions about whether the variance-bounds violations are empirically the same thing as mean reversion. At this writing these questions remain unresolved.

VI. *Nonmartingale Models*

Documenting the existence of systematic empirical departures from the martingale model may seem to be entirely beside the point. After all, Samuelson's derivation of the martingale model assumed risk neutrality, whereas in fact people are risk-averse. So why should one be surprised when the martingale model does not work empirically? Aware of this point, analysts were led to look for an analogue to the martingale model that would remain valid if agents were risk-averse. It has not proved difficult to formulate such extensions theoretically, but, as will be reported in this section, it has turned out to be very difficult to correlate the departures from the martingale that these theories lead one to expect with the departures that one sees in the data. Therefore allowing for risk aversion does not in practice go far toward resolving the empirical puzzles that attend the martingale model. Consequently, not much is lost empirically by ignoring risk aversion, which is why that was done in the preceding sections.

Samuelson was not aware that his derivation of the martingale model depended critically on the assumption of risk neutrality: He conjectured that risk aversion could be handled simply by including a risk premium in the discount factor used to calculate present values. However, it is easy to see why asset returns will not generally be a fair game if agents are risk-averse. Suppose that risk covaries positively over time, so that big price changes (positive or negative) are likely to be followed by big changes and small changes by small changes.[18] If agents are risk-averse, they will hold risky assets only if expected returns vary so as to compensate them for these changes in risk. One would expect that returns therefore will in general be partly forecastable: If the current realization of Φ_t implies high risk over the near future, should it not also imply high expected return?

To formalize this reasoning, one would like to have in hand a model that allows for risk-averse agents and that can generate an intertemporal sequence of equilibrium prices and returns. The problem in incorporating risk aversion into efficient-markets theory was that as of about 20 years ago the only equilibrium asset pricing model extant in which risk and risk aversion were adequately handled was the equilibrium version of the CAPM of William Sharpe (1964), John Lintner (1965), and Jan Mossin (1966). (General analytical frameworks like the Arrow-Debreu contingent claims setup are, of course, capable in principle of dealing with risk aversion, but unless suitably restricted, are too general to be of much use in applied work.) The CAPM takes the mean and variance of next-period price as exogenous and determines current asset prices as those prices that just induce agents to bear existing risk willingly. Price, in other words, equals discounted expected return less a correction that reflects risk and risk aversion. Now, the fact that next-period expected price and the variance of next-period return are given exogenously in the CAPM means that even though the CAPM determines the current risk premium endogenously, it does not give a complete general equilibrium determination of returns on multiperiod assets such as stock. In multiperiod models it makes little sense to determine current risk premia endogenously while taking future risk premia, as embodied in expected next-period price, as exogenous.

What was needed was a model that would generate price from the probability distribution of next-period returns, and that would simultaneously characterize agents' probability distribution of next-period returns in a manner that is consistent with agents' expectations that price will be determined in a similar fashion when the next period arrives. This required a new concept of equilibrium. In my (1971) dissertation and (1973) paper, equilibrium was defined to consist of a single function simultaneously mapping current dividends into current price and next-period dividends into next-period price such that if agents have rational expectations about future dividends and optimize, then markets clear for any level of dividends.[19] The solution method then was to specify a general class of price functions and derive the appropriate equilibrium condition under the assumption that both current and next-period price conform to this function. The equilibrium price function was that for which this equilibrium condition is satisfied *as an identity in dividends* (it would contradict the exogeneity of dividends if markets failed to clear for some values

[18] Empirical evidence supports this specification (for example, Poterba and Summers 1986).

[19] Merton (1973) reported an intertemporal extension of the CAPM at the same time. Neither LeRoy (1973) nor Merton (1973) provided a full general equilibrium analysis. For example, in both models the risk-free interest rate is taken as exogenous rather than determined from preferences and technology. However, the former paper pointed more clearly in the direction of general equilibrium by contributing the idea that equilibrium can be characterized as a stable function linking exogenous state variables to asset prices, an idea not found in the latter paper. General equilibrium versions of LeRoy's and Merton's models were provided by Lucas (1978) and Cox, Ingersoll, and Stephen Ross (1985), respectively.

of dividends, hence the need for the equilibrium condition to hold as an identity).

As it turned out, the identical concept, which came to be called *rational expectations equilibrium,* was being developed at the same time in the macroeconomics literature. Further, exactly the same "undetermined coefficients" solution method—seeking coefficients such that the equilibrium condition holds as an identity—came into use in linear rational expectations macroeconomic models (Robert Lucas 1973).

In the intertemporal version of CAPM just described, the conditional expected return per dollar fluctuates over time as dividends change. Because dividends are autocorrelated, conditional expected returns are autocorrelated as well, implying that actual returns are partly forecastable. This forecastability goes contrary to the martingale model. It is, however, consistent with equilibrium because equilibrium stock prices are such that the fluctuations in risk per dollar invested induced by dividends fluctuations correlate with the fluctuations in expected returns so as to leave agents just willing to hold existing assets. In other words, even though the existence of serial dependence in conditional expected returns implies that different formulas for trading bonds and stock will generate different expected returns, because of risk, these alternative trading rules are utility-decreasing relative to the optimal buy-and-hold strategy. Of course, if as a special case it is assumed that agents are risk-neutral, these effects disappear and the martingale model obtains.

These considerations made clear that, in general, risk aversion will lead to departures from the martingale model. It does not follow from this that risk neutrality is the only case in which conditionally expected returns will be constant. In his (1977) comment on my (1973) paper, James Ohlson showed that if dividend growth rates are serially independent and agents have constant (but not necessarily zero) relative risk aversion, then the conditional expected rate of return on stock will be constant and returns will be unforecastable. In a sense Ohlson's case was very specialized because if agents are risk-averse the martingale requires restrictions both on return distributions and risk aversion, rather than just the latter as in the risk-neutrality case. However, neither of Ohlson's assumptions is as wildly at odds with reality as the assumption of risk neutrality. The practical implication of Ohlson's result is that even though the conditions under which he derived an exact martingale are restrictive, the assumption that these conditions are satisfied to a tolerable approximation may not be so implausible.

The foregoing discussion has concerned asset prices that are or are not martingales with respect to the probabilities that agents actually have—more precisely, with respect to the probabilities that, under the axioms of choice under uncertainty, are implicit in agents' orderings over portfolios. Suppose, however, that we start from the other end by assuming that asset prices always follow martingales with respect to some probabilities. It is easy to show that there always exist such probabilities: They are readily derived by repackaging the Arrow-Debreu prices that underlie any equilibrium (Stephen Ross, 1977, was the first clearly to appreciate this point; see also Ross 1978; J. M. Harrison and D. M. Kreps 1979; Harrison and S. R. Pliska 1981).[20] These probabilities are

[20] As a sidelight, it is interesting to note that in the finance literature Ross' (1977) paper is almost universally incorrectly referred to as having been published in 1976. This practice was started by Ross, who deliberately misdated references to this paper in order to encourage readers interested in the arbitrage pricing theory to read it before taking on his more difficult, less intuitive, and more rigorous (1976)

called *risk-neutral probabilities* in the finance literature because asset prices can always be expressed as discounted expected returns—as would be appropriate if agents were risk-neutral—if the expectation is taken with respect to these probabilities rather than the probabilities implicit in agents' orderings of portfolios. In other words, asset prices can be analyzed as if agents are risk-neutral, but take expectations with respect to the risk-neutral probabilities rather than their actual probabilities. The risk-neutral probabilities coincide with actual subjective probabilities if agents are in fact risk-neutral—otherwise they contain in addition adjustments for risk aversion.

The fact that there always exist martingale representations of asset prices is very convenient for theoretical work. It is also useful in such applied work as the pricing of redundant assets, the central problem of applied finance.[21] For the study of capital market efficiency, however, this line of research is not directly relevant. Given that market efficiency includes rational expectations (Fama 1976a), the subjective probabilities implied by agents' orderings over portfolios must be identifiable with the objective probabilities specified to obtain in the model under discussion. In the present setting it is therefore of no help to know that returns are always fair games with respect to some fictional probability measure that has no directly observable counterpart.

Both my (1973) paper and Ohlson's (1977) comment were essentially counterexamples, the former to the proposition that capital market efficiency necessarily implies martingales, and the latter to the proposition that risk neutrality is required for martingales. As such, there is nothing wrong with the fact that they are highly specialized. For general analysis, however, more powerful methods are needed so as to derive equilibria in more general settings. These were supplied in Lucas' (1978) paper. (Related material, developed independently, was presented in Douglas Breeden, 1979, and in John Cox, Jonathan Ingersoll, and Stephen Ross' 1985 paper, which was circulating as a working paper in the mid-1970s.) Lucas assumed that identical infinitely lived agents maximize the utility function $\Sigma(1 + \rho)^{-\tau}U(c_{t+\tau})$, which allows for risk aversion (U strictly concave) as well as risk neutrality (U linear). Using dynamic programming, Lucas demonstrated the existence and uniqueness of a pricing function similar to that of my (1973) paper. Even though the equilibrium pricing function is nonlinear in Lucas' model and is usually not amenable to closed-form representation, many of its properties can be derived analytically.

In Lucas' model equilibrium prices satisfy the stochastic Euler equation

$$p_tU_t' = (1 + \rho)^{-1}E_t(p_{t+1} + d_{t+1})U_{t+1}' \quad (6.1)$$

Here the marginal utilities U_t' and U_{t+1}' are evaluated at the endowment, reflecting the equilibrium condition that consumption must equal the endowment in an exchange economy. To understand the Euler equation (6.1), suppose that an investor is considering selling one share of stock and consuming the proceeds. The utility gain is p_tU_t'. Assuming

treatment of the arbitrage pricing theory. The (1977) paper was actually written in 1971. Most subsequent writers on the arbitrage pricing theory followed Ross' lead in dating the (1977) paper as 1976. An exception is Ingersoll (1987), who, going Ross one better, referred to the publication date of Ross' (1977) paper as 1975.

[21] For example, Cox, Ross, and Rubinstein (1979) presented an intuitive derivation of the Black-Scholes model of option pricing using martingale representations. Specifically, they derived risk-neutral probabilities from the assumed price of stock and the interest rate, and then calculated the price of an option on the stock by discounting its expected return, where the expectation was calculated using the risk-neutral probabilities.

that consumption at dates other than t and $t+1$ remains unchanged, the budget constraint implies a drop in consumption at $t+1$ of $p_{t+1} + d_{t+1}$. The right-hand side of (6.1) gives the expected utility cost of the decline in consumption, discounted back to t. If the investor is at an optimum, the utility gain at t must just equal the expected utility loss at $t+1$.

Equation (6.1) agrees with the martingale model

$$p_t = (1+\rho)^{-1}E_t(p_{t+1}+d_{t+1}) \qquad (3.4)$$

except that in (6.1) price at t is weighted by current marginal utility and next-period price by next-period marginal utility. Under risk neutrality U'_t and U'_{t+1} are equal to a common constant, so (6.1) and (3.4) agree. Lucas therefore again pointed out that martingales generally would obtain only under risk neutrality. Also, Lucas' work made clear that the connection between risk neutrality and martingales obtains without qualification only in exchange economies. In production economies in which corner solutions are possible, prices will reflect the technology as well as preferences whenever corner solutions occur, so risk neutrality by itself is insufficient to generate the martingale. This qualification was not stated in Samuelson's paper or mine. In production economies like that of William A. Brock (1982) in which the technology excludes corner solutions, on the other hand, risk neutrality is sufficient for the martingale model without qualification.

An immediate payoff of Lucas' model was that it provided an analytical framework in which to determine whether the violations of the variance-bounds theorems reflect the unrealism of the underlying risk-neutrality assumption. It was shown by LeRoy and C. J. LaCivita (1981), Grossman and Shiller (1981), and Ronald Michener (1982) that in Lucas' model there is a general presumption that the more risk-averse agents are, the more volatile asset prices will be. The argument is very simple. In an economy with no production, agents must consume their randomly fluctuating endowment (taking account of capital and intertemporal production would complicate the story, but would not alter its fundamentals). The price system must induce them to do so willingly. Highly risk-averse agents, however, will want very much to smooth their consumption streams over time. This they cannot do in the aggregate. To induce them not to save (by buying stock) in periods of prosperity, and not to dissave (by selling stock) in periods of shortage, stock prices must be very high in periods of prosperity and very low in periods of shortage. Thus the more risk-averse agents are, the more volatile equilibrium stock prices will be. However, this argument is not completely general. As Ohlson (1977) showed, if dividend growth rates are independently distributed, then prices will follow a martingale for any degree of (constant relative) risk aversion.[22] In such settings risk aversion cannot be the explanation for asset price volatility in excess of that implied by the martingale model. See Kevin Salyer (1988) for a general discussion of price volatility in models like Ohlson's.

These theoretical developments raised the possibility that the variance-bounds violations (or, equivalently, the partial forecastability of intermediate-term returns) reflected departures from the mar-

[22] Ohlson's model is not a special case of Lucas' because dividend levels are nonstationary in the former. However, Mehra and Prescott (1985) formulated a general framework analogous to Lucas' except that dividend growth rates rather than levels are stationary. Ohlson's model is a special case of Mehra and Prescott's. In Mehra and Prescott's setting there is no simple connection between risk aversion and asset price volatility (Salyer 1988).

tingale model induced by risk-aversion. Grossman and Shiller (1981) and Lars Hansen and Kenneth Singleton (1982, 1983), among others, attempted to determine whether asset price fluctuations could be interpreted as reflecting risk-averse agents' attempts to smooth consumption over time. Results to date have been disappointing (see Singleton 1987 for a survey of this literature). The problem is that consumption-based models of asset pricing, at least in their simplest form, imply that stock returns will be positively and strongly correlated with consumption growth, and this turns out not to be true empirically. Therefore, introducing risk aversion does not generally improve the performance of the predicted price series much in tracking actual prices relative to the martingale model. However, this pessimistic evaluation is not universally shared: Kleidon (1988b), for example, expressed doubt that the variance-bounds violations reflect anything deeper than an unjustified assumption of a constant rate of time discount (and perhaps, given the econometric problems, not even that). Also, more sophisticated representations of risk aversion (for example, George Constantinides' 1988 non-time separable utilities) may improve the results.

In fact, rather than resolving the difficulties attending the martingale model, passing to the consumption-based asset pricing model has given rise to new problems. Rajnish Mehra and Edward Prescott (1985), studying a representative-agent model, showed that no reasonable specification of agents' rates of time preference and risk aversion was able to generate real returns on bonds as low as those measured, while at the same time generating real returns on stock as high as those measured. It is true that Mehra and Prescott's model is highly simplified, but the dramatic failure of the consumption-based model of asset prices to explain the equity premium cannot be easily dismissed.[23]

There remains the fads model proposed by Shiller (1981a, 1984). Here, of course, we are dealing with an alternative to the efficient capital markets model, not with a modification of it. Most economists are extremely reluctant to resort to fads models because doing so would involve relaxing the stable-preferences assumption that many economists regard as an indispensable part of their outlook (George Stigler and Gary Becker 1977). In any case, pending a theory of what causes fads to come and go or a specification of potential phenomena that would be inconsistent with a fads model, it is not clear that anything is gained by characterizing an unexplained variation in asset prices as a fad. One is reminded of Robert Solow's (1957) labeling as technological change the unexplained residual in output growth after allowing for increase in inputs: Precisely because the residual is unobserved, one is free to accept or reject the interpretation; nothing is at stake either way. Advocacy of a fads model is perhaps best interpreted as a statement of belief that the most fruitful avenues of future research will involve social or cognitive psychology, rather than as referring to any well-formed model that is now available.

VII. *Other Evidence*

The discussion of empirical evidence in the preceding two sections was narrowly concentrated on the time structure of asset returns and such closely related topics as variance bounds. This restricted focus was adopted to avoid spreading the discussion too thin. But there is no point in basing conclusions on only a small sub-

[23] Proposed resolutions to Mehra and Prescott's equity premium puzzle have been suggested by Rietz (1988), Constantinides (1988), and Nason (1988).

set of the available evidence. This section briefly acknowledges the existence of other types of evidence that bear on the question of capital market efficiency. For more extensive reviews, see the papers in Elroy Dimson (1988) (especially Donald Keim 1988), G. William Schwert (1983), Richard Thaler (1987a, 1987b, 1988), Josef Lakonishok and Seymour Smidt (1988), and Ross Clark and William Ziemba (1987).

There always existed a subculture within the finance profession that rejected the majority conclusion in favor of efficiency. These heretics pointed to the "P-E anomaly": stock with low price-earnings ratios appeared systematically to outperform those with high price-earnings ratios (Francis Nicholson 1968; Sanjoy Basu 1977, 1983; Marc Reinganum 1981; David Dreman 1982). Recently Werner DeBondt and Thaler (1985, 1987) documented the related proposition that "losers"—stocks that had recently undergone large drops—appear systematically to generate higher returns than winners. Another similar result is that the ratio of price to book value is a predictor of returns (Barr Rosenberg, Kenneth Reid, and Ronald Lanstein 1985). This evidence of systematic overreaction to current information may be related to the excess volatility documented in the variance-bounds literature. Also, the apparent success of some investors—Warren Buffett—and some investment services—Value Line—in outperforming the market is difficult to reconcile with capital market efficiency. Proponents of market efficiency have always minimized such evidence. It is true that the correspondence of the Value Line stock rankings with subsequent performance appears too strong to have occurred by chance if Value Line is thought of as a single prespecified observation. But suppose that Value Line is thought of as the best performing of *n* investment advisory services. If *n* is large, one would expect the best of *n* services to perform extremely well purely by chance. And surely the population of investment services is large, especially if, as is appropriate, one counts the services that drop out because of a poor track record.[24]

The advent of cheap computing and large financial data bases brought new anomalies. The consensus now is that the anomalies pose a serious problem which cannot be shrugged off, as had been presumed earlier. The best known of these is the "January effect" (see Thaler 1987a or Clark and Ziemba 1987 for surveys). Michael Rozeff and William Kinney (1976) found that stock returns averaged 3.5 percent in January, while other months averaged 0.5 percent, a pattern which, being nonstationary, is inconsistent with a martingale. Subsequent studies (for example, Reinganum 1981, 1982, 1983, and Richard Roll 1983) replicated and refined the January effect. Rolf Banz (1981) found that small firms have higher returns than is consistent with their riskiness. Keim (1983) showed that the small-firm effect and the January effect may be the same thing: The January effect appears only in samples that include and give equal weight to small and large firms (see also Lakonishok and Smidt 1988 and

[24] One is reminded of the story about an entrepreneur who wanted to sell recommendations to football bettors. He divided a list of 16,000 potential customers into two sublists of 8,000 names each. He informed the first sublist of his prediction that the Redskins would beat the 49ers on Sunday, while the second sublist was given the reverse prediction. When the Redskins did beat the 49ers, he threw out the second list. The next week he divided the first list into two new sublists of 4,000 names each. He reminded both that he had correctly predicted the outcome of last week's game. For the first sublist he picked the Giants over the Eagles; the second sublist received the reverse prediction. After four weeks he was left with 1,000 names. He then wrote to these reminding them that he had correctly called the past four games, and expressed a willingness to tell them the outcome of the next game in exchange for $10,000.

Mustafa Gultekin and N. Bulent Gultekin 1987), as opposed to samples that weight firms by value.

Not only is the January effect an anomaly in its own right, but it contaminates the one regularity that finance theory (specifically the CAPM) predicts should be found in the data: the relation between risk and expected return. Fama and James MacBeth (1973) and others had earlier confirmed the CAPM (or commonsense) prediction that riskier stocks should earn higher average returns. Seha Tinic and Richard West (1984) were motivated by the findings just summarized to analyze the monthly patterns in the risk-return relation. Incredibly, they found that the risk-return trade-off occurs entirely in January: They could not reject the hypothesis that during the other eleven months investors are not compensated at all for bearing risk (however, see also Tinic and West 1986).

The January effect is only one of several calendar-based anomalies that have been unearthed in recent years. Another is the "weekend effect" (Frank Cross 1973; French 1980; Keim and Robert Stambaugh 1984; Lakonishok and Maurice Levi 1982; R. Rogalski 1984; Jeffrey Jaffe and Randolph Westerfield 1985; Lawrence Harris 1986), which finds that stock returns are on average negative from the close of trading on Fridays to the opening of trading on Mondays. A similar effect exists for bonds (Michael Gibbons and Patrick Hess 1981). Further, we have the "Wednesday effect": In 1968 the New York Stock Exchange was closed on Wednesdays in order to ease the paperwork backlog at brokerage houses. French and Roll (1986) found that the volatility of prices from Tuesday to Thursday was lower than over other two-day intervals, suggesting that prices fluctuate more when markets are open than when they are closed. Because, presumably, as much news about fundamentals is generated on Wednesdays as other weekdays, this "Wednesday effect" suggests that it is the trading process itself rather than news about fundamentals that generates price changes.[25] The Wednesday effect, like the January effect and assorted other calendar effects, appears difficult to reconcile with the martingale model. Finally, Robert Ariel (1987) showed that returns are positive on average only in the first half of the calendar month.

It is difficult to know how seriously to take these asset pricing anomalies. As Robert Merton (1987) and many others have noted, there is a problem of selection bias in these results. An analyst who conducts an empirical study investigating a purported correlation between stock returns and the stage of the moon, for example, and finds no correlation is unlikely to succeed in reporting this result in the journals. Therefore the published literature is skewed toward interesting, that is, anomalous, results, and away from boring confirmations of the absence of anomaly. A related problem is that anomalies are typically tested on the same data on which they are discovered, and analysts frequently construct their classifications so as to maximize the anomalous nature of the finding. For example, Ariel (1987) included the last day of the preceding month along with the first half of the current month because returns on the last day of the month are very high, implying an increased reported disparity between returns in the first half of the month and returns in the second half (see Lakonishok and Smidt 1988 for discussion).

Different types of evidence bear more directly on the assumptions of rationality and rational expectations that underlie

[25] However, see Slezak (1988) for an alternative explanation for the Wednesday effect which is consistent with (a sophisticated version of) the efficient markets model.

market efficiency (and, consequently, are less closely related to martingales). For example, there is some evidence that asset prices are subject to "winner's curse" (Edward Miller 1977; Stuart Theil 1988; Kenneth Hendricks and Robert Porter 1988; S. Michael Giliberto and Nikhil Varaiya 1989). If agents have different opinions about the value of some asset to be sold at auction, and if their bids are naively based on these opinions, the winner will be the bidder with the most inflated estimate of the asset's value. On average, winners will overpay. Winner's curse is inconsistent with full rationality: Each bidder's strategy should make allowance for the possibly biased nature of his own appraisal of value (R. Preston McAfee and John McMillan 1987). Richard Thaler (1988) interpreted the finding of Walter Mead, Asbjorn Moseidjord, and Philip Sorensen (1983, 1984) that winning bidders on wildcat offshore oil leases overpay on average as evidence of winner's curse.[26]

A very striking piece of evidence conflicting with market efficiency is the high volume of trade on organized securities exchanges. For some reason this is seldom listed in the finance literature as one of the major anomalies of efficient capital markets. Paul Milgrom and Nancy Stokey's (1982) paper and Jean Tirole's (1982) paper (see also Harrison and Kreps 1978) showed that rational agents with asymmetric information will not offer to trade securities based on a naive interpretation of their private information. Rather, they will take account of the fact that if they are able to consummate a trade, that will occur because some other agent with different but perhaps equally accurate information is willing to take the other side of the trade. Such transactions, being a zero-sum (or negative-sum, if brokerage charges and costs of information acquisition are included) game, are pure risk uncompensated by positive expected gain. Risk-averse agents will reject such trades. Contrary to the prediction of Milgrom, Stokey, and Tirole's model, large numbers of investors forsake the buy-and-hold strategy that efficient-markets theory dictates in favor of actively betting their information against other investors' information. Of course, it is not the fact that the volume of trade is positive that causes the problem: Milgrom, Stokey, and Tirole's theorem depends on assumptions that are not even approximately satisfied empirically—for example, that agents have common priors (see Hal Varian 1985, 1989 for analyses of models in which agents have heterogeneous priors) and that the pretrade allocation of securities is Pareto-optimal. Given market incompleteness, rational investors will want to buy or sell securities to provide for or finance large expenditures or adjust risk exposure. However, it is clear that only a small percentage of stock market trades can be rationalized in this way. The majority of trades appear to reflect belief on the part of each investor that he can outwit other investors, which is inconsistent with common knowledge of rationality.

The Milgrom, Stokey, and Tirole re-

[26] However, Thaler did not note that these authors suggested an explanation different from winner's curse for the low returns to successful bidders on wildcat leases. The successful bidder on a wildcat lease—a lease for which there exists no drilling data that would indicate potential productivity—acquires valuable proprietary information about oil reserves in neighboring tracts. When drainage leases—leases on tracts adjoining tracts from which oil is already being extracted—on these neighboring tracts come up for auction, the holder of the wildcat lease can modify his bid in light of this privileged information. Mead, Moseidjord, and Sorensen (1983, 1984) showed that, as this argument leads one to expect, returns to successful bidders on drainage leases were exceptionally high when these bidders were those who had already leased neighboring tracts. Mead, Moseidjord, and Sorensen suggested that the low returns to successful bidders on wildcat tracts are consistent with market efficiency when allowance is made for the value of the information gained by the successful bidder about neighboring tracts.

sult poses a problem: Either analysts of financial markets must ignore the existence of high volumes of securities trading or they must incorporate irrationality into their models, at least when analyzing complete-market environments. Given the traditional hostility toward irrationality as manifested, for example, in Shiller's fad variables, neither alternative is attractive. Fortunately, Fischer Black (1986) came to the rescue. By renaming irrational trading "noise trading" Black avoided the I-word, thereby sanitizing irrationality and rendering it palatable to many analysts who in other settings would not be receptive to such a specification. The economic effects of noise traders is now an active research area (Campbell and Albert Kyle 1986).

Inasmuch as efficient-markets theory attributes asset price changes exclusively to information about fundamentals, it implies that returns should be explainable ex post by fundamentals. Curiously, financial economists have until recently displayed a marked lack of interest in testing this implication of market efficiency, strongly preferring instead to concentrate their attention on testing the martingale implication that returns should not be explainable by fundamentals ex ante (see Summers 1985 for discussion). However, two recent studies by Roll are distinguished exceptions. After persuasively arguing that information on weather in Florida—specifically, information bearing on the probability of a freeze, which would adversely affect the orange crop—should be the dominant influence on orange juice futures prices, Roll (1984) showed that weather information could explain empirically only a small fraction of the variation in these prices. He could not identify any variable that explained the remainder of the variation. In his presidential address to the American Finance Association, Roll (1988) continued along the same lines, showing empirically that it is difficult to explain ex post more than a small fraction of the variation in individual stock prices, even using data like industry average prices and market price indices as explanatory variables.

It would seem almost self-evident that the recent wave of leveraged buyouts provides strong evidence against market efficiency: The astronomical fees to investment bankers that these mergers generate are difficult to reconcile with any nontautologous version of market efficiency, as are the stock price gyrations that accompany leveraged buyouts. Mergers themselves, of course, are consistent with efficiency; indeed, they are implied by efficiency if they result in synergies in operations or serve to remove bad management. However, most students of corporate takeovers believe that such effects are of secondary importance. On Roll's (1986) account, takeovers may be consistent with market efficiency even if motivated solely by the "hubris" of the acquiring group. Roll interpreted the stock price declines that typically follow takeovers as validating the pretakeover valuation of the firm on the part of the large majority of investors, and as invalidating the runup that occurs upon takeover. The majority of traders, then, value the firm correctly; only the acquirer is led by "hubris" to overpay. Roll argued from this that "the market," which he identified with the majority of traders, is efficient. This argument will not do at all. The simplest efficient-markets reasoning implies that no systematic pattern of price decline should occur in the wake of a publicly known event like a successful takeover. Further, as proponents of market efficiency themselves insist in other contexts, the market price of a company is the price that the firm trades at, no more and no less. Even (in fact, especially) within the logic of efficient capital market theory, which rejects any distinction between market price and "true value," no case whatever can be made for discounting the price runup on the grounds that only a minority of traders are involved.

Finally, we have the October 19, 1987, stock market selloff. As readers are well aware, stock values dropped half a trillion dollars on that single day in the complete absence of news that can plausibly be related to market fundamentals. The undeniable and spectacular presence of nonfundamental factors affecting stock prices on Black Monday renders more credible the presence, and perhaps dominance, of similar factors when the stock market is functioning normally.

VIII. *Conclusion*

The central idea of efficient capital market theory is that securities prices are determined by the interaction of self-interested rational agents. At this most basic level, the assertion that capital markets are efficient therefore reduces to the assertion that it is economic theory rather than any other discipline that provides the analytical tools appropriate for understanding securities pricing. The intuitive presentation of efficient capital market theory in the introduction was intended to convey its essential identity with economic theory. Empirical tests of capital market efficiency, however, are in practice usually tests of the martingale model. This survey should by now have made amply clear that the transition between the intuitive idea of market efficiency and the martingale model is far from direct. Few financial economists, surprisingly, have taken direct issue with the prevailing practice in the finance literature of identifying market efficiency with the validity of a particular specialized model of equilibrium in financial markets.[27]

The failure of many financial economists to appreciate the extent of the gulf separating market efficiency interpreted as economic equilibrium and market efficiency interpreted as the martingale model has led them to vacillate between viewing market efficiency, on one hand, as hard-wired into their intellectual capital and unfalsifiable and, on the other hand, as consisting of a specific class of falsifiable models of asset prices. In abstract discussions, financial economists almost always characterize market efficiency as a specific theory which in principle is falsifiable, but which in practice turns out not to be falsified empirically. At an applied level, however, they frequently find it difficult to specify concretely what evidence would in principle contradict the theory. This is most evident in Fama's (1970) discussion, where market efficiency was described as a substantive theory generating falsifiable predictions, but where at the same time the mathematical formulation of the market efficiency was tautologous. Further, it was noted in Section IV that several pieces of evidence that seemed to contradict market efficiency were dismissed by Fama for reasons that were not made clear.

There is no shortage of other examples of lack of clarity and consistency in discussions of capital market efficiency.

[27] Ross (1987) is an exception. Ross proposed as if it were self-evident that the intuition of market efficiency is essentially that of no arbitrage, rather than the martingale model or rational expectations. Because (loosely) any equilibrium price system implies satisfaction of the no-arbitrage condition, and satisfaction of the no-arbitrage condition implies the existence of a consistent equilibrium price system, Ross' identification of market efficiency with the absence of arbitrage opportunities is essentially equivalent to our identification in the introduction of market efficiency with economic equilibrium. Now, most economists regard the proposition that the data they observe were generated by some, as opposed to a particular, equilibrium model as an untestable expression of a preferred research method. If so, Ross' definition implies that market efficiency is untestable, and that therefore the entire empirical literature on market efficiency is beside the point. Despite the considerable merits of Ross' characterization of market efficiency, it is seen to be at odds with the received practice, which emphasizes the testability of market efficiency.

Merton (1987) went out of his way to emphasize that the hypothesis of stock market rationality is not tautologous: Market efficiency is "not consistent with models or empirical facts which imply that either stock prices depend in an important way on factors other than the fundamentals . . . or that . . . investors can systematically identify significant differences between stock prices and fundamental value." Yet Terry Marsh and Merton (1986) interpreted the variance-bounds violations, which would seem to raise questions about the empirical validity of both these attributes of market efficiency, as constituting evidence against the assumed stationarity of dividends rather than as conflicting with market efficiency. Apparently when the evidence is favorable, market efficiency is supported, but when the evidence is unfavorable, market efficiency is treated as part of the maintained hypothesis, insulated from falsification. Another example of the extreme reluctance, bordering on inability, of proponents of efficient capital markets to acknowledge contrary evidence is Roll's (1986) "hubris" hypothesis of corporate takeovers, discussed in the preceding section.

Several attributes of financial economists' outlook help explain the extraordinary durability of the widely held opinion that the bulk of the empirical evidence favors capital market efficiency. As observed in Section VII, financial economists at once insist on the central importance of their contention that asset prices are determined exclusively by fundamentals, and at the same time have been unreceptive to attempts to determine empirically whether price changes are in fact traceable to fundamentals, at least until recently. Accordingly, it has been only recently that they have come to appreciate that fundamentals appear to explain ex post only a small portion of price changes. Further, financial economists have always displayed a strong preference for empirical tests in which market efficiency implies the absence of a pattern, such as return autocorrelation tests, over tests that do not have such a characterization, such as variance-bounds tests. Therefore they have been led to dismiss out of hand some of the most important evidence bearing on market efficiency. Finally, financial economists' preference for arbitrage-based over equilibrium-based arguments (together with the predilection noted above for tautologous formulations of market efficiency) has diverted them from attempting to specify intellectually coherent alternatives to market efficiency, and from analyzing the econometric properties of these alternatives relative to the null hypothesis of market efficiency. Thus they have not seriously considered the possibility that many of the econometric tests that favor market efficiency have little power to reject reasonable alternative hypotheses.

The foregoing discussion suggests that financial economists have not always succeeded in applying to efficient capital market theory the same high standards of rigor and consistency that they have exhibited in other areas of finance. As a result, they have for the most part been able to avoid confronting the conclusion that is warranted by the evidence: However attractive (to economists) capital market efficiency is on methodological grounds, it is extraordinarily difficult to formulate nontrivial and falsifiable implications of capital market efficiency that are not in fact falsified.

Empirical rejection of the martingale model suggests that there exist trading rules that increase expected returns relative to buy-and-hold. It is this implication that advocates of market efficiency have always found implausible: Even if it is conceded that some or most traders act irrationally, why would rational traders not exploit the patterns, and in so doing bid them away? The simplest answer to this question is that optimal trading by rational agents will completely reverse the effects of irrational trades on prices only if the rational agents are well financed and risk-neutral. The need for substantial wealth on the part of rational agents is obvious: The existence of a lower bound (zero) on any agent's consumption in any state implies the existence of bounds on that agent's security purchases and sales.[28] Existence of these bounds is consistent with rational agents completely offsetting the effect on prices of irrational agents' trades only if the bounds are not binding, which will occur only if the rational agents' wealth is large. The need for risk neutrality is equally obvious: If rational agents are risk-averse, they will find that the portfolio they would have to acquire in order completely to reverse the effects of irrational trades imply excessive risk.

A related argument for full rationality is sometimes put in sociobiological terms. Traders who act irrationally will, it is suggested, lose wealth on average. Like any group of individuals whose ability to survive and reproduce is impaired by a dysfunctional genetic mutation, the irrational agents will eventually disappear from the population. In a series of recent papers, Bradford De Long et al. (1988a, 1988b, 1989a, 1989b), however, questioned this reasoning. If the irrational behavior of the nonoptimizers consists of taking risks based on unrealistically optimistic appraisals of possible outcomes, this irrationality may have effects that are indistinguishable from low risk aversion. Because in a population of risk-averse agents the average rewards to risk takers exceed those to risk avoiders, the law of large numbers implies (in some settings) that the risk takers as a whole do better than the risk avoiders, even though individual risk takers will suffer bad outcomes with higher frequency than individuals who are fully rational. Thus irrationality may actually be rewarded in the aggregate.

Market efficiency is a complex joint hypothesis. Some elements of this joint hypothesis are central to economists' way of thinking, like rationality and rational expectations, while others are no more than convenient auxiliary assumptions, like the martingale model. Rejection of market efficiency requires that one or more of these elements of the joint hypothesis be replaced. Understandably, economists have focused their critical attention on those elements that can be discarded with the least damage to their research programs. We have already seen that the effort to generalize the martingale model to allow for risk aversion has not succeeded empirically so far. While it is possible that this work will succeed better in the future than it has in the past, several considerations suggest that the problems with market efficiency go deeper.

The high volume of trade on organized securities markets poses a serious problem; no minor tinkering with efficient-markets models seems likely to provide an intelligible reason why rational agents would exchange securities as much as real-world market participants do. The willingness of investors to pay for information is equally problematic: As noted in the introduction, if the purchased information makes profitable trades possible, securities markets cannot be informationally efficient, while if it does, agents are irrationally wasting their money. Neither is consistent with efficiency. These considerations suggest that a large number of market participants act as if they do not believe that the market is efficient. While there may be some

[28] It is true that by borrowing agents can acquire investments that exceed their total assets in value, but insofar as borrowings are secured by future wealth, their amount remains bounded.

sense in which securities markets can be efficient even though most agents act as if they believe them to be inefficient, the argument is far from transparent, to say the least. Regrettably, it appears as if it is the assumptions of rationality and rational expectations that require reformation.

The recent literature on cognitive psychology (e.g., Kenneth Arrow 1982; Daniel Kahneman, Paul Slovic, and Amos Tversky 1982; Robin Hogarth and Melvin Reder 1987; Mark Machina 1987) provides a promising avenue for future research. Cognitive psychologists have documented systematic biases in the way people use information and make decisions. Some of these biases are easy to connect, at least informally, with securities market behavior. For example, agents allow their decisions to be distorted by the presence of points of reference that should be irrelevant ("anchoring"). Further, they systematically overweight current information and underweight background information relative to what Bayes' theorem implies. To be sure, most of the evidence for these biases comes from experiments and questionnaires. Economists have in the past confidently assumed that these biases would disappear in settings where the stakes are high, as in real-world securities markets. However, this line is beginning to wear thin, particularly in light of economists' continuing inability to explain asset prices using models that assume away cognitive biases.

The problem with the cognitive psychology literature is that it is more successful in providing after-the-fact explanations for observed behavior than in generating testable predictions. Economists require from their theories a clear statement of what observed phenomena would be inconsistent with these theories, and so far this has not been forthcoming from the psychologists. Models that make indiscriminate use of irrationality and nonrational expectations cannot impose discipline on economists' thinking about securities markets. Nonetheless, there is no reason in principle to believe that these objections cannot be met. It is a task to which economists, working with psychologists, would do well to turn their attention.

If it is accepted that successful models of securities prices will require a broader analytical framework than has been adopted up to now, it follows that the routine use of efficient-markets reasoning will require reassessment. Some arguments based on appeal to market efficiency will remain valid, while others will have to be discarded. The most fundamental insight of market efficiency—the reminder that asset prices reflect the interaction of self-interested agents—will remain. However, the contention that no successful trading rule can be based on publicly available information may have to go; it is this strict version of market efficiency that produces the empirical implications that the evidence contradicts.

The most radical revision in efficient-markets reasoning will involve those implications of market efficiency that depend on asset prices equaling or closely approximating fundamental values. The evidence suggests that, contrary to the assertion of this version of efficient markets theory, such large discrepancies between price and fundamental value regularly occur.[29] The implication is that there may be a constructive role for government in altering or regulating the operation of securities markets. Those who think of governments as engines of Pareto optimality will interpret the evidence summarized here as in fact justifying such

[29] Black (1986), in tacit recognition of the frequency with which major discrepancies between prices and values occur, defined a market as efficient if price is within a factor of two of value, and estimated that U.S. capital markets are efficient on the order of 90 percent of the time.

an enlarged role for government. The rest of us, however, will continue to reject major changes along these lines, while acknowledging that the case against such changes is not as clear-cut as it once seemed.

REFERENCES

ALEXANDER, SIDNEY. "Price Movements in Speculative Markets: Trends or Random Walks?" (1961) in COOTNER, 1964(a), pp. 199–218.

______. "Price Movements in Speculative Markets: Trends or Random Walks, no. 2," (1964) in COOTNER 1964(b), pp. 338–72.

ARIEL, ROBERT A. "A Monthly Effect in Stock Returns," *J. Finan. Econ.*, 1987, *18*(1), pp. 161–74.

ARROW, KENNETH J. "Risk Perception in Psychology and Economics," *Econ. Inquiry*, Jan. 1982, *20*(1), pp. 1–9.

BACHELIER, LOUIS. "Theory of Speculation," in COOTNER 1964, pp. 17–78 (first published 1900).

BANZ, ROLF. "The Relationship Between Return and Market Value of Common Stocks," *J. Finan. Econ.*, Mar. 1981, 9(1), pp. 3–18.

BASU, SANJOY. "Investment Performance of Common Stocks in Relation to Their Price-Earnings Ratios: A Test of the Efficient Market Hypothesis," *J. Finance*, June 1977, *32*(3), pp. 663–82.

______. "The Relationship Between Earnings' Yield, Market Value and Returns for NYSE Common Stocks: Further Evidence," *J. Finan. Econ.*, June 1983, *12*(1), pp. 129–56.

BLACK, FISCHER. "Noise," *J. Finance*, 1986, *41*(3), 529–43.

BREEDEN, DOUGLAS. "An Intertemporal Asset Pricing Model with Stochastic Consumption and Investment Opportunities," *J. Finan. Econ.*, Sept. 1979, 7(3), pp. 265–96.

BROCK, WILLIAM, A. "Asset Prices in a Production Economy," in *The economics of information and uncertainty*. Ed.: JOHN J. MCCALL. Amsterdam: North-Holland, 1982, pp. 1–42.

CAMPBELL, JOHN Y. AND KYLE, ALBERT. "Smart Money, Noise Trading and Stock Price Behavior." Unpublished ms., Princeton U., 1986.

CAMPBELL, JOHN Y. AND SHILLER, ROBERT J. "The Dividend-Price Ratio and Expectations of Future Dividends and Discount Factors," *Rev. Finan. Stud.*, 1988a, *1*, pp. 195–228.

______. "Stock Prices, Earnings, and Expected Dividends," *J. Finance*, 1988b, *43*(3), pp. 661–76.

CLARK, ROSS AND ZIEMBA, WILLIAM T. "Playing the Turn-of-the-Year Effect with Index Futures," *Operations Research*, Nov./Dec. 1987, *35*(6), pp. 799–813.

COCHRANE, JOHN H. "How Big Is the Random Walk in GNP?" *J. Polit. Econ.*, 1988, *96*(5), pp. 893–920.

CONSTANTINIDES, GEORGE M. "Habit Formation: A Resolution of the Equity Premium Puzzle." Unpublished ms., U. of Chicago, Dec. 1988.

COOTNER, PAUL H., ed. *The random character of stock market prices*. Cambridge: MIT Press, 1964.

COPELAND, THOMAS E. AND WESTON, J. FRED. *Financial theory and corporate policy*. 2nd ed. Reading, MA: Addison-Wesley, 1983.

COWLES, ALFRED. "Can Stock Market Forecasters Forecast?" *Econometrica*, July 1933, *1*(4), 309–24.

COX, JOHN; INGERSOLL, JONATHAN E. AND ROSS, STEPHEN A. "A Theory of the Term Structure of Interest Rates," *Econometrica*, Mar. 1985, *53*(2), pp. 385–407.

COX, JOHN: ROSS, STEPHEN A. AND RUBINSTEIN, MARK. "Option Pricing: A Simplified Approach," *J. Finan. Econ.*, Sept. 1979, 7(3), pp. 229–63.

CROSS, FRANK. "The Behavior of Stock Prices on Fridays and Mondays," *Financial Analysts J.*, Nov./Dec. 1973, *29*(6), pp. 67–69.

DANTHINE, JEAN-PIERRE. "Martingale, Market Efficiency and Commodity Prices," *Europ. Econ. Rev.*, Oct. 1977, *10*(1), pp. 1–17.

DEBONDT, WERNER F. M. AND THALER, RICHARD. "Does the Stock Market Overreact?" *J. Finance*, July 1985, *40*(3), pp.793–805.

______. "Further Evidence on Investor Overreaction and Stock Market Seasonality," *J. Finance*, July 1987, *42*(3), pp. 557–81.

DE LONG, J. BRADFORD ET AL. "The Survival of Noise Traders in Financial Markets," NBER Working Paper No. 2715, Sept. 1988a.

______. "Noise Trader Risk in Financial Markets," reproduced, Harvard U., 1988b.

______. "The Size and Incidence of the Losses From Noise Trading," *J. Finance*, July 1989a, *44*(3), pp. 681–96.

______. "Positive Feedback Investment Strategies and Destabilizing Rational Speculation," NBER Working Paper No. 2880, Mar. 1989b.

DIEBOLD, FRANCIS X. "Testing for Bubbles, Reflecting Barriers and Other Anomalies," *J. Econ. Dynam. Control*, Mar. 1988, *12*(1), pp. 63–70.

DIMSON, ELROY, ed. *Stock market anomalies*. Cambridge: Cambridge U. Press, 1988.

DREMAN, DAVID. *The new contrarian investment strategy*. NY: Random House, 1982.

FAMA, EUGENE F. "Efficient Capital Markets: A Review of Theory and Empirical Work," *J. Finance*, May 1970, 25(2), pp. 383–417.

______. *Foundations of finance*. NY: Basic Books, 1976a.

______. "Efficient Capital Markets: Reply," *J. Finance*, Oct. 1976b, *3*(4), pp. 143–45

FAMA, EUGENE F. AND BLUME, MARSHALL. "Filter Rules and Stock Market Trading," *J. Bus.*, Jan. 1966, *39*(1), pp. 226–41.

FAMA, EUGENE F. ET AL. "The Adjustment of Stock Prices to New Information," *Int. Econ. Rev.*, Feb. 1969, *10*(1), pp. 1–21.

FAMA, EUGENE F. AND FRENCH, KENNETH R. "Permanent and Temporary Components of Stock Prices," *J. Polit. Econ.*, Apr. 1988a, *96*(2), pp. 246–73.

______. "Dividend Yields and Expected Stock Returns," *J. Finan. Econ.*, 1988b, 22(1), pp. 3–25.

FAMA, EUGENE F. AND MACBETH, JAMES D. "Risk,

Return, and Equilibrium: Empirical Tests," *J. Polit. Econ.*, May/June 1973, *81*(3), pp. 607–36.

FLAVIN, MARJORIE A. "Excess Volatility in the Financial Markets: A Reassessment of the Empirical Evidence," *J. Polit. Econ.*, Dec. 1983, *91*(6), pp. 929–56.

FRENCH, KENNETH. "Stock Returns and the Weekend Effect," *J. Finan. Econ.*, Mar. 1980, *8*(1), pp. 55–69.

FRENCH, KENNETH AND ROLL, RICHARD W. "Stock Return Variances: The Arrival of Information and the Reaction of Traders," *J. Finan. Econ.*, Sept. 1986, *17*(1), pp. 5–26.

GIBBONS, MICHAEL AND HESS, PATRICK. "Day of the Week Effects and Asset Returns," *J. Bus.*, Oct. 1981, *54*(4), pp. 579–96.

GILIBERTO, S. MICHAEL AND VARAIYA, NIKHIL P. "The Winner's Curse and Bidder Competition in Acquisitions: Evidence from Failed Bank Auctions," *J. Finance*, Mar. 1989, *44*(1), pp. 59–76.

GILLES, CHRISTIAN. "Charges as Equilibrium Prices and Asset Bubbles," *J. Math. Econ.*, forthcoming.

GILLES, CHRISTIAN AND LEROY, STEPHEN F. "A Note on The Local Expectations Hypothesis: A Discrete-Time Exposition," *J. Finance*, Sept. 1986, *41*(4), pp. 975–79.

______. "Econometric Aspects of the Variance-Bounds Tests." Reproduced, U. of California, Santa Barbara, Jan. 1988a.

______. "Bubbles and Charges." Reproduced, U. of California, Santa Barbara, 1988b.

GRAHAM, BENJAMIN AND DODD, DAVID L. *Security analysis*. NY: McGraw-Hill, 1934.

GRANGER, CLIVE W. J. AND MORGENSTERN, OSKAR. "Spectral Analysis of New York Stock Market Prices," (1963) in COOTNER 1964, pp. 162–88.

GROSSMAN, SANFORD J. "Further Results on the Informational Efficiency of Competitive Stock Markets," *J. Econ. Theory*, June 1978, *18*(1), pp. 81–101.

GROSSMAN, SANFORD AND SHILLER, ROBERT J. "The Determinants of the Variability of Stock Market Prices," *Amer. Econ. Rev.*, May 1981, *71*(2), pp. 222–27.

GROSSMAN, SANFORD AND STIGLITZ, JOSEPH E. "Information and Competitive Price Systems," *Amer. Econ. Rev.*, May 1976, *66*(2), pp. 246–53.

______. "On the Impossibility of Informationally Efficient Markets," *Amer. Econ. Rev.*, June 1980, *70*(3), pp. 393–408.

GULTEKIN, MUSTAFA N. AND GULTEKIN, N. BULENT. "Stock Return Anomalies and the Tests of the APT," *J. Finance*, Dec. 1987, *42*(5), pp. 1213–24.

HANSEN, LARS AND SINGLETON, KENNETH J. "Generalized Instrumental Variables Estimation of Nonlinear Rational Expectations Models," *Econometrica*, Sept. 1982, *50*(5), pp. 1269–86.

______. "Stochastic Consumption, Risk Aversion, and the Temporal Behavior of Asset Returns," *J. Polit. Econ.*, Apr. 1983, *91*(2), pp. 249–65.

HARRIS, LAWRENCE. "A Transaction Data Study of Weekly and Intradaily Patterns in Stock Returns," *J. Finan. Econ.*, May 1986, *16*(1), pp. 99–117.

HARRISON, J. MICHAEL AND KREPS, DAVID M. "Speculative Investor Behavior in a Stock Market with Heterogeneous Expectations," *Quart. J. Econ.*, May 1978, *92*(2), pp. 323–36.

______. "Martingales and Arbitrage in Multiperiod Securities Markets," *J. Econ. Theory*, June 1979, *20*, pp. 381–408.

HARRISON, J. MICHAEL AND PLISKA, S. R. "Martingales and Stochastic Integrals in the Theory of Continuous Trading," *Stochastic Processes and Their Applications*, 1981, *11*, pp. 215–60.

HENDRICKS, KENNETH AND PORTER, ROBERT H. "Empirical Study of an Auction with Asymmetric Information," *Amer. Econ. Rev.*, Dec. 1988, *78*(5), pp. 865–83.

HOGARTH, ROBIN M. AND REDER, MELVIN W. *Rational choice: The contrast between economics and psychology*. Chicago: U. of Chicago Press, 1987.

HUANG, CHI-FU AND LITZENBERGER, ROBERT H. *Foundations for financial economics*. NY: North-Holland, 1988.

INGERSOLL, JONATHAN E., JR. *Theory of financial decision-making*. Totowa, NJ: Rowman and Littlefield, 1987.

JAFFE, JEFFREY AND WESTERFIELD, RANDOLPH. "The Week-End Effect in Common Stock Returns: The International Evidence," *J. Finance*, June 1985, *40*(2), pp. 433–54.

JENSEN, MICHAEL. "The Performance of Mutual Funds in the Period 1945–1964," *J. Finance*, May 1968, *23*(2), pp. 389–416.

______. "Risk, the Pricing of Capital Assets, and the Evaluation of Investment Portfolios," *J. Bus.*, Apr. 1969, *42*(2), pp. 167–247.

JORDAN, JAMES. "On the Efficient Markets Hypothesis," *Econometrica*, Sept. 1983, *51*(5), pp. 1325–43.

KAHNEMAN, DANIEL; SLOVIC, PAUL AND TVERSKY, AMOS. *Judgment under uncertainty: Heuristics and biases*. Cambridge: Cambridge U. Press, 1982.

KEIM, DONALD B. "Size-Related Anomalies and Stock Return Seasonality," *J. Finan. Econ.*, 1983, *12*(1), pp. 13–32.

______. "Stock Market Regularities: A Synthesis of the Evidence and Explanations," in DIMSON 1988, pp. 16–39.

KEIM, DONALD B. AND STAMBAUGH, ROBERT F. "A Further Investigation of the Weekend Effect in Stock Returns," *J. Finance*, July 1984, *39*(3), pp. 819–37.

KENDALL, MAURICE G. "The Analysis of Economic Time-Series, Part I: Prices," (1953) in COOTNER 1964, pp. 85–99.

KEYNES, JOHN MAYNARD. *General theory of employment, interest and money*. NY: Harcourt, Brace, 1936.

KIM, MYUNG JIG; NELSON, CHARLES R. AND STARTZ, RICHARD. "Mean Reversion in Stock Prices? A Reappraisal of the Empirical Evidence." Reproduced, U. of Washington, May 1988.

KLEIDON, ALLAN W. "Variance Bounds Tests and Stock Price Valuation Models," *J. Polit. Econ.*, Oct. 1986a, *94*(5), pp. 953–1001.

______. "Bias in Small Sample Tests of Stock Price Rationality," *J. Bus.*, Apr. 1986b, *59*(2), pp. 237–61.

______. "The Probability of Gross Violations of a Present Value Variance Inequality: Reply," *J. Polit. Econ.*, Oct. 1988a, *96*(5), pp. 1093–96.

______. "Bubbles, Fads and Stock Price Volatility Tests: A Partial Evaluation: Discussion," *J. Finance* 1988b, *43*(3), pp. 656–59.

LAKONISHOK, JOSEF AND LEVI, MAURICE. "Weekend Effects on Stock Returns: A Note," *J. Finance*, June 1982, *37*(3), pp. 883–89.

LAKONISHOK, JOSEF AND SMIDT, SEYMOUR. "Volume and Turn-of-the-Year Behavior," *J. Finan. Econ.*, Sept. 1984, *13*(3), pp. 435–55.

______. "Are Seasonal Anomalies Real?: A Ninety-Year Perspective," *Rev. Finan. Stud.*, Winter 1988, *1*(4), pp. 403–25.

LEROY, STEPHEN F. *The determination of stock prices*. Unpub. PhD dissertation, U. of Pennsylvania, 1971.

______. "Risk Aversion and the Martingale Property of Stock Prices," *Int. Econ. Rev.*, June 1973, *14*(2), pp. 436–46.

______. "Efficient Capital Markets: Comment," *J. Finance*, Mar. 1976, *3*(1), pp. 139–41.

______. "Expectations Models of Asset Prices: A Survey of Theory," *J. Finance*, Mar. 1982, *37*(1), pp. 185–217.

______. "Efficiency and the Variability of Asset Prices," *Amer. Econ. Rev.*, May 1984, *74*(2), pp. 183–87.

LEROY, STEPHEN F. AND LACIVITA, C. J. "Risk Aversion and the Dispersion of Asset Prices," *J. Bus.*, Oct. 1981, *54*(4), pp. 535–47.

LEROY, STEPHEN F. AND PARKE, WILLIAM C. "Stock Price Volatility: An Inequality Test Based on the Geometric Random Walk." Reproduced, U. of California, Santa Barbara, May 1988.

LEROY, STEPHEN F. AND PORTER, RICHARD D. "The Present-Value Relation: Tests Based on Implied Variance Bounds," *Econometrica*, May 1981, *49*(3), pp. 555–74.

LINTNER, JOHN. "The Valuation of Risk Assets and the Selection of Risky Investments in Stock Portfolios and Capital Budgets," *Rev. Econ. Stat.*, Feb. 1965, *47*(1), pp. 13–37.

LO, ANDREW W. AND MACKINLAY, A. CRAIG. "Stock Market Prices Do Not Follow Random Walks: Evidence from a Simple Specification Test," *Rev. Finan. Stud.*, Spring 1988, *1*(1), pp. 41–66.

LUCAS, ROBERT E., JR. "Some International Evidence on Output-Inflation Tradeoffs," *Amer. Econ. Rev.*, June 1973, *63*(3), pp. 326–34.

______. "Asset Prices in an Exchange Economy," *Econometrica*, Nov. 1978, *46*(6), pp. 1429–45.

MACHINA, MARK. "Choice under Uncertainty: Problems Solved and Unsolved," *J. Econ. Perspectives*, Summer 1987, *1*(1), pp. 121–54.

MANDELBROT, BENOIT. "Forecasts of Future Prices, Unbiased Markets, and 'Martingale' Models," *J. Bus.*, Jan. 1966, *39*(1), pp. 242–55.

MANKIW, N. GREGORY; ROMER, DAVID AND SHAPIRO, MATTHEW D. "An Unbiased Reexamination of Stock Market Volatility," *J. Finance*, July 1985, *40*(3), pp. 677–87.

MARSH, TERRY AND MERTON, ROBERT C. "Dividend Variability and Variance Bounds Tests for the Rationality of Stock Market Prices," *Amer. Econ. Rev.*, June 1986, *76*(3), pp. 483–98.

MCAFEE, R., PRESTON AND MCMILLAN, JOHN. "Auctions and Bidding," *J. Econ. Lit.*, June 1987, *25*(2), pp. 699–738.

MCCLOSKEY, DONALD N. *The writing of economics*. NY: Macmillan, 1987.

MEAD, WALTER J.; MOSEIDJORD, ASBJORN AND SORENSEN, PHILIP E. "The Rate of Return Earned by Lessees under Cash Bonus Bidding for OCS Oil and Gas Leases," *Energy J.*, Oct. 1983, *4*(2), pp. 37–52.

______. "Competitive Bidding under Asymmetrical Information: Behavior and Performance in Gulf of Mexico Drainage Lease Sales, 1959–1969," *Rev. Econ. Statist.*, Aug. 1984, *66*(3), pp. 505–08.

MEHRA, RAJNISH AND PRESCOTT, EDWARD C. "The Equity Premium: A Puzzle," *J. Monet. Econ.*, Mar. 1985, *15*(2), pp. 145–61.

MERTON, ROBERT C. "An Intertemporal Capital Asset Pricing Model," *Econometrica*, Sept. 1973, *41*(5), pp. 867–87.

______. "On the Current State of the Stock Market Rationality Hypothesis," in *Macroeconomics and finance: Essays in honor of Franco Modigliani*. Ed.: STANLEY FISCHER ET AL. Cambridge: MIT Press, 1987.

MICHENER, RONALD W. "Variance Bounds in a Simple Model of Asset Pricing," *J. Polit. Econ.*, Feb. 1982, *90*(1), 166–75.

MILGROM, PAUL AND STOKEY, NANCY. "Information, Trade and Common Knowledge," *J. Econ. Theory*, Feb. 1982, *26*(1), pp. 17–27.

MILLER, EDWARD M. "Risk, Uncertainty, and Divergence of Opinion," *J. Finance*, Sept. 1977, *32*(4), pp. 1151–68.

MOSSIN, JAN. "Equilibrium in a Capital Asset Market," *Econometrica*, Oct. 1966, *34*(4), pp. 768–83.

NASON, J. "The Equity Premium and Time-Varying Risk Behavior." Reproduced, Federal Reserve Board, 1988.

NICHOLSON, FRANCIS. "Price Ratios in Relation to Investment Results," *Financial Analysts J.*, Jan./Feb. 1968, *24*(1), pp. 105–09.

NIEDERHOFFER, VICTOR AND OSBORNE, M. F. M. "Market Making and Reversal of the Stock Exchange," *J. Amer. Statist. Assoc.*, Dec. 1966, *61*(316), pp. 897–916.

OHLSON, JAMES. "Risk-Aversion and the Martingale Property of Stock Prices: Comments," *Int. Econ. Rev.*, Feb. 1977, *18*(1), pp. 229–34.

POTERBA, JAMES AND SUMMERS, LAWRENCE. "The Persistence of Volatility and Stock Market Fluctuations," *Amer. Econ. Rev.*, Dec. 1986, *76*(5), pp. 1142–51.

______. "Mean Reversion in Stock Prices: Evidence and Implications," *J. Finan. Econ.*, Oct. 1988, *22*(1), pp. 27–59.

REINGANUM, MARC. "Misspecification of Capital Asset Pricing: Empirical Anomalies Based on Earnings' Yields and Market Values," *J. Finan. Econ.*, Mar. 1981, 9, pp. 19–46.

______. "A Direct Test of Roll's Conjecture on the Firm Size Effect," *J. Finance*, Mar. 1982, *37*(1), pp. 27–35.

______. "The Anomalous Stock Market Behavior of Small Firms in January: Empirical Tests for Tax-loss Selling Effects," *J. Finan. Econ.*, June 1983, *12*(1), pp. 89–104.

RICARDO, DAVID. *Principles of political economy and taxation*. London: Aldine, [1817] 1960.

RIETZ, THOMAS A. "The Equity Risk Premium: A Solution," *J. Monet. Econ.*, July 1988, *22*(1), pp. 117–31.

ROBERTS, HARRY V. "Stock-Market 'Patterns' and Financial Analysis: Methodological Suggestions," (1959) in COOTNER 1964, pp. 7–16.

ROGALSKI, ROBERT. "New Findings Regarding Day-of-the-Week Returns Over Trading and Non-Trading Periods: A Note," *J. Finance*, Dec. 1984, *39*(5), pp. 1603–14.

ROLL, RICHARD. "Vas Ist Das? The Turn-of-the-Year Effect and the Return Premia of Small Firms," *J. Portfol. Manage.*, Winter 1983, *9*(2), pp. 18–28.

______. "Orange Juice and Weather," *Amer. Econ. Rev.*, Dec. 1984, *74*(5), pp. 861–80.

______. "The Hubris Hypothesis of Corporate Takeovers," *J. Bus.*, Apr. 1986, *59*(2), pp. 197–216.

______. "R^2," *J. Finance*, July 1988, *43*(2), pp. 541–66.

ROSENBERG, BARR; REID, KENNETH AND LANSTEIN, RONALD. "Persuasive Evidence of Market Inefficiency," *J. Portfol. Manage.*, Spring 1985, *11*(3), pp. 9–16.

ROSS, STEPHEN A. "The Arbitrage Theory of Capital Asset Pricing," *J. Econ. Theory*, Dec. 1976, *13*(3), pp. 341–60.

______. "Return, Risk, and Arbitrage," in *Risk and return in finance*, Vol. I. Eds.: IRWIN FRIEND AND JAMES L. BICKSLER. Cambridge: Lippincott, 1977, pp. 189–218.

______. "A Simple Approach to the Valuation of Risky Streams," *J. Bus.*, July 1978, *51*(3), pp. 453–75.

______. "The Interrelations of Finance and Economics: Theoretical Perspectives," *Amer. Econ. Rev.*, May 1987, *77*(2), pp. 29–34.

ROZEFF, MICHAEL S. AND KINNEY, WILLIAM R., JR., "Capital Market Seasonality: The Case of Stock Returns," *J. Finan. Econ.*, Oct. 1976, *3*(4), pp. 379–402.

RUBINSTEIN, MARK. "Securities Market Efficiency in an Arrow-Debreu Economy," *Amer. Econ. Rev.*, Dec. 1975, *65*(5), pp. 812–24.

SALYER, KEVIN D. "Risk Aversion and Stock Price Volatility When Dividends Are Difference Stationary," *Econ. Letters*, 1988, *28*(3), pp. 251–54.

SAMUELSON, PAUL A. "Proof That Properly Anticipated Prices Fluctuate Randomly," *Ind. Manage. Rev.*, 1965, *6*, pp. 41–49.

______. "Proof That Properly Discounted Present Values of Assets Vibrate Randomly," *Bell J. Econ.*, Autumn 1973, *4*(2), pp. 369–74.

SCHWERT, G. WILLIAM. "Size and Stock Returns, and Other Empirical Regularities," *J. Finan. Econ.*, June 1983, *12*(1), pp. 3–12.

SHARPE, WILLIAM F. "Capital Asset Prices: A Theory of Market Equilibrium under Conditions of Risk," *J. Finance*, Sept. 1964, *19*(4), pp. 425–42.

SHILLER, ROBERT J. "The Volatility of Long-Term Interest Rates and Expectations Models of the Term Structure," *J. Polit. Econ.*, Dec. 1979, *87*(6), pp. 1190–1219.

______. "The Use of Volatility Measures in Assessing Market Efficiency," *J. Finance*, May 1981a, *36*(2), pp. 291–304.

______. "Do Stock Prices Move Too Much to Be Justified by Subsequent Changes in Dividends?" *Amer. Econ. Rev.*, June 1981b, *71*(3), pp. 421–36.

______. "Stock Prices and Social Dynamics," *Brookings Pap. Econ. Act.*, 1984, 2, pp. 457–98.

______. "The Probability of Gross Violations of a Present Value Variance Inequality," *J. Polit. Econ.*, Oct. 1988, *96*(5), pp. 1089–92.

SIMS, CHRISTOPHER J. "Martingale-Like Behavior of Prices and Interest Rates." Discussion Paper No. 205. U. of Minnesota Center for Economic Research, 1984.

SINGLETON, KENNETH J. "Specification and Estimation of Intertemporal Asset Pricing Models," in *Handbook of monetary economics*. Eds.: B. FRIEDMAN AND F. HAHN, Amsterdam: North-Holland, 1987.

SLEZAK, STEVE L. "The Effect of Market Interruptions on Equilibrium Asset Return Distributions in Dynamic Economies with Asymmetrically Informed Traders." Reproduced, U. of California, San Diego, 1988.

SMITH, ADAM. *The money game*. NY: Random House, 1968.

SOLOW, ROBERT M. "Technical Change and the Aggregate Production Function," *Rev. Econ. Statist.*, Aug. 1957, *39*(3), pp. 312–20.

STIGLER, GEORGE J. AND BECKER, GARY S. "De Gustibus Non Est Disputandum," *Amer. Econ. Rev.*, Mar. 1977, *67*(2), pp. 76–90.

SUMMERS, LAWRENCE. "On Economics and Finance," *J. Finance*, July 1985, *40*(3), pp. 633–35.

______. "Does the Stock Market Rationally Reflect Fundamental Values?" *J. Finance*, July 1986, *41*(3), pp. 591–601.

THALER, RICHARD H. "Anomalies: The January Effect," *J. Econ. Perspectives*, Summer 1987a, *1*(1), pp. 197–201.

______. "Anomalies: Seasonal Movements in Security Prices II: Weekend, Hoiliday, Turn of the Month, and Intraday Effects," *J. Econ. Perspectives*, Fall 1987b, *1*(2), pp. 169–78.

______. "Anomalies: The Winner's Curse," *J. Econ. Perspectives*, Winter 1988, *2*(1), pp. 191–202.

THIEL, STUART E. "Some Evidence on the Winner's Curse," *Amer. Econ. Rev.*, Dec. 1988, *78*(5), pp. 884–95.

TINIC, SEHA M. AND WEST, RICHARD R. "Risk and Return: January vs. the Rest of the Year," *J. Finan. Econ.*, Dec. 1984, *13*(4), pp. 561–74.

______. "Risk, Return, and Equilibrium: A Revisit," *J. Polit. Econ.*, Feb. 1986, *94*(1), pp. 126–47.

TIROLE, JEAN. "On the Possibility of Speculation Under Rational Expectations," *Econometrica*, Sept. 1982, *50*(5), pp. 1163–81.

VARIAN, HAL R. "Divergence of Opinion in Complete Markets: A Note," *J. Finance*, Mar. 1985, *40*(1), pp. 309–17.

______. "Differences of Opinion in Financial Markets," in *Financial risk: Theory, evidence and implications*. Ed.: COURTENAY C. STONE. Boston: Kluwer Academic Publishers, 1989, pp. 3–37.

WEST, KENNETH D. "Dividend Innovations and Stock Price Volatility," *Econometrica*, Jan. 1988a, *56*(1), pp. 37–61.

______. "Bubbles, Fads and Stock Price Volatility Tests: A Partial Evaluation," *J. Finance*, 1988b, *43*(3), pp. 639–60.

WILLIAMS, J. B. *The theory of investment value*. Cambridge: Harvard U. Press, 1938.

WORKING, HOLBROOK. A Random Difference Series for Use in the Analysis of Time Series," *J. Amer. Statist. Assoc.*, 1934, *29*, pp. 11–24.

______. "The Investigation of Economic Expectations," *Amer. Econ. Rev.*, May 1949, *39*(3), pp. 150–66.

______. "Note on the Correlation of First Differences of Averages in a Random Chain," (1960) in COOTNER 1964, pp. 129–31.

Part II
Market Inefficiency and Stock Price Predictability

[5]

Permanent and Temporary Components of Stock Prices

Eugene F. Fama and Kenneth R. French

University of Chicago

A slowly mean-reverting component of stock prices tends to induce negative autocorrelation in returns. The autocorrelation is weak for the daily and weekly holding periods common in market efficiency tests but stronger for long-horizon returns. In tests for the 1926–85 period, large negative autocorrelations for return horizons beyond a year suggest that predictable price variation due to mean reversion accounts for large fractions of 3–5-year return variances. Predictable variation is estimated to be about 40 percent of 3–5-year return variances for portfolios of small firms. The percentage falls to around 25 percent for portfolios of large firms.

I. Introduction

Early tests of market efficiency examined autocorrelations of daily and weekly stock returns. Sample sizes for such short return horizons are typically large, and reliable evidence of nonzero autocorrelation is common. Since the estimated autocorrelations are usually close to 0.0, however, most studies conclude that the implied predictability of returns is not economically significant. Fama (1970) summarizes this early work, which largely concludes that the stock market is efficient.

Summers (1986) challenges this interpretation of the autocorrelation of short-horizon returns. He argues that the claim in common

The comments of Craig Ansley, David Booth, John Cochrane, John Huizinga, Shmuel Kandel, Robert Kohn, Richard Leftwich, Merton Miller, Sam Peltzman, Charles Plosser, Rex Sinquefield, and, especially, G. William Schwert are gratefully acknowledged. This research is supported by the National Science Foundation (Fama), the Center for Research in Security Prices (French), and Batterymarch Financial Management (French).

[*Journal of Political Economy*, 1988, vol. 96, no. 2]

models of an inefficient market is that prices take long temporary swings away from fundamental values, which he translates into the statistical hypothesis that prices have slowly decaying stationary components. He shows that autocorrelations of short-horizon returns can give the impression that such mean-reverting components of prices are of no consequence when in fact they account for a substantial fraction of the variation of returns.

Our tests are based on the converse proposition that the behavior of long-horizon returns can give a clearer impression of the importance of mean-reverting price components. Specifically, a slowly decaying component of prices induces negative autocorrelation in returns that is weak for the daily and weekly holding periods common in market efficiency tests. But such a temporary component of prices can induce strong negative autocorrelation in long-horizon returns.

We examine autocorrelations of stock returns for increasing holding periods. In the results for the 1926–85 sample period, large negative autocorrelations for return horizons beyond a year are consistent with the hypothesis that mean-reverting price components are important in the variation of returns. The estimates for industry portfolios suggest that predictable variation due to mean reversion is about 35 percent of 3–5-year return variances. Returns are more predictable for portfolios of small firms. Predictable variation is estimated to be about 40 percent of 3–5-year return variances for small-firm portfolios. The percentage falls to around 25 percent for portfolios of large firms.

Our results add to mounting evidence that stock returns are predictable (see, e.g., Bodie 1976; Jaffe and Mandelker 1976; Nelson 1976; Fama and Schwert 1977; Fama 1981; Campbell 1987; French, Schwert, and Stambaugh 1987). Again, this work focuses on short return horizons (De Bondt and Thaler [1985] are an exception), and the common conclusion is that predictable variation is a small part (usually less than 3 percent) of the variation of returns. There is little in the literature that foreshadows our estimates that 25–45 percent of the variation of 3–5-year stock returns is predictable from past returns.

There are two competing economic stories for strong predictability of long-horizon returns due to slowly decaying price components. Such price behavior is consistent with common models of an irrational market in which stock prices take long temporary swings away from fundamental values. But the predictability of long-horizon returns can also result from time-varying equilibrium expected returns generated by rational pricing in an efficient market. Poterba and Summers (1987) show formally how these opposite views can imply the same price behavior. The intuition is straightforward.

Expected returns correspond roughly to the discount rates that relate a current stock price to expected future dividends. Suppose that investor tastes for current versus risky future consumption and the stochastic evolution of the investment opportunities of firms result in time-varying equilibrium expected returns that are highly autocorrelated but mean-reverting. Suppose that shocks to expected returns are uncorrelated with shocks to rational forecasts of dividends. Then a shock to expected returns has no effect on expected dividends or expected returns in the distant future. Thus the shock has no long-term effect on expected prices. The cumulative effect of a shock on expected returns must be exactly offset by an opposite adjustment in the current price.

In this scenario, autocorrelated equilibrium expected returns lead to slowly decaying components of prices that are indistinguishable from the temporary price components of an inefficient market, at least with univariate tests like those considered here. More informed choices between the competing explanations of return predictability will require models that restrict the variation of expected returns in plausible ways, for example, models that restrict the relations between the behavior of macroeconomic driving variables and equilibrium expected returns.

Finally, tests on long-horizon returns can provide a better impression of the importance of slowly decaying stationary price components, but the cost is statistical imprecision. The temporary component of prices must account for a large fraction of return variation to be identified in the univariate properties of long-horizon returns. We find "reliable" evidence of negative autocorrelation only in tests on the entire 1926–85 sample period, and the evidence is clouded by the statistical issues (changing parameters, heteroscedasticity, etc.) that such a long time period raises.

II. A Simple Model for Stock Prices

Let $p(t)$ be the natural log of a stock price at time t. We model $p(t)$ as the sum of a random walk, $q(t)$, and a stationary component, $z(t)$,

$$p(t) = q(t) + z(t), \quad (1)$$

$$q(t) = q(t - 1) + \mu + \eta(t), \quad (2)$$

where μ is expected drift and $\eta(t)$ is white noise. Summers (1986) argues that the long temporary price swings assumed in models of an inefficient market imply a slowly decaying stationary price component. As an example, he suggests a first-order autoregression (AR1),

$$z(t) = \phi z(t - 1) + \epsilon(t), \tag{3}$$

where $\epsilon(t)$ is white noise and ϕ is close to but less than 1.0.

The model (1)–(3) is just one way to represent a mix of random-walk and stationary price components. The general hypothesis is that stock prices are nonstationary processes in which the permanent gain from each month's price shock is less than 1.0. Our tests are relevant for the general class of models in which part of each month's shock is permanent and the rest is gradually eliminated. The tests center on the fact that the temporary part of the shock implies predictability (negative autocorrelation) of returns.

A. *The Implications of a Stationary Price Component*

Since $p(t)$ is the natural log of the stock price, the continuously compounded return from t to $t + T$ is

$$\begin{aligned} r(t, t + T) &= p(t + T) - p(t) \\ &= [q(t + T) - q(t)] + [z(t + T) - z(t)]. \end{aligned} \tag{4}$$

The random-walk price component produces white noise in returns. We show next that the mean reversion of the stationary price component $z(t)$ causes negative autocorrelation in returns.

The slope in the regression of $z(t + T) - z(t)$ on $z(t) - z(t - T)$, the first-order autocorrelation of T-period changes in $z(t)$, is

$$\rho(T) = \frac{\text{cov}[z(t + T) - z(t), z(t) - z(t - T)]}{\sigma^2[z(t + T) - z(t)]}. \tag{5}$$

The numerator covariance is

$$\begin{aligned} \text{cov}[z(t + T) - z(t), z(t) - z(t - T)] = &-\sigma^2(z) + 2\,\text{cov}[z(t), z(t + T)] \\ &- \text{cov}[z(t), z(t + 2T)]. \end{aligned} \tag{6}$$

The stationarity of $z(t)$ implies that the covariances on the right of (6) approach 0.0 as T increases, so the covariance on the left approaches $-\sigma^2(z)$. The variance in the denominator of the slope,

$$\sigma^2[z(t + T) - z(t)] = 2\sigma^2(z) - 2\,\text{cov}[z(t + T), z(t)], \tag{7}$$

approaches $2\sigma^2(z)$. We can infer from (6) and (7) that the slope in the regression of $z(t + T) - z(t)$ on $z(t) - z(t - T)$ approaches -0.5 for large T.

The slope $\rho(T)$ has an interesting interpretation used often in the empirical work of later sections. If $z(t)$ is an AR1, the expected change from t to T is

$$E_t[z(t + T) - z(t)] = (\phi^T - 1)z(t), \tag{8}$$

and the covariance in the numerator of $\rho(T)$ is

$$\begin{aligned} \text{cov}[z(t + T) - z(t), z(t) - z(t - T)] &= (-1 + 2\phi^T - \phi^{2T})\sigma^2(z) \\ &= -(1 - \phi^T)^2\sigma^2(z). \end{aligned} \tag{9}$$

With (8) and (9) we can infer that the covariance is minus the variance of the T-period expected change, $-\sigma^2[E_t z(t + T) - z(t)]$. Thus, when $z(t)$ is an AR1, the slope in the regression of $z(t + T) - z(t)$ on $z(t) - z(t - T)$ is (minus) the ratio of the variance of the expected change in $z(t)$ to the variance of the actual change. This interpretation of the slope is a valid approximation for any slowly decaying stationary process.[1]

Equation (8) shows that when ϕ is close to 1.0, the expected change in an AR1 slowly approaches $-z(t)$ as T increases. Likewise, the slope $\rho(T)$ is close to 0.0 for short return horizons and slowly approaches -0.5. This illustrates Summers's (1986) point that slow mean reversion can be missed with the short return horizons common in market efficiency tests. Our tests are based on the converse insight that slow mean reversion can be more evident in long-horizon returns.

B. *The Properties of Returns*

Since we do not observe $z(t)$, we infer its existence and properties from the behavior of returns. Let $\beta(T)$ be the slope in the regression of the return $r(t, t + T)$ on $r(t - T, t)$. If changes in the random-walk and stationary components of stock prices are uncorrelated,

$$\beta(T) = \frac{\text{cov}[r(t, t + T), r(t - T, t)]}{\sigma^2[r(t - T, t)]} \tag{10}$$

$$= \frac{\rho(T)\sigma^2[z(t + T) - z(t)]}{\sigma^2[z(t + T) - z(t)] + \sigma^2[q(t + T) - q(t)]} \tag{10a}$$

[1] For long return horizons, the interpretation of the slope as the proportion of the variance of the change in $z(t)$ due to the expected change is valid for any stationary process. If $z(t)$ is a stationary process with a zero mean, the expected change from t to T approaches $-z(t)$ as T increases, and the variance of the expected change approaches $\sigma^2(z)$. The ratio of the long-horizon variance of the expected change in $z(t)$, $\sigma^2(z)$, to the long-horizon variance of the actual change, $2\sigma^2(z)$, is thus 0.5, the negative of the long-horizon value of $\rho(T)$.

$$\approx \frac{-\sigma^2[E_t z(t + T) - z(t)]}{\sigma^2[r(t - T, t)]}. \tag{10b}$$

Expression (10b) highlights the result that $\beta(T)$ measures the proportion of the variance of T-period returns explained by (or predictable from) the mean reversion of a slowly decaying price component $z(t)$. Expression (10a) helps predict the behavior of the slopes for increasing values of T. If the price does not have a stationary component, the slopes are 0.0 for all T. If the price does not have a random-walk component, $\beta(T) = \rho(T)$ and the slopes approach -0.5 for large values of T.

Predictions about the slope $\beta(T)$ are more complicated if the stock price has both random-walk and stationary components. The mean reversion of the stationary component tends to push the slopes toward -0.5 for long return horizons, while the variance of the white-noise component, $q(t + T) - q(t)$, pushes the slopes toward 0.0. Since the variance of $z(t + T) - z(t)$ approaches $2\sigma^2(z)$ as the return horizon increases and the white-noise variance grows like T, the white-noise component eventually dominates. Thus, if stock prices have both random-walk and slowly decaying stationary components, the slopes in regressions of $r(t, t + T)$ on $r(T - t, t)$ might form a U-shaped pattern, starting around 0.0 for short horizons, becoming more negative as T increases, and then moving back toward 0.0 as the white-noise variance begins to dominate at long horizons.

Finally, existing evidence (e.g., Fama and Schwert 1977; Keim and Stambaugh 1986; Fama and French 1987; French et al. 1987) suggests that expected returns are positively autocorrelated. The negative autocorrelation of long-horizon returns due to a stationary component of prices is consistent with positively autocorrelated expected returns. For example, the model (1)–(3) implies negatively autocorrelated returns. Poterba and Summers (1987) show, however, that if the stationary price component $z(t)$ in (3) is an AR1 with parameter $\phi > 0.0$, the expected return is an AR1 with parameter ϕ and so is positively autocorrelated. The economic intuition is that shocks to expected returns (discount rates) can generate opposite shocks to current prices, and returns can be negatively autocorrelated when expected returns are positively autocorrelated.

III. The Autocorrelation of Industry and Decile Portfolio Returns

A. *The Data*

The mix of random-walk and stationary components in stock prices can differ across stocks. Firm size and industry are dimensions known to capture differences in return behavior (see King 1966; Banz 1981; Huberman and Kandel 1985). We examine results for industry portfolios and for portfolios formed on the basis of size.

The basic data are 1-month returns for all New York Stock Exchange (NYSE) stocks for the 1926–85 period from the Center for Research in Security Prices. At the end of each year, stocks are ranked on the basis of size (shares outstanding times price per share) and grouped into ten (decile) portfolios. One-month portfolio returns, with equal weighting of securities, are calculated and transformed into continuously compounded returns. These nominal returns are adjusted for the inflation rate of the U.S. Consumer Price Index (CPI) and then summed to get overlapping monthly observations on longer-horizon returns. Unless otherwise noted, return henceforth implies a continuously compounded real return.

There is a problem with the decile portfolios. Stocks with unusually high or low returns tend to move across deciles from one year to the next. If unusual returns are caused by temporary price swings, subsequent reversals may be missed—the tests may understate the importance of stationary price components—because of the movement of stocks across deciles. Since the problem is less severe for portfolios that include all stocks, we also show results for the equal- and value-weighted portfolios of all NYSE stocks. The value-weighted market portfolio summarizes the return behavior of large stocks, while the equal-weighted portfolio is tilted more toward small stocks.

Using Standard Industrial Classification codes, we also form 17 industry portfolios, with equal weighting of the stocks in a portfolio. One criterion in defining an industry is that it contains firms in similar activities. The other criterion is that the industry produces diversified portfolios during the 1926–85 period. Each of the 17 industries always has at least seven firms (15 after 1929), and the number of firms per industry is usually greater than 30. Within industries, there is little concentration of firms by size. For example, the average of the decile ranks of the firms in an industry is typically between 4.0 and 7.0. Thus size and industry are not proxies, and size and industry portfolios can provide independent evidence on the behavior of long-horizon returns. (Details on the industry portfolios are available from the authors.)

The tests center on slopes in regressions of $r(t, t + T)$ on $r(t - T, t)$. The slopes are first-order autocorrelations of T-year returns. Ordinary least squares (OLS) estimates have a bias that depends on the true slopes, sample sizes, and the overlap of monthly data on long-horizon returns (see Kendall 1954; Marriot and Pope 1954; Huizinga 1984). Proper bias adjustments when the true slopes are 0.0 (prices do not have stationary components) are difficult to determine analytically. We use simulations, constructed to mimic properties of stock returns, to estimate the bias adjustments (see the Appendix). The simulations also show that when prices have stationary components that generate negative autocorrelations on the order of those observed here, simple OLS slopes have little bias. We examine both OLS and bias-adjusted slopes.

B. Regression Slopes for the 1926–85 Sample Period

Industries

Table 1 shows slopes in regressions of $r(t, t + T)$ on $r(t - T, t)$ for return horizons from 1 to 10 years, using the industry portfolio data for the 1926–85 sample period. As predicted by the hypothesis that prices have stationary components, negative slopes are the rule. The bias-adjusted slopes are uniformly negative for return horizons from 2 to 5 years. The unadjusted slopes are almost always negative for all horizons. The slopes reach minimum values for 3–5-year returns, and they become less negative for return horizons beyond 5 years. This U-shaped pattern is consistent with the hypothesis that stock prices also have random-walk components that eventually dominate long-horizon returns. Estimated slopes (not shown) for nominal returns are usually within 0.04 of those for real returns.

The slopes for 3-, 4-, and 5-year returns are large in magnitude and relative to their standard errors. The average values of the bias-adjusted slopes for 3-, 4-, and 5-year returns are −0.30, −0.34, and −0.32; the averages of the unadjusted slopes are −0.38, −0.45, and −0.45. Expression (10b) says that the slope measures the proportion of the variance of T-year returns due to time-varying expected returns generated by slowly decaying stationary price components. The slopes for the industry portfolios thus suggest that these time-varying expected returns average between 30 percent and 45 percent of the variances of 3–5-year returns.

Moreover, the limiting argument for the slopes in Section II says that the variance of the expected change in the stationary price component $z(t)$ approaches half the variance of the long-horizon change in $z(t)$. Thus regression slopes that average between −0.30 and −0.45 estimate that, on average, between 60 percent and 90 percent of the variances of 3–5-year industry returns are due to the stationary price component $z(t)$.

A caveat is in order. The hypothesis that prices contain both random-walk and slowly decaying stationary components predicts a U-shaped pattern of slopes for increasing return horizons. This provides some justification for leaning toward extreme slopes to estimate

TABLE 1

OLS and Bias-adjusted Slopfs for Industry Portfolios: 1926–85

$r(t, t + T) = \alpha(T) + \beta(T)r(t - T, t) + \epsilon(t, t + T)$

	Return Horizon (Years)							
	1	2	3	4	5	6	8	10
	OLS Slopes β(T)							
Food	−.04	−.28*	−.41*	−.46*	−.47*	−.30	−.21	−.20
Apparel	−.11	−.23	−.27	−.37*	−.43*	−.37	−.43	−.56*
Drugs	−.04	−.19	−.25	−.22	−.26	−.22	−.31	−.50
Retail	−.03	−.22	−.37*	−.42*	−.46*	−.34	−.32	−.31
Durables	.00	−.19	−.34*	−.43*	−.43*	−.25	−.20	−.15
Autos	−.07	−.27	−.43*	−.52*	−.48*	−.29*	−.26	−.30
Construction	−.03	−.17	−.34*	−.51*	−.55*	−.36*	−.06	−.04
Finance	−.04	−.22	−.33*	−.35*	−.28	−.09	.00	.06
Miscellaneous	−.04	−.18	−.32*	−.45*	−.50*	−.34	−.22	−.17
Utilities	−.07	−.21	−.35*	−.32*	−.15	.08	−.08	−.18
Transportation	−.12	−.25	−.34*	−.44*	−.45*	−.33	−.30	−.27
Business equipment	−.01	−.26	−.46*	−.51*	−.49*	−.35*	−.17	−.15
Chemicals	−.06	−.38*	−.50*	−.48*	−.50*	−.34*	−.21	−.17
Metal products	−.02	−.25	−.45*	−.59*	−.65*	−.53*	−.38*	−.33*
Metal industries	−.10	−.32*	−.43*	−.46*	−.48*	−.33*	−.04	−.01
Mining	−.11	−.33*	−.44*	−.54*	−.61*	−.44*	−.20	−.21
Oil	−.04	−.28*	−.36*	−.52*	−.53*	−.36*	−.05	−.01
Average β(T)	−.06	−.25	−.38	−.45	−.45	−.30	−.20	−.21

continued overleaf

	Bias-adjusted Slopes $\beta(T)$							
Food	−.01	−.24	−.34*	−.36*	−.34*	−.15	.01	.08
Apparel	−.08	−.18	−.20	−.27	−.30	−.21	−.21	−.27
Drugs	−.02	−.14	−.18	−.12	−.13	−.06	−.09	−.22
Retail	−.01	−.17	−.30	−.32*	−.33*	−.18	−.10	−.02
Durables	.02	−.14	−.26	−.33*	−.30*	−.09	.02	.13
Autos	−.05	−.22	−.36*	−.42*	−.35*	−.13	−.04	−.02
Construction	−.01	−.13	−.27	−.41*	−.42*	−.21	.16	.24
Finance	−.01	−.17	−.26	−.25	−.15	.07	.22	.35
Miscellaneous	−.02	−.13	−.25	−.35*	−.37*	−.18	.00	.12
Utilities	−.05	−.16	−.27	−.22	−.02	.24	.14	.10
Transportation	−.10	−.20	−.26*	−.33*	−.32	−.18	−.09	.02
Business equipment	.01	−.22	−.39*	−.41*	−.36*	−.19	.05	.13
Chemicals	−.04	−.33*	−.43*	−.38*	−.37*	−.19	.01	.12
Metal products	.01	−.20	−.38*	−.49*	−.52*	−.37*	−.16	−.05
Metal industries	−.08	−.27*	−.36*	−.36*	−.35*	−.17	.18	.28
Mining	−.09	−.29*	−.37*	−.44*	−.48*	−.28*	.02	.08
Oil	−.02	−.23	−.29	−.42*	−.40*	−.20	.17	.27
Average $\beta(T)$	−.03	−.20	−.30	−.34	−.32	−.14	.02	.08
Average $s(\beta)$	.11	.14	.15	.14	.15	.17	.23	.26

NOTE.—The corrections for the bias of the OLS slopes used in the bias-adjusted slopes are discussed in the Appendix. The standard errors of the slopes are adjusted for the residual autocorrelation due to overlap of monthly observations on longer-horizon returns with the method of Hansen and Hodrick (1980). Averages of the slopes and their standard errors—average $\beta(T)$ and average $s(\beta)$—are computed across the 17 industries. Returns are real (CPI-adjusted).

* Indicates that slope is more than 2.0 standard errors from 0.0.

proportions of return variances due to the two components of prices. Since we do not predict the return horizons likely to produce extreme slopes, however, using the observed extremes to estimate proportions of variance probably overstates the importance of stationary components of prices.

Moreover, a pervasive characteristic of the tests is that small effective sample sizes imply imprecise slope estimates for long-horizon returns. The large standard errors of the industry slopes (averaging 0.11 for 1-year returns and 0.26 for 10-year returns) leave much uncertainty about the true slopes and thus about the proportions of variance due to the random-walk and stationary components of prices. (See the Appendix for pertinent details.)

Deciles

There is no obvious pattern in the variation of the regression slopes across industries. There is a clearer pattern in the slopes for the decile portfolios in table 2. Like the industry slopes, the decile slopes are negative and large for 2–5-year returns. However, the minimum values of the slopes tend to be more extreme for lower (smaller-firm) deciles. All the bias-adjusted slopes less than −0.30 and all the unadjusted slopes less than −0.37 are generated by the equal-weighted market portfolio and deciles 1–7. Most of the 4- and 5-year bias-adjusted slopes for these portfolios are more than 2.0 standard errors below 0.0. The value-weighted market and the larger-firm deciles 9 and 10 produce no bias-adjusted slopes more than 2.0 standard errors below 0.0.

Again, perspective is in order. The large standard errors of the decile slopes—between 0.13 and 0.20 for 3–5-year returns—mean that if stock prices have stationary components, they must generate large negative slopes (and account for large fractions of variance) to be identified reliably, even when the estimates use the entire 1926–85 sample period. Nevertheless, every decile produces a simple OLS slope for 3-, 4-, or 5-year returns more than 2.0 standard errors below 0.0. And the U-shaped pattern of the slopes across return horizons predicted by the hypothesis that prices have both random-walk and slowly decaying stationary components is observed for all the deciles, the industry portfolios, and the two market portfolios.

We conclude that the tests for 1926–85 are consistent with the hypothesis that stock prices have both random-walk and stationary components. The estimates suggest that stationary price components account for large fractions of the variation of returns and that they are relatively more important for small-stock portfolios. We recognize, however, that the imprecision of the tests implies substantial uncertainty about any interpretation of the results. The relevance of this caveat is obvious in the subperiod results that follow.

C. *Subperiod Autocorrelations*

Because the regression slopes are not estimated precisely, the results for the 1926–85 period are in principle the strongest test of the hypothesis that stock prices have stationary components. There are, however, reasons to examine subperiods. First, return variances drop substantially after 1940 (see Officer 1973; French et al. 1987). The variance changes make inference less precise even if the autocorrelations of returns are stationary. Moreover, the high variances of the early years are associated with large price swings. It is possible that the large negative autocorrelations estimated for 1926–85 are a consequence of the early years.

We have estimated the slopes in the regression of $r(t, t + T)$ on $r(t - T, t)$ for the 30-year splits, 1926–55 and 1956–85, and for the longer 1946–85 and 1941–85 periods. The estimates for 1941–85 are in tables 3 and 4. We choose 1941–85 because it is the longest period of roughly constant return variances. The regression slopes it produces are similar in magnitude and pattern to those for 1946–85 and 1956–85.

Like 1926–85, the 1941–85 period produces a general pattern of negative autocorrelation of returns that is consistent with the hypothesis that prices have stationary components. However, the 1941–85 bias-adjusted slopes are typically closer to 0.0, and they do not produce the strong U-shaped pattern across return horizons observed for 1926–85. Moreover, large standard errors (averaging 0.13 for 1-year industry portfolio returns and 0.27 for 8-year returns) make the hypothesis that prices contain no stationary components (the true slopes are 0.0) difficult to reject.

Large standard errors make most hypotheses about subperiods difficult to reject. For example, slope estimates for 1926–55 (not shown) have an even stronger U-shaped pattern than those for 1926–85, while estimates for 1956–85 (also not shown) are much like those for 1941–85. However, the hypothesis that the slopes for 1926–55 and 1956–85 are equal cannot be rejected; indeed, large standard errors make the hypothesis essentially untestable.

In short, the preponderance of negative slopes observed for all periods (shown and not shown) is consistent with the hypothesis that stock prices have stationary components that generate negative autocorrelation in long-horizon returns. Subperiod slopes suggest that the negative autocorrelation is weaker (stationary price components are less important in the variation of returns) after 1940. But reliable

TABLE 2

OLS and Bias-adjusted Slopes for the Decile Portfolios and the Equal- and Value-weighted NYSE Market Portfolios: 1926–85

$$r(t, t + T) = \alpha(T) + \beta(T)r(t - T, t) + \epsilon(t, t + T)$$

	Return Horizon (Years)							
	1	2	3	4	5	6	8	10
	OLS Slopes β(T)							
Equal	−.07	−.26	−.39*	−.46*	−.47*	−.29	−.14	−.06
Decile 1	−.01	−.18	−.30	−.46*	−.45*	−.21	.13	.27
Decile 2	−.01	−.16	−.32*	−.51*	−.58*	−.42*	−.24	−.20
Decile 3	−.06	−.20	−.34*	−.46*	−.48*	−.35*	−.30	−.33
Decile 4	−.04	−.23	−.37*	−.48*	−.52*	−.39*	−.30	−.24
Decile 5	−.08	−.27	−.37*	−.42*	−.46*	−.32	−.23	−.16
Decile 6	−.07	−.25	−.38*	−.41*	−.41*	−.26	−.18	−.16
Decile 7	−.09	−.32*	−.42*	−.38*	−.35*	−.18	−.10	−.12
Decile 8	−.08	−.28*	−.37*	−.30*	−.26	−.10	−.07	−.13
Decile 9	−.06	−.26	−.34*	−.24	−.14	.05	.08	−.04
Decile 10	−.08	−.27*	−.35*	−.20	−.08	.09	.12	−.03
Value	−.05	−.24	−.32*	−.19	−.07	.09	.10	−.08
Average	−.06	−.24	−.36	−.39	−.37	−.21	−.11	−.12

continued overleaf

	Bias-adjusted Slopes β(*T*)							
Equal	−.05	−.22	−.32*	−.36*	−.34*	−.13	.08	.22
Decile 1	.01	−.13	−.23	−.36*	−.32	−.05	.35	.56
Decile 2	.01	−.12	−.25	−.41*	−.45*	−.26	−.02	.09
Decile 3	−.04	−.16	−.27	−.35*	−.35*	−.19	−.08	−.04
Decile 4	−.02	−.19	−.29	−.38*	−.39*	−.23	−.08	.05
Decile 5	−.06	−.23	−.29*	−.32*	−.33*	−.16	−.01	.13
Decile 6	−.05	−.20	−.31*	−.31*	−.28	−.10	.04	.13
Decile 7	−.07	−.27*	−.35*	−.28*	−.22	−.02	.12	.16
Decile 8	−.05	−.23	−.30*	−.20	−.13	.06	.15	.15
Decile 9	−.04	−.21	−.27	−.13	−.01	.21	.30	.25
Decile 10	−.06	−.23	−.27	−.10	.05	.25	.34	.25
Value	−.03	−.20	−.25	−.09	.06	.25	.31	.21
Average	−.04	−.19	−.28	−.28	−.24	−.05	.11	.17
	Standard Errors							
Equal	.11	.14	.14	.13	.14	.17	.24	.28
Value	.11	.14	.15	.16	.20	.23	.34	.43
Average	.11	.14	.15	.14	.16	.19	.25	.31

NOTE.—The corrections for the bias of the OLS slopes used in the bias-adjusted slopes are discussed in the Appendix. The standard errors of the slopes are adjusted for the residual autocorrelation due to overlap of monthly observations on longer-horizon returns with the method of Hansen and Hodrick (1980). Averages of the slopes and their standard errors are computed across the 10 deciles. Returns are real (CPI-adjusted).

* Indicates that the slope is more than 2.0 standard errors from 0.0.

TABLE 3

OLS and Bias-adjusted Slopes for Industry Portfolios: 1941–85

$r(t, t + T) = \alpha(T) + \beta(T)r(t - T, t) + \epsilon(t, t + T)$

	Return Horizon (Years)						
	1	2	3	4	5	6	8
	OLS Slopes $\beta(T)$						
Food	−.03	−.24	−.27	−.26	−.29	−.32	−.43
Apparel	−.08	−.22	−.13	−.14	−.26	−.35	−.51
Drugs	−.02	−.13	−.07	−.01	−.11	−.16	−.30
Retail	−.03	−.21	−.23	−.22	−.32	−.34	−.41
Durables	−.03	−.26	−.30	−.27	−.24	−.22	−.24
Autos	−.06	−.36*	−.39*	−.35	−.33*	−.29	−.33
Construction	−.06	−.23	−.24	−.29	−.31	−.28	−.10
Finance	−.02	−.11	−.10	−.12	−.14	−.08	.05
Miscellaneous	.00	−.18	−.23	−.27	−.34	−.34	−.29
Utilities	−.03	−.18	−.30	−.21	−.12	.01	−.05
Transportation	−.10	−.20	−.25	−.33	−.40*	−.42*	−.29
Business equipment	−.10	−.26	−.24	−.28	−.35	−.33	−.18
Chemicals	−.25*	−.47*	−.32*	−.22	−.22	−.24	−.21
Metal products	−.06	−.29	−.39*	−.44*	−.49*	−.49*	−.40
Metal industries	−.19	−.26	−.22	−.19	−.21	−.18	.00
Mining	−.18	−.36*	−.41*	−.46*	−.54*	−.51*	−.32
Oil	−.17	−.27	−.25	−.33	−.32	−.32	−.12
Average $\beta(T)$	−.08	−.25	−.26	−.26	−.29	−.29	−.24

continued overleaf

	Bias-adjusted Slopes $\beta(T)$						
Food	.00	−.18	−.17	−.13	−.13	−.13	−.17
Apparel	−.05	−.16	−.04	−.02	−.10	−.16	−.26
Drugs	.01	−.06	.03	.12	.05	.03	−.04
Retail	.00	−.15	−.13	−.09	−.16	−.15	−.16
Durables	.00	−.20	−.20	−.14	−.09	−.03	.01
Autos	−.03	−.30	−.30	−.22	−.17	−.10	−.07
Construction	−.03	−.17	−.15	−.16	−.16	−.09	.15
Finance	.01	−.04	−.00	.00	.02	.11	.30
Miscellaneous	.03	−.12	−.13	−.14	−.18	−.14	−.03
Utilities	.00	−.12	−.21	−.08	.04	.20	.21
Transportation	−.07	−.13	−.16	−.21	−.24	−.23	−.04
Business equipment	−.07	−.20	−.15	−.15	−.19	−.14	.08
Chemicals	−.22	−.41*	−.22	−.09	−.06	−.05	.05
Metal products	−.03	−.22	−.29	−.31	−.33*	−.30	−.15
Metal industries	−.16	−.20	−.12	−.06	−.05	.01	.25
Mining	−.15	−.30*	−.31	−.33	−.39*	−.32	−.06
Oil	−.14	−.21	−.16	−.20	−.16	−.12	.13
Average $\beta(T)$	−.05	−.19	−.16	−.13	−.14	−.09	.01
Average $s(\beta)$	.13	.16	.19	.20	.21	.23	.27

NOTE.—The corrections for the bias of the OLS slopes used in the bias-adjusted slopes are discussed in the Appendix. The standard errors of the slopes are adjusted for the residual autocorrelation due to overlap of monthly observations on longer-horizon returns with the method of Hansen and Hodrick (1980). Averages of the slopes and their standard errors—average $\beta(T)$ and average $s(\beta)$—are computed across the 17 industries. Returns are real (CPI-adjusted).

* Indicates that the slope is more than 2.0 standard errors from 0.0.

TABLE 4

OLS AND BIAS-ADJUSTED SLOPES FOR THE DECILE PORTFOLIOS AND THE EQUAL- AND VALUE-WEIGHTED NYSE MARKET PORTFOLIOS: 1941–85

$$r(t, t+T) = \alpha(T) + \beta(T)r(t-T, t) + \epsilon(t, t+T)$$

	Return Horizon (Years)						
	1	2	3	4	5	6	8
	OLS Slopes $\beta(T)$						
Equal	−.09	−.24	−.23	−.22	−.26	−.24	−.18
Decile 1	.02	−.05	−.13	−.29	−.36*	−.30	−.15
Decile 2	.00	−.14	−.22	−.33*	−.44*	−.48	−.42
Decile 3	−.05	−.22	−.24	−.27	−.33	−.36	−.39
Decile 4	−.05	−.24	−.26	−.31	−.39	−.42	−.36
Decile 5	−.08	−.27	−.24	−.18	−.26	−.29	−.26
Decile 6	−.06	−.23	−.22	−.17	−.22	−.22	−.19
Decile 7	−.13	−.32*	−.23	−.11	−.11	−.10	−.10
Decile 8	−.15	−.31*	−.21	−.04	−.06	−.05	−.13
Decile 9	−.10	−.19	−.05	.13	.15	.15	.10
Decile 10	−.12	−.23	−.04	.22	.26	.22	.15
Value	−.09	−.22	−.03	.19	.22	.18	.09
Average	−.07	−.22	−.18	−.14	−.17	−.18	−.17

continued overleaf

	Bias-adjusted Slopes $\beta(T)$						
Equal	−.06	−.18	−.13	−.09	−.10	−.05	.08
Decile 1	.05	.01	−.03	−.16	−.20	−.11	.11
Decile 2	.03	−.08	−.12	−.21	−.28	−.28	−.17
Decile 3	−.02	−.16	−.15	−.14	−.17	−.17	−.13
Decile 4	−.02	−.17	−.17	−.18	−.23	−.22	−.11
Decile 5	−.05	−.21	−.15	−.06	−.10	−.10	−.01
Decile 6	−.03	−.17	−.13	−.04	−.06	−.03	.07
Decile 7	−.10	−.26	−.14	.02	.05	.09	.16
Decile 8	−.12	−.25	−.11	.09	.10	.14	.12
Decile 9	−.07	−.12	.04	.26	.31	.35	.35
Decile 10	−.09	−.17	.05	.34	.42	.41	.41
Value	−.06	−.16	.06	.32	.38	.37	.35
Average	−.04	−.16	−.09	−.01	−.02	.01	.08
	Standard Errors						
Equal	.13	.16	.19	.21	.21	.24	.29
Value	.13	.16	.19	.23	.27	.31	.41
Average	.13	.16	.19	.21	.22	.25	.30

Note.—The corrections for the bias of the OLS slopes used in the bias-adjusted slopes are discussed in the Appendix. The standard errors of the slopes are adjusted for the residual autocorrelation due to overlap of monthly observations on longer-horizon returns with the method of Hansen and Hodrick (1980). Averages of the slopes and their standard errors are computed across the 10 deciles. Returns are real (CPI-adjusted).

* Indicates that the slope is more than 2.0 standard errors from 0.0.

contrasts across periods are impossible. Perhaps stationary price components are less important after 1940. Perhaps prices no longer have such temporary components. Only time (and lots of it) will tell.[2]

IV. Negative Autocorrelation: Common or Firm-specific Factors?

An important economic question is whether the negative autocorrelation of long-horizon returns is due to common or firm-specific factors. Evidence that the autocorrelation is due to common factors would raise the possibility that it can be traced to common macroeconomic driving variables. On the other hand, evidence that the autocorrelation is firm-specific would raise the possibility that expected returns have firm-specific components. Such a finding would challenge the relevance of parsimonious equilibrium pricing models. We summarize briefly some preliminary work on these issues.

A. *Portfolios*

Evidence that a single portfolio absorbs the negative autocorrelation of returns for all the industry and decile portfolios would suggest that the negative autocorrelation of the 1926–85 period is due to one common factor. We have estimated residual autocorrelations for regressions of the decile and industry portfolio returns on the return to decile 1. We choose decile 1 as the explanatory portfolio because of the evidence in table 2 that the general negative autocorrelation of portfolio returns is a larger fraction of the variation of returns on portfolios of small firms.

For the 1926–85 period, the residual autocorrelations for the industry and decile portfolios are more often positive than negative, but they are typically close to 0.0. Results for other periods are similar. The evidence suggests that the general negative autocorrelation of portfolio returns is largely due to a common macroeconomic phenomenon.

[2] We have also tested the autocorrelation of returns by examining return variances for increasing horizons (see Alexander 1961; Cochrane 1986; French and Roll 1986; Lo and MacKinlay 1986). Return variances for the industry and decile portfolios behave as predicted by the hypothesis that stock prices have stationary components that induce negative autocorrelation in returns. In particular, the variances grow less than in proportion to the return horizon. Unlike the regression slopes in tables 1 and 2, however, the variance tests for the 1926–85 period do not reliably identify negative autocorrelation in long-horizon returns. We mention the variance tests to emphasize that different univariate approaches to identifying slowly decaying stationary components of price have the common problem of low statistical power—a point treated in detail in Poterba and Summers (1987).

B. *Individual Securities*

Since the decile and industry portfolios are diversified, firm-specific factors contribute little to the variation of their returns. Tests for autocorrelation due to firm-specific factors must use individual stocks. A problem, however, is that reliable inferences about long-horizon returns require long sample periods, but the population of NYSE stocks changes through time. Our preliminary solution is to study the 82 stocks listed for the entire 1926–85 period.

The equal-weighted portfolio of the 82 stocks produces a strong U-shaped pattern of autocorrelations like that observed for the equal-weighted portfolio of all stocks in table 2. The bias-adjusted autocorrelations for 2-, 3-, and 4-year returns on this portfolio are −0.26, −0.36, and −0.28, and they are at least 1.99 standard errors below 0.0. The autocorrelation of returns on the 82 individual stocks is weaker. The averages of the (82) 2-, 3-, and 4-year bias-adjusted slopes are −0.10, −0.16, and −0.10, and the slopes are, on average, −0.78, −1.09, and −0.76 standard errors from 0.0. Moreover, even the weak negative autocorrelation in the individual stock returns disappears in the residuals from regressions of the returns on decile 1. The average bias-adjusted residual autocorrelations for the 82 stocks are close to 0.0 for all return horizons, and the cross-sectional distributions of the autocorrelations are roughly symmetric about 0.0. Tests on the 230 stocks listed for the 1941–85 period yield similar results.

Heavy-handed conclusions from these rather special samples of survivors are inappropriate. But the fact that returns on portfolios of the survivors have autocorrelations similar to those of the equal-weighted market portfolio gives some confidence in the individual stock evidence that firm-specific components of long-horizon stock returns have no autocorrelation. The results are heartening for proponents of parsimonious equilibrium pricing models.

V. Conclusions

First-order autocorrelations of industry and decile portfolio returns for the 1926–85 period form a U-shaped pattern across increasing return horizons. The autocorrelations become negative for 2-year returns, reach minimum values for 3–5-year returns, and then move back toward 0.0 for longer return horizons. This pattern is consistent with the hypothesis that stock prices have a slowly decaying stationary component. The negative autocorrelation of returns generated by a slowly decaying component of prices is weak at the short return horizons common in empirical work, but it becomes stronger as the return horizon increases. Eventually, however, random-walk price components begin to dominate the variation of returns, and long-horizon autocorrelations move back toward 0.0.

Autocorrelation may reflect market inefficiency or time-varying equilibrium expected returns generated by rational investor behavior. Neither view suggests, however, that patterns of autocorrelation should be stable for a sample period as long as 60 years. Although a tendency toward negative autocorrelation of long-horizon returns is always observed, subperiod results suggest that the strong negative autocorrelation of the 1926–85 period may be largely due to the first 15 years. Autocorrelations for periods after 1940 are closer to 0.0, and they do not show the U-shaped pattern of the overall period. Because sample sizes for long-horizon returns are small, however, sample autocorrelations cannot identify changes in the time-series properties of returns. Stationary price components may be less important after 1940, or perhaps prices no longer have such temporary components. Resolution of this issue will require more powerful statistical techniques.

Appendix

Simulations

The simulations mimic properties of NYSE returns. Monthly simulated returns are summed to get overlapping monthly observations on T-year returns, $r(t, t + T)$. We estimate regressions of simulated returns $r(t, t + T)$ on lagged returns $r(t, t - T)$ to obtain sampling distributions of the slopes. The simulations use 720 observations per replication, matching the number of months in the 1926–85 sample period.

We simulate two models in which the true slopes are 0.0. One is a random walk in the log price with normal (0, 1) monthly returns. The second is a random walk in which return variances change every 2 years to approximate changes in stock return variances (see table A1). We also simulate constant and changing variance versions of the model (1)–(3) in which the log price has both a random-walk and an AR1 component (see table A2).

A. The Random-Walk Simulations

Table A1 summarizes estimates of regression slopes for the random-walk models. The negative bias of OLS slopes is apparent from the average slopes in the first line of the table. The bias increases with the return horizon because effective sample sizes are smaller for longer horizons and because the increased overlap of the observations increases serial dependence.

The second line of the table shows average bias-adjusted slopes. The bias correction is the average slope for each return horizon from 10,000 preliminary replications of the constant-variance random-walk model. These bias corrections are used whenever we refer to bias-adjusted slopes for the 1926–85 period for NYSE returns or for the simulations. Since the average bias-adjusted slopes in table A1 are close to 0.0, the preliminary simulations give good estimates of bias when monthly returns are white noise. The bias corrections for the 1941–85 period (540 months) used in the text are also average slopes from 10,000 preliminary replications of the random-walk model, but with 540 rather than 720 observations per replication.

The standard deviation of the sample of slopes for each return horizon in table A1 estimates the standard error of the slope. The standard deviations are large, for example, 0.24 for 5-year returns. Since 720 months yield 12 nonoverlapping 5-year returns, the slope standard error for nonoverlapping returns would be $(1/11)^{.5} = 0.30$. The standard error 0.24 for 600 monthly observations on 5-year returns implies an effective sample size of 18.4 non-overlapping returns.

The t's in table A1 for tests of bias-adjusted slopes against 0.0 use standard errors adjusted for residual autocorrelation due to return overlap (see Hansen and Hodrick 1980). Lower fractiles of the t's are estimates of critical values for tests of the hypothesis that the slope is 0.0 (prices are random walks) against the alternative that the slope is negative because the price has a temporary component. The t's for the changing-variance random walk are most relevant, given the changing variances of stock returns. For 3–5-year returns, the .10, .05, and .01 fractiles of the t's are around −1.8, −2.3, and −3.5. These are more extreme than the same fractiles of the unit normal, −1.28, −1.65, and −2.33. Standard deviations around 1.3 also show that the simulation t's have more dispersion than the unit normal.

Comparison with part A of table A1 shows that the higher dispersion of the t's in part B is due to changing variances. We have estimated slope standard errors using the method of White (1980) and Hansen (1982) to jointly correct for autocorrelation and heteroscedasticity. Resulting t's show more dispersion and more extreme negative lower fractiles than t's based on Hansen and Hodrick's (1980) standard errors. In the NYSE returns, we use Hansen and Hodrick's standard errors.

B. The Mixed AR1–Random-Walk Simulations

Table A2 summarizes simulations of the mixed AR1–random-walk model. True slopes that drop from −0.10 for 1-year returns to −0.27 for 5-year returns are similar to the slopes estimated for the value-weighted NYSE market portfolio in table 1. We view the simulations as evidence about the power of the tests to reject the random-walk model when prices have stationary components that imply slopes in the 3–5-year range like those observed for NYSE returns.

Under the random-walk hypothesis, t's for tests of bias-adjusted slopes against 0.0 are relevant. Average t's in part B of table A2 are only around −1.18 for 3–5-year returns. Likewise, the fractiles of the slopes for the mixed AR1–random-walk model in part B of table A2 are somewhat to the left of those for the random-walk model in part B of table A1, but the overlap of the distributions is substantial. In short, large standard errors for the slopes (the standard deviation of the 5-year slopes in pt. B of table A2 is 0.18) mean that the regression tests have little power to reject the random-walk model when prices have a stationary component that accounts for 27 percent of the variance of 5-year returns. Stationary components of stock prices must generate large negative slopes to be identified reliably in our tests.

Finally, consistent with Kendall (1954) and Marriot and Pope (1954), table

TABLE A1

SUMMARY OF SIMULATIONS WHEN PRICES ARE PURE RANDOM WALKS
$r(t, t+T) = \alpha + \beta r(t-T, t) + \epsilon(t, t+T)$

	Return Horizon (Years)							
	1	2	3	4	5	6	8	10
	A. $\epsilon(t, t+T)$ Homoscedastic (Constant Variance): Mean and Standard Deviation of β (OLS and Bias-adjusted)							
$\bar{\beta}$ (OLS)	−.03	−.04	−.07	−.10	−.13	−.16	−.24	−.30
$\bar{\beta}$ (adjusted)	−.01	.00	.00	.00	.00	.00	−.02	−.01
$s(\beta)$	.11	.15	.19	.22	.24	.26	.28	.30
	Mean, Standard Deviation, and Fractiles of t's for Test of Bias-adjusted β = 0.0							
Mean	−.09	−.01	−.03	−.05	−.09	−.12	−.25	−.23
Standard deviation	1.06	1.00	1.09	1.12	1.13	1.10	1.10	1.12
Fractile:								
.01	−2.62	−2.56	−2.78	−2.93	−2.85	−2.65	−2.76	−4.04
.05	−2.12	−1.51	−1.81	−2.04	−1.95	−2.00	−2.07	−1.92
.10	−1.56	−1.24	−1.42	−1.50	−1.56	−1.58	−1.66	−1.53
.25	−.78	−.76	−.74	−.76	−.83	−.88	−1.03	−.87

continued overleaf

	B. $\epsilon(t, t+T)$ HETEROSCEDASTIC (Changing Variance): Mean and Standard Deviation of β (OLS and Bias-adjusted); Fractiles (Bias-adjusted)							
$\overline{\beta}$ (OLS)	−.01	−.05	−.08	−.10	−.11	−.13	−.11	−.11
$\overline{\beta}$ (adjusted)	.01	−.00	−.01	.00	.02	.03	.11	.17
$s(\beta)$	.15	.19	.20	.22	.23	.25	.25	.28
Fractile:								
.01	−.27	−.45	−.43	−.48	−.47	−.45	−.43	−.40
.05	−.24	−.31	−.34	−.35	−.35	−.34	−.30	−.24
.10	−.19	−.23	−.27	−.28	−.28	−.28	−.20	−.19
.25	−.10	−.14	−.16	−.16	−.15	−.17	−.08	−.02
.50	.00	−.02	.00	.00	.00	.01	.08	.12
.75	.10	.14	.14	.16	.18	.21	.26	.30
.90	.19	.26	.25	.28	.34	.37	.44	.56
.95	.24	.33	.32	.35	.42	.45	.53	.70
.99	.38	.44	.48	.53	.54	.60	.69	.90
	Mean, Standard Deviation, and Fractiles of t's for Test of Bias-adjusted $\beta = 0.0$							
Mean	.01	−.09	−.12	−.10	−.03	.05	.50	.84
Standard deviation	1.43	1.39	1.24	1.31	1.37	1.45	1.51	1.61
Fractile:								
.01	−2.87	−3.77	−3.29	−3.51	−3.62	−3.22	−3.40	−2.56
.05	−2.39	−2.53	−2.30	−2.48	−2.30	−2.25	−1.67	−1.21
.10	−1.90	−1.75	−1.78	−1.74	−1.83	−1.81	−1.13	−.84
.25	−1.02	−.99	−.96	−.88	−.83	−.91	−.38	−.10

NOTE.—The number of monthly returns per replication is 720. Monthly returns are summed to get overlapping monthly observations on T-year returns, $r(t, t+T)$, $T = 1, 2, \ldots, 10$. Sampling distributions of the slopes are based on 200 replications for the 1-, 2-, 8-, and 10-year regressions and 1,000 for the 3–6-year regressions. The log price in pt. A is a random walk with normal (0, 1) monthly returns. The log price in pt. B is a heteroscedastic random walk that changes the standard deviation of the white-noise returns every 2 years to approximate variation through time in stock return variances. Specifically, in each replication, the normal (0, 1) monthly returns in nonoverlapping 2-year periods, generated for the homoscedastic random walk, are multiplied by the standard deviation of the monthly returns on the equal-weighted NYSE market portfolio for the corresponding 2-year period.

TABLE A2

SUMMARY OF SIMULATIONS WHEN PRICES HAVE AR1 AND RANDOM-WALK COMPONENTS

$r(t, t + T) = \alpha + \beta r(t - T, t) + \epsilon(t, t + T)$

	Return Horizon (Years)							
	1	2	3	4	5	6	8	10
	A. $\epsilon(t, t + T)$ Homoscedastic (Constant Variance)							
β (true)	−.10	−.17	−.22	−.25	−.27	−.27	−.28	−.27
	Mean and Standard Deviation of β (OLS and Bias-adjusted)							
$\bar{\beta}$ (OLS)	−.12	−.20	−.24	−.28	−.31	−.33	−.36	−.38
$\bar{\beta}$ (adjusted)	−.10	−.15	−.17	−.18	−.18	−.17	−.14	−.10
$s(\beta)$	.10	.11	.15	.16	.18	.19	.22	.23
	Mean and Standard Deviation of t's for Test of OLS or Bias-adjusted β = 0.0							
Mean (OLS)	−1.22	−1.55	−1.59	−1.64	−1.66	−1.71	−1.82	−1.77
Standard deviation	.99	.92	1.08	1.10	1.13	1.14	1.41	1.37
Mean (adjusted)	−1.04	−1.21	−.92	−1.08	−1.00	−.90	−.84	−.58
Standard deviation	.99	.90	1.04	1.04	1.05	1.03	1.20	1.10
	B. $\epsilon(t, t + T)$ Heteroscedastic (Changing Variance)							
β (true)	−.10	−.17	−.22	−.25	−.27	−.27	−.28	−.27

continued overleaf

	Mean and Standard Deviation of β (OLS and Bias-adjusted); Fractiles (Bias-adjusted)							
$\bar{\beta}$ (OLS)	−.12	−.19	−.24	−.27	−.30	−.31	−.30	−.28
$\bar{\beta}$ (adjusted)	−.10	−.14	−.17	−.17	−.17	−.15	−.08	.01
$s(\beta)$	.14	.16	.17	.17	.18	.19	.22	.23
Fractile:								
.01	−.44	−.51	−.51	−.51	−.52	−.52	−.55	−.48
.05	−.34	−.40	−.43	−.44	−.45	−.44	−.41	−.34
.10	−.27	−.34	−.37	−.39	−.39	−.38	−.34	−.28
.25	−.19	−.26	−.28	−.29	−.29	−.29	−.23	−.18
.50	−.10	−.14	−.17	−.18	−.18	−.17	−.13	−.03
.75	−.01	−.04	−.04	−.06	−.06	−.03	.03	.10
.90	.10	.07	.06	.06	.07	.08	.18	.30
.95	.14	.13	.12	.12	.13	.18	.34	.40
.99	.18	.21	.25	.25	.27	.32	.44	.55
	Mean and Standard Deviation of t's for Test of OLS or Bias-adjusted β = 0.0							
Mean (OLS)	−1.23	−1.54	−1.62	−1.80	−1.96	−2.01	−1.82	−1.74
Standard deviation	1.50	1.33	1.30	1.31	1.37	1.47	1.42	1.51
Mean (adjusted)	−1.04	−1.19	−1.14	−1.18	−1.17	−1.06	−.58	−.13
Standard deviation	1.49	1.30	1.24	1.23	1.24	1.30	1.28	1.34
	Mean and Standard Deviation of t's for Test of OLS or Bias-adjusted β = −0.5							
Mean (OLS)	3.74	2.17	1.59	1.29	1.11	1.03	1.13	1.28
Standard deviation	1.19	1.00	.95	.95	1.00	1.09	1.24	1.40
Mean (adjusted)	3.93	2.52	2.08	1.91	1.90	1.98	2.36	2.89
Standard deviation	1.18	.98	.91	.91	.97	1.10	1.33	1.68

NOTE.—The AR1 parameter for the stationary component of the simulated monthly returns is .975, the monthly AR1 and random-walk shocks are independent, and the AR1 shock has twice the standard deviation of the random-walk shock. The model in pt. B is a heteroscedastic version of the model in pt. A, in which the standard deviations of both the random-walk and AR1 shocks change within each replication, as described for the second random-walk model in table A1.

A2 shows that simple OLS slopes are less biased when the true slopes are negative, and bias corrections relevant when the true slopes are 0.0 produce estimates biased toward 0.0. For example, the true 5-year slope in part B of table A2 is −0.27, the average of simple OLS slopes is −0.30, and the average bias-adjusted slope is −0.17. Thus simple OLS slopes are closer to unbiased when the log price has an important AR1 component.

References

Alexander, Sidney S. "Price Movements in Speculative Markets: Trends or Random Walks." *Indus. Management Rev.* 2 (May 1961): 7–26.

Banz, Rolf W. "The Relationship between Return and Market Value of Common Stocks." *J. Financial Econ.* 9 (March 1981): 3–18.

Bodie, Zvi. "Common Stocks as a Hedge against Inflation." *J. Finance* 31 (May 1976): 459–70.

Campbell, John Y. "Stock Returns and the Term Structure." *J. Financial Econ.* 18 (June 1987): 373–400.

Cochrane, John. "How Big Is the Random Walk Component in GNP?" Mimeographed. Chicago: Univ. Chicago, Dept. Econ., April 1986.

De Bondt, Werner F. M., and Thaler, Richard. "Does the Stock Market Overreact?" *J. Finance* 40 (July 1985): 793–805.

Fama, Eugene F. "Efficient Capital Markets: A Review of Theory and Empirical Work." *J. Finance* 25 (May 1970): 383–417.

———. "Stock Returns, Real Activity, Inflation, and Money." *A.E.R.* 71 (September 1981): 545–65.

Fama, Eugene F., and French, Kenneth R. "Dividend Yields and Expected Stock Returns." Mimeographed. Chicago: Univ. Chicago, Grad. School Bus., March 1987.

Fama, Eugene F., and Schwert, G. William. "Asset Returns and Inflation." *J. Financial Econ.* 5 (November 1977): 115–46.

French, Kenneth R., and Roll, Richard. "Stock Return Variances: The Arrival of Information and the Reaction of Traders." *J. Financial Econ.* 17 (September 1986): 5–26.

French, Kenneth R.; Schwert, G. William; and Stambaugh, Robert F. "Expected Stock Returns and Volatility." *J. Financial Econ.* 19 (September 1987): 3–30.

Hansen, Lars Peter. "Large Sample Properties of Generalized Method of Moments Estimators." *Econometrica* 50 (July 1982): 1029–54.

Hansen, Lars Peter, and Hodrick, Robert J. "Forward Exchange Rates as Optimal Predictors of Future Spot Rates: An Econometric Analysis." *J.P.E.* 88 (October 1980): 829–53.

Huberman, Gur, and Kandel, Shmuel. "A Size Based Stock Returns Model." Working Paper no. 148. Chicago: Univ. Chicago, Grad. School Bus., Center Res. Security Prices, October 1985.

Huizinga, John. "Tests of Market Efficiency in Models with Multiperiod Forecasts." Mimeographed. Chicago: Univ. Chicago, Grad. School Bus., February 1984.

Jaffe, Jeffrey F., and Mandelker, Gershon. "The 'Fisher Effect' for Risky Assets: An Empirical Investigation." *J. Finance* 31 (May 1976): 447–58.

Keim, Donald B., and Stambaugh, Robert F. "Predicting Returns in the Stock and Bond Markets." *J. Financial Econ.* 17 (December 1986): 357–90.

Kendall, M. G. "Note on Bias in the Estimation of Autocorrelation." *Biometrika* 41, pts. 3, 4 (1954): 403–4.

King, Benjamin F. "Market and Industry Factors in Stock Price Behavior." *J. Bus.* 39 (January 1966): 139–90.

Lo, Andrew W., and MacKinlay, A. Craig. "Stock Market Prices Do Not Follow Random Walks: Evidence from a Simple Specification Test." Mimeographed. Philadelphia: Univ. Pennsylvania, Wharton School, December 1986.

Marriot, F. H. C., and Pope, J. A. "Bias in the Estimation of Autocorrelations." *Biometrika* 41, pts. 3, 4 (1954): 390–402.

Nelson, Charles R. "Inflation and Rates of Return on Common Stocks." *J. Finance* 31 (May 1976): 471–83.

Officer, Robert R. "The Variability of the Market Factor of the New York Stock Exchange." *J. Bus.* 46 (July 1973): 434–53.

Poterba, James M., and Summers, Lawrence. "Mean Reversion in Stock Returns: Evidence and Implications." Mimeographed. Cambridge, Mass.: NBER, March 1987.

Summers, Lawrence H. "Does the Stock Market Rationally Reflect Fundamental Values?" *J. Finance* 41 (July 1986): 591–601.

White, Halbert. "A Heteroskedasticity-Consistent Covariance Matrix Estimator and a Direct Test for Heteroskedasticity." *Econometrica* 48 (May 1980): 817–38.

[6]

ECONOMETRICA

VOLUME 49 MAY, 1981 NUMBER 3

THE PRESENT-VALUE RELATION: TESTS BASED ON IMPLIED VARIANCE BOUNDS[1]

BY STEPHEN F. LEROY AND RICHARD D. PORTER[2]

This paper investigates the implications for asset price dispersion of conventional security valuation models. Successively sharper variance bounds on asset prices are derived. Large-sample tests of the bounds are determined and applied to aggregated and disaggregated price and earnings data of U.S. corporations.

1. INTRODUCTION AND SUMMARY OF CONCLUSIONS

CONSIDER A SCALAR TIME SERIES $\{x_t\}$ which is generated jointly with a vector time series $\{\underline{z}_t\}$ as a stationary multivariate linear stochastic process. We then may define $\{y_t\}$ as another scalar time series related to $\{x_t\}$ and $\{\underline{z}_t\}$ by

$$y_t = \sum_{j=0}^{n} \beta^j x_t^e(j), \tag{1}$$

where $x_t^e(j)$ denotes $E(x_{t+j} \mid I_t)$, I_t is the realization of $\{x_t\}$ and $\{\underline{z}_t\}$ up to and including time t, and $\beta < 1$. The multivariate time series $\{x_t, \underline{z}_t\}$ may be labeled the independent-variable series, its distribution being taken as exogenous, and $\{y_t\}$ the dependent-variable series. Equation (1) is the present-value relation. It states that the distribution of the dependent-variable process is related to that of the independent-variable process in such a way that the current realization of the dependent-variable process equals the present discounted expected value of one element of the independent-variable process, (x_t), where the expectation is conditional on all information currently available.

The present-value relation is repeatedly encountered in economic theory. The most familiar application is to the theory of stock prices, where $\{x_t\}$ refers to some corporation's earnings, $\{\underline{z}_t\}$ to any variables other than past earnings which are used to predict its future earnings, $\{y_t\}$ to the price of stock, and β to the discount factor.[3] In expectations theories of the term structure of interest rates, the present-value relation also appears (with a finite upper limit in the summation in (1)), although its validity in such applications is based on a linear

[1]The analyses and conclusions set forth are those of the authors and do not necessarily indicate concurrence by other members of the research staffs, by the Board of Governors, or by the Federal Reserve Banks.

[2]We wish to thank Evelyn Flynn, Gregory Connor, Juan Perea, and Birch Lee for able assistance and William Barnett, Fischer Black, Christopher Sims, Michael Dooley, Donald Hester, Agustin Maravall, Bennett McCallum, Darrel Parke, David Pierce, William Poole, Jack Rutner, and especially Robert Shiller, and two anonymous referees for helpful criticism. Thanks are also due to Susan Fay Eubank for typing innumerable drafts.

[3]As is well known in the finance literature, the representation of stock prices as the present value of discounted earnings involves double counting if any earnings are retained, since in that case both retained earnings and the revenues generated subsequently by these retentions are counted. However, in our model the maintained hypothesis that earnings are stationary implicitly presumes no retention. In the empirical work examined below an adjustment to the data to correct for earnings retention will be required.

approximation (Shiller [**15**]). Finally, the permanent income hypothesis of Friedman [**2**] may also be cast in the framework of equation (1).

In Section 2 of the present paper we state and prove three theorems about the variance of the dependent-variable process as it relates to that of the independent-variable process. The theorems embody successively sharper restrictions on the parameters of the independent and dependent variable processes. Theorem 1 asserts that the coefficient of dispersion (i.e., the ratio of the standard deviation to the mean) of $\{y_t\}$ is less than that of $\{x_t\}$. The second theorem involves two new time series $\{\hat{y}_t\}$ and $\{y_t^*\}$ which are generated by altering the amount of information assumed available about the future innovations of $\{x_t\}$ from that implicit in the specified joint distribution of $\{x_t\}$ and $\{\underline{z}_t\}$. If it is assumed that there is no information about the future innovations in $\{x_t\}$, the derived present value series is defined to be $\{\hat{y}_t\}$. On the other hand, if the future innovations in $\{x_t\}$ are taken as known, the derived present value series is labeled $\{y_t^*\}$. The dependent-variable series of primary interest, $\{y_t\}$, is in a sense an intermediate case since the realizations of $\{\underline{z}_t\}$ may be viewed as in general providing some information about the innovations in the univariate process for $\{x_t\}$, but not complete information. Theorem 2 exploits this fact, asserting that the variances of $\{\hat{y}_t\}$ and $\{y_t^*\}$ constitute lower and upper bounds, respectively, on the variance of $\{y_t\}$. Theorem 3, unlike Theorems 1 and 2 which state that the variance of $\{y_t\}$ lies within an interval, is the basis for an asymptotic point test of the null hypothesis defined by the present-value relation. If $\{\pi_t\}$ is defined as the present value of the forecast errors for $\{x_t\}$, we show that $\text{var}(y_t) + \text{var}(\pi_t) = \text{var}(y_t^*)$. Theorem 3 asserts that the three terms of this variance decomposition can all be estimated from observations on x_t and y_t and, therefore, forms the basis for a large-sample test of the present-value equation.

These theorems furnish a basis for constructing tests of the validity of the present-value relation. Such theorems are necessary because the present-value relation cannot be tested directly without also specifying the variables $\underline{z}_t$ used to predict x_t and then determining the joint distribution of $\{x_t, \underline{z}_t\}$, since in the absence of such a procedure the $x_t^e(j)$ are not measurable. Consequently, direct tests of the present-value relation are always conditional on the specification of the set of variables used to predict x_t, and the difficulty of specifying these variables exhaustively greatly weakens the plausibility of any conclusions based on such direct tests. By contrast, our three theorems are valid for general specifications of the joint distribution of $\{x_t, \underline{z}_t\}$, and do not require identification of the distribution of $\{x_t, \underline{z}_t\}$, or even specification of what the variables $\underline{z}_t$ are. Thus even though we do not measure the expectations $x_t^e(j)$ or the discounted forecast errors π_t, our theorems constitute testable implications of the present-value relation. The fact that the maintained assumptions required for our indirect tests are so much weaker than those required for the direct tests adds to the appeal of our results. Statistical tests of the three theorems are derived in Section 3.

In Section 4 we consider the application of our results to the theory of stock prices. First it is shown that the efficient capital markets hypothesis as conventionally formulated implies (and is implied by) the present-value relation between earnings and stock prices. Consequently, the hypothesis of capital market efficiency implies the validity of the theorems, and the latter may therefore be used to construct tests of market efficiency. That capital market efficiency implies restrictions on the volatility of stock prices is at first surprising because the most commonly-cited implication of market efficiency is that stock prices should move instantaneously rather than gradually in response to news. However, the result that if markets are efficient the coefficient of dispersion of stock prices should be less than that of earnings (Theorem 1) makes sense if it is observed that the present-value equation defines stock prices as a kind of weighted average of earnings, and an average is generally less volatile than its components. Another consideration strengthens this conclusion. Since stock prices are an average of expected rather than actual earnings, and since expected earnings can plausibly be assumed to regress toward a mean (correcting for trend) in the increasingly distant future, it follows that expected earnings should show less dispersion than actual earnings, further reducing the anticipated dispersion of stock prices.

Our first data set is based on Standard & Poor's Composite Index of stock prices and the related earnings and dividends series. The observations are quarterly over the interval 1955 to 1973, and the data are corrected for trend.[4] The estimated coefficients of dispersion of earnings and stock prices are 0.172 and 0.452, indicating that the inequality of Theorem 1 is contradicted (Table III). The point estimates on which the tests of Theorems 2 and 3 are based imply an even more flagrant violation of the model; for example, the estimated variance of y_t is 4.89, whereas the estimated variance of y_t^*, which theoretically should exceed that of y_t, is 0.255. These results, while dramatic, are difficult to interpret in the absence of any indication of the reliability of the test statistics. To provide such an indication, we calculated formal tests based on the asymptotic distribution of the parameter estimates, as described in Section 3. Because the test statistics measuring departures from the null hypothesis are all insignificant, the derived confidence intervals suggest that our statistical tests may have very little power.

The outcome of these tests may reflect the fact that they are based on aggregate data, whereas the theory applies to individual firms; a simple argument (presented in detail in Section 2) demonstrates the possible existence of bias in our tests due to aggregation error across firms. If the earnings of each firm consist of a common factor and an individual uncorrelated term, and if the common factor is forecastable whereas the individual term is not, then our tests will be biased in favor of rejection of market efficiency. In the reverse case, our tests will be biased in favor of acceptance. We do not know which case, if either, is more plausible than the intermediate case under which these biases approximately cancel, but the example provides strong motivation to examine data for individual firms. We collected quarterly earnings and price data for three large

[4]For a detailed description of the data, the complete derivation of the statistical tests, and for the data themselves, see LeRoy and Porter [**9**]; this paper is available upon request from the authors.

corporations—American Telephone & Telegraph, General Electric, and General Motors—then adjusted them for trend in the same way as the aggregate data, and calculated the test statistics for the three theorems.

The empirical results for the firm data show, as might be expected, that sharper hypotheses are more often rejected than blunt hypotheses. The point estimates for the tests of Theorem 1 were somewhat closer to being consistent with the null hypothesis of market efficiency for the individual firms than for the aggregate data. For one firm (GM) the coefficient of dispersion of earnings exceeded that of stock prices, as implied by the theory, while for another (GE) the two were virtually identical. Only AT&T was similar to the aggregate data in that earnings were considerably less volatile than stock prices, although for AT&T as with the aggregate data the test statistic did not allow rejection of the null hypothesis of Theorem 1 at the usual significance levels. Contrary to the implication of Theorem 2, however, the variance of y_t exceeded that of y_t^* by a wide margin for each of the three firms as with the aggregate data. Further, the relevant test statistic was significant for one firm (GE) and of borderline significance for another (GM), although it was insignificant for the third (AT&T). Finally, the test statistics for the more restrictive Theorem 3 all indicated rejection of the null hypothesis at the one per cent level.

Comparison of the results for the three firms with those for the Standard & Poor's series gives no clear reason to suspect that aggregation over firms biases aggregate tests either way, although, of course, this conclusion is not unequivocal since the Standard & Poor's series cannot be viewed as a simple aggregate of the three firms alone. As with the aggregate data, the point estimates for the firms are not consistent with the efficient markets model, although they are somewhat closer to those expected from theory than those for the aggregate data. However, the confidence intervals for the firms are more prone to indicate rejection of the null hypothesis; the smaller confidence regions for the firm data suggest that tests based on firm data may be somewhat more powerful than those for aggregate data.

We see that based on both aggregated and disaggregated data, stock prices appear to be more volatile than is consistent with the efficient capital markets model. This conclusion differs from that of most studies of market efficiency, such as that of Fama [**1**]. In many studies of market efficiency, it is observed that the martingale assumption requires that measured rates of return be serially uncorrelated; consequently, the efficient capital markets model may be tested by determining whether it is possible to reject the joint hypothesis that all the autocorrelations of rates of return are zero. Typically this null hypothesis cannot be rejected at the usual significance levels; we show this to be the case also for the rates of return earned on the stock of our three firms. Since these tests of the nonautocorrelatedness of rates of return are derivable consequences of the same model used to generate our variance restrictions, we are led to inquire why the nonautocorrelatedness implication is apparently satisfied, whereas the variance implications are not. Although it is possible that the difference in the outcomes of the dispersion and autocorrelation tests is due to differing sensitivity to specification or measurement error, an explanation that appears more attractive to us is that the dispersion tests have greater power than the autocorrelation tests against the hypothesis of market efficiency, given that alternative hypothesis which actually generated the data. This argument suggests that a promising way to investigate the stock market would be to ascertain what kinds of structures in earnings and prices would lead to deviations from market efficiency that would be more readily detected by a dispersion test than by an autocorrelation test. We have not yet pursued this line, however.

It is not clear how to interpret our rejection of the hypothesis we have characterized as "market efficiency." It should be recognized that our theorems are actually tests of a joint hypothesis, some elements of which have only tenuous support. The most important elements in our joint hypothesis are (i) the present-value relation (or, in the stock market application, the equivalent martingale assumption), (ii) the assumption that the real conditional expected rate of return on stock is constant over time, and (iii) the assumption of rational expectations. If our tests are not subject to econometric or measurement difficulties, then our rejection of the theorems implies that one or more of these elements of the joint hypothesis must be rejected. There is no reason to doubt that with further work it will be possible to distinguish which of the components of the rejected joint hypothesis must be revised.

In an important recent paper, Shiller **[16]** has independently derived and conducted tests of expectations models of the term structure of interest rates based on implied restrictions on the admissible dispersion of long rates relative to short. These restrictions are similar to our Theorems 1 and 2; in addition, Shiller obtained some important frequency-domain implications of the model. Although Shiller's tests, unlike ours, are based on point estimates rather than confidence intervals, implying that there is no way to determine statistical significance, he finds that the expectations model of the term structure appears to be violated, long rates being too volatile relative to short rates. The fact that Shiller's results on interest rates so closely parallel ours on stock prices suggests that neither set of results can be dismissed as a statistical accident. Rather, in our view, the fact that asset prices appear to fluctuate more than is consistent with most financial models in current use should be regarded as a major challenge to those models. As yet, however, it is impossible to determine what changes in financial theory may turn out to be necessary to accommodate our results and those of Shiller.

2. THREE THEOREMS ON THE VARIANCE OF THE DEPENDENT-VARIABLE PROCESS[5]

It is assumed that the $p \times 1$ vector $\{x_t, \underline{z}_t\}$ follows a multivariate linearly regular stationary stochastic process:

$$(2) \quad \begin{bmatrix} x_t \\ \underline{z}_t \end{bmatrix} = \underline{c} + \underline{\epsilon}_t + D_1 \underline{\epsilon}_{t-1} + D_2 \underline{\epsilon}_{t-2} + \cdots = \underline{c} + D(B)\underline{\epsilon}_t,$$

[5]In the remainder of this paper we let the upper limit (n) in the summation in (1) be infinite, as is appropriate for application to the stock market.

where the innovations sequence $\{\underline{\epsilon}_t\}$ is a set of serially uncorrelated vector random variables with zero mean and positive definite covariance matrix Σ, where $\underline{c}$ is a $p \times 1$ vector, the D_i are square matrices of order p, and where B is the lag operator, defined by $B^j \epsilon_t = \epsilon_{t-j}$.[6] If we delete all but the first element of the vector equation (2), we obtain

$$(3) \qquad x_t = c + \underline{\delta}_0' \underline{\epsilon}_t + \underline{\delta}_1' \underline{\epsilon}_{t-1} + \cdots = c + \underline{\delta}'(B)\underline{\epsilon}_t,$$

where c is the first element of $\underline{c}$ and $\underline{\delta}_i'$ is the first row of D_i.[7] We incur no loss of generality by ignoring the distribution of $\underline{z}$ since the information content of current and past values of $\underline{z}$ is contained in the current and past values of $\underline{\epsilon}$, which are known. The conditional expected future values of x are given by

$$(4) \qquad x_t^e(j) = c + \underline{\delta}'_j \underline{\epsilon}_t + \underline{\delta}'_{j+1} \underline{\epsilon}_{t-1} + \cdots .$$

In general, the forecasts $x_t^e(j)$ depend on the $\underline{z}_t$ as well as the x_t, since both are needed to construct the lagged $\underline{\epsilon}_t$. In this case the series $\{\underline{z}_t\}$ is said to be a leading indicator of $\{x_t\}$, in Pierce's [11] usage; see also Granger [3]. In the special case in which all the elements of $\underline{\delta}_j$ are zero except the first, efficient forecasts of $\{x_t\}$ can be constructed from past realizations of $\{x_t\}$ alone since in that case $\{\underline{z}_t\}$ is not a leading indicator of $\{x_t\}$. In this special case $\underline{\epsilon}_t$ and $\underline{\delta}_j$ can be taken as scalars without loss of generality. More generally, when $\underline{z}_t$ is a leading indicator of x_t, we can express the dependent-variable series in terms of the (vector) innovations in the independent-variable series. By substituting (4) into (1), it is easily verified that we have

$$(5) \qquad y_t = \frac{c}{1-\beta} + \sum_{j=0}^{\infty} \left[\sum_{k=j}^{\infty} \beta^{k-j} \underline{\delta}'_k \right] \underline{\epsilon}_{t-j} \equiv \frac{c}{1-\beta} + \underline{a}'(B)\underline{\epsilon}_t,$$

where $\underline{a}_j' = \sum_{k=j}^{\infty} \beta^{k-j} \underline{\delta}_k'$.

We now state and prove the three theorems restricting the variance of $\{y_t\}$.

THEOREM 1: *The coefficient of dispersion of* $\{y_t\}$ *is less than that of* $\{x_t\}$ *for any distribution obeying* (2).

The proof of Theorem 1 is most conveniently presented later. At this point, it is useful to consider a special case in order to render Theorem 1 as intuitive as possible. Suppose that $\{\underline{z}_t\}$ is not a leading indicator of $\{x_t\}$ and that $\{x_t\}$ is distributed by a first-order autoregressive process,

$$x_t - c = \phi(x_{t-1} - c) + \epsilon_t, \qquad |\phi| < 1,$$

which has the moving-average representation

$$x_t = c + \epsilon_t + \phi\epsilon_{t-1} + \phi^2\epsilon_{t-2} + \cdots .$$

[6] $D(B) = D_0 + D_1 B + D_2 B^2 + \cdots$, with $D_0 = I$.

[7] That is, $\delta(B) = \underline{\delta}_0 + \underline{\delta}_1 B + \underline{\delta}_2 B^2 + \cdots$ where $\underline{\delta}_0' = (1, 0, 0, \ldots, 0)$. See Rozanov [12] or Hannan [4] for a general discussion of the statistical properties of (2).

It is easily verified that the ratio of the coefficients of dispersion takes the simple form

$$\frac{CD(y_t)}{CD(x_t)} = \frac{1-\beta}{1-\beta\phi}, \tag{6}$$

which is always less than one since β is bounded by zero and one. Equation (6) shows that the lower ϕ is and the higher β is, the lower will be the ratio of the coefficients of dispersion. The reason is that if ϕ is near zero, expected x_t regresses rapidly toward the trend value c, which means that y_t is approximately equal to current x_t plus the discounted value of a series of constants. The addition of constants to x_t raises the mean of y_t without increasing its standard deviation, thereby lowering its coefficient of dispersion. Similarly, if β is near 1, relatively more weight is given to future expected x_t than to current x_t, compared to the case when β is near zero. Since for any value of ϕ expected future x_t has less dispersion than current x_t, the effect of larger values of β is to lower the ratio of the coefficients of dispersion.

Depending on the actual distribution of $\{x_t\}$, the test implied by Theorem 1 may not be very powerful statistically. Thus, if β is near one in the population and the distribution of $\{x_t\}$ incorporates strong damping, the efficient markets model might imply that the coefficient of dispersion of $\{y_t\}$ is a small fraction of that of $\{x_t\}$, say, one-quarter. In that case, the test implied by Theorem 1 that the ratio of coefficients of dispersion is less than unity would with high probability indicate acceptance of the null hypothesis even when it should be rejected (for example, if in the population the ratio of coefficients of dispersion were 1/2 or 3/4). Again, it is impossible to test this conjecture directly without knowledge of the joint distribution of $\{x_t\}$ and $\{\underline{z}_t\}$. We seek to derive restrictions on the dispersion of $\{y_t\}$ stronger than those implied by Theorem 1, but still without specifying the distribution of $\{\underline{z}_t\}$.

To do so we observe that so far we have used only one function of the parameters of the marginal distribution of $\{x_t\}$: its coefficient of dispersion. It might be expected that stronger restrictions on the behavior of $\{y_t\}$ could be derived if all the parameters of the distribution of $\{x_t\}$ were employed. To show that this is in fact possible we consider once again the general leading indicator case under which there exist variables $\underline{z}_t$ which figure in the forecasts of future x_t, but which do not predict x_t perfectly. Now fix the marginal distribution of $\{x_t\}$ and consider two polar cases: one under which there exist variables $\underline{z}_t$ which in addition to past x_t allow perfect forecasting of x_t, and the other in which $\{\underline{z}_t\}$ is not a leading indicator of $\{x_t\}$ (i.e., in which there are no variables other than lagged x_t which assist in the forecasting of future x_t). Define $\{y_t^*\}$ and $\{\hat{y}_t\}$ as the series generated when the present-value relation operates on $\{x_t\}$ in each of these cases, and note that the distributions of these hypothetical price variables, unlike that of $\{y_t\}$, are completely determined by the marginal distribution of $\{x_t\}$.

THEOREM 2: *When $\underline{z}_t$ is a leading indicator of $\{x_t\}$ the coefficient of dispersion of $\{y_t\}$ is greater than or equal to that of $\{\hat{y}_t\}$, and less than that of $\{y_t^*\}$.*[8]

Theorem 2 gives bounds on the variance of any series $\{y_t\}$ that is generated by some joint distribution of x_t and $\underline{z}_t$, and these bounds can be calculated from the marginal distribution of $\{x_t\}$ alone, implying that, as required, the general leading indicator case be tested without actually estimating the joint distribution of $\{x_t\}$ and $\{\underline{z}_t\}$.

The proof of Theorem 2 is direct. By definition, y_t^* is expressible as

$$y_t^* = x_t + \beta x_{t+1} + \beta^2 x_{t+2} + \cdots . \tag{7}$$

Now define π_t, the discounted value of forecast errors, as

$$\pi_t = \sum_{j=1}^{\infty} \beta^j (x_{t+j} - x_t^e(j)), \tag{8}$$

where the $x_t^e(j)$ are the forecasts made under the general leading indicator model, as before. Then we have

$$y_t^* = y_t + \pi_t.$$

Now y_t depends only on the innovations in x_t and $\underline{z}_t$ up to and including period t, while π_t depends only on the innovations occurring after period t. Accordingly, they are statistically independent, and we have

$$\text{var}(y_t^*) = \text{var}(y_t) + \text{var}(\pi_t). \tag{9}$$

Equation (9) shows that the higher the variance of the discounted sum of forecast errors, the lower the variance of $\{y_t\}$. Consequently, the variance of $\{y_t^*\}$ provides an upper bound for the variance of $\{y_t\}$. Also, assuming as throughout that the information set always contains at least the past history of $\{x_t\}$, the variance of $\{\hat{y}_t\}$ furnishes a lower bound for the variance of $\{y_t\}$, since the presence of forecasting variables $\underline{z}_t$ in the information set can never increase the variance of discounted forecasting errors. Stating this conclusion in terms of coefficients of dispersion, we have

$$CD(\hat{y}_t) \leqslant CD(y_t) < CD(y_t^*).$$

Note that the right-hand side strict inequality follows from the fact that the model is one in which uncertainty cannot be entirely eliminated.

[8] As Singleton [18] observed, the proof to follow applies without modification in the case when y_t is given by

$$\sum_{k=1}^{K} \sum_{j=0}^{\infty} \beta_k^j x_{kt}^e(j), \tag{1'}$$

that is, when y_t is the sum of K terms of the form of (1). Since this vector extension is immediate, our proof is restricted to the case $K = 1$. Note also that in economic applications of the present-value relation discussed in this paper, equation (1) is sufficiently general.

We are now in a position to prove Theorem 1. By virtue of Theorem 2, it is sufficient to show that the coefficient of dispersion of $\{y_t^*\}$ is less than that of $\{x_t\}$. But that result may be developed directly from equation (7). We have

$$\operatorname{var}(y_t^*) = E\left[(x_t - c) + \beta(x_{t+1} - c) + \beta^2(x_{t+2} - c) + \cdots\right]^2$$

or

$$\operatorname{var}(y_t^*) = \frac{1}{1-\beta^2}\left[\gamma_x(0) + 2\beta\gamma_x(1) + 2\beta^2\gamma_x(2) + \cdots\right], \tag{10}$$

where $\gamma_x(i) \equiv$ covariance (x_t, x_{t-i}) for all t. From the Cauchy-Schwartz inequality and stationarity, $\gamma_x(i) < \gamma_x(0)$ if $i > 0$, so

$$\operatorname{var}(y_t^*) < \gamma_x(0)\left[\frac{1}{1-\beta^2} + \frac{2\beta}{(1-\beta)(1-\beta^2)}\right] = \frac{\gamma_x(0)}{(1-\beta)^2}. \tag{11}$$

From (11) it follows immediately that

$$\frac{\sqrt{\gamma_y^*(0)}}{c/(1-\beta)} < \frac{\sqrt{\gamma_x(0)}}{c}.$$

THEOREM 3: *When $\{\underline{z}_t\}$ is a leading indicator of $\{x_t\}$, the variance of $\{y_t^*\}$ is equal to the variance of $\{y_t\}$ plus the variance of $\{\pi_t\}$, the discounted forecast error. Further, all these variances may be estimated directly using only measurements on $\{x_t\}$ and $\{y_t\}$.*[9]

We have already proved the first part of Theorem 3 (see equation (9)). Thus the significant assertion of Theorem 3 is that equation (9) may be used to construct a point test of the efficient markets model which can be applied without specifying the variables $\underline{z}_t$ and estimating their joint distribution with x_t. This is not obvious since the forecasts $x_t^e(j)$ which are used to calculate the π_t are not directly observable, nor can they be calculated without knowledge of the joint distribution of $\{\underline{z}_t\}$ and $\{x_t\}$. However, it happens that even though π_t is not directly observable, its variance can be calculated from the distribution of $\{x_t\}$ and $\{y_t\}$ alone, and this is the content of Theorem 3.

To show this, substitute (3) and (4) into (8) to obtain

$$\pi_t = \beta\underline{\delta}_0'\underline{\epsilon}_{t+1} + \beta^2(\underline{\delta}_0'\underline{\epsilon}_{t+2} + \underline{\delta}_1'\underline{\epsilon}_{t+1})$$
$$+ \beta^3(\underline{\delta}_0'\underline{\epsilon}_{t+3} + \underline{\delta}_1'\underline{\epsilon}_{t+2} + \underline{\delta}_2'\underline{\epsilon}_{t+1}) + \cdots.$$

[9] Singleton [**18**] also obtained a vector extension of Theorem 3; see footnote 8 supra. His extension, however, assumes that the $\beta_k (k = 1, 2, \ldots K)$ are known, whereas in our model β is estimable.

Collecting terms, squaring, and taking expectations gives

$$\text{(12)} \qquad \operatorname{var}(\pi_t) = \frac{\beta^2 \underline{a}_0' \Sigma \underline{a}_0}{1-\beta^2},$$

where $\underline{a}_0$ is as defined in (5). Although $\underline{a}_0$ is not directly estimable, its weighted length is. Equation (5) may be used to derive

$$\text{(13)} \qquad \underline{a}_0' \underline{\epsilon}_{t+1} = y_{t+1} + \frac{x_t - y_t}{\beta},$$

from which we calculate an expression for $\underline{a}_0' \Sigma \underline{a}_0$:

$$\text{(14)} \qquad \underline{a}_0' \Sigma \underline{a}_0 = \operatorname{var}\left[y_{t+1} + 1/\beta(x_t - y_t) \right].$$

Since Σ is positive definite, $\operatorname{var}(\pi_t) > 0$. Combining equations (12) and (14), we have

$$\text{(15)} \qquad \operatorname{var}(\pi_t) = \frac{\operatorname{var}(\beta y_{t+1} + x_t - y_t)}{1-\beta^2}$$

which is directly measurable. Since the variances of $\{\hat{y}_t\}$ and $\{y_t^*\}$ are functions of β and a univariate representation for $\{x_t\}$, they are, of course, directly estimable from observations on x_t and y_t.[10]

The theorems just proved apply to individual firms; can they be tested on cross-section averages? A simple example[11] shows that aggregation bias may be a problem, depending on the covariance of x_{it} among firms and on the assumption made about the forecastability of x_{it}. Suppose that x_{it} depends linearly on a common factor z_t, which is perfectly forecastable, and a white noise term w_{it}:

$$x_{it} = \alpha(z_t + w_{it}).$$

Further, suppose that w_{it} is independent across firms, is independent of z_t, has common variance across firms, and is not forecastable. Since the forecastable component of each x_{it} is identical across firms, we have $CD(y_t) = CD(y_{it})$ for all i, as is readily verified. However, upon aggregation, the cancellation of the white noise terms, w_{it}, implies that $CD(y_t^*) < CD(y_{it}^*)$ for all i. If $CD(y_t^*)$ were viewed as an estimate of $CD(y_{it}^*)$, it would be biased toward zero, and a test of the null hypothesis, $CD(y_{it}) < CD(y_{it}^*)$ based on the inequality $CD(y_t) < CD(y_t^*)$ would be biased toward rejection. More generally, the example suggests that our tests will be biased toward rejection if the common component of x_{it} is more forecastable than the independent components. We do not know if this assumption is more reasonable than its opposite, in which case our tests are biased

[10] Observe that $E(x_t) = c$ and $E(y_t) = c/(1-\beta)$ so that β may be readily estimated from the means of the two observed processes.

[11] We are indebted to a referee for this example.

toward acceptance. However, since we do not wish to prejudge the question by presuming that the two components are equally forecastable, as must be implicitly assumed under tests based on aggregated data, we are motivated to conduct our tests on both disaggregated and aggregated data, and thereby to avoid the issue of aggregation error.

3. TEST STATISTICS

The three theorems developed in Section 2 impose nonlinear restrictions on the expected value and autocovariance function of the bivariate process for x_t and y_t. To restate these restrictions in a way that is convenient for testing, we first define

$$\gamma_{xy}(k) = E\left[(x_t - c)(y_{t-k} - c/(1-\beta))\right] \tag{16}$$

for $k = 0, \pm 1, \pm 2$, and so forth. Theorem 1 states that

$$f_1 > 0, \tag{17}$$

where

$$f_1 = \frac{\left[\gamma_x(0)\right]^{1/2}}{c} - \frac{\left[\gamma_y(0)\right]^{1/2}}{c/(1-\beta)}. \tag{18}$$

Theorem 3 imposes the restriction

$$f_3 = 0, \tag{19}$$

where

$$\begin{aligned} f_3 &= \gamma_y^*(0) - \gamma_y(0) - \gamma_\pi(0) \\ &= \frac{1}{1-\beta^2}\left[\gamma_x(0) + 2\sum_{j=1}^{\infty} \beta^j \gamma_x(j)\right] - \gamma_y(0) \\ &\quad - \frac{1}{1-\beta^2}\left[(1+\beta^2)\gamma_y(0) + \gamma_x(0) + 2\beta\gamma_{xy}(-1) - 2\beta\gamma_y(1) - 2\gamma_{xy}(0)\right], \end{aligned} \tag{20}$$

in view of (10) and (15). The upper bound in Theorem 2 may be written as

$$f_2^u > 0, \tag{21}$$

where

$$\begin{aligned} f_2^u &= \frac{\left[\gamma_{y^*}(0)\right]^{1/2}}{c/(1-\beta)} - \frac{\left[\gamma_y(0)\right]^{1/2}}{c/(1-\beta)} \\ &= \frac{(1-\beta)}{c(1-\beta^2)^{1/2}}\left[\gamma_x(0) + \sum_{k=1}^{\infty} 2\beta^k \gamma_x(k)\right]^{1/2} - \frac{\left[\gamma_y(0)\right]^{1/2}}{c/(1-\beta)}. \end{aligned} \tag{22}$$

Finally, the lower bound restriction in Theorem 2 is

$$(23)\qquad f_2^l \geqslant 0,$$

where

$$(24)\qquad f_2^l = \frac{[\gamma_{y}(0)]^{1/2}}{c/(1-\beta)} - \frac{[\gamma_{\hat{y}}(0)]^{1/2}}{c/(1-\beta)}$$

and

$$\gamma_{\hat{y}}(0) = \sum_{j=0}^{\infty}\left[\sum_{k=j}^{\infty}\beta^{k-j}b_k\right]^2\sigma_v^2$$

where σ_v^2 and $b(B)(=1+b_1B+b_2B^2+\cdots)$ may be obtained by factoring the autocovariance generating function of $\{x_t\}$.[12]

Large-sample tests of the nonlinear restrictions in (17), (19), (21), and (23) on the functions in (18), (20), (22), and (24), respectively, may be constructed in a straightforward manner. First, a bivariate stationary and invertible ARMA representation for x and y is specified.[13] To estimate the ARMA model parameters, Wilson's **[20]** quasi-maximum likelihood algorithm is used except that the means are estimated first and then treated as if they are known.[14] The form of the estimated model is thus

$$\begin{bmatrix}\phi_{11}(B) & \phi_{12}(B)\\ \phi_{21}(B) & \phi_{22}(B)\end{bmatrix}\begin{bmatrix}x_t-\bar{x}\\ y_t-\bar{y}\end{bmatrix} = \begin{bmatrix}\theta_{11}(B) & \theta_{12}(B)\\ \theta_{21}(B) & \theta_{22}(B)\end{bmatrix}\underline{\zeta}_t,$$

where $\phi_{ij}(B)$ and $\theta_{ij}(B)$ are polynomials of order p_{ij} and q_{ij}, respectively,

$$\phi_{ij}(B) = k_{ij} - \sum_{s=1}^{p_{ij}}\phi_{ij,s}B^s,$$

$$\theta_{ij}(B) = k_{ij} - \sum_{s=1}^{q_{ij}}\theta_{ij,s}B^s,$$

[12] That is, σ_v^2 and $b(B)$ are solutions to

$$\sigma_v^2 b(B)b(B^{-1}) = \sum_{j=-\infty}^{\infty}\gamma_x(j)B^j.$$

[13] See Wilson **[19** and **20]** for a description of multiple ARMA models. From (3) and (5) it will be seen that the bivariate process for y and x is a linear regular stationary process so that there exists an infinite order moving average representation (Wold decomposition). We assume that this representation can be approximated by a finite parameter bivariate ARMA representation; see Sims **[17]** for a proof that rational functions provide a mean square approximation to such linear regular processes. We also assume that under the alternative hypothesis, x and y are generated by a linear regular process which can be approximated as under the null hypothesis by a finite parameter ARMA model.

[14] Wilson's procedure maximizes the logarithm of the likelihood function under a normality assumption concerning the error, neglecting effects of initial conditions. The sample means x and y are used to estimate the population means c and $c/(1-\beta)$, respectively.

$k_{ij} = 1$ if $i = j$ and is 0 otherwise, and $\{\underline{\zeta}_t\}$ is a set of serially uncorrelated bivariate random variables with zero mean and covariance matrix V. Let $\underline{\omega}$ be the vector of ARMA parameters (including intercepts and distinct elements of V) with $\hat{\underline{\omega}}$ denoting the estimate of $\underline{\omega}$. Under general conditions $\hat{\underline{\omega}}$ is asymptotically normally distributed with mean $\underline{\omega}$ and covariance matrix Ω.[15] Next, given $\hat{\underline{\omega}}$ and an estimate of Ω, the associated function $f_i(\underline{\omega})$, i.e., the functions in (18), (20), (22), and (24), and its asymptotic standard error may be evaluated. Since each of the test functions, f_i, is continuous, the ratio of $f_i(\hat{\underline{\omega}})$ to its estimated asymptotic standard error will have a $N(0, 1)$ distribution under the null hypothesis. That is,

$$\sqrt{T}(f_i(\hat{\underline{\omega}}) - f_i(\underline{\omega})) \rightarrow N(0, \underline{j}_i'\Omega \underline{j}_i),$$

where

$$\underline{j}_i = \frac{\partial f_i(\underline{\omega})}{\partial \underline{\omega}}$$

and T denotes the sample size.

4. APPLICATION TO THE EFFICIENT MARKETS MODEL OF STOCK PRICES

The efficient markets model may be characterized by the restriction that the (real) rate of return on stock $\{r_t\}$ is a time series obeying the relation

$$(25) \qquad E(r_t \mid I_t) = \rho$$

for all I_t, where ρ is a positive constant. This relation is the basis for most empirical tests of market efficiency, since it implies that no information contained in I_t is of any assistance in predicting future expected rates of return.[16] The analytical justification for identifying such a restriction with some economic notion of market efficiency, such as Pareto-optimal resource allocation or costless dissemination of information, is not immediate. This point is not pursued here; see, however, LeRoy **[6, 7, 8]**, Lucas **[10]**, Rubinstein **[13]**, and Woodward **[21]** for discussion. If all (real) earnings on stock x_t are paid out in dividends and the payout is assumed to occur at the beginning of the period, the rate of return

[15] See LeRoy and Porter **[9]** for a detailed examination of the conditions and our estimate of the Ω based on $\hat{\omega}$. We assume that the fourth cumulants of ζ_t are zero in estimating the covariance matrix of V.

[16] In Fama's review article on the efficient capital markets theory **[1]**, the efficient markets model when $\{\underline{z}_t\}$ is a leading indicator of x_t is termed the semi-strong-form constant-return model, while the case in which $\underline{z}_t$ is the empty set is called the weak-form constant return model. In his context, the terminology is appropriate since it appears to be natural to view a model in which the expected return is constant conditional on the broader set of information as involving a stronger restriction on reality. Here, however, these usages would be misleading since in fact neither model is generally a special case of the other. Further, we will derive results that apply over all multivariate stationary earnings distributions, and therefore a fortiori over all distributions in which $\underline{z}_t$ is not a leading indicator. Thus in Fama's terminology, some of our weak-form results follow as a special case of the strong-form results. We see that Fama's definition, while analytically equivalent to our usage, would be misleading in the present context.

is

$$r_t = \frac{y_{t+1}}{y_t - x_t} - 1, \tag{26}$$

where y_t is the (real) price of stock. Taking expectations conditional on I_t and using (25), this becomes

$$y_t = x_t + \frac{y_t^e(1)}{1+\rho}.$$

Repeating this procedure and assuming convergence, we obtain the present-value relation (1), with $\beta = (1+\rho)^{-1}$.[17]

The fact that stock prices are expressible as the present value of expected earnings means that the theorems derived in Section 2 are consequences of capital market efficiency as defined by (25). These results provide insights into the functions of capital markets that are interesting and not altogether obvious. For example, Theorem 1 says that the coefficient of dispersion of stock prices is necessarily less than that of earnings; this fact was noted and interpreted in the introduction. Additionally, equations (9), (13), and (15) show that the greater the accuracy with which individuals are able to forecast earnings, the higher the variance of stock prices, but the lower the variance of the rate of return on stock. These results are surprisingly powerful considering the generality with which the distribution of earnings has been specified. However, our primary interest is in constructing statistical tests of market efficiency, and not in providing extended interpretation of the properties of efficient markets, so we turn now to the empirical implementation.

Earnings and price data for Standard & Poor's Composite Index, AT&T, GE, and GM were assembled, and an attempt was made to correct for trends induced by inflation and earnings retention.[18] The question remains whether the resulting

[17] This argument, of course, does no more than motivate the connection between equation (25) defining an efficient capital market and the present-value relation. A formal derivation is found in Samuelson [**14**]. Note that even though under certainty the present-value relation is an immediate consequence of the definition of the rate of return, under uncertainty the strong restriction (25) on the distribution of rates of return is required in order to derive the present-value relation from the definition of the rate of return. Under general conditions of uncertainty (i.e., without assuming (25)), the present-value relation does not obtain.

[18] To correct for inflation, we divided all variables by the GNP deflator. The correction for retained earnings was somewhat more involved. First, we calculated a new variable, k_t, which may be viewed as a quantity index of the physical capital to which corporate equity is title. This index was assumed to equal unity at the initial time period and was augmented in proportion to the amount of retained corporate earnings in each quarter:

$$k_t = \begin{cases} 1, & t = 1, \\ k_{t-1} + \dfrac{E_t - D_t}{P_0}, & t = 2, 3, \ldots, \end{cases}$$

where E_t is real earnings, D_t is real dividends, and P_t is real stock value. Finally, the adjusted earnings and equity value series, x_t and y_t, were calculated by dividing the actual earnings and equity value series by k_t:

$$x_t = E_t / k_t, \qquad y_t = P_t / k_t.$$

See LeRoy and Porter [**9**] for the original data and adjusted series.

series can be assumed to obey the stationarity requirement. There appears to be some evidence of downward trends, although they are not clearly significant. We have decided to neglect such evidence and simply assume that the series are stationary since otherwise it is necessary to address such difficult questions as ascertaining to what degree stockholders can be assumed to have foreseen the assumed trend in earnings. It seems preferable to assume instead that there exist long cycles in the earnings series, implying that a sample of only a few decades may well appear nonstationary. On this interpretation, no correction for nonstationarity is indicated, but we must expect that, as with any statistical test based on a small sample, high Type II error will occur. We do not argue that this treatment is entirely adequate, nor do we in any way minimize the problem of nonstationarity; the dependence of our results on the assumption of stationarity is probably their single most severe limitation.

Table I presents the bivariate ARMA estimates for the four different data sets as well as the large-sample standard errors.[19] Table II shows the chi-square statistics $C(i, j)$ for the overall adequacy of the bivariate model.[20] The results in Table II suggest that the overall specification is adequate. The lefthand panel of Table III displays estimates of the four statistics f_1, f_2^l, f_2^u, and f_3, and of the asymptotic standardized normal ratios (z ratios) for f_1, f_2^u, and f_3, namely:

$$z_1 = f_1 \Big/ \left(\hat{\underline{j}}_1' \left(\frac{1}{T} \right) \hat{\Omega} \hat{\underline{j}}_1 \right)^{1/2}, \qquad z_2^u = f_2^u \Big/ \left(\hat{\underline{j}}_2^{u\prime} \left(\frac{1}{T} \right) \hat{\Omega} \hat{\underline{j}}_2^u \right)^{1/2},$$

$$z_3 = f_3 \Big/ \left(\hat{\underline{j}}_3' \left(\frac{1}{T} \right) \hat{\Omega} \hat{\underline{j}}_3 \right)^{1/2}.$$ [21]

The middle and right panels of Table III present estimates of the variance and coefficients of dispersion, respectively, of y_t, $\hat{y}_t$, y_t^*, and π_t. For GM the coefficient of dispersion of earnings exceeds that of prices, as required by Theorem 1. However, for GE the two statistics are virtually identical, while for AT&T and the Standard & Poor's Index the coefficients of dispersion of prices are several times higher that those of earnings. Despite these apparently pronounced inequalities, none of the three z-statistics for the associated test $H_0: f_1 = 0$ are even nearly significant, so we can conclude that at the 5 percent level the data are consistent with Theorem 1. These results indicate that, as reported in the introduction, our tests have very wide confidence intervals. As expected, the hypothesis $H_0: f^l > 0$ that stock price variance exceeds its theoretical lower bound is accepted; since the point estimate indicates acceptance, it is unnecessary to calculate the z statistics associated with f^l.

[19] As indicated earlier, a circumflex over a parameter denotes an estimate. Only the nonzero lags are reported in Table I. Selection of the nonzero lags followed the identification procedures suggested by Haugh [**5**].

[20] See Wilson [**19, 20**].

[21] To conserve space we have listed the estimates of $\underline{j}_i$ and Ω in LeRoy and Porter [**9**]. The sample periods for the four data sets were 1955:1 to 1973:4 (Standard & Poor), 1955:1 to 1977:4 (AT&T); 1955:1 to 1978:2 (GE); and 1955:4 to 1977:4 (GM). To let starting transients damp out, the first ten observations in each sample were used to provide initial conditions; see Wilson [**19**]. The sample means $\bar{x}$ and $\bar{y}$ were also based on this truncated sample.

TABLE I

PARAMETER ESTIMATES OF THE BIVARIATE ARMA PROCESS

Firm or Aggregate	$\bar{x}$	$\bar{y}$	$\hat{\beta}$	$\hat{v}_{11}$	$\hat{v}_{12}$	$\hat{v}_{22}$	$\hat{\phi}_{11}$		$\hat{\theta}_{11}$		$\hat{\theta}_{12}$		$\hat{\theta}_{21}$		$\hat{\phi}_{22}$		$\hat{\theta}_{22}$	
Standard and Poor							Lag	Coeff.	Lag	Coeff.	Lag	Coeff.	Lag	Coeff.	Lag	Coeff.	Lag	Coeff.
Estimate	.285	4.89	.942	$.542 \times 10^{-3}$	$.990 \times 10^{-2}$	.280	1	.814	4	−.182					1	.761	3	.158
Standard Error	.0343	3.79	.0456					.072		.082						.068		.062
Estimate							4	.099	5	.338					4	.240	4	.082
Standard Error								.068		.082						.072		.080
Estimate									12	−.237							5	.447
Standard Error										.072								.075
									17	.268							12	−.306
										.076								.079
																	17	.246
																		.086
American Telephone and Telegraph							Lag	Coeff.	Lag	Coeff.	Lag	Coeff.	Lag	Coeff.	Lag	Coeff.	Lag	Coeff.
Estimate	.783	46.8	.983	3.21×10^{-3}	-3.28×10^{-2}	1.09×10^{-2}	1	.988	7	.231			3	-4.85×10^{-2}	1	.966	1	−.298
Standard Error	.095	13.7	5.29×10^{-3}					.022		.086				1.64×10^{-2}		.032		.102
Estimate									13	−.179			14	-3.06×10^{-2}			3	−.265
Standard Error										.087				1.58×10^{-2}				.103
Estimate													16	3.67×10^{-2}				
Standard Error														1.61×10^{-2}				
General Electric							Lag	Coeff.	Lag	Coeff.	Lag	Coeff.	Lag	Coeff.	Lag	Coeff.	Lag	Coeff.
Estimate	.497	44.7	.989	.0139	.0416	18.1	1	.273	9	.288	8	−.008	3	12.16	1	.944	12	−.290
Standard Error	.00173	6.91	.00169					.090		.095		.002		3.63		.048		.100
Estimate									11	.194			5	5.37			13	.359
Standard Error										.100				3.48				.102
Estimate									12	−.451			10	5.04				
Standard Error										.094				3.36				
Estimate													11	9.75				
Standard Error														3.41				
General Motors							Lag	Coeff.	Lag	Coeff.	Lag	Coeff.	Lag	Coeff.	Lag	Coeff.	Lag	Coeff.
Estimate	1.37	69.5	.980	.217	.590	41.5	4	.632	1	−.144	2	−.0209			1	.965	6	−.147
Standard Error	.104	18.2	4.86×10^{-3}					.082		.114		.0082				.029		.105
Estimate									9	.262	3	−.0181					9	.066
Standard Error										.118		.0083						.102
Estimate									10	.178	16	−.0158						
Standard Error										.121		.0082						

TABLE II

"CHI-SQUARE" STATISTICS FOR OVERALL ADEQUACY OF BIVARIATE SPECIFICATION

Firm or Aggregate	Chi-Square Statistics $C(1, 1)$	$C(1, 2)$	$C(2, 1)$	$C(2, 2)$
Standard & Poor	49.3 (38)	32.2 (38)	28.7 (38)	20.7 (38)
AT&T	30.2 (46)	27.2 (46)	28.4 (46)	22.2 (46)
GE	35.2 (47)	35.8 (47)	27.1 (47)	21.8 (47)
GM	22.0 (44)	41.2 (44)	21.0 (44)	32.8 (44)

NOTE:

$$C(i, j) = T\left(\sum_{k=1}^{df} r_{ij}^2(k)\right)$$

where

$$r_{ij}(k) = \frac{1}{T}\left(\sum_{t=1}^{T-k} \hat{\xi}_{it}\hat{\xi}_{jt+k}\right)$$

and df, the degrees of freedom, is reported in parentheses beneath each "chi-square" statistic.

On the basis of point estimates, the Theorem 2 upper bound test, $\gamma_y(0) < \gamma_y^*(0)$, or, equivalently, $f_2^u > 0$, is flagrantly violated for all four data sets. However, as before, the asymptotic variances of the test statistics are very high—only for GE is rejection of the null hypothesis clearly called for. GM is a borderline case at the 5 per cent level, while for AT&T and the Standard & Poor's Index acceptance is indicated. Finally, for the more restrictive Theorem 3 test that $\gamma_y^*(0) = \gamma_y(0) + \gamma_\pi(0)$, the z statistic for the hypothesis H_0: $f_3 = 0$ indicates clear rejection of market efficiency for the three firms; for the aggregate index the test statistic was not significantly different from zero.

Our results may be summarized as follows: the point estimates corresponding to our three theorems all indicate that the bounds on price dispersion implied by the efficient markets model are dramatically violated empirically, although the confidence intervals on our tests are so wide that the departures are not always statistically significant. This conclusion differs from that of most tests of restriction (25), which generally indicate acceptance of the null hypothesis (Fama [1]).[22]

In order to interpret this discrepancy, we computed the standard autocorrelation test of the sort that has led to the acceptance of market efficiency (Table IV). The statistic appropriate for testing the joint hypothesis that the population autocorrelation of the rate of return up to lag k equal zero is

$$\text{(27)} \qquad \chi^2(k) = T\sum_{i=1}^{k}\left[\hat{\gamma}_r(i)/\hat{\gamma}_r(0)\right]^2,$$

[22] It should be noted that we have tested the model in real terms in contrast to most work in which nominal magnitudes are examined.

TABLE III

TEST STATISTICS, VARIANCES, AND COEFFICIENTS OF DISPERSION

Firm or Aggregate Index	Test Statistics				Variances				Coefficients of Dispersion			
	f_1	f_2^l	f_2^u	f_3	$\gamma_y(0)$	$\gamma_{\hat{y}}(0)$	$\gamma_y^*(0)$	$\gamma_\pi(0)$	$CD(x)$	$CD(\hat{y})$	$CD(y)$	$CD(y^*)$
Standard & Poor	$-.280$	.396	$-.348$	-8.63	4.89	1.64×10^{-1}	.255	3.99	.172	8.28×10^{-2}	.452	.052
z Statistic	$-.193$	——	$-.242$	$-.254$								
AT&T	$-.281$	.420	$-.314$	-828.7	385.7	9.77×10^{-6}	24.6	467.6	.139	6.68×10^{-5}	.420	.106
z Statistic	-1.096	——	-1.223	-2.006								
GE	-6.84×10^{-4}	.288	$-.264$	-1478.4	165.9	3.81×10^{-4}	1.12	1313.6	.287	4.36×10^{-4}	.288	.024
z Statistic	$-.0056$	——	-2.57	-4.41								
GM	.103	.375	$-.314$	-1773.9	690.5	3.37×10^{-2}	19.90	1103.3	.481	2.64×10^{-3}	.378	.064
z Statistic	.596	——	-1.84	-2.76								

TABLE IV
TESTS OF OVERALL MARKET EFFICIENCY

Firm or Aggregate	Chi-Square Statistics for Rates of Return $\chi^2(12)$	$\chi^2(24)$
Standard & Poor	88.0	155.4
American Telephone and Telegraph	9.4	15.2
General Electric	10.2	17.0
General Motors	10.8	14.4

where the term in brackets is the sample autocorrelation of rates of return, equation (26), at lag i. Under the null hypothesis of market efficiency, (27) is distributed as a chi-square statistic with k degrees of freedom. We calculated $\chi^2(k)$ for $k = 12$ and $k = 24$; for $k = 12$ ($k = 24$) the critical value of the chi-square statistic at the twenty-five per cent level is 14.8 (28.2), while at the one per cent level the critical value is 26.2 (43.0). Comparison of the sample statistics with the critical values indicates that the hypotheses that all lagged autocorrelations in rates of return are zero is accepted at the 25 per cent level for either $k = 12$ or $k = 24$ for the firm data, although it is rejected at the one per cent level for the Standard & Poor's Index for either $k = 12$ or $k = 24$.

As indicated earlier in Section 1, we are not able to resolve this difference between our results in which market efficiency is rejected with the standard results in which the opposite conclusion is reached. As suggested in the introduction, one possibility is that our test has greater power than the standard test for the particular dispersion restriction embodied in Theorem 3.[23]

University of California, Santa Barbara and Federal Reserve Board

Manuscript received March, 1978; revision received January, 1980.

[23] Both our test and the standard test may be derived from (13). Theorem 3 tests only one of the restrictions contained in (13), while the standard test is a simultaneous test of all the restrictions. The situation is analogous to a multivariate test that all the coefficients in a linear model are simultaneously zero versus a t test on an individual coefficient. If one particular coefficient is nonzero, the t test for that coefficient would have greater power than the multivariate test.

REFERENCES

[1] FAMA, EUGENE F.: "Efficient Capital Markets: A Review of Theory and Empirical Work," *Journal of Finance*, 25 (1970), 383–416.

[2] FRIEDMAN, MILTON: *A Theory of the Consumption Function*. Princeton: Princeton University Press, 1957.

[3] GRANGER, C. W. J.: "Investigating Causal Relations by Econometric Models and Cross-Spectral Methods," *Econometrica*, 37 (1969), 424–438.

[4] HANNAN, E. J.: *Multiple Time Series*. New York: John Wiley and Sons, 1970.

[5] HAUGH, LARRY D.: *The Identification of Time Series Interrelationships with Special Reference to Dynamic Regression Models*, Ph.D. Dissertation, Department of Statistics, University of Wisconsin, 1972.

[6] LEROY, STEPHEN F.: "Risk Aversion and the Martingale Property of Stock Prices," *International Economic Review*, 14 (1973), 436–446.

[7] ———: "Efficient Capital Markets: Comment," *Journal of Finance*, 31 (1976), 139–141.

[8] ———: "Securities Prices Under Risk-Neutrality and Near Risk-Neutrality," reproduced, University of Chicago, 1979.

[9] LEROY, STEPHEN F., AND RICHARD D. PORTER: "The Present-Value Relation: Tests Based on Implied Variance Bounds," Federal Reserve Board Special Studies Paper, 1980.

[10] LUCAS, ROBERT E., JR.: "Asset Prices in an Exchange Economy," *Econometrica*, 46 (1978), 1426–1446.

[11] PIERCE, DAVID A.: "Forecasting Dynamic Models with Stochastic Regressors," *Journal of Econometrics*, 3 (1975), 349–374.

[12] ROZANOV, YU. A.: *Stationary Random Processes*, Tr. by A. Feinstein. San Francisco: Holden-Day, 1963.

[13] RUBINSTEIN, MARK: "Securities Market Efficiency in an Arrow-Debreu Economy," *American Economic Review*, 65 (1975), 812–824.

[14] SAMUELSON, PAUL A.: "Proof that Properly Anticipated Prices Fluctuate Randomly," *Industrial Management Review*, 6 (1965), 41–49.

[15] SHILLER, ROBERT J.: *Rational Expectations and the Structure of Interest Rates*, unpublished Ph.D. dissertation, Department of Economics, M.I.T., 1972.

[16] ———: "The Volatility of Long-Term Interest Rates and Expectations of the Term Structure," *Journal of Political Economy*, 87 (1979), 1190–1219.

[17] SIMS, CHRISTOPHER A.: "Approximate Price Restrictions in Distributed Lag Estimation," *Journal of the American Statistical Association*, 67 (1972), 169–175.

[18] SINGLETON, KENNETH J.: "Expectations Models of the Term Structure and Implied Variance Bounds," *Journal of Political Economy*, 88 (1980), 1159–1176.

[19] WILSON, G. TUNNICLIFFE: Unpublished Ph.D. dissertation, Lancaster University, 1970.

[20] ———: "The Estimation of Parameters in Multivariate Time Series Models," *Journal of the Royal Statistical Society*, Series B, 35 (1973), 76–85.

[21] WOODWARD, S. E.: "Properly Anticipated Prices Do Not, In General, Fluctuate Randomly," reproduced, University of California, Santa Barbara, 1979.

[7]

THE JOURNAL OF FINANCE • VOL. L, NO. 4 • SEPTEMBER 1995

Predictability of Stock Returns: Robustness and Economic Significance

M. HASHEM PESARAN AND ALLAN TIMMERMANN*

ABSTRACT

This article examines the robustness of the evidence on predictability of U.S. stock returns, and addresses the issue of whether this predictability could have been historically exploited by investors to earn profits in excess of a buy-and-hold strategy in the market index. We find that the predictive power of various economic factors over stock returns changes through time and tends to vary with the volatility of returns. The degree to which stock returns were predictable seemed quite low during the relatively calm markets in the 1960s, but increased to a level where, net of transaction costs, it could have been exploited by investors in the volatile markets of the 1970s.

MANY RECENT STUDIES CONCLUDE that stock returns can be predicted by means of publicly available information, such as time series data on financial and macroeconomic variables with an important business cycle component.[1] This conclusion seems to hold across international stock markets as well as over different time horizons. Variables identified by these studies to have been statistically important for predicting stock returns include interest rates, monetary growth rates, changes in industrial production, inflation rates, earnings-price ratios, and dividend yields. However, the economic interpretation of these results is controversial and far from evident. First, it is possible that the predictable components in stock returns reflect time-varying expected returns, in which case predictability of stock returns is, in principle, consistent with an efficient stock market. A second interpretation takes expected returns as roughly constant and regards predictability of stock returns as evidence of stock market inefficiency. It is, however, clear that predictability of excess returns on its own does not imply stock market inefficiency, and can be

* Pesaran is from Trinity College, Cambridge. Timmermann is from University of California, San Diego. This is a substantially revised and abridged version of the paper "The Use of Recursive Model Selection Strategies in Forecasting Stock Returns," *Department of Applied Economics Working paper No. 9406, March 1994,* University of Cambridge. We would like to thank a referee and the editor, René Stulz, as well as seminar participants at The London School of Economics, The University of Exeter, The Bank of England, University of Southern California, and University of California at San Diego for helpful comments on the earlier version. The first author gratefully acknowledges financial support from the Economic and Social Research Council and the Newton Trust of Trinity College, Cambridge.

[1] See, for instance, the articles by Balvers, Cosimano, and McDonald (1990), Breen, Glosten, and Jagannathan (1990), Campbell (1987), Cochrane (1991), Fama and French (1989), Ferson and Harvey (1993), French, Schwert, and Stambaugh (1987), Glosten, Jagannathan, and Runkle (1993), Pesaran and Timmermann (1994a).

interpreted only in conjunction with, and in relation to, an intertemporal equilibrium model of the economy. Inevitably, all theoretical attempts at interpretation of excess return predictability will be model-dependent, and hence inconclusive (see Fama (1991)).

An alternative approach to evaluating the economic significance of stock market predictability would be to see if the evidence could have been exploited successfully in investment strategies. This can be done in two ways: One method would be to evaluate the track records of portfolio managers in "real time," and see if these portfolios systematically generate excess returns. The main strength of this approach lies in the fact that it ensures that investors' portfolio decisions are based exclusively on historically available information. However, it does not provide much information on which specific factors have been responsible for predicting stock returns, nor does it guarantee that the information used by portfolio managers has been publicly available. An alternative approach, which explicitly addresses these issues, is to simulate investors' decisions in real time using publicly available information on a set of factors thought a priori to have been relevant to forecasting stock returns. Clearly, caution needs to be exercised when following this research strategy. In particular, it is important that, as far as possible, rules for prediction of stock returns are formulated and estimated without the benefit of hindsight. Most articles in the finance literature report excess return regressions estimated on the basis of the entire sample of available observations or on substantial subsamples of the data, which, for the purpose of trading, is clearly inappropriate, as in "real time" no investor could have obtained parameter estimates based on the entire sample. A similar consideration also applies to the choice of the forecasting model. Any analysis of stock market predictability that focuses on a particular forecasting model, taken as known with certainty over the whole sample period, can be criticized for ignoring the problem of "model uncertainty" and the impact this is likely to have on investors' portfolio strategy in "real time." When the same forecasting model is used over the whole sample period, it inevitably raises the possibility that the choice of the model could have been made with the benefit of hindsight.

The purpose of this article is to assess the economic significance of the predictability of U.S. stock returns, explicitly accounting for the forecasting uncertainty faced by investors who only have access to historical information. Rather than assuming that investors somehow historically knew that a specific forecasting model was going to perform well, we make a much weaker assumption about investors' beliefs over the sort of business cycle and financial variables thought as being potentially important in forecasting stock returns. Based on these beliefs, we assume that agents establish a base set of potential forecasting variables and, at each point in time, search for a reasonable model specification, capable of predicting stock returns, across this set. Notably, this procedure assumes that, at each point in time, investors use only historically available information to select a model according to a predefined model selection criterion and then use the chosen model to make one-period ahead predictions of excess returns. The recursive forecasts are then employed in a portfolio switching strategy according to which shares or bonds are held depending on whether excess returns on stocks are predicted to be positive or negative.

A third factor that needs to be taken into account when simulating investors' portfolio decisions in "real time" is transaction costs. We analyze portfolio returns for zero, low, and high transaction cost scenarios to shed light on whether the predictable components in stock returns are economically exploitable net of transaction costs. Finally, we also consider the public availability of statistical methods and computer technology used by investors to compute one-step ahead forecasts of excess returns. In developing our forecasting equations we use simple statistical and computing techniques that clearly were publicly available to any investor throughout the sample period analyzed in this paper. We also provide evidence based on forecasting techniques that were not available until well into the seventies, since this offers important insights into the potential usefulness of our methodology for forecasting of stock returns in the future. The availability of different model selection criteria also raises the issue of uncertainty over the choice of model selection criteria. This problem is addressed in an Appendix where a new profit-based hyper-selection procedure is proposed.

The plan of the article is as follows: Section I discusses how to identify predictability of stock returns. Section II sets up the real time simulation experiments and reports the main prediction results for the monthly observations on U.S. stock returns. The economic significance of the predictions is assessed through their use in a trading strategy in Section III, and Section IV provides a discussion of the main findings.

I. Identifying Predictability of Stock Returns: A Recursive Modeling Approach

Consider an investor who believes that stock returns can be predicted by means of a set of financial and macroeconomic indicators, but does not know the "true" form of the underlying specification, let alone the "true" parameter values. Under these circumstances the best the investor can do is to search for a suitable model specification among the set of models believed a priori to be capable of predicting stock returns. As time progresses and the historical observations available to investors increase, the added information is likely to lead the investor to change the forecasting equation unless, of course, the investor holds very strong prior beliefs in a specific model. Here we consider an open-minded investor with no strong beliefs in any particular model. The evolution of forecasting models over time may reflect the learning process of the investor or the changing nature of the underlying data generating process, or both. In practice it will be difficult to disentangle these two effects.[2]

[2] A similar recursive modelling strategy has also been considered by Phillips (1992) and Phillips and Ploberger (1994) in the context of univariate autoregressive-moving average processes. However, their work is best viewed as recursive estimation of the order of the Autoregressive Moving Average process, and does not involve searching over subset of regressors as we do in this paper. Also see the discussion of the hyper-selection criterion in the Appendix, where the recursive modelling strategy is further extended to allow for the uncertainty over the choice of model selection criterion itself.

Suppose that, at each point in time, t, an investor searches over a base set of κ factors or regressors to make one period ahead forecasts of excess returns using only information that are publicly available at the time.[3] We simulate investor's search for a forecasting model by applying standard statistical criteria for model selection, as well as financial criteria, to the set of regression models spanned by all possible permutations of the κ factors/regressors $\{x_1, x_2, \ldots, x_\kappa\}$ in the base set.[4] This gives a total of 2^κ different models, each of which is uniquely identified by a number, i, between 1 and 2^κ. Consider a $\kappa \times 1$ selection vector, ν_i, composed of ones and zeros where a one in its jth element means that the jth regressor is included in the model, whereas a zero in its jth element means that this regressor is excluded from the model. Then model i (denoted by M_i) can be represented by the κ-digit string of zeros and ones corresponding to the binary code of its number. Denoting the number of regressors included in model M_i by κ_i, then $\kappa_i = e'\nu_i$, where e is a $\kappa \times 1$ vector of ones. Suppose that ρ_τ, the excess return at time τ, is forecast by means of linear regressions

$$M_i : \rho_{\tau+1} = \beta_i' X_{\tau,i} + \varepsilon_{\tau+1,i} \qquad \tau = 1, 2, \ldots, t-1. \tag{1}$$

where $X_{\tau,i}$ is a $(\kappa_i + 1) \times 1$ vector of regressors under model M_i, obtained as a subset of the base set of regressors, X_τ, chosen by the investor at the beginning of the experiments, plus a vector of ones for the intercept term. Conditional on model M_i and given the observations $\rho_{\tau+1}, X_{\tau,i}, \tau = 1, 2, \ldots, t-1$ (with $t \geq \kappa + 2$), parameters of model M_i can be estimated by the ordinary least squares (OLS) method. Denoting these estimates by $\hat{\beta}_{t,i}$ we have

$$\hat{\beta}_{t,i} = \left(\sum_{\tau=0}^{t-1} X_{\tau,i} X'_{\tau,i} \right)^{-1} \sum_{\tau=0}^{t-1} X_{\tau,i} \rho_{\tau+1}, \qquad \begin{array}{ll} \text{for} & t = \kappa+2, \kappa+3, \ldots, T, \\ \text{and} & i = 1, \ldots, 2^\kappa. \end{array} \tag{2}$$

The OLS estimates are fairly simple to compute (even in the early 1960s) and, in view of the Gauss-Markov Theorem, are reasonably robust even in the presence of nonnormal errors in the excess return equation.

The particular choice of $X_{\tau,i}$ to be used in forecasting of $\rho_{\tau+1}$ can be based on a number of statistical model selection criteria suggested in the literature, such as the $\bar{R}^2$, Akaike's Information Criterion (AIC) (Akaike (1973)), or Schwarz's Bayesian Information Criterion (BIC) (Schwarz (1978)).[5] These

[3] In this article we shall make the simplifying assumption that the base regressors remain in effect over the whole sample period. However, in principle, one can also consider the possibility of revising the base set once clear indications of "regime switches" are established.

[4] An intercept term is included in all the excess return regressions considered by the investor.

[5] There are, of course, other criteria that could be used for choosing the subset of regressors used to compute the forecasts. Prominent examples are Mallows' (1973) C_p criterion, Amemiya's (1980) prediction criterion, and the Posterior Information Criterion recently proposed by Phillips (1992) and Phillips and Ploberger (1994). However, in this article we focus on the more often used and familiar model selection criteria.

criteria are likelihood-based and assign different weights to the "parsimony" and "fit" of the models. The "fit" is measured by the maximized value of the log-likelihood function ($\widehat{\mathrm{LL}}$), and the "parsimony" by the number of freely estimated coefficients. At time t, and under model M_i, we have

$$\widehat{\mathrm{LL}}_{t,i} = \frac{-t}{2}\{1 + \log(2\pi\hat{\sigma}^2_{t,i})\}, \tag{3}$$

where

$$\hat{\sigma}^2_{t,i} = \sum_{\tau=0}^{t-1} (\rho_{\tau+1} - X'_{\tau,i}\hat{\beta}_{t,i})^2/t. \tag{4}$$

The Akaike and Schwarz model selection criteria can be written as

$$\mathrm{AIC}_{t,i} = \widehat{\mathrm{LL}}_{t,i} - (\kappa_i + 1), \tag{5}$$

$$\mathrm{BIC}_{t,i} = \widehat{\mathrm{LL}}_{t,i} - \tfrac{1}{2}(\kappa_i + 1)\log(t). \tag{6}$$

The $\bar{\mathrm{R}}^2$ criterion, originally suggested by Theil (1958) as a criterion for selecting regressors in a linear regression model, is given by

$$\bar{R}^2_{t,i} = 1 - \frac{\tilde{\sigma}^2_{t,i}}{S^2_{\rho,t}} \tag{7}$$

where $\tilde{\sigma}^2_{t,i}$ is the unbiased estimator of σ^2 given by $\tilde{\sigma}^2_{t,i} = \sum_{\tau=0}^{t-1} (\rho_{\tau+1} - X'_{\tau,i}\hat{\beta}_{t,i})^2/(t - \kappa_i - 1)$, and $S^2_{\rho,t} = \sum_{\tau=1}^{t} (\rho_\tau - \bar{\rho}_t)^2/(t - 1)$ is the sample variance for the first t observations on ρ, and $\bar{\rho}_t = t^{-1}\sum_{\tau=1}^{t} \rho_\tau$. The $\bar{\mathrm{R}}^2$ criterion can also be written explicitly as a trade-off between fit and parsimony:

$$\mathrm{TC}_{t,i} = \widehat{\mathrm{LL}}_{t,i} - \tfrac{1}{2}\log\left(\frac{t}{t - k_i - 1}\right). \tag{8}$$

It is easy to show that, in the context of linear regression models, the $\bar{\mathrm{R}}^2_{t,i}$ and the $\mathrm{TC}_{t,i}$ criteria are equivalent, in the sense that they select the same model.

We also considered a model selection criterion based on a measure of directional accuracy, on the grounds that investors in practice often are interested in predicting the switches in the sign of the excess return function and not necessarily the magnitude of changes in the excess returns. The derivation of the 'sign' criterion (SC) based on the directional accuracy of the forecasts involves two steps. In the first step, one finds the set of regressors that maximize the proportion of correctly predicted signs of the excess returns given by

$$\mathrm{SC}_{t,i} = \frac{1}{t}\sum_{\tau=1}^{t} \{\mathrm{I}(\rho_\tau)\mathrm{I}(\hat{\rho}_{\tau,i}) + (1 - \mathrm{I}(\rho_\tau))(1 - \mathrm{I}(\hat{\rho}_{\tau,i}))\}, \tag{9}$$

where $I(\rho_\tau)$ is an indicator function that takes the value of unity if $\rho_\tau > 0$, and zero otherwise, and $\hat{\rho}_{\tau,i}$ is the forecast of ρ_τ based on model M_i. In the case of a draw, i.e., when two or more models correctly predict the same (maximum) proportion of signs of excess returns, a second step selects a model recursively according to the $\bar{R}^2$ criterion.

From the point of view of assessing the market value of predictability of stock returns, the above statistical criteria can, however, be criticized on the grounds that they do not take account of transaction costs, and are not necessarily in accordance with the investor's loss function. To deal with these shortcomings, we use a forecasting strategy that directly maximizes financial criteria. In particular we consider a "recursive wealth" criterion and a recursive Sharpe ratio.[6] The recursive wealth criterion maximizes the cumulated wealth obtained using forecasts from model M_i in a switching portfolio, which we refer to as portfolio i, at time t. The cumulative wealth from such a portfolio at time t is given by

$$W_{t,i} = W_0 \prod_{\tau=1}^{t} (1 + r_{\tau,i}), \tag{10}$$

where $r_{\tau,i}$ is the period τ return (net of transaction costs) on portfolio i, constructed on the basis of the excess return forecasts from model M_i. The returns $r_{\tau,i}$ depend on the nature of the trading rule, the transaction costs and the whole sequence of excess return forecasts, risk free interest rates, stock prices and dividends prior to period τ. For an example of the sort of trading rule that we have in mind, see Section III.

The Recursive Sharpe Criterion maximizes the ratio of the mean excess return on portfolio i to its standard deviation:

$$\text{Sharpe}_{t,i} = \frac{\frac{1}{t}\sum_{\tau=1}^{t}(r_{\tau,i} - I1_{\tau-1})}{\sqrt{\frac{1}{t-1}\sum_{\tau=1}^{t}(r_{\tau,i} - \bar{r}_{t,i})^2}}, \tag{11}$$

where I1 is the return on a 1-month T-bill held from the end of one month to the next, and $\bar{r}_{t,i} = t^{-1}\sum_{\tau=1}^{t} r_{\tau,i}$.

We applied all the above model selection criteria to the linear regressions. For each of the criteria, and based on data up to period t, the model with the highest value for the criterion function was chosen to forecast excess returns for period $t + 1$. For example, in the case of the recursive Sharpe criterion, the selected model was that which maximized $\text{Sharpe}_{t,i}$ given by (11) over all of the 2^k portfolios, $i = 1, 2, 3, \ldots, 2^k$. Notice that our approach makes only very

[6] We are grateful to a referee for drawing our attention to this work.

weak assumptions about the underlying data generating process (DGP). We do not assume that the DGP is necessarily fixed throughout the sample period, and at each point in time we use the different model selection criteria simply as a tool for obtaining an *approximate* forecasting equation. This procedure treats all models under consideration as equally likely. Choosing a particular model at time t does not necessarily restrict the model choice at subsequent periods.

When interpreting the results reported in Sections II and III below, however, it is important to recognize that neither the AIC nor the BIC was publicly available until well into the 1970s. The main property of the BIC criterion is that, under certain regularity conditions, it will asymptotically select the "true" model, provided of course that the 'true' model is contained in the set of models over which the search is conducted.[7] Neither Akaike's criterion nor the $\bar{R}^2$ criterion is consistent, in the sense of selecting the "true" model, as the sample size increases without bounds. In the context of forecasting stock returns where the "true" model or the correct list of regressors is clearly unknown and may be changing over time, the consistency property of a model selection criterion is not as important as it may appear at first. Both the $\bar{R}^2$ and the AIC, although statistically inconsistent, have the important property of yielding an approximate model. The primary aim is to select a forecasting equation that could be viewed *at the time* as being a reasonable approximation to the data generating process. Akaike's criterion has been shown by Shibata (1976) to strike a good balance between giving biased estimates when the order of the model is too low, and the risk of increasing the variance when too many regressors are included. Finally, for the purpose of our exercise, the $\bar{R}^2$ has the advantage of being extensively used by economists to evaluate model performance.

II. Recursive Predictions of U.S. Stock Returns

When simulating the historical process through which an investor may attempt to forecast stock returns, it is important to establish the sort of variables the investor is likely to consider using in modeling stock returns, the criteria he/she adopts to select a particular forecasting model, and the estimation procedure applied.

In this section we explain the choice of the base variables that we assume will be considered by investors in forecasting stock returns, and in the next section we explain the estimation and forecasting procedure in more detail. The starting point of our analysis is the long tradition in finance that links movements in stock returns to business cycle indicators. For instance, in his book *Investment for Appreciation. Forecasting Movements in Security Prices. Techniques of Trading in Shares for Profit* published in 1936, Angas writes that "The major determinant of price movements on the stock exchange is the business cycle." (p. 15). Other examples of early studies that emphasize the

[7] See, for example, Pötscher (1991) and the references cited therein.

systematic variation of stock returns over the business cycle include Prime (1946). Dowrie and Fuller (1950), Rose (1960), and Morgan and Thomas (1962). Variables suggested by these studies to be systematically linked with stock returns include short and long interest rates, dividend yields, industrial production, company earnings, liquidity measures, and the inflation rate.

Based on a review of the early literature (see Pesaran and Timmermann (1994c)) we established a benchmark set of regressors over which the search for a "satisfactory" prediction model could be conducted by a potential investor. The set consists of a constant, which is always included in the model, as well as nine regressors, namely $X_t = \{YSP_{t-1}, EP_{t-1}, I1_{t-1}, I1_{t-2}, I12_{t-1}, I12_{t-2}, \Pi_{t-2}, \Delta IP_{t-2}, \Delta M_{t-2}\}$, where YSP is the dividend yield, EP is the earnings-price ratio, I1 is the 1-month T-bill rate, I12 is the 12-month T-bond rate, Π is the year-on-year rate of inflation, ΔIP is the year-on-year rate of change in industrial output, and ΔM is the year-on-year growth rate in the narrow money stock. All variables computed using macroeconomic indicators, such as, ΔIP and ΔM, were measured using 12-month moving averages to decrease the impact of historical data revisions on the results.

The early studies of stock returns are not always clear on what they consider to be the appropriate time lags between the changes in the business cycle variables and stock returns. Here, following standard practice in finance, we decided to include the most recently available values of the macroeconomic variables in the base set of regressors. The lag associated with the publication of macroeconomic indicators means that these variables must be included in the base set with a 2-month time lag. Since the dividend and earning yields are based on 12-month moving averages, only a one period lag of these variables was included in the base set. To allow for the possibility, often mentioned in financial studies, that changes in interest rates rather than their absolute levels affect stock returns, we also included a two month as well as a one month lagged value of the interest variables.

A. Data Sources

All variables were measured at monthly frequencies over the period 1954(1) to 1992(12), and the data sources were as follows: Stock prices were measured by the Standard & Poor's 500 index at close on the last trading day of each month. These stock indices, as well as a monthly average of annualized dividends and earnings, were taken from Standard & Poor's Statistical Service. The 1-month T-bill rate was measured on the last trading day of the month and computed as the average of the bid and ask yields. The source was the Fama-Bliss risk free rates file on the Center for Research in Security Prices (CRSP) tapes. Similarly, the 12-month discount bond rate was measured on the last trading day of the month, using the Fama-Bliss discount bonds file on the CRSP tapes as the data source. The inflation rate was computed using the producer price index for finished goods (source: Citibase), and the rate of change in industrial production was based on a seasonally adjusted index for industrial production (source: Citibase). The monetary series were based on the narrow monetary aggregates published by the Federal Reserve Bank of St. Louis and provided by Citibase. Finally, the dependent variable, excess returns on stocks, ρ_t, was computed as $\rho_t = (P_t + D_t - P_{t-1})/P_{t-1} - I1_{t-1}$, where P_t is the stock price, D_t is dividends and $I1_{t-1}$ is the return from holding a 1-month T-bill from the end of month $t - 1$ to the end of month t.

The recursive model selection and estimation strategy was based on monthly observations over the period 1954(1) to 1992(12). The year 1954 was chosen as the start of the sample for estimation, since reliable monthly measures for most macroeconomic time series start to become available only after the Second World War. Also, it was only after the "accord" between the Fed and the Treasury in March 1951, and after the presidential election in 1952, that the Fed stopped pegging interest rates and began to pursue an independent monetary policy (see Mishkin (1992), p. 453). As far as trading in stocks and bonds are concerned, we took a rather conservative stand and commenced with the trading at the start of 1960, thus using 6 years of monthly observations as a preliminary "training" period for estimation. As noted above, by the early 1960s, a number of studies had already suggested the possibility that stock returns may be varying systematically over the course of the business cycle.

In each case the model selection criteria set out in Section I were applied to linear regression models using the excess returns on the S & P 500 portfolio as the dependent variable and subsets of the base set of regressors as the independent variables. For our set of nine regressors, this means comparing $2^9 = 512$ models at each point in time, and over the period 1959(12) to 1992(11) this gives a total of 202,752 regressions to be computed. Of course, we do not literally assume that investors proceeded with these computations, but we emphasize the simplicity of the individual steps involved in such a forecasting procedure: OLS estimation of the models, followed by model selection using simple choice criteria and then computation of a one-step-ahead forecast. We also computed forecasts of monthly excess returns based on a model that included the entire set of regressors. There is no specification uncertainty associated with this last procedure, according to which only the parameter estimates are updated recursively in light of new monthly observations.

To summarize, the recursive model specification proceeds as follows: in 1959(12) the values of the selection criteria are computed for each of the 512 possible combinations of regressors from the base set using monthly data over the period 1954(1) to 1959(12). An intercept term is included in all the regressions. The model that maximizes the discriminant function of a given model selection criterion is chosen, and the parameter values estimated with observations over the 1954(1) to 1959(12) period are used to forecast excess returns for 1960(1). To forecast monthly excess returns for 1960(2), the procedure is repeated for all the 512 models using monthly data over the period 1954(1) to 1960(1), and so on. Thus, although computationally demanding, our selection procedure clearly simulates the search procedure which an investor could have carried out in real time. It also captures the possibility that an investor may switch from one model to another in light of new empirical evidence obtained as the sample size expands.

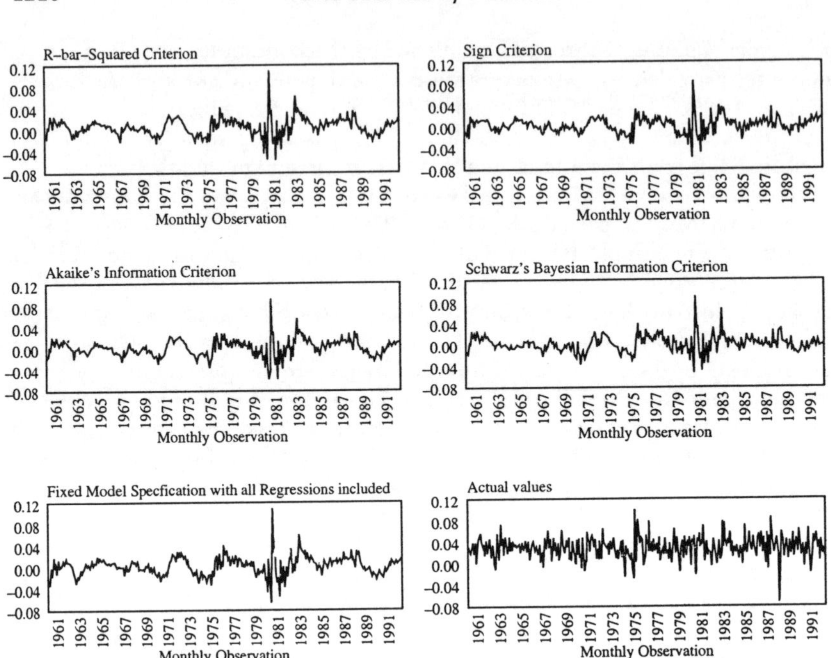

Figure 1. Recursive excess return forecasts under alternative model selection strategies, 1960(1) to 1992(12).

B. Empirical Results: How Robust is the Predictability of Stock Returns?

As the previous section makes clear, we estimated a total of 202,752 models over the 1959(12) to 1992(1) period. Clearly, we cannot supply the reader with all the details of the estimation results.[8] Here we provide some graphic displays of the main results.

Figure 1 shows the predicted excess returns based on the linear regression models estimated by OLS and selected recursively according to the four model selection criteria, namely $\bar{R}^2$, AIC, BIC, and SC. The bottom panel of this figure also shows the actual values of the excess returns and predictions from a recursively estimated equation with all the nine variables in the base set included as regressors.[9] The recursive predictions based on the various model selection criteria have very similar patterns showing quite a high degree of volatility, especially during the early 1980s. This coincides with the period of high volatility of nominal interest rates resulting from changes in the operat-

[8] The data files and the details of the estimations and forecasting results are available from the authors on request.

[9] Notice, however, that the figures giving the recursive forecasts have a different vertical scale than the actual values of the excess returns. Due to the relatively high variance of actual excess returns plotting the excess return forecasts and their realizations on the same scale would have obscured the differences that exist between the different recursive forecasts.

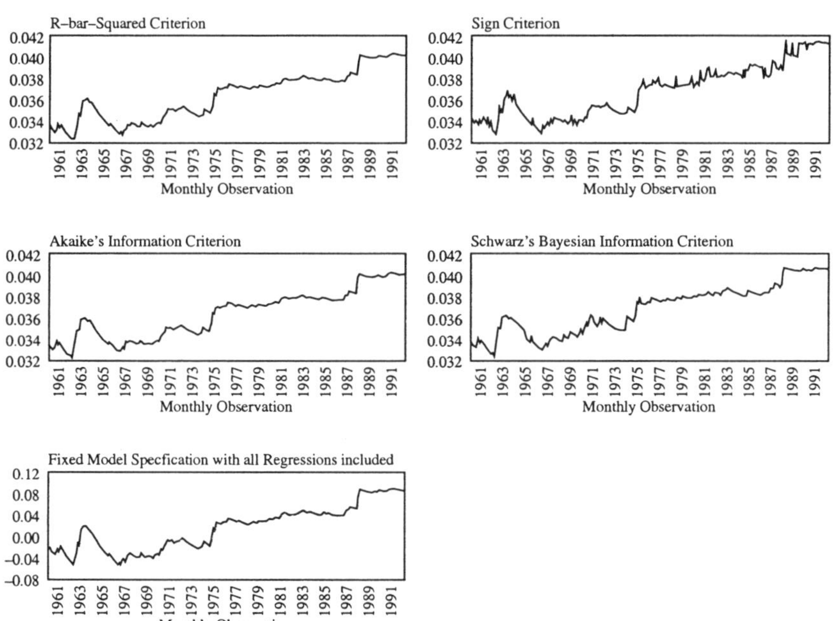

Figure 2. Standard errors of recursive excess return equations under alternative model selection strategies, 1960(1) to 1992(12).

ing procedures followed by the Federal Reserve between September 1979 and October 1982. Not surprisingly, the volatility of the predictions is much smaller than the volatility of the actual excess returns.

Figure 2 shows the standard errors of recursive excess return regressions under the different model selection strategies. In all cases, the recursively estimated standard errors have a tendency to increase over time. In particular, substantial increases in the estimated standard errors can be clearly seen in 1962, 1974, and after the October 1987 stock market crash.[10] Important information on the ex ante forecasting performance of the different model selection strategies is also provided in Figure 3, which displays the recursively computed squared values of the simple correlation coefficient (r^2) between the recursive forecasts obtained under the different model selection criteria and the actual excess returns. The fit of the recursive forecasts is relatively high in the early 1960s (with values of the r^2 being around 0.20), and increases substantially during 1962, but then starts to decline until the early 1970s. With increased volatility of the markets in 1974, the fit of the recursive

[10] The recursive standard error estimates in Figure 2 show the trend in volatility of excess returns conditional on the information in the base set of regressors. Similar trends can also be seen in unconditional measures of volatility, such as the recursively estimated standard deviations of the actual excess return series.

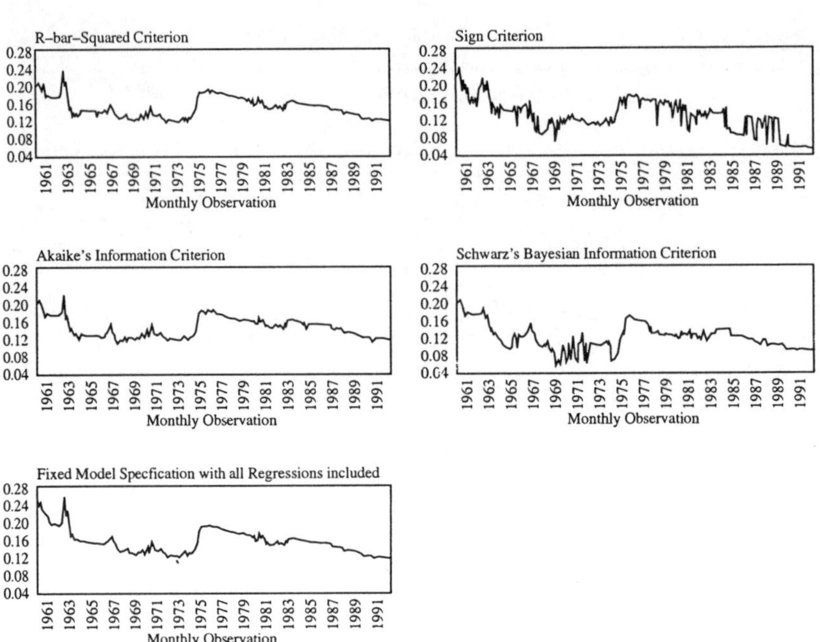

Figure 3. Fit of recursive excess return equations, 1960(1) to 1992(12). Note: The fit is measured by the recursively computed squared correlation coefficient between the recursive forecasts (from Figure 1) and the actual values of the excess returns.

forecasts, as measured by r^2, jumps from around 0.12 to around 0.18, and then once again starts to decline steadily up to the end of the sample, where it takes a value of around 0.12 for models selected according to the $\bar{R}^2$ and the Akaike Criteria, and 0.10 for models selected using the Schwarz criterion.

Taken together, Figures 2 and 3 show that although the volatility in the U.S. stock market increased significantly around 1974, the predictability of stock returns, as measured by the fit of the recursive forecasts relative to the actual values, also increased in this period. This suggests that predictability of stock returns may indeed be particularly pronounced in periods of economic "regime switches" where the markets are relatively unsettled and investors are particularly uncertain of which forecasting model to use for trading. The episode early in 1962 where the volatility in the stock market also went up leads to a similar conclusion. In contrast, the significant increase in the standard errors of the recursive forecasting equations after the October 1987 stock market crash coincided with a decline in the value of r^2 for all the model selection criteria, indicating that this episode was somewhat different from the ones in 1962 and 1974.

For each of the variables in the base set of regressors Table I presents the percentage of periods where a regressor is included in the recursively selected models. As to be expected, on balance the $\bar{R}^2$ and the Akaike criteria tend to

Table I

Percentage of Periods Where a Regressor is Included in Forecasting Equations

The results are based on monthly excess return equations selected and estimated recursively over the period 1960(1) to 1992(12). Each month the set of regressors that maximizes a given model selection criterion was determined and used to forecast stock returns one month ahead. For a definition of the statistical model selection criteria, see Section II of the article. The regressors are YSP(−1) = dividend yield lagged one period, EP(−1) = earnings-price ratio lagged one period I1(−1) = one-month T-bill rate lagged one period, I1(−2) = one-month T-bill rate lagged two periods, I12(−1) = twelve-month T-bill rate lagged one period, I12(−2) = twelve-month T-bill rate lagged two periods, Π(−2) = inflation rate lagged two periods, ΔIP(−2) = change in industrial production lagged two periods, and ΔM(−2) = monetary growth rate lagged two periods.

Selection	Percentages								
Criteria	YSP(−1)	EP(−1)	I1(−1)	I1(−2)	I12(−1)	I12(−2)	Π(−2)	ΔIP(−2)	ΔM(−2)
Akaike	70.5	9.6	98.5	25.0	27.0	31.3	51.8	74.7	84.6
Schwarz	62.9	0.0	93.9	22.0	2.8	34.8	0.0	8.8	28.3
$\bar{R}^2$	69.7	20.5	99.2	23.0	44.7	42.9	55.8	87.9	89.6
Sign	62.4	44.2	72.5	54.8	49.7	50.0	59.6	58.6	76.5

select more regressors than does the Schwarz criterion. The latter criterion imposes a much heavier penalty for inclusion of an additional regressor than do the former criteria, and this difference becomes particularly marked as the sample size is increased from 72 to 468 observations over the 1960 to 1992 period.

An alternative, and in many respects more comprehensive, method of examining the robustness of the factors contributing to the predictability of stock returns would be to consider the time-profile of the inclusion frequencies of the different factors in the forecasting model. The graphs in Figure 4 provide such time-profiles for the $\bar{R}^2$ criterion, and show the periods in which a regressor is included (the graph takes a value of 1) or excluded (the graph takes a value of 0) from the model used for the one-period ahead prediction of excess returns. Similar graphs for the other model selection criteria are also available from the authors, and are not presented here to save space.[11] Since we are searching for a model specification over a large number of time periods and across different combinations of regressors, it is possible that a regressor occasionally gets included by chance and not because it is statistically significant for prediction of excess returns. In such cases, however, it is unlikely that the regressor under consideration will be included in the forecasting equation for long in subsequent periods. In contrast, when a regressor is selected in a large proportion of the time periods and on a continuous basis, then it is reasonable to

[11] The results for the Akaike criterion were very close to those for the $\bar{R}^2$ criterion. The Sign criterion did not provide much information about periods in which specific regressors are included. Because of the discontinuous nature of this criterion, the number of switches between periods where a variable is included in the model and periods where it is excluded from the model is much higher for the Sign criterion than for any of the other model selection criteria.

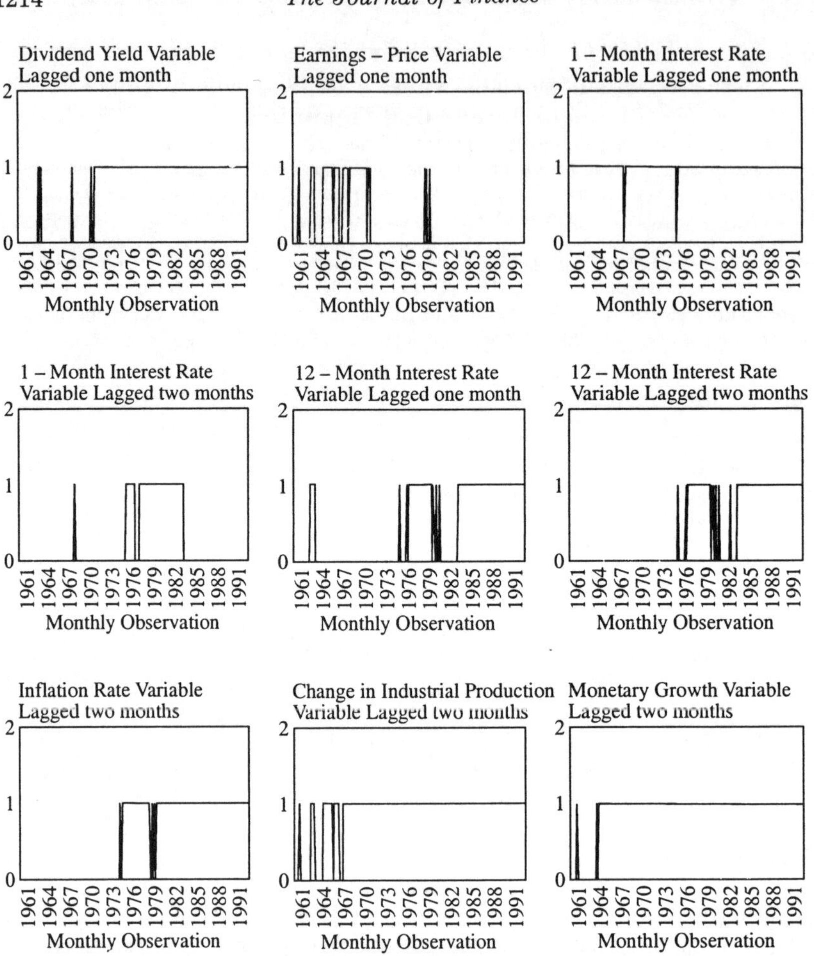

Figure 4. Inclusion frequency of the variables in the base set under the $\bar{R}^2$ model selection criterion, 1960(1) to 1992(12). Note: The inclusion of the variable in the regression model is depicted by unity, and zero otherwise.

expect the regressor in question to be an important factor in generating the observed predictability of stock returns.

Figure 4 shows that the dividend yield variable is selected in most periods from 1970 onwards. This finding supports the many recent studies that find the yield variable to be statistically significant in predicting stock returns (e.g., Campbell (1987), Fama and French (1989)). Our results, however, suggest that the correlation between yields and excess returns has become particularly strong only after 1970.[12] Compared to the dividend yield variable, the earnings-price ratio lagged one month is not selected as often in the forecasting models; in fact, this regressor is never chosen by the Schwarz criterion.

The 1-month interest rate variable lagged one month is excluded in the forecasting models in most periods (see Figure 4), whereas the two-month lagged value of the 1-month interest rate, $I1_{t-2}$, is included as a regressor in the forecasting models mainly during the 1975 to 1982 period. In the case of the longer interest rate lagged one month, $I12_{t-1}$, it is clear from Figure 4 that this variable is selected by the $\bar{R}^2$ criterion (but not by the Schwarz criterion), during the 1976 to 1979 periods, and again after 1982. This is an interesting finding since the periods when the $I12_{t-1}$ variable is not included in the forecasting model coincide closely with the period from October 1979 to September 1982, when the Federal Reserve ceased to target interest rates. It suggests that the 12-month interest rate has predictive power over excess returns in regimes where the Federal Reserve targets interest rates, but not in regimes where monetary aggregates are targeted. A similar conclusion also emerges with respect to the 12-month interest rate lagged two months, $I12_{t-2}$.

Using the $\bar{R}^2$ model selection criterion, the inflation variable lagged two periods (Π_{t-2}) is included in the forecasting equations primarily after the first oil shock. In contrast, the Schwarz criterion does not select this variable at all. Figure 4 also shows that the rate of change in industrial production lagged two periods (ΔIP_{t-2}) tends to be included in the forecasting models from 1964 onwards, when the $\bar{R}^2$ model selection criterion is adopted. Once again, by comparison the Schwarz criterion rarely selects the ΔIP_{t-2} variable. Finally, using the $\bar{R}^2$ criterion, the money growth variable, ΔM_{t-2}, gets selected continuously from 1964 onwards, but the same is not true when the Schwarz criterion is considered, which selects the money growth variable 28 percent of the times.

The different outcomes obtained under the $\bar{R}^2$ and the Akaike Criteria on the one hand, and under the Schwarz criterion on the other, lies in the fact that the Schwarz criterion penalizes inclusion of variables more heavily than either the Akaike or the $\bar{R}^2$ criteria. This may be a drawback for the Schwarz criterion since, in the event of a structural break in the underlying data generating process, this criterion may detect the change at a slower rate than the other criteria.

In a recent study, Bossaerts and Hillion (1994)[13] also find evidence supporting the conclusion that the best prediction model for monthly stock returns changes over time. Bossaerts and Hillion compare the in-sample and out-of-sample forecasting performance of models selected according to a variety of standard model selection criteria and develop a new model selection criterion

[12] On this point see also the recent papers by Goetzmann and Jorion (1993) and Nelson and Kim (1993), who find that, after correcting for lagged endogenous variable bias, the correlation between lagged values of the dividend yield and excess returns on stocks is particularly strong after the Second World War.

[13] We are grateful to an anonymous referee for bringing this research to our attention.

that can be used to detect nonstationarities in the underlying data generating process. Based on an examination of the out-of-sample forecasts of monthly returns in 15 countries over the period 1989 to 1993, Bossaerts and Hillion conclude that there is strong evidence of nonstationarities in stock returns in the U.S. and several other markets. Notice that an important difference between our study and theirs is that we explicitly allow the forecasting model to change through time.

C. The Market Timing Value of The Recursive Forecasts

In a recent study, Leitch and Tanner (1991) found that traditional measures of forecasting performance, such as the $\bar{R}^2$, were not as strongly correlated with profits from a trading strategy based on a set of predictions as were a measure of the directional accuracy (e.g., the proportion of times the sign of excess returns is correctly predicted) of the forecasts. In Pesaran and Timmermann (1992, 1994b) we have developed a new market timing test statistic that is based on the directional accuracy of the forecasts and hence may provide important information on the economic value of the recursive forecasts. In the present case with only two directions, our test statistic is asymptotically equivalent to the Henriksson and Merton (1981) test. (Pesaran and Timmermann (1994b)).[14] Values of this market timing test statistic, which are asymptotically normally distributed, are reported in Table II. For a one-sided test of the null of no market timing against the alternative of market timing skills, the 5 percent critical value is 1.64. Using the whole sample, 1960(1) to 1992(12), the null hypothesis is strongly rejected for the predictions based on models recursively selected according to all criteria except for the Schwarz criterion. Predictability seems particularly high during the 1970s and is not statistically significant during the other two decades. This suggests that the forecasting performance is not primarily a function of the length of the "learning period" of the models, as one might have suspected if the underlying data-generating process had remained constant over time.

The percentage of correctly predicted signs of the excess returns also conveys important information to an investor. Once again, with the exception of the Schwarz criterion, the recursive predictions get the sign of the excess returns right in at least 58 percent of all months over the 1960 to 1992 period. The results over the three subperiods, 1960 to 1969, 1970 to 1979 and 1980 to 1989, also show the substantially higher proportion of correct signs achieved by all the recursive forecasts over the 1970s as compared to the other two subperiods.

III. Assessing the Economic Significance of Predictability of Excess Returns in a Simple Trading Strategy

In the finance literature, the efficient market hypothesis is often interpreted as the impossibility of constructing a trading rule, based on publicly available

[14] The largest deviation between the values of our test statistic and the values of the nonparametric Henriksson-Merton test statistic reported in Table II was 0.03.

Table II

Predictive Accuracy of Excess Return Forecasts over 1960(1) to 1992(12) and Three Sub-Periods

The *PT* statistic is the nonparametric test statistic for market timing proposed in Pesaran and Timmermann (1992). This test, which is asymptotically equivalent to the Henriksson-Merton (1981) test of market-timing, has a standardized normal distribution in large samples. All selection criteria were applied recursively (see Section II). The hyper-selection criterion is described in the Appendix. The recursive wealth procedure uses as a forecasting model the one that, at each point in time, generated the largest wealth (net of transaction costs) when its forecasts were used in a simple trading strategy. The recursive Sharpe criterion is based on a similar procedure with the difference that it is now the Sharpe ratio corresponding to trading results based on the set of predictions generated by a particular regression model that is being maximized recursively.

	1960 to 1992		1960 to 1969		1970 to 1979		1980 to 1989	
Selection Criteria	PT-Statistics	Proportion of Correct Signs	PT-Statistics	Proportion of Correct Signs	PT-Statistics	Proportion of Correct Signs	PT-Statistics	Proportion of Correct Signs
Panel A: Statistical Selection Criteria								
$\bar{R}^2$	3.39*	59.6	1.64†	58.3	2.64*	61.7	0.76	56.7
Akaike	2.88*	58.3	1.33	56.7	2.67*	61.7	0.43	55.0
Schwarz	1.34	53.3	−1.20	43.3	2.39*	60.8	0.73	54.2
Sign	2.93*	58.3	1.92†	59.2	1.88†	58.3	0.79	55.8
All Regressors	3.41*	59.6	1.14	56.7	2.81*	62.5	1.11	57.5
Panel B: Hyper-Selection Procedure								
Transaction Costs								
Zero	2.88*	58.1	1.92†	59.2	1.88†	58.3	0.85	55.8
Medium	3.06*	58.6	1.92†	59.2	1.71†	57.5	0.95	56.7
High	3.06*	58.6	1.92†	59.2	1.51	56.7	1.11	57.5
Panel C: Financial Criteria								
Recursive Wealth Procedure								
Transaction Costs								
Zero	3.73*	60.4	0.98	55.8	2.64*	61.7	1.67†	60.0
Medium	3.51*	59.6	1.39	56.7	2.25*	60.0	1.51	59.2
High	3.27*	58.8	1.39	56.7	1.88†	58.3	1.58	58.3
Recursive Sharpe Procedure								
Transaction Costs								
Zero	3.71*	60.4	1.29	57.5	2.62*	61.7	1.90†	60.8
Medium	3.14*	58.8	1.14	56.7	2.62*	61.7	1.07	56.7
High	3.31*	59.1	0.98	55.8	2.62*	61.7	1.20	56.7

* Indicates statistically significant evidence of market timing at the 10 percent level.
† Indicates statistically significant evidence of market timing at the 1 percent level.

information, that is capable of yielding positive excess profits (discounted at an appropriate risk-adjusted rate). Jensen (1978) puts it this way: "A market is efficient with respect to information set Ω_t if it is impossible to make economic profits by trading on the basis of information set Ω_t."

Predictability of stock returns in itself does not, however, guarantee that an investor can earn profits from a trading strategy based on such forecasts. First, monthly excess returns on stocks do not follow a standard distribution but are considerably more leptokurtic than, say, the normal distribution. Standard measures of predictive performance, such as the $\bar{R}^2$, may not be reliable in terms of indicating opportunities for profit-making. Secondly, transaction costs may erode the profits from trading in the financial markets based on recursive forecasts of excess returns. Compared to the natural benchmark of a buy-and-hold strategy in the market portfolio, which is a relatively passive investment strategy and hence incurs low transaction costs, an investment strategy based on recursive forecasts is likely to incur considerably higher transaction costs and may not be as profitable as the buy-and-hold strategy when transaction costs are appropriately taken into account.

To find out if our recursive predictions could have been used to generate a higher profit than that earned from following a buy-and-hold strategy in the market portfolio, we used our predictions in a simple switching strategy that has been employed extensively in the finance literature. According to this strategy, investors should hold equity in periods where the business cycle indicators suggest that equity returns are going to outperform returns from holding bonds (i.e., the predicted excess return on stocks is positive), and otherwise hold bonds. We do not allow for short-selling of assets, nor do we assume that investors can use leverage when selecting their portfolios. Also, in the absence of a published time series on transaction costs during the period 1960 to 1992, we made the simplifying assumption that these are constant through time and symmetric with respect to whether the investor is buying or selling assets. We further assume that transaction costs are proportional to the value of the trade, letting c_1 and c_2 be the percentage transaction costs on shares and bonds, respectively.[15]

To analyze how the value of the investor's portfolio evolves through time, we first introduce some notations. Let W_t be the funds available to the investor at the end of period t, N_t the numbers of shares held at the end of period t (after trading), P_t the price of shares at the end of period t, D_t the dividends per share paid during period t, r_t the rate of return on bonds in period t, B_t the investor's position in bonds at the end of period t (after trading), and $I_{t+1}(\hat{\rho}_{t+1})$ the indicator variable, as defined earlier, which takes the value 1 or 0 according to the predicted sign of excess returns in period $t + 1$, namely: $I_{t+1}(\hat{\rho}_{t+1}) = 1$, if $\hat{\rho}_{t+1} > 0$, and $I_{t+1}(\hat{\rho}_{t+1}) = 0$, otherwise. For simplicity we also refer to this function as I_{t+1}.

At a particular point in time, t, we assume that the funds are held entirely either in bonds or in stocks, according to the value predicted for I_{t+1}. Net of transaction costs the investor can allocate the funds either to shares or to bonds:

$$N_t = W_t I_{t+1}(1 - c_1)/P_t, \tag{12}$$

$$B_t = W_t(1 - I_{t+1})(1 - c_2). \tag{13}$$

[15] For a more detailed discussion of transaction costs and their relation to commission fees and bid-ask spreads, see Pesaran and Timmermann (1994a).

For period $t + 1$, the budget constraint of the investor becomes

$$W_{t+1} = N_t(P_{t+1} + D_{t+1}) + B_t(1 + r_t). \tag{14}$$

Based on the forecast of excess returns for period $t + 2$, the portfolio allocation procedure is repeated at the end of period $t + 1$. The size of the transaction costs incurred through the reallocation of funds depends on the composition of the investor's existing portfolio in bonds (B_t) or in stocks (N_t), and on the selected portfolio composition for period $t + 1$. This gives four different cases to be considered:

Case I (Reinvest Cash Dividends in Shares)

$$\begin{gathered} \mathrm{I}_{t+1} = 1 \quad \text{and} \quad \mathrm{I}_{t+2} = 1, \\ N_{t+1} = N_t + N_t D_{t+1}(1 - c_1)/P_{t+1}, \\ B_{t+1} = 0. \end{gathered}$$

Case II (Sell Stocks and Buy Bonds)

$$\begin{gathered} \mathrm{I}_{t+1} = 1 \quad \text{and} \quad \mathrm{I}_{t+2} = 0, \\ N_{t+1} = 0, \\ B_{t+1} = (1 - c_2)[(1 - c_1)N_t P_{t+1} + N_t D_{t+1}]. \end{gathered}$$

Case III (Bonds Mature, Buy Shares)

$$\begin{gathered} \mathrm{I}_{t+1} = 0 \quad \text{and} \quad \mathrm{I}_{t+2} = 1, \\ N_{t+1} = (1 - c_1)B_t(1 + r_t)/P_{t+1}, \\ B_{t+1} = 0. \end{gathered}$$

Case IV (Bonds Mature, Buy Bonds)

$$\begin{gathered} \mathrm{I}_{t+1} = 0 \quad \text{and} \quad \mathrm{I}_{t+2} = 0, \\ N_{t+1} = 0, \\ B_{t+1} = (1 - c_2)(1 + r_t)B_t. \end{gathered}$$

Using these formulae the value of the investor's funds at the end of period $t + 2$ becomes

$$W_{t+2} = N_{t+1}(P_{t+2} + D_{t+2}) + B_{t+1}(1 + r_{t+1}). \tag{15}$$

Extension of these rules to subsequent periods is straightforward.

A. Empirical Results from Trading Based on the Recursive Forecasts

Table III presents the trading results for a number of switching portfolios constructed using forecasts from models selected recursively according to the different selection strategies. Table III also reports the Sharpe index for the various portfolios. These computations assume that investors start off with \$100 at the beginning of 1960 and reinvest the portfolio income every month. In the case of the market and bond portfolios, only the dividends or interests

Table III

Performance Measures for the S&P 500 Switching Portfolio Relative to the Market Portfolio and T-Bills (Monthly Results: 1960(1) to 1992(12))

The switching portfolios are based on recursive least squares regressions of excess returns on an intercept term and a subset of regressors selected from a base set of 9 variables according to different statistical model selection criteria and financial performance criteria. See Section II of the article for a definition of the statistical and financial selection criteria. The hyper-selection criterion is described in the Appendix. The columns headed Zero, Low, and High refer to the portfolio returns under the three transaction costs scenarios described in Section III. *A* of the article. The final wealth figures assume that investors start off with $100 at the beginning of 1960 and reinvest portfolio income every month. The recursive wealth procedure uses as a forecasting model the one that, at each point in time, generated the largest wealth (net of transaction costs) when its forecasts were used in a simple trading strategy. The recursive Sharpe criterion is based on a similar procedure with the only difference that it is now the Sharpe ratio corresponding to trading results based on the set of predictions generated by a particular regression model that is being maximized recursively. S.D. is standard deviation.

Panel A: Benchmarks, Statistical Selection Criteria

Transaction costs	Market Portfolio			Bonds			Akaike			Schwarz		
	Zero	Low	High	Zero	Low	High	Zero	Low	High	Zero	Low	High
Mean return	11.39	11.34	11.29	5.92	4.66	4.66	14.06	12.51	11.48	11.68	9.46	7.91
S.D. of return	15.71	15.72	15.73	2.61	2.59	2.59	11.16	11.47	11.69	10.73	10.85	10.95
Sharpe's index	0.35	0.43	0.42	—	—	—	0.73	0.69	0.58	0.54	0.44	0.30
Final wealth ($)	**2503**	**2463**	**2424**	**660**	**445**	**445**	**6601**	**4144**	**3024**	**3305**	**1687**	**1049**

Panel B: Statistical Selection Criteria

Transaction costs	$\bar{R}^2$			Sign			All Regressors			Hyper-Selection Criterion		
	Zero	Low	High	Zero	Low	High	Zero	Low	High	Zero	Low	High
Mean return	14.83	13.22	12.13	13.69	11.70	10.25	14.46	12.85	11.78	13.58	12.32	11.28
S.D. of return	11.37	11.51	11.58	9.06	9.24	9.40	11.61	11.79	11.91	9.78	10.32	10.77
Sharpe's index	0.78	0.74	0.65	0.86	0.76	0.60	0.74	0.70	0.60	0.74	0.74	0.62
Final wealth ($)	**8218**	**5113**	**3694**	**6236**	**3452**	**2233**	**7329**	**4556**	**3288**	**5943**	**4044**	**2932**

Panel C: Financial Criteria

Transaction costs	Recursive Wealth Procedure			Recursive Sharpe Procedure		
	Zero	Low	High	Zero	Low	High
Mean return	14.00	11.76	10.83	15.14	11.81	10.73
S.D. of return	12.24	11.98	11.22	11.60	10.66	10.97
Sharpe's index	0.66	0.59	0.55	0.79	0.67	0.55
Final wealth ($)	**6242**	**3247**	**2508**	**8859**	**3429**	**2458**

are reinvested on a monthly basis. In contrast, the switching portfolios may reallocate funds between bonds and shares, depending on whether a change in the sign of the excess return is predicted.

First consider the results based on zero transaction costs. The mean annual return on the market index over the period 1960 to 1992 is 11.39 percent, and is smaller than the mean return on all the switching portfolios under consideration. Comparing the performance of the switching portfolios based on forecasts using different model selection criteria, the portfolio based on Schwarz's criterion only pays a marginally higher mean return than the buy-and-hold strategy in the market index. At the other end of the performance spectrum, the portfolios based on the forecasts using the Akaike, the $\bar{R}^2$, and the recursive Sharpe criteria pay mean returns of 14.06, 14.83, and 15.14 percent, respectively, which are substantially above the mean return on the market index. Interestingly, the annual mean return on the switching portfolio based on predictions maximizing recursive wealth is smaller than the annual mean returns on most of the other switching portfolios. Clearly, there are important differences in the performance of the model selection criteria in identifying predictability of stock returns. A possible method of resolving the uncertainty surrounding the choice of model selection criterion is discussed in the Appendix.

These differences in mean returns are reflected in the end-of-period wealth accrued to the investment strategies based on reinvesting the funds in either bonds or shares at the end of every month. Under the zero transaction cost scenario, the end-of-period funds of the switching portfolios were approximately twice as large as the end-of-period funds of the market portfolio (in the case of the Akaike, Sign, and recursive wealth criteria) or three times as large (in the case of the $\bar{R}^2$, the recursive Sharpe criterion and the fixed model specification that includes all regressors). The fact that the recursive predictions based on models selected according to the $\bar{R}^2$ or the recursive Sharpe criterion perform better than the recursive predictions from the model that included all regressors suggests that it may pay off for investors to engage in an active search process to find an adequate forecasting equation rather than just basing their forecasts on a fixed model specification that includes the entire set of regressors.[16]

Turning next to the standard deviation of the returns on the switching portfolios, these lie in the range from 9.1 to 12.2 percent per annum, which is substantially lower than the standard deviation of returns on the market portfolio (15.7 percent). The standard deviation of the returns on the switching portfolio selected on the basis of predictions using the sign criterion is particularly low. Taken together, the higher mean and lower standard deviation of the returns on the switching portfolios result in high values of the Sharpe ratio of these portfolios. Notice that the switching portfolio based on recursively maximizing the Sharpe ratio does not produce the highest Sharpe statistic among all the switching portfolios.

Allowing for "low" transaction costs of 0.5 of a percent on trading in shares (c_1 = 0.005) and 0.1 of a percent on trading in bonds (c_2 = 0.001), the mean payoffs on the switching portfolios decline by between 1.6 and 3.3 percent per

[16] This should be compared to the findings in Phillips (1992) which report that a model specification that includes a large number of autoregressive lags, as well as deterministic trends, tends to produce worse predictions than models selected recursively according to his Bayesian Posterior Information Criterion.

annum. Thus, under the low transaction cost scenario, mean returns on the switching portfolios based on predictions from models selected according to Schwarz's criterion are now lower than the mean returns on the market portfolio. In comparison, transaction costs hardly affect the mean return on the buy-and-hold strategy, since the only turnover associated with this portfolio arises from reinvestment of the dividends. Even so, under this low transaction cost scenario, the switching portfolios based on the forecasts produced by models that either included all regressors or were recursively selected according to any of the criteria (apart from the Schwarz's criterion) continue to pay higher mean returns with a lower standard deviation than the market index. This is the case despite the fact that the number of portfolio switches is between two and three per year, depending on which set of forecasts is used.

With "high" transaction costs of 1 percent on shares and 0.1 of a percent on bonds, the mean return on the switching portfolios based on forecasts using the $\bar{R}^2$ and the Akaike criteria still exceed the mean return on the market portfolio. Furthermore, as witnessed by the values of the Sharpe ratios, even with high transaction costs the switching portfolios based on predictions using these model selection criteria still offer a better risk-return trade-off than the market portfolio. Notice the sharp decline in the performance of the switching portfolios based on financial criteria as transaction costs are introduced. This suggests that a two-step procedure using statistical model selection criteria to compute recursive forecasts of stock returns and then trading on the basis of these forecasts may be better at identifying predictability in the stock market than a more direct procedure based on a forecasting model selected according to a financial criterion.

Using the test statistic suggested by Gibbons, Ross, and Shanken (GRS) (1989), we computed the joint significance of the intercept terms in regressions of monthly excess returns of the eight switching portfolios on a constant and the excess return on the market portfolio. In the case of zero transaction costs the value of the GRS test statistic was 3.26 (0.001). But as to be expected, the GRS test statistic declined to 2.36 (0.017) and 1.96 (0.05) for the low and high transaction cost scenarios, respectively. Rejection probability values are provided in brackets after the value of the test statistics.[17] Clearly, the mean-variance efficiency of the buy-and-hold strategy is rejected.

We also analyzed the performance of the switching portfolios over the sub-periods 1960 to 1969, 1970 to 1979 and 1980 to 1989 (see Table IV). For all three subperiods, the portfolios based on forecasts using the Akaike, $\bar{R}^2$, or the sign criteria paid a higher mean return than the buy-and-hold strategy under the zero transaction cost scenario. The switching portfolios based on the remaining model selection criteria only paid a higher mean return than the market during the 1970s and 1980s, while the switching portfolio using the Schwarz criterion paid a higher mean return than the market index only during the 1970s. When transaction costs are introduced, it becomes even

[17] Under the null hypothesis that the market portfolio is mean-variance efficient the Gibbons, Ross, and Shanken (1989) test statistic has a central F distribution.

Table IV

Risk and Returns of Different Portfolios for Subperiods: 1960s, 1970s, and 1980s

	Zero Transaction Costs			Low Transaction Costs			High Transaction Costs		
Risk and Returns	1960 to 1969	1970 to 1979	1980 to 1989	1960 to 1969	1970 to 1979	1980 to 1989	1960 to 1969	1970 to 1979	1980 to 1989
	Panel A: Mean (Annualized)								
Portfolios									
Market	8.63	7.42	18.06	8.56	7.40	18.03	8.49	7.38	18.01
Bond	3.71	6.02	8.23	2.47	4.76	6.94	2.47	4.76	6.94
Akaike	8.78	13.35	19.14	7.37	12.06	17.03	6.55	11.31	15.40
Schwarz	5.20	11.94	16.70	3.28	10.13	14.09	2.09	8.96	12.15
$\bar{R}^2$	9.17	14.22	20.28	7.45	12.87	18.25	6.31	12.09	16.69
Sign	11.04	11.19	18.37	9.03	9.79	15.55	7.67	8.96	13.31
All regressors	8.13	15.03	19.26	6.29	13.64	17.42	4.99	12.84	16.08
Hyper selection	11.04	11.19	18.53	9.03	9.38	17.17	7.67	7.89	16.71
Recursive wealth proc.	7.81	14.26	18.07	6.90	11.44	15.16	6.28	9.84	14.57
Recursive sharpe proc.	8.49	15.06	21.25	6.61	13.55	13.96	4.28	12.64	13.43
	Panel B: Standard Deviation (Annual)								
Portfolios									
Market	14.36	19.24	12.65	14.39	19.24	12.65	14.42	19.24	12.65
Bond	1.32	1.80	2.66	1.31	1.78	2.63	1.31	1.78	2.63
Akaike	8.30	10.64	12.90	9.16	10.62	13.41	9.72	10.56	13.88
Schwarz	9.92	9.29	10.07	10.53	9.24	10.53	10.97	9.10	11.02
$\bar{R}^2$	8.99	12.52	10.99	9.70	12.10	11.34	10.20	11.64	11.68
Sign	8.62	7.69	8.94	9.39	7.94	8.78	9.99	8.02	8.75
All regressors	7.14	13.17	12.29	8.37	12.60	12.46	9.36	12.03	12.54
Hyper selection	8.62	7.69	10.81	9.39	9.32	10.79	9.99	8.53	11.67
Recursive wealth proc.	10.51	13.44	10.81	11.49	13.02	10.21	11.77	13.10	7.27
Recursive sharpe proc.	10.60	11.91	10.07	11.02	11.13	8.88	11.92	10.47	8.47
	Panel C: Sharpe Ratio								
Portfolios									
Market	0.342	0.073	0.776	0.424	0.137	0.877	0.418	0.136	0.875
Bond	-	-	-	-	-	-	-	-	-
Akaike	0.610	0.689	0.846	0.535	0.688	0.752	0.420	0.621	0.609
Schwarz	0.150	0.637	0.842	0.078	0.581	0.679	−0.034	0.461	0.473
$\bar{R}^2$	0.607	0.655	1.097	0.513	0.670	0.998	0.376	0.630	0.835
Sign	0.849	0.672	1.130	0.699	0.633	0.980	0.521	0.524	0.727
All regressors	0.619	0.683	0.898	0.456	0.705	0.841	0.269	0.672	0.729
Hyper selection	0.849	0.672	0.952	0.699	0.496	0.948	0.521	0.367	0.837
Recursive wealth proc.	0.390	0.613	0.910	0.386	0.513	0.805	0.324	0.388	1.050
Recursive sharpe proc.	0.450	0.759	1.290	0.376	0.790	0.790	0.152	0.753	0.766

See the notes to Table III for details of the various procedures.

clearer that the higher mean returns on the switching portfolios are concentrated in the 1970s. Since the standard deviation of returns in the stock market was particularly high during the 1970s, these results seem to indicate that, if ever there was a possibility that investors could improve their market timing based on a simple forecasting procedure similar to ours, this was during the volatile periods in the 1970s where macroeconomic risks and volatility in nominal magnitudes, such as the rate of inflation and nominal interest rates, mattered the most.

Because the portfolios based on forecasts using models recursively selected according to the $\bar{R}^2$, Akaike, and the Sign criteria were quite successful, while portfolios based on the Schwarz criterion were not as successful in terms of the values generated for the financial performance measures, it raises the issue of whether our results can be explained by uncertainty over the choice of model selection criterion. This problem is addressed in the Appendix, where it is shown that the switching portfolios continue to strongly outperform the buy-and-hold strategy, even if the choice of the model selection criterion is made endogenous to the forecasting and the trading processes. The hyper-selection procedure advanced in the Appendix for the resolution of the uncertainties over the choice of model selection criteria and the forecasting model can also be viewed as an artificial intelligence system capable of detecting unexploited profit opportunities in the market. Clearly, it would be possible to devise more comprehensive and sophisticated artificial intelligence systems for the analysis of stock market predictability. However, a comparative analysis of such systems fall outside the scope of the present paper.

IV. Concluding Remarks and a Discussion of the Main Results

We have proposed in this article a new approach for simulating the behavior of an investor in real time, using as little hindsight as possible and specifically accounting for the effect of model specification uncertainty which is crucially important to any investor trying to forecast asset returns in real time.

As far as the issue of robustness of the predictability of U.S. stock returns is concerned, our plots of the inclusion frequency of the different factors in the forecasting models clearly show the importance of allowing for changes in the underlying process of excess returns in the U.S. stock market that seem to have taken place during the 1960 to 1992 period. The only variable to be included in the forecasting models throughout the entire sample period 1960 to 1992 is the one-month lagged value of the one-month T-bill rate. Monetary growth and industrial production are included in the forecasting models more or less continuously from the mid and late 1960s, respectively, and the dividend yield variable starts to get included as a regressor in the forecasting models around 1970. The frequency with which the inflation rate variable and the 12-month interest rate are included in the forecasting equations is, however, closely related to economic "regime switches": the inflation rate gets included after the first oil shock while, according to the models selected by the

$\bar{R}^2$ criterion, the 12-month interest rate is selected from the mid-seventies onwards during periods where the Federal Reserve targeted interest rates.

Thus, in general our findings confirm the results of recent research which has emphasized the importance of predictable components in stock returns related to the business cycle, (see the references cited in Footnote 1). But we find that predictability of stock returns of a magnitude that is economically exploitable seems to depend not just on the evolution of the business cycle, but also on the magnitude of the shocks. Also there does not seem to be a robust forecasting model in the sense that the determinants of the predictability of stock returns in the U.S. seem to have undergone important changes throughout the period under consideration. The timing of the episodes where many of the regressors get included in the forecasting model seems to be linked to macroeconomic events such as the oil price shock in 1974 and the Fed's change in its operating procedures during the 1979 to 1982 period. If we are right in our conclusion that important episodes of predictability of stock returns are closely linked to incidence of sudden shocks to the economy, then in analyzing stock return predictability it is advisable to use forecasting procedures that allow for possible regime changes.

Another conclusion emerging from our study is that there appears to be a relation between periods with high volatility in the markets and periods with higher-than-normal predictability of excess returns on shares. Our results suggest that during the relatively calm markets of the 1960s, there were no excess returns to be gained from following a switching strategy based on forecasts using the recursively selected regression models. In contrast, during the more volatile 1970s there seems to have been important gains to be made from following such a forecasting and trading strategy, while in the 1980s the gains were much smaller. This finding could be consistent both with incomplete learning in the aftermath of a large shock to the economy (see Timmermann (1993)) as well as with a story where the predictability of excess returns is reflecting time-varying risk premia. In the context of the latter it is, however, difficult to explain why return on the switching portfolio exceeds the return on the market when the markets are volatile. It is well known that there is no theoretical reason why required returns on stocks cannot be lower during periods with relatively high volatility. For instance, risk averse investors may want to increase their savings, thereby bidding down the equilibrium return on stocks when the markets are particularly volatile. Furthermore, it is quite possible that the price of risk is time-varying so that there is no constant, proportional relationship between the first and second conditional moments of stock returns. Given the existence of a risk-free T-bill rate, which establishes a lower bound for the nominal return, it seems difficult, however, in the context of an equilibrium model to explain the predictions of negative risk premia on the market portfolio apparent in the 1970s.[18] On the other hand,

[18] One possibility is that, during the periods of high volatility and high inflation in the early 1970s, stocks acted as an inflation hedge making investors more willing to accept low or even negative expected excess returns of stocks. For a more detailed discussion of the equilibrium conditions under which the predicted excess return on stocks can be negative in certain states, see Pesaran and Potter (1993).

it is quite possible that in the event of a major regime switch in the economy, such as the one induced by the first oil shock in 1973, learning may take longer than usual to complete as investors would need extra time to model, say, the new relationship between inflation, nominal interest rates, and stock returns. Learning about the market is a continuous process that involves both the routine updating of the parameter estimates of a given model as well as searching for new models when there are clear signs that the old established relations are no longer valid. It is this latter form of learning that is likely to be time consuming, and seems to account for the increased predictability of stock returns in periods with large and sudden shocks and important regime switches.

Finally, our results do not appear to be sensitive to the particular choice of trading rule. In fact, we investigated the returns from following a trading rule that explicitly accounts for the prediction uncertainty. According to this rule, investors stay in the stock market unless their predictions indicate that there is at least 90 percent probability that bonds will pay a higher return than stocks. This is a relatively conservative trading rule in the sense that the investor stays in the stock market unless he is fairly confident that it will be better to stay in bonds. Consequently this rule generates fewer switches between the two types of assets, and transaction costs are much lower. We found that this trading rule would generate returns with a higher mean and lower standard deviation than the market index, provided transaction costs are zero or low. Under high transaction costs the mean return on the switching portfolio was similar to the market, whereas the volatility of returns was much lower.

Appendix

Uncertainty Over the Choice of Model Selection Criterion—A Profit-Based Hyper-Selection Criterion

It is clear from the empirical results reported in Section III that although most of the model selection criteria considered generate a profit relative to the market index, this is not the case for the Schwarz criterion under the low or high transaction cost scenarios. Without some rule for choosing a model selection criterion an investor could not, without the benefit of hindsight, have been guaranteed to choose one of the more successful selection criteria. In this Appendix we address this issue and consider the problem of how an investor could resolve the uncertainty surrounding the choice of model selection criterion.

In view of the objective of the exercise we consider a profit-based hyper-selection criterion that we employ recursively to choose the model selection criterion to be used subsequently for selecting the forecasting model. The idea is similar to choosing a subset of regressors from the base set of regressors explained in detail in Section II. Here, however, there are two levels at which the search for a suitable forecasting equation needs to be conducted. First, a model selection criterion needs to be chosen from the base set consisting of the five statistical model selection criteria, namely the $\bar{R}^2$, Akaike, Schwarz, and the Sign criteria, as well as the general model specification that includes all the regressors. Having chosen a model selection criterion we then proceed to select the subset of the regressors from the base set for computing one-period ahead forecasts. More specifically, the profit-based hyper-selection criterion works as follows: at each point in time we calculate the funds that would have been generated by using the forecasts from the models selected according to the various model selection criteria. Then the model selection criterion corresponding to the fund with the highest cumulative wealth is chosen to select the model to be used for forecasting the excess return for the next period.

In application of the hyper-selection rule we used information up to 1959(12) to choose a forecasting model and parameter estimates according to the five different ways of selecting a model. Generating in-sample forecasts for the period 1954(1) to 1959(12) and using these in a trading strategy beginning in 1954(1), we computed the value of the funds for the five different portfolios (associated with the five different model selection criteria) at the end of 1959(12). The model selection criterion for which the simulated wealth at this point was highest was then used to select a model to forecast excess returns for 1960(1). Given the dependence of the portfolio values on transaction costs, it is clear that the choice of the model selection criterion will in general also depend on the assumed level of transaction costs. In the low transaction costs scenario, which is likely to be the most relevant one in practice, the final wealth of the switching portfolio selected using the profit-based hyper-selection criterion was 4044 dollars. This compares with final funds of 2463 dollars for the market index under the low transaction cost scenario. (See the results for the Hyper-Selection Criterion in Table III).

In the case of zero transaction costs, the Sign criterion was chosen by the profit-based hyper-selection criterion from 1960 to 1986. Thereafter, the $\bar{R}^2$ criterion was chosen up to 1992, apart from a brief spell in 1990, when the Sign criterion was again chosen. Under the low transaction costs scenario, the Sign criterion was again chosen by the hyper-selection criterion over the periods 1960 to 1975 and 1980 to 1985, while the $\bar{R}^2$ criterion was chosen in the remaining years. These findings are in accordance with the subsample results reported in Table IV, which show that the switching portfolio based on the forecasts using the Sign criterion paid the highest return during the 1960s, but did less well relative to other selection criteria during the 1970s and 1980s.

REFERENCES

Akaike, H., 1973, Information theory and an extension of the maximum likelihood principle, in B.N. Petrov and F. Csaki, Eds., *Second International Symposium on Information Theory*, Akademiai Kiado, (Budapest, Hungary), 267–281.

Amemiya, T., 1980, Selection of regressors, *International Economic Review* 21, 331–345.

Angas, L.L.B., 1936, Investment for appreciation. Forecasting movements in security prices. *Technique of Trading in Shares for Profit* (Macmillan, London).

Balvers, R.J., T.F. Cosimano, and B. McDonald, 1990, Predicting stock returns in an efficient market, *Journal of Finance* 45, 1109–1128.

Bossaerts, P., and P. Hillion, 1994, Implementing statistical criteria to select return forecasting models, Working paper, Caltech.

Breen, W., L.R. Glosten, and R. Jagannathan, 1990, Predictable variations in stock index returns, *Journal of Finance* 44, 1177–1189.

Campbell, J.Y., 1987, Stock returns and the term structure, *Journal of Financial Economics* 18, 373–399.

Cochrane, J.H., 1991, Production-based asset pricing and the link between stock returns and economic fluctuations, *Journal of Finance* 46, 209–238.

Dowrie, G.W. and D.R. Fuller, 1950, *Investments* (second ed.). (John Wiley, New York).

Fama, E.F., 1991, Efficient capital markets: II, *Journal of Finance* 46, 1575–1617.

Fama, E.F., and K.R. French, 1989, Business conditions and expected returns on stocks and bonds, *Journal of Financial Economics* 25, 23–49.

Ferson, W.E., and C.R. Harvey, 1993, The risk and predictability of international equity returns, *Review of Financial Studies* 6, 527–566.

French, K.R., G.S. Schwert, and R.F. Stambaugh, 1987, Expected stock returns and volatility, *Journal of Financial Economics* 19, 3–30.

Gibbons, M.R., S.A. Ross, and J. Shanken, 1989, A test of the efficiency of a given portfolio, *Econometrica* 57, 1121–1152.

Glosten, C.R., R. Jagannathan, and D.E. Runkle, 1993, On the relation between the expected value and the volatility of the nominal excess returns on stocks, *Journal of Finance* 48, 1779–1802.

Goetzmann, W.N., and P. Jorion, 1993, Testing the predictive power of dividend yields, *Journal of Finance* 48, 663–680.

Henriksson, R.D., and R.C. Merton, 1981, On market timing and investment performance. II. Statistical procedures for evaluating forecasting skills, *Journal of Business* 54, 513–533.

Jensen, M.C., 1978, Some anomalous evidence regarding market efficiency, *Journal of Financial Economics* 6, 95–101.

Leitch, G., and J.E. Tanner, 1991, Economic forecast evaluation: Profits versus the conventional error measures, *American Economic Review* 81, 580–590.

Mallows, C.P., 1973, Some comments on C_p, *Technometrics* 15, 661–675.

Mishkin, F.S., 1992, The economics of money, banking, and financial markets, Third ed. (Harper Collins Publishers, New York).

Morgan, E.V., and W.A. Thomas, 1962, The stock exchange. Its history and functions, (Elek Books, London).

Nelson, C.R., and M.J. Kim, 1993, Predictable stock returns: The role of small sample bias, *Journal of Finance* 48, 641–662.

Pesaran, M.H., and S. Potter, 1993, Equilibrium asset pricing models and predictability of excess returns, Department of Applied Economics, Working paper, Cambridge University.

Pesaran, M.H., and A. Timmermann, 1992, A simple nonparametric test of predictive performance, *Journal of Business and Economic Statistics* 10, 461–465.

Pesaran, M.H., and A. Timmermann, 1994a, Forecasting stock returns. An examination of stock market trading in the presence of transaction costs, *Journal of Forecasting* 13, 335–367.

Pesaran, M.H., and A. Timmermann, 1994b, A generalisation of the nonparametric Henriksson-Merton test of market timing, *Economics Letters* 44, 1–7.

Pesaran, M.H., and A. Timmermann, 1994c, The use of recursive model selection strategies in forecasting stock returns, Department of Applied Economics, University of Cambridge, Working paper No. 9406.

Phillips, P.C.B., 1992, Bayesian model selection and prediction with empirical applications. Cowles Foundation Discussion Paper No. 1023, Yale University.

Phillips, P.C.B., and Ploberger, 1994, Posterior odds testing for a unit root with data-based model selection, *Econometric Theory* 10, 744–808.

Pötscher, B.M., 1991, Effects of model selection on inference, *Econometric Theory* 7, 163–185.

Prime, J.H., 1946, Investment analysis (Prentice Hall, New York).

Rose, H.B., 1960, The economic background to investment (Cambridge University Press).

Schwarz, G., 1978, Estimating the dimension of a model, *Annals of Statistics* 6, 461–464.

Shibata, R., 1976, Selection of the order of an autoregressive model by Akaike's information criterion, *Biometrika* 63, 117–126.

Theil, H., 1958, Economic forecasts and policy, (Amsterdam, North Holland).

Timmermann, A., 1993, How learning in financial markets generates excess volatility and predictability in stock prices, *Quarterly Journal of Economics*, 108, 1135–1145.

[8]

Journal of Financial Economics 22 (1988) 27–59. North-Holland

MEAN REVERSION IN STOCK PRICES
Evidence and Implications*

James M. POTERBA

Massachusetts Institute of Technology, Cambridge, MA 02139, USA
National Bureau of Economic Research, Cambridge, MA 02138, USA

Lawrence H. SUMMERS

Harvard University, Boston, MA 02138, USA
National Bureau of Economic Research, Cambridge, MA 02138, USA

Received August 1987, final version received March 1988

This paper investigates transitory components in stock prices. After showing that statistical tests have little power to detect persistent deviations between market prices and fundamental values, we consider whether prices are mean-reverting, using data from the United States and 17 other countries. Our point estimates imply positive autocorrelation in returns over short horizons and negative autocorrelation over longer horizons, although random-walk price behavior cannot be rejected at conventional statistical levels. Substantial movements in required returns are needed to account for these correlation patterns. Persistent, but transitory, disparities between prices and fundamental values could also explain our findings.

1. Introduction

The extent to which stock prices exhibit mean-reverting behavior is crucial in assessing assertions such as Keynes' (1936) that 'all sorts of considerations enter into market valuation which are in no way relevant to the prospective yield' (p. 152). If market and fundamental values diverge, but beyond some range the differences are eliminated by speculative forces, then stock prices will revert to their mean. Returns must be negatively serially correlated at

*We are grateful to Changyong Rhee, Jeff Zweibel and, especially, David Cutler for excellent research assistance, to Ben Bernanke, Fischer Black, Olivier Blanchard, John Campbell, Robert Engle, Eugene Fama, Terence Gorman, Pete Kyle, Andrew Lo, Greg Mankiw, Robert Merton, Julio Rotemberg, Kenneth Singleton, Mark Watson, an anonymous referee, and the editor, William Schwert, for helpful comments, and to James Darcel and Matthew Shapiro for data assistance. This research was supported by the National Science Foundation and a Batterymarch Financial Fellowship to the first author, and is part of the NBER Programs in Economic Fluctuations and Financial Markets. A data appendix is on file with the ICPSR in Ann Arbor, Michigan.

some frequency if 'erroneous' market moves are eventually corrected.[1] Merton (1987) notes that reasoning of this type has been used to draw conclusions about market valuation from failure to reject the absence of negative serial correlation in returns. Conversely, the presence of negative autocorrelation may signal departures from fundamental values, although it could also arise from variation in risk factors over time.

Our investigation of mean reversion in stock prices is organized as follows. Section 2 evaluates alternative statistical tests for transitory price components. We find that variance-ratio tests of the type used by Fama and French (1986a) and Lo and MacKinlay (1988) are close to the most powerful tests of the null hypothesis of market efficiency with constant required returns against plausible alternative hypotheses such as the fads model suggested by Shiller (1984) and Summers (1986). These tests nevertheless have little power, even with monthly data for a 60-year period. We conclude that a sensible balancing of Type I and Type II errors suggests using critical values above the conventional 0.05 level.

Section 3 examines the extent of mean reversion in stock prices. For the U.S. we analyze monthly data on real and excess New York Stock Exchange (NYSE) returns since 1926, as well as annual returns data for the 1871–1985 period. We also analyze 17 other equity markets and study the mean-reverting behavior of individual corporate securities in the U.S. The results consistently suggest the presence of transitory components in stock prices, with returns showing positive autocorrelation over short periods but negative autocorrelation over longer periods.

Section 4 uses our variance-ratio estimates to gauge the significance of transitory price components. For the U.S. we find the standard deviation of the transitory price component varies between 15% and 25% of value, depending on our assumption about its persistence. The point estimates imply that transitory components account for more than half of the monthly return variance, a finding confirmed by international evidence.

Section 5 investigates whether observed patterns of mean reversion and the associated movements in *ex ante* returns are better explained by shifts in required returns due to changes in interest rates or market volatility or as byproducts of noise trading.[2] We argue that it is difficult to account for observed transitory components on the basis of changes in discount rates. The

[1]Stochastic speculative bubbles, considered by Blanchard and Watson (1982), could create deviations between market prices and fundamental values without negative serial correlation in returns. In the presence of any limits on valuation errors set by speculators or real investment opportunities, however, such bubbles could not exist.

[2]Noise traders are investors whose demands for securities are best treated as exogenous, rather than the result of maximizing a conventional utility function using rational expectations of the return distribution. Black (1986), Campbell and Kyle (1986), DeLong et al. (1987), and Shiller (1984) discuss a variety of possible models for noise trader behavior.

conclusion discusses some implications of our results and directions for future research.

2. Methodological issues involved in testing for transitory components

A vast literature dating at least to Kendall (1953) has tested the efficient-markets/constant-required-returns model by examining individual autocorrelations in security returns. The early literature, surveyed in Fama (1970), found little evidence of patterns in security returns and is frequently adduced in support of the efficient-markets hypothesis. Recent work by Shiller and Perron (1985) and Summers (1986) has shown that such tests have relatively little power against interesting alternatives to the null hypothesis of market efficiency with constant required returns. Several recent studies using new tests for serial dependence have nonetheless rejected the random-walk model.[3]

This section begins by describing several possible tests for the presence of stationary stock-price components, including those used in recent studies. We then present Monte Carlo evidence on each test's power against plausible alternatives to the null hypothesis of serially independent returns. Even the most powerful tests have little power against these alternatives to the random walk when we specify the conventional size of 0.05. We conclude with a discussion of test design when the data can only weakly differentiate alternative hypotheses, addressing in particular the degree of presumption that should be accorded to our null hypothesis of serially independent returns.

2.1. Test methods

Recent studies use different but related tests for mean reversion. Fama and French (1986a) and Lo and MacKinlay (1988) compare the relative variability of returns over different horizons using variance-ratio tests. Fama and French (1988b) use regression tests that also involve studying the serial correlation in multiperiod returns. Campbell and Mankiw (1987) study the importance of transitory components in real output using parametric ARMA models. Each of these approaches involves using a particular function of the sample autocorrelations to test the hypothesis that all autocorrelations equal zero.

The variance-ratio test exploits the fact that if the logarithm of the stock price, including cumulated dividends, follows a random walk, the return

[3]Fama (1976) acknowledges the difficulty of distinguishing the random-walk model from some alternative specifications. In addition to the recent work of Fama and French (1988b) and Lo and MacKinlay (1988), O'Brien (1987) demonstrates the presence of negative serial correlation at very long (up to twenty-year) horizons. Huizinga (1987) provides a spectral interpretation of the variance-ratio estimator and reports evidence that exchange rates also show long-horizon deviations from random-walk behavior.

variance should be proportional to the return horizon.[4] We study the variability of returns at different horizons, in relation to the variation over a one-year period.[5] For monthly returns, the variance-ratio statistic is therefore

$$VR(k) = \frac{\operatorname{var}(R_t^k)}{k} \Bigg/ \frac{\operatorname{var}(R_t^{12})}{12}, \tag{1}$$

where

$$R_t^k = \sum_{i=0}^{k-1} R_{t-i},$$

R_t denoting the total return in month t. This statistic converges to unity if returns are uncorrelated through time. If some of the price variation is due to transitory factors, however, autocorrelations at some lags will be negative and the variance ratio will fall below one. The statistics reported below are corrected for small-sample bias by dividing by $\mathrm{E}[VR(k)]$.[6]

The variance ratio is closely related to earlier tests based on estimated autocorrelations. Using Cochrane's (1988) result that the ratio of the k-month return variance to k times the one-month return variance is approximately equal to a linear combination of sample autocorrelations, (1) can be written

$$VR(k) \cong 1 + 2\sum_{j=1}^{k-1}\left(\frac{k-j}{k}\right)\hat{\rho}_j - 2\sum_{j=1}^{11}\left(\frac{12-j}{12}\right)\hat{\rho}_j. \tag{2}$$

The variance ratio places increasing positive weight on autocorrelations up to and including lag 11, with declining positive weight thereafter. Our variance ratios for k-period annual returns place declining weight on all autocorrelations up to order k.

A second test for mean reversion, used by Fama and French (1988b), regresses multiperiod returns on lagged multiperiod returns. If $\tilde{R}_t^k$ denotes the

[4] Testing the relationship between the variability of returns at different horizons has a long tradition: see Osborne (1959) and Alexander (1961).

[5] We use twelve-month returns in the denominator of the variance ratio to permit comparability with our results using annual returns data. With annual data, the variance-ratio denominator is $\operatorname{var}(R_t)$.

[6] Kendall and Stuart (1976) show that under weak restrictions, the expected value of the jth sample autocorrelation is $-1/(T-j)$. Using this result, we compute $\mathrm{E}[VR(k)]$. When the horizon of the variance ratio is large in relation to the sample size, this can be substantially less than unity. For example, with $T = 720$ and $k = 60$, the bias is -0.069. It rises to -0.160 if $k = 120$. Detailed Monte Carlo analysis of the variance-ratio statistic may be found in Lo and MacKinlay (1988).

de-meaned k-period return, the regression coefficient is

$$\hat{\beta}_k = \sum_{t=2k}^{T} \left(\tilde{R}_t^k \tilde{R}_{t-k}^k\right) \Big/ \sum_{t=2k}^{T} \left(\tilde{R}_{t-k}^k\right)^2. \tag{3}$$

This statistic applies negative weight to autocorrelations up to order $2k/3$, followed by increasing positive weight up to lag k, followed by decaying positive weights.[7] Fama and French (1988b) report regression tests because they reject the null hypothesis of serially independent returns more strongly than the variance-ratio test. This is the result of the actual properties of the returns data, not a general rule about the relative power of the two tests. We show below that returns display positive, then negative, serial correlation as the horizon lengthens. In this case the regression test, by virtue of its negative, then positive, weights on sample autocorrelations, will reject the null hypothesis of serial independence more often than the variance-ratio test.

A third method of detecting mean reversion involves estimating parametric time-series models for returns, or computing likelihood-ratio tests of the null hypothesis of serial independence against particular parametric alternatives. Because returns are nearly white noise under both the null hypothesis and the alternatives we consider, standard ARMA techniques often fail.[8] When they are feasible, however, the Neyman–Pearson lemma dictates that the likelihood-ratio test is the most powerful test of the null of serial independence against the particular alternative that generated the data, so its Type II error rate is a lower bound on the error rates that other tests with the same size could achieve. In practice, this bound is unlikely to be achieved, since we do not know the precise data-generation process.

2.2. Power calculations

We analyze the power of tests for transitory components against the alternative hypotheses that Summers (1986) suggests, where the logarithm of stock prices (p_t) embodies both a permanent (p_t^*) and a transitory (u_t)

[7] Further details on the relationship between regression tests and the sample autocorrelogram are presented in an earlier draft, available on request.

[8] We tried estimating ARMA models for the pseudo-returns generated in our Monte Carlo study. Although these data were generated by an ARMA(1,1) model with first-order autoregressive and moving-average coefficients of roughly equal but opposite signs, standard ARMA estimation packages (i.e., RATS) had difficulty recovering this process. For example, with three-quarters of the variation in returns due to transitory factors, the estimation package encountered noninvertibilities in the moving-average polynomial and therefore broke down in more than a third of all Monte Carlo runs. Less than 10% of the cases led to well-estimated parameters that were close to those from the data-generation process.

component. We assume that $p_t = p_t^* + u_t$. If the stationary component is an AR(1) process

$$u_t = \rho_1 u_{t-1} + \nu_t, \tag{4}$$

and $\varepsilon_t = p_t^* - p_{t-1}^*$ denotes the innovation to the nonstationary component, then

$$\Delta p_t = \varepsilon_t + (1 - L)(1 - \rho_1 L)^{-1} \nu_t. \tag{5}$$

If ν_t and ε_t are independent, Δp_t follows an ARMA (1,1) process.[9] This description of returns allows us to capture in a simple way the possibility that stock prices contain transitory, but persistent, components. The parameter ρ_1 determines the persistence of the transitory component, and the share of return variation due to transitory factors is determined by the relative size of σ_ε^2 and σ_ν^2.

We perform Monte Carlo experiments by generating 25,000 sequences of 720 returns, the number of monthly observations in the Center for Research in Securities Prices (CRSP) data base.[10] We set $\sigma_\varepsilon^2 = 1$ so that the variance of returns (Δp_t) equals $1 + 2\sigma_\nu^2/(1 + \rho_1)$ and set parameters for the return-generating process by choosing ρ_1 and $\delta = 2\sigma_\nu^2/(1 + \rho_1 + 2\sigma_\nu^2)$. The parameter δ denotes the share of return variance accounted for by the stationary component; δ and ρ_1 determine σ_ν^2. We consider cases where δ equals 0.25 and 0.75. We set ρ_1 equal to 0.98 for both cases, implying that innovations in the transitory price component have a half-life of 2.9 years.

In evaluating Type II error rates, the probability of failing to reject the null hypothesis when it is false, we use the empirical distribution of the test statistic generated with $\delta = 0$ to determine the critical region for a one-sided 0.05 test of the random-walk null against the mean-reverting alternative. The panels of table 1 report Type II error rates for each test when the data are generated by the process indicated at the column head. The mean value of the test statistic under the alternative hypothesis is also reported.

The first row in table 1 analyzes a test based on the first-order autocorrelation coefficient. As Shiller and Perron (1985) and Summers (1986) observe, this

[9]The parameters of the ARMA(1,1) model $(1 - \phi L)\Delta p_t = (1 + \theta L) w_t$ are

$$\phi = \rho_1,$$

$$\theta = \left\{ -\left(1 + \rho_1^2\right) - 2\sigma_\nu^2 + (1 - \rho_1)\left[4\sigma_\nu^2 + (1 + \rho_1)^2\right]^{1/2} \right\} / \left(2\sigma_\nu^2 + 2\rho_1\right),$$

$$\sigma_w^2 = -\left(\rho_1 + \sigma_\nu^2\right)/\theta.$$

[10]In practice we draw 720 *pairs* of random variables, associate them with (ε_t, ν_t), and then construct Δp_t.

Table 1

Simulated Type II error rates of alternative tests for transitory components in security returns.

Each row describes the statistical properties of a particular test for mean reversion. All tabulations are based on one set of 25,000 Monte Carlo experiments using 720 monthly returns generated by the process described at the column heading. Both underlying processes are ARMA(1,1), with parameters set by δ, the share of return variation due to transitory components, and ρ_1, the monthly serial correlation of the transitory component. Each test we analyze has size 0.05.

Test statistic and return measurement interval	Parameters of return-generating process			
	$\rho_1 = 0.98$ $\delta = 0.25$		$\rho_1 = 0.98$ $\delta = 0.75$	
	Type II error rate	Mean value of test statistic	Type II error rate	Mean value of test statistic
First-order autocorrelation	0.941	−0.002	0.924	−0.007
Variance ratio				
24 months	0.933	0.973	0.863	0.927
36 months	0.931	0.952	0.844	0.867
48 months	0.929	0.935	0.839	0.815
60 months	0.927	0.920	0.820	0.771
72 months	0.925	0.906	0.814	0.733
84 months	0.927	0.894	0.814	0.700
96 months	0.929	0.884	0.813	0.670
Return regression				
12 months	0.933	−0.044	0.863	−0.089
24 months	0.929	−0.080	0.842	−0.158
36 months	0.929	−0.112	0.841	−0.210
48 months	0.934	−0.141	0.856	−0.250
60 months	0.934	−0.167	0.868	−0.282
72 months	0.941	−0.194	0.887	−0.308
84 months	0.941	−0.221	0.903	−0.332
96 months	0.943	−0.250	0.914	−0.354
LR test	0.924	1.244	0.760	4.497

test has minimal power against the alternative hypotheses we consider. The Type II error rate for a size 0.05 test is 0.941 (0.924) when one-quarter (three-quarters) of the variation in returns is from the stationary component (i.e., $\delta = 0.25$ and $\delta = 0.75$).

The next panel in table 1 considers variance-ratio tests comparing return variances for several different horizons, indexed by k, with one-period return variances. The variance-ratio tests are more powerful than tests based on first-order autocorrelation coefficients, but they still have little power to detect persistent, but transitory, return components. When one-quarter of the return variation is due to transitory factors ($\delta = 0.25$), the Type II error rate never falls below 0.81. It is useful in considering the empirical results below to note that when the transitory component in prices has a half-life of less than three years and accounts for three-quarters of the variation in returns ($\delta = 0.75$), the variance ratio at 96 months is 0.67.

The next panel in table 1 shows Type II error rates for the long-horizon regression tests. The results are similar to those for variance ratios, although the regression tests appear to be somewhat less powerful against our alternative hypotheses. For example, the best variance-ratio test against the $\delta = 0.25$ case has a Type II error rate of 0.925, compared with 0.929 for the most powerful regression test.

The final panel of the table presents results on likelihood-ratio tests.[11] Although these are more powerful than the variance-ratio tests, with Type II error rates of 0.922 in the $\delta = 0.25$ case and 0.760 in the $\delta = 0.75$ case, the error rates are still high. Even the best possible tests therefore have little power to distinguish the random-walk model of stock prices from alternatives that imply highly persistent, yet transitory, price components.

One potential shortcoming of our Monte Carlo analysis is our assumption of homoskedasticity in the return-generating process. To investigate its importance, we fit a first-order autoregressive model to monthly data on the logarithm of volatility.[12] We expand our Monte Carlo experiments to allow σ_ε^2 to vary through time according to this process. The Type II error calculations from the resulting simulations are similar to those in table 1. Fig. 1 illustrates this, showing the empirical distribution function for the 96-month variance ratio in both the homoskedastic and heteroskedastic cases.

2.3. *Evaluating statistical significance*

For most of the tests described above, the Type II error rate would be between 0.85 and 0.95 if the Type I error rate were set at the conventional 0.05 level. Leamer (1978) echoes a point made in most statistics courses when he writes that 'the [popular] rule of thumb, setting the significance level arbitrarily at 0.05, is... deficient in the sense that from every reasonable viewpoint the significance level should be a decreasing function of sample size' (p. 92). For the case where three-quarters of the return variation is due to transitory

[11] The likelihood value under each hypothesis is evaluated using Harvey's (1981) exact maximum likelihood method. Because estimating the mean induces a small-sample bias toward negative autocorrelations, even under the null hypothesis of serial independence the mean likelihood ratios for each alternative hypothesis are above one.

[12] The estimated volatility process that we use for our simulations is

$$\log(\sigma_t^2) = -2.243 + 0.7689 * \log(\sigma_{t-1}^2) + \omega_t,$$

where ω_t has a normal distribution with mean zero and standard deviation 0.691. The monthly volatility data are described in French, Schwert, and Stambaugh (1987).

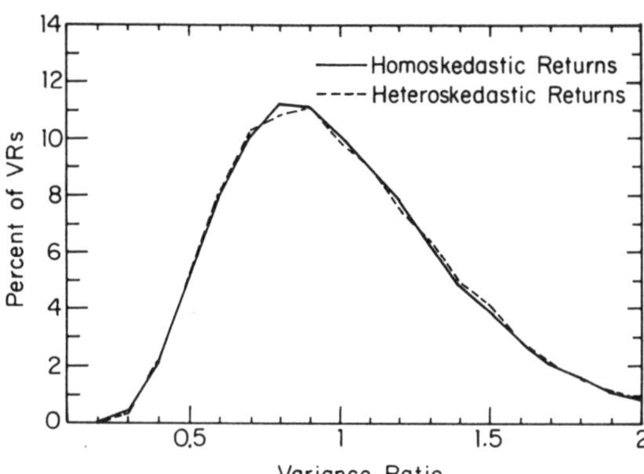

Fig. 1. Empirical distribution of 96-month variance-ratio statistic with homoskedastic and heteroskedastic returns.

The solid curve shows the empirical distribution of the 96-month variance-ratio statistic, calculated from 25,000 replications of 720-observation time series under the null hypothesis of serially independent draws from an identical distribution. The broken curve presents a similar empirical distribution calculated from the same number of Monte Carlo draws, but allowing for heteroskedasticity in the simulated returns. The logarithm of the simulated return variance evolves through time as noted in footnote 12.

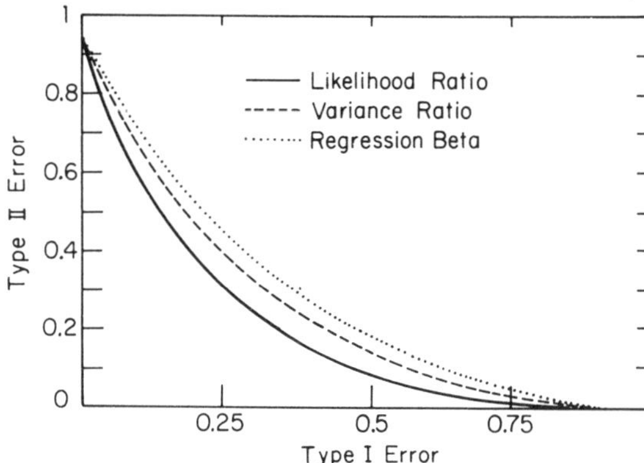

Fig. 2. Type II versus Type I error rates for three alternative tests of mean reversion.

Each curve displays the tradeoff between Type I and Type II error rates for a particular test of mean reversion in stock returns. Critical regions for each test are found using simulated empirical distributions for the variance-ratio, regression-beta, and likelihood-ratio tests under the null hypothesis of serially independent, homoskedastic returns. The Type II error rate for each test under the alternative hypothesis of $\delta = 0.75$, $\rho_1 = 0.98$ is calculated using another set of simulated empirical distributions. Under both the null and the alternative hypothesis, the empirical distributions are calculated using 25,000 replications of 720-observation time series for synthetic returns. For variance-ratio, regression-beta, and likelihood-ratio tests with given Type I error rates shown along the horizontal axis, the figure shows the associated Type II error rate against the alternative hypothesis.

factors, fig. 2 depicts the attainable tradeoff between Type I and Type II errors for the most powerful variance-ratio and regression tests, as well as for the likelihood-ratio test. The Type II error curve for the variance-ratio test lies between the frontiers attainable using regression and likelihood-ratio tests. For the variance-ratio test, a 0.40 significance level is appropriate if the goal is to minimize the sum of Type I and Type II errors. To justify using the conventional 0.05 test, one would have to assign three times as great a cost to Type I as to Type II errors.

Since there is little theoretical basis for strong attachment to the null hypothesis that stock prices follow a random walk, significance levels in excess of 0.05 seem appropriate in evaluating the importance of transitory components in stock prices. Many asset-pricing models, involving rational and irrational behavior, suggest the presence of transitory components and time-varying returns. Furthermore, the same problems of statistical power that plague our search for transitory components complicate investors' lives, so it may be difficult for speculative behavior to eliminate these components. The only solution to the problem of low power is the collection of more data. In the next section, we bring to bear as much data as possible in evaluating the importance of transitory components.

3. Statistical evidence on mean reversion

This section uses variance-ratio tests to analyze the importance of stationary components in stock prices. We analyze excess and real returns using four major data sets: monthly returns on the NYSE for the period since 1926, annual returns on the Standard and Poor's–Cowles stock price indices for the period since 1871, post-World War II monthly stock returns for 17 stock markets outside the U.S., and returns on individual firms in the U.S. for the post-1926 period.

3.1. Monthly NYSE returns, 1926–1985

We begin by analyzing monthly returns on both the value-weighted and equal-weighted NYSE indices from the CRSP data base for the 1926–1985 period. We consider excess returns with the risk-free rate measured as the Treasury bill yield, as well as real returns measured using the Consumer Price Index (CPI) inflation rate. The variance-ratio statistics for these series are shown in table 2. We confirm the Fama and French (1988b) finding that both real and excess returns at long horizons show negative serial correlation. Eight-year returns are about four rather than eight times as variable as one-year returns. Despite the low power of our tests, the null hypothesis of serial independence is rejected at the 0.08 level for value-weighted excess

Table 2

Variance ratios for U.S. monthly data, 1926–1985.

Calculations are based on the monthly returns for the value-weighted and equal-weighted NYSE portfolios, as reported in the CRSP monthly returns file. The variance-ratio statistic is defined as $VR(k) = (12/k) * \text{var}(R^k)/\text{var}(R^{12})$, where R^j denotes returns over a j-period measurement interval. Values in parentheses are Monte Carlo estimates of the standard error of the variance ratio, based on 25,000 replications under the null hypothesis of serially independent returns. Each variance ratio is corrected for small-sample bias by dividing by the mean value from Monte Carlo experiments under the null hypothesis of no serial correlation.

Data series	Annual return standard deviation	Return measurement interval							
		1 month	24 months	36 months	48 months	60 months	72 months	84 months	96 months
Value-weighted real returns	20.6%	0.797 (0.150)	0.973 (0.108)	0.873 (0.177)	0.747 (0.232)	0.667 (0.278)	0.610 (0.320)	0.565 (0.358)	0.575 (0.394)
Value-weighted excess returns	20.7%	0.764 (0.150)	1.036 (0.108)	0.989 (0.177)	0.917 (0.232)	0.855 (0.278)	0.781 (0.320)	0.689 (0.358)	0.677 (0.394)
Equal-weighted real returns	29.6%	0.809 (0.150)	0.963 (0.108)	0.835 (0.177)	0.745 (0.232)	0.642 (0.278)	0.522 (0.320)	0.400 (0.358)	0.353 (0.394)
Equal-weighted excess returns	29.6%	0.785 (0.150)	1.010 (0.108)	0.925 (0.177)	0.878 (0.232)	0.786 (0.278)	0.649 (0.320)	0.487 (0.358)	0.425 (0.394)

returns and at the 0.005 level for equal-weighted excess returns.[13] Mean reversion is more pronounced for the equal-weighted than for the value-weighted returns, but the variance ratios at long horizons are well below unity for both.

The variance ratios also suggest positive return autocorrelation at horizons shorter than one year. The variance of the one-month return on the equal-weighted index is only 0.79 times as large as the variability of twelve-month returns implies it should be. A similar conclusion applies to the value-weighted index. This finding of first positive then negative serial correlation parallels Lo and MacKinlay's (1988) result that variance ratios exceed unity in their weekly data, whereas variance ratios fall below one in other studies concerned with longer horizons.[14]

One potential difficulty in interpreting our finding of positive serial correlation at short horizons concerns nontrading effects. If some of the securities in

[13] These p-values are calculated from the empirical distribution of our test statistic, based on Monte Carlo results. They permit rejection at lower levels than would be possible using the normal approximation to the distribution of the variance ratio, along with the Monte Carlo estimates of the standard deviation of the variance ratio. Further details are available on request.

[14] French and Roll (1986) apply variance-ratio tests to daily returns for a sample of NYSE and AMEX stocks for the period 1963–1982. They find evidence of negative serial correlation, especially among smaller securities. The divergence between their findings and those of Lo and MacKinlay (1988) is presumably due to differences in the two data sets.

the market index trade infrequently, returns will show positive serial correlation. We doubt this explanation of our results since we are analyzing monthly returns. Nontrading at this frequency is likely to affect only a small fraction of securities, whereas accounting for the degree of positive correlation we observe would require that one security in ten typically did not trade in a given month. We also investigated the incidence of nontrading in a portfolio similar to the value-weighted index by analyzing daily returns on the Standard and Poor's Index [see Poterba and Summers (1986)] for the period 1928–1986. The first-order autocorrelation coefficient for daily returns is only 0.064, and grouping returns into nonoverlapping five-day periods yields a first-order autocorrelation coefficient of −0.009. This suggests that autocorrelation patterns in monthly returns are not likely to be due to infrequent trading.

A second issue that arises in analyzing the post-1926 data is the sensitivity of the findings to inclusion or exclusion of the Depression years. A number of previous studies, such as Officer (1973), have documented the unusual behavior of stock price volatility during the early 1930s. One could argue for excluding these years from analyses designed to shed light on current conditions, although the sharp increase in market volatility in the last quarter of 1987 undercuts this view. The counterargument suggesting inclusion of this period is that the 1930s, by virtue of the large movements in prices, contain a great deal of information about the persistence of price shocks. We explored the robustness of our findings by truncating the sample period at both the beginning and the end. Excluding the first ten years weakens the evidence for mean reversion at long horizons. The results for both equal-weighted real and excess returns are robust to the sample choice, with variance ratios of 0.587 and 0.736 at the 96-month horizon, but the long-horizon variance ratios on the value-weighted index rise to 0.97 and 1.10, respectively. The one-month variance ratios are not substantially changed by treatment of the early years. For the post-1936 period, the one-month variance ratios are 0.782 and 0.825 for value- and equal-weighted real returns and 0.833 and 0.851 for value- and equal-weighted excess returns.[15] Truncating the sample to exclude the last ten years of data strengthens the evidence for mean reversion.

3.2. Historical data for the United States

The CRSP data are the best available for analyzing recent U.S. experience, but the low power of available statistical tests and data-mining risks stressed by Merton (1987) suggest the value of examining other data as well. We

[15]We also experimented with crude techniques for accounting for time-varying stock market volatility in estimating variance ratios. Estimating sample autocorrelations with a heteroskedasticity correction based on French, Schwert, and Stambaugh's (1987) estimate of the previous month's return volatility effectively reduces the weight of the early Depression years, yielding variance-ratio estimates closer to unity.

Table 3

Variance ratios for U.S. data, 1871–1985.

Each entry is a bias-adjusted variance ratio with a mean of unity under the null hypothesis. The variance-ratio statistic is defined as $VR(k) = (12/k) * \text{var}(R^k)/\text{var}(R^{12})$, where R^j denotes the return measured over a j-month interval. Values in parentheses are Monte Carlo standard deviations of the variance ratio, based on 25,000 replications under the null hypothesis of serial independence. The underlying data are annual returns on the Standard and Poor's composite stock index, backdated to 1871 using the Cowles data as reported in Wilson and Jones (1987).

Data series	Annual return standard deviation	Return measurement interval						
		24 months	36 months	48 months	60 months	72 months	84 months	96 months
Excess returns 1871–1925	16.2%	0.915 (0.140)	0.612 (0.210)	0.591 (0.265)	0.601 (0.313)	0.464 (0.358)	0.425 (0.398)	0.441 (0.436)
Real returns 1871–1925	17.2%	0.996 (0.140)	0.767 (0.210)	0.806 (0.265)	0.847 (0.313)	0.737 (0.358)	0.737 (0.398)	0.807 (0.436)
Excess returns 1871–1985	18.9%	1.047 (0.095)	0.922 (0.143)	0.929 (0.179)	0.913 (0.211)	0.856 (0.240)	0.821 (0.266)	0.833 (0.290)
Real returns 1871–1985	19.0%	1.035 (0.095)	0.880 (0.143)	0.876 (0.179)	0.855 (0.211)	0.797 (0.240)	0.769 (0.266)	0.781 (0.290)

therefore consider real and excess returns based on the Standard and Poor's–Cowles Commission stock price indices, revised by Wilson and Jones (1987), which are available beginning in 1871. These data have rarely been used in studies of the serial correlation properties of stock returns, although they have been used in some studies of stock market volatility, such as Shiller (1981).

The results are presented in table 3. For the pre-1925 period, excess returns display negative serial correlation at long horizons. For real returns, however, the pattern is weaker. Although the explanation for this phenomenon is unclear, it appears to result from the volatility of the CPI inflation rate in the years before 1900. This may make the *ex post* inflation rate an unreliable measure of expected inflation during this period. The two lower rows in table 3 present results for the full 1871–1985 sample period. Both series show negative serial correlation at long lags, but real and excess returns provide less evidence of mean reversion than the monthly post-1925 CRSP data.[16]

3.3. Equity markets outside the United States

Additional evidence on mean reversion can be obtained by analyzing the behavior of equity markets outside the U.S. We analyze returns in Canada for

[16]The variance ratio for the full sample (1871–1985) period is not a simple weighted average of the variance ratios for the two subperiods, pre- and post-1926. The 96-month variance ratios for the post-1926 period excess and real S&P data, for example, are 0.463 and 0.731, respectively.

Table 4

Variance ratios for international data on real monthly returns.

Each entry reports the variance-ratio statistic (or in the bottom panel, average of variance-ratio statistics) for a particular nation and return horizon. The variance ratio is defined by $VR(k) = (12/k) * \mathrm{var}(R^k)/\mathrm{var}(R^{12})$, where R^j denotes the real return over a j-month measurement interval. Data underlying the variance ratios are real dividend-exclusive returns, calculated from share price indices in the International Monetary Funds' *International Financial Statistics*. For most countries the monthly IMF data span the period 1957:1–1986:12; other data ranges are noted. Values in parentheses are Monte Carlo standard deviations of the variance-ratio statistics (and standard deviations for the averages in the last three rows). For the averages, these are computed allowing for a constant correlation across countries. If this correlation was estimated to be negative, we assume it is zero. In all cases except those marked with an asterisk (*) the data are monthly averages of daily or weekly values. The U.K. data are point-sampled but only at the end of each year. The variance ratios are corrected for the time aggregation induced by averaging closing values of the index within each month.

Return series Country/sample	Annual return standard deviation	Return measurement interval							
		1 month	24 months	36 months	48 months	60 months	72 months	84 months	96 months
Canada/1919–1986 (capital gains only)	20.1%	0.711* (0.141)	1.055 (0.102)	0.998 (0.166)	0.912 (0.218)	0.799 (0.261)	0.692 (0.301)	0.617 (0.336)	0.575 (0.370)
U.K./1939–1986	20.9%	0.832 (0.167)	0.987 (0.125)	0.868 (0.198)	0.740 (0.259)	0.752 (0.317)	0.807 (0.358)	0.806 (0.400)	0.794 (0.440)
Austria/1957–1986 (capital gains only)	21.4%	0.663 (0.214)	1.205 (0.156)	1.206 (0.254)	1.132 (0.334)	0.864 (0.403)	0.666 (0.464)	0.582 (0.518)	0.502 (0.566)
Belgium/1957–1986 (capital gains only)	17.0%	0.718* (0.214)	1.054 (0.156)	1.137 (0.254)	1.121 (0.334)	1.060 (0.403)	0.876 (0.464)	0.807 (0.518)	0.776 (0.566)
Colombia/1959–1983 (capital gains only)	21.4%	1.223 (0.214)	0.822 (0.156)	0.743 (0.254)	0.724 (0.334)	0.583 (0.403)	0.477 (0.464)	0.386 (0.518)	0.180 (0.566)
Germany/1957–1986 (capital gains only)	23.8%	0.610 (0.214)	1.309 (0.156)	1.251 (0.254)	0.987 (0.334)	0.747 (0.403)	0.687 (0.464)	0.581 (0.518)	0.462 (0.566)
Finland/1957–1986 (capital gains only)	22.1%	0.504 (0.214)	1.141 (0.156)	1.262 (0.254)	1.396 (0.334)	1.463 (0.403)	1.381 (0.464)	1.215 (0.518)	1.014 (0.566)

France/1957–1986 (capital gains only)	23.6%	0.874* (0.214)	0.961 (0.156)	0.914 (0.254)	0.865 (0.334)	0.607 (0.403)	0.460 (0.464)	0.433 (0.518)	0.438 (0.566)
India/1957–1986 (capital gains only)	15.6%	0.752 (0.214)	0.985 (0.156)	0.974 (0.254)	0.942 (0.334)	0.823 (0.403)	0.767 (0.464)	0.619 (0.518)	0.596 (0.566)
Japan/1957–1986 (capital gains only)	20.0%	0.870 (0.214)	1.135 (0.155)	1.015 (0.254)	0.927 (0.334)	0.803 (0.403)	0.691 (0.464)	0.595 (0.518)	0.538 (0.567)
Netherlands/1957–1986 (capital gains only)	20.0%	0.710 (0.214)	1.238 (0.155)	1.263 (0.254)	1.217 (0.334)	1.083 (0.403)	1.047 (0.464)	0.894 (0.518)	0.741 (0.567)
Norway/1957–1986 (capital gains only)	24.2%	0.601 (0.214)	1.033 (0.155)	0.961 (0.254)	0.926 (0.334)	0.844 (0.403)	0.825 (0.464)	0.840 (0.518)	0.784 (0.567)
Phillipines/1957–1986 (capital gains only)	29.7%	0.910 (0.214)	0.908 (0.155)	0.749 (0.254)	0.707 (0.334)	0.703 (0.403)	0.839 (0.464)	0.898 (0.518)	0.887 (0.567)
South Africa/1957–1986 (capital gains only)	23.2%	0.767 (0.214)	1.515 (0.155)	1.063 (0.254)	0.963 (0.334)	0.980 (0.403)	1.090 (0.464)	1.131 (0.518)	1.151 (0.567)
Spain/1961–1986 (capital gains only)	27.7%	0.603 (0.230)	1.289 (0.166)	1.584 (0.273)	1.831 (0.359)	2.008 (0.433)	2.246 (0.498)	2.347 (0.5556)	2.373 (0.609)
Sweden/1957–1986 (capital gains only)	21.1%	0.728 (0.214)	0.898 (0.155)	0.822 (0.254)	0.901 (0.334)	0.885 (0.403)	0.916 (0.464)	0.760 (0.518)	0.629 (0.567)
Switzerland/1957–1986 (capital gains only)	21.5%	0.789 (0.214)	1.343 (0.155)	1.395 (0.254)	1.300 (0.334)	1.034 (0.403)	0.749 (0.464)	0.489 (0.518)	0.382 (0.567)
U.S./1957–1986 (capital gains only)	16.6%	0.813 (0.214)	0.814 (0.155)	0.653 (0.254)	0.656 (0.334)	0.696 (0.403)	0.804 (0.464)	0.803 (0.518)	0.800 (0.567)
Average value		0.760 (0.140)	1.074 (0.036)	1.048 (0.062)	1.014 (0.164)	0.930 (0.212)	0.890 (0.228)	0.822 (0.266)	0.757 (0.312)
Average value (excluding U.S.)		0.757 (0.135)	1.089 (0.024)	1.071 (0.100)	1.035 (0.173)	0.943 (0.204)	0.895 (0.207)	0.824 (0.243)	0.754 (0.290)
Average value (excluding U.S., Spain)		0.766 (0.135)	1.077 (0.042)	1.039 (0.155)	0.985 (0.259)	0.877 (0.331)	0.811 (0.392)	0.728 (0.447)	0.653 (0.494)

the period since 1919, in Britain since 1939, and in 15 other nations for a shorter postwar period.

The Canadian data consist of monthly capital gains on the Toronto Stock Exchange. The British data are monthly returns, inclusive of dividends, on the *Financial Times*–Actuaries Share Price Index. The first two rows of table 4 show that both markets display mean reversion at long horizons. The 96-month variance ratio for the Canadian data is 0.585, while for the British data it is 0.794. Both markets also display statistically significant positive serial correlation at lags of less than 12 months. For Canada, the one-month variance is 0.718 times the value that would be predicted on the basis of the 12-month variance. For Britain, the comparable value is 0.832.

The variance ratios for the 15 other stock markets are calculated from monthly returns based on stock price indices in the International Monetary Fund's *International Financial Statistics*. The IMF does not tabulate dividend yields, so the reported returns correspond to capital gains alone. To assess the importance of this omission, we reestimated the variance ratios for dividend-exclusive CRSP and British stock market returns. The results, available from the authors on request, show only minor differences as a result of dividend omission. For example, the 96-month variance ratio for real value-weighted CRSP returns inclusive of dividends is 0.575 and that for dividend-exclusive returns is 0.545. We suspect that yield-inclusive data, although superior to the returns we use, would affect our results in only minor ways.[17]

Table 4 presents the variance ratios for individual countries, based typically on data starting in 1957. Most of the countries display negative serial correlation at long horizons. In Germany, for example, the 96-month variance ratio is 0.462; in France it is 0.438. Only three of the fifteen countries have 96-month variance ratios that exceed unity, and many are substantially below one. Evidence of positive serial correlation at short horizons is also pervasive. Only one country, Colombia, has a one-month variance ratio greater than unity. The short data samples, and associated large standard errors, make it difficult to reject the null hypothesis of serial independence for any individual country. The similarity of the results across nations nevertheless supports our earlier finding of substantial transitory price components.

Average variance ratios are shown in the last three rows of the table for all countries, all countries except the U.S., and all countries except the U.S. and Spain. The mean 96-month variance ratio is 0.754 when all countries are

[17]In some cases, the monthly stock index data from the IFS are time averages of daily or weekly index values. Working (1960) showed that the first difference of a time-averaged random walk would exhibit positive serial correlation, with a first-order autocorrelation coefficient of 0.25 as the number of observations in the average becomes large. This will bias our estimated variance ratios. For the countries with time aggregated data we therefore modify our small-sample bias correction. Instead of taking the expected value of the first-order autocorrelation to be $-1/(T-1)$ when evaluating $E[VR(k)]$ we use $0.25-1/(T-1)$. The reported variance ratios have been bias-adjusted by dividing by the resulting expected value.

aggregated and 0.653 when we exclude Spain, an outlier because of the unusual pattern of hyperinflation followed by deflation that it experienced during our sample period. By averaging across many countries, we also obtain a more precise estimate of the long-horizon variance ratio, although the efficiency gain is attenuated because the results for different countries are not independent.[18]

3.4. *Individual firm data*

Arbitrageurs should be better at trading in individual securities to correct mispricing than at taking positions in the entire market to offset persistent misvaluations. Although we expect transitory components to be less likely in the relative prices of individual stocks than in the market as a whole, some previous work has suggested that individual stock returns may show negative serial correlation over some horizons [Lehmann (1987), DeBondt and Thaler (1985)]. We examine the 82 firms in the CRSP monthly master file that have no missing return information between 1926 and 1985. This is a biased sample, weighted toward large firms that have been traded actively over the entire period. Firms that went bankrupt or began trading during the sample period are necessarily excluded.

We compute variance ratios using both real and excess returns for these 82 firms. Because the returns for different firms are not independent, we also examine the returns on portfolios formed by buying one dollar of each firm and short-selling $82 of the aggregate market. That is, we examine properties of the time series $R_{it} - R_{mt}$ where R_{mt} is the value-weighted NYSE return. Table 5 reports the mean values of the individual-firm variance ratios, along with standard errors that take account of cross-firm correlation. The results suggest some long-horizon mean reversion for individual stock prices in relation to the overall market or a risk-free asset. The point estimates suggest that 12% of the eight-year variance in excess returns is due to stationary factors, and the increased precision gained by studying returns for many independent firms enables us to reject the null hypothesis that all of the price variation arises from nonstationary factors. The last row, which reports variance-ratio calculations using the residuals from market-model equations estimated for each firm (assuming a constant β for the entire period), shows

[18]The standard errors for the cross-country averages allow for correlation between the variance ratios for different countries. If all nations have a constant pairwise correlation τ between their variance ratios and these variance ratios have constant variance σ_x^2, then the expected value of the sample variance of the variance-ratio statistics is $E(s_n^2) = \sigma_x^2(1-\tau)$. Replacing the expected sample variance with the actual value, we estimate τ as $1 - s_n^2/\sigma_x^2$. The variance of the sample mean for N observations, each with the same variance σ_x^2 but constant cross-correlation τ, is $\sigma_x^2[1+(N-1)\tau]/N$. We use our estimate of τ to evaluate this expression, generalized to allow for different sampling variances for different variance ratios on the basis of our Monte Carlo standard errors from table 4.

Table 5

Average variance ratios for individual company monthly returns, 1926–1985.

Each entry reports the average of variance ratios calculated for the 82 firms on the monthly CRSP returns file with continuous data between 1926 and 1985. The variance-ratio statistic is defined as $VR(k) = (12/k) * \text{var}(R^k)/\text{var}(R^{12})$, where R^j denotes returns over a j-period measurement interval. Values in parentheses are Monte Carlo estimates of the standard error on the variance ratio, based on 25,000 replications under the null hypothesis of serially independent returns. Each variance ratio is correlated for small-sample bias by dividing the average Monte Carlo value under the null hypothesis of no serial correlation. For the returns in relation to the risk-free rate the standard errors take account of estimated contemporaneous correlation among variance ratios, using the techniques described in footnote 18.

	Return measurement interval							
Return concept	1 month	24 months	36 months	48 months	60 months	72 months	84 months	96 months
Excess returns in relation to risk-free rate	0.942 (0.063)	1.035 (0.063)	1.000 (0.100)	0.950 (0.135)	0.888 (0.166)	0.820 (0.198)	0.755 (0.236)	0.739 (0.258)
Excess returns in relation to value-weighted NYSE	1.088 (0.017)	1.034 (0.012)	1.019 (0.020)	1.002 (0.026)	0.968 (0.031)	0.928 (0.035)	0.898 (0.040)	0.886 (0.044)
Residuals from market model	1.107 (0.017)	1.055 (0.012)	1.065 (0.020)	1.057 (0.026)	1.034 (0.031)	1.008 (0.035)	0.995 (0.040)	0.985 (0.044)

less evidence of serial correlation than the results that subtract the market return. These results suggest that transitory factors account for a smaller share of the variance in relative returns for individual stocks than for the market as a whole.

3.5. Summary

Our point estimates generally suggest that over long horizons return variance increases less than proportionally with time, and in many cases they imply more mean reversion than our examples in the last section, where transitory factors accounted for three-fourths of the variation in returns. Many of the results reject the null hypothesis of serial independence at the 0.15 level, a level that may be appropriate given our previous discussion of size versus power tradeoffs. Furthermore, each of the different types of data we analyze provides evidence of departure from serial independence in stock returns. Taken together, the results are stronger than any individual finding, although not by as much as they would be if the various data sets were independent.

There is some tendency for more mean reversion in less broad-based and sophisticated equity markets. The U.S. data before 1925 show greater evidence of mean reversion than the post-1926 data. The equal-weighted portfolio of NYSE stocks shows more mean reversion than the value-weighted portfolio.[19] In recent years, mean reversion is more pronounced in smaller foreign equity markets than in the U.S.

4. The substantive importance of transitory components in stock prices

This section assesses the substantive importance of mean reversion in stock prices. One possible approach would involve calibrating models of the class considered in the first section. We do not follow this strategy because our finding of positive autocorrelation over short intervals implies that the AR(1) specification of the transitory component is inappropriate and because of our difficulties in estimating the ARMA(1, 1) models implied by this approach. Instead, we use an approach that does not require us to specify a process for the transitory component, but nevertheless allows us to focus on its standard deviation and the fraction of the one-period return variance that can be attributed to it.

[19] We conjectured that the greater mean reversion in the equal-weighted than the value-weighted portfolio might be because the less heavily traded equal-weighted portfolio experienced larger swings in required returns or fluctuated more in relation to fundamental values than the value-weighted portfolio. Assuming similar-sized movements in the permanent component of the two indices, this conjecture can be tested by analyzing the degree of mean reversion in the *relative* returns on the two indices. These returns show positive serial correlation at all lags, contrary to our conjecture.

We treat the logarithm of the stock price as the sum of a permanent and a transitory component. The permanent component evolves as a random walk and the transitory component follows a stationary process. This decomposition may be given two (not necessarily exclusive) interpretations. The transitory component may reflect fads – speculation-induced deviations of prices from fundamental values – or it may be a consequence of changes in required returns. In either case, describing the stochastic properties of the stationary price component is a way of characterizing the part of stock price movements that cannot be explained by changing expectations about future cash flows.

Given our assumptions, the variance of T-period returns is

$$\sigma_T^2 = T\sigma_\varepsilon^2 + 2(1-\rho_T)\sigma_u^2, \tag{6}$$

where σ_ε^2 is the variance of innovations to the permanent price component, σ_u^2 is the variance of the stationary component, and ρ_T is the T-period autocorrelation of the stationary component. Given data on the variance of returns over two horizons T and T' and assumptions about ρ_T and $\rho_{T'}$, a pair of equations with the form (6) can be solved to yield estimates of σ_ε^2 and σ_u^2. Using σ_R^2 for the variance of one-period returns, and $VR(T)$ for the T-period variance ratio in relation to one-period returns, estimates of σ_ε^2 and σ_u^2 are given by

$$\sigma_\varepsilon^2 = \frac{\sigma_R^2[VR(T)(1-\rho_{T'})T - VR(T')(1-\rho_T)T']}{(1-\rho_{T'})T-(1-\rho_T)T'}, \tag{7a}$$

$$\sigma_u^2 = \frac{\sigma_R^2 T'[VR(T)-VR(T')]T}{2[(1-\rho_T)T'-(1-\rho_{T'})T]}. \tag{7b}$$

Many pairs of variance ratios and assumptions about the serial correlation properties of u_t could be analyzed by using (7a)–(7b). We begin by postulating that u_t is serially uncorrelated at the horizon of 96 months. For various degrees of serial correlation at other horizons, we can then estimate the variance of the transitory component, σ_u^2, and the share of the return variation due to transitory components, $1-\sigma_\varepsilon^2/\sigma_R^2$. We present estimates based on values of 0, 0.35, and 0.70 for ρ_{12}, the twelve-month autocorrelation in u_t. The findings are insensitive to our choice of ρ_{96}; we report values of 0, 0.15, and 0.30.

Table 6 presents estimates of the standard deviation of the transitory component in stock prices for the value-weighted and equal-weighted NYSE portfolios over the period 1926–1985 for various values of ρ_{12}, assuming $\rho_{96}=0$. For the equal-weighted portfolio, the transitory component accounts

Table 6

Permanent and transitory return components, U.S. monthly data.

Each entry reports the standard deviation of the transitory component of prices, measured at annual rates (σ_u), as well as the share of return variation due to transitory factors, calculated from eqs. (7a) and (7b) to match the observed pattern of variances in long- and short-horizon returns. The variance-ratio estimates that underlie this table are drawn from the entires for 96-month variance ratios for excess returns in table 2. The different cases of ρ_{12} (ρ_{96}) correspond to different assumptions about the 12-month (96-month) autocorrelation in the transitory price component.

	$\rho_{12}=0.0$		$\rho_{12}=0.35$		$\rho_{12}=0.70$	
	σ_u	$1-\sigma_\varepsilon^2/\sigma_R^2$	σ_u	$1-\sigma_\varepsilon^2/\sigma_R^2$	σ_u	$1-\sigma_\varepsilon^2/\sigma_R^2$
			Value-weighted excess returns			
$\rho_{96}=0.00$	9.7%	0.369	12.5%	0.400	21.6%	0.554
$\rho_{96}=0.15$	–	–	12.3%	0.386	20.5%	0.500
$\rho_{96}=0.30$	–	–	12.1%	0.373	19.6%	0.456
			Equal-weighted excess returns			
$\rho_{96}=0.00$	16.8%	0.657	21.7%	0.712	37.7%	0.986
$\rho_{96}=0.15$	–	–	21.4%	0.687	35.8%	0.890
$\rho_{96}=0.30$	–	–	21.0%	0.664	34.2%	0.812

for between 43% and 99% of the variance in equal-weighted monthly returns, depending on our serial correlation assumption, and it has a standard deviation of between 14% and 37%. Results for value-weighted returns also suggest a substantial, though smaller, transitory component. Since other nations and historical periods show patterns of variance-ratio decline similar to those in U.S. data, we do not present parallel calculations for them. As one would expect, nations with 96-month variance ratios lower than those for the U.S. have larger transitory components.

Table 6 indicates that increasing the assumed persistence of the transitory component raises both its standard deviation and its contribution to the return variance. More persistent transitory components are less able to account for declining variance ratios at long horizons. To rationalize a given long-horizon variance ratio, increasing the transitory component's persistence requires increasing the weight on the transitory component in relation to the permanent component. Sufficiently persistent transitory components will be unable to account for low long-horizon variance ratios, even if they account for all of the return variation. A transitory component that is almost as persistent as a random walk, for example, will be unable to explain very much long-horizon mean reversion.

Which cases in table 6 are most relevant? As an *a priori* matter, it is difficult to argue for assuming that transitory components should die out rapidly.

Previous claims that there are fads in stock prices have typically suggested half-lives of several years, implying that the elements in the table corresponding to $\rho_{12}=0.70$ are most relevant. With geometric decay, this suggests a half-life of two years. One other consideration supports large values for ρ_{12}. For given values of σ_ε^2 and σ_u^2, eq. (6) permits us to calculate ρ_T over any horizon. A reasonable restriction, that ρ_T not be very negative over periods of up to 96 months, is satisfied only for cases where ρ_{12} is large. For example, with $\rho_{96}=0$, imposing $\rho_{12}=0.35$ yields an implied autocorrelation for the stationary component of -0.744 at 36 months, -1.27 at 60 months, and -0.274 at 84 months. In contrast, when $\rho_{12}=0.70$ and $\rho_{96}=0$, the implied values of ρ_{36} and ρ_{60} are 0.168 and -0.173, respectively. Similar results obtain for other large values of ρ_{12}. This is because actual variance ratios decline between long and longer horizons, and as eq. (6) demonstrates, rationalizing this requires declining values of ρ_T. If ρ_T starts small, it must become negative to account for the observed pattern. Larger autocorrelations at short horizons do not necessitate such patterns.

Insofar as the evidence in the last section and in Fama and French (1988b) is persuasive in suggesting the presence of transitory components in stock prices, this section's results confirm Shiller's (1981) conclusion that models assuming constant *ex ante* returns cannot account for all of the variance in stock market returns. Since our analysis does not rely on the present-value relation between stock prices and expected future dividends, it does not suffer from some of the problems that have been highlighted in the volatility-test debate.[20]

5. The source of the transitory component in stock prices

Transitory components in stock prices imply variation in *ex ante* returns.[21] Any stochastic process for the transitory price component can be mapped into a stochastic process for *ex ante* returns, and any pattern for *ex ante* returns can be represented by describing the associated transitory price component. The central issue is whether variations in *ex ante* returns are better explained

[20]Shiller's conclusion that market returns are too volatile to be reconciled with valuation models assuming constant required returns is controversial; see West (1988) for a survey of recent work.

[21]Several recent studies have considered the extent to which equity returns can be predicted using various information sets. Keim and Stambaugh (1986) find that between 8% and 13% of the variation in returns for a portfolio of stocks in the bottom quintile of the NYSE can be predicted using lagged information. A much smaller share of the variation in returns to larger companies can be accounted for in this way. Campbell (1987) finds that approximately 11% of the variation in excess returns can be explained on the basis of lagged information derived from the term structure. Fama and French (1988a) find that lagged dividend yields can predict a much higher fraction of returns over longer horizons.

by changes in interest rates and volatility, or instead as byproducts of price deviations caused by noise traders.[22] This section notes two considerations that incline us toward the latter view.

First, we calibrate the variation in expected returns that risk factors would have to generate to account for the observed transitory components in stock prices. We assume for simplicity that the transitory component follows an AR(1) process as postulated in Summers (1986). This has the virtue of tractability, although it is inconsistent with the observation that actual returns show positive, then negative, serial correlation. If required returns show positive autocorrelation, then an innovation that raises required returns will reduce share prices. This will induce a holding period loss, followed by higher returns. The appendix shows that when required returns follow an AR(1) process,[23] *ex post* returns (R_t) are given by

$$R_t - \bar{R} \cong \frac{1+\bar{g}}{1+\bar{r}-\rho_1(1+\bar{g})}(r_t - \bar{r}) - \frac{(1+\bar{r})^{-1}(1+\bar{g})^2}{1+\bar{r}-\rho_1(1+\bar{g})}(r_{t+1} - \bar{r}) + \zeta_t, \tag{8}$$

where ζ_t, a serially uncorrelated innovation that is orthogonal to innovations about the future path of required returns (ξ_t), reflects revisions in expected future dividends. The average dividend yield and dividend growth rate are $\bar{d}$ and $\bar{g}$, respectively; in steady state, $\bar{r} = \bar{d} + \bar{g}$.

If changes in required returns and profits are positively correlated, then the assumption that ξ_t and ζ_t are orthogonal will *understate* the variance in *ex ante* returns needed to rationalize mean reversion in stock prices. It is possible to construct theoretical examples in which profits and interest rates are negatively related, as in Campbell (1986), but the empirical finding of weak

[22] Lucas (1978) and Cox, Ingersoll, and Ross (1985) study the pricing of assets with time-varying required returns. Several recent papers, including Black (1986), Campbell and Kyle (1986), DeLong et al. (1987), and Shiller (1984), have discussed the possible influence of noise traders on security prices and required returns. Fama and French (1986b) show that the negative serial correlation in different stocks may be attributable to a common factor, and interpret this finding as support for the time-varying returns view of mean reversion.

[23] The possibility of negative expected excess returns is an unattractive feature of the simple model we have analyzed. In principle the analysis could be repeated using Merton's (1980) model, which requires the expected excess return to be positive. The exact parallel between the time-varying returns model and the fads model would not hold in this case, however.

positive correlation between bond and stock returns suggests either positive or weak negative correlation between shocks to cash flows and required returns.[24]

Our assumption that required returns are given by $r_t - \bar{r} = (1 - \rho_1 L)^{-1}\xi_t$ enables us to rewrite (8), defining

$$\tilde{\xi}_t \equiv -\xi_{t+1}(1+\bar{r})^{-1}(1+\bar{g})^2/[1+\bar{r}-\rho_1(1+\bar{g})],$$

as

$$(1-\rho_1 L)(R_t - \bar{R}) \cong \tilde{\xi}_t + \zeta_t - (1+\bar{d})\tilde{\xi}_{t-1} - \rho_1\zeta_{t-1}. \qquad (9)$$

The first-order autocovariance of the expression on the right-hand side of (9) is nonzero, but all higher-order autocovariances equal zero.[25] Provided $\sigma_\xi^2 > 0$, returns follow an ARMA(1,1) process; if $\sigma_\xi^2 = 0$, then returns are white noise.

The simple model of stationary and nonstationary price components summarized in eq. (5) also yields an ARMA(1,1) representation for returns. This allows us to calculate the variation in required returns that is needed to generate the same time-series process for observed returns as fads of various sizes. In the appendix we show that the required return variance corresponding to a given fad variance is

$$\sigma_r^2 - \frac{[1+\bar{r}-\rho_1(1+\bar{g})]^2(1-\rho_1)^2(1+\bar{r})^2}{\{(1+\bar{d})(1+\rho_1^2)-\rho_1[1+(1+\bar{d})^2]\}(1+\bar{g})^2}\sigma_u^2. \qquad (10)$$

Table 7 reports calculations based on (10). It shows the standard deviation of required excess returns, measured on an annual basis, implied by a variety of fad models. We calibrate the calculations using the average excess return (8.9% per year) on the NYSE equal-weighted share price index over the 1926–1985 period. The dividend yield on these shares averages 4.5%, implying an average dividend growth rate of 4.4%. We use estimates of the variance ratio at 96 months to calibrate the degree of mean reversion.

Substantial variability in required returns is needed to explain mean reversion in prices. For example, if we postulate that the standard deviation of the transitory price component is 20%, then even when required return shocks have a half-life of 2.9 years, the standard deviation of *ex ante* returns must be 5.8% per annum. Even larger amounts of required return variation are needed

[24] Campbell (1987) estimates that the correlation between excess returns on long-term bonds and corporate equities was 0.22 for the 1959–1979 period and 0.36 for the more recent 1979–1983 period.

[25] Ansley, Spivey, and Wrobleski (1977) prove that an autocorrelogram with zero entries beyond order k implies an MA(k) process.

Table 7

Amount of variation in required returns needed to account for mean reversion in stock prices.

Each entry answers the question: 'If both required returns and price fads follow first-order autoregressions with half-lives indicated in the row margin, and the amount of mean reversion in observed returns is consistent with a price fad with a standard deviation (σ_u) given in the column heading, what would the standard deviation of required returns need to be to generate the same time-series process for *ex post* returns?' Our calculations employ the fact that with AR(1) required returns, the *ex post* returns process is given by eq. (8). Similarly the price fad is assumed to follow an AR(1) that yields a process like (5) for *ex post* returns. We then ask what value of σ_r (or implicitly σ_ξ) is needed to generate a given size transitory price pattern implied by σ_u. The calculations are calibrated using data on excess returns for the equal-weighted NYSE index over the 1926–1985 period and are based on eq. (10) in the text. The average excess return for this period is 8.9% per year, with a dividend yield of 4.5%.

	Standard deviation of transitory component			
Half-life	15.0%	20.0%	25.0%	30.0%
1.4 years	7.9%	10.6%	13.2%	15.8%
1.9 years	6.1%	8.2%	10.2%	12.3%
2.9 years	4.4%	5.8%	7.3%	8.7%

to explain the same size price fads when required return shocks are less persistent. These estimates of the standard deviation of required returns are large in relation to the mean of *ex post* excess returns and imply that if *ex ante* returns are never negative they must frequently exceed 20%.

It is difficult to think of risk factors that could account for such variation in required returns. Campbell and Shiller (1987), using data on real interest rates and market volatilities, find no evidence that stock prices help to forecast future movements in discount rates, as they should if stock price movements are caused by fluctuations in these factors.[26] Although they show that stock prices do forecast consumption fluctuations, the sign is counter to the theory's prediction. On the other hand, if the transitory components are viewed as a reflection of mispricing, they are also large in relation to traditional views of market efficiency.

The second difficulty in explaining the observed correlation patterns with models of time-varying returns arises from our finding of positive followed by negative serial correlation. Models with first-order autoregressive transitory components can rationalize the second but not the first of these observations. It is instructive to consider what type of expected returns behavior is necessary to account for both observations.

[26]Contrary evidence suggesting that stock returns do predict future volatility patterns is provided by French, Schwert, and Stambaugh (1987).

There are two potential explanations for the positive autocorrelation in observed returns at short lags. First, contrary to our maintained specification, shocks to required returns and to prospective dividends may be positively correlated. This could lead to positive autocorrelation at short horizons because increases in expected dividends, which would raise share prices, would be followed by higher *ex ante* returns. We explored this possibility by forming monthly 'dividend innovations' ($IDIV_t$) for the 1926–1985 period as the residuals from a regression of real dividends (on the value-weighted NYSE portfolio) on twelve lagged values of real dividends, a time trend, and a set of monthly dummy variables. We then regressed real returns on the value-weighted index on lagged values of $IDIV_t$. A representative equation, including six lagged values, is shown below. R_t is measured in percentage points and standard errors are given in parentheses:

$$\begin{aligned} R_t = {} & \underset{(0.040)}{1.568} + \underset{(1.380)}{0.844} * IDIV_{t-1} - \underset{(1.380)}{0.109} * IDIV_{t-2} \\ & - \underset{(1.380)}{3.667} * IDIV_{t-3} - \underset{(1.380)}{0.904} * IDIV_{t-4} \\ & - \underset{(1.377)}{1.061} * IDIV_{t-5} - \underset{(1.374)}{1.769} * IDIV_{t-6}, \end{aligned}$$

$$R^2 = 0.037, \qquad 1927{:}7\text{–}1985{:}12.$$

The coefficients on lagged values of *IDIV* should be positive if required returns and prospective dividends are positively correlated, but the results provide no support for this view. If anything, they suggest a negative but statistically insignificant relationship between dividend innovations and subsequent returns. This would suggest that positive dividend news is followed by lower required returns, a pattern that should be reflected in negative autocorrelation of *ex post* returns over short horizons.

The second potential explanation for positive serial correlation is that the autocorrelogram of *ex post* returns reflects the dynamics of required returns. Some required-return processes could generate positive, followed by negative, return autocorrelation. The required-return processes with this feature that we have identified all show increasing coefficients in some part of their moving average representation.[27] We are unaware of evidence suggesting that observ-

[27]Two examples of required return processes are twelfth-order moving-average processes with the following coefficients: 1, −1.5, −0.75, −0.5, −0.5, 0.75, 0.75, 0.75, 0.75, 0.75, 0.75, 0.75, 0.75 and 1, 1.5, 2, 2.5, 3, 3.5, 4, 4.5, 5, 4, 3, 2, 1. The autocorrelogram of the former process displays positive, then negative, correlation in required returns, while the second process exhibits positive autocorrelation at all lags. Both processes generate positive, then negative, autocorrelation in *ex post* returns.

able proxies for required returns display such stochastic properties. Studies of volatility such as French, Schwert, and Stambaugh (1987) or Poterba and Summers (1986) suggest that shocks are persistent but that their moving-average representations show declining coefficients. An alternative possibility is that movements in required returns are due to changes in the equity demands of noise traders. For example, assume that the required return of sophisticated traders is equal to $\alpha + \beta S_t$, where S_t is the fraction of the outstanding common stock that these investors must hold. Equity demands of noise traders (which in equilibrium must equal $1 - S_t$) that follow a moving-average process similar to one of those for required returns that generate positive, then negative, autocorrelation in *ex post* returns will also generate this pattern in *ex post* returns. The notion that noise trading impulses intensify and then decline comports with qualitative discussions of fads, but further work is clearly necessary to evaluate this conjecture.

6. Conclusions

Our results suggest that stock returns show positive serial correlation over short periods and negative correlation over longer intervals. This conclusion emerges from data on equal-weighted and value-weighted NYSE returns over the 1926–1985 period, and is corroborated by data from other nations and time periods. Although individual data sets do not consistently permit rejection of the random-walk hypothesis at high significance levels, the various data sets together strengthen the case against its validity. Our point estimates suggest that transitory price components account for a substantial part of the variance in returns.

Our finding of significant transitory price components has potentially important implications for financial practice. If stock price movements contain large transitory components, then for long-horizon investors the stock market may be less risky than it appears to be when the variance of single-period returns is extrapolated using the random-walk model. Samuelson (1988) demonstrates that in the presence of mean reversion, an investor's horizon will influence his portfolio decisions. If the investor's relative risk aversion is greater (less) than unity, as his horizon lengthens he will invest more (less) in equities than he would with serially independent returns. The presence of transitory price components also suggests the desirability of investment strategies, such as those considered by DeBondt and Thaler (1985), involving the purchase of securities that have recently declined in value. It may also justify some institutions' practice of spending on the basis of a weighted average of their past endowment values, rather than current market value.

Although the temptation to apply more sophisticated statistical techniques to stock return data in an effort to extract more information about the magnitude and structure of transitory components is ever present, we doubt that a great deal can be learned in this way. Even the broad characteristics of the data examined in this paper cannot be estimated precisely. As the debate over volatility tests has illustrated, sophisticated statistical results are often very sensitive to maintained assumptions that are difficult to evaluate. We have validated the statistical procedures in this paper by applying them to pseudo data conforming to the random-walk model. Our suspicion, supported by Kleidon's (1986) results, is that such Monte Carlo analysis of much of the more elaborate work on stock-price volatility would reveal poor statistical properties.

We suggest in the paper's final section that noise trading, trading by investors whose demand for shares is determined by factors other than their expected return, provides a plausible explanation for the transitory components in stock prices.[28] Pursuing this will involve constructing and testing theories of noise trading, as well as theories of changing risk factors, that could account for the characteristic stock return autocorrelogram documented here. Evaluating such theories is likely to require information other than stock returns, such as data on fundamental values, proxies for noise trading such as the net purchases by odd-lot traders, turnover, or the level of participation in investment clubs, and indicators of risk factors such as *ex ante* volatilities implied by stock options. Only by comparing models based on the presence of noise traders with models based on changing risk factors can we judge whether financial markets are efficient in the sense of rationally valuing assets, as well as precluding the generation of excess profits.

Appendix

Derivation of ex post return process when required returns are AR(1)

The price of a common stock, P_t, equals

$$P_t = \mathrm{E}_t\left\{ \sum_{j=0}^{\infty} \left[\prod_{i=0}^{j-1} (1 + r_{t+i})^{-1}(1 + g_{t+i}) \right] D_t \right\}, \tag{A.1}$$

where r_{t+i} denotes the required real return in period $t+i$, D_t is the dividend paid in period t, g_{t+i} is the real dividend growth rate between periods $t+i$ and $t+i+1$, and $\mathrm{E}_t\{\cdot\}$ designates expectations formed using information available as of period t. We linearize inside the expectation operator in r_{t+i}

[28] Cutler, Poterba, and Summers (1988) document the difficulty of explaining a significant fraction of return variation on the basis of observable news about future cash flows or discount rates.

and g_{t+i}:

$$P_t \cong \mathrm{E}_t\left\{\sum_{j=1}^{\infty}\left(\frac{1+\bar{g}}{1+\bar{r}}\right)^{j-1} D_t + \sum_{j=0}^{\infty}\frac{\partial P_t}{\partial r_{t+j}}[r_{t+j}-\bar{r}] + \sum_{j=0}^{\infty}\frac{\partial P_t}{\partial g_{t+j}}[g_{t+j}-\bar{g}]\right\}$$

$$= \frac{D_t(1+\bar{r})}{\bar{r}-\bar{g}} - \frac{D_t(1+\bar{g})}{(1+\bar{r})(\bar{r}-\bar{g})}\mathrm{E}_t\left\{\sum_{j=0}^{\infty}\beta^j[r_{t+j}-\bar{r}]\right\} + \frac{D_t}{\bar{r}-\bar{g}}\mathrm{E}_t\left\{\sum_{j=0}^{\infty}\beta^j[g_{t+j}-\bar{g}]\right\}, \tag{A.2}$$

where $\beta=(1+\bar{g})/(1+\bar{r})$. We denote $D_t(1+\bar{r})/(\bar{r}-\bar{g})$ as $\overline{P}_t$. In the special case of

$$(r_t-\bar{r}) = \rho_1(r_{t-1}-\bar{r}) + \xi_t, \tag{A.3}$$

we can simplify the second term in (A.2) to obtain

$$P_t - \overline{P}_t \cong \frac{-D_t(1+\bar{g})}{(1+\bar{r})(\bar{r}-\bar{g})}\sum_{j=0}^{\infty}\beta^j\rho_1^j[r_t-\bar{r}] + \frac{D_t}{\bar{r}-\bar{g}}\mathrm{E}_t\left\{\sum_{j=0}^{\infty}\beta^j[g_{t+j}-\bar{g}]\right\}, \tag{A.4}$$

$$= \frac{-D_t(1+\bar{g})(r_t-\bar{r})}{(\bar{r}-\bar{g})(1+\bar{r}-\rho_1(1+g))} + \frac{D_t}{\bar{r}-\bar{g}}\mathrm{E}_t\left\{\sum_{j=0}^{\infty}\beta^j[g_{t+j}-\bar{g}]\right\}.$$

Now recall that the holding period return, R_t, is given by

$$R_t = \frac{P_{t+1}+D_t}{P_t} - 1. \tag{A.5}$$

It can be linearized around P_t and P_{t+1} as follows:

$$R_t \cong \bar{R} + \frac{P_{t+1} - \bar{P}_{t+1}}{\bar{P}_t} - \frac{(\bar{P}_{t+1} + D_t)}{\bar{P}_t^2}(P_t - \bar{P}_t), \tag{A.6}$$

where $\bar{P}_{t+1} = (1+\bar{g})\bar{P}_t$ and $\bar{R} = \bar{r}(1+\bar{g})/(1+\bar{r})$. Substituting (A.4) into (A.6) yields

$$\begin{aligned} R_t - \bar{R} \cong{} & \frac{-D_{t+1}(1+\bar{g})}{\bar{P}_t(\bar{r}-\bar{g})[1+\bar{r}-\rho_1(1+\bar{g})]}(r_{t+1}-\bar{r}) \\ & + \frac{D_{t+1}}{\bar{P}(\bar{r}-\bar{g})}\sum_{j=0}^{\infty}\beta^j \mathrm{E}_{t+1}\{g_{t+1+j}-\bar{g}\} \\ & + \frac{D_t(1+\bar{r})(1+\bar{g})}{\bar{P}_t(\bar{r}-\bar{g})[1+\bar{r}-\rho_1(1+\bar{g})]}(r_t-\bar{r}) \\ & - \frac{D_t(1+\bar{r})}{\bar{P}_t(\bar{r}-\bar{g})}\sum_{j=0}^{\infty}\beta^j \mathrm{E}_t\{g_{t+j}-\bar{g}\}. \end{aligned} \tag{A.7}$$

This can be rewritten as

$$\begin{aligned} R_t - \bar{R} \cong{} & -\frac{D_t(1+\bar{g})^2}{\bar{P}_t(\bar{r}-\bar{g})(1+\bar{r}-\rho_1(1+\bar{g}))} \\ & \times\left[(r_{t+1}-\bar{r}) - \beta^{-1}(r_t-\bar{r})\right] + \zeta_t \\ ={} & -\frac{\beta(1+\bar{g})}{1+\bar{r}-\rho_1(1+g)} \\ & \times\left[(1-\rho_1 L)^{-1}\xi_{t+1} - \beta(1-\rho_1 L)^{-1}\xi_t\right] + \zeta_t, \end{aligned} \tag{A.8}$$

where ζ_t reflects changes in expected future dividend growth rates between t and $t+1$, and the last expression exploits the fact that $(1-\rho_1 L)(r_t - \bar{r}) = \xi_t$. Now defining $\{\beta(1+\bar{g})/[1+\bar{r}-\rho_1(1+\bar{g})]\}\xi_{t+1} = \tilde{\xi}_t$, we can multiply through by $(1-\rho_1 L)$ so that

$$(1-\rho_1 L)(R_t - \bar{R}) \cong \tilde{\xi}_t - \left(\frac{1+\bar{r}}{1+\bar{g}}\right)\tilde{\xi}_{t-1} + \zeta_t - \rho_1\zeta_{t-1}. \tag{A.9}$$

This yields an ARMA(1, 1) representation of returns. Since $(1+\bar{r})/(1+\bar{g}) \approx (1+\bar{d})$, this is eq. (8) in the text.

We now explore the parallel between the time-varying returns model and the fad model, which postulates that returns evolve according to

$$(1-\rho_1 L)(R_t-\bar{R}) \cong \varepsilon_t-\rho_1\varepsilon_{t-1}+\nu_t-\nu_{t-1}. \tag{A.10}$$

For this ARMA(1, 1) process to be the same as (A.9), two restrictions must be satisfied. We find them by equating the variances and first-order autocovariance of the right-hand sides of (A.9) and (A.10):

$$\left[1+(1+\bar{d})^2\right]\sigma_\xi^2+\left(1+\rho_1^2\right)\sigma_\zeta^2=2\sigma_\nu^2+\left(1+\rho_1^2\right)\sigma_\varepsilon^2, \tag{A.11}$$

$$(1+\bar{d})\sigma_\xi^2+\rho_1\sigma_\zeta^2=\sigma_\nu^2+\rho_1\sigma_\varepsilon^2. \tag{A.12}$$

Using (A.12) to eliminate σ_ζ^2 from (A.11) we find

$$\sigma_\xi^2=\frac{(1-\rho_1)^2}{(1+\bar{d})\left(1+\rho_1^2\right)-\rho_1\left[1+(1+\bar{d})^2\right]}\sigma_\nu^2. \tag{A.13}$$

Recall that the variance of the fad, σ_u^2, equals $\sigma_\nu^2/(1-\rho_1^2)$. Using this and the definition of ξ_t, we find from (A.13) that the variance of required returns corresponding to a given fad variance is

$$\sigma_r^2=\frac{\left[1+\bar{r}-\rho_1(1+\bar{g})\right]^2(1-\rho_1)^2(1+r)^2}{\left\{(1+\bar{d})\left(1+\rho_1^2\right)-\rho_1\left[1+(1+\bar{d})^2\right]\right\}(1+\bar{g})^2}\sigma_u^2. \tag{A.14}$$

This leads immediately to (10) in the text.

References

Alexander, Sidney S., 1961, Price movements in speculative markets: Trends or random walks, Industrial Management Review 2, 7–26.

Ansley, Craig, W. Allen Spivey, and William Wrobleski, 1977, On the structure of moving average processes, Journal of Econometrics 6, 121–134.

Black, Fischer, 1986, Noise, Journal of Finance 41, 529–543.

Blanchard, Olivier J. and Mark Watson, 1982, Bubbles, crashes, and rational expectations, in: P. Wachtel, ed., Crises in the economic and financial structure (Lexington Books, Lexington, MA) 295–315.

Campbell, John Y., 1986, Bond and stock returns in a simple exchange model, Quarterly Journal of Economics 102, 785–803.

Campbell, John Y., 1987, Stock returns and the term structure, Journal of Financial Economics 18, 373–400.

Campbell, John Y. and Albert S. Kyle, 1986, Smart money, noise trading, and stock price behavior, Unpublished manuscript (Princeton University, Princeton, NJ).
Campbell, John Y. and N. Gregory Mankiw, 1987, Are output fluctuations transitory?, Quarterly Journal of Economics 102, 857–880.
Campbell, John Y. and Robert J. Shiller, 1987, The dividend–price ratio and expectations of future dividends and discount factors, Mimeo. (Yale University, New Haven, CT).
Cochrane, John H. 1988, How big is the random walk in GNP?, Journal of Political Economy, forthcoming.
Cox, John C., Jonathan Ingersoll, and Stephen Ross, 1985, An intertemporal general equilibrium model of asset prices, Econometrica 53, 363–384.
Cutler, David C., James M. Poterba, and Lawrence H. Summers, 1988, What moves stock prices?, Journal of Portfolio Management, forthcoming.
DeBondt, Werner and Richard Thaler, 1985, Does the stock market overreact, Journal of Finance 40, 793–805.
DeLong, J. Bradford, Andrei Shleifer, Lawrence Summers, and Robert Waldman, 1987, The economic consequences of noise traders, National Bureau of Economic Research working paper no. 2395 (NBER, Cambridge, MA).
Fama, Eugene F., 1970, Efficient capital markets: A review of theory and empirical work, Journal of Finance 25, 383–417.
Fama, Eugene F., 1976, Foundations of finance (Basic Books, New York, NY).
Fama, Eugene F. and Kenneth R. French, 1986a, Permanent and temporary components of stock prices, Center for Research in Security Prices working paper no. 178 (University of Chicago, Chicago, IL).
Fama, Eugene F. and Kenneth R. French, 1986b, Common factors in the serial correlation of stock returns, Center for Research in Security Prices working paper no. 200 (University of Chicago, Chicago, IL).
Fama, Eugene F. and Kenneth R. French, 1988a, Dividend yields and expected stock returns, Journal of Financial Economics, this issue.
Fama, Eugene F. and Kenneth R. French, 1988b, Permanent and temporary components of stock prices, Journal of Political Economy 96, 246–273.
French, Kenneth R. and Richard Roll, 1986, Stock return variances: The arrival of information and the reaction of traders, Journal of Financial Economics 17, 5–26.
French, Kenneth R., William Schwert, and Robert Stambaugh, 1987, Expected stock returns and stock market volatility, Journal of Financial Economics 19, 3–30.
Harvey, Andrew, 1981, Time series models (Philip Allan, Oxford).
Huizinga, John, 1987, An empirical investigation of the long run behavior of real exchange rates, Carnegie–Rochester Conference Series on Public Policy 27, 149–214.
Kendall, Maurice G., 1953, The analysis of economic time series – Part I: Prices, Journal of the Royal Statistical Society A 96, 11–25.
Kendall, Maurice G. and Alan Stuart, 1976, The advanced theory of statistics, Vol. 3, 3rd ed. (Griffin, London).
Keim, Donald B. and Robert F. Stambaugh, 1986, Predicting returns in the stock and bond markets, Journal of Financial Economics 17, 357–390.
Keynes, John M., 1936, The general theory of employment, interest, and money (Harcourt, Brace, and Company, New York, NY).
Kleidon, Allan, 1986, Variance bounds tests and stock price valuation models, Journal of Political Economy, 94, 953–1001.
Leamer, Edward, 1978, Specification searches: Ad hoc inferences with nonexperimental data (Wiley, New York, NY).
Lehmann, Bruce N., 1987, Fads, martingales, and market efficiency, Mimeo. (Columbia University, Graduate School of Business, New York, NY).
Lo, Andrew W. and A. Craig MacKinlay, 1987, A simple specification test of the random walk hypothesis, Rodney L. White Center for Financial Research discussion paper no. 13-87 (Wharton School, University of Pennsylvania, Philadelphia, PA).
Lo, Andrew W. and A. Craig MacKinlay, 1988, Stock market prices do not follow random walks: Evidence from a simple specification test, Review of Financial Studies, 1, 41–66.

Lucas, Robert, 1978, Asset prices in an exchange economy, Econometrica 66, 1429–1445.

Merton, Robert C., 1980, On estimating the expected return on the market, Journal of Financial Economics 8, 323–361.

Merton, Robert C., 1987, On the state of the efficient market hypothesis in financial economics, in: R. Dornbusch, S. Fischer, and J. Bossons, eds., Macroeconomics and finance: Essays in honor of Franco Modigliani (MIT Press, Cambridge, MA) 93–124.

O'Brien, James M., 1987, Testing for transitory elements in stock prices, Mimeo. (Board of Governors of the Federal Reserve, Washington, DC).

Officer, Robert R., 1973, The variability of the market factor of the New York Stock Exchange, Journal of Business 46, 434–453.

Osborne, M.F., 1959, Brownian motion in the stock market, Operations Research 7, 145–173.

Poterba, James M. and Lawrence H. Summers, 1986, The persistence of volatility and stock market returns, American Economic Review 76, 1142–1151.

Samuelson, Paul A., 1988, Longrun risk tolerance when equity returns are mean regressing: Pseudoparadoxes and vindication of 'business man's risk', Mimeo. (Massachusetts Institute of Technology, Cambridge, MA).

Shiller, Robert J., 1981, Do stock prices move too much to be justified by subsequent changes in dividends?, American Economic Review 71, 421–436.

Shiller, Robert J., 1984, Stock prices and social dynamics, Brookings Papers on Economic Activity 2, 457–498.

Shiller, Robert J. and P. Perron, 1985, Testing the random walk hypothesis: Power versus frequency of observation, Economics Letters 18, 381–386.

Summers, Lawrence H., 1986, Does the stock market rationally reflect fundamental values?, Journal of Finance 41, 591–601.

West, Kenneth, 1988, Bubbles, fads, and stock price volatility: A partial evaluation, Journal of Finance 43, 639–655.

Wilson, Jack W. and Charles Jones, 1987, A comparison of annual common stock returns: 1871–1925 with 1926–1985, Journal of Business 60, 239–258.

Working, Holbrook, 1960, Note on the correlation of first differences of averages in a random chain, Econometrica 28, 916–918.

[9]

Do Stock Prices Move Too Much to be Justified by Subsequent Changes in Dividends?

By ROBERT J. SHILLER*

A simple model that is commonly used to interpret movements in corporate common stock price indexes asserts that real stock prices equal the present value of rationally expected or optimally forecasted future real dividends discounted by a constant real discount rate. This valuation model (or variations on it in which the real discount rate is not constant but fairly stable) is often used by economists and market analysts alike as a plausible model to describe the behavior of aggregate market indexes and is viewed as providing a reasonable story to tell when people ask what accounts for a sudden movement in stock price indexes. Such movements are then attributed to "new information" about future dividends. I will refer to this model as the "efficient markets model" although it should be recognized that this name has also been applied to other models.

It has often been claimed in popular discussions that stock price indexes seem too "volatile," that is, that the movements in stock price indexes could not realistically be attributed to any objective new information, since movements in the price indexes seem to be "too big" relative to actual subsequent events. Recently, the notion that financial asset prices are too volatile to accord with efficient markets has received some econometric support in papers by Stephen LeRoy and Richard Porter on the stock market, and by myself on the bond market.

To illustrate graphically why it seems that stock prices are too volatile, I have plotted in Figure 1 a stock price index p_t with its *ex post* rational counterpart p_t^* (data set 1).[1] The stock price index p_t is the real Standard and Poor's Composite Stock Price Index (detrended by dividing by a factor proportional to the long-run exponential growth path) and p_t^* is the present discounted value of the actual subsequent real dividends (also as a proportion of the same long-run growth factor).[2] The analogous series for a modified Dow Jones Industrial Average appear in Figure 2 (data set 2). One is struck by the smoothness and stability of the *ex post* rational price series p_t^* when compared with the actual price series. This behavior of p^* is due to the fact that the present value relation relates p^* to a long-weighted moving average of dividends (with weights corresponding to discount factors) and moving averages tend to smooth the series averaged. Moreover, while real dividends did vary over this sample period, they did not vary long enough or far enough to cause major movements in p^*. For example, while one normally thinks of the Great Depression as a time when business was bad, real dividends were substantially below their long-run exponential growth path (i.e., 10–25 percent below the

*Associate professor, University of Pennsylvania, and research associate, National Bureau of Economic Research. I am grateful to Christine Amsler for research assistance, and to her as well as Benjamin Friedman, Irwin Friend, Sanford Grossman, Stephen LeRoy, Stephen Ross, and Jeremy Siegel for helpful comments. This research was supported by the National Bureau of Economic Research as part of the Research Project on the Changing Roles of Debt and Equity in Financing U.S. Capital Formation sponsored by the American Council of Life Insurance and by the National Science Foundation under grant SOC-7907561. The views expressed here are solely my own and do not necessarily represent the views of the supporting agencies.

[1] The stock price index may look unfamiliar because it is deflated by a price index, expressed as a proportion of the long-run growth path and only January figures are shown. One might note, for example, that the stock market decline of 1929–32 looks smaller than the recent decline. In real terms, it was. The January figures also miss both the 1929 peak and 1932 trough.

[2] The price and dividend series as a proportion of the long-run growth path are defined below at the beginning of Section I. Assumptions about public knowledge or lack of knowledge of the long-run growth path are important, as shall be discussed below. The series p^* is computed subject to an assumption about dividends after 1978. See text and Figure 3 below.

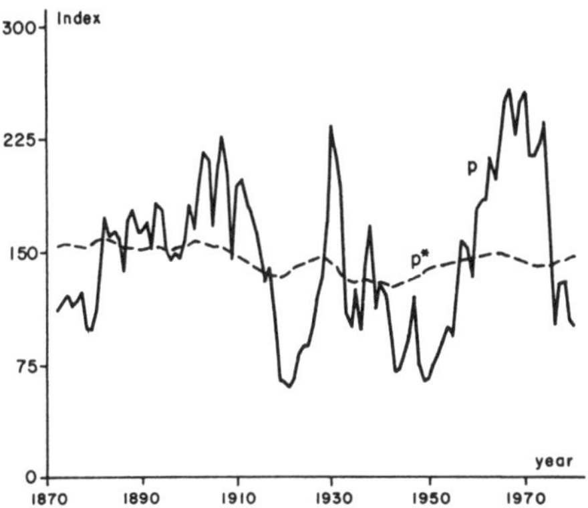

FIGURE 1

Note: Real Standard and Poor's Composite Stock Price Index (solid line p) and *ex post* rational price (dotted line p^*), 1871–1979, both detrended by dividing a long-run exponential growth factor. The variable p^* is the present value of actual subsequent real detrended dividends, subject to an assumption about the present value in 1979 of dividends thereafter. Data are from Data Set 1, Appendix.

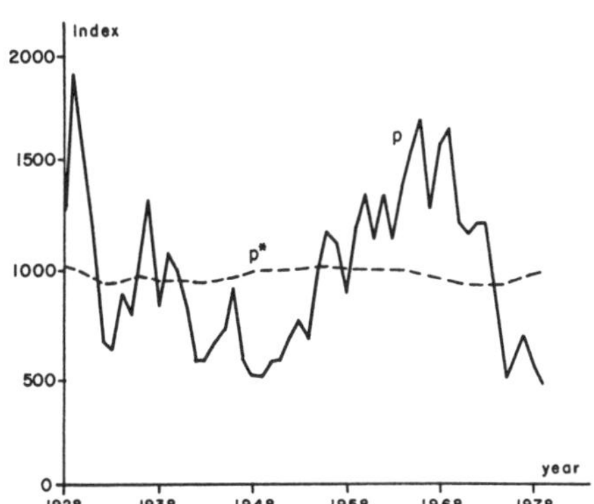

FIGURE 2

Note: Real modified Dow Jones Industrial Average (solid line p) and *ex post* rational price (dotted line p^*), 1928-1979, both detrended by dividing by a long-run exponential growth factor. The variable p^* is the present value of actual subsequent real detrended dividends, subject to an assumption about the present value in 1979 of dividends thereafter. Data are from Data Set 2, Appendix.

growth path for the Standard and Poor's series, 16–38 percent below the growth path for the Dow Series) only for a few depression years: 1933, 1934, 1935, and 1938. The moving average which determines p^* will smooth out such short-run fluctuations. Clearly the stock market decline beginning in 1929 and ending in 1932 could not be rationalized in terms of subsequent dividends! Nor could it be rationalized in terms of subsequent earnings, since earnings are relevant in this model only as indicators of later dividends. Of course, the efficient markets model does not say $p=p^*$. Might one still suppose that this kind of stock market crash was a rational mistake, a forecast error that rational people might make? This paper will explore here the notion that the very volatility of p (i.e., the tendency of big movements in p to occur again and again) implies that the answer is no.

To give an idea of the kind of volatility comparisons that will be made here, let us consider at this point the simplest inequality which puts limits on one measure of volatility: the standard deviation of p. The efficient markets model can be described as asserting that $p_t=E_t(p_t^*)$, i.e., p_t is the mathematical expectation conditional on all information available at time t of p_t^*. In other words, p_t is the optimal forecast of p_t^*. One can define the forecast error as $u_t=p_t^*-p_t$. A fundamental principle of optimal forecasts is that the forecast error u_t must be uncorrelated with the forecast; that is, the covariance between p_t and u_t must be zero. If a forecast error showed a consistent correlation with the forecast itself, then that would in itself imply that the forecast could be improved. Mathematically, it can be shown from the theory of conditional expectations that u_t must be uncorrelated with p_t.

If one uses the principle from elementary statistics that the variance of the sum of two uncorrelated variables is the sum of their variances, one then has $var(p^*)=var(u)+var(p)$. Since variances cannot be negative, this means $var(p)\leqslant var(p^*)$ or, converting to more easily interpreted standard deviations,

$$\sigma(p)\leqslant\sigma(p^*) \tag{1}$$

This inequality (employed before in the

papers by LeRoy and Porter and myself) is violated dramatically by the data in Figures 1 and 2 as is immediately obvious in looking at the figures.[3]

This paper will develop the efficient markets model in Section I to clarify some theoretical questions that may arise in connection with the inequality (1) and some similar inequalities will be derived that put limits on the standard deviation of the innovation in price and the standard deviation of the change in price. The model is restated in innovation form which allows better understanding of the limits on stock price volatility imposed by the model. In particular, this will enable us to see (Section II) that the standard deviation of Δp is highest when information about dividends is revealed smoothly and that if information is revealed in big lumps occasionally the price series may have higher kurtosis (fatter tails) but will have *lower* variance. The notion expressed by some that earnings rather than dividend data should be used is discussed in Section III, and a way of assessing the importance of time variation in real discount rates is shown in Section IV. The inequalities are compared with the data in Section V.

This paper takes as its starting point the approach I used earlier (1979) which showed evidence suggesting that long-term bond yields are too volatile to accord with simple expectations models of the term structure of interest rates.[4] In that paper, it was shown how restrictions implied by efficient markets on the cross-covariance function of short-term and long-term interest rates imply inequality restrictions on the spectra of the long-term interest rate series which characterize the smoothness that the long rate should display. In this paper, analogous implications are derived for the volatility of stock prices, although here a simpler and more intuitively appealing discussion of the model in terms of its innovation representation is used. This paper also has benefited from the earlier discussion by LeRoy and Porter which independently derived some restrictions on security price volatility implied by the efficient markets model and concluded that common stock prices are too volatile to accord with the model. They applied a methodology in some ways similar to that used here to study a stock price index and individual stocks in a sample period starting after World War II.

It is somewhat inaccurate to say that this paper attempts to contradict the extensive literature of efficient markets (as, for example, Paul Cootner's volume on the random character of stock prices, or Eugene Fama's survey).[5] Most of this literature really examines different properties of security prices. Very little of the efficient markets literature bears directly on the characteristic feature of the model considered here: that expected *real* returns for the aggregate stock market are constant through time (or approximately so). Much of the literature on efficient markets concerns the investigation of nominal "profit opportunities" (variously defined) and whether transactions costs prohibit their exploitation. Of course, if real stock prices are "too volatile" as it is defined here, then there may well be a sort of real profit opportunity. Time variation in expected real interest rates does not itself imply that any

[3]Some people will object to this derivation of (1) and say that one might as well have said that $E_t(p_t)=p_t^*$, i.e., that forecasts are correct "on average," which would lead to a reversal of the inequality (1). This objection stems, however, from a misinterpretation of conditional expectations. The subscript t on the expectations operator E means "taking as given (i.e., nonrandom) all variables known at time t." Clearly, p_t is known at time t and p_t^* is not. In practical terms, if a forecaster gives as his forecast anything other than $E_t(p_t^*)$, then high forecast is not optimal in the sense of expected squared forecast error. If he gives a forecast which equals $E_t(p_t^*)$ only on average, then he is adding random noise to the optimal forecast. The amount of noise apparent in Figures 1 or 2 is extraordinary. Imagine what we would think of our local weather forecaster if, say, actual local temperatures followed the dotted line and his forecasts followed the solid line!

[4]This analysis was extended to yields on preferred stocks by Christine Amsler.

[5]It should not be inferred that the literature on efficient markets uniformly supports the notion of efficiency put forth there, for example, that no assets are dominated or that no trading rule dominates a buy and hold strategy, (for recent papers see S. Basu; Franco Modigliani and Richard Cohn; William Brainard, John Shoven and Lawrence Weiss; and the papers in the symposium on market efficiency edited by Michael Jensen).

trading rule dominates a buy and hold strategy, but really large variations in expected returns might seem to suggest that such a trading rule exists. This paper does not investigate this, or whether transactions costs prohibit its exploitation. This paper is concerned, however, instead with a more interesting (from an economic standpoint) question: what accounts for movements in real stock prices and can they be explained by new information about subsequent real dividends? If the model fails due to excessive volatility, then we will have seen a new characterization of how the simple model fails. The characterization is not equivalent to other characterizations of its failure, such as that one-period holding returns are forecastable, or that stocks have not been good inflation hedges recently.

The volatility comparisons that will be made here have the advantage that they are insensitive to misalignment of price and dividend series, as may happen with earlier data when collection procedures were not ideal. The tests are also not affected by the practice, in the construction of stock price and dividend indexes, of dropping certain stocks from the sample occasionally and replacing them with other stocks, so long as the volatility of the series is not misstated. These comparisons are thus well suited to existing long-term data in stock price averages. The robustness that the volatility comparisons have, coupled with their simplicity, may account for their popularity in casual discourse.

I. The Simple Efficient Markets Model

According to the simple efficient markets model, the real price P_t of a share at the beginning of the time period t is given by

$$(2) \qquad P_t = \sum_{k=0}^{\infty} \gamma^{k+1} E_t D_{t+k} \qquad 0<\gamma<1$$

where D_t is the real dividend paid at (let us say, the end of) time t, E_t denotes mathematical expectation conditional on information available at time t, and γ is the constant real discount factor. I define the constant real interest rate r so that $\gamma = 1/(1+r)$. Information at time t includes P_t and D_t and their lagged values, and will generally include other variables as well.

The one-period holding return $H_t \equiv (\Delta P_{t+1} + D_t)/P_t$ is the return from buying the stock at time t and selling it at time $t+1$. The first term in the numerator is the capital gain, the second term is the dividend received at the end of time t. They are divided by P_t to provide a rate of return. The model (2) has the property that $E_t(H_t) = r$.

The model (2) can be restated in terms of series as a proportion of the long-run growth factor: $p_t = P_t/\lambda^{t-T}$, $d_t = D_t/\lambda^{t+1-T}$ where the growth factor is $\lambda^{t-T} = (1+g)^{t-T}$, g is the rate of growth, and T is the base year. Dividing (2) by λ^{t-T} and substituting one finds[6]

$$(3) \qquad p_t = \sum_{k=0}^{\infty} (\lambda\gamma)^{k+1} E_t d_{t+k}$$

$$= \sum_{k=0}^{\infty} \bar{\gamma}^{k+1} E_t d_{t+k}$$

The growth rate g must be less than the discount rate r if (2) is to give a finite price, and hence $\bar{\gamma} \equiv \lambda\gamma < 1$, and defining $\bar{r}$ by $\bar{\gamma} \equiv 1/(1+\bar{r})$, the discount rate appropriate for the p_t and d_t series is $\bar{r} > 0$. This discount rate $\bar{r}$ is, it turns out, just the mean dividend divided by the mean price, i.e, $\bar{r} = E(d)/E(p)$.[7]

[6]No assumptions are introduced in going from (2) to (3), since (3) is just an algebraic transformation of (2). I shall, however, introduce the assumption that d_t is jointly stationary with information, which means that the (unconditional) covariance between d_t and z_{t-k}, where z_t is any information variable (which might be d_t itself or p_t), depends only on k, not t. It follows that we can write expressions like $var(p)$ without a time subscript. In contrast, a realization of the random variable the *conditional* expectation $E_t(d_{t+k})$ is a function of time since it depends on information at time t. Some stationarity assumption is necessary if we are to proceed with any statistical analysis.

[7]Taking unconditional expectations of both sides of (3) we find

$$E(p) = \frac{\bar{\gamma}}{1-\bar{\gamma}} E(d)$$

using $\bar{\gamma} = 1/1+\bar{r}$ and solving we find $\bar{r} = E(d)/E(p)$.

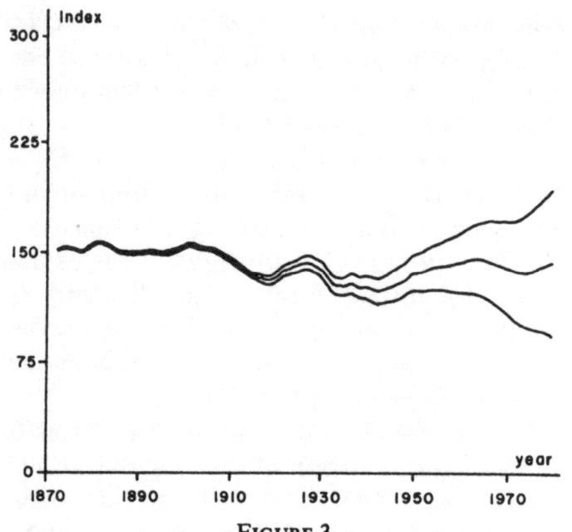

FIGURE 3

Note: Alternative measures of the *ex post* rational price p^*, obtained by alternative assumptions about the present value in 1979 of dividends thereafter. The middle curve is the p^* series plotted in Figure 1. The series are computed recursively from terminal conditions using dividend series d of Data Set 1.

TABLE 1—DEFINITIONS OF PRINCIPAL SYMBOLS

γ = real discount factor for series before detrending; $\gamma = 1/(1+r)$

$\bar{\gamma}$ = real discount factor for detrended series; $\bar{\gamma} \equiv \lambda\gamma$

D_t = real dividend accruing to stock index (before detrending)

d_t = real detrended dividend; $d_t \equiv D_t/\lambda^{t+1-T}$

Δ = first difference operator $\Delta x_t \equiv x_t - x_{t-1}$

δ_t = innovation operator; $\delta_t x_{t+k} \equiv E_t x_{t+k} - E_{t-1} x_{t+k}$; $\delta x \equiv \delta_t x_t$

E = unconditional mathematical expectations operator. $E(x)$ is the true (population) mean of x.

E_t = mathematical expectations operator conditional on information at time t; $E_t x_t \equiv E(x_t | I_t)$ where I_t is the vector of information variables known at time t.

λ = trend factor for price and dividend series; $\lambda \equiv 1+g$ where g is the long-run growth rate of price and dividends.

P_t = real stock price index (before detrending)

p_t = real detrended stock price index; $p_t = P_t/\lambda^{t-T}$

p_t^* = *ex post* rational stock price index (expression 4)

r = one-period real discount rate for series before detrending

$\bar{r}$ = real discount rate for detrended series; $\bar{r} = (1-\bar{\gamma})/\bar{\gamma}$

$\bar{r}_2$ = two-period real discount rate for detrended series; $\bar{r}_2 = (1+\bar{r})^2 - 1$

t = time (year)

T = base year for detrending and for wholesale price index; $p_T = P_T$ = nominal stock price index at time T

We may also write the model as noted above in terms of the *ex post* rational price series p_t^* (analogous to the *ex post* rational interest rate series that Jeremy Siegel and I used to study the Fisher effect, or that I used to study the expectations theory of the term structure). That is, p_t^* is the present value of actual subsequent dividends:

$$p_t = E_t(p_t^*) \tag{4}$$

where $$p_t^* = \sum_{k=0}^{\infty} \bar{\gamma}^{k+1} d_{t+k}$$

Since the summation extends to infinity, we never observe p_t^* without some error. However, with a long enough dividend series we may observe an approximate p_t^*. If we choose an arbitrary value for the terminal value of p_t^* (in Figures 1 and 2, p^* for 1979 was set at the average detrended real price over the sample) then we may determine p_t^* recursively by $p_t^* = \bar{\gamma}(p_{t+1}^* + d_t)$ working backward from the terminal date. As we move back from the terminal date, the importance of the terminal value chosen declines. In data set (1) as shown in Figure 1, $\bar{\gamma}$ is .954 and $\bar{\gamma}^{108} = .0063$ so that at the beginning of the sample the terminal value chosen has a negligible weight in the determination of p_t^*. If we had chosen a different terminal condition, the result would be to add or subtract an exponential trend from the p^* shown in Figure 1. This is shown graphically in Figure 3, in which p^* is shown computed from alternative terminal values. Since the only thing we need know to compute p^* about dividends after 1978 is p^* for 1979, it does not matter whether dividends are "smooth" or not after 1978. Thus, Figure 3 represents our uncertainty about p^*.

There is yet another way to write the model, which will be useful in the analysis which follows. For this purpose, it is convenient to adopt notation for the innovation in a variable. Let us define the innovation operator $\delta_t \equiv E_t - E_{t-1}$ where E_t is the conditional expectations operator. Then for any variable X_t the term $\delta_t X_{t+k}$ equals $E_t X_{t+k} - E_{t-1} X_{t+k}$ which is the change in the conditional expectation of X_{t+k} that is made in response to new information arriving between $t-1$ and t. The time subscript t may be dropped so that δX_k denotes $\delta_t X_{t+k}$ and

δX denotes δX_0 or $\delta_t X_t$. Since conditional expectations operators satisfy $E_j E_k = E_{min(j,k)}$ it follows that $E_{t-m}\delta_t X_{t+k} = E_{t-m}(E_t X_{t+k} - E_{t-1}X_{t+k}) = E_{t-m}X_{t+k} - E_{t-m}X_{t+k} = 0$, $m \geq 0$. This means that $\delta_t X_{t+k}$ must be uncorrelated for all k with all information known at time $t-1$ and must, since lagged innovations are information at time t, be uncorrelated with $\delta_{t'} X_{t+j}$, $t' < t$, all j, i.e., innovations in variables are serially uncorrelated.

The model implies that the innovation in price $\delta_t p_t$ is observable. Since (3) can be written $p_t = \bar{\gamma}(d_t + E_t p_{t+1})$, we know, solving, that $E_t p_{t+1} = p_t/\bar{\gamma} - d_t$. Hence $\delta_t p_t \equiv E_t p_t - E_{t-1}p_t = p_t + d_{t-1} - p_{t-1}/\bar{\gamma} = \Delta p_t + d_{t-1} - \bar{r}p_{t-1}$. The variable which we call $\delta_t p_t$ (or just δp) is the variable which Clive Granger and Paul Samuelson emphasized should, in contrast to $\Delta p_t \equiv p_t - p_{t-1}$, by efficient markets, be unforecastable. In practice, with our data, $\delta_t p_t$ so measured will approximately equal Δp_t.

The model also implies that the innovation in price is related to the innovations in dividends by

$$(5) \qquad \delta_t p_t = \sum_{k=0}^{\infty} \bar{\gamma}^{k+1} \delta_t d_{t+k}$$

This expression is identical to (3) except that δ_t replaces E_t. Unfortunately, while $\delta_t p_t$ is observable in this model, the $\delta_t d_{t+k}$ terms are not directly observable, that is, we do not know when the public gets information about a particular dividend. Thus, in deriving inequalities below, one is obliged to assume the "worst possible" pattern of information accrual.

Expressions (2)–(5) constitute four different representations of the same efficient markets model. Expressions (4) and (5) are particularly useful for deriving our inequalities on measures of volatility. We have already used (4) to derive the limit (1) on the standard deviation of p given the standard deviation of p^*, and we will use (5) to derive a limit on the standard deviation of δp given the standard deviation of d.

One issue that relates to the derivation of (1) can now be clarified. The inequality (1) was derived using the assumption that the forecast error $u_t = p_t^* - p_t$ is uncorrelated with p_t. However, the forecast error u_t is not serially uncorrelated. It is uncorrelated with all information known at time t, but the lagged forecast error u_{t-1} is not known at time t since p_{t-1}^* is not discovered at time t. In fact, $u_t = \sum_{k=1}^{\infty} \bar{\gamma}^k \delta_{t+k} p_{t+k}$, as can be seen by substituting the expressions for p_t and p_t^* from (3) and (4) into $u_t = p_t^* - p_t$, and rearranging. Since the series $\delta_t p_t$ is serially uncorrelated, u_t has first-order autoregressive serial correlation.[8] For this reason, it is inappropriate to test the model by regressing $p_t^* - p_t$ on variables known at time t and using the ordinary t-statistics of the coefficients of these variables. However, a generalized least squares transformation of the variables would yield an appropriate regression test. We might thus regress the transformed variable $u_t - \bar{\gamma}u_{t+1}$ on variables known at time t. Since $u_t - \bar{\gamma}u_{t+1} = \bar{\gamma}\delta_{t+1}p_{t+1}$, this amounts to testing whether the innovation in price can be forecasted. I will perform and discuss such regression tests in Section V below.

To find a limit on the standard deviation of δp for a given standard deviation of d_t, first note that d_t equals its unconditional expectation plus the sum of its innovations:

$$(6) \qquad d_t = E(d) + \sum_{k=0}^{\infty} \delta_{t-k} d_t$$

If we regard $E(d)$ as $E_{-\infty}(d_t)$, then this expression is just a tautology. It tells us, though, that d_t $t=0,1,2,\ldots$ are just different linear combinations of the same innovations in dividends that enter into the linear combination in (5) which determine $\delta_t p_t$ $t = 0,1,2,\ldots$. We can thus ask how large var (δp) might be for given $var(d)$. Since innovations are serially uncorrelated, we know from (6) that the variance of the sum is

[8]It follows that $var(u) = var(\delta p)/(1-\bar{\gamma}^2)$ as LeRoy and Porter noted. They base their volatility tests on our inequality (1) (which they call theorem 2) and an equality restriction $\sigma^2(p) + \sigma^2(\delta p)/(1-\bar{\gamma}^2) = \sigma^2(p^*)$ (their theorem 3). They found that, with postwar Standard and Poor earnings data, both relations were violated by sample statistics.

the sum of the variances:

$$(7) \quad var(d) = \sum_{k=0}^{\infty} var(\delta d_k) = \sum_{k=0}^{\infty} \sigma_k^2$$

Our assumption of stationarity for d_t implies that $var(\delta_{t-k} d_t) \equiv var(\delta d_k) \equiv \sigma_k^2$ is independent of t.

In expression (5) we have no information that the variance of the sum is the sum of the variances since all the innovations are time t innovations, which may be correlated. In fact, for given $\sigma_0^2, \sigma_1^2, \ldots$, the maximum variance of the sum in (5) occurs when the elements in the sum are perfectly positively correlated. This means then that so long as $var(\delta d) \neq 0$, $\delta_t d_{t+k} = a_k \delta_t d_t$, where $a_k = \sigma_k / \sigma_0$. Substituting this into (6) implies

$$(8) \quad \hat{d}_t = \sum_{k=0}^{\infty} a_k \varepsilon_{t-k}$$

where a hat denotes a variable minus its mean: $\hat{d}_t \equiv d_t - E(d)$ and $\varepsilon_t \equiv \delta_t d_t$. Thus, if $var(\delta p)$ is to be maximized for given $\sigma_0^2, \sigma_1^2, \ldots$, the dividend process must be a moving average process in terms of its own innovations.[9] I have thus shown, rather than assumed, that if the variance of δp is to be maximized, the forecast of d_{t+k} will have the usual ARIMA form as in the forecast popularized by Box and Jenkins.

We can now find the maximum possible variance for δp for given variance of d. Since the innovations in (5) are perfectly positively correlated, $var(\delta p) = (\Sigma_{k=0}^{\infty} \bar{\gamma}^{k+1} \sigma_k)^2$. To maximize this subject to the constraint $var(d) = \Sigma_{k=0}^{\infty} \sigma_k^2$ with respect to $\sigma_0, \sigma_1, \ldots$, one may set up the Lagrangean:

$$(9) \quad L = \left(\sum_{k=0}^{\infty} \bar{\gamma}^{k+1} \sigma_k \right)^2 + \nu \left(var(d) - \sum_{k=0}^{\infty} \sigma_k^2 \right)$$

[9] Of course, all indeterministic stationary processes can be given linear moving average representations, as Hermann Wold showed. However, it does not follow that the process can be given a moving average representation in terms of its own innovations. The true process may be generated nonlinearly or other information besides its own lagged values may be used in forecasting. These will generally result in a less than perfect correlation of the terms in (5).

where ν is the Lagrangean multiplier. The first-order conditions for $\sigma_j, j = 0, \ldots \infty$ are

$$(10) \quad \frac{\partial L}{\partial \sigma_j} = 2 \left(\sum_{k=0}^{\infty} \bar{\gamma}^{k+1} \sigma_k \right) \bar{\gamma}^{j+1} - 2\nu \sigma_j = 0$$

which in turn means that σ_j is proportional to $\bar{\gamma}^j$. The second-order conditions for a maximum are satisfied, and the maximum can be viewed as a tangency of an isoquant for $var(\delta p)$, which is a hyperplane in $\sigma_0, \sigma_1, \sigma_2, \ldots$ space, with the hypersphere represented by the constraint. At the maximum $\sigma_k^2 = (1 - \bar{\gamma}^2) var(d) \bar{\gamma}^{2k}$ and $var(\delta p) = \bar{\gamma}^2 var(d)/(1 - \bar{\gamma}^2)$ and so, converting to standard deviations for ease of interpretation, we have

$$(11) \quad \sigma(\delta p) \leqslant \sigma(d)/\sqrt{\bar{r}_2}$$

where $\quad \bar{r}_2 = (1 + \bar{r})^2 - 1$.

Here, $\bar{r}_2$ is the two-period interest rate, which is roughly twice the one-period rate. The maximum occurs, then, when d_t is a first-order autoregressive process, $\hat{d}_t = \bar{\gamma} \hat{d}_{t-1} + \varepsilon_t$, and $E_t \hat{d}_{t+k} = \bar{\gamma}^k \hat{d}_t$, where $\hat{d} \equiv d - E(d)$ as before.

The variance of the innovation in price is thus maximized when information about dividends is revealed in a smooth fashion so that the standard deviation of the new information at time t about a future dividend d_{t+k} is proportional to its weight in the present value formula in the model (5). In contrast, suppose all dividends somehow became known years before they were paid. Then the innovations in dividends would be so heavily discounted in (5) that they would contribute little to the standard deviation of the innovation in price. Alternatively, suppose nothing were known about dividends until the year they are paid. Here, although the innovation would not be heavily discounted in (5), the impact of the innovation would be confined to only one term in (5), and the standard deviation in the innovation in price would be limited to the standard deviation in the single dividend.

Other inequalities analogous to (11) can also be derived in the same way. For example, we can put an upper bound to the standard deviation of the change in price (rather than the innovation in price) for given standard deviation in dividend. The only difference induced in the above procedure is that Δp_t is a different linear combination of innovations in dividends. Using the fact that $\Delta p_t = \delta_t p_t + \bar{r} p_{t-1} - d_{t-1}$ we find

$$(12) \qquad \Delta p_t = \sum_{k=0}^{\infty} \bar{\gamma}^{k+1} \delta_t d_{t+k}$$

$$+ \bar{r} \sum_{j=1}^{\infty} \delta_{t-j} \sum_{k=0}^{\infty} \bar{\gamma}^{k+1} d_{t+k-1} - \sum_{j=1}^{\infty} \delta_{t-j} d_{t-1}$$

As above, the maximization of the variance of δp for given variance of d requires that the time t innovations in d be perfectly correlated (innovations at different times are necessarily uncorrelated) so that again the dividend process must be forecasted as an ARIMA process. However, the parameters of the ARIMA process for d which maximize the variance of Δp will be different. One finds, after maximizing the Lagrangean expression (analogous to (9)) an inequality slightly different from (11),

$$(13) \qquad \sigma(\Delta p) \leqslant \sigma(d)/\sqrt{2\bar{r}}$$

The upper bound is attained if the optimal dividend forecast is first-order autoregressive, but with an autoregressive coefficient slightly different from that which induced the upper bound to (11). The upper bound to (13) is attained if $\hat{d}_t = (1-\bar{r})\hat{d}_{t-1} + \varepsilon_t$ and $E_t d_{t+k} = (1-\bar{r})^k \hat{d}_t$, where, as before, $\hat{d}_t \equiv d_t - E(d)$.

II. High Kurtosis and Infrequent Important Breaks in Information

It has been repeatedly noted that stock price change distributions show high kurtosis or "fat tails." This means that, if one looks at a time-series of observations on δp or Δp, one sees long stretches of time when their (absolute) values are all rather small and then an occasional extremely large (absolute) value. This phenomenon is commonly attributed to a tendency for new information to come in big lumps infrequently. There seems to be a common presumption that this information lumping might cause stock price changes to have high or infinite variance, which would seem to contradict the conclusion in the preceding section that the variance of price is limited and is maximized if forecasts have a simple autoregressive structure.

High sample kurtosis does not indicate infinite variance if we do not assume, as did Fama (1965) and others, that price changes are drawn from the stable Paretian class of distributions.[10] The model does not suggest that price changes have a distribution in this class. The model instead suggests that the existence of moments for the price series is implied by the existence of moments for the dividends series.

As long as d is jointly stationary with information and has a finite variance, then p, p^*, δp, and Δp will be stationary and have a finite variance.[11] If d is normally distributed, however, it does not follow that the price variables will be normally distributed. In fact, they may yet show high kurtosis.

To see this possibility, suppose the dividends are serially independent and identically normally distributed. The kurtosis of the price series is defined by $K = E(\hat{p})^4 / (E(\hat{p})^2)^2$, where $p \equiv \hat{p} - E(p)$. Suppose, as an example, that with a probability of $1/n$

[10]The empirical fact about the unconditional distribution of stock price changes in not that they have infinite variance (which can never be demonstrated with any finite sample), but that they have high kurtosis in the sample.

[11]With any stationary process X_t, the existence of a finite $var(X_t)$ implies, by Schwartz's inequality, a finite value of $cov(X_t, X_{t+k})$ for any k, and hence the entire autocovariance function of X_t, and the spectrum, exists. Moreover, the variance of $E_t(X_t)$ must also be finite, since the variance of X equals the variance of $E_t(X_t)$ plus the variance of the forecast error. While we may regard real dividends as having finite variance, innovations in dividends may show high kurtosis. The residuals in a second-order autoregression for d_t have a studentized range of 6.29 for the Standard and Poor series and 5.37 for the Dow series. According to the David-Hartley-Pearson test, normality can be rejected at the 5 percent level (but not at the 1 percent level) with a one-tailed test for both data sets.

the public is told d_t at the beginning of time t, but with probability $(n-1)/n$ has no information about current or future dividends.[12] In time periods when they are told d_t, $\hat{p}_t$ equals $\bar{\gamma}\hat{d}_t$, otherwise $\hat{p}_t=0$. Then $E(\hat{p}_t^4)=E((\bar{\gamma}\hat{d}_t)^4)/n$ and $E(\hat{p}_t^2)=E((\bar{\gamma}\hat{d}_t)^2)/n$ so that kurtosis equals $nE(\bar{\gamma}\hat{d}_t)^4)/E((\bar{\gamma}\hat{d}_t)^2)$ which equals n times the kurtosis of the normal distribution. Hence, by choosing n high enough one can achieve an arbitrarily high kurtosis, and yet the variance of price will always exist. Moreover, the distribution of $\hat{p}_t$ conditional on the information that the dividend has been revealed is also normal, in spite of high kurtosis of the unconditional distribution.

If information is revealed in big lumps occasionally (so as to induce high kurtosis as suggested in the above example) $var(\delta p)$ or $var(\Delta p)$ are not especially large. The variance loses more from the long interval of time when information is not revealed than it gains from the infrequent events when it is. The highest possible variance for given variance of d indeed comes when information is revealed smoothly as noted in the previous section. In the above example, where information about dividends is revealed one time in n, $\sigma(\delta p)=\bar{\gamma}n^{1/2}\sigma(d)$ and $\sigma(\Delta p)=\bar{\gamma}(2/n)^{1/2}\sigma(d)$. The values of $\sigma(\delta p)$ and $\sigma(\Delta p)$ implied by this example are for all n strictly below the upper bounds of the inequalities (11) and (13).[13]

III. Dividends or Earnings?

It has been argued that the model (2) does not capture what is generally meant by efficient markets, and that the model should be replaced by a model which makes price the present value of expected earnings rather than dividends. In the model (2) earnings may be relevant to the pricing of shares but only insofar as earnings are indicators of future dividends. Earnings are thus no different from any other economic variable which may indicate future dividends. The model (2) is consistent with the usual notion in finance that individuals are concerned with returns, that is, capital gains plus dividends. The model implies that expected total returns are constant and that the capital gains component of returns is just a reflection of information about future dividends. Earnings, in contrast, are statistics conceived by accountants which are supposed to provide an indicator of how well a company is doing, and there is a great deal of latitude for the definition of earnings, as the recent literature on inflation accounting will attest.

There is no reason why price per share ought to be the present value of expected earnings per share if some earnings are retained. In fact, as Merton Miller and Franco Modigliani argued, such a present value formula would entail a fundamental sort of double counting. It is incorrect to include in the present value formula both earnings at time t and the later earnings that accrue when time t earnings are reinvested.[14] Miller and Modigliani showed a formula by which price might be regarded as the present value of earnings corrected for investments, but that formula can be shown, using an accounting identity to be identical to (2).

Some people seem to feel that one cannot claim price as present value of expected dividends since firms routinely pay out only a fraction of earnings and also attempt somewhat to stabilize dividends. They are right in the case where firms paid out *no* dividends, for then the price p_t would have to grow at the discount rate $\bar{r}$, and the model (2) would not be the solution to the difference equation implied by the condition $E_t(H_t)=r$. On the other hand, if firms pay out a fraction of dividends or smooth short-run fluctuations in dividends, then the price of the firm will grow at a rate less than the

[12] For simplicity, in this example, the assumption elsewhere in this article that d_t is always known at time t has been dropped. It follows that in this example $\delta_t p_t \neq \Delta p_t + d_{t-1} - rp_{t-1}$ but instead $\delta_t p_t = \hat{p}_t$.

[13] For another illustrative example, consider $\hat{d}_t=\bar{\gamma}\hat{d}_{t-1}+\varepsilon_t$ as with the upper bound for the inequality (11) but where the dividends are announced for the next n years every $1/n$ years. Here, even though $\hat{d}_t$ has the autoregressive structure, ε_t is not the innovation in d_t. As n goes to infinity, $\sigma(\delta p)$ approaches zero.

[14] LeRoy and Porter do assume price as present value of earnings but employ a correction to the price and earnings series which is, under additional theoretical assumptions not employed by Miller and Modigliani, a correction for the double counting.

discount rate and (2) is the solution to the difference equation.[15] With our Standard and Poor data, the growth rate of real price is only about 1.5 percent, while the discount rate is about 4.8%+1.5%=6.3%. At these rates, the value of the firm a few decades hence is so heavily discounted relative to its size that it contributes very little to the value of the stock today; by far the most of the value comes from the intervening dividends. Hence (2) and the implied p^* ought to be useful characterizations of the value of the firm.

The crucial thing to recognize in this context is that once we know the terminal price and intervening dividends, we have specified all that investors care about. It would not make sense to define an *ex post* rational price from a terminal condition on price, using the same formula with earnings in place of dividends.

IV. Time-Varying Real Discount Rates

If we modify the model (2) to allow real discount rates to vary without restriction through time, then the model becomes untestable. We do not observe real discount rates directly. Regardless of the behavior of P_t and D_t, there will always be a discount rate series which makes (2) hold identically. We might ask, though, whether the movements in the real discount rate that would be required aren't larger than we might have expected. Or is it possible that small movements in the current one-period discount rate coupled with new information about such movements in future discount rates could account for high stock price volatility?[16]

[15] To understand this point, it helps to consider a traditional continuous time growth model, so instead of (2) we have $P_0=\int_0^\infty D_t e^{-rt}dt$. In such a model, a firm has a constant earnings stream I. If it pays out all earnings, then $D=I$ and $P_0=\int_0^\infty Ie^{-rt}dt=I/r$. If it pays out only s of its earnings, then the firm grows at rate $(1-s)r$, $D_t=sIe^{(1-s)rt}$ which is less than I at $t=0$, but higher than I later on. Then $P_0=\int_0^\infty sIe^{(1-s)rt}e^{-rt}dt=\int_0^\infty sIe^{-srt}dt=sI/(rs)$. If $s\neq 0$ (so that we're not dividing by zero) $P_0=I/r$.

[16] James Pesando has discussed the analogous question: how large must the variance in liquidity premia be in order to justify the volatility of long-term interest rates?

The natural extension of (2) to the case of time varying real discount rates is

$$P_t=E_t\left(\sum_{k=0}^{\infty} D_{t+k}\prod_{j=0}^{k}\frac{1}{1+r_{t+j}}\right) \tag{14}$$

which has the property that $E_t((1+H_t)/(1+r_t))=1$. If we set $1+r_t=(\partial U/\partial C_t)/(\partial U/\partial C_{t+1})$, i.e., to the marginal rate of substitution between present and future consumption where U is the additively separable utility of consumption, then this property is the first-order condition for a maximum of expected utility subject to a stock market budget constraint, and equation (14) is consistent with such expected utility maximization at all times. Note that while r_t is a sort of *ex post* real interest rate not necessarily known until time $t+1$, only the conditional distribution at time t or earlier influences price in the formula (14).

As before, we can rewrite the model in terms of detrended series:

$$p_t=E_t(p_t^*) \tag{15}$$

where $$p_t^*\equiv\sum_{k=0}^{\infty} d_{t+k}\prod_{j=0}^{k}\frac{1}{1+\bar{r}_{t+j}}$$

$$1+\bar{r}_{t+j}\equiv(1+r_t)/\lambda$$

This model then implies that $\sigma(p_t)\leqslant\sigma(p_t^*)$ as before. Since the model is nonlinear, however, it does not allow us to derive inequalities like (11) or (13). On the other hand, if movements in real interest rates are not too large, then we can use the linearization of p_t^* (i.e., Taylor expansion truncated after the linear term) around $d=E(d)$ and $\bar{r}=E(\bar{r})$; i.e.,

$$\hat{p}_t^*\cong\sum_{k=0}^{\infty}\bar{\gamma}^{k+1}\hat{d}_{t+k}-\frac{E(d)}{E(\bar{r})}\sum_{k=0}^{\infty}\bar{\gamma}^{k+1}\hat{\bar{r}}_{t+k} \tag{16}$$

where $\bar{\gamma}=1/(1+E(\bar{r}))$, and a hat over a variable denotes the variable minus its mean. The first term in the above expression is just the expression for p_t^* in (4) (demeaned). The second term represents the effect on p_t^* of movements in real discount rates. This second term is identical to the expression for $\hat{p}^*$ in (4) except that d_{t+k} is replaced by $\bar{r}_{t+k}$ and the expression is premultiplied by $-E(d)/E(\bar{r})$.

It is possible to offer a simple intuitive interpretation for this linearization. First note that the derivative of $1/(1+\bar{r}_{t+k})$, with respect to $\bar{r}$ evaluated at $E(\bar{r})$ is $-\bar{\gamma}^2$. Thus, a one percentage point increase in $\bar{r}_{t+k}$ causes $1/(1+\bar{r}_{t+k})$ to drop by $\bar{\gamma}^2$ times 1 percent, or slightly less than 1 percent. Note that all terms in (15) dated $t+k$ or higher are premultiplied by $1/(1+\bar{r}_{t+k})$. Thus, if $\bar{r}_{t+k}$ is increased by one percentage point, all else constant, then all of these terms will be reduced by about $\bar{\gamma}^2$ times 1 percent. We can approximate the sum of all these terms as $\bar{\gamma}^{k-1}E(d)/E(\bar{r})$, where $E(d)/E(\bar{r})$ is the value at the beginning of time $t+k$ of a constant dividend stream $E(d)$ discounted by $E(\bar{r})$, and $\bar{\gamma}^{k-1}$ discounts it to the present. So, we see that a one percentage point increase in $\bar{r}_{t+k}$, all else constant, decreases p_t^* by about $\bar{\gamma}^{k+1}E(d)/E(\bar{r})$, which corresponds to the kth term in expression (16). There are two sources of inaccuracy with this linearization. First, the present value of all future dividends starting with time $t+k$ is not exactly $\bar{\gamma}^{k-1}E(d)/E(\bar{r})$. Second, increasing $\bar{r}_{t+k}$ by one percentage point does not cause $1/(1+\bar{r}_{t+k})$ to fall by exactly $\bar{\gamma}^2$ times 1 percent. To some extent, however, these errors in the effects on p_t^* of $\bar{r}_t, \bar{r}_{t+1}, \bar{r}_{t+2}, \ldots$ should average out, and one can use (16) to get an idea of the effects of changes in discount rates.

To give an impression as to the accuracy of the linearization (16), I computed p_t^* for data set 2 in two ways: first using (15) and then using (16), with the same terminal condition p_{1979}^*. In place of the unobserved $\bar{r}_t$ series, I used the actual four–six-month prime commercial paper rate plus a constant to give it the mean $\bar{r}$ of Table 2. The commercial paper rate is a *nominal* interest rate, and thus one would expect its fluctuations represent changes in inflationary expectations as well as real interest rate movements. I chose it nonetheless, rather arbitrarily, as a series which shows much more fluctuation than one would normally expect to see in an expected *real* rate. The commercial paper rate ranges, in this sample, from 0.53 to 9.87 percent. It stayed below 1 percent for over a decade (1935–46) and, at the end of the sample, stayed generally well above 5 percent for over a decade. In spite of this erratic behavior, the correlation coefficient between p^* computed from (15) and p^* computed from (16) was .996, and $\sigma(p_t^*)$ was 250.5 and 268.0 by (15) and (16), respectively. Thus the linearization (16) can be quite accurate. Note also that while these large movements in $\bar{r}_t$ cause p_t^* to move much more than was observed in Figure 2, $\sigma(p^*)$ is still less than half of $\sigma(p)$. This suggests that the variability $\bar{r}_t$ that is needed to save the efficient

TABLE 2—SAMPLE STATISTICS FOR PRICE AND DIVIDEND SERIES

	Data Set 1: Standard and Poor's	Data Set 2: Modified Dow Industrial
Sample Period:	1871–1979	1928–1979
1) $E(p)$	145.5	982.6
$E(d)$	6.989	44.76
2) $\bar{r}$	.0480	0.456
$\bar{r}_2$	.0984	.0932
3) $b = ln\lambda$	.0148	.0188
$\hat{\sigma}(b)$	(.0011)	(1.0035)
4) $cor(p, p^*)$	.3918	.1626
$\sigma(d)$	1.481	9.828
Elements of Inequalities:		
Inequality (1)		
5) $\sigma(p)$	50.12	355.9
6) $\sigma(p^*)$	8.968	26.80
Inequality (11)		
7) $\sigma(\Delta p + d_{-1} - \bar{r}p_{-1})$	25.57	242.1
$min(\sigma)$	23.01	209.0
8) $\sigma(d)/\sqrt{\bar{r}_2}$	4.721	32.20
Inequality (13)		
9) $\sigma(\Delta p)$	25.24	239.5
$min(\sigma)$	22.71	206.4
10) $\sigma(d)/\sqrt{2\bar{r}}$	4.777	32.56

Note: In this table, E denotes sample mean, σ denotes standard deviation and $\hat{\sigma}$ denotes standard error. $Min(\sigma)$ is the lower bound on σ computed as a one-sided χ^2 95 percent confidence interval. The symbols p, d, $\bar{r}$, $\bar{r}_2$, b, and p^* are defined in the text. Data sets are described in the Appendix. Inequality (1) in the text asserts that the standard deviation in row 5 should be less than or equal to that in row 6, inequality (11) that σ in row 7 should be less than or equal to that in row 8, and inequality (13) that σ in row 9 should be less than that in row 10.

markets model is much larger yet, as we shall see.

To put a formal lower bound on $\sigma(\bar{r})$ given the variability of Δp, note that (16) makes $\hat{p}_t^*$ the present value of $z_t, z_{t+1}, \ldots$ where $z_t \equiv \hat{d}_t - \hat{r}_t E(d)/E(\bar{r})$. We thus know from (13) that $2E(\bar{r})var(\Delta p) \leqslant var(z)$. Moreover, from the definition of z we know that $var(z) \leqslant var(d) + 2\sigma(d)\sigma(\bar{r})E(d)/E(\bar{r}) + var(\bar{r})E(d)^2/E(\bar{r})^2$ where the equality holds if d_t and $\bar{r}_t$ are perfectly negatively correlated. Combining these two inequalities and solving for $\sigma(\bar{r})$ one finds

(17)

$$\sigma(\bar{r}) \geqslant \left(\sqrt{2E(\bar{r})}\,\sigma(\Delta p) - \sigma(d)\right) E(\bar{r})/E(d)$$

This inequality puts a lower bound on $\sigma(\bar{r})$ proportional to the discrepancy between the left-hand side and right-hand side of the inequality (13).[17] It will be used to examine the data in the next section.

V. Empirical Evidence

The elements of the inequalities (1), (11), and (13) are displayed for the two data sets (described in the Appendix) in Table 2. In both data sets, the long-run exponential growth path was estimated by regressing $ln(P_t)$ on a constant and time. Then λ in (3) was set equal to e^b where b is the coefficient of time (Table 2). The discount rate $\bar{r}$ used to compute p^* from (4) is estimated as the average d divided by the average p.[18] The terminal value of p^* is taken as average p.

With data set 1, the nominal price and dividend series are the real Standard and Poor's Composite Stock Price Index and the associated dividend series. The earlier observations for this series are due to Alfred Cowles who said that the index is

> intended to represent, ignoring the elements of brokerage charges and taxes, what would have happened to an investor's funds if he had bought, at the beginning of 1871, all stocks quoted on the New York Stock Exchange, allocating his purchases among the individual stocks in proportion to their total monetary value and each month up to 1937 had by the same criterion redistributed his holdings among all quoted stocks. [p. 2]

In updating his series, Standard and Poor later restricted the sample to 500 stocks, but the series continues to be value weighted. The advantage to this series is its comprehensiveness. The disadvantage is that the dividends accruing to the portfolio at one point of time may not correspond to the dividends forecasted by holders of the Standard and Poor's portfolio at an earlier time, due to the change in weighting of the stocks. There is no way to correct this disadvantage without losing comprehensiveness. The original portfolio of 1871 is bound to become a relatively smaller and smaller sample of *U.S.* common stocks as time goes on.

With data set 2, the nominal series are a modified Dow Jones Industrial Average and associated dividend series. With this data set, the advantages and disadvantages of data set 1 are reversed. My modifications in the Dow Jones Industrial Average assure that this series reflects the performance of a single unchanging portfolio. The disadvantage is that the performance of only 30 stocks is recorded.

Table 2 reveals that all inequalities are dramatically violated by the sample statistics for both data sets. The left-hand side of the inequality is always at least five times as great as the right-hand side, and as much as thirteen times as great.

The violation of the inequalities implies that "innovations" in price as we measure them can be forecasted. In fact, if we regress $\delta_{t+1}p_{t+1}$ onto (a constant and) p_t, we get significant results: a coefficient of p_t of $-.1521$ ($t = -3.218$, $R^2 = .0890$) for data set 1 and a coefficient of $-.2421$ ($t = -2.631$, $R^2 = .1238$) for data set 2. These results are

[17] In deriving the inequality (13) it was assumed that d_t was known at time t, so by analogy this inequality would be based on the assumption that r_t is known at time t. However, without this assumption the same inequality could be derived anyway. The maximum contribution of $\bar{r}_t$ to the variance of ΔP occurs when $\bar{r}_t$ is known at time t.

[18] This is not equivalent to the average dividend price ratio, which was slightly higher (.0514 for data set 1, .0484 for data set 2).

not due to the representation of the data as a proportion of the long-run growth path. In fact, if the holding period return H_t is regressed on a constant and the dividend price ratio D_t/P_t, we get results that are only slightly less significant: a coefficient of 3.533 (t=2.672, R^2=.0631) for data set 1 and a coefficient of 4.491 (t=1.795, R^2=.0617) for data set 2.

These regression tests, while technically valid, may not be as generally useful for appraising the validity of the model as are the simple volatility comparisons. First, as noted above, the regression tests are not insensitive to data misalignment. Such low R^2 might be the result of dividend or commodity price index data errors. Second, although the model is rejected in these very long samples, the tests may not be powerful if we confined ourselves to shorter samples, for which the data are more accurate, as do most researchers in finance, while volatility comparisons may be much more revealing. To see this, consider a stylized world in which (for the sake of argument) the dividend series d_t is absolutely constant while the price series behaves as in our data set. Since the actual dividend series is fairly smooth, our stylized world is not too remote from our own. If dividends d_t are absolutely constant, however, it should be obvious to the most casual and unsophisticated observer by volatility arguments like those made here that the efficient markets model must be wrong. Price movements cannot reflect new information about dividends if dividends never change. Yet regressions like those run above will have limited power to reject the model. If the alternative hypothesis is, say, that $\hat{p}_t = \rho\hat{p}_{t-1} + \varepsilon_t$, where ρ is close to but less than one, then the power of the test in short samples will be very low. In this stylized world we are testing for the stationarity of the p_t series, for which, as we know, power is low in short samples.[19] For example, if postwar data from, say, 1950–65 were chosen (a period often used in recent financial markets studies) when the stock market was drifting up, then clearly the regression tests will not reject. Even in periods showing a reversal of upward drift the rejection may not be significant.

Using inequality (17), we can compute how big the standard deviation of real discount rates would have to be to possibly account for the discrepancy $\sigma(\Delta p) - \sigma(d)/(2\bar{r})^{1/2}$ between Table 2 results (rows 9 and 10) and the inequality (13). Assuming Table 2 $\bar{r}$ (row 2) equals $E(\bar{r})$ and that sample variances equal population variances, we find that the standard deviation of $\bar{r}_t$ would have to be at least 4.36 percentage points for data set 1 and 7.36 percentage points for data set 2. These are very large numbers. If we take, as a normal range for $\bar{r}_t$ implied by these figures, a ± 2 standard deviation range around the real interest rate $\bar{r}$ given in Table 2, then the real interest rate $\bar{r}_t$ would have to range from -3.91 to 13.52 percent for data set 1 and -8.16 to 17.27 percent for data set 2! And these ranges reflect lowest possible standard deviations which are consistent with the model only if the real rate has the first-order autoregressive structure and perfect negative correlation with dividends!

These estimated standard deviations of *ex ante* real interest rates are roughly consistent with the results of the simple regressions noted above. In a regression of H_t on D_t/P_t and a constant, the standard deviation of the fitted value of H_t is 4.42 and 5.71 percent for data sets 1 and 2, respectively. These large standard deviations are consistent with the low R^2 because the standard deviation of H_t is so much higher (17.60 and 23.00 percent, respectively). The regressions of $\delta_t p_t$ on p_t suggest higher standard deviations of expected real interest rates. The standard deviation of the fitted value divided by the average detrended price is 5.24 and 8.67 percent for data sets 1 and 2, respectively.

VI. Summary and Conclusions

We have seen that measures of stock price volatility over the past century appear to be far too high—five to thirteen times too

[19] If dividends are constant (let us say $d_t = 0$) then a test of the model by a regression of $\delta_{t+1}p_{t+1}$ on p_t amounts to a regression of p_{t+1} on p_t with the null hypothesis that the coefficient of p_t is $(1+\bar{r})$. This appears to be an explosive model for which t-statistics are not valid yet our true model, which in effect assumes $\sigma(d) \neq 0$, is nonexplosive.

high—to be attributed to new information about future real dividends if uncertainty about future dividends is measured by the sample standard deviations of real dividends around their long-run exponential growth path. The lower bound of a 95 percent one-sided χ^2 confidence interval for the standard deviation of annual changes in real stock prices is over five times higher than the upper bound allowed by our measure of the observed variability of real dividends. The failure of the efficient markets model is thus so dramatic that it would seem impossible to attribute the failure to such things as data errors, price index problems, or changes in tax laws.

One way of saving the general notion of efficient markets would be to attribute the movements in stock prices to changes in expected real interest rates. Since expected real interest rates are not directly observed, such a theory can not be evaluated statistically unless some other indicator of real rates is found. I have shown, however, that the movements in expected real interest rates that would justify the variability in stock prices are very large—much larger than the movements in nominal interest rates over the sample period.

Another way of saving the general notion of efficient markets is to say that our measure of the uncertainty regarding future dividends—the sample standard deviation of the movements of real dividends around their long-run exponential growth path—understates the true uncertainty about future dividends. Perhaps the market was rightfully fearful of much larger movements than actually materialized. One is led to doubt this, if after a century of observations nothing happened which could remotely justify the stock price movements. The movements in real dividends the market feared must have been many times larger than those observed in the Great Depression of the 1930's, as was noted above. Since the market did not know in advance with certainty the growth path and distribution of dividends that was ultimately observed, however, one cannot be sure that they were wrong to consider possible major events which did not occur. Such an explanation of the volatility of stock prices, however, is "academic," in that it relies fundamentally on unobservables and cannot be evaluated statistically.

Appendix

A. *Data Set 1*: *Standard and Poor Series*

Annual 1871–1979. The price series P_t is Standard and Poor's Monthly Composite Stock Price index for January divided by the Bureau of Labor Statistics wholesale price index (January *WPI* starting in 1900, annual average *WPI* before 1900 scaled to 1.00 in the base year 1979). Standard and Poor's Monthly Composite Stock Price index is a continuation of the Cowles Commission Common Stock index developed by Alfred Cowles and Associates and currently is based on 500 stocks.

The Dividend Series D_t is total dividends for the calendar year accruing to the portfolio represented by the stocks in the index divided by the average wholesale price index for the year (annual average *WPI* scaled to 1.00 in the base year 1979). Starting in 1926 these total dividends are the series "Dividends per share... 12 months moving total adjusted to index" from Standard and Poor's statistical service. For 1871 to 1925, total dividends are Cowles series Da-1 multiplied by .1264 to correct for change in base year.

B. *Data Set 2*: *Modified Dow Jones Industrial Average*

Annual 1928–1979. Here P_t and D_t refer to real price and dividends of the portfolio of 30 stocks comprising the sample for the Dow Jones Industrial Average when it was created in 1928. Dow Jones averages before 1928 exist, but the 30 industrials series was begun in that year. The published Dow Jones Industrial Average, however, is not ideal in that stocks are dropped and replaced and in that the weighting given an individual stock is affected by splits. Of the original 30 stocks, only 17 were still included in the Dow Jones Industrial Average at the end of our sample. The published Dow Jones Industrial Average is the simple sum of the price per share of the 30 companies divided by a divisor which changes through time. Thus, if a stock splits two for one, then Dow Jones continues to include only one share but changes the divisor to prevent a sudden drop in the Dow Jones average.

To produce the series used in this paper, the *Capital Changes Reporter* was used to trace changes in the companies from 1928 to 1979. Of the original 30 companies of the Dow Jones Industrial Average, at the end of our sample (1979), 9 had the identical names, 12 had changed only their names, and 9 had been acquired, merged or consolidated. For these latter 9, the price and dividend series are continued as the price and dividend of the shares exchanged by the acquiring corporation. In only one case was a cash payment, along with shares of the acquiring corporation, exchanged for the shares of the acquired corporation. In this case, the price and dividend series were continued as the price and dividend of the shares exchanged by the acquiring corporation. In four cases, preferred shares of the acquiring corporation were among shares exchanged. Common shares of equal value were substituted for these in our series. The number of shares of each firm included in the total is determined by the splits, and effective splits effected by stock dividends and merger. The price series is the value of all these shares on the last trading day of the preceding year, as shown on the Wharton School's Rodney White Center Common Stock tape. The dividend series is the total for the year of dividends and the cash value of other distributions for all these shares. The price and dividend series were deflated using the same wholesale price indexes as in data set 1.

REFERENCES

C. Amsler, "An American Consol: A Reexamination of the Expectations Theory of the Term Structure of Interest Rates," unpublished manuscript, Michigan State Univ. 1980.

S. Basu, "The Investment Performance of Common Stocks in Relation to their Price-Earnings Ratios: A Test of the Efficient Markets Hypothesis," *J. Finance*, June 1977, *32*, 663–82.

G. E. P. Box and G. M. Jenkins, *Time Series Analysis for Forecasting and Control*, San Francisco: Holden-Day 1970.

W. C. Brainard, J. B. Shoven, and L. Weiss, "The Financial Valuation of the Return to Capital," *Brookings Papers,* Washington 1980, *2*, 453–502.

Paul H. Cootner, *The Random Character of Stock Market Prices*, Cambridge: MIT Press 1964.

Alfred Cowles and Associates, *Common Stock Indexes, 1871–1937*, Cowles Commission for Research in Economics, Monograph No. 3, Bloomington: Principia Press 1938.

E. F. Fama, "Efficient Capital Markets: A Review of Theory and Empirical Work," *J. Finance*, May 1970, *25*, 383–420.

______, "The Behavior of Stock Market Prices," *J. Bus., Univ. Chicago*, Jan. 1965, *38*, 34–105.

C. W. J. Granger, "Some Consequences of the Valuation Model when Expectations are Taken to be Optimum Forecasts," *J. Finance*, Mar. 1975, *30*, 135–45.

M. C. Jensen et al., "Symposium on Some Anomalous Evidence Regarding Market Efficiency," *J. Financ. Econ.*, June/Sept. 1978, *6*, 93–330.

S. LeRoy and R. Porter, "The Present Value Relation: Tests Based on Implied Variance Bounds," *Econometrica*, forthcoming.

M. H. Miller and F. Modigliani, "Dividend Policy, Growth and the Valuation of Shares," *J. Bus., Univ. Chicago*, Oct. 1961, *34*, 411–33.

F. Modigliani and R. Cohn, "Inflation, Rational Valuation and the Market," *Financ. Anal. J.*, Mar./Apr. 1979, *35*, 24–44.

J. Pesando, "Time Varying Term Premiums and the Volatility of Long-Term Interest Rates," unpublished paper, Univ. Toronto, July 1979.

P. A. Samuelson, "Proof that Properly Discounted Present Values of Assets Vibrate Randomly," in Hiroaki Nagatani and Kate Crowley, eds., *Collected Scientific Papers of Paul A. Samuelson*, Vol. IV, Cambridge: MIT Press 1977.

R. J. Shiller, "The Volatility of Long-Term Interest Rates and Expectations Models of the Term Structure," *J. Polit. Econ.*, Dec. 1979, *87*, 1190–219.

______ **and J. J. Siegel,** "The Gibson Paradox and Historical Movements in Real Interest Rates," *J. Polit. Econ.*, Oct. 1979, *85*, 891–907.

H. Wold, "On Prediction in Stationary Time Series," *Annals Math. Statist.* 1948, *19*, 558–67.

Commerce Clearing House, *Capital Changes Reporter*, New Jersey 1977.

Dow Jones & Co., *The Dow Jones Averages 1855–1970*, New York: Dow Jones Books 1972.

Standard and Poor's *Security Price Index Record*, New York 1978.

Part III
Noise Traders, Investor Sentiment and Behavioral Finance

THE JOURNAL OF FINANCE • VOL. XLI, NO. 3 • JULY 1986

Noise

FISCHER BLACK*

ABSTRACT

The effects of noise on the world, and on our views of the world, are profound. Noise in the sense of a large number of small events is often a causal factor much more powerful than a small number of large events can be. Noise makes trading in financial markets possible, and thus allows us to observe prices for financial assets. Noise causes markets to be somewhat inefficient, but often prevents us from taking advantage of inefficiencies. Noise in the form of uncertainty about future tastes and technology by sector causes business cycles, and makes them highly resistant to improvement through government intervention. Noise in the form of expectations that need not follow rational rules causes inflation to be what it is, at least in the absence of a gold standard or fixed exchange rates. Noise in the form of uncertainty about what relative prices would be with other exchange rates makes us think incorrectly that changes in exchange rates or inflation rates cause changes in trade or investment flows or economic activity. Most generally, noise makes it very difficult to test either practical or academic theories about the way that financial or economic markets work. We are forced to act largely in the dark.

I USE THE WORD "noise" in several senses in this paper.

In my basic model of financial markets, noise is contrasted with information. People sometimes trade on information in the usual way. They are correct in expecting to make profits from these trades. On the other hand, people sometimes trade on noise as if it were information. If they expect to make profits from noise trading, they are incorrect. However, noise trading is essential to the existence of liquid markets.

In my model of the way we observe the world, noise is what makes our observations imperfect. It keeps us from knowing the expected return on a stock or portfolio. It keeps us from knowing whether monetary policy affects inflation or unemployment. It keeps us from knowing what, if anything, we can do to make things better.

In my model of inflation, noise is the arbitrary element in expectations that leads to an arbitrary rate of inflation consistent with expectations. In my model of business cycles and unemployment, noise is information that hasn't arrived yet. It is simply uncertainty about future demand and supply conditions within and across sectors. When the information does arrive, the number of sectors where there is a good match between tastes and technology is an index of economic activity. In my model of the international economy, changing relative prices become noise that makes it difficult to see that demand and supply

* Goldman, Sachs & Co. I am grateful for comments on earlier drafts by Peter Bernstein, Robert Merton, James Poterba, Richard Roll, Hersh Shefrin, Meir Statman, Lawrence Summers, and Laurence Weiss.

conditions are largely independent of price levels and exchange rates. Without these relative price changes, we would see that a version of purchasing power parity holds most of the time.

I think of these models as equilibrium models. Not rational equilibrium models, because of the role of noise and because of the unconventional things I allow an individual's utility to depend on, but equilibrium models nonetheless. They were all derived originally as part of a broad effort to apply the logic behind the capital asset pricing model to markets other than the stock market and to behavior that does not fit conventional notions of optimization.

These models are in very different fields: finance, econometrics, and macroeconomics. Do they have anything in common other than the use of the word "noise" in describing them? The common element, I think, is the emphasis on a diversified array of unrelated causal elements to explain what happens in the world. There is no single factor that causes stock prices to stray from theoretical values, nor even a small number of factors. There is no single variable whose neglect causes econometric studies to go astray. And there is no simple single or multiple factor explanation of domestic or international business fluctuations.

While I have made extensive use of the work of others, I recognize that most researchers in these fields will regard many of my conclusions as wrong, or untestable, or unsupported by existing evidence. I have not been able to think of any conventional empirical tests that would distinguish between my views and the views of others. In the end, my response to the skepticism of others is to make a prediction: someday, these conclusions will be widely accepted. The influence of noise traders will become apparent. Conventional monetary and fiscal policies will be seen as ineffective. Changes in exchange rates will come to provoke no more comment than changes in the real price of an airline ticket.

Perhaps most important, research will be seen as a process leading to reliable and relevant conclusions only very rarely, because of the noise that creeps in at every step.

If my conclusions are not accepted, I will blame it on noise.

I. Finance

Noise makes financial markets possible, but also makes them imperfect.[1]

If there is no noise trading, there will be very little trading in individual assets.[2] People will hold individual assets, directly or indirectly, but they will rarely trade them. People trading to change their exposure to broad market risks will trade in mutual funds, or portfolios, or index futures, or index options. They will have

[1] The concept of noise trading and its role in financial markets that I develop in this paper was developed through conversations with James Stone.

[2] Jaffe and Winkler [31] have a model where the traders who make speculative markets stable are those who trade to adjust their risk level or who misperceive their forecasting ability or who trade for reasons other than maximizing expected return for a given level of risk. Figlewski [23] has a model where there are two types of traders who differ in forecasting ability. Since neither kind of trader explicitly takes into account the information the other kind of trader has, each is to some degree trading on noise.

little reason to trade in the shares of an individual firm.[3] People who want cash to spend or who want to invest cash they have received will increase or decrease their positions in short term securities, or money market accounts, or money market mutual funds, or loans backed by real estate or other assets.

A person with information or insights about individual firms will want to trade, but will realize that only another person with information or insights will take the other side of the trade. Taking the other side's information into account, is it still worth trading? From the point of view of someone who knows what both the traders know, one side or the other must be making a mistake.[4] If the one who is making a mistake declines to trade, there will be no trading on information.

In other words, I do not believe it makes sense to create a model with information trading but no noise trading where traders have different beliefs and one trader's beliefs are as good as any other trader's beliefs. Differences in beliefs must derive ultimately from differences in information.[5] A trader with a special piece of information will know that other traders have their own special pieces of information, and will therefore not automatically rush out to trade.

But if there is little or no trading in individual shares, there can be no trading in mutual funds or portfolios or index futures or index options, because there will be no practical way to price them. The whole structure of financial markets depends on relatively liquid markets in the shares of individual firms.

Noise trading provides the essential missing ingredient. Noise trading is trading on noise as if it were information. People who trade on noise are willing to trade even though from an objective point of view they would be better off not trading. Perhaps they think the noise they are trading on is information. Or perhaps they just like to trade.[6]

With a lot of noise traders in the market, it now pays for those with information to trade. It even pays for people to seek out costly information which they will then trade on. Most of the time, the noise traders as a group will lose money by trading, while the information traders as a group will make money.

[3] Rubinstein [54], Milgrom and Stokey [50], and Hakansson, Kunkel, and Ohlson [30] show in a state preference world that differences in information may affect prices without causing people to trade. Grossman and Stiglitz [28] show that there may be no equilibrium when rational investors trade in the market portfolio. Grossman [27] shows the same thing for a world with trading in individual assets. Diamond and Verrecchia [21] redefine a rational expectations equilibrium in the presence of noise and show the conditions under which their equilibrium exists. In Tirole's model [61], "speculation" relies on inconsistent plans, and thus is ruled out by rational expectations. Kyle [36], [37], [38] and Grinblatt and Ross [26] look at quite different models of equilibrium where traders have market power. Kyle specifically examines the effects of changing the number of noise traders in both kinds of equilibrium.

[4] This assumes that the traders start with well diversified portfolios. In Admati [1], the traders start with suboptimal portfolios of assets.

[5] Varian [64] distinguishes between "opinions" and "information." He says that only differences in opinions will generate trading. In the kind of model he is working with, I think that differences of opinion will not exist.

[6] In Laffont [39], traders gather costly information because it has direct utility for reasons other than trading. Once they have it, they trade on it. If people start with efficient portfolios, though, even the arrival of free information may not make them want to trade. We may need to introduce direct utility of trading to explain the existence of speculative markets.

The more noise trading there is, the more liquid the markets will be, in the sense of having frequent trades that allow us to observe prices. But noise trading actually puts noise into the prices. The price of a stock reflects both the information that information traders trade on and the noise that noise traders trade on.

As the amount of noise trading increases, it will become more profitable for people to trade on information, but only because the prices have more noise in them. The increase in the amount of information trading does not mean that prices are more efficient. Not only will more information traders come in, but existing information traders will take bigger positions and will spend more on information. Yet prices will be less efficient.[7] What's needed for a liquid market causes prices to be less efficient.

The information traders will not take large enough positions to eliminate the noise. For one thing, their information gives them an edge, but does not guarantee a profit. Taking a larger position means taking more risk. So there is a limit to how large a position a trader will take. For another thing, the information traders can never be sure that they are trading on information rather than noise. What if the information they have has already been reflected in prices? Trading on that kind of information will be just like trading on noise.[8] Because the actual return on a portfolio is a very noisy estimate of expected return, even after adjusting for returns on the market and other factors, it will be difficult to show that information traders have an edge. For the same reason, it will be difficult to show that noise traders are losing by trading. There will always be a lot of ambiguity about who is an information trader and who is a noise trader.

The noise that noise traders put into stock prices will be cumulative, in the same sense that a drunk tends to wander farther and farther from his starting point. Offsetting this, though, will be the research and actions taken by the information traders. The farther the price of a stock gets from its value, the more aggressive the information traders will become. More of them will come in, and they will take larger positions. They may even initiate mergers, leveraged buyouts, and other restructurings.

Thus the price of a stock will tend to move back toward its value over time.[9] The move will often be so gradual that it is imperceptible. If it is fast, technical traders will perceive it and speed it up. If it is slow enough, technical traders will not be able to see it, or will be so unsure of what they see that they will not take large positions.[10]

Still, the farther the price of a stock moves away from value, the faster it will tend to move back. This limits the degree to which it is likely to move away from

[7] This result is specific to a model where noise traders trade on noise as if it were information. In Kyle's [36], [37], [38] model, having more noise traders can make markets more efficient.

[8] Arrow [4] says that excessive reaction to current information characterizes all the securities and futures markets. If this is true, it could be caused by trading on information that has already been discounted.

[9] Merton [47] describes a model where long run prices are efficient but short run prices need not be.

[10] Summers [60] emphasizes the difficulty in telling whether markets are efficient or not. This difficulty affects market participants and researchers alike.

value. All estimates of value are noisy, so we can never know how far away price is from value.

However, we might define an efficient market as one in which price is within a factor of 2 of value, i.e., the price is more than half of value and less than twice value.[11] The factor of 2 is arbitrary, of course. Intuitively, though, it seems reasonable to me, in the light of sources of uncertainty about value and the strength of the forces tending to cause price to return to value. By this definition, I think almost all markets are efficient almost all of the time. "Almost all" means at least 90%.

Because value is not observable, it is possible for events that have no information content to affect price. For example, the addition of a stock to the Standard & Poors 500 index will cause some investors to buy it. Their buying will force the price up for a time. Information trading will force it back, but only gradually.[12]

Similarly, when a firm with two classes of common stock issues more of one class, the price of the class of stock issued will decline relative to the price of the class of stock not issued.[13]

Both price and value will look roughly like geometric random walk processes with non-zero means. The means of percentage change in price and value will change over time. The mean of the value process will change because tastes and technology and wealth change. It may well decline when value rises, and rise when value declines. The mean of the price process will change because the relation between price and value changes (and because the mean of the value process changes). Price will tend to move toward value.

The short term volatility of price will be greater than the short term volatility of value. Since noise is independent of information in this context, when the variance of the percentage price moves caused by noise is equal to the variance of the percentage price moves caused by information, the variance of percentage price moves from day to day will be roughly twice the variance of percentage value moves from day to day. Over longer intervals, though, the variances will converge. Because price tends to return to value, the variance of price several years from now will be much less than twice the variance of value several years from now.

Volatilities will change over time. The volatility of the value of a firm is affected by things like the rate of arrival of information about the firm and the firm's leverage. All the factors affecting the volatility of a firm's value will change. The volatility of price will change for all these reasons and for other reasons as well. Anything that changes the amount or character of noise trading will change the volatility of price.

Noise traders must trade to have their influence. Because information traders trade with noise traders more than with other information traders, cutting back on noise trading also cuts back on information trading. Thus prices will not move

[11] I think this puts me between Merton [49] and Shiller [57], [58]. Deviations from efficiency seem more significant in my world than in Merton's, but much less significant in my world than in Shiller's.

[12] This effect was discovered independently by Shleifer [59] and Gurel and Harris [29].

[13] Loderer and Zimmermann [43] discovered this effect in connection with offerings in Switzerland, where multiple classes of stock are common.

as much when the market is closed as they move when the market is open.[14] The relevant market here is the market on which most of the noise traders trade.

Noise traders may prefer low-priced stocks to high-priced stocks. If they do, then splits will increase both the liquidity of a stock and its day-to-day volatility. Low-priced stocks will be less efficiently priced than high-priced stocks.[15]

The price of a stock will be a noisy estimate of its value. The earnings of a firm (multiplied by a suitable price-earnings ratio) will give another estimate of the value of the firm's stock.[16] This estimate will be noisy too. So long as noise traders do not always look at earnings in deciding how to trade, the estimate from earnings will give information that is not already in the estimate from price.[17]

Because an estimate of value based on earnings will have so much noise, there will be no easy way to use price-earnings ratios in managing portfolios. Even if stocks with low price-earnings ratios have higher expected returns than other stocks, there will be periods, possibly lasting for years, when stocks with low price-earnings ratios have lower returns than other comparable stocks.

In other words, noise creates the opportunity to trade profitably, but at the same time makes it difficult to trade profitably.

II. Econometrics

Why do people trade on noise?

One reason is that they like to do it. Another is that there is so much noise around that they don't know they are trading on noise. They think they are trading on information.[18]

Neither of these reasons fits into a world where people do things only to maximize expected utility of wealth, and where people always make the best use of available information. Once we let trading enter the utility function directly (as a way of saying that people like to trade), it's hard to know where to stop. If anything can be in the utility function, the notion that people act to maximize expected utility is in danger of losing much of its content.

So we want to be careful about letting things into the utility function. We want to do it only when the evidence is compelling. I believe that this is such a case.

[14] French and Roll [25] find that the volatilities of stock returns are much lower across periods when markets are closed than across periods when markets are open.

[15] Ohlson and Penman [53] find that when stocks split, their return volatilities go up on the ex-split date by an average of about 30%. This may be due to a higher proportion of noise traders, though they also find no increase in trading volume on the ex-split date. Amihud [3] feels that another possible explanation for this result is the increase in the bid-asked spread following a stock split.

[16] For a discussion of the relation between earnings and stock price, see Black [13].

[17] Basu [5] summarizes the evidence that stocks with high earnings-price ratios have higher expected returns than stocks with low earnings-price ratios, even after controlling for size of firm and risk. DeBondt and Thaler [20] give more evidence on the existence of temporary dislocations in price, and on the psychological factors that may influence the noise traders who create these opportunities.

[18] Kahneman and Tversky [32] have a more sophisticated model of why people make decisions for what are seemingly non-rational reasons. Their theory may help describe the motivation of noise traders. For applications of their theory to economics and finance, see Russell and Thaler [55].

Another such case is dividend payments by firms. Given our tax laws, it seems clear that share repurchase in a non-systematic way is better than payment of dividends. If people want to maximize only expected utility of after-tax wealth, there will be no reason for firms to pay regular dividends. And when they do pay dividends, they will apologize to the stockholders (at least to individual stockholders) for causing them the discomfort of extra taxes.[19]

The idea that dividends convey information beyond that conveyed by the firm's financial statements and public announcements stretches the imagination.[20] It is especially odd that some firms pay dividends while making periodic offerings of common stock that raise more money than the firms are paying in dividends. For such firms, we cannot say that dividends force the firm to go through the rigors of a public offering of stock. Even if they pay no dividends, they will still be issuing common stock.[21]

I think we must assume that investors care about dividends directly. We must put dividends into the utility function.

Perhaps we should be happy that we can continue to think in terms of expected utility at all. There is considerable evidence now that people do not obey the axioms of expected utility. Of special concern is the finding that people will take certain gambles to avoid losses, but will refuse the same gambles when they involve prospective gains. Can this be consistent with risk aversion?[22]

I think that noise is a major reason for the use of decision rules that seem to violate the normal axioms of expected utility. Because there is so much noise in the world, people adopt rules of thumb. They share their rules of thumb with each other, and very few people have enough experience with interpreting noisy evidence to see that the rules are too simple. Over time, I expect that the transmission through the media and through the schools of scientific ways of interpreting evidence will gradually make the rules of thumb more sophisticated, and will thus make the expected utility model more valid.

Even highly trained people, though, seem to make certain kinds of errors consistently. For example, there is a strong tendency in looking at data to assume that when two events frequently happen together, one causes the other. There is an even stronger tendency to assume that the one that occurs first causes the one that occurs second. These tendencies are easy to resist in the simplest cases. But they seem to creep back in when econometric studies become more complex. Sometimes I wonder if we can draw any conclusions at all from the results of regression studies.

Because there is so much noise in the world, certain things are essentially unobservable.

For example, we cannot know what the expected return on the market is. There is every reason to believe that it changes over time, and no particular

[19] In Black [11], I described the dividend puzzle. The solution to the puzzle, I now believe, is that we must put dividends directly into the utility function. For one way of putting dividends into the utility function, see Shefrin and Statman [56]. For another way of resolving the dividend puzzle, and of relating it to the capital structure puzzle, see Myers [52].

[20] For a statement of the case that dividends do convey information, see Miller [51].

[21] Kalay and Shimrat [33] observe, however, that firms issuing common stock do tend to reduce their dividends.

[22] This phenomenon is discussed extensively by Tversky and Kahneman [63].

reason to believe that the changes occur smoothly. We can use the average past return as an estimate of the expected return, but it is a very noisy estimate.[23]

Similarly, the slopes of demand and supply curves are so hard to estimate that they are essentially unobservable. Introspection seems as good a method as any in trying to estimate them. One major problem is that no matter how many variables we include in an econometric analysis, there always seem to be potentially important variables that we have omitted, possibly because they too are unobservable.[24]

For example, wealth is often a key variable in estimating any demand curve. But wealth is itself unobservable. It's not even clear how to define it. The market value of traded assets is part of it, but the value of non-traded assets and especially of human capital is a bigger part for most individuals. There is no way to observe the value of human capital for an individual, and it is not clear how we might go about adding up the values of human capital for individuals to obtain a value of human capital for a whole economy.

I suspect that if it were possible to observe the value of human capital, we would find it fluctuating in much the same way that the level of the stock market fluctuates. In fact, I think we would find fluctuations in the value of human capital to be highly correlated with fluctuations in the level of the stock market, though the magnitude of the fluctuations in the value of human capital is probably less than the magnitude of the fluctuations in the level of the stock market.[25]

It's actually easier to list observables than unobservables, since so many things are unobservable. The interest rate is observable. If there were enough trading in CPI futures, the real interest rate would be observable. So far, though, there are not enough noise traders in CPI futures to make it a viable market.

Stock prices and stock returns are observable. The past volatility of a stock's returns is observable, and by using daily returns we can come close to observing the current volatility of a stock's returns. We can also come close to observing the correlations among the returns on different stocks.

Economic variables seem generally less observable than financial variables. The prices of goods and services are hard to observe, because they are specific to location and terms of trade much more than financial variables. Quantities are hard to observe, because what is traded differs from place to place and through time.

Thus econometric studies involving economic variables are hard to interpret for two reasons: first, the coefficients of regressions tell us little about causal relations even when the variables are observable; and second, the variables are subject to lots of measurement error, and the measurement errors are probably related to the true values of the variables.

Perhaps the easiest economic variable to observe is the money stock, once we agree on a definition for it. I think that accounts for some of the fascination it holds for economic theorists. In my view, though, this easiest to observe of

[23] Merton [48] shows how difficult it is to estimate the expected return on the market.

[24] Leamer [40] and Black [16] discuss the profound difficulties with conventional econometric analyses.

[25] Fama and Schwert [22] study the relation between human capital and the stock market. They do not find a close relation.

economic variables has no important role in the workings of the economy. Money is important, but the money stock is not.

Still, the money stock is correlated with every measure of economic activity, because the amount of money used in trade is related to the volume of trade. This correlation implies neither that the government can control the money stock nor that changes in the money stock influence economic activity.[26]

Empirical studies in finance are easier to do than empirical studies in economics, because data on security prices are of generally higher quality than the available data in economics. But there are major pitfalls in trying to interpret even the results of studies of security prices.

For example, many recent empirical studies in finance have taken the form of "event studies," which look at stock price reactions to announcements that affect a firm.[27] If there were no noise in stock prices, this would be a very reliable way to find out how certain events affect firms. In fact, though, the stock price reaction tells us only how investors think the events will affect firms, and investors' thoughts include both noise and information.

Moreover, if investors care directly about certain attributes of a firm (such as its dividend yield) independently of how those attributes affect its value, event studies will pick up these preferences along with the effects of the events on value. When a firm increases its dividend, its price may go up because investors like dividends, even though the present value of its future dividends in a world where the marginal investor is taxed may have gone down.

Is there any solution to these problems? No single, simple solution, I believe. Correlations among economic and financial variables do give us some information of value. Experimental studies in economics and finance have value. Analysis of "stylized facts" is often useful. Unusual events can provide special insight. In the end, a theory is accepted not because it is confirmed by conventional empirical tests, but because researchers persuade one another that the theory is correct and relevant.[28]

III. Macroeconomics

If business cycles were caused by unanticipated shifts in the general price level or in the level of government spending, we might not call that kind of uncertainty noise. It's too simple. Because it is so simple, I don't think this kind of uncertainty can play a major role in business cycles. I have not seen any models with all the kinds of markets we have in the economy where shifts in the general price level or in the level of government spending are large enough or powerful enough or unanticipated enough to cause significant business cycles.[29]

On the other hand, if business cycles are caused by unanticipated shifts in the

[26] King and Plosser [35] look at the possibility that economic activity influences the money stock rather than the other way around.

[27] For a typical event study, together with discussion of a factor that may make event studies hard to interpret properly, see Kalay and Loewenstein [34].

[28] This point of view is taken in part from McCloskey [46].

[29] For a review of research in business cycle theory, see Zarnowitz [65]. For an attempt to explain large business cycles with seemingly innocent changes in the price level, see Mankiw [45].

entire pattern of tastes and technologies across sectors, we might call that uncertainty noise. I believe that these shifts are significant for the economy as a whole because they do not cancel in any meaningful sense. The number of sectors in which there is a match between tastes and technology varies a lot over time. When it is high, we have an expansion. When it is low, we have a recession.[30]

One reason the shifts do not cancel is that they are not independent across sectors. When the costs of producing goods and services that require oil are high, they will be high across many related sectors. When demand for vacation homes is high, it will be high for many kinds of related services at the same time. The more we divide sectors into subsectors, the more related the subsectors will be to one another.

It is not clear whether the increasing diversity and specialization that go along with the transition from a simple economy to a complex modern economy will be associated with larger or smaller business cycles. On the one hand, the diversity in a more complex economy means that a single crop failure or demand shock cannot have such a devastating effect; but on the other hand, the specialization in a more complex economy means that when there is a mismatch between tastes and technology, it is costly to move skills and machines between sectors to correct the mismatch.

Money and prices play no role in this explanation. Everything is real.[31] For a small sample of the kind of thing I have in mind, suppose I gear up to produce dolls, while you gear up to produce art books. If it turns out that you want dolls and I want art books, we will have a boom. We will both work hard, and will exchange our outputs and will have high consumption of both dolls and art books. But if it turns out that you want action toys and I want science books, we will have a bust. The relative price of toys and books may be the same as before, but neither of us will work so hard because we will not value highly that which we can exchange our outputs for.

This is just one kind of example. The variations can occur in use of machines as well as in use of people, and the underlying uncertainty can concern what we can make as well as what we want.

Unanticipated shifts in tastes and technology within and across sectors is what we call information in discussing financial markets. In economic markets, it seems more appropriate to call these shifts noise, to contrast them with shifts in the aggregates that conventional macroeconomic models focus on. In other words, the cause of business cycles is not a few large things that can be measured and controlled, but many small things that are difficult to measure and essentially impossible to control.

Noise or uncertainty has its effects in economic markets because there are costs in shifting physical and human resources within and between sectors. If skills and capital can be shifted without cost after tastes and technology become

[30] For a more extensive discussion of this point of view, see Black [15], [16].

[31] The most closely related work in the more conventional business cycle literature is Long and Plosser [44] and Lilien [41]. Bernanke [6] has an entirely real explanation for swings in the production of durable goods: it is sectoral in the sense that specific investments are irreversible. Topel and Weiss [62] use uncertainty about employment conditions in different sectors to help explain unemployment; their methods can also be applied, I think, to explaining cyclical fluctuations in unemployment.

known, mismatches between what we can do and what we want to do will not occur.

The costs of shifting real resources are clearly large, so it is plausible that these costs might play a role in business cycles. The costs of putting inflation adjustments in contracts or of publicizing changes in the money stock or the price level seem low, so it is not plausible that these costs play a significant role in business cycles.

Presumably the government does not have better information about the details of future supply and demand conditions within and between sectors than the people working in those sectors. Thus there is little the government can do to help the economy avoid recessions. These unknown future details are noise to the workers and managers involved, and they are noise twice over to government employees, even those who collect statistics on individual industries.

I cannot think of any conventional econometric tests that would shed light on the question of whether my business cycle theory is correct or not. One of its predictions, though, is that real wages will fluctuate with other measures of economic activity. When there is a match between tastes and technology in many sectors, income will be high, wages will be high, output will be high, and unemployment will be low. Thus real wages will be procyclical. This is obviously true over long periods, as from the Twenties to the Thirties and from the Thirties to the Forties, but is also seems true over shorter periods, especially when overtime and layoffs are taken into account.[32]

How do inflation and money fit into this picture?

I believe that monetary policy is almost completely passive in a country like the U.S.[33] Money goes up when prices go up or when income goes up because demand for money goes up at those times. I have been unable to construct an equilibrium model in which changes in money cause changes in prices or income, but I have had no trouble constructing an equilibrium model in which changes in prices or income cause changes in money.[34]

Changes in money often precede changes in income, but this is not surprising, since demand for money can depend on expected income as well as current income. Changes in wealth (measured at market value) also precede changes in income.

In the conventional story, open market operations change perceived wealth, which leads to a change in demand for existing assets, and thus to a change in the price level. But open market operations have no effect on wealth when wealth is measured at market value. They merely substitute one form of wealth for another. Some say that open market operations cause a change in interest rates, which then have further effects on the economy. But this cannot happen in an equilibrium model. There is no temporary equilibrium, with the price level and rate of inflation unchanged, where a different interest rate will be equal to the certain component of the marginal product of capital. If we allow the price level

[32] Bils [7] reviews previous work in this area, and gives evidence that real wages are indeed procyclical.

[33] My views are explained more fully in Black [8], [9], [10].

[34] For an analysis of possible explanations for some of the correlations between money and other variables, see Cornell [18].

and rate of inflation to change, then there are many equilibria, but there are no rules to tell us how one is chosen over another. There is no logical story explaining how the change in money will cause a shift from one equilibrium to another.

If monetary policy doesn't cause changes in inflation, what does?

I think that the price level and rate of inflation are literally indeterminate. They are whatever people think they will be. They are determined by expectations, but expectations follow no rational rules. If people believe that certain changes in the money stock will cause changes in the rate of inflation, that may well happen, because their expectations will be built into their long term contracts.

Another way to make the same point is this. Within a sector, the prices of inputs and outputs are largely taken as given. Decisions on what and how much to produce are made taking these prices as given. Thus each sector assumes that the rates of inflation of its input and output prices are given. In my models, this includes the government sector in its role as supplier of money. If we are in an equilibrium with one expected rate of inflation (assuming neither gold prices or exchange rates are fixed), and everyone shifts to a lower expected rate of inflation, we will have (with only minor modifications) a new equilibrium.

One way to describe this view is to say that noise causes changes in the rate of inflation.

If we have a gold standard, where the price of gold is adjusted over time to make the general price level follow a desired path, and where the government stands ready to buy or sell gold at the temporarily fixed price without allowing its inventory to fluctuate much, then inflation will be controlled rather than random.[35] But it seems unlikely that we will adopt a gold standard of this kind or of any other kind anytime soon.

Similarly, if a small country adopts a policy of varying its exchange rate with a large country to make its price level follow a desired path, where its government stands ready to buy or sell foreign exchange at the temporarily fixed rate without allowing its foreign exchange inventory to fluctuate much, then its inflation rate will be controlled rather than random. This is possible for any country that has wealth and stable taxing power, because the country can always sell assets for foreign exchange, and can then buy the assets back (almost) with the foreign currency it obtains.

However, it is not clear what is gained by controlling the price level. If business cycles are caused by real factors rather than by things that are affected by the rate of inflation, then many of the reasons for controlling inflation vanish.

In my view, then, there is a real international equilibrium that is largely unaffected by price levels or monetary policies, except in countries with unstable financial markets or national debt that is large compared with taxable wealth. This real equilibrium involves a world business cycle and national business cycles driven by the degree to which there is a match between tastes and technology.

The real equilibrium also involves changing relative prices for all kinds of

[35] For an old version of this argument, see Fisher [24]. For a new version, together with discussion of the possibility of keeping gold inventories roughly fixed while controlling the price of gold and the price level, see Black [14].

goods and services, including relative prices for the "same" goods and services in different locations. Different locations can be around the corner or around the world. Since information and transportation are so costly (especially information), there is no form of arbitrage that will force the prices of similar goods and services in different locations to be similar.

Moreover, the real equilibrium involves constantly changing trade flows for various pairs of countries. There is no reason for trade to be balanced between any pair of countries either in the short run or in the long run. And an imbalance in trade has no particular welfare implications.[36]

Since the real equilibrium is fixed at a point in time, though it is continually changing through time, a higher domestic currency price for an item at one point in time will mean a higher domestic currency price for all items at that same point in time. There will be some lags in making price changes, and many lags in posting or reporting price changes, but these will not affect the equilibrium significantly.

If we were able to observe the economy at a given point in time with two different domestic price levels, we would see that the real equilibrium is largely independent of price levels and exchange rates, and we might call this situation "purchasing power parity." Since we must actually observe the economy as it evolves over time, we cannot see that purchasing power parity holds. We see relative price changes occurring, and fluctuations in the level of economic activity, while exchange rates and money stocks are changing. We think that exchange rates and money are causing relative price changes and business fluctuations.[37]

But that is only because the noise in the data is clouding our vision.

[36] This is a common result in international economics. For my treatment of it, see Black [12].

[37] Davutyan and Pippenger [19] suggest some ways in which standard tests of purchasing power parity may be flawed. Moreover, our tests of purchasing power parity are inadequate unless we consider transport costs, as Aizenman [2] notes. Transport costs can be very large for services and some goods.

REFERENCES

1. Admati, Anat R. "A Noisy Rational Expectations Equilibrium for Multi-Asset Securities Markets." *Econometrica* 53 (May 1985), 629–657.
2. Aizenman, Joshua. "Testing Deviations from Purchasing Power Parity (PPP)." National Bureau of Economic Research Working Paper No. 1475, October, 1984.
3. Amihud, Yakov. "Biases in Computed Return Variance: An Application to Volatility Increases Subsequent to Stock Splits." Unpublished manuscript, December, 1985.
4. Arrow, Kenneth J. "Risk Perception in Psychology and Economics." *Economic Inquiry* 20 (January 1982), 1–9.
5. Basu, Sanjoy. "The Relationship between Earnings' Yield, Market Value and Return for NYSE Common Stocks: Further Evidence." *Journal of Financial Economics* 12 (June 1983), 129–156.
6. Bernanke, Ben S. "Irreversibility, Uncertainty, and Cyclical Investment." *Quarterly Journal of Economics* (February 1983), 85–106.
7. Bils, Mark J., "Real Wages over the Business Cycle: Evidence from Panel Data." *Journal of Political Economy* 93 (August 1985), 666–689.
8. Black, Fischer. "Banking and Interest Rates in a World Without Money: The Effects of Uncontrolled Banking." *Journal of Bank Research* 1 (Autumn 1970), 8–20.
9. ———. "Active and Passive Monetary Policy in a Neoclassical Model." *Journal of Finance* 27 (September 1972), 801–814.

10. ———. "Uniqueness of the Price Level in Monetary Growth Models with Rational Expectations." *Journal of Economic Theory* 7 (January 1974), 53–65.
11. ———. "The Dividend Puzzle." *Journal of Portfolio Management* 2 (Winter 1976), 5–8.
12. ———. "The Ins and Outs of Foreign Investment." *Financial Analysts Journal* 34 (May/June 1978), 25–32.
13. ———. "The Magic in Earnings: Economic Earnings Versus Accounting Earnings." *Financial Analysts Journal* 36 (November/December 1980), 19–24.
14. ———. "A Gold Standard with Double Feedback and Near Zero Reserves." Unpublished manuscript, 1981.
15. ———. "The ABCs of Business Cycles." *Financial Analysts Journal* 37 (November/December 1981), 75–80.
16. ———. "The Trouble with Econometric Models." *Financial Analysts Journal* 38 (March/April 1982), 29–37.
17. ———. "General Equilibrium and Business Cycles." National Bureau of Economic Research Working Paper No. 950, August, 1982.
18. Cornell, Bradford. "The Money Supply Announcements Puzzle: Review and Interpretation." *American Economic Review* 73 (September 1983), 644–657.
19. Davutyan, Nurhan, and John Pippenger. "Purchasing Power Parity Did Not Collapse During the 1970's." *American Economic Review* 75 (December 1985), 1151–1158.
20. DeBondt, Werner F. M., and Richard Thaler. "Does the Stock Market Overreact?" *Journal of Finance* 40 (July 1985), 793–805.
21. Diamond, Douglas W., and Robert E. Verrecchia. "Information Aggregation in Noisy Rational Expectations Economy." *Journal of Financial Economics* 9 (September 1981), 221–235.
22. Fama, Eugene F., and G. William Schwert. "Human Capital and Capital Market Equilibrium." *Journal of Financial Economics* 4 (January 1977), 95–125.
23. Figlewski, Stephen. "Market 'Efficiency' in a Market with Heterogeneous Information." *Journal of Political Economy* 86 (August 1978), 581–597.
24. Fisher, Irving. *Stabilizing the Dollar.* New York: Macmillan, 1920.
25. French, Kenneth R., and Richard Roll. "Stock Return Variances: the Arrival of Information and the Reaction of Traders." Graduate School of Management, UCLA Working Paper, July, 1985.
26. Grinblatt, Mark S., and Stephen A. Ross. "Market Power in a Securities Market with Endogenous Information." *Quarterly Journal of Economics* 100 (November 1985), 1143–1167.
27. Grossman, Sanford. "Further Results on the Informational Efficiency of Competitive Stock Markets." *Journal of Economic Theory* 18 (June 1978), 81–101.
28. ———, and Joseph E. Stiglitz. "On the Impossibility of Informationally Efficient Markets." *American Economic Review* 70 (June 1980), 393–408.
29. Gurel, Eitan, and Lawrence Harris. "Price and Volume Effects Associated with Changes in the S&P 500 List: New Evidence for the Existence of Price Pressures." Unpublished manuscript, April, 1985.
30. Hakansson, Nils, J. Gregory Kunkel, and James Ohlson. "Sufficient and Necessary Conditions for Information to have Social Value in Pure Exchange." *Journal of Finance* 37 (December 1982), 1169–1181.
31. Jaffe, Jeffrey F., and Robert L. Winkler. "Optimal Speculation Against an Efficient Market." *Journal of Finance* 31 (March 1976), 49–61.
32. Kahneman, Daniel, and Amos Tversky. "Prospect Theory: An Analysis of Decision Under Risk." *Econometrica* 47 (March 1979), 263–291.
33. Kalay, Avner, and Adam Shimrat. "On the Payment of Equity Financed Dividends." Unpublished manuscript, December, 1985.
34. Kalay, Avner, and Uri Loewenstein. "Predictable Events and Excess Returns: The Case of Dividend Announcements." *Journal of Financial Economics* 14 (September 1985), 423–449.
35. King, Robert G., and Charles I. Plosser. "Money, Credit, and Prices in a Real Business Cycle." *American Economic Review* 74 (June 1984), 360–380.
36. Kyle, Albert S. "Market Structure, Information, Futures Markets, and Price Formation." in Gary G. Storey, Andrew Schmitz, and Alexander H. Sarris, eds. *International Agricultural Trade* (Boulder and London: Westview Press, 1984), pp. 45–63.

37. ———. "Continuous Auctions and Insider Trading." *Econometrica* 53 (November 1985), 1315–1335.
38. ———. "Informed Speculation with Imperfect Competition." Unpublished manuscript, December, 1985.
39. Laffont, Jean-Jacques. "On the Welfare Analysis of Rational Expectations Equilibria with Asymmetric Information." *Econometrica* 53 (January 1985), 1–29.
40. Leamer, Edward E. "Let's Take the Con Out of Econometrics." *American Economic Review* 73 (March 1983), 31–43.
41. Lilien, David M. "Sectoral Shifts and Cyclical Unemployment." *Journal of Political Economy* 90 (July/August 1982), 777–793.
42. ———. "A Sectoral Model of the Business Cycle." USC Modelling Research Group Working Paper #8231, December, 1982.
43. Loderer, Claudio, and Heinz Zimmermann. "Rights Issues in Switzerland: Some Findings to Consider in the Debate over Financing Decisions." Unpublished manuscript, July, 1985.
44. Long, John B., and Charles I. Plosser. "Real Business Cycles." *Journal of Political Economy* 91 (February 1983), 39–69.
45. Mankiw, N. Gregory. "Small Menu Costs and Large Business Cycles." *Quarterly Journal of Economics* 100 (May 1985), 529–538.
46. McCloskey, Donald N. "The Rhetoric of Economics." *Journal of Economic Literature* 21 (June 1983), 481–517.
47. Merton, Robert C. "Optimum Consumption and Portfolio Rules in a Continuous-Time Model." *Journal of Economic Theory* 3 (December 1971), 373–413.
48. ———. "On Estimating the Expected Return on the Market: An Exploratory Investigation." *Journal of Financial Economics* 8 (December 1980), 323–361.
49. ———. "On the Current State of the Stock Market Rationality Hypothesis." Sloan School of Management Working Paper #1717-85, October, 1985.
50. Milgrom, Paul, and Nancy Stokey. "Information, Trade and Common Knowledge." *Journal of Economic Theory* 26 (January 1982), 17–27.
51. Miller, Merton H. "The Information Content of Dividends." Unpublished manuscript, July, 1985.
52. Myers, Stewart C. "The Capital Structure Puzzle." *Journal of Finance* 39 (July 1984), 575–592.
53. Ohlson, James A., and Stephen H. Penman. "Volatility Increases Subsequent to Stock Splits: An Empirical Aberration." *Journal of Financial Economics* 14 (June 1985), 251–266.
54. Rubinstein, Mark. "Security Market Efficiency in an Arrow-Debreu Economy." *American Economic Review* 65 (December 1975), 812–824.
55. Russell, Thomas, and Richard Thaler. "The Relevance of Quasi Rationality in Competitive Markets." *American Economic Review* 75 (December 1985), 1071–1082.
56. Shefrin, Hersh, and Meir Statman. "Comparing Two Theories of Dividend Function." Unpublished manuscript, April, 1985.
57. Shiller, Robert J. "Do Stock Prices Move Too Much to be Justified by Subsequent Changes in Dividends?" *American Economic Review* 71 (June 1981), 421–436.
58. ———. "Stock Prices and Social Dynamics." *Brookings Papers on Economic Activity* 2 (December 1984), 457–498.
59. Shleifer, Andrei. "Do Demand Curves for Stocks Slope Down?" *Journal of Finance* 41 (July 1986), 579–590.
60. Summers, Lawrence H. "Do We Really Know That Financial Markets are Efficient?" *Journal of Finance* 41 (July 1986), 591–602.
61. Tirole, Jean. "On the Possibility of Speculation under Rational Expectations." *Econometrica* 50 (September 1982), 1163–1181.
62. Topel, Robert, and Laurence Weiss. "Sectoral Uncertainty and Unemployment." University of California at San Diego Economics Department Discussion Paper 85-27, September, 1985.
63. Tversky, Amos, and Daniel Kahneman. "The Framing of Decisions and the Psychology of Choice." *Science* 211 (30 January 1981), 453–458.
64. Varian, Hal R. "Differences of Opinion and the Volume of Trade." University of Michigan Department of Economics Discussion Paper C-67, June, 1985.
65. Zarnowitz, Victor. "Recent Work on Business Cycles in Historical Perspective: A Review of Theories and Evidence." *Journal of Economic Literature* 23 (June 1985), 523–580.

[11]

THE JOURNAL OF FINANCE • VOL. XL, NO. 3 • JULY 1985

Does the Stock Market Overreact?

WERNER F. M. De BONDT and RICHARD THALER*

ABSTRACT

Research in experimental psychology suggests that, in violation of Bayes' rule, most people tend to "overreact" to unexpected and dramatic news events. This study of market efficiency investigates whether such behavior affects stock prices. The empirical evidence, based on CRSP monthly return data, is consistent with the overreaction hypothesis. Substantial weak form market inefficiencies are discovered. The results also shed new light on the January returns earned by prior "winners" and "losers." Portfolios of losers experience exceptionally large January returns as late as five years after portfolio formation.

AS ECONOMISTS INTERESTED IN both market behavior and the psychology of individual decision making, we have been struck by the similarity of two sets of empirical findings. Both classes of behavior can be characterized as displaying *overreaction*. This study was undertaken to investigate the possibility that these phenomena are related by more than just appearance. We begin by describing briefly the individual and market behavior that piqued our interest.

The term overreaction carries with it an implicit comparison to some degree of reaction that is considered to be appropriate. What is an appropriate reaction? One class of tasks which have a well-established norm are probability revision problems for which Bayes' rule prescribes the correct reaction to new information. It has now been well-established that Bayes' rule is not an apt characterization of how individuals actually respond to new data (Kahneman et al. [14]). In revising their beliefs, individuals tend to overweight recent information and underweight prior (or base rate) data. People seem to make predictions according to a simple matching rule: "The predicted value is selected so that the standing of the case in the distribution of outcomes matches its standing in the distribution of impressions" (Kahneman and Tversky [14, p. 416]). This rule-of-thumb, an instance of what Kahneman and Tversky call the representativeness heuristic, violates the basic statistical principal that the extremeness of predictions must be moderated by considerations of predictability. Grether [12] has replicated this finding under incentive compatible conditions. There is also considerable evidence that the actual expectations of professional security analysts and economic forecasters display the same overreaction bias (for a review, see De Bondt [7]).

One of the earliest observations about overreaction in markets was made by J. M. Keynes:"... day-to-day fluctuations in the profits of existing investments,

* University of Wisconsin at Madison and Cornell University, respectively. The financial support of the C.I.M. Doctoral Fellowship Program (Brussels, Belgium) and the Cornell Graduate School of Management is gratefully acknowledged. We received helpful comments from Seymour Smidt, Dale Morse, Peter Bernstein, Fischer Black, Robert Jarrow, Edwin Elton, and Ross Watts.

which are obviously of an ephemeral and nonsignificant character, tend to have an altogether excessive, and even an absurd, influence on the market" [17, pp. 153–154]. About the same time, Williams noted in this *Theory of Investment Value* that "prices have been based too much on current earning power and too little on long-term dividend paying power" [28, p. 19]. More recently, Arrow has concluded that the work of Kahneman and Tversky "typifies very precisely the exessive reaction to current information which seems to characterize all the securities and futures markets" [1, p. 5]. Two specific examples of the research to which Arrow was referring are the excess volatility of security prices and the so-called price earnings ratio anomaly.

The excess volatility issue has been investigated most thoroughly by Shiller [27]. Shiller interprets the Miller-Modigliani view of stock prices as a constraint on the likelihood function of a price-dividend sample. Shiller concludes that, at least over the last century, dividends simply do not vary enough to rationally justify observed aggregate price movements. Combining the results with Kleidon's [18] findings that stock price movements are strongly correlated with the following year's earnings changes suggests a clear pattern of overreaction. In spite of the observed trendiness of dividends, investors seem to attach disproportionate importance to short-run economic developments.[1]

The price earnings ratio (P/E) anomaly refers to the observation that stocks with extremely low P/E ratios (i.e., lowest decile) earn larger risk-adjusted returns than high P/E stocks (Basu [3]). Most financial economists seem to regard the anomaly as a statistical artifact. Explanations are usually based on alleged misspecification of the capital asset pricing model (CAPM). Ball [2] emphasizes the effects of omitted risk factors. The P/E ratio is presumed to be a proxy for some omitted factor which, if included in the "correct" equilibrium valuation model, would eliminate the anomaly. Of course, unless these omitted factors can be identified, the hypothesis is untestable. Reinganum [21] has claimed that the small firm effect subsumes the P/E effect and that both are related to the same set of missing (and again unknown) factors. However, Basu [4] found a significant P/E effect after controlling for firm size, and earlier Graham [11] even found an effect within the thirty Dow Jones Industrials, hardly a group of small firms!

An alternative behavioral explanation for the anomaly based on investor overreaction is what Basu called the "price-ratio" hypothesis (e.g., Dreman [8]). Companies with very low P/E's are thought to be temporarily "undervalued" because investors become excessively pessimistic after a series of bad earnings reports or other bad news. Once future earnings turn out to be better than the unreasonably gloomy forecasts, the price adjusts. Similarly, the equity of companies with very high P/E's is thought to be "overvalued," before (predictably) falling in price.

While the overreaction hypothesis has considerable a priori appeal, the obvious question to ask is: How does the anomaly survive the process of arbitrage? There

[1] Of course, the variability of stock prices may also reflect changes in real interest rates. If so, the price movements of other assets—such as land or housing—should match those of stocks. However, this is not actually observed. A third hypothesis, advocated by Marsh and Merton [19], is that Shiller's findings are a result of his misspecification of the dividend process.

is really a more general question here. What are the equilibria conditions for markets in which some agents are not rational in the sense that they fail to revise their expectations according to Bayes' rule? Russell and Thaler [24] address this issue. They conclude that the existence of some rational agents is not sufficient to guarantee a rational expectations equilibrium in an economy with some of what they call quasi-rational agents. (The related question of market equilibria with agents having heterogeneous expectations is investigated by Jarrow [13].) While we are highly sensitive to these issues, we do not have the space to address them here. Instead, we will concentrate on an empirical test of the overreaction hypothesis.

If stock prices systematically overshoot, then their reversal should be predictable from past return data alone, with no use of any accounting data such as earnings. Specifically, two hypotheses are suggested: (1) Extreme movements in stock prices will be followed by subsequent price movements in the opposite direction. (2) The more extreme the initial price movement, the greater will be the subsequent adjustment. Both hypotheses imply a violation of weak-form market efficiency.

To repeat, our goal is to test whether the overreaction hypothesis is *predictive*. In other words, whether it does more for us than merely to explain, ex post, the P/E effect or Shiller's results on asset price dispersion. The overreaction effect deserves attention because it represents a behavioral principle that may apply in many other contexts. For example, investor overreaction possibly explains Shiller's earlier [26] findings that when long-term interest rates are high relative to short rates, they tend to move down later on. Ohlson and Penman [20] have further suggested that the increased volatility of security returns following stock splits may also be linked to overreaction. The present empirical tests are to our knowledge the first attempt to use a behavioral principle to predict a new market anomaly.

The remainder of the paper is organized as follows. The next section describes the actual empirical tests we have performed. Section II describes the results. Consistent with the overreaction hypothesis, evidence of weak-form market inefficiency is found. We discuss the implications for other empirical work on asset pricing anomalies. The paper ends with a brief summary of conclusions.

I. The Overreaction Hypothesis: Empirical Tests

The empirical testing procedures are a variant on a design originally proposed by Beaver and Landsman [5] in a different context. Typically, tests of semistrong form market efficiency start, at time $t = 0$, with the formation of portfolios on the basis of some event that affects all stocks in the portfolio, say, an earnings announcement. One then goes on to investigate whether later on ($t > 0$) the estimated residual portfolio return $\hat{u}_{pt}$—measured relative to the single-period CAPM—equals zero. Statistically significant departures from zero are interpreted as evidence consistent with semistrong form market inefficiency, even though the results may also be due to misspecification of the CAPM, misestimation of the relevant alphas and/or betas, or simply market inefficiency of the weak form.

In contrast, the tests in this study assess the extent to which systematic nonzero residual return behavior in the period after portfolio formation ($t > 0$) is associated with systematic residual returns in the preformation months ($t < 0$). We will focus on stocks that have experienced either extreme capital gains or extreme losses over periods up to five years. In other words, "winner" (W) and "loser" portfolios (L) are formed *conditional upon past excess returns*, rather than some firm-generated informational variable such as earnings.

Following Fama [9], the previous arguments can be formalized by writing the efficient market's condition,

$$E(\tilde{R}_{jt} - E_m(\tilde{R}_{jt} \mid F_{t-1}^m) \mid F_{t-1}) = E(\tilde{u}_{jt} \mid F_{t-1}) = 0$$

where F_{t-1} represents the complete set of information at time $t - 1$, $\tilde{R}_{jt}$ is the return on security j at t, and $E_m(\tilde{R}_{jt} \mid F_{t-1}^m)$ is the expectation of $\tilde{R}_{jt}$, assessed by the market on the basis of the information set F_{t-1}^m. The efficient market hypothesis implies that $E(\tilde{u}_{Wt} \mid F_{t-1}) = E(\tilde{u}_{Lt} \mid F_{t-1}) = 0$. As explained in the introduction, the overreaction hypothesis, on the other hand, suggests that $E(\tilde{u}_{Wt} \mid F_{t-1}) < 0$ and $E(\tilde{u}_{Lt} \mid F_{t-1}) > 0$.

In order to estimate the relevant residuals, an equilibrium model must be specified. A common procedure is to estimate the parameters of the market model (see e.g., Beaver and Landsman [5]). What will happen if the equilibrium model is misspecified? As long as the variation in $E_m(\tilde{R}_{jt} \mid F_{t-1}^m)$ is small relative to the movements in $\tilde{u}_{jt}$, the exact specification of the equilibrium model makes little difference to tests of the efficient market hypothesis. For, even if we knew the "correct" model of $E_m(\tilde{R}_{jt} \mid F_{t-1}^m)$, it would explain only small part of the variation in $\tilde{R}_{jt}$.[2]

Since this study investigates the return behavior of specific portfolios over extended periods of time (indeed, as long as a decade), it cannot be merely *assumed* that model misspecification leaves the conclusions about market efficiency unchanged. Therefore, the empirical analysis is based on three types of return residuals: market-adjusted excess returns; market model residuals; and excess returns that are measured relative to the Sharpe-Lintner version of the CAPM. However, since all three methods are single-index models that follow from the CAPM, misspecification problems may still confound the results. De Bondt [7] formally derives the econometric biases in the estimated market-adjusted and market model residuals if the "true" model is multifactor, e.g., $\tilde{R}_{jt} = A_j + B_j\tilde{R}_{mt} + C_j\tilde{X}_t + \tilde{e}_{jt}$. As a final precaution, he also characterizes the securities in the extreme portfolios in terms of a number of financial variables. If there were a persistent tendency for the portfolios to differ on dimensions that may proxy for "risk," then, again, we cannot be sure whether the empirical results support market efficiency or market overreaction.

It turns out that, whichever of the three types of residuals are used, the results

[2] Presumably, this same reasoning underlies the common practice of measuring abnormal security price performance by way of easily calculable mean-adjusted excess returns [where, by assumption, $E(\tilde{R}_j)$ equals a constant K_j], market-adjusted excess returns (where, by assumption, $\alpha_j = 0$ and $\beta_j = 1$ for all j), rather than more complicated market model residuals, let along residuals relative to some multifactor model.

of the empirical analysis are similar and that the choice does not affect our main conclusions. Therefore, we will only report the results based on market-adjusted excess returns. The residuals are estimated as $\hat{u}_{jt} = R_{jt} - R_{mt}$. There is no risk adjustment except for movements of the market as a whole and the adjustment is identical for all stocks. Since, for any period t, the same (constant) market return R_{mt} is subtracted from all R_{jt}'s, the results are interpretable in terms of raw (dollar) returns. As shown in De Bondt [7], the use of market-adjusted excess returns has the further advantage that it is likely to bias the research design *against* the overreaction hypothesis.[3] Finally, De Bondt shows that winner and loser portfolios, formed on the basis of market-adjusted excess returns, do not systematically differ with respect to either market value of equity, dividend yield or financial leverage.

We will now describe the basic research design used to form the winner and loser portfolios and the statistical test procedures that determine which of the two competing hypotheses receives more support from the data.

A. Test Procedures: Details

Monthly return data for New York Stock Exchange (NYSE) common stocks, as compiled by the Center for Research in Security Prices (CRSP) of the University of Chicago, are used for the period between January 1926 and December 1982. An equally weighted arithmetic average rate of return on all CRSP listed securities serves as the market index.

1. For every stock j on the tape with at least 85 months of return data (months 1 through 85), without any missing values in between, and starting in January 1930 (month 49), the next 72 monthly residual returns u_{jt} (months 49 through 120) are estimated. If some or all of the raw return data beyond month 85 are missing, the residual returns are calculated up to that point. The procedure is repeated 16 times starting in January 1930, January 1933, . . . , up to January 1975. As time goes on and new securities appear on the tape, more and more stocks qualify for this step.
2. For every stock j, starting in December 1932 (month 84; the "portfolio formation date") ($t = 0$), we compute the cumulative excess returns $CU_j = \sum_{t=-35}^{t=0} u_{jt}$ for the prior 36 months (the "portfolio formation" period, months 49 through 84). The step is repeated 16 times for all nonoverlapping three-year periods between January 1930 and December 1977. On each of the 16 relevant portfolio formation dates (December 1932, December 1935, . . . , December 1977), the CU_j's are ranked from low to high and portfolios are formed. Firms in the top 35 stocks (or the top 50 stocks, or the top decile) are assigned to the winner portfolio W; firms in the bottom 35 stocks (or the bottom 50 stocks, or the bottom decile) to the loser portfolio L. Thus, the portfolios are formed conditional upon excess return behavior prior to $t = 0$, the portfolio formation date.
3. For both portfolios in each of 16 nonoverlapping three-year periods (n =

[3] We will come back to this bias in Section II.

1, . . . , N; $N = 16$), starting in January 1933 (month 85, the "starting month") and up to December 1980, we now compute the cumulative average residual returns of all securities in the portfolio, for the next 36 months (the "test period," months 85 through 120), i.e., from $t = 1$ through $t = 36$. We find $CAR_{W,n,t}$ and $CAR_{L,n,t}$. If a security's return is missing in a month subsequent to portfolio formation, then, from that moment on, the stock is permanently dropped from the portfolio and the CAR is an average of the available residual returns. Thus, whenever a stock drops out, the calculations involve an implicit rebalancing.[4]

4. Using the CAR's from all 16 test periods, *average* CAR's are calculated for both portfolios and each month between $t = 1$ and $t = 36$. They are denoted $ACAR_{W,t}$ and $ACAR_{L,t}$. The overreaction hypothesis predicts that, for $t > 0$, $ACAR_{W,t} < 0$ and $ACAR_{L,t} > 0$, so that, by implication, $[ACAR_{L,t} - ACAR_{W,t}] > 0$. In order to assess whether, at any time t, there is indeed a statistically significant difference in investment performance, we need a pooled estimate of the population variance in CAR_t,

$$S_t^2 = [\sum_{n=1}^{N}(CAR_{W,n,t} - ACAR_{W,t})^2 + \sum_{n=1}^{N}(CAR_{L,n,t} - ACAR_{L,t})^2]/2(N-1).$$

With two samples of equal size N, the variance of the difference of sample means equals $2S_t^2/N$ and the t-statistic is therefore

$$T_t = [ACAR_{L,t} - ACAR_{W,t}]/\sqrt{2S_t^2/N}.$$

Relevant t-statistics can be found for each of the 36 postformation months but they do not represent independent evidence.

5. In order to judge whether, for any month t, the average residual return makes a contribution to either $ACAR_{W,t}$ or $ACAR_{L,t}$, we can test whether it is significantly different from zero. The sample standard deviation of the winner portfolio is equal to

$$s_t = \sqrt{\sum_{n=1}^{N}(AR_{W,n,t} - AR_{W,t})^2/N-1}.$$

Since $s_t/\sqrt{N}$ represents the sample estimate of the standard error of $AR_{W,t}$, the t-statistic equals

$$T_t = AR_{W,t}/(s_t/\sqrt{N}).$$

Similar procedures apply for the residuals of the loser portfolio.

B. Discussion

Several aspects of the research design deserve some further comment. The choice of the data base, the CRSP Monthly Return File, is in part justified by

[4] Since this study concentrates on companies that experience extraordinary returns, either positive or negative, there may be some concern that their attrition rate sufficiently deviates from the "normal" rate so as to cause a survivorship bias. However, this concern is unjustified. When a security is delisted, suspended or halted, CRSP determines whether or not it is possible to trade at the last listed price. If no trade is possible, CRSP tries to find a subsequent quote and uses it to compute a return for the last period. If no such quote is available because the stockholders receive nothing for their shares, the return is entered as minus one. If trading continues, the last return ends with the last listed price.

our concern to avoid certain measurement problems that have received much attention in the literature. Most of the problems arise with the use of daily data, both with respect to the risk and return variables. They include, among others, the "bid-ask" effect and the consequences of infrequent trading.

The requirement that 85 subsequent returns are available before any firm is allowed in the sample biases the selection towards large, established firms. But, if the effect under study can be shown to apply to them, the results are, if anything, more interesting. In particular, it counters the predictable critique that the overreaction effect may be mostly a small-firm phenomenon. For the experiment described in Section A, between 347 and 1,089 NYSE stocks participate in the various replications.

The decision to study the CAR's for a period of 36 months after the portfolio formation date reflects a compromise between statistical and economic considerations, namely, an adequate number of independent replications versus a time period long enough to study issues relevant to asset pricing theory. In addition, the three-year period is also of interest in light of Benjamin Graham's contention that "the interval required for a substantial underevaluation to correct itself averages approximately 1½ to 2½ years" [10, p. 37). However, for selected experiments, the portfolio formation (and testing) periods are one, two, and five years long. Clearly, the number of independent replications varies inversely with the length of the formation period.

Finally, the choice of December as the "portfolio formation month" (and, therefore, of January as the "starting month") is essentially arbitrary. In order to check whether the choice affects the results, some of the empirical tests use May as the portfolio formation month.

II. The Overreaction Hypothesis: Empirical Results

A. Main Findings

The results of the tests developed in Section I are found in Figure 1. They are consistent with the overreaction hypothesis. Over the last half-century, loser portfolios of 35 stocks outperform the market by, on average, 19.6%, thirty-six months after portfolio formation. Winner portfolios, on the other hand, earn about 5.0% less than the market, so that the difference in cumulative average residual between the extreme portfolios, $[ACAR_{L,36} - ACAR_{W,36}]$ equals 24.6% (t-statistic: 2.20). Figure 1 shows the movement of the ACAR's as we progress through the test period.

The findings have other notable aspects. First, the overreaction effect is asymmetric; it is much larger for losers than for winners. Secondly, consistent with previous work on the turn-of-the-year effect and seasonality, most of the excess returns are realized in January. In months $t = 1$, $t = 13$, and $t = 25$, the loser portfolio earns excess returns of, respectively, 8.1% (t-statistic: 3.21), 5.6% (3.07), and 4.0% (2.76). Finally, in surprising agreement with Benjamin Graham's claim, the overreaction phenomenon mostly occurs during the second and third year of the test period. Twelve months into the test period, the difference in performance between the extreme portfolios is a mere 5.4% (t-statistic: 0.77).

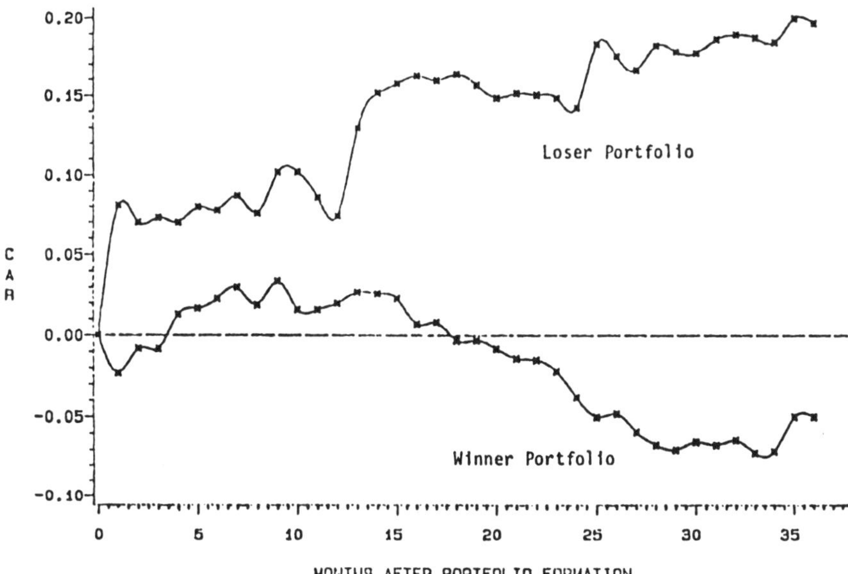

Figure 1. Cumulative Average Residuals for Winner and Loser Portfolios of 35 Stocks (1–36 months into the test period)

While not reported here, the results using market model and Sharpe-Lintner residuals are similar. They are also insensitive to the choice of December as the month of portfolio formation (see De Bondt [7]).

The overreaction hypothesis predicts that, as we focus on stocks that go through more (or less) extreme return experiences (during the formation period), the subsequent price reversals will be more (or less) pronounced. An easy way to generate more (less) extreme observations is to lengthen (shorten) the portfolio formation period; alternatively, for any given formation period (say, two years), we may compare the test period performance of less versus more extreme portfolios, e.g., decile portfolios (which contain an average 82 stocks) versus portfolios of 35 stocks. Table I confirms the prediction of the overreaction hypothesis. As the cumulative average residuals (during the formation period) for various sets of winner and loser portfolios grow larger, so do the subsequent price reversals, measured by $[ACAR_{L,t} - ACAR_{W,t}]$ and the accompanying t-statistics. For a formation period as short as one year, no reversal is observed at all.

Table I and Figure 2 further indicate that the overreaction phenomenon is qualitatively different from the January effect and, more generally, from season-

Table I

Differences in Cumulative Average (Market-Adjusted) Residual Returns Between the Winner and Loser Portfolios at the End of the Formation Period, and 1, 12, 13, 18, 24, 25, 36, and 60 Months into the Test Period

Portfolio Selection Procedures: Length of the Formation Period and No. of Independent Replications	Average No. of Stocks	CAR at the End of the Formation Period: Winner Portfolio	CAR at the End of the Formation Period: Loser Portfolio	Difference in CAR (*t*-Statistics), Months After Portfolio Formation: 1	12	13	18	24	25	36	60
10 five-year periods	50	1.463	−1.194	0.070 (3.13)	0.156 (2.04)	0.248 (3.14)	0.256 (3.17)	0.196 (2.15)	0.228 (2.40)	0.230 (2.07)	0.319 (3.28)
16 three-year periods	35	1.375	−1.064	0.105 (3.29)	0.054 (0.77)	0.103 (1.18)	0.167 (1.51)	0.181 (1.71)	0.234 (2.19)	0.246 (2.20)	NA*
24 two-year periods[a]	35	1.130	−0.857	0.062 (2.91)	−0.006 (−0.16)	0.074 (1.53)	0.136 (2.02)	0.101 (1.41)	NA	NA	NA
25 two-year periods[b]	35	1.119	−0.866	0.089 (3.98)	0.011 (0.19)	0.092 (1.48)	0.107 (1.47)	0.115 (1.55)	NA	NA	NA
24 two-year periods[a] (deciles)	82	0.875	−0.711	0.051 (3.13)	0.006 (0.19)	0.066 (1.71)	0.105 (1.99)	0.083 (1.49)	NA	NA	NA
25 two-year periods[b] (deciles)	82	0.868	−0.714	0.068 (3.86)	0.008 (0.19)	0.071 (1.46)	0.078 (1.41)	0.072 (1.29)	NA	NA	NA
49 one-year periods	35	0.774	−0.585	0.042 (2.45)	−0.076 (−2.32)	−0.006 (−0.15)	0.007 (0.14)	−0.005 (−0.09)	NA	NA	NA

[a] The formation month for these portfolios is the month of December in all uneven years between 1933 and 1979.

[b] The formation month for these portfolios is the month of December in all even years between 1932 and 1980.

* NA, not applicable.

ality in stock prices. Throughout the test period, the difference in ACAR for the experiment with a three-year formation period (the upper curve) exceeds the same statistic for the experiments based on two- and one-year formation periods (middle and lower curves). But all three experiments are clearly affected by the same underlying seasonal pattern.

In Section I, it was mentioned that the use of market-adjusted excess returns is likely to bias the research design against the overreaction hypothesis. The bias can be seen by comparing the CAPM-betas of the extreme portfolios. For all the experiments listed in Table I, the average betas of the securities in the winner portfolios are significantly larger than the betas of the loser portfolios.[5] For example, for the three-year experiment illustrated in Figure 1, the relevant numbers are respectively, 1.369 and 1.026 (*t*-statistic on the difference: 3.09). Thus, the loser portfolios not only outperform the winner portfolios; if the CAPM is correct, they are also significantly less risky. From a different viewpoint, therefore, the results in Table I are likely to *underestimate* both the true magnitude and statistical significance of the overreaction effect. The problem is particularly severe with respect to the winner portfolio. Rather than 1.369, the residual return calculations assume the CAPM-beta of that portfolio to equal

[5] The CAPM-betas are found by estimating the market model over a period of 60 months prior to portfolio formation.

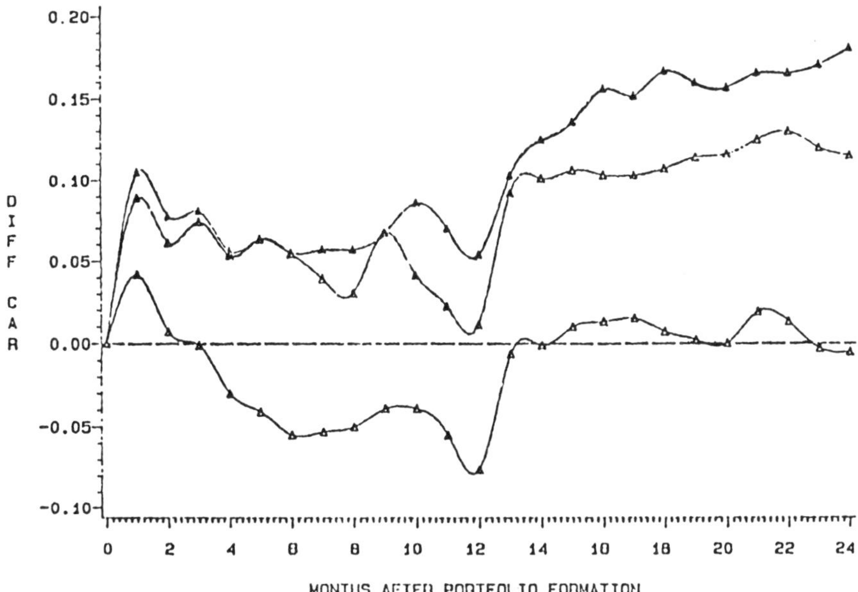

Figure 2. Differences in Cumulative Average Residual Between Winner and Loser Portfolios of 35 Stocks (formed over the previous one, two, or three years; 1–24 months into the test period)

1.00 only. This systematic bias may be responsible for the earlier observed asymmetry in the return behavior of the extreme portfolios.

To reiterate, the previous findings are broadly consistent with the predictions of the overreaction hypothesis. However, several aspects of the results remain without adequate explanation. Most importantly, the extraordinarily large positive excess returns earned by the loser portfolio in January.

One method that allows us to further accentuate the strength of the January effect is to increase the number of replications. Figure 3 shows the ACAR's for an experiment with a five-year-long test period. Every December between 1932 and 1977, winner and loser portfolios are formed on the basis of residual return behavior over the previous five years. Clearly, the successive 46 yearly selections are not independent. Therefore, no statistical tests are performed. The results in Figure 3 have some of the properties of a "trading rule." They represent the average (cumulative) excess return (before transaction costs) that an investor, aware of the overreaction phenomenon, could expect to earn following any

Average of 46 Yearly Replications
Starting Every January Between 1933 and 1978
Length of Formation Period: Five Years

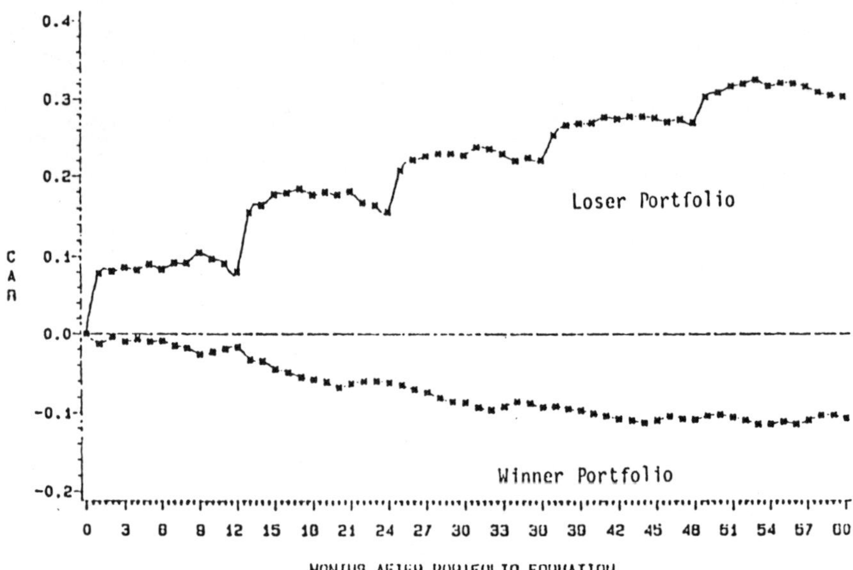

Figure 3. Cumulative Average Residuals for Winner and Loser Portfolios of 35 Stocks (1–60 months into the test period)

December in which he chose to try the strategy. The effect of multiplying the number of replications is to remove part of the random noise.

The outstanding feature of Figure 3 is, once again, the January returns on the loser portfolio. The effect is observed as late as five Januaries after portfolio formation! Careful examination of Figure 3 also reveals a tendency, on the part of the loser portfolio, to decline in value (relative to the market) between October and December. This observation is in agreement with the naive version of the tax-loss selling hypothesis as explained by, e.g., Schwert [25]. The winner portfolio, on the other hand, gains value at the end of the year and loses some in January (for more details, see De Bondt [7]).

B. Implications for Other Empirical Work

The results of this study have interesting implications for previous work on the small firm effect, the January effect and the dividend yield and P/E effects. Blume and Stambaugh [6], Keim [16], and Reinganum [21] have studied the interaction between the small firm and January effects. Their findings largely redefine the small firm effect as a "losing firm" effect around the turn-of-the-year.[6] Our own results lend further credence to this view. Persistently, losers earn exceptionally large January returns while winners do not. However, the companies in the extreme portfolios do not systematically differ with respect to market capitalization.

The January phenomenon is usually explained by tax-loss selling (see, e.g., Roll [23]). Our own findings raise new questions with respect to this hypothesis. First, if in early January selling pressure disappears and prices "rebound" to equilibrium levels, why does the loser portfolio—even while it outperforms the market—"rebound" once again in the second January of the test period? And again, in the third and fourth Januaries? Secondly, if prices "rebound" in January, why is that effect so much larger in magnitude than the selling pressure that "caused" it during the final months of the previous year? Possible answers to these questions include the argument that investors may wait for years before realizing losses, and the observed seasonality of the market as a whole.

With respect to the P/E effect, our results support the price-ratio hypothesis discussed in the introduction, i.e., high P/E stocks are "overvalued" whereas low P/E stocks are "undervalued." However, this argument implies that the P/E effect is also, for the most part, a January phenomenon. At present, there is no evidence to support that claim, except for the persistent positive relationship between dividend yield (a variable that is correlated with the P/E ratio) and January excess returns (Keim [15]).

III. Conclusions

Research in experimental psychology has suggested that, in violation of Bayes' rule, most people "overreact" to unexpected and dramatic news events. The question then arises whether such behavior matters at the market level.

Consistent with the predictions of the overreaction hypothesis, portfolios of prior "losers" are found to outperform prior "winners." Thirty-six months after portfolio formation, the losing stocks have earned about 25% more than the winners, even though the latter are significantly more risky.

Several aspects of the results remain without adequate explanation; most importantly, the large positive excess returns earned by the loser portfolio every January. Much to our surprise, the effect is observed as late as five years after portfolio formation.

[6] Even after purging the data of tax-loss selling effects, Reinganum [22] finds a (considerably smaller) January seasonal effect related to company size. This result may be due to his particular definition of the tax-loss selling measure. The measure is related to the securities' relative price movements over the last *six months* prior to portfolio formation only. Thus, if many investors choose to wait longer than six months before realizing losses, the portfolio of small firms may still contain many "losers."

REFERENCES

1. K. J. Arrow. "Risk Perception in Psychology and Economics." *Economic Inquiry* 20 (January 1982), 1–9.

2. R. Ball. "Anomalies in Relationships Between Securities' Yields and Yield-Surrogates." *Journal of Financial Economics* 6 (June–September 1978), 103–26.
3. S. Basu. "Investment Performance of Common Stocks in Relation to Their Price-Earnings Ratios: A Test of the Efficient Market Hypothesis." *Journal of Finance* 3 (June 1977), 663–82.
4. ———. "The Relationship Between Earnings' Yield, Market Value and Return for NYSE Common Stocks: Further Evidence." *Journal of Financial Economics* 12 (June 1983), 129–56.
5. W. Beaver and W. R. Landsman. "Note on the Behavior of Residual Security Returns for Winner and Loser Portfolios." *Journal of Accounting and Economics* 3 (December 1981), 233–41.
6. M. Blume and R. Stambaugh. "Biases in Computed Returns: An Application to the Size Effect." *Journal of Financial Economics* 12 (November 1983), 387–404.
7. W. F. M. De Bondt. "Does the Stock Market Overreact to New Information?" Unpublished Ph.D. dissertation, Cornell University, 1985.
8. D. N. Dreman. *The New Contrarian Investment Strategy*. New York: Random House, 1982.
9. E. F. Fama. *Foundations of Finance*. New York: Basic Books, Inc., 1976.
10. B. Graham. *The Intelligent Investor, A Book of Practical Counsel*, 3rd ed. New York: Harper & Brothers Publishers, 1959.
11. ———. *The Intelligent Investor, A Book of Practical Counsel*, 4th rev. ed. New York: Harper & Brothers Publishers, 1973.
12. D. M. Grether. "Bayes Rule as a Descriptive Model: The Representativeness Heuristic." *Quarterly Journal of Economics* 95 (November 1980), 537–57.
13. R. Jarrow. "Beliefs, Information, Martingales, and Arbitrage Pricing." Working Paper, Johnson Graduate School of Management, Cornell University, November 1983.
14. D. Kahneman and A. Tversky. "Intuitive Prediction: Biases and Corrective Procedures." In D. Kahneman, P. Slovic, and A. Tversky, (eds.), *Judgment Under Uncertainty: Heuristics and Biases*. London: Cambridge University Press, 1982.
15. D. Keim. "Further Evidence on Size Effects and Yield Effects: The Implications of Stock Return Seasonality." Working Paper, Graduate School of Business, University of Chicago, April 1982.
16. ———. "Size-Related Anomalies and Stock Return Seasonality: Further Empirical Evidence." *Journal of Financial Economics* 12 (June 1983), 13–32.
17. J. M. Keynes. *The General Theory of Employment, Interest and Money*. London: Harcourt Brace Jovanovich, 1964 (reprint of the 1936 edition).
18. A. W. Kleidon. "Stock Prices as Rational Forecasters of Future Cash Flows." Working Paper, Graduate School of Business, University of Chicago, November 1981.
19. T. A. Marsh and R. C. Merton. "Aggregate Dividend Behavior and Its Implications for Tests of Stock Market Rationality." Working Paper No. 1475–83, Sloan School of Management, MIT, September 1983.
20. J. A. Ohlson and S. H. Penman. "Variance Increases Subsequent to Stock Splits: An Empirical Aberration." Working Paper, Graduate School of Business, Columbia University, September 1983.
21. M. R. Reinganum. "Misspecification of Capital Asset Pricing: Empirical Anomalies Based on Earnings' Yields and Market Values." *Journal of Financial Economics* 9 (March 1981), 19–46.
22. ———. "The Anomalous Stock Market Behavior of Small Firms in January." *Journal of Financial Economics* 12 (June 1983), 89–104.
23. R. Roll. "Vas ist das?". *Journal of Portfolio Management* 10 (Winter 1983), 18–28.
24. T. Russell and R. Thaler. "The Relevance of Quasi-Rationality in Competitive Markets." *American Economic Review* 75 (1985), forthcoming.
25. G. W. Schwert. "Size and Stock Returns, and Other Empirical Regularities." *Journal of Financial Economics* 12 (June 1983), 3–12.
26. R. J. Shiller. "The Volatility of Long-Term Interest Rates and Expectations Models of the Term Structure." *Journal of Political Economy* 87 (December 1979), 1190–1219.
27. ———. "Do Stock Prices Move Too Much to be Justified by Subsequent Changes in Dividends?" *American Economic Review* 71 (June 1981), 421–36.
28. J. B. Williams. *The Theory of Investment Value*. Amsterdam: North-Holland, 1956 (reprint of 1938 edition).

[12]

Noise Trader Risk in Financial Markets

J. Bradford De Long

Harvard University and National Bureau of Economic Research

Andrei Shleifer

University of Chicago and National Bureau of Economic Research

Lawrence H. Summers

Harvard University and National Bureau of Economic Research

Robert J. Waldmann

European University Institute

We present a simple overlapping generations model of an asset market in which irrational noise traders with erroneous stochastic beliefs both affect prices and earn higher expected returns. The unpredictability of noise traders' beliefs creates a risk in the price of the asset that deters rational arbitrageurs from aggressively betting against them. As a result, prices can diverge significantly from fundamental values even in the absence of fundamental risk. Moreover, bearing a disproportionate amount of risk that they themselves create enables noise traders to earn a higher expected return than rational investors do. The model sheds light on a number of financial anomalies, including the excess volatility of asset prices, the mean reversion of stock returns, the underpricing of closed-end mutual funds, and the Mehra-Prescott equity premium puzzle.

We would like to thank the National Science, Russell Sage, and Alfred P. Sloan foundations for financial support. We have benefited from comments from Robert Barsky, Fischer Black, John Campbell, Andrew Caplin, Peter Diamond, Miles Kimball, Bruce Lehmann, Charles Perry, Robert Vishny, Michael Woodford, and especially from Kevin M. Murphy and Barry Nalebuff.

[*Journal of Political Economy*, 1990, vol. 98, no. 4]

> If the reader interjects that there must surely be large profits to be gained . . . in the long run by a skilled individual who . . . purchase[s] investments on the best genuine long-term expectation he can frame, he must be answered . . . that there are such serious-minded individuals and that it makes a vast difference to an investment market whether or not they predominate. . . . But we must also add that there are several factors which jeopardise the predominance of such individuals in modern investment markets. Investment based on genuine long-term expectation is so difficult . . . as to be scarcely practicable. He who attempts it must surely . . . run greater risks than he who tries to guess better than the crowd how the crowd will behave. [Keynes 1936, p. 157]

There is considerable evidence that many investors do not follow economists' advice to buy and hold the market portfolio. Individual investors typically fail to diversify, holding instead a single stock or a small number of stocks (Lewellen, Schlarbaum, and Lease 1974). They often pick stocks through their own research or on the advice of the likes of Joe Granville or "Wall Street Week." When investors do diversify, they entrust their money to stock-picking mutual funds that charge them high fees while failing to beat the market (Jensen 1968). Black (1986) believes that such investors, with no access to inside information, irrationally act on noise as if it were information that would give them an edge. Following Kyle (1985), Black calls such investors "noise traders."

Despite the recognition of the abundance of noise traders in the market, economists feel safe ignoring them in most discussions of asset price formation. The argument against the importance of noise traders for price formation has been forcefully made by Friedman (1953) and Fama (1965). Both authors point out that irrational investors are met in the market by rational arbitrageurs who trade against them and in the process drive prices close to fundamental values. Moreover, in the course of such trading, those whose judgments of asset values are sufficiently mistaken to affect prices lose money to arbitrageurs and so eventually disappear from the market. The argument "that speculation is . . . destabilizing . . . is largely equivalent to saying that speculators lose money, since speculation can be destabilizing in general only if speculators on . . . average sell . . . low . . . and buy . . . high" (Friedman 1953, p. 175). Noise traders thus cannot affect prices too much and, even if they can, will not do so for long.

In this paper we examine these arguments by focusing explicitly on the limits of arbitrage dedicated to exploiting noise traders' misperceptions. We recognize that arbitrageurs are likely to be risk averse and to have reasonably short horizons. As a result, their willingness to take positions against noise traders is limited. One source of risk that limits the power of arbitrage—fundamental risk—is well understood. Figlewski (1979) shows that it might take a very long time for noise traders to lose most of their money if arbitrageurs must bear fundamental risk in betting against them and so take limited positions. Shiller (1984) and Campbell and Kyle (1987) focus on arbitrageurs' aversion to fundamental risk in discussing the effect of noise traders on stock market prices. Their results show that aversion to fundamental risk can by itself severely limit arbitrage, even when arbitrageurs have infinite horizons.

But there is another important source of risk borne by short-horizon investors engaged in arbitrage against noise traders: the risk that noise traders' beliefs will not revert to their mean for a long time and might in the meantime become even more extreme. If noise traders today are pessimistic about an asset and have driven down its price, an arbitrageur buying this asset must recognize that in the near future noise traders might become even more pessimistic and drive the price down even further. If the arbitrageur has to liquidate before the price recovers, he suffers a loss. Fear of this loss should limit his original arbitrage position.

Conversely, an arbitrageur selling an asset short when bullish noise traders have driven its price up must remember that noise traders might become even more bullish tomorrow, and so must take a position that accounts for the risk of a further price rise when he has to buy back the stock. This risk of a further change of noise traders' opinion away from its mean—which we refer to as "noise trader risk"—must be borne by any arbitrageur with a short time horizon and must limit his willingness to bet against noise traders.

Because the unpredictability of noise traders' future opinions deters arbitrage, prices can diverge significantly from fundamental values even when there is no fundamental risk. Noise traders thus create their own space. All the main results of our paper come from the observation that arbitrage does not eliminate the effects of noise because noise itself creates risk.[1]

The risk resulting from stochastic changes in noise traders' opinions raises the possibility that noise traders who are on average bullish

[1] Our paper is related to other examinations of Friedman's arguments, including Hart and Kreps (1986), Ingram (1987), and Stein (1987). Also relevant are Haltiwanger and Waldman (1985) and Russell and Thaler (1985). We discuss these papers after presenting our model.

earn a higher expected return than rational, sophisticated investors engaged in arbitrage against noise trading. This result obtains because noise trader risk makes assets less attractive to risk-averse arbitrageurs and so drives down prices. If noise traders on average overestimate returns or underestimate risk, they invest more in the risky asset on average than sophisticated investors and may earn higher average returns. This result is more interesting than the point that if noise traders bear more fundamental risk they earn higher returns: our point is that noise traders can earn higher expected returns solely by bearing more of the risk that they themselves create. Noise traders can earn higher expected returns from their own destabilizing influence, not because they perform the useful social function of bearing fundamental risk.

Our model also has several implications for asset price behavior. Because noise trader risk limits the effectiveness of arbitrage, prices in our model are excessively volatile. If noise traders' opinions follow a stationary process, there is a mean-reverting component in stock returns. Our model also shows how assets subject to noise trader risk can be underpriced relative to fundamental values. We apply this idea to explain the underpricing of closed-end mutual funds, as well as the long-run underpricing of stocks known as the Mehra-Prescott (1985) puzzle. Finally, our model has several implications for the optimal investment strategy of sophisticated investors and for the possible role of long-term investors in stabilizing asset prices.

We develop our two main arguments—that bearing noise trader risk raises noise traders' returns and that noise trader risk can explain several financial anomalies—in five sections. Section I presents a model of noise trader risk and shows how prices can diverge significantly from fundamental values. Section II calculates the relative expected returns of noise traders and of sophisticated investors. Section III analyzes the persistence of noise traders in an extended model in which successful investors are imitated (as in Denton [1985]). Section IV presents qualitative implications of the model for the behavior of asset prices and market participants. Section V presents conclusions.

I. Noise Trading as a Source of Risk

The model contains noise traders and sophisticated investors. Noise traders falsely believe that they have special information about the future price of the risky asset. They may get their pseudosignals from technical analysts, stockbrokers, or economic consultants and irrationally believe that these signals carry information. Or in formulating their investment strategies, they may exhibit the fallacy of excessive subjective certainty that has been repeatedly demonstrated in experimental contexts since Alpert and Raiffa (1982). Noise traders select their portfolios on the basis of such incorrect beliefs. In response to noise traders' actions, it is optimal for sophisticated investors to exploit noise traders' irrational misperceptions. Sophisticated traders buy when noise traders depress prices and sell when noise traders push prices up. Such active contrarian investment strategies push prices toward fundamentals, but not all the way.

A. *The Model*

Our basic model is a stripped-down overlapping generations model with two-period-lived agents (Samuelson 1958). For simplicity, there is no first-period consumption, no labor supply decision, and no bequest. As a result, the resources agents have to invest are exogenous. The only decision agents make is to choose a portfolio when young.

The economy contains two assets that pay identical dividends. One of the assets, the safe asset s, pays a fixed real dividend r. Asset s is in perfectly elastic supply: a unit of it can be created out of, and a unit of it turned back into, a unit of the consumption good in any period. With consumption each period taken as numeraire, the price of the safe asset is always fixed at one. The dividend r paid on asset s is thus the riskless rate. The other asset, the unsafe asset u, always pays the same fixed real dividend r as asset s. But u is not in elastic supply: it is in fixed and unchangeable quantity, normalized at one unit. The price of u in period t is denoted p_t. If the price of each asset were equal to the net present value of its future dividends, then assets u and s would be perfect substitutes and would sell for the same price of one in all periods. But this is not how the price of u is determined in the presence of noise traders.

We usually interpret s as a riskless short-term bond and u as aggregate equities. It is important for the analysis below that noise trader risk be marketwide rather than idiosyncratic. If noise traders' misperceptions of the returns to individual assets are uncorrelated and if each asset is small relative to the market, arbitrageurs would eliminate any possible mispricing for the same reasons that idiosyncratic risk is not priced in the standard capital asset pricing model.

There are two types of agents: sophisticated investors (denoted i) who have rational expectations and noise traders (denoted n). We assume that noise traders are present in the model in measure μ, that sophisticated investors are present in measure $1 - \mu$, and that all agents of a given type are identical. Both types of agents choose their portfolios when young to maximize perceived expected utility given their own beliefs about the ex ante mean of the distribution of the price of u at $t + 1$. The representative sophisticated investor young in period t accurately perceives the distribution of returns from holding the risky asset, and so maximizes expected utility given that distribution. The representative noise trader young in period t misperceives the expected price of the risky asset by an independent and identically distributed normal random variable ρ_t:

$$\rho_t \sim N(\rho^*, \sigma_\rho^2). \tag{1}$$

The mean misperception ρ^* is a measure of the average "bullishness" of the noise traders, and σ_ρ^2 is the variance of noise traders' misperceptions of the expected return per unit of the risky asset.[2] Noise traders thus maximize their own expectation of utility given the next-period dividend, the one-period variance of p_{t+1}, and their false belief that the distribution of the price of u next period has mean ρ_t above its true value.

Each agent's utility is a constant absolute risk aversion function of wealth when old:

$$U = -e^{-(2\gamma)w}, \tag{2}$$

where γ is the coefficient of absolute risk aversion. With normally distributed returns to holding a unit of the risky asset, maximizing the expected value of (2) is equivalent to maximizing

$$\bar{w} - \gamma\sigma_w^2, \tag{3}$$

where w is the expected final wealth, and σ_w^2 is the one-period-ahead variance of wealth. The sophisticated investor chooses the amount λ_t^i of the risky asset u held to maximize

$$\begin{aligned} E(U) &= \bar{w} - \gamma\sigma_w^2 \\ &= c_0 + \lambda_t^i[r + {}_tp_{t+1} - p_t(1 + r)] - \gamma(\lambda_t^i)^2({}_t\sigma_{p_{t+1}}^2), \end{aligned} \tag{4}$$

where c_0 is a function of first-period labor income, an anterior subscript denotes the time at which an expectation is taken, and we define

$${}_t\sigma_{p_{t+1}}^2 = E_t\{[p_{t+1} - E_t(p_{t+1})]^2\} \tag{5}$$

to be the one-period variance of p_{t+1}. The representative noise trader maximizes

$$\begin{aligned} E(U) &= \bar{w} - \gamma\sigma_w^2 \\ &= c_0 + \lambda_t^n[r + {}_tp_{t+1} - p_t(1 + r)] - \gamma(\lambda_t^n)^2({}_t\sigma_{p_{t+1}}^2) + \lambda_t^n(\rho_t). \end{aligned} \tag{6}$$

[2] The assumption that noise traders misperceive the expected price hides the fact that the expected price is itself a function of the parameters ρ^* and σ_ρ^2. Thus we are implicitly assuming that noise traders know how to factor the effect of future price volatility into their calculations of values. This assumption is made for simplicity. We have also solved a more complicated model that parameterizes noise traders' beliefs by their expectations of future prices, not by their misperceptions of future returns. The thrust of the results is the same.

The only difference between (4) and (6) is the last term in (6), which captures the noise traders' misperception of the expected return from holding λ_t^n units of the risky asset.

Given their beliefs, all young agents divide their portfolios between u and s. The quantities λ_t^n and λ_t^i of the risky asset purchased are functions of its price p_t, of the one-period-ahead distribution of the price of u, and (in the case of noise traders) of their misperception ρ_t of the expected price of the risky asset. When old, agents convert their holdings of s to the consumption good, sell their holdings of u for price p_{t+1} to the new young, and consume all their wealth.

One can think of alternative ways of specifying noise trader demands.[3] There are well-defined mappings between misperceptions of returns ρ_t and (*a*) noise traders' fixing a price p_t at which they will buy and sell, (*b*) noise traders' purchasing a fixed quantity λ_t^n of the risky asset, or (*c*) noise traders' mistaking the variance of returns (taking them to be σ^{2*} instead of σ^2). The equilibrium in which noise traders matter found in our basic model exists regardless of which primitive specification of noise traders' behavior is assumed.

Solving (4) and (6) yields expressions for agents' holdings of u:

$$\lambda_t^i = \frac{r + {}_tp_{t+1} - (1 + r)p_t}{2\gamma({}_t\sigma^2_{p_{t+1}})}, \tag{7}$$

$$\lambda_t^n = \frac{r + {}_tp_{t+1} - (1 + r)p_t}{2\gamma({}_t\sigma^2_{p_{t+1}})} + \frac{\rho_t}{2\gamma({}_t\sigma^2_{p_{t+1}})}. \tag{8}$$

We allow noise traders' and sophisticated investors' demands to be negative; they can take short positions at will. Even if investors hold only positive amounts of both assets, the fact that returns are unbounded gives each investor a chance of having negative final wealth. We use a standard specification of returns at the cost of allowing consumption to be negative with positive probability.[4]

Under our assumptions on preferences and the distribution of re-

[3] Let noise traders set

$$p_t = 1 - \frac{2\gamma}{r}\sigma^2 + \frac{\mu\rho^*}{r} + \frac{\mu(\rho_t - \rho^*)}{1 + r},$$

where σ^2 is the total variance—the sum of "fundamental" dividend variance, noise trader–generated price variance, and any covariance terms—associated with holding the risky asset u for one period. Alternatively, let noise traders set the quantity of the risky asset that they buy—whatever its price—as $\lambda_t^n = 1 + [\rho_t/(2\gamma)\sigma^2]$ or let the noise traders misperceive the variance of returns on the risky asset, taking as the variance

$$\sigma^{2*} = \sigma^2\left(\frac{\gamma\sigma^2 - \rho_t}{\gamma\sigma^2 + \rho_t}\right).$$

[4] An appendix of our working paper (De Long et al. 1987) presents an example in which asset prices and consumption are always positive.

turns, the demands for the risky asset are proportional to its perceived excess return and inversely proportional to its perceived variance. The additional term in the demand function of noise traders comes from their misperception of the expected return. When noise traders overestimate expected returns, they demand more of the risky asset than sophisticated investors do; when they underestimate the expected return, they demand less. Sophisticated investors exert a stabilizing influence in this model since they offset the volatile positions of the noise traders.

The variance of prices appearing in the denominators of the demand functions is derived solely from noise trader risk. Both noise traders and sophisticated investors limit their demand for asset u because the price at which they can sell it when old depends on the uncertain beliefs of next period's young noise traders. This uncertainty about the price for which asset u can be sold afflicts all investors, no matter what their beliefs about expected returns, and so limits the extent to which they are willing to bet against each other. If the price next period were certain, then noise traders and sophisticated investors would hold with certainty different beliefs about expected returns; they would therefore try to take infinite bets against each other. An equilibrium would not exist. Noise trader risk limits all investors' positions and in particular keeps arbitrageurs from driving prices all the way to fundamental values.

B. *The Pricing Function*

To calculate equilibrium prices, observe that the old sell their holdings, and so the demands of the young must sum to one in equilibrium. Equations (7) and (8) imply that

$$p_t = \frac{1}{1 + r}[r + {}_tp_{t+1} - 2\gamma({}_t\sigma^2_{p_{t+1}}) + \mu\rho_t]. \tag{9}$$

Equation (9) expresses the risky asset's price in period t as a function of period t's misperception by noise traders (ρ_t), of the technological (r) and behavioral (γ) parameters of the model, and of the moments of the one-period-ahead distribution of p_{t+1}. We consider only steady-state equilibria by imposing the requirement that the unconditional distribution of p_{t+1} be identical to the distribution of p_t. The endogenous one-period-ahead distribution of the price of asset u can then be eliminated from (9) by solving recursively:[5]

[5] The model cannot have stationary bubble equilibria, for the safe asset is formally equivalent to a storage technology that pays a rate of return r greater than the growth rate of the economy. The number of stationary equilibria in the model does, however,

$$p_t = 1 + \frac{\mu(\rho_t - \rho^*)}{1 + r} + \frac{\mu\rho^*}{r} - \frac{2\gamma}{r} ({}_t\sigma^2_{p_{t+1}}). \tag{10}$$

Inspection of (10) reveals that only the second term is variable, for γ, ρ^*, and r are all constants, and the one-step-ahead variance of p_t is a simple unchanging function of the constant variance of a generation of noise traders' misperception ρ_t:

$$_t\sigma^2_{p_{t+1}} = \sigma^2_{p_{t+1}} = \frac{\mu^2\sigma^2_\rho}{(1 + r)^2}. \tag{11}$$

The final form of the pricing rule for u, in which the price depends only on exogenous parameters of the model and on public information about present and future misperception by noise traders, is

$$p_t = 1 + \frac{\mu(\rho_t - \rho^*)}{1 + r} + \frac{\mu\rho^*}{r} - \frac{(2\gamma)\mu^2\sigma^2_\rho}{r(1 + r)^2}. \tag{12}$$

C. *Interpretation*

The last three terms that appear in (12) and (10) show the impact of noise traders on the price of asset u. As the distribution of ρ_t converges to a point mass at zero, the equilibrium pricing function (12) converges to its fundamental value of one.

The second term in (12) captures the fluctuations in the price of the risky asset u due to the variation of noise traders' misperceptions. Even though asset u is not subject to any fundamental uncertainty and is so known by a large class of investors, its price varies substantially as noise traders' opinions shift. When a generation of noise traders is more bullish than the average generation, they bid up the price of u. When they are more bearish than average, they bid down the price. When they hold their average misperception—when $\rho_t = \rho^*$—the term is zero. As one would expect, the more numerous noise traders are relative to sophisticated investors, the more volatile asset prices are.

The third term in (12) captures the deviations of p_t from its fundamental value due to the fact that the average misperception by noise traders is not zero. If noise traders are bullish on average, this "price pressure" effect makes the price of the risky asset higher than it

depend on the primitive specification of noise traders' behavior. For example, if noise traders randomly pick each period the price p_t at which they will buy and sell unlimited quantities of the risky asset, then (trivially) there is only one equilibrium. If the noise traders randomly pick the quantity λ_t^i that they purchase, then the fundamental solution in which p_t is always equal to one is an equilibrium in addition to the equilibrium in which noise traders matter.

would otherwise be. Optimistic noise traders bear a greater than average share of price risk. Since sophisticated investors bear a smaller share of price risk the higher ρ^* is, they require a lower expected excess return and so are willing to pay a higher price for asset u.

The final term in (12) is the heart of the model. Sophisticated investors would not hold the risky asset unless compensated for bearing the risk that noise traders will become bearish and the price of the risky asset will fall. Both noise traders and sophisticated investors present in period t believe that asset u is mispriced, but because p_{t+1} is uncertain, neither group is willing to bet too much on this mispricing. At the margin, the return from enlarging one's position in an asset that everyone agrees is mispriced (but different types think is mispriced in different directions) is offset by the additional price risk that must be run. Noise traders thus "create their own space": the uncertainty over what next period's noise traders will believe makes the otherwise riskless asset u risky and drives its price down and its return up. This is so despite the fact that both sophisticated investors and noise traders always hold portfolios that possess the same amount of fundamental risk: zero. Any intuition to the effect that investors in the risky asset "ought" to receive higher expected returns because they perform the valuable social function of risk bearing neglects to consider that noise traders' speculation is the only source of risk. For the economy as a whole, there is no risk to be borne.

The reader might suspect that our results are critically dependent on the overlapping generations structure of the model, but this is not quite accurate. Equilibrium exists as long as the returns to holding the risky asset are always uncertain. In the overlapping generations structure, this is assured by the absence of a last period. For if there is a last period in which the risky asset pays a nonstochastic dividend and is liquidated, then both noise traders and sophisticated investors will seek to exploit what they see as riskless arbitrage. If, say, the liquidation value of the risky asset is $1 + r$, previous-period sophisticated investors will try to trade arbitrarily large amounts of asset u at any price other than one, and noise traders will try to trade arbitrarily large amounts at any price other than

$$p_t = 1 + \frac{\rho_t}{1 + r}. \qquad (13)$$

The excess demand function for the risky asset will be undefined and the model will have no equilibrium. But in a model with fundamental dividend risk the assumption that there is no last period and, hence, the overlapping generations structure are not necessary. With fundamental dividend risk, no agent is ever subjectively certain what the return on the risky asset will be, and so the qualitative properties of equilibrium in our model are preserved even with a known terminal date. The overlapping generations structure is therefore not needed when fundamental dividend risk is present.

The infinitely extended overlapping generations structure of the basic model does play another function. It assures that each agent's horizon is short. No agent has any opportunity to wait until the price of the risky asset recovers before selling. Such an overlapping generations structure may be a fruitful way of modeling the effects on prices of a number of institutional features, such as frequent evaluations of money managers' performance, that may lead rational, long-lived market participants to care about short-term rather than long-term performance. In our model, the horizon of the typical investor is important. If sophisticated investors' horizons are long relative to the duration of noise traders' optimism or pessimism toward risky assets, then they can buy low, confident that they will be able to sell high when prices revert to the mean. As we show below, as the horizon of agents becomes longer, arbitrage becomes less risky and prices approach fundamental values. Noise trader risk is an important deterrent to arbitrage only when the duration of noise traders' misperceptions is of the same order of magnitude as or longer than the horizon of sophisticated investors.

II. Relative Returns of Noise Traders and Sophisticated Investors

We have demonstrated that noise traders can affect prices even though there is no uncertainty about fundamentals. Friedman (1953) argues that noise traders who affect prices earn lower returns than the sophisticated investors they trade with, and so economic selection works to weed them out. In our model, it need not be the case that noise traders earn lower returns. Noise traders' collective shifts of opinion increase the riskiness of returns to assets. If noise traders' portfolios are concentrated in assets subject to noise trader risk, noise traders can earn a higher average rate of return on their portfolios than sophisticated investors.

A. Relative Expected Returns

The conditions under which noise traders earn higher expected returns than sophisticated investors are easily laid out. All agents earn a certain net return of r on their investments in asset s. The difference between noise traders' and sophisticated investors' total returns given equal initial wealth is the product of the difference in their holdings of the risky asset u and of the excess return paid by a unit of the risky asset u. Call this difference in returns to the two types of agents ΔR_{n-i}:

$$\Delta R_{n-i} = (\lambda_t^n - \lambda_t^i)[r + p_{t+1} - p_t(1 + r)]. \tag{14}$$

The difference between noise traders' and sophisticated investors' demands for asset u is

$$\lambda_t^n - \lambda_t^i = \frac{\rho_t}{(2\gamma)_t\sigma^2_{p_{t+1}}} = \frac{(1 + r)^2\rho_t}{(2\gamma)\mu^2\sigma^2_\rho}. \tag{15}$$

Note that as μ becomes small, (15) becomes large: noise traders and sophisticated investors take enormous positions of opposite signs because the small amount of noise trader risk makes each group think that it has an almost riskless arbitrage opportunity. In the limit in which $\mu = 0$, equilibrium no longer exists (in the absence of fundamental risk) because the two groups try to place infinite bets against each other.

The expected value of the excess return on the risky asset u as of time t is

$${}_t[r + p_{t+1} - p_t(1 + r)] = (2\gamma)_t\sigma^2_{p_{t+1}} - \mu\rho_t = \frac{(2\gamma)\mu^2\sigma^2_\rho}{(1 + r)^2} - \mu\rho_t. \tag{16}$$

And so

$${}_t(\Delta R_{n-i}) = \rho_t - \frac{(1 + r)^2(\rho_t)^2}{(2\gamma)\mu\sigma^2_\rho}. \tag{17}$$

The expected excess total return of noise traders is positive only if both noise traders are optimistic (ρ_t is positive, which makes [15] positive) and the risky asset is priced below its fundamental value (which makes [16] positive).

Taking the global unconditional expectation of (17) yields

$$E(\Delta R_{n-i}) = \rho^* - \frac{(1 + r)^2(\rho^*)^2 + (1 + r)^2\sigma^2_\rho}{(2\gamma)\mu\sigma^2_\rho}. \tag{18}$$

Equation (18) makes obvious the requirement that for noise traders to earn higher expected returns, the mean misperception ρ^* of returns on the risky asset must be positive. The first ρ^* on the right-hand side of (18) increases noise traders' expected returns through what might be called the "hold more" effect. Noise traders' expected returns relative to those of sophisticated investors are increased when noise traders on average hold more of the risky asset and earn a larger share of the rewards to risk bearing. When ρ^* is negative, noise traders' changing misperceptions still make the fundamentally riskless asset u risky and still push up the expected return on asset u, but the rewards to risk bearing accrue disproportionately to sophisticated investors, who on average hold more of the risky asset than the noise traders do.

The first term in the numerator in (18) incorporates the "price pressure" effect. As noise traders become more bullish, they demand more of the risky asset on average and drive up its price. They thus reduce the return to risk bearing and, hence, the differential between their returns and those of sophisticated investors.

The second term in the numerator incorporates the buy high–sell low or "Friedman" effect. Because noise traders' misperceptions are stochastic, they have the worst possible market timing. They buy the most of the risky asset u just when other noise traders are buying it, which is when they are most likely to suffer a capital loss. The more variable noise traders' beliefs are, the more damage their poor market timing does to their returns.

The denominator incorporates the "create space" effect central to this model. As the variability of noise traders' beliefs increases, the price risk increases. To take advantage of noise traders' misperceptions, sophisticated investors must bear this greater risk. Since sophisticated investors are risk averse, they reduce the extent to which they bet against noise traders in response to this increased risk. If the create space effect is large, then the price pressure and buy high–sell low effects inflict less damage on noise traders' average returns relative to sophisticated investors' returns.

Two effects—hold more and create space—tend to raise noise traders' relative expected returns. Two effects—the Friedman and price pressure effects—tend to lower noise traders' relative expected returns. Neither pair clearly dominates. Noise traders cannot earn higher average returns if they are on average bearish, for if ρ^* does not exceed zero, there is no hold more effect and (18) must be negative. Nor can noise traders earn higher average returns if they are too bullish, for as ρ^* gets large the price pressure effect, which increases with $(\rho^*)^2$, dominates. For intermediate degrees of average bullishness, noise traders earn higher expected returns. And it is clear from (18) that the larger γ is, that is, the more risk averse agents are, the larger is the range of ρ^* over which noise traders earn higher average returns.

B. Relative Utility Levels

The higher expected returns of the noise traders come at the cost of holding portfolios with sufficiently higher variance to give noise traders lower expected utility (computed using the true distribution of wealth when old). Since sophisticated investors maximize true expected utility, any trading strategy alternative to theirs that earns a higher mean return must have a variance sufficiently higher to make it unattractive. The average amount of asset s that must be given to old noise traders to give them the ex ante expected utility of sophisticated investors can be shown to be

$$\frac{(1 + r)^2}{(4\gamma)\mu^2}\left(1 + \frac{\rho^{*2}}{\sigma_\rho^2}\right). \tag{19}$$

This amount is decreasing in the variance and increasing in the square of the mean of noise traders' misperceptions. The size of their mistakes grows with ρ^*, but the risk penalty for attempting to exploit noise traders' mistakes grows with σ_ρ^2. Noise traders receive the same average realized utility when $\rho^* = x$ as when $\rho^* = -x$, but when $\rho^* > 0$, they may receive higher average returns. When $\rho^* < 0$, noise traders receive both lower realized utility levels and lower average returns.

Sophisticated investors are necessarily better off when noise traders are present in this model. In the absence of noise traders, sophisticated investors' opportunities are limited to investing at the riskless rate r. The presence of noise traders gives sophisticated investors a larger opportunity set, in that they can still invest all they want at the riskless rate r, but they can also trade in the unsafe asset. Access to a larger opportunity set clearly raises sophisticated investors' expected utility.[6]

Noise traders receive higher average consumption than sophisticated investors, and sophisticated investors receive higher average consumption than in fundamental equilibrium. Yet the productive resources available to society—its labor income per period, its ability to create the productive asset s, and the unit amount of asset u yielding its dividend r per period—are unchanged by the presence of noise trading. The source of extra returns is made clear by the following thought experiment. Imagine that before some date τ there are no noise traders. Up until time τ, both assets sell at a price of one. At τ it is unexpectedly announced that in the next generation noise traders will appear. The price p_τ of the asset u drops; those who hold asset u in period τ suffer a capital loss. This capital loss is the source of the excess returns and of the higher consumption in the equilibrium with noise. The period τ young have more to invest in s because they pay less to the old for the stock of asset u. If at time ω it became known

[6] If the stock of the risky asset is endogenous—if there is a nontrivial capital supply decision—sophisticated investors can be worse off with noise traders present. If noise traders make capital riskier and reduce the price of risk, they reduce the opportunity set of sophisticated investors and their welfare (De Long et al. 1989).

that noise traders had permanently withdrawn, then those who held u at time ω would capture the present value of what would otherwise have been future excess returns as p_ω jumped to one. The same supernormal return would also be received by a generation that suddenly acquired the opportunity to "bust up" the risky asset by turning it into an equivalent quantity of the safe asset. The fact that the generation that suffers from the arrival of noise traders is pushed off to negative infinity in the model creates the appearance of a free lunch.[7]

C. A Comparison with Other Work

The fact that bullish noise traders can earn higher returns in the market than sophisticated traders implies that Friedman's simple "market selection" argument is incomplete.[8] Since noise traders' wealth can increase faster than sophisticated investors', it is not possible to make any blanket statement that noise traders lose money and eventually become unimportant. One should not overinterpret our result. The greater variance of noise traders' returns might give them in the long run a high probability of having low wealth and a low probability of having very high wealth. Market selection might work against such traders even if their expected value of wealth is high since they would be poor virtually for certain. A more appropriate selection criterion would take this into account, but we have not found a tractable way to implement such a selection criterion in a model in which noise traders affect prices.[9]

At this point we can compare our results with recent discussions of Friedman's argument that destabilizing speculation is unprofitable, and so profitable speculation must be stabilizing. Hart and Kreps (1986) point out that an injection of rational investors able to perform profitable intertemporal trade could destabilize prices. In our model, rational speculation is always stabilizing, but average returns earned by rational speculators need not be as high as those earned by noise traders. In Stein (1987), speculators' access to private information allows for profitable destabilizing speculation. In our model, arbitrageurs know exactly the way in which noise traders are confused today, and noise traders have no private information. The uncer-

[7] In practice, the cost of future noise trader risk in a security will be paid for by whoever sells it to the public. In the case of a stock, the cost will be paid by the entrepreneur.

[8] The key difference from Friedman's (1953) model is that here the demand curve of sophisticated investors shifts in response to the addition of noise traders and the resulting increase in risk. Because of this shift, sophisticated investors' expected returns may fall even though their expected utility rises.

[9] De Long et al. (1988) consider the evolution of the wealth distribution in a model in which noise traders have no effect on prices.

tainty that affects noise traders and sophisticated investors equally concerns the behavior of noise traders tomorrow. Haltiwanger and Waldman (1985) and Russell and Thaler (1985) study the effects of irrational behavior on prices in the presence of externalities and of restrictions on trade, respectively. Our model is related to Russell and Thaler's, in that the short horizon of arbitrageurs can be interpreted as a form of restriction on trade.

III. Imitation of Beliefs

We have already observed that noise traders earn higher expected returns than sophisticated investors. This at least raises the possibility that their importance does not diminish over time. Our two-period model does not permit us to examine the accumulation of wealth by noise traders. As an alternative approach, we consider two rules describing the emulative behavior of new generations of traders. While it is possible to think of the succession of generations of investors in our model as families, a more relevant image of a new investor entering the market is that of a pension fund searching for a new money manager. Our new investors collect information about the performance of the past generation and decide which strategy to follow. The first approach is to postulate that new investors respond only to recent returns achieved by different investment strategies and are not able to accurately assess the ex ante risks undertaken. For this case, we show that noise traders' effects on prices do not inevitably diminish over time. In our second approach, new investors select their investment strategies on the basis of recent utility levels realized by these strategies. For this case, we show that noise traders' influence necessarily diminishes over time. We stress, however, that even readers preferring the second imitation rule should consider the *empirical* implications of our model. Under the P. T. Barnum rule that a noise trader is born every minute, a steady supply of new noise traders enters the market every period (as in our basic model) even if their strategies are not imitated.

A. *A Model of Imitation Based on Realized Returns without Fundamental Risk*

Each generation of investors earns exogenous labor income when young and consumes all its wealth when old. Each generation has the same number of investors following noise trader and sophisticated investor strategies as the previous one, except a few investors in each generation change type on the basis of the past relative performance of the two strategies. If noise traders earn a higher return in any period, a fraction of the young who would otherwise have been sophisticated investors become noise traders, and vice versa if noise traders earn a lower return. Moreover, the higher the difference in realized returns in any period, the more people switch. Letting μ_t be the share of the population that are noise traders and R_t^n and R_t^s be the realized returns of noise traders and sophisticated investors, we assume that

$$\mu_{t+1} = \max\{0, \min[1, \mu_t + \zeta(R_n - R_i)]\}, \tag{20}$$

where ζ is the rate at which additional new investors become noise traders per unit difference in realized returns.[10]

Equation (20) says that success breeds imitation: investment strategies that made their followers richer win converts. Underlying this imitation rule is the idea that new money entering the market is not completely sure which investment strategy to pursue. If sophisticated investors have earned a high return recently, new investors try to allocate their wealth mimicking sophisticated investors, or perhaps even entrusting their wealth to sophisticated money managers. If noise trader strategies have earned a higher return recently, new investors imitate those strategies to a greater extent. One way to interpret this imitation rule is that *some* new investors use what Black (1986) calls pseudosignals, such as the past return, to decide which strategy to follow.

This model can be easily solved only if ζ is very close to zero. If ζ is significantly different from zero at the scale of any one generation, then those investing in period t have to calculate the effect of the realization of returns on the division of those young in period $t + 1$ between noise traders and sophisticated investors. If ζ is sufficiently small, then returns can be calculated under the approximation that the noise trader share will be unchanged.

Equation (12), the pricing rule with a constant number of noise traders, with μ changed to μ_t, gives the limit as ζ converges to zero of the pricing rule for the model with imitation:

$$p_t = 1 + \frac{\mu_t(\rho_t - \rho^*)}{1 + r} + \frac{\mu_t\rho^*}{r} - \frac{(2\gamma)\mu_t^2\sigma_\rho^2}{r(1 + r)^2}. \tag{21}$$

The expected return gap between noise traders and sophisticated investors is equation (17) when the proportion of noise traders is fixed

[10] An alternative learning rule, studied by Bray (1982), would make the conversion parameter ζ a function of time: $\zeta_t = \zeta_0/t$. Under this alternative conversion rule, the noise trader share would converge to an element of the set $\{0, 1\}$ in the model without fundamental risk and to an element of the set $\{\mu_L, 1\}$ in the model with fundamental risk studied in the following subsection.

at μ. With the proportion μ_t variable, the limit of the expected return gap as ζ converges to zero is given by

$$E_t(\Delta R_{n-i}) = \rho_t - \frac{(1 + r)^2(\rho_t)^2}{(2\gamma)\mu_t\sigma_\rho^2}. \tag{22}$$

Over time, μ_t tends to grow or shrink as (22) is greater or less than zero. It is then clear that although there is a value for μ_t at which $E_t(\mu_{t+1}) = \mu_t$, this value is unstable. As the share of noise traders declines, sophisticated investors' willingness to bet against them rises. Sophisticated investors then earn more money from their exploitation of noise traders' misperceptions, and the gap between the expected returns earned by noise traders and those earned by sophisticated investors becomes negative. If the noise trader share μ_t is below

$$\mu^* = \frac{(\rho^{*2} + \sigma_\rho^2)(1 + r)^2}{2\rho^*(\gamma\sigma_\rho^2)}, \tag{23}$$

then μ_t tends to shrink. If μ_t is greater than μ^*, noise traders create so much price risk as to make sophisticated investors very reluctant to speculate against them. Noise traders then earn higher average returns than sophisticated investors and grow in number. In the long run, noise traders dominate the market or effectively disappear, as shown in figure 1.

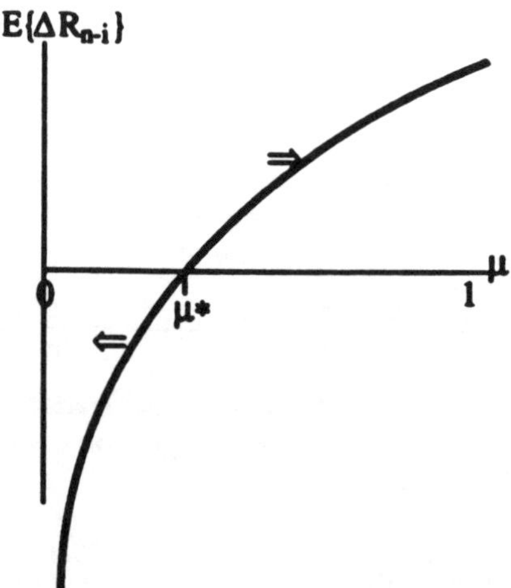

FIG. 1.—Dynamics of the noise trader share with no fundamental risk

B. An Extension with Fundamental Risk

This subsection extends our model of imitation to the case of fundamentally risky returns on the unsafe asset. We show that the long-run distribution of the share of noise traders is very different from the case without fundamental risk. Specifically, for sufficiently small values of ζ, the expected noise trader share for the steady-state distribution of μ_t is always bounded away from zero.

Let asset u pay not a certain dividend r but an uncertain dividend

$$r + \epsilon_t, \tag{24}$$

where ϵ_t is serially independent, normally distributed with zero mean and constant variance, and, for simplicity, uncorrelated with noise traders' opinions ρ_t. Asset demands then become

$$\lambda_t^i = \frac{r + E_t p_{t+1} - (1 + r)p_t}{2\gamma(\sigma_{p_{t+1}}^2 + \sigma_\epsilon^2)} \tag{25}$$

and

$$\lambda_t^n = \frac{r + E_t p_{t+1} - (1 + r)p_t}{2\gamma(\sigma_{p_{t+1}}^2 + \sigma_\epsilon^2)} + \frac{\rho_t}{2\gamma(\sigma_{p_{t+1}}^2 + \sigma_\epsilon^2)} \tag{26}$$

instead of (7) and (8). The only change is the appearance in the denominators of the asset demand functions of the total risk involved from asset u—the sum of noise trader price risk and fundamental dividend risk—instead of simply noise trader–generated price risk.

The pricing function if there is fundamental risk is transformed from (21) into

$$p_t = 1 + \frac{\mu_t \rho^*}{r} - \frac{2\gamma}{r}\left[\sigma_\epsilon^2 + \frac{\mu^2\sigma_\rho^2}{(1 + r)^2}\right] + \frac{\mu_t(\rho_t - \rho^*)}{1 + r} \tag{27}$$

in the limit as ζ converges to zero. The noise trader risk term is replaced by the total risk associated with holding u. The difference between expected returns of noise traders and those of sophisticated investors becomes

$$E[\Delta R_{n-i}(\mu)] = \rho^* - \frac{\rho^{*2} + \sigma_\rho^2}{2\gamma\left[\frac{\sigma_\rho^2\mu}{(1 + r)^2} + \frac{\sigma_\epsilon^2}{\mu}\right]} \tag{28}$$

if μ is greater than zero and

$$E[\Delta R_{n-i}(0)] = \rho^*. \tag{29}$$

While the hold more, average price pressure, and Friedman effects are not changed by the addition of fundamental risk, the create space effect—the denominator of the second term on the right-hand side of (28)—is increased. Since holding asset u is now more risky, sophisticated investors are less willing to trade in order to exploit noise traders' mistakes. We continue to assume that $\zeta = 0$ in the calculation of prices, so that (27) is the pricing rule for this model and (28) is the difference in expected returns.

Equation (12) shows that, in the absence of fundamental risk, a sequence of economies in which μ approaches zero also has $E(\Delta R_{n-i})$ approach negative infinity. By contrast, equation (28) shows that, with fundamental risk present, $E(\Delta R_{n-i})$ approaches ρ^* as μ approaches zero. There is an intuitive explanation for the substantially different dynamics for $\sigma_\epsilon^2 = 0$ and $\sigma_\epsilon^2 > 0$. If $\sigma_\epsilon^2 > 0$, then noise traders' and sophisticated investors' demands remain bounded as μ approaches zero. For a sufficiently small noise trader share, therefore, sophisticated investors must have positive holdings of the risky asset—the very small number of noise traders cannot hold it all—and so the risky asset must offer an expected return higher than the safe rate in equilibrium. If $\sigma_\epsilon^2 = 0$, then noise traders' and sophisticated investors' demands become unbounded as μ approaches zero and the unsafe asset loses its risk. Noise traders' positions then lose them arbitrarily large amounts each period.

For parameter values that satisfy both $\rho^* > 0$ and

$$\sigma_\epsilon^2 > \frac{(1 + r)^2(\rho^* + \sigma_\rho^2)^2}{16\gamma^2\rho^{*2}\sigma_\rho^2}, \tag{30}$$

equation (28) has no real roots and noise traders always earn higher expected returns. In this case, for sufficiently small values of ζ the expected long-run noise trader share is close to one.

For parameter values such that (30) fails, (28) has two positive real roots. If the lower root $\mu_L < 1$, noise traders do not always earn higher expected returns and the expected long-run noise trader share is not in general close to one. For this case, we have proved the following proposition.

PROPOSITION. Let the pricing rule be given by (27) and the imitation rule by (20). Suppose that the equation $E[\Delta R(\mu)] = 0$ has at least one real root for $\mu \in [0, 1]$. Consider a sequence of economies indexed by n, differing only in their values of the imitation parameter ζ_n, such that $\zeta_n \rightarrow 0$ as $n \rightarrow \infty$. Then there is a $\delta > 0$ such that $E(\mu_t) \rightarrow \mu \geq \delta$ as $n \rightarrow \infty$, where the expectation is taken over the steady-state distribution of μ_t.

An appendix containing a proof is available from the authors on request.

When imitation is based on realized returns, for some parameter values the expected noise trader share of the population approaches

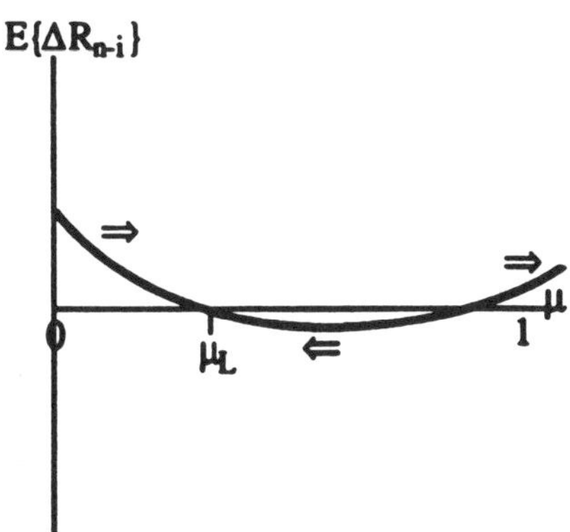

Fig. 2.—Dynamics of the noise trader share with fundamental risk

one as ζ approaches zero. The proposition above shows, and figure 2 illustrates, that if asset u is fundamentally risky, there are no parameter values for which the expected noise trader share of the population approaches zero as ζ becomes small. This result suggests that at least one plausible form of dynamics ensures that noise traders matter and affect prices in the long run.

C. *Imitation Based on Utility*

The imitation rule (20) is based on the assumption that the rate of conversion depends on the difference in realized *returns* and not on the difference in realized *utilities*. It implicitly assumes that converts do not take account of the greater risk that noise traders bear to earn higher returns. This form of imitation requires investors to use past investors' realized returns as a proxy for success even though their own objective is to maximize not wealth but utility.

An alternative imitation rule is to make the number of new noise traders depend on the difference in *utilities* realized last period from sophisticated investor and noise trader strategies. This rule is different from (20): with concave utility, there is more switching away from a strategy in response to past low returns than switching toward a strategy in response to past high returns. Under this imitation rule, the share of noise traders in the economy in fact converges to zero as ζ approaches zero, in contrast to our result under (20). Since sophisticated investors maximize true expected utility, on average the realized utility of a sophisticated investor is higher than the realized utility of a noise trader. That is, under this imitation rule the higher variance of noise traders' returns costs them in terms of winning converts because it costs them in terms of average utility. For each initial state of the system, the noise trader share tends to fall under a utility difference–based imitation rule until it reaches the neighborhood of the reflecting barrier at $\mu = 0$. The expected noise trader share for the steady-state distribution of μ is no longer bounded away from zero as ζ approaches zero.

This alternative rule has considerable appeal in that imitation is based on the realization of agents' true objectives. Nonetheless, there are two reasons to prefer the wealth-based imitation rule (20). First, we find it plausible that many investors attribute the higher return of an investment strategy to the market timing skills of its practitioners and not to its greater risk. This consideration may be particularly important when we ask whether individuals change their own investment strategies that have just earned them a high return. When people imitate investment strategies, they appear to focus on standard metrics such as returns relative to market averages and do not correct for ex ante risk. As long as enough investors use the pseudosignal of realized returns to choose their own investment strategy, noise traders will persist. The second reason to focus on returns-based imitation is that Friedman (1953) argued that noise traders must earn lower average *returns* and so become unimportant. He did not argue that money-making noise traders would fail to attract imitators because potential imitators would attribute their success to luck rather than to skill. Our focus on an imitation rule in which higher wealth wins converts is closer to Friedman's argument.

IV. Noise Trading and Asset Market Behavior

This section describes some implications of our model for financial markets (see also Black 1986). We show that in the presence of noise trader risk, asset returns exhibit the mean reversion documented by a great deal of empirical work, asset prices diverge on average from fundamental values as suggested by Mehra and Prescott (1985) and by the comparison of the portfolio and market values of closed-end mutual funds, and long-term investors stabilize prices. Finally, we discuss the effects of noise trader risk on corporate finance.

A. *Volatility and Mean Reversion in Asset Prices*

In our model with noise traders absent—with both ρ^* and σ_ρ^2 set equal to zero—the price of u is always equal to its fundamental value of one. When noise traders are present, the price of u—identical to s in all fundamental respects—is excessively volatile in the sense that it moves more than can be explained on the basis of changes in fundamental values. None of the variance in the price of u can be justified by changes in fundamentals: there are no changes in expected future dividends in our model or in any fundamental determinant of required returns.

Accumulating evidence suggests that it is difficult to account for all the volatility of asset prices in terms of news. Although Shiller's (1981) claim that the stock market wildly violated variance bounds imposed by the requirement that prices be discounted present values relied on controversial statistical procedures (Kleidon 1986), other evidence that asset price movements do not all reflect changes in fundamental values is more clear-cut. Roll (1984) considers the orange juice futures market, where the principal source of relevant news is weather. He demonstrates that a substantial share of the movement in prices cannot be attributed to news about the weather that bears on fundamental values. Campbell and Kyle (1987) conclude that a large fraction of market movements cannot be attributed to news about future dividends and discount rates.

Such excess volatility becomes even easier to explain if we relax our assumption that all market participants are either noise traders or sophisticated investors who bet against them. A more reasonable assumption is that many traders pursue passive strategies, neither responding to noise nor betting against noise traders. If a large fraction of investors allocate a constant share of their wealth to stocks, then even a small measure of noise traders can have a large impact on prices. When noise traders try to sell, only a few sophisticated investors are willing to hold extra stock, and consequently prices must fall considerably for them to do so. The fewer sophisticated investors there are relative to the noise traders, the larger is the impact of noise.[11]

If asset prices respond to noise and if the errors of noise traders are temporary, then asset prices revert to the mean. For example, if noise traders' misperceptions follow an AR(1) process, then the serial correlation in returns decays geometrically as in the "fads" example of Summers (1986), who stresses that even with long time series it is difficult to detect slowly decaying transitory components in asset prices. Since the same problems of identification that plague econometricians affect speculators, actual market forces are likely to be less effective in limiting the effects of noise trading than in our model, where rational investors fully understand the process governing the behavior of noise traders.

[11] A simple example may help to make our point. Suppose that all investors are convinced that the market is efficient. They will hold the market portfolio. Now suppose that one investor decides to commit his wealth disproportionately to a single security. Its price will be driven to infinity.

Moreover, even if sophisticated investors accurately diagnose the process describing the behavior of noise traders, if misperceptions are serially correlated, they will not be willing to bet nearly as heavily against noise traders: the risk of a capital loss remains and is balanced by a smaller expected return since the next-period price is not expected to move all the way back to its fundamental value. A high unconditional variance of prices can coexist with only a small opportunity to exploit noise traders.

For an example of how rapidly unconditional price variance grows as misperceptions become persistent, assume that misperceptions follow an AR(1) process with innovation η_t and autoregressive parameter ϕ. In this case the unconditional variance of the price of u is[12]

$$\sigma_p^2 = \frac{\mu^2\sigma_\rho^2}{[r + (1 - \phi)]^2} = \frac{\mu^2\sigma_\eta^2}{[r + (1 - \phi)]^2(1 - \phi^2)}. \tag{31}$$

Noise traders who earn higher expected returns than sophisticated investors can thus cause larger deviations of prices from fundamental values if misperceptions are serially correlated. The difference in expected returns is given by

$$E(\Delta R_{n-i}) = \rho^* - \frac{[r + (1 - \phi)]^2(\rho^*)^2}{(2\gamma)\mu\sigma_\eta^2} - \frac{[r + (1 - \phi)]^2}{(2\gamma)\mu(1 - \phi^2)}. \tag{32}$$

Highly persistent transitory components in asset prices can be very large and still consistent with noise traders' earning higher returns than sophisticated investors.

There is significant evidence that stock prices indeed exhibit mean-reverting behavior. Fama and French (1988*b*) and Poterba and Summers (1988) demonstrate that long-horizon stock returns exhibit negative serial correlation. The fact that prices revert to the mean also implies that measures of scale have predictive power for asset returns: when prices are above p^*—that is, are high relative to their historical average multiple of dividends—prices are likely to fall in our model. In fact, Campbell and Shiller (1987), Fama and French (1988*a*), and other studies find that dividend/price and earnings/price ratios appear to contain substantial power for detecting transitory components in stock prices.

Many studies including Mankiw and Summers (1984) and Mankiw

[12] Demand for assets depends not on the unconditional price variances but on the conditional one-step-ahead price risk. The variance of the price of u about its one-step-ahead anticipated value is

$$\sigma_{p_{t+1}}^2 = \frac{\mu^2\sigma_\eta^2}{[r + (1 - \phi)]^2}$$

in the case of serially correlated misperceptions.

(1986) note that anomalies exactly paralleling the dividend/price ratio anomaly are present in the bond market. Long rates have predictive power for future short rates, but it is nonetheless the case that when long rates exceed short rates, they tend to fall and not to rise as predicted by the expectations hypothesis. While convincing stories about changing risk factors are yet to be provided, this behavior is exactly what one would expect if noise trading distorted long bond yields. Specifically, if we think of the short-term bond as asset s and the long-term bond as asset u, then the price of u exhibits the mean-reverting behavior observed in the data on long-term bonds.

In a world with mean-reverting noise traders' misperceptions, the optimal investment strategy is very different from the buy and hold strategy of the standard investment model. The optimal strategy for sophisticated investors is a *market timing* strategy that calls for increased exposure to stocks after they have fallen and decreased exposure to stocks after they have risen in price. The strategy of betting against noise traders is a contrarian investment strategy: it requires investment in the market at times when noise traders are bearish, in anticipation that their sentiment will recover. The fundamentalist investment strategies of Graham and Dodd (1934) seem to be based on largely the same idea, although they are typically described in terms of individual stocks. The evidence on mean reversion in stock returns suggests that, over the long run, such contrarian strategies pay off.

As our model shows, successful pursuit of such contrarian investment strategies can require a long time horizon, and such strategies are by no means safe because of the noise trader risk that must be run (see the quotation from Keynes at the beginning of this article). In fact, our model shows precisely why apparent anomalies such as the high dollar of the mid 1980s and the extraordinary price/earnings ratios on Japanese stocks in 1987–89 can persist for so long even when many investors recognize these anomalies. Betting against such perceived mispricing requires bearing a lot of risk. Even if the price is too high now, it can always go higher in the short run, leading to the demise of an arbitrageur with limited resources or a short time horizon.

Contrarian investment strategies work because arbitrageurs can take advantage of mean reversion in noise traders' beliefs. An alternative rational investment strategy would be to gather information about future noise trader demand shifts and to trade in anticipation of such shifts. Such information can come from examining trading volume, price patterns, buy/sell ratios, and other "chartist" indicators. Trading based on forecasting the behavior of others is not modeled here, but we consider it elsewhere (De Long et al. 1990). With short horizons, it may well be more attractive for smart money to pursue these anticipatory strategies than to wait for the reversion of noise traders' beliefs to their mean (Shleifer and Vishny 1990). In this case, we anticipate that many sophisticated investors will try to "guess better than the crowd how the crowd will behave" rather than pursue contrarian long-term arbitrage.

B. *Asset Prices and Fundamental Values: Closed-End Mutual Funds*

The efficient markets hypothesis states that assets ought to sell for their fundamental values. In most cases, fundamental value is difficult to measure, and so this prediction cannot be directly tested. But the fundamental value of a closed-end fund is easily assessed: the fund pays dividends equal to the sum of the dividends paid by the stocks in its portfolio and so should sell for the market price of its portfolio. Yet closed-end funds sell and have sold at large and substantially fluctuating discounts (Malkiel 1977; Herzfeld 1980), which have been relatively small during the bull markets of the late 1960s and the 1980s and large during the bear markets of the 1970s.

Available explanations of discounts on closed-end funds are not completely satisfactory. Two of the most prominent explanations rely on the agency costs of fund management and on the miscalculation of net asset value because of a failure to deduct the fund's capital gains tax liability. The agency theory for discounts, however, cannot explain how closed-end funds are ever rationally formed since the original investors throw away the present value of future agency costs without earning higher returns. The agency explanation is also inconsistent with the evidence that funds with higher transaction costs and stock turnover do not sell at higher discounts (Malkiel 1977) and with the correlated variability of discounts across funds (Herzfeld 1980). With respect to tax-based theories, Brauer (1984) and Brickley and Schallheim (1985) find that prices of closed-end funds rise on the announcement of open-ending or of liquidation. This result is difficult to interpret if the closed-end fund's discount reflects its unrealized capital gain tax liability since, if anything, discounts should *widen* when the fund is open-ended and tax payments can no longer be deferred. Nor can the capital gains story explain how funds trade at a premium when they get started.

The concept of noise trader risk can explain both the persistent and variable discounts on closed-end funds and the creation of such funds.[13] Think of the safe asset s in our model as the stocks in the closed-end fund and of the unsafe asset u as the fund itself. As in our

[13] It does not explain why such funds are not broken up immediately once a discount appears.

model, the two securities are perfect substitutes as far as dividends are concerned and so should sell at the same price in equilibrium without noise traders. Note that it does not matter for our purposes if there is noise trading in the stocks themselves and therefore a mispricing of s as well. All we need is additional noise trader misperception of returns on the closed-end fund u that is separate from their misperception of returns on the underlying stocks. Finally, we need to assume that noise traders' misperceptions of returns on closed-end funds are correlated with other (possibly irrational) sources of systematic risk since idiosyncratic noise trader risk is not priced in our model.

Under these assumptions, the results from our basic model can be directly applied to closed-end funds. Noise traders' misperceptions about the returns on the funds become a source of risk for any short-horizon investor trying to arbitrage the difference between the fund and its underlying assets. Thus when an investor buys the fund u and sells short the underlying stocks s, he bears the risk that at the time he wants to liquidate his position the discount will be wider. Just as in our model, noise traders can become more bearish on the fund in the future than they are today, and so an arbitrageur will suffer a loss. Such risk of changes in noise traders' opinions of closed-end funds leads to the market's discounting of their price on average relative to the net asset value even if noise traders themselves are neither bullish nor bearish on average, that is, $\rho^* = 0$. The discount arises solely because holding the fund entails additional noise trader risk: we do not assume that noise traders are on average bearish about closed-end funds.[14]

This theory of discounts on closed-end funds makes several accurate predictions. First, it explains how the funds can get started even when on average they will be underpriced. Closed-end funds get started when noise traders are unusually optimistic about the returns

[14] One can see how the fact that closed-end fund shares are subject not only to fundamental risk (risk affecting the value of the fund's portfolio) but also to noise trader risk (risk that the closed-end fund discount might change) affects investment decisions in the investment advice given by Malkiel (1973, 1975, 1985, 1989). He confidently recommended in 1973 that investors purchase then heavily discounted (20–30 percent) closed-end fund shares: such an investor would do better than by picking stocks or investing in an open-end fund unless "the discount widened in the future." The confidence of Malkiel's recommendation stemmed from his belief that "this . . . risk is minimized . . . [since] discounts [now] . . . are about as large as they have ever been historically" (1975, p. 263). And the obverse is his belief that the holder of a closed-end fund should be prepared to sell if the discount narrowed, not only if the discount disappeared, but also if the discount narrowed. The 4th ed. of *A Random Walk down Wall Street* does not recommend the purchase of closed-end fund shares in spite of the fact that many closed-end funds still sell at discounts. The noise trader risk that discounts may widen again in the future is a disadvantage that apparently weighs heavily against the relatively small advantages given by the small then-current discount. The 5th ed. once again recommends the purchase of closed-end funds now that the discount has widened.

on closed-end funds, that is, when ρ_t *for the funds* is unusually high. In such a case, it would pay entrepreneurs to buy stocks (asset s), repackage them as closed-end funds (asset u), and sell the closed-end funds to optimistic noise traders at a premium. This result has the implication, which has not yet been tested, that new closed-end funds are formed in clusters at the times when other closed-end funds sell at a premium.

The fluctuations in noise trader opinion of the expected return on the funds also explain why the discounts fluctuate, widening at some times and turning into premiums at others (when the funds get started). Fluctuations in discounts are in fact the reason that there is an average discount. No other theory of discounts predicts that closed-end funds sometimes sell at a premium, that changes in discounts are correlated across funds, or that new funds are started when old closed-end funds sell at a premium.

Two key assumptions must be made for this theory of closed-end fund discounts to be coherent. First, noise trader risk on the funds should be systematic and not idiosyncratic. Consistent with this assumption, discounts on different closed-end funds do seem to fluctuate together (Herzfeld 1980). Second, investors in the economy must have horizons that are with some probability shorter than the time to liquidation of the fund. If some investors on the contrary have very long horizons, they can buy the closed-end fund and sell short the underlying securities, wait until the fund is liquidated, and so lock in a capital gain without bearing any risk. Consistent with this observation, discounts become much narrower on the announcement of the open-ending of a closed-end fund (Brauer 1984). The application of our model to closed-end funds illustrates the essential role played by the finite horizon of investors.

C. *Asset Prices and Fundamental Values: The Mehra-Prescott Puzzle*

In our model, if noise traders earn higher expected returns than sophisticated investors, then the average price of u must be below its fundamental value. The expected value of p_t is

$$E(p) = p^* = 1 - \frac{2\gamma\mu\sigma_\rho^2}{r(1+r)^2} + \frac{\mu\rho^*}{r}. \tag{33}$$

Since noise traders hold more of the risky asset and earn negative capital gains on average, they can earn higher expected returns than sophisticated investors only if the dividend on the unsafe asset amounts to a higher rate of return on average than the same dividend on the safe asset. For this to hold, the unsafe asset must sell at an average price below its fundamental value of one.

The result that noise traders earn a higher expected return whenever the unsafe asset is priced below its fundamental value may shed some light on the well-known Mehra-Prescott puzzle. Mehra and Prescott (1985) show that the realized average return on U.S. equities over the last 60 years has been around 8 percent, and the realized real return on safe bonds only around zero. Such a risk premium seems to be inconsistent with the standard representative consumer model applied to U.S. data unless that consumer has an implausibly large coefficient of risk aversion.

If we interpret asset u in our model as the aggregate stock market and asset s as short-term bonds, our model can shed light on the Mehra-Prescott puzzle. Since noise trader risk drives down the price of u, equities yield a higher return in our model than the riskless asset does. Moreover, this difference in yields obtains despite the fact that aggregate consumption does not vary too much with the expected return on equities. The reason is that the consumption of sophisticated investors satisfies the Euler equation with respect to the true distribution of expected returns exactly, but the consumption of noise traders does not. In fact, the share of wealth invested (and thus not consumed) by noise traders is low when the true expected return is high, and high when the true expected return is low. The presence of noise traders thus makes aggregate consumption less sensitive to the variation of true expected returns than it should be. A large equity premium can thus coexist with a low covariance of returns on equities with aggregate consumption. Although the mechanics of our model are very different from the model in Ingram (1987), this particular implication works similarly to her explanation of the equity premium, which relies on the insensitivity of the consumption of a group of rule-of-thumb agents to expected returns.

It is important to stress that our model sheds light on the Mehra-Prescott puzzle only if equities are underpriced, which is itself a necessary condition for noise traders to earn higher expected returns. In other words, the fact that the Mehra-Prescott equity premium obtains in an economy is evidence for the proposition that the expected returns of noise traders are likely to be higher than those of sophisticated investors. In the context of our model, the existence of an equity premium in the U.S. economy suggests that American noise traders are on average bullish on the assets that they disturb and may earn higher average returns than American arbitrageurs.

D. *Long Horizons*

Noise trader risk makes coherent a widely held view of the relative social merits of "speculation" and "investment" that has found little academic sympathy. Many participants in financial markets have argued that the presence of traders who are looking for only short-term profits is socially destructive. The standard economist's refutation of this argument relies on recursion: If one seeks to buy a stock now to sell in an hour, one must calculate its price in an hour. But its price in an hour depends on what those who will purchase it think its price will be a further hour down the road. Anyone who buys an asset, no matter how short the holding period, must perform the same present value calculation as someone who intends to hold the asset for 50 years. Since a linked chain of short-term "traders" performs the same assessment of values as a single "investor," the claim that trading is bad and investing good cannot be correct. Prices will be unaffected by the horizon of the agent as long as the rate of discount and willingness to bear risk are unchanged.

In our model this analysis does not apply. The horizon of agents matters. If agents live for more than two periods, the equilibrium is closer to the "fundamental" equilibrium than if agents live for two periods. As an example, consider an infinitesimal measure of infinitely lived but risk-averse sophisticated traders. Suppose that p_t is less than one. An infinitely lived agent can sell short a unit of s and buy a unit of u. He collects a gain of $1 - p_t$, and he has incurred no liability in any state of the world. The dividend on u will always offset the dividend owed on s. The fact that an infinitely lived agent can arbitrage assets s and u without ever facing a settlement date implies that any infinitely lived sophisticated investor could push the price of u to its fundamental value of one.

Although arbitrage is not riskless for long but finite-lived agents, their asset demands are more responsive to price movements than those of two-period-lived agents. There are two reasons for this. First, even if an $n > 2$ period-lived sophisticated investor can liquidate his position in asset u only in the last period of his life, he bears the same amount of resale price risk as his two-period-lived counterpart but gets some insurance from dividends. If, for example, he buys an undervalued asset u, he receives a high dividend yield for several periods before he sells. Because as the horizon expands so does the share of dividends in expected returns, agents with longer horizons buy more at the start. Second, a long-lived sophisticated investor has in fact many periods to liquidate his position. Since he makes money on arbitrage if the price reverts to the mean at any time before his death, having several opportunities to liquidate reduces his risk. For these two reasons, raising sophisticated investors' horizons makes them more aggressive and brings the price of u closer to fundamentals.

The embedding of the financial market in an overlapping generations model in which agents die after two periods is a device to give rational utility maximizers short horizons. This device may adequately model institutional features of asset markets—triennial performance evaluations of pension fund money managers, for example—that may lead even fully rational agents to have short horizons. Realistically, even an agent with a horizon long in terms of time may have a horizon "short" in the context of this model. If dividend risk is great enough and if noise trader misperceptions are persistent, then agents might well find it unattractive to buy stocks and hold them for a long time hoping that the market someday recognizes their value. For in the meantime, during which the assets might have to be sold, market prices may deviate even further from fundamental values. The claim that short horizons are bad for the economy is both coherent and true in our model.

E. *Observations on Corporate Finance*

Throughout this paper, we have focused on the implications of marketwide noise trader risk. The reason is that in our model, just as in a standard asset valuation model, idiosyncratic risk is unpriced. A number of implications of noise trading, however, including those stressed by Black (1986), rely on misperceptions of firm-specific returns. To allow such idiosyncratic misperceptions to matter, the model must include transactions costs that limit the universe of stocks that each sophisticated investor holds (Mayshar 1983). Although such a model is beyond the scope of this paper, we mention a few issues that idiosyncratic risk raises in the context of corporate finance.

In a model with noise traders the Modigliani-Miller theorem does not necessarily apply. To see this, consider the standard homemade leverage proof of the theorem. This proof demonstrates that a rational investor can undo any effects of firm leverage and maintain the same real position regardless of a firm's payout policy. It does not suggest that less than rational traders will do so. Given that noise traders in general affect prices, it follows that unless they happen to trade so as to undo the effects of changes in leverage, the Modigliani-Miller theorem will not hold.

It is plausible to think that noise traders do not get confused about the value of assets that have a certain and immediate liquidation value. Noise traders are more likely to become confused about assets that offer fundamentally risky payouts in the distant future. Assets of long duration that promise fundamentally uncertain as opposed to immediate and certain cash payouts may thus be subject to an especially great amount of noise trader risk. In this case, a firm might choose to pay dividends rather than reinvest even if there are tax costs to dividends. If dividends make equity look more like a safe short-term bond to noise traders, then paying dividends can reduce the total amount of noise trader risk borne by a firm's securities. Paying dividends might raise the value of equity if the reduction in the discount entailed by noise trader risk exceeds additional shareholder tax liability. Moreover, dividends are not equivalent to share repurchases unless *noise traders* perceive the two to be complete substitutes. If investors believe that future stock repurchases are of uncertain value because noise traders disturb the price of equity, then the equity of a firm repurchasing shares can be subject to greater undervaluation than that of a firm paying dividends. A bird in the hand is truly better than one in the bush.

Jensen (1986) summarizes evidence showing that the more constrained the allocation of the firm's cash flows, the higher its valuation by the market. For example, share prices rise when a firm raises dividends, swaps debt for equity, or buys back shares. In contrast, share prices fall when a firm cuts dividends or issues new shares. These results are consistent with our model if making the returns to equity more determinate reduces the noise trader risk that it bears. Increases in dividends that make equity look safer to noise traders may reduce noise trader risk and raise share prices. Swaps of debt for equity have the same effect, as do share buybacks. As long as a change in capital structure convinces noise traders that a firm's total capital is more like asset s and less like asset u than they had previously thought, changes in capital structure raise value.

The discussion above suggests that noise trader risk is a cost that an issuer of a security that will be publicly traded must bear. Both traded equity and traded long-term debt will be underpriced relative to fundamentals if their prices are subject to the whims of noise traders' opinions. Why then are securities traded publicly? Put differently, why don't all firms go private to avoid noise trader risk? Presumably firms have publicly traded securities if the benefits, such as a broader base from which to draw capital, a larger pool to use to diversify systematic risk, and liquidity, exceed the costs of the noise trader–generated undervaluation. Assets for which these benefits of public ownership are the highest relative to the costs of noise trader risk are the assets that will be issued into markets with public trading. While the issuers of these securities will try to minimize the costs of noise trader risk by "packaging" the securities appropriately, they will not be able to eliminate such risk entirely.

V. Conclusion

We have shown that risk created by the unpredictability of unsophisticated investors' opinions significantly reduces the attractiveness of arbitrage. As long as arbitrageurs have short horizons and so must worry about liquidating their investment in a mispriced asset, their aggressiveness will be limited even in the absence of fundamental risk. In this case noise trading can lead to a large divergence between market prices and fundamental values. Moreover, noise traders may be compensated for bearing the risk that they themselves create and so earn higher returns than sophisticated investors even though they distort prices. As we discuss in the paper, this result at the least calls for a closer scrutiny of the standard argument that destabilizing speculation must be unprofitable and so noise traders will not persist in the market.

This paper has also argued that a number of financial market anomalies can be explained by the idea of noise trader risk. These anomalies include the excess volatility of and mean reversion in stock market prices, the failure of the expectations hypothesis of the term structure, the Mehra-Prescott equity premium, the undervaluation of closed-end mutual funds, and several others. The essential assumption we use is that the opinions of noise traders are unpredictable and arbitrage requires bearing the risk that their misperceptions become even more extreme tomorrow than they are today. Since "unpredictability" seems to be a general property of the behavior of irrational investors, we believe that our conclusions are not simply a consequence of a particular parameterization of noise trader actions.

Our model suggests that much of the behavior of professional arbitrageurs can be seen as a response to noise trading rather than as trading on fundamentals. Many professional arbitrageurs spend their resources examining and predicting the pseudosignals noise traders follow in order to bet against them more successfully. These pseudosignals include volume and price patterns, sentiment indices, and the forecasts of Wall Street gurus. Just as it pays entrepreneurs to build casinos to exploit gamblers, it pays rational investors to spend considerable resources to exploit noise traders. In both cases, private returns to the activity probably exceed social returns.

Our focus on irrationality in financial markets departs from that of earlier studies of rational but heterogeneously informed investors (Grossman and Stiglitz 1980; Townsend 1983; Varian 1986; Stein 1987). Many of the results in this paper could perhaps be derived using a fully rational model with differentially informed investors, provided that one gets away from the "no-trade" theorems (Milgrom and Stokey 1982).

Apart from the question of tractability, we have focused on models of irrationality for three reasons. First, in the context of fluctuations in the aggregate market, we find the idea of privately informed investors somewhat implausible. While one can always think of a person's opinion as private information, this seems like playing with words. Speaking of the private information of a market timer like Joe Granville—who himself insists that he has a "system" rather than an informational advantage—makes little sense to us. Second, given the traditional argument that the stock market price aggregates information and opinions, it is important to examine the extent to which there is a tendency of prices to reflect "good" rather than "bad" opinions. Even more than Figlewski's (1979) result that "bad" opinions can influence market prices for a long time, our paper suggests skepticism about the long-run irrelevance of "bad" opinions. Third, our analysis illustrates the point that studying irrational behavior does not always require specifying its content. We have shown that something can be learned about financial markets simply by looking at the effect of *unpredictability* of irrational behavior on the opportunities of rational investors. The idea of noise trader risk is much more general than our particular examples. In future research, it would be valuable to consider asset markets with more primitive descriptions of irrationality. One advantage of such an approach would be to generate more restrictive predictions that are easier to reject.

References

Alpert, Marc, and Raiffa, Howard. "A Progress Report on the Training of Probability Assessors." In *Judgment under Uncertainty: Heuristics and Biases,* edited by Daniel Kahneman, Paul Slovic, and Amos Tversky. Cambridge: Cambridge Univ. Press, 1982.

Black, Fischer. "Noise." *J. Finance* 41 (July 1986): 529–43.

Brauer, Gregory A. " 'Open-ending' Closed-End Funds." *J. Financial Econ.* 13 (December 1984): 491–507.

Bray, Margaret M. "Learning, Estimation, and the Stability of Rational Expectations." *J. Econ. Theory* 26 (April 1982): 318–39.

Brickley, James A., and Schallheim, James S. "Lifting the Lid on Closed-End Investment Companies: A Case of Abnormal Returns." *J. Financial and Quantitative Analysis* 20 (March 1985): 107–17.

Campbell, John Y., and Kyle, Albert. "Smart Money, Noise Trading, and Stock Price Behavior." Manuscript. Princeton, N.J.: Princeton Univ., 1987.

Campbell, John Y., and Shiller, Robert J. "Cointegration and Tests of Present Value Models." *J.P.E* 95 (October 1987): 1062–88.

De Long, J. Bradford; Shleifer, Andrei; Summers, Lawrence H.; and Waldmann, Robert J. "Noise Trader Risk in Financial Markets." Working Paper no. 2395. Cambridge, Mass.: NBER, October 1987.

———. "The Survival of Noise Traders in Financial Markets." Working Paper no. 2715. Cambridge, Mass.: NBER, September 1988.

———. "The Size and Incidence of the Losses from Noise Trading." *J. Finance* 44 (July 1989): 681–96.

———. "Positive Feedback Investment Strategies and Destabilizing Rational Speculation." *J. Finance* 45 (June 1990).

Denton, Frank T. "The Effect of Professional Advice on the Stability of a Speculative Market." *J.P.E.* 93 (October 1985): 977–93.

Fama, Eugene F. "The Behavior of Stock Market Prices." *J. Bus.* 38 (January 1965): 34–105.

Fama, Eugene F., and French, Kenneth R. "Dividend Yields and Expected Stock Returns." *J. Financial Econ.* 22 (October 1988): 3–25. (*a*)

———. "Permanent and Temporary Components of Stock Prices." *J.P.E.* 96 (April 1988): 246–73. (*b*)

Figlewski, Stephen. "Subjective Information and Market Efficiency in a Betting Market." *J.P.E.* 87 (February 1979): 75–88.

Friedman, Milton. "The Case for Flexible Exchange Rates." In *Essays in Positive Economics.* Chicago: Univ. Chicago Press, 1953.

Graham, Benjamin, and Dodd, David L. *Security Analysis.* New York: McGraw-Hill, 1934.

Grossman, Sanford J., and Stiglitz, Joseph E. "On the Impossibility of Informationally Efficient Markets." *A.E.R.* 70 (June 1980): 393–408.

Haltiwanger, John C., and Waldman, Michael. "Rational Expectations and the Limits of Rationality: An Analysis of Heterogeneity." *A.E.R.* 75 (June 1985): 326–40.

Hart, Oliver D., and Kreps, David M. "Price Destabilizing Speculation." *J.P.E.* 94 (October 1986): 927–52.

Herzfeld, Thomas J. *The Investor's Guide to Closed-End Funds: The Herzfeld Edge.* New York: McGraw-Hill, 1980.

Ingram, Beth Fisher. "Equilibrium Modelling of Asset Prices: Rationality v. Rules of Thumb." Manuscript. Ithaca, N.Y.: Cornell Univ., 1987.

Jensen, Michael C. "The Performance of Mutual Funds in the Period 1945–1964." *J. Finance* 23 (May 1968): 389–416.

———. "Agency Costs of Free Cash Flow, Corporate Finance, and Takeovers." *A.E.R. Papers and Proc.* 76 (May 1986): 323–29.

Keynes, John Maynard. *The General Theory of Employment, Interest and Money.* London: Macmillan, 1936.

Kleidon, Allan W. "Anomalies in Financial Economics: Blueprint for Change?" *J. Bus.* 59, no. 4, pt. 2 (October 1986): S469–S499.

Kyle, Albert S. "Continuous Auctions and Insider Trading." *Econometrica* 53 (November 1985): 1315–35.

Lewellen, Wilbur G.; Schlarbaum, Gary E.; and Lease, Ronald C. "The Individual Investor: Attributes and Attitudes." *J. Finance* 29 (May 1974): 413–33.

Malkiel, Burton G. *A Random Walk down Wall Street.* New York: Norton, 1973; 2d ed., 1975; 4th ed., 1985; 5th ed., 1989.

———. "The Valuation of Closed-End Investment-Company Shares." *J. Finance* 32 (June 1977): 847–59.

Mankiw, N. Gregory. "The Term Structure of Interest Rates Revisited." *Brookings Papers Econ. Activity,* no. 1 (1986), pp. 61–110.

Mankiw, N. Gregory, and Summers, Lawrence H. "Do Long-Term Interest Rates Overreact to Short-Term Interest Rates?" *Brookings Papers Econ. Activity,* no. 1 (1984), pp. 223–42.

Mayshar, Joram. "On Divergence of Opinion and Imperfections in Capital Markets." *A.E.R.* 73 (March 1983): 114–28.

Mehra, Rajnish, and Prescott, Edward C. "The Equity Premium: A Puzzle." *J. Monetary Econ.* 15 (March 1985): 145–61.

Milgrom, Paul, and Stokey, Nancy. "Information, Trade and Common Knowledge." *J. Econ. Theory* 26 (February 1982): 17–27.

Poterba, James M., and Summers, Lawrence H. "Mean Reversion in Stock Prices: Evidence and Implications." *J. Financial Econ.* 22 (October 1988): 27–59.

Roll, Richard. "Orange Juice and Weather." *A.E.R.* 74 (December 1984): 861–80.

Russell, Thomas, and Thaler, Richard H. "The Relevance of Quasi Rationality in Competitive Markets." *A.E.R.* 75 (December 1985): 1071–82.

Samuelson, Paul A. "An Exact Consumption-Loan Model of Interest with or without the Social Contrivance of Money." *J.P.E.* 66 (December 1958): 467–82.

Shiller, Robert J. "Do Stock Prices Move Too Much to Be Justified by Subsequent Changes in Dividends?" *A.E.R.* 71 (June 1981): 421–36.

———. "Stock Prices and Social Dynamics." *Brookings Papers Econ. Activity*, no. 2 (1984), pp. 457–98.

Shleifer, Andrei, and Vishny, Robert. "Equilibrium Short Horizons of Investors and Firms." *A.E.R. Papers and Proc.* 80 (May 1990).

Stein, Jeremy C. "Informational Externalities and Welfare-reducing Speculation." *J.P.E.* 95 (December 1987): 1123–45.

Summers, Lawrence H. "Does the Stock Market Rationally Reflect Fundamental Values?" *J. Finance* 41 (July 1986): 591–601.

Townsend, Robert M. "Forecasting the Forecasts of Others." *J.P.E.* 91 (August 1983): 546–88.

Varian, Hal. "Differences of Opinion and the Volume of Trade." Manuscript. Ann Arbor: Univ. Michigan, 1986.

[13]

ELSEVIER Journal of Financial Economics 49 (1998) 283–306

Market efficiency, long-term returns, and behavioral finance[1]

Eugene F. Fama*

Graduate School of Business, University of Chicago, Chicago, IL 60637, USA

Received 17 March 1997; received in revised form 3 October 1997

Abstract

Market efficiency survives the challenge from the literature on long-term return anomalies. Consistent with the market efficiency hypothesis that the anomalies are chance results, apparent overreaction to information is about as common as underreaction, and post-event continuation of pre-event abnormal returns is about as frequent as post-event reversal. Most important, consistent with the market efficiency prediction that apparent anomalies can be due to methodology, most long-term return anomalies tend to disappear with reasonable changes in technique. © 1998 Elsevier Science S.A. All rights reserved.

JEL classification: G14; G12

Keywords: Market efficiency; Behavioral finance

1. Introduction

Event studies, introduced by Fama et al. (1969), produce useful evidence on how stock prices respond to information. Many studies focus on returns in a short window (a few days) around a cleanly dated event. An advantage of this approach is that because daily expected returns are close to zero, the model for expected returns does not have a big effect on inferences about abnormal returns.

* Corresponding author. Tel.: 773 702 7282; fax: 773 702 9937; e-mail: eugene.fama@gsb.uchicago.edu.

[1] The comments of Brad Barber, David Hirshleifer, S.P. Kothari, Owen Lamont, Mark Mitchell, Hersh Shefrin, Robert Shiller, Rex Sinquefield, Richard Thaler, Theo Vermaelen, Robert Vishny, Ivo Welch, and a referee have been helpful. Kenneth French and Jay Ritter get special thanks.

PII S0304-405X(98)00026-9

The assumption in studies that focus on short return windows is that any lag in the response of prices to an event is short-lived. There is a developing literature that challenges this assumption, arguing instead that stock prices adjust slowly to information, so one must examine returns over long horizons to get a full view of market inefficiency.

If one accepts their stated conclusions, many of the recent studies on long-term returns suggest market inefficiency, specifically, long-term underreaction or overreaction to information. It is time, however, to ask whether this literature, viewed as a whole, suggests that efficiency should be discarded. My answer is a solid no, for two reasons.

First, an efficient market generates categories of events that individually suggest that prices over-react to information. But in an efficient market, apparent underreaction will be about as frequent as overreaction. If anomalies split randomly between underreaction and overreaction, they are consistent with market efficiency. We shall see that a roughly even split between apparent overreaction and underreaction is a good description of the menu of existing anomalies.

Second, and more important, if the long-term return anomalies are so large they cannot be attributed to chance, then an even split between over- and underreaction is a pyrrhic victory for market efficiency. We shall find, however, that the long-term return anomalies are sensitive to methodology. They tend to become marginal or disappear when exposed to different models for expected (normal) returns or when different statistical approaches are used to measure them. Thus, even viewed one-by-one, most long-term return anomalies can reasonably be attributed to chance.

A problem in developing an overall perspective on long-term return studies is that they rarely test a specific alternative to market efficiency. Instead, the alternative hypothesis is vague, market inefficiency. This is unacceptable. Like all models, market efficiency (the hypothesis that prices fully reflect available information) is a faulty description of price formation. Following the standard scientific rule, however, market efficiency can only be replaced by a better specific model of price formation, itself potentially rejectable by empirical tests.

Any alternative model has a daunting task. It must specify biases in information processing that cause the same investors to under-react to some types of events and over-react to others. The alternative must also explain the range of observed results better than the simple market efficiency story; that is, the expected value of abnormal returns is zero, but chance generates deviations from zero (anomalies) in both directions.

Since the anomalies literature has not settled on a specific alternative to market efficiency, to get the ball rolling, I assume reasonable alternatives must choose between overreaction or underreaction. Using this perspective, Section 2 reviews existing studies, without questioning their inferences. My conclusion is that, viewed as a whole, the long-term return literature does not identify overreaction or underreaction as the dominant phenomenon. The random split predicted by market efficiency holds up rather well.

Two recent papers, Barberis et al. (1998) and Daniel et al. (1997), present behavioral models that accommodate overreaction and underreaction. To their credit, these models present rejectable hypotheses. Section 3 argues that, not surprisingly, the two behavioral models work well on the anomalies they are designed to explain. Other anomalies are, however, embarrassing. The problem is that both models predict post-event return reversals in response to long-term pre-event abnormal returns. In fact, post-event return continuation is about as frequent as reversal – a result that is more consistent with market efficiency than with the two behavioral models.

Section 4 examines the problems in drawing inferences about long-term returns. Foremost is an unavoidable bad-model problem. Market efficiency must be tested jointly with a model for expected (normal) returns, and all models show problems describing average returns. The bad-model problem is ubiquitous, but it is more serious in long-term returns. The reason is that bad-model errors in expected returns grow faster with the return horizon than the volatility of returns. Section 4 also argues that theoretical and statistical considerations alike suggest that formal inferences about long-term returns should be based on averages or sums of short-term abnormal returns (AARs or CARs) rather than the currently popular buy-and-hold abnormal returns (BHARs).

In categorizing studies on long-term returns, Sections 2 and 3 do not question their inferences. Dissection of individual studies takes place in Section 5. The bottom line is that the evidence against market efficiency from the long-term return studies is fragile. Reasonable changes in the approach used to measure abnormal returns typically suggest that apparent anomalies are methodological illusions.

2. Overreaction and underreaction: An overview

One of the first papers on long-term return anomalies is DeBondt and Thaler (1985). They find that when stocks are ranked on three- to five-year past returns, past winners tend to be future losers, and vice versa. They attribute these long-term return reversals to investor overreaction. In forming expectations, investors give too much weight to the past performance of firms and too little to the fact that performance tends to mean-revert. DeBondt and Thaler seem to argue that overreaction to past information is a general prediction of the behavioral decision theory of Kahneman and Tversky (1982). Thus, one could take overreaction to be the prediction of a behavioral finance alternative to market efficiency. For the most part, however, the anomalies literature has not accepted the discipline of an alternative hypothesis.

An exception is Lakonishok et al. (1994). They argue that ratios involving stock prices proxy for past performance. Firms with high ratios of earnings to price (E/P), cashflow to price (C/P), and book-to-market equity (BE/ME) tend to have poor past earnings growth, and firms with low E/P, C/P, and BE/ME tend to have strong past earnings growth. Because the market over-reacts to past growth, it is surprised when earnings growth mean reverts. As a result, high E/P, C/P, and BE/ME stocks (poor past performers) have high future returns, and low E/P, C/P, and BE/ME stocks (strong past performers) have low future returns.

I also classify the poor long-term post-event returns of initial public offerings (IPOs) (Ritter, 1991; Loughran and Ritter, 1995) and seasoned equity offerings (SEOs) (Loughran and Ritter, 1995; Spiess and Affleck-Graves, 1995) in the overreaction camp. Mitchell and Stafford (1997) show that SEOs have strong stock returns in the three years prior to the issue. It seems safe to presume that these strong returns reflect strong earnings. It also seems safe to presume that IPOs have strong past earnings to display when going public. If the market does not understand that earnings growth tends to mean revert, stock prices at the time of the equity issue (IPO or SEO) are too high. If the market only gradually recognizes its mistakes, the overreaction to past earnings growth is corrected slowly in the future. Finally, Dharan and Ikenberry (1995) argue that the long-term negative post-listing abnormal stock returns of firms that newly list on the NYSE or Amex are due to overreaction. Firms list their stocks to take advantage of the market's overreaction to their recent strong performance.

If apparent overreaction was the general result in studies of long-term returns, market efficiency would be dead, replaced by the behavioral alternative of DeBondt and Thaler (1985). In fact, apparent underreaction is about as frequent. The granddaddy of underreaction events is the evidence that stock prices seem to respond to earnings for about a year after they are announced (Ball and Brown, 1968; Bernard and Thomas, 1990). More recent is the momentum effect identified by Jegadeesh and Titman (1993); stocks with high returns over the past year tend to have high returns over the following three to six months.

Other recent event studies also produce long-term post-event abnormal returns that suggest underreaction. Cusatis et al. (1993) find positive post-event abnormal returns for divesting firms and the firms they divest. They attribute the result to market underreaction to an enhanced probability that, after a spinoff, both the parent and the spinoff are likely to become merger targets, and the recipients of premiums. Desai and Jain (1997) and Ikenberry et al. (1996) find that firms that split their stock experience long-term positive abnormal returns both before and after the split. They attribute the post-split returns to market underreaction to the positive information signaled by a split. Lakonishok and Vermaelen (1990) find positive long-term post-event abnormal returns when firms tender for their stock. Ikenberry et al. (1995) observe similar results for open-market share repurchases. The story in both cases is that the market under-reacts to the positive signal in share repurchases about future performance. Finally, Michaely et al. (1995) find that stock prices seem to under-react to the negative information in dividend omissions and the positive information in initiations.

Some long-term return anomalies are difficult to classify. For example, Asquith (1983) and Agrawal et al. (1992) find negative long-term abnormal returns to acquiring firms following mergers. This might be attributed to market underreaction to a poor investment decision (Roll, 1986) or overreaction to the typically strong performance of acquiring firms in advance of mergers, documented in Mitchell and Stafford (1997). Ikenberry and Lakonishok (1993) find negative post-event abnormal returns for firms involved in proxy contests. One story is that stock prices under-react to the poor performance of these firms before the proxy contest, but another is that prices over-react to the information in a proxy that something is likely to change.

Given the ambiguities in classifying some anomalies, and given that the review above is surely incomplete, I shall not do a count of underreaction versus overreaction studies. The important point is that the literature does not lean cleanly toward either as the behavioral alternative to market efficiency. This is not lost on behavioral finance researchers who acknowledge the issue:

> We hope future research will help us understand why the market appears to overreact in some circumstances and underreact in others. (Michaely et al., 1995, p. 606).

The market efficiency hypothesis offers a simple answer to this question – chance. Specifically, the expected value of abnormal returns is zero, but chance generates apparent anomalies that split randomly between overreaction and underreaction.

Is the weight of the evidence on long-term return anomalies so overwhelming that market efficiency is not a viable working model even in the absence of an alternative that explains both under- and overreaction? My answer to this question is no, for three reasons.

First, I doubt that the literature presents a random sample of events. Splashy results get more attention, and this creates an incentive to find them. That dredging for anomalies is a rewarding occupation is suggested by the fact that the anomalies literature shows so little sensitivity to the alternative hypothesis problem. The same authors, viewing different events, are often content with overreaction or underreaction, and are willing to infer that both warrant rejecting market efficiency.

Second, some apparent anomalies may be generated by rational asset pricing. Fama and French (1996) find that the long-term return reversals of DeBondt and Thaler (1985) and the contrarian returns of Lakonishok et al. (1994) are captured by a multifactor asset pricing model. In a nutshell, return covariation among long-term losers seems to be associated with a risk premium that can explain why they have higher future average returns than long-term winners. Fama and French (1996) discuss the quarrels with their multifactor model, but their results suffice to illustrate an important point: Inferences about market efficiency can be sensitive to the assumed model for expected returns.

Finally, but most important, a roughly even split between overreaction and underreaction would not be much support for market efficiency if the long-term return anomalies are so large they cannot possibly be attributed to chance. Section 5 argues, however, that even viewed individually, most anomalies are shaky. They tend to disappear when reasonable alternative approaches are used to measure them.

3. Behavioral models of underreaction and overreaction

Before examining individual long-term return studies, I first consider two behavioral models, recently proposed by Barberis, Shleifer, and Vishny (BSV 1998) and Daniel, Hirshleifer, and Subramanyam (DHS 1997), to explain how the judgment biases of investors can produce overreaction to some events and underreaction to others.

The BSV model is motivated by evidence from cognitive psychology of two judgment biases. (i) The representativeness bias of Kahneman and Tversky (1982): People give too much weight to recent patterns in the data and too little to the properties of the population that generates the data. (ii) Conservatism, attributed to Edwards (1968): The slow updating of models in the face of new evidence.

In the model of stock prices proposed by BSV to capture the two judgment biases, earnings are a random walk, but investors falsely perceive that there are two earnings regimes. In regime A, which investors assume is more likely, earnings are mean-reverting. When investors decide regime A holds, a stock's price under-reacts to a change in earnings because investors mistakenly think the change is likely to be temporary. When this expectation is not confirmed by later earnings, stock prices show a delayed response to earlier earnings. In regime B, which investors think is less likely, a run of earnings changes of the same sign leads investors to perceive that a firm's earnings are trending. Once investors are convinced that the trending regime B holds, they incorrectly extrapolate the trend and the stock price over-reacts. Because earnings are a random walk, the overreaction is exposed by future earnings, leading to reversal of long-term returns.

Regime A in the BSV model is motivated by the evidence of short-term momentum in stock returns (Jegadeesh and Titman, 1993) and the evidence of delayed short-term responses of stock prices to earnings announcements (Ball and Brown, 1968; Bernard and Thomas, 1990). Regime B is meant to explain the long-term return reversals of DeBondt and Thaler (1985) and the returns to the contrarian investment strategies of Lakonishok et al. (1994). How does the model do on other anomalies?

The prediction of regime B is reversal of long-term abnormal returns. Specifically, persistent long-term pre-event returns are evidence of market overreaction which should eventually be corrected in post-event returns. In addition to DeBondt and Thaler (1985) and Lakonishok et al. (1994), other events consistent with this prediction are seasoned equity offerings (Loughran and Ritter, 1995; Mitchell and Stafford, 1997), new exchange listings (Dharan and Ikenberry, 1995), and returns to acquiring firms in mergers (Asquith, 1983). All these events are characterized by positive long-term abnormal returns before the event and negative abnormal returns thereafter.

But long-term return reversal is not the norm. Events characterized by long-term post-event abnormal returns of the same sign as long-term pre-event returns include dividend initiations and omissions (Michaely et al., 1995), stock splits (Ikenberry et al., 1996; Desai and Jain, 1997), proxy contests (Ikenberry and Lakonishok, 1993), and spinoffs (Miles and Rosenfeld, 1983; Cusatis et al., 1993).

In short, and not surprisingly, the BSV model does well on the anomalies it was designed to explain. But its prediction of long-term return reversal does not capture the range of long-term results observed in the literature. On the whole, the long-term return literature seems more consistent with the market efficiency prediction that long-term return continuation and long-term return reversal are equally likely chance results.

The DHS model has different behavioral foundations than the BSV model. In DHS there are informed and uninformed investors. The uninformed are not subject to judgment biases. But stock prices are determined by the informed investors, and they are subject to two biases, overconfidence and biased self-attribution. Overconfidence leads them to exaggerate the precision of their private signals about a stock's value. Biased self-attribution causes them to downweight public signals about value, especially when the public signals contradict their private signals. Overreaction to private information and under-reaction to public information tend to produce short-term continuation of stock returns but long-term reversals as public information eventually overwhelms the behavioral biases. Thus, though based on different behavioral premises, the DHS predictions are close to those of BSV, and the DHS model shares the empirical successes and failures of the BSV model. This last comment also applies to Hong and Stein (1997).

DHS make a special prediction about what they call selective events. These are events that occur to take advantage of the mispricing of a firm's stock. For example, managers announce a new stock issue when a firm's stock price is too high, or they repurchase shares when the stock price is too low. This public signal produces an immediate price reaction that absorbs some of the mispricing. But in the DHS model, the announcement period price response is incomplete because informed investors overweight their prior beliefs about the stock's value. (The conservatism bias of the BSV model would produce a similar result.)

Eventually, the mispricing is fully absorbed as further public information confirms the information implied by the event announcement. The general prediction for selective events is thus momentum; stock returns after an event announcement will tend to have the same sign as the announcement period return.

Does the DHS prediction about selective events stand up to the data? Table 1 summarizes the signs of short-term announcement returns and long-term

Table 1
Signs of long-term pre-event, announcement, and long-term post-event returns for various long-term return studies

Event	Long-term pre-event return	Announcement return	Long-term post-event return
Initial public offerings (IPOs) (Ibbotson, 1975; Loughran and Ritter, 1995)	Not available	+	–
Seasoned equity offerings (Loughran and Ritter, 1995)	+	–	–
Mergers (acquiring firm) (Asquith, 1983; Agrawal et al., 1992)	+	0	–
Dividend initiations (Michaely et al., 1995)	+	+	+
Dividend omissions (Michaely et al., 1995)	–	–	–
Earnings announcements (Ball and Brown, 1968; Bernard and Thomas, 1990)	Not available	+	+
New exchange listings (Dharan and Ikenberry, 1995)	+	+	–
Share repurchases (open market) (Ikenberry et al., 1995; Mitchell and Stafford, 1997)	0	+	+
Share repurchases (tenders) (Lakonishok and Vermaelen, 1990; Mitchell and Stafford, 1997)	0	+	+
Proxy fights (Ikenberry and Lakonishok, 1993)	–	+	– (or 0)
Stock splits (Dharan and Ikenberry, 1995; Ikenberry et al., 1996)	+	+	+
Spinoffs (Miles and Rosenfeld, 1983; Cusatis et al., 1993)	+	+	+ (or 0)

post-announcement returns for the major long-term return studies. Except for earnings announcements, all these events seem selective. As predicted by DHS, announcement and post-announcement returns have the same sign for SEOs, dividend initiations and omissions, share repurchases, stock splits, and spinoffs. But announcement and post-announcement returns have opposite signs for new exchange listings and proxy fights, and the negative post-event returns to acquiring firms in mergers are not preceded by negative announcement returns. Most embarrassing for the DHS prediction, the long-term negative post-event returns of IPOs (the premier long-term return anomaly) are preceded by positive returns for a few months following the event (Ibbotson, 1975; Ritter, 1991).

Finally, given the demonstrated ingenuity of the theory branch of finance, and given the long litany of apparent judgment biases unearthed by cognitive psychologists (DeBondt and Thaler, 1995), it is safe to predict that we will soon see a menu of behavioral models that can be mixed and matched to explain specific anomalies. My view is that any new model should be judged (as above) on how it explains the big picture. The question should be: Does the new model produce rejectable predictions that capture the menu of anomalies better than market efficiency? For existing behavioral models, my answer to this question (perhaps predictably) is an emphatic no.

The main task that remains is to examine the long-term return anomalies one at a time to see if they deliver on their claims. We set the stage with a discussion of some of the general problems that arise in tests on long-term returns.

4. Drawing inferences from long-term returns

Fama (1970) emphasizes that market efficiency must be tested jointly with a model for expected (normal) returns. The problem is that all models for expected returns are incomplete descriptions of the systematic patterns in average returns during any sample period. As a result, tests of efficiency are always contaminated by a bad-model problem.

The bad-model problem is less serious in event studies that focus on short return windows (a few days) since daily expected returns are close to zero and so have little effect on estimates of unexpected (abnormal) returns. But the problem grows with the return horizon. A bad-model problem that produces a spurious abnormal average return of $x\%$ per month eventually becomes statistically reliable in cumulative monthly abnormal returns (CARs). The reason is that the mean of the CAR increases like N, the number of months summed, but the standard error of the CAR increases like $N^{1/2}$. In AARs (averages of monthly abnormal returns), the pricing error is constant at $x\%$, but the standard error of the AAR decreases like $N^{-1/2}$. Bad-model problems are most acute with long-term buy-and-hold abnormal returns (BHARs), which compound (multiply) an expected-return model's problems in explaining short-term returns.

This section discusses various approaches that attempt to limit bad-model problems. It also discusses a related issue, the relevant return metric in tests on long-term returns. I argue that theoretical and statistical considerations alike suggest that CARs (or AARs) should be used, rather than BHARs.

4.1. Bad-model problems

Bad-model problems are of two types. First, any asset pricing model is just a model and so does not completely describe expected returns. For example, the CAPM of Sharpe (1964) and Lintner (1965) does not seem to describe expected returns on small stocks (Banz, 1981). If an event sample is tilted toward small stocks, risk adjustment with the CAPM can produce spurious abnormal returns. Second, even if there were a true model, any sample period produces systematic deviations from the model's predictions, that is, sample-specific patterns in average returns that are due to chance. If an event sample is tilted toward sample-specific patterns in average returns, a spurious anomaly can arise even with risk adjustment using the true asset pricing model.

One approach to limiting bad-model problems bypasses formal asset pricing models by using firm-specific models for expected returns. For example, the stock split study of Fama et al. (1969) uses the market model to measure abnormal returns. The intercept and slope from the regression of a stock's return on the market return, estimated outside the event period, are used to estimate the stock's expected returns conditional on market returns during the event period. Masulis's (1980) comparison period approach uses a stock's average return outside the event period as the estimate of its expected return during the event period.

Unlike formal asset pricing models, the market model and the comparison period approach produce firm-specific expected return estimates; that is, a stock's expected return is estimated without constraining the cross-section of expected returns. Thus, these approaches can be used to study the reaction of stock prices to firm-specific events (splits, earnings, etc.). But they cannot identify anomalies in the cross-section of average returns, like the size effect of Banz (1981), since such anomalies must be measured relative to predictions about the cross-section of average returns.

The hypothesis in studies that focus on long-term returns is that the adjustment of stock prices to an event may be spread over a long post-event period. For many events, long periods of unusual pre-event returns are common. Thus, the choice of a normal period to estimate a stock's expected return or its market model parameters is problematic. Perhaps because of this problem, event studies often control for expected returns with approaches that constrain the cross-section of expected returns. An advantage of these approaches is that they do not require out-of-sample parameter estimates. A disadvantage is that constraints on the cross-section of expected returns always produce imperfect descriptions of average returns, and so can lead to bad-model problems.

For example, one approach estimates an abnormal return as the difference between an event firm's return and the return on a non-event firm or portfolio that is similar on characteristics known to be related to average returns. The hope in this matching approach is to control for cross-firm variation in average returns due both to differences in expected returns and to chance sample-specific patterns in average returns. For example, following Banz' (1981) evidence that small stocks have higher average returns than predicted by the CAPM, an event stock's abnormal return is often estimated as the difference between its return and the return on non-event stocks matched to the event stock on size. Following the evidence of Fama and French (1992) that average stock returns are also related to book-to-market equity (*BE*/*ME*), it is now common to estimate abnormal returns by matching event stocks with non-event stocks similar in terms of size and *BE*/*ME*.

When we analyze individual event studies, we shall see that matching on size can produce much different abnormal returns than matching on size and *BE*/*ME*. And size and *BE*/*ME* surely do not capture all relevant cross-firm variation in average returns due to expected returns or sample-specific patterns in average returns. In short, the matching approach is not a panacea for bad-model problems in studies of long-term abnormal returns.

Another method of estimating abnormal returns is to use an asset pricing model to estimate expected returns. Early studies of long-term abnormal returns (Jaffe, 1974; Mandelker, 1974; Asquith, 1983) use the CAPM. Some recent studies use the three-factor model of Fama and French (1993). Like all asset pricing models, however, the CAPM and the Fama–French model are incomplete descriptions of average returns. The shortcomings of the CAPM are well known (Fama and French, 1992). Fama and French (1993) show that their three-factor model does not even provide a full explanation of average returns on portfolios formed on size and *BE*/*ME*, the dimensions of average returns that the model's risk factors are designed to capture.

In short, bad-model problems are unavoidable, and they are more serious in tests on long-term returns. When we review individual studies in Section 5, the tracks of the bad-model problem will be clear. Different models for expected returns produce different estimates of long-term abnormal returns. And a reasonable change of models often causes an anomaly to disappear. I argue that when this happens, the anomaly is not much evidence against market efficiency.

4.2. The return metric

Studies of long-term returns are also sensitive to the way the tests are done. Average monthly abnormal returns (AARs or CARs) can produce different inferences than buy-and-hold abnormal returns (BHARs). Equal-weight returns produce different results than value-weight returns. And failure to account for the cross-correlation of event firm returns during long post-event periods can affect inferences. These implementation issues are discussed next.

4.2.1. The return metric: theoretical issues

In principle, the model of market equilibrium jointly tested with market efficiency specifies the unit of time for returns. For example, if the model defines equilibrium in terms of monthly expected returns, average monthly returns should be the metric used to test market efficiency. To examine how prices respond over periods longer than a month, one can average (AARs) or sum (CARs) the average monthly abnormal returns. Beginning with Fama et al. (1969), AARs and CARs are a common approach to examining long-term returns.

A criticism of this approach is that an average monthly return does not accurately measure the return to an investor who holds a security for a long post-event period. Long-term investor experience is better captured by compounding short-term returns to obtain long-term buy-and-hold returns. Much of the recent literature tests buy-and-hold abnormal returns for periods up to five years after an event.

Investor experience is interesting, and long-term BHARs are thus interesting. But formal tests for abnormal returns should use the return metric called for by the model invoked to estimate expected (normal) returns. The problem, of course, is that discrete-time asset pricing models are silent on the relevant interval for expected returns. Nevertheless, there are at least three theoretical reasons to lean toward shorter intervals:

(i) Asset pricing models, like the Sharpe (1964)–Lintner (1965) CAPM and the discrete-time version of Merton's (1973) ICAPM, commonly assume normally distributed returns. Normality is a better approximation for short horizons like a month than for longer horizons, where skewness becomes increasingly important (Fama, 1976, 1996).

(ii) The empirical tests of asset pricing models, invoked to justify applying the models in tests of market efficiency, typically use monthly returns. I know of no tests of asset pricing models on five-year returns.

(iii) Mitchell and Stafford (1997) point out that BHARs can give false impressions of the speed of price adjustment to an event. The reason is that BHARs can grow with the return horizon even when there is no abnormal return after the first period. For example, suppose returns for the first year after the event are 10% for event firms and zero for benchmark firms, so the first-year abnormal return is 10%. Suppose event and benchmark firms both have a 100% buy-and-hold return over the next four years. Although there is no abnormal return after the first year, the BHAR after five years grows to 20% [i.e., $(1.1 \times 2.0) - (1.0 \times 2.0)$].

4.2.2. The return metric: statistical issues

AARs and CARs also pose fewer statistical problems than long-term BHARs. Barber and Lyon (1997) provide the most complete discussion of the inference problems in tests on long-term returns. [See also Kothari and Warner (1997).] Barber and Lyon favor BHARs, but their tests show that inferences are less problematic for average monthly returns (AARs or CARs). In a follow-up paper, Lyon et al. (1997) develop elaborate techniques for correcting some of the inference problems of BHARs. But they acknowledge that their improved methods for BHARs produce inferences no more reliable than simpler methods applied to monthly AARs or CARs. The reason is that average monthly returns avoid the problems (e.g., extreme skewness) produced by compounding monthly returns to get long-term BHARs.

Brav (1997) emphasizes that all existing methods for drawing inferences from BHARs, including those in Lyon et al. (1997), fail to correct fully for the correlation of returns across events not absorbed by the model used to adjust for expected returns. The problem is more severe in long-term BHARs because more firms have events within, say, a given five-year window than within a three-day window. Brav (1997) presents an elaborate scheme to adjust for the cross-correlation of long-term BHARs in special cases (e.g., when it is due to industry effects). But a full solution is not typically available because the number of return covariances to be estimated is greater than the number of time-series observations.

In contrast, if average monthly returns are used, there has long been a full solution to the cross-correlation problem. Suppose the post-event period of interest is five years. For each calendar month, calculate the abnormal return on each stock that had an event in the last five years. (Abnormal returns can be estimated in any reasonable way, for example, with a matching firm or matching portfolio approach, or with an asset pricing model.) Then average the abnormal returns for the calendar month across stocks to get the abnormal return for the month on the portfolio of stocks with an event in the last five years. Re-form the portfolio every month. The time-series variation of the monthly abnormal return on this portfolio accurately captures the effects of the correlation of returns across event stocks missed by the model for expected returns. The mean and variance of the time series of abnormal portfolio returns can be used to test the average monthly response of the prices of event stocks for five years following the event. The approach can also be refined to allow for heteroskedasticity of the portfolio's abnormal return due to changes through time in the composition of the portfolio. This rolling portfolio approach (with refinements) was first used by Jaffe (1974) and Mandelker (1974).

A referee suggests that the portfolio approach described above can cause an anomaly to be understated if events bunch in time because firms exploit pricing errors during windows of opportunity. For example, Loughran and Ritter (1995) suggest that IPOs bunch because particular industries tend to be overvalued at specific times. This criticism of the portfolio approach is valid if monthly abnormal portfolio returns are weighted equally in calculating an overall average monthly abnormal return. One solution to the problem is to adjust for heteroskedasticity. Specifically, following Jaffe (1974) and Mandelker (1974), divide the abnormal portfolio return for each month by an estimate of its standard deviation. The overall abnormal return is then estimated by averaging the standardized monthly abnormal returns. This approach is attractive because it weights each month's abnormal return by its statistical precision, which seems like the right way to capture the increased information due to event bunching. More generally, however, one can weight the portfolio abnormal return for a month in any way that captures the economic hypothesis of interest.

4.2.3. The return metric: value weights versus equal weights

In the review of individual studies that follows, we find that apparent anomalies in long-term post-event returns typically shrink a lot and often disappear when event firms are value-weighted rather than equal-weighted. One can argue that value-weight returns give the right perspective on an anomaly because they more accurately capture the total wealth effects experienced by investors. But I am more concerned about bad-model problems. All the common asset pricing models, including the Fama–French (1993) three-factor model, have systematic problems explaining the average returns on categories of small stocks. Since equal-weight portfolio returns give more weight to small stocks, bad-model problems are more severe in inferences from equal-weight returns.

Many readers suggest that more serious mispricing of small stocks is a general prediction of behavioral finance. It is thus worth noting that the two behavioral pricing models reviewed in Section 3 do not produce this prediction. In Barberis et al. (1998), pricing is dominated by a representative investor, and there is no prediction that the judgment biases of this investor are more severe for small stocks. In Daniel et al. (1997), pricing is dominated by informed investors subject to judgment biases. Uninformed investors have no such biases. Thus, if large stocks attract more interest from informed investors (e.g., security analysts), mispricing problems might be more severe for large stocks.

Most important, the cognitive psychology literature does not seem to say that different classes of people are more subject to judgment biases. The same biases that plague college students (the subjects of most cognitive psychology experiments) also occur among experts (see the references in Barberis et al.). Thus, cognitive psychology, the basis of behavioral finance, does not seem to provide a basis for the common presumption that small stocks are more likely to be mispriced.

5. The reliability of individual studies

The summary of long-term return studies in Sections 2 and 3 accepts the conclusions of the papers at face value. Now the gloves come off. Examining long-term return anomalies one at a time, I argue that most are fragile. Abnormal returns often disappear with reasonable changes in the way they are measured.

5.1. IPOs and SEOs

Among the more striking of the long-term return anomalies is the study of initial public offerings (IPOs) and seasoned equity offerings (SEOs) by Loughran and Ritter (1995). They find that the total wealth generated at the end of five years if one invests $1 in each IPO or SEO immediately following the event is about 70% of that produced by the same buy-and-hold strategy applied to a sample of stocks matched to the IPOs and SEOs on size.

IPOs and SEOs clearly have poor long-term returns during the Loughran–Ritter sample period (1970–1990). The interesting question is whether the returns are really abnormal or whether they are shared with non-event firms similar on characteristics related to average returns. During the Loughran–Ritter period, variables known to be related to average stock return include size and book-to-market equity (Fama and French, 1992), and short-term past return (Jegadeesh and Titman, 1993). Since the long-term buy-and-hold returns in Loughran and Ritter only control for size, their results might be affected by other variables that are systematically related to average return.

Following up on this possibility, Brav and Gompers (1997) compare five-year buy-and-hold returns on IPOs with the returns on portfolios that match the IPOs on size and book-to-market equity (BE/ME) but exclude SEOs as well as IPOs. The five-year wealth relative (the ratio of five-year buy-and-hold wealth for IPOs to five-year buy-and-hold wealth for the benchmarks) rises from about 0.7 with the Loughran–Ritter size benchmarks to a bit more than 1.0 (that is, the anomaly disappears) when the benchmarks control for BE/ME as well as size. Similarly, Brav et al. (1995) find that the five-year buy-and-hold returns on SEOs are close to those of non-event portfolios matched on size and BE/ME.

Brav (1997) and Mitchell and Stafford (1997) show that IPOs and SEOs are typically small growth stocks. Fama and French (1993) show that such stocks have low returns during the post-1963 period. The results of Brav and Gompers (1997) and Brav et al. (1995) then suggest that explaining the IPO-SEO anomaly reduces to explaining why small growth stocks in general have poor returns during the IPO-SEO sample period. In other words, if there is a mispricing problem, it is not special to IPO-SEO stocks.

Brav and Gompers (1997) and Brav et al. (1995) also find that when IPOs and SEOs are value-weighted, five-year abnormal buy-and-hold returns shrink a lot, whatever the benchmark. For IPOs, value-weight five-year wealth relatives are 0.86 or greater for all benchmarks, and four of six benchmarks produce wealth relatives in excess of 0.9. For SEOs, value-weight five-year wealth relatives are 0.88 or greater for all benchmarks; three of six are in excess of 0.98. The message is that many IPO and SEO stocks are tiny, and they are influential in the returns observed when sample firms are equal-weighted. This result is general. We shall see that apparent anomalies typically shrink a lot when viewed in terms of value-weight returns.

Loughran and Ritter (1995), Brav and Gompers (1997), and Brav et al. (1995) do not engage in the treacherous game of drawing statistical inferences from long-term buy-and-hold returns. Their inferences are based on average monthly returns. Every month they calculate the return on a portfolio that contains all firms with an IPO or SEO in the last five years. The three-factor model of Fama and French (FF 1993) is then used to estimate the portfolio's abnormal returns. The average monthly abnormal return during the five-year post-event period is the intercept, α_p, of the time-series regression

$$R_{pt} - R_{ft} = a_P + b_p[R_{Mt} - R_{ft}] + s_p\text{SMB} + h_p\text{HML} + \varepsilon_{pt}, \tag{1}$$

where R_{pt} is the monthly return on the IPO or SEO portfolio, R_{ft} is the one-month Treasury bill rate, R_{Mt} is the monthly return on a value-weight market portfolio of NYSE, Amex, and Nasdaq stocks, SMB is the difference between the returns on portfolios of small and big stocks (below or above the NYSE median), and HML is the difference between the returns on portfolios of high- and low-*BE*/*ME* stocks (above and below the 0.7 and 0.3 fractiles of *BE*/*ME*).

Brav et al. (1995) estimate the intercepts in (1) for equal- and value-weight portfolios of the SEOs of their 1975–92 sample period. The intercept for the equal-weight portfolio is -0.42% per month ($t = -4.8$), but the intercept for the value-weight portfolio is -0.14% per month ($t = -1.18$). Similarly, Brav and Gompers (1997) find that the intercepts for equal- and value-weight portfolios of IPOs that are not backed by venture capitalists are -0.52% ($t = -2.80$) and -0.29% ($t = -1.84$). For IPOs backed by venture capitalists, the intercepts are slightly positive. Loughran and Ritter (1995) only show regressions that combine IPOs and SEOs, but their results are similar: Equal-weight portfolios produce reliably negative intercepts, but abnormal returns for value-weight portfolios are economically and statistically close to zero.

Since inferences about abnormal returns from estimates of (1) on rolling post-event portfolio returns are common in the recent anomalies literature, it is important to note three potential problems.

First, since the firms in the event portfolio change through time, the true slopes on the risk factors in (1) are time-varying. Mitchell and Stafford (1997) confirm that for three important events (mergers, share repurchases, and SEOs), changes in the composition of the event portfolio generate substantial variation in the slopes in (1). For SEOs, they find that the intercepts for their 1960–93 period for equal- and value-weight portfolios drop from -0.38 ($t = 4.47$) and -0.14 ($t = -1.51$) in the constant slope regressions, to -0.24 ($t = -3.64$) and -0.07 ($t = -0.81$) in the regressions that allow the slopes to vary through time.

Second, the number of firms in the event portfolio changes through time, creating residual heteroskedasticity that can affect inferences about the intercept. [Solutions to this problem like those in Jaffe (1974) and Mandelker (1974) are apparently a lost technology.]

Third, but most important, Fama and French (1993) show that the three-factor model is not a perfect story for average returns. This bad-model problem can produce spurious anomalies in event studies. For example, IPOs and SEOs tend to be small, low-*BE*/*ME* firms. Fama and French (1993) show that the three-factor model overestimates average returns on such firms during the IPO-SEO sample periods. This bad-model problem can explain why estimates of (1) on equal-weight IPO and SEO portfolios produce reliably negative intercepts, but estimates on value-weight portfolios produce intercepts close to zero. It can also explain why the intercepts in (1), which control for loadings on risk factors related to size and *BE*/*ME*, suggest abnormal post-event returns for equal-weight IPO and SEO portfolios. But with direct benchmark matching on size and *BE*/*ME*, the abnormal returns largely disappear.

I emphasize, however, that the results for IPOs and SEOs do not imply that benchmark matching on size and *BE*/*ME* is always superior to estimating abnormal returns as the intercepts from (1). All methods for estimating abnormal returns are subject to bad-model problems, and no method is likely to minimize bad-model problems for all classes of events. The important general message from the IPO-SEO results is one of caution: Two approaches that seem closely related (both attempt to control for variation in average returns related to size and *BE*/*ME*) can produce much different estimates of long-term abnormal returns.

In sum, I read Brav and Gompers (1997) and Brav et al. (1995) as showing that the poor long-term buy-and-hold returns following IPOs and SEOs are not a special anomaly. The low returns are shared with other firms similar on two dimensions, size and *BE*/*ME*, known to be related to average return. Moreover, when IPOs and SEOs are value-weighted, abnormal returns shrink for all benchmarks, and they are not reliably different from zero. Thus, if there is an IPO-SEO anomaly, it seems to be largely restricted to tiny firms.

5.2. Mergers

Asquith (1983) and Agrawal et al. (1992) find negative abnormal returns for acquiring firms for up to five years following merger announcements. Using a comprehensive sample of mergers for 1960–93, Mitchell and Stafford (1997) also find negative long-term abnormal returns for acquiring firms. Since these studies produce similar results, I focus on Mitchell and Stafford (MS 1997).

MS find that the three-year post-event buy-and-hold return for equal-weighted acquiring firms is on average 4% lower than for portfolios matched to acquiring firms on size and BE/ME. In economic terms, this is not a dramatic anomaly. For formal inferences, MS estimate the three-factor model (1) on the monthly returns on a rolling portfolio that includes firms with acquisitions during the preceding three years. When the acquirers are equal-weighted, the intercept in Eq. (1), that is, the average monthly abnormal return for the three years after a merger, is -0.25% per month (-25 basis points, $t = -3.49$), which is larger than but roughly consistent with the BH returns. When acquiring firms are value-weighted, the intercept in Eq. (1) drops to -0.11% per month ($t = -1.55$). Thus, if there is an anomaly, it is more important for smaller acquiring firms. Finally, MS and Loughran and Vijh (1997) show that abnormal post-announcement average returns to acquiring firms are limited to mergers financed with stock, that is, mergers that are also SEOs. When mergers are financed without issuing stock, the negative abnormal post-event returns disappear. This suggests that there is no distinct merger anomaly. Any merger anomaly may be the SEO anomaly in disguise.

5.3. Stock splits

Desai and Jain (1997) and Ikenberry et al. (1996) find that for the 17-year 1975–91 period, stock splits are followed by positive abnormal returns of about 7% in the year after the split. Abnormal returns are calculated relative to benchmarks that control for size, BE/ME, and, in Desai and Jain, past one-year return.

One way to test whether such an anomaly is real or the sample-specific result of chance is to examine a different sample period. Fama et al. (1969) examine splits during the 33-year 1927–59 period. They find no drift in cumulative abnormal returns during the 30 months following splits. Since the split anomaly fails the out-of-sample test provided by FFJR, it seems reasonable to conclude that the 1975–91 anomaly is not real, unless the market has recently become inefficient.

Desai and Jain (1997) and Ikenberry et al. (1996) do provide neat evidence on one of the pitfalls in using buy-and-hold abnormal returns to judge the long-term return drift associated with an event. As noted earlier, Mitchell and Stafford (1997) point out that BHARs are likely to grow with the return horizon even when there is no abnormal return after the first period. For the 1975–91 period, the abnormal return is about 7% for the first year following stock splits, but it is close to zero in the following two years (slightly negative in the second and slightly positive in the third). BHARs, however, rise from 7% to about 12% after three years.

One way to avoid the distorted perspective on long-term drift produced by BHARs is to examine ratios rather than differences of the cumulative wealths generated by event and benchmark firms, as in Ritter (1991) and Loughran and Ritter (1995). Another is the time-worn CAR approach of FFJR, which sums returns rather than compounding them, or the rolling portfolio average monthly abnormal return (AAR) approach of Jaffe (1974) and Mandelker (1974).

5.4. *Self-tenders and share repurchases*

Lakonishok and Vermaelen (1990) examine long-term returns following self-tender offers (tenders by firms for their own shares) during the 1962–86 period. Ikenberry et al. (1995) examine long-term returns following share repurchases during the 1980–90 period. Mitchell and Stafford (1997) study both self-tenders and repurchases for the 1960–93 period. Since the MS results are similar to but more comprehensive than those in the earlier papers, the discussion focuses on them.

MS find that three-year post-event BHARs, computed relative to matching portfolios that control for size and BE/ME, are 9% for self-tenders (475 events) and 19% for the much larger sample of 2,542 repurchases. When they estimate the three-factor regression (1) for the monthly returns on an equal-weight portfolio that contains all self-tenders and repurchases in the last three years, however, the average abnormal monthly return is puny, 0.11% per month ($t = 1.62$). Any hint of significance, economic or statistical, disappears entirely when the stocks in the rolling portfolio are value-weighted. The intercept for the value-weight portfolio of self-tenders and repurchases is -0.03% (-3 basis points per month, $t = -0.34$). In short, viewed from the perspective of the three-factor model of Eq. (1), there is no share repurchase anomaly.

Note, once again, that two apparently similar methods for estimating abnormal returns, (i) a matching portfolio control for size and BE/ME and (ii) an asset pricing regression that adjusts for sensitivity to risk factors related to size and BE/ME, produce somewhat different results. This again illustrates that estimates of long-term abnormal returns can be sensitive to apparently small changes in technique.

5.5. *Exchange listings*

Dharan and Ikenberry (1995) find that during the 1962–90 period, stocks that newly list on the NYSE, or move from Nasdaq to Amex, have negative post-listing abnormal returns. When returns are risk-adjusted using matching portfolios formed on size and BE/ME, the three-year average abnormal return is -7.02%. The t-statistic for this CAR is -2.78, but this is without a full adjustment for the correlation of abnormal returns across firms. Moreover, Dharan and Ikenberry show that the negative post-listing abnormal returns are limited to firms below the NYSE-Amex median in size. Thus, once again, an apparent anomaly is limited to small stocks.

Mitchell and Stafford (1997) offer concrete perspective on how significance levels can be overstated because of the failure to adjust for the correlation across firms of post-event abnormal returns. Using the three-factor model (1), they calculate the standard deviations of abnormal returns for portfolios of firms with an event during the most recent 36 months. The proportions vary somewhat through time and across their three event classes (mergers, share repurchases, and SEOs), but on average the covariances of event-firm abnormal returns account for about half the standard deviation of the event portfolio's abnormal return. Thus, if the covariances are ignored, the standard error of the abnormal portfolio return is too small by about 50%! This estimate need not apply intact to the exchange listings of Dharan and Ikenberry (1995), but it suggests that a full adjustment for the cross-correlation of post-listing abnormal returns could cause the statistical reliability ($t = -2.78$) of their -7.02% post-event three-year CAR to disappear.

Dharan and Ikenberry's explanation of their negative post-listing abnormal returns is that firms are opportunistic, and they list their stocks to take advantage of the market's overreaction to their recent good times. This explanation seems shaky, however, given that any overreaction to past performance has already occurred and will soon be reversed. Moreover, standard signaling theory (e.g., Ross, 1977) does not predict that firms will incur costs to make a false signal whose price effects are soon obliterated. On the contrary, since listing involves costs, it should be a signal that the firm is under-valued.

5.6. Dividend initiations and omissions

Michaely et al. (1995) find that during the 1964–88 period, firms that initiate dividends have positive abnormal stock returns for three years after the event, and firms omitting dividends have negative abnormal returns. For the same sample, Brav (1997) finds that the three-year post-event abnormal return following initiations disappears with benchmarks that control for size and BE/ME. Michaely et al. (1995) show that the negative three-year abnormal returns following omissions, confirmed by Brav (1997), are largely concentrated in the second half of their 1964–88 sample period. All this suggests that inferences about long-term returns following changes in dividends should probably await an out-of-sample test.

The finding that stock prices under-react to dividend announcements is suspect on other grounds. It seems reasonable that underreaction would occur because the market underestimates the information in dividends about future earnings. However, from Watts (1973) to Benartzi et al. (1997), there is little evidence that changes in dividends predict changes in earnings.

5.7. Spinoffs

Cusatis et al. (1993) study the post-event returns of spinoffs and their parents for the 1965–88 period. The benchmarks are firms matched to the event firms on size and industry, and abnormal returns are BHARs. Both parents and spinoffs have positive abnormal returns in the three years after the event. The abnormal returns are, however, limited to event firms (parents and spinoffs) acquired in mergers. The conclusion is that the market does not properly assess the increased probability of takeover (and the attendant buyout premiums) following spinoffs.

The t-statistics for the three-year BHARs for spinoffs range from 0.58 to 2.55, hardly overwhelming. Moreover, in calculating the t-statistics, the BHARs of the event firms are assumed to be independent. It would not take a large adjustment for cross-correlation to produce t-statistics that suggest no real anomaly.

5.8. Proxy contests

Ikenberry and Lakonishok (1993) examine stock returns following proxy contests during the 1968–87 period. They find negative post-event abnormal returns relative to benchmarks that control for market β and size. In the results for all proxy contests, the post-event abnormal returns are not statistically reliable. The negative post-event returns are only statistically reliable for the 50-odd proxy contests in which the dissidents win board representation. Since this result is not an ex ante prediction, the weak evidence for the overall sample seems more relevant, and it does not suggest a reliable anomaly. This is more or less the conclusion of the authors.

5.9. Summary

If a reasonable change in the method of estimating abnormal returns causes an anomaly to disappear, the anomaly is on shaky footing, and it is reasonable to suggest that it is an illusion. Included in this category are IPOs, SEOs, self-tenders, share repurchases, and dividend initiations. Moreover, the doubts about these anomalies are the result of replication and robustness checks that followed publication of the original studies. Other anomalies will likely fall prey to the same process.

Other long-term return anomalies are economically or statistically marginal. The negative post-event abnormal returns to acquiring firms in mergers are economically small. For exchange listings, spinoffs, and proxy contests, a full correction for the cross-correlation of long-term post-event abnormal returns could easily reduce them to former anomalies.

Some anomalies do not stand up to out-of-sample replication. Foremost (in my mind) is the stock split anomaly observed after 1975, which is contradicted by the earlier FFJR study. The long-term negative post-event returns of dividend-omitting firms also seem sensitive to sample period.

Whenever value-weight returns are examined, apparent anomalies shrink a lot and typically become statistically unreliable. At a minimum, this suggests that anomalies are largely limited to small stocks. But a reasonable alternative explanation is that small stocks are just a sure source of bad-model problems. Small stocks always pose problems in tests of asset pricing models, so they are prime candidates for bad-model problems in tests of market efficiency on long-term returns.

Which anomalies are above suspicion? The post-earnings-announcement drift first reported by Ball and Brown (1968) has survived robustness checks, including extension to more recent data (Bernard and Thomas, 1990; Chan et al., 1996). Again, though, the anomaly is stronger for small stocks. The short-term continuation of returns documented by Jegadeesh and Titman (1993) is also an open puzzle, but it is still rather new and further tests are in order.

6. Conclusions

The recent finance literature seems to produce many long-term return anomalies. Subjected to scrutiny, however, the evidence does not suggest that market efficiency should be abandoned. Consistent with the market efficiency hypothesis that the anomalies are chance results, apparent overreaction of stock prices to information is about as common as underreaction. And post-event continuation of pre-event abnormal returns is about as frequent as post-event reversal. Most important, the long-term return anomalies are fragile. They tend to disappear with reasonable changes in the way they are measured.

References

Agrawal, A., Jaffe, Mandelker, G., 1992. The post-merger performance of acquiring firms: a re-examination of an anomaly. Journal of Finance 47, 1605–1621.

Asquith, P., 1983. Merger bids, uncertainty and stockholder returns. Journal of Financial Economics 11, 51–83.

Ball, R., Brown, P., 1968. An empirical evaluation of accounting income numbers. Journal of Accounting Research 6, 159–178.

Banz, R., 1981. The relationship between return and market value of common stocks. Journal of Financial Economics 9, 3–18.

Barber, B., Lyon, J., 1997. Detecting long-horizon abnormal stock returns: the empirical power and specification of test statistics. Journal of Financial Economics 43, 341.

Barberis, N., Shleifer, A., Vishny, R., 1998. A model of investor sentiment. Journal of Financial Economics 49, 307–343 (this issue).

Benartzi, S., Michaely, R., Thaler, R., 1997. Do dividend changes signal the future or the past. Journal of Finance 52, 1007–1034.

Bernard, V., Thomas, J., 1990. Evidence that stock prices do not fully reflect the implications of current earnings for future earnings. Journal of Accounting and Economics 13, 305.

Brav, A., 1997. Inference in long-horizon event studies: a re-evaluation of the evidence. Unpublished working paper. Graduate School of Business, University of Chicago.

Brav, A., Gompers, P., 1997. Myth or reality? The long-run underperformance of initial public offerings: evidence from venture and nonventure capital-backed companies. Journal of Finance 52, 1791–1821.

Brav, A., Geczy, C., Gompers, P., 1995. The long-run underperformance of seasoned equity offerings revisited. Unpublished working paper. Graduate School of Business, University of Chicago.

Chan, L., Jegadeesh, N., Lakonishok, J., 1996. Momentum strategies. Journal of Finance 51, 1681–1713.

Cusatis, P., Miles, J., Woolridge, J., 1993. Restructuring through spinoffs. Journal of Financial Economics 33, 293–311.

Daniel, K., Hirshleifer, D., Subrahmanyam, A., 1997. A theory of overconfidence, self-attribution, and security market under- and over-reactions. Unpublished working paper. University of Michigan.

DeBondt, W., Thaler, R., 1985. Does the stock market overreact? Journal of Finance 40, 793–805.

DeBondt, W., Thaler, R., 1995. Financial decision-making in markets and firms: a behavioral perspective. In: Jarrow, R. et al. (Eds.), Handbooks in OR and MS, vol. 9, Elsevier, Amsterdam, pp. 385–410.

Desai, H., Jain, P., 1997. Long-run common stock returns following splits and reverse splits. Journal of Business 70, 409–433.

Dharan, B., Ikenberry, D., 1995. The long-run negative drift of post-listing stock returns. Journal of Finance 50, 1547–1574.

Edwards, W., 1968. Conservatism in human information processing. In: Kleinmutz, B. (Ed.), Formal Representation of Human Judgement. Wiley, New York.

Fama, E., 1970. Efficient capital markets: a review of theory and empirical work. Journal of Finance 25, 383–417.

Fama, E., 1976. Foundations of Finance. Basic Books, New York.

Fama, E., 1996. Discounting under uncertainty. Journal of Business 69, 415–428.

Fama, E., Fisher, L., Jensen, M., Roll, R., 1969. The adjustment of stock prices to new information. International Economic Review 10, 1–21.

Fama, E., French, K., 1992. The cross-section of expected stock returns. Journal of Finance 47, 427–465.

Fama, E., French, K., 1993. Common risk factors in the returns on stocks and bonds. Journal of Financial Economics 33, 3–56.

Fama, E., French, K., 1996. Multifactor explanations of asset pricing anomalies. Journal of Finance 51, 55–84.

Hong, H., Stein, J., 1997. A unified theory of underreaction, momentum trading, and overreaction in asset markets. Unpublished working paper. Sloan School of Management, Massachusetts Institute of Technology.

Ibbotson, R., 1975. Price performance of common stock new issues. Journal of Financial Economics 2, 235–272.

Ikenberry, D., Lakonishok, J., 1993. Corporate governance through the proxy contest: evidence and implications. Journal of Business 66, 405–435.

Ikenberry, D., Lakonishok, J., Vermaelen, T., 1995. Market underreaction to open market share repurchases. Journal of Financial Economics 39, 181–208.

Ikenberry, D., Rankine, G., Stice, E., 1996. What do stock splits really signal? Journal of Financial and Quantitative Analysis 31, 357–377.

Jaffe, J., 1974. Special information and insider trading. Journal of Business 47, 410–428.

Jegadeesh, N., Titman, S., 1993. Returns to buying winners and selling losers: implications for stock market efficiency. Journal of Finance 48, 65–91.

Kahneman, D., Tversky, A., 1982. Intuitive predictions: biases and corrective procedures. Reprinted in Kahneman, Slovic, and Tversky, Judgement under Uncertainty: Heuristics and Biases. Cambridge University Press, Cambridge, England.

Kothari, S., Warner, J., 1997. Measuring long-horizon security price performance. Journal of Financial Economics 43, 301–339.

Lakonishok, J., Shleifer, A., Vishny, R., 1994. Contrarian investment, extrapolation, and risk. Journal of Finance 49, 1541–1578.

Lakonishok, J., Vermaelen, T., 1990. Anomalous price behavior around repurchase tender offers. Journal of Finance 45, 455–477.

Lintner, J., 1965. The valuation of risk assets and the selection of risky investments in stock portfolios and capital budgets. Review of Economics and Statistics 47, 13–37.

Loughran, T., Ritter, J., 1995. The new issues puzzle. Journal of Finance 50, 23–51.

Loughran, T., Vijh, A., 1997. Do long-term shareholders benefit from corporate acquisitions? Journal of Finance 52, 1765–1790.

Lyon, J., Barber, B., Tsai, C., 1997. Improved methods for tests of long-run abnormal returns. Unpublished working paper. Graduate School of Management, University of California, Davis.

Mandelker, G., 1974. Risk and return: the case of merging firms. Journal of Financial Economics 1, 303.

Masulis, R., 1980. The effects of capital structure changes on security prices: a study of exchange offers. Journal of Financial Economics 8, 139–177.

Merton, R., 1973. An intertemporal capital asset pricing model. Econometrica 41, 867–887.

Michaely, R., Thaler, R., Womack, K., 1995. Price reactions to dividend initiations and omissions. Journal of Finance 50, 573–608.

Miles, J., Rosenfeld, J., 1983. The effect of voluntary spinoff announcements on shareholder wealth. Journal of Finance 38, 1597–1606.

Mitchell, M., Stafford, E., 1997. Managerial decisions and long-term stock price performance. Unpublished working paper. Graduate School of Business, University of Chicago.

Ritter, J., 1991. The long-term performance of initial public offerings. Journal of Finance 46, 3–27.

Roll, R., 1986. The hubris hypothesis of corporate takeovers. Journal of Business 59, 197–216.

Ross, S., 1977. The determinants of financial structure: the incentive signaling approach. Bell Journal of Economics 8, 23–40.

Sharpe, W., 1964. Capital asset prices: a theory of market equilibrium under conditions of risk. Journal of Finance 19, 425.

Spiess, D., Affleck-Graves, J., 1995. Underperformance in long-run stock returns following seasoned equity offerings. Journal of Financial Economics 38, 243–267.

Watts, R., 1973. The information content of dividends. Journal of Business 46, 191–211.

[14]

ROBERT J. SHILLER
Yale University

Stock Prices and Social Dynamics

Fashion is the great governor of this world; it presides not only in matters of dress and amusement, but in law, physic, politics, religion, and all other things of the gravest kind; indeed, the wisest of men would be puzzled to give any better reason why particular forms in all these have been at certain times universally received, and at others universally rejected, than that they were in or out of fashion.

Henry Fielding[1]

INVESTING in speculative assets is a social activity. Investors spend a substantial part of their leisure time discussing investments, reading about investments, or gossiping about others' successes or failures in investing. It is thus plausible that investors' behavior (and hence prices of speculative assets) would be influenced by social movements. Attitudes or fashions seem to fluctuate in many other popular topics of conversation, such as food, clothing, health, or politics. These fluctuations in attitude often occur widely in the population and often appear without any apparent logical reason. It is plausible that attitudes or fashions regarding investments would also change spontaneously or in arbitrary social reaction to some widely noted events.

Most of those who buy and sell in speculative markets seem to take it for granted that social movements significantly influence the behavior of prices. Popular interpretations of the recurrent recessions that we observe often include ideas that the shifts in, say, consumer confidence

John Pound provided research assistance. This research was supported by the National Science Foundation under grant SES-8408565 and the Sloan Foundation.

1. Henry Fielding, *The True Patriot*, no. 1, 1745, in James P. Browne, ed., *The Works of Henry Fielding, Esq.*, vol. 8 (London: Bickers and Son, 1903), p. 69.

or optimism are also at work in other aspects of the business cycle, such as interest rates, inventories, and so on. Academic research on market psychology, however, appears to have more or less died out in the 1950s, at about the time the expected-utility revolution in economics was born. Those academics who write about financial markets today are usually very careful to dissociate themselves from any suggestion that market psychology might be important, as if notions of market psychology have been discredited as unscientific.[2] There is instead an enormous recent literature in finance that takes one of the various forms of the efficient markets hypothesis for motivation and a related literature in macroeconomics that is based on the assumption of rational expectations. In academic circles there has certainly been an interest in speculative bubbles, but pursued within the framework of rational expectations models with unchanging tastes.[3]

It is hard to find in the large literature on the efficient markets hypothesis any discussion of an alternative hypothesis involving social psychology in financial markets.[4] Yet the impression persists in the literature and in casual discussions that there are very powerful arguments against such social-psychological theories. Arguments confined to an oral tradition, tacitly accepted by all parties, and not discussed in the scholarly literature are particularly vulnerable to error. It is thus important to consider explicitly these arguments against a major role for mass psychology in financial markets.

Returns on speculative assets are nearly unforecastable; this fact is the basis of the most important argument in the oral tradition against a role for mass psychology in speculative markets. One form of this

2. The recent literature on behavioral economics associated with survey research has apparently not touched substantially on speculative markets. Some of their findings are relevant and will be cited below.

3. For example, David Cass and Karl Shell refer to market psychology in motivating their discussion of extraneous uncertainty, but they then assume economic agents are expected-utility maximizers with unchanging tastes. There is, however, a sense in which they and others are wrestling with some of the same issues that are of concern in this paper. See Cass and Shell, "Do Sunspots Matter?" *Journal of Political Economy*, vol. 91 (April 1983), pp. 193–227.

4. There are some casual arguments in the literature against such a role for mass psychology. The most-cited reference may be Eugene F. Fama, "The Behavior of Stock Market Prices," *Journal of Business*, vol. 38 (January 1965), pp. 34–105. The argument consists of no more than a few paragraphs pointing out that "sophisticated traders" might eliminate profit opportunities, thereby tending to make "actual prices closer to intrinsic values" (p. 38).

argument claims that because real returns are nearly unforecastable, the real price of stocks is close to the intrinsic value, that is, the present value with constant discount rate of optimally forecasted future real dividends. This argument for the efficient markets hypothesis represents one of the most remarkable errors in the history of economic thought. It is remarkable in the immediacy of its logical error and in the sweep and implications of its conclusion. I will discuss this and other arguments for the efficient markets hypothesis and claim that mass psychology may well be the dominant cause of movements in the price of the aggregate stock market.

I have divided my discussion into four major sections: arguments from a social-psychological standpoint for the importance of fashions in financial markets, a critique of the argument for the efficient markets hypothesis, a proposed alternative model based on social psychology, and some exploratory data analysis suggested by the alternative model.

The first section discusses what we know about changing fashions or attitudes in light of everyday experience, research in social psychology and sociology, and evidence from postwar stock market history. This will not be direct evidence that people violate the principle of expected-utility maximization, nor is the evidence of great value in judging how far we should carry the assumption of rationality in other areas of economics (although I think it is of value in understanding the business cycle). Rather, I will be motivated here by the relatively narrow question of why speculative asset prices fluctuate as much as they do.

The second section sets forth and evaluates the efficient markets model and the presumed evidence against a role for social psychology in determining prices. The fundamental issue is the power of statistical tests in distinguishing the efficient markets model from the important alternatives. If statistical tests have little power, then we ought to use the sort of qualitative evidence discussed in the first section to evaluate the efficient markets model.

The third section offers a simple though rather incomplete alternative model of stock prices that admits the importance of social-psychological factors. This model involves "smart-money investors" and "ordinary investors" and is intended to demonstrate how models of financial markets might better accommodate the econometric evidence on the near unforecastability of returns, evidence that is widely interpreted as favoring the efficient markets model.

The fourth section uses U.S. stock market data to explore some relations suggested by the alternative model. Using Standard and Poor's composite stock price index, I examine various forecasting equations for real returns. I consider whether stock price movements seem to follow simple patterns, as in an overreaction to dividends or earnings news, and whether this overreaction induces a sort of forecastability for returns. In doing this I present a time series model of the aggregate real dividend series associated with Standard and Poor's composite stock price index. I also propose a hypothetical scenario using the alternative model that shows for recent U.S. history what the smart-money investors may have been doing, the fraction of total trading volume that might have been accounted for by smart-money trades in and out of the market, and the extent to which ordinary investors may have influenced stock prices.

Evidence on Fashions and Financial Markets

FASHIONS IN EVERYDAY LIFE

Isn't it plausible that those who are so enlightened as to be readers of *BPEA* might find themselves caught up in capricious fashion changes? Those of us involved in the current fashion of running for exercise may say that we do it because it is good for our health, but the health benefits of such exercise were known decades ago.[5] Talking with runners suggests that far more is at work in this movement than the logical reaction to a few papers in medical journals. Why wasn't the joy of running appreciated twenty years ago? Why are we thinking about running these days and not about once-popular leisure activities now in decline, such as leading Boy Scout troops or watching western movies?[6]

Fashions in one country may often move in one direction while those

5. A few minutes spent with an index to periodical literature will confirm that the idea that regular exercise helps prevent heart disease was part of the conventional wisdom by the mid-1950s.

6. There seems to be the same superabundance of theories to explain the decline of boy scouting since 1973 as for the decline in the stock market over the same period. See "Whatever Happened to . . . Boy Scouts: Trying to Make a Comeback," *U.S. News and World Report* (May 7, 1979), pp. 86–87. Those who think that people simply got tired of westerns will have to explain why it took a generation for them to do so.

in another country are moving in a different direction. In politics, for instance, we have seen in the last decade a drift toward conservatism in some Western countries and a drift toward socialism in others. The objective evidence for or against socialism cannot have moved both ways. Something about the social environment, collective memories, or leadership is different and changing through time differently in these countries. Is there any reason to think that social movements affect investments any less strongly than they do these other activities? We know that attitudes toward investments are very different across cultures. In West Germany today investors are notably cautious; it is hard to raise venture capital, and the stock market itself is very small. Isn't it plausible that attitudes that change across countries should also change within a country through time?

Some may argue that investing is less likely than other activities to be influenced by fashions because people make investment choices privately, based on their perception of the prospects for return, and usually not with any concern for what people will think. It is, however, plausible that these perceptions of return themselves represent changing fashions. The changing fashions in "physic" that Fielding noted are analogous. Sick people in Fielding's day asked physicians to bleed them because they thought they would get well as a result and not because they thought that they would impress other people by having it done. Therapeutic bleeding is an excellent example of a fashion because there has never been any scientific basis for it; the belief in its efficacy arose entirely from the social milieu.

WHO CONTROLS EQUITY INVESTMENTS?

It is important first to clarify the identity of investors in corporate stock. It is widely and mistakenly believed that (1) institutional investors hold most stocks, (2) most wealthy individuals have delegated authority to manage their investments, and (3) smart money dominates the market. By suggesting that the market is more professionalized than it is, these misconceptions lend spurious plausibility to the notion that markets are very efficient.

It is true that the importance of institutional investors has been growing in the postwar period. Institutional holdings of New York Stock

Exchange stocks as a percent of the total value of the stocks rose from 15.0 percent in 1955 to 35.4 percent in 1980.[7] Still, nearly 65 percent of all New York Stock Exchange stocks were held by individuals in 1980.

Most individually held corporate stock belongs to the wealthy. In 1971, the 1 percent of U.S. families (including single individuals) with the largest personal income accounted for 51 percent of the market value of stock owned by all families, while the 10 percent of families with the largest income accounted for 74 percent of market value.[8] Wealthy individuals are of course part of the same society as the rest of us. They read the same newspapers and watch the same television programs. They are different, however, in one important way. For them, information costs are quite low relative to the income from their investments. One might be inclined to think that they would in practice delegate to experts the authority over their investments.

A 1964 Brookings study interviewed 1,051 individuals with 1961 incomes of more than $10,000 (or about $34,000 in 1984 prices) concerning their investment habits, among other things. The 1961 median income for the sample was about $40,000 (or about $135,000 in 1984 prices). "Only one-tenth reported delegating some or all authority over their investments, and this proportion reached one-fourth only for those with incomes over $300,000. Only 2 percent of the entire high-income group said they delegated 'all' authority."[9] Instead of delegating authority, most made their own investment decisions with some advice: "About three-fourths of the high income respondents who managed their own assets said that they got advice from others in making their investment decisions. One in three of those seeking advice said they 'always' sought

7. See New York Stock Exchange, *New York Stock Exchange Fact Book 1983* (NYSE, 1983), p. 52. This source says that institutional investors accounted for 65 percent of all public volume on the New York Stock Exchange in the fourth quarter of 1980 (p. 54). Thus, institutional investors trade much more frequently than do individual investors. Data that are probably more accurate on institutional holdings are in Irwin Friend and Marshall Blume, *The Changing Role of the Institutional Investor* (Wiley, 1978); they estimated that 24.9 percent of all stock was held by institutions and foreigners in 1971, up from 17.9 percent in 1960 (p. 32).

8. See Marshall E. Blume, Jean Crockett, and Irwin Friend, "Stockownership in the United States: Characteristics and Trends," *Survey of Current Business*, vol. 54 (November 1974), pp. 16–40. In 1981, 7.2 percent of households had income above $50,000 (*Statistical Abstract of the United States, 1982–83*, p. 430).

9. Robin Barlow, Harvey E. Brazer, and James N. Morgan, *Economic Behavior of the Affluent* (Brookings, 1966), p. 26.

advice when investing, while two out of three said they did 'occasionally.' "[10] Two-thirds of the investors said they tried to keep informed, and more than half said they made use of business magazines, but "only one-tenth of those trying to keep informed said that they read the financial statements and other reports issued by the corporations in which they were considering an investment."[11]

What is really important for one's view of financial markets is not directly the extent to which institutional investors or wealthy individuals dominate the market, but the extent to which smart money dominates the market. One commonly expressed view is that intelligent individuals can be assumed to take control of the market by accumulating wealth through profitable trading. This argument overlooks the fact that individuals consume their wealth and eventually also die. When they die they bequeath it to others who have perhaps only a small probability of being smart investors as well. In assessing this probability, one must bear in mind that the class of smart-money investors does not correspond closely to the intelligent segment of the population. What is at work behind smart money is not just intelligence but also interest in investments and timeliness. Presumably the probability is fairly low that heirs are smart investors.[12]

There are several factors that serve to mitigate the effects of higher returns on the average wealth of smart-money investors. One is that most people do not acquire most of their maximum wealth until fairly late in the life cycle and thus do not have as much time to accumulate. Another factor is that in a growing population, younger persons, whose portfolios have had less time to accumulate, will figure more prominently in the aggregate of wealth. Yet another factor is that saving early in the life cycle tends for institutional reasons to take the form of investing in a house rather than in speculative assets.

Roughly speaking, one can expect to live thirty years after receiving a bequest on the death of one's parents. A representative smart-money heir who earns and accumulates at a rate n greater than a representative ordinary investor in the middle of the thirty years will thus have on

10. Ibid., p. 68.

11. Ibid., p. 71. These findings were also confirmed in other surveys. See George Katona, *Psychological Economics* (Elsevier, 1975), p. 269.

12. The median correlation (from 12 studies) between IQs of natural parents and of their children is 0.50. See H. J. Eysenck and Leon Kamin, *The Intelligence Controversy* (Wiley, 1980), p. 50.

average, if original bequests were equal, roughly $(1 + n)^{15}$ times as much wealth. If n is 2 percent per year, this is 1.3; if 5 percent per year, this is 2.1. As long as the percentage of smart investors is small, returns that are higher by this order of magnitude will not cause the smart money to take over the market.

Of course, it is unlikely that smart-money investors are pure accumulators; because we lack data on their savings patterns versus the savings patterns of ordinary investors, it is impossible to say anything concrete about how much money smart investors accumulate. If the smart investors behave like good trustees of the family estate and consume at exactly the rate that would preserve the real value of the family wealth, then smart money will not accumulate at all, regardless of the return it earns.

THE AMBIGUITY OF STOCK VALUE

Stock prices are likely to be among the prices that are relatively vulnerable to purely social movements because there is no accepted theory by which to understand the worth of stocks and no clearly predictable consequences to changing one's investments.

Ordinary investors have no model or at best a very incomplete model of the behavior of prices, dividends, or earnings of speculative assets. Do projections of large future deficits in the federal budget imply that the price of long-term bonds will go up or down? Does the election of a conservative U.S. president imply that earnings of General Motors will go up or down? Does a rise in the price of oil cause the price of IBM stock to go up or down? Ordinary investors have no objective way of knowing.

Ordinary investors are faced with what Frank Knight in 1921 called "uncertainty" rather than "risk":

> The practical difference between the two categories, risk and uncertainty, is that in the former the distribution of the outcome in a group of instances is known (either from calculation *a priori* or from statistics of past experience), while in the case of uncertainty this is not true, the reason being in general that it is impossible to form a group of instances, because the situation dealt with is in a high degree unique. . . . It is this *true uncertainty* which by preventing the theoretically perfect outworking of the tendencies of competition gives the characteristic form of "enterprise" to economic organization as a whole and accounts for the peculiar income of the entrepreneur.[13]

13. Frank H. Knight, *Risk, Uncertainty and Profit* (Augustus M. Kelley, 1964), pp. 232–33.

Ordinary investors also cannot judge the competence of investment counselors in the way they can that of other professionals. It is very easy to learn whether a map company is producing correct maps; we can therefore take it for granted that others have done this and that any map that is sold will serve to guide us. It is much harder to evaluate investment advisers who counsel individual investors on the composition of their portfolios and who claim to help them make investments with high returns. Most investors lack data on past outcomes of a counselor's advice and on whether the current advice is based on the same approach that produced these outcomes. Moreover, most investors do not understand data analysis or risk correction, necessary knowledge for evaluating the data.

It is also much easier to change one's mind on one's investments than on one's consumption of commodities. The former has no apparent immediate effect on one's well being, whereas to change one's consumption of commodities, one must give up some habit or consume something one formerly did not enjoy.

SUGGESTIBILITY AND GROUP PRESSURE

Since investors lack any clear sense of objective evidence regarding prices of speculative assets, the process by which their opinions are derived may be especially social. There is an extensive literature in social psychology on individual suggestibility and group pressure. Much of this literature seeks to quantify, by well-chosen experiments, how individual opinions are influenced by the opinions of others. A good example of such experiments is Muzafer Sherif's classic work using the "autokinetic effect."[14] In this experiment, subjects were seated in a totally darkened room and asked to view at a distance of five meters a point of light seen through a small hole in a metal box. They were told that the point of light would begin to move and were asked to report to the experimenter the magnitude, in inches, of its movements. In fact, the point was not moving, and the viewer had no frame of reference, in the total darkness, to decide how it was moving. When placed in groups so that they could hear answers of others in the group, the individuals arrived, without any discussion, at consensuses (differing across groups)

14. See Muzafer Sherif, "An Experimental Approach to the Study of Attitudes," *Sociometry*, vol. 1 (1937), pp. 90–98.

on the amount of movement. Subjects, interviewed afterward, showed little awareness of the influence of the group on their individual decision.

In another well-known experiment, Solomon Asch had individuals alone and in groups compare the lengths of line segments. The lengths were sufficiently different that, when responding alone, subjects gave very few wrong answers. Yet when placed in a group in which all other members were coached to give the same wrong answers, individual subjects also frequently gave wrong answers.[15] Through follow-up questions, Asch found that even though the subject was often aware of the correct answer, and the answer was completely inoffensive, the subject was afraid to contradict the group.

The research shows evidence of flagrant decision errors under social pressure but not of abandonment of rational individual judgment. It does help provide some understanding of possible origins of swings in public opinion. The Asch experiment suggests that group pressures do serve at the very least to cause individuals to remain silent when their own views appear to deviate from the group's, and their silence will prevent the dissemination of relevant information that might establish the dissenters' views more firmly.

THE DIFFUSION OF OPINIONS

The dynamic process by which social movements take place is the subject of an extensive literature by social psychologists and sociologists, and the basic mechanisms are well known. The ideas that represent a movement may be latent in people's minds long before the movement begins. An idea may not become a matter of conviction or active thought until the individual hears the idea from several friends or from public authorities. This process takes time. The process may be helped along if some vivid news event causes people to talk about related matters or slowed if a news event distracts their attention.

Social movements can take place in a matter of hours after so vivid an event as the onset of a war. Or changes in attitudes can take decades to diffuse through the population, as evidenced by the fact that many fashion changes in dress seem to happen very slowly. The communications media may, if attention is given to some event, speed the rate of

15. See Solomon E. Asch, *Social Psychology* (Prentice Hall, 1952).

diffusion. However, the general finding of research on persuasion is that "any impact that the mass media have on opinion change is less than that produced by informal face-to-face communication of the person with his primary groups, his family, friends, coworkers, and neighbors."[16] This fact is recognized by television advertisers who, in promoting their products, often try to create with actors the illusion of such communication. Katona has used the term *social learning* to refer to the slow process of "mutual reinforcement through exchange of information among peer groups by word of mouth, a major condition for the emergence of a uniform response to new stimuli by very many people."[17] Thus, it is not surprising that in surveys in the 1950s and 1960s "the answers to the two questions 'Do you own any stocks' and 'Do you have any friends or colleagues who own any stocks' were practically identical."[18]

Such diffusion processes for news or rumor have been modeled more formally by mathematical sociologists drawing on the mathematical theory of epidemics.[19] For example, in what has been referred to as the "general epidemic model,"[20] it is assumed, first, that new carriers of news (as of a disease) are created at a rate equal to an "infection rate" β times the number of carriers times the number of susceptibles and, second, that carriers cease being carriers at a "removal rate" τ. The first assumption is that of the familiar model which gives rise to the logistic curve; and the second assumption causes any epidemic or social movement eventually to come to an end. In this model a new infectious agent or an event interpreted as important news can have either of two basic consequences. If the infection rate is less than a threshold equal to the removal rate divided by the number of susceptibles, the number of carriers will decline monotonically. If the infection rate is above the threshold, the number of carriers will have a hump-shaped pattern, rising at first and then declining.

16. William J. McGuire, "The Nature of Attitudes and Attitude Change," in Gardner Lindzey and Elliot Aronson, eds., *Handbook of Social Psychology* (Addison Wesley, 1969), p. 231.

17. See Katona, *Psychological Economics*, p. 203.

18. Ibid., p. 267.

19. See for example David J. Bartholomew, *Stochastic Models for Social Processes* (Wiley, 1967).

20. See Norman T. Bailey, *The Mathematical Theory of Epidemics* (London: C. Griffin, 1957).

The removal rate and the infection rate may differ dramatically from one social movement to another depending on the characteristics of the sources, media, and receivers. One survey of the literature on removal rates after persuasive communications concluded that "the 'typical' persuasive communication has a half-life of six months" but that different experiments produced widely different half-lives.[21] Changes in the infection rate or removal rate may be what accounts for the sudden appearance of some social movements. A rise in the infection rate, for example, may cause an attitude long latent in people's minds to snowball into a movement.

We might expect then to see a variety of patterns in social movements: long-lasting "humps" that build slowly (low removal and infection rate) or that rise and fall quickly (high removal and infection rate); news events with a subsequent monotonic decline of infectives (zero infection rate) or followed by a monotonically increasing number of infectives (zero removal rate). Of course, such patterns may not be seen directly in prices of speculative assets, as the "alternative model" I present later in the paper will show.

SOCIAL MOVEMENTS AND THE POSTWAR STOCK MARKET

The real price of corporate stocks, as measured by a deflated Standard and Poor's composite stock price index (figure 1), shows what appears to be a pronounced uptrend between the late 1940s and the late 1960s and since then a downtrend (or, more accurately, a single major drop between 1973 and 1975). The postwar uptrend period, the last great bull market, has often been characterized as one of contagious and increasingly excessive optimism. Is there any evidence of such a social movement then? Is there evidence that such a social movement came to an end after the late 1960s?

Such evidence will not take the form of proof that people should have known better than to price stocks as they did. The postwar period was one of rapidly growing real earnings and real dividends, and that the

21. McGuire, "The Nature of Attitudes," pp. 253–54. A description of recent research in marketing journals on the removal rate is in Richard P. Bagozzi and Alvin J. Silk, "Recall, Recognition, and the Measurement of Memory for Print Advertisements," *Marketing Science*, vol. 2 (Spring 1983), pp. 95–134. See Bartholomew, *Stochastic Models*, for a discussion of empirical work on the infection rate.

Figure 1. Standard and Poor's Stock Price Data, 1926–84[a]

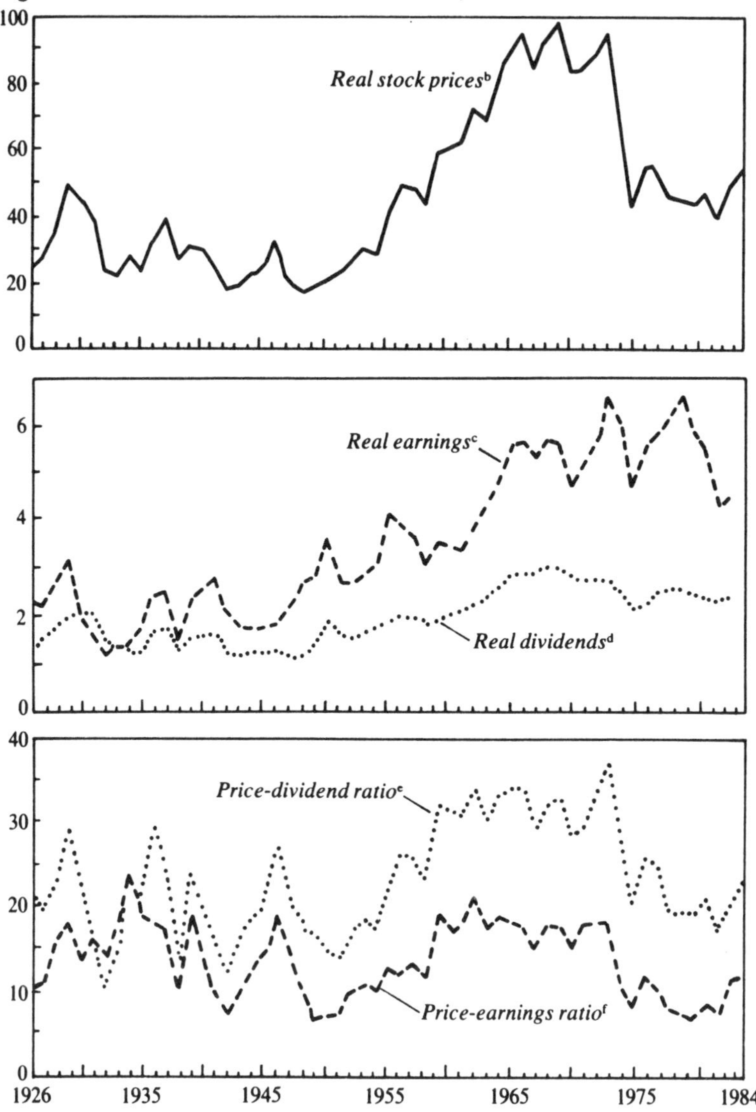

Source: Calculated from data from Standard and Poor's Statistical Service and the U.S. Bureau of Labor Statistics.

a. Annual data, fifty-nine observations from 1926 to 1984. The stock price index is Standard and Poor's composite stock price index.

b. Stock price index for January (1941–43 = 100) divided by the January producer price index, all items, times 100.

c. Four-quarter total for the fourth quarter of Standard and Poor's earnings per share adjusted to the stock price index, divided by the January producer price index, times 100.

d. Four-quarter total for the fourth quarter of Standard and Poor's dividends per share adjusted to the stock price index, divided by the January producer price index, times 100.

e. Computed by dividing the stock price series by the dividends series for the preceding year (in nominal terms).

f. Computed as for the price-dividend ratio, with earnings in place of dividends.

growth should be expected to continue was an idea backed by plausible reasons, such as:

the constant speed-up in business research in order to cut costs and bring out ever newer and more competitive products; the extension of business expansion planning farther and farther into the future, which means that such plans are carried forward regardless of any jiggles in the trend of business; the improvement in business techniques that offset the effects of seasonal fluctuations; the advance in methods of monetary management by the Federal Reserve Board; and the similar advance in general understanding of the effects of the Government's tax and other economic policies.[22]

How was anyone to know whether these reasons were right or not?

The evidence for a social movement driving the bull market will come instead from other sources. The evidence will be the growing numbers of individuals who participated in, were interested in, or knew about the market; the changes in relations between investor and agent; and the changes in attitudes that might plausibly affect the valuation of stocks. The evidence is not intended to provide a tight theory of the movements of stock prices but to show that large social movements appear to have occurred that might plausibly have had a great impact on stock prices. In fact, there is a superabundance of plausible reasons for the movements of the market.

Evidence for the growing numbers of individuals who participated in the market can of course be found most directly in the rising quantity of stocks held by institutional investors. The most important component of this increase was pension funds. The rise of employer pension funds in the postwar period might even be considered a social movement that probably caused an increased demand for shares. Individuals may, by saving less themselves, offset the saving done on their behalf by firms; but because most people do not hold any stocks, it is not possible for them (without short sales) to offset the institutional demand for stocks by holding fewer shares. Such changes in demand by institutions are likely to be important in determining asset prices but are not my main concern here. Others have studied such changes using flow-of-funds methodology.[23]

22. George Shea, *Wall Street Journal*, October 12, 1955, reprinted in *Forty Years on Wall Street* (Princeton, N.J.: Dow Jones, 1968), pp. 42–43.

23. For a recent example, see Benjamin M. Friedman, "Effects of Shifting Saving Patterns on Interest Rates and Economic Activity," *Journal of Finance*, vol. 37 (March 1982), pp. 37–62.

The period of rising stock prices also corresponds roughly with a period of a dramatic increase in the number of people who participated directly (not through institutions) in the stock market. The New York Stock Exchange shareownership surveys showed that the total number of individual shareowners as a percent of the U.S. population rose from 4 percent in 1952 to 7 percent in 1959 to a peak of 15 percent in 1970.[24] The corresponding numbers for 1975, 1980, and 1981 varied from 11 percent to 12 percent.[25]

The increase in individual stockownership appears to correspond to an increase in knowledge about and interest in the market. The 1954 New York Stock Exchange investor attitude survey, consisting of interviews of several thousand individuals, was motivated by the question, Why is it that "4 out of 5 doctors, lawyers, major and minor executives, engineers and salesmen *do not own* stock in publicly owned corporations?"[26] What came out of the survey was a sense of lack of information or interest in the stock market and vague senses of prejudice against the stock market. Only 23 percent of the adult population knew enough to define corporate stock as "a share in profit," "bought and sold by public, anyone can buy," or "not preferred or a bond."

By 1959 there appeared a "much better understanding of the functions of the Stock Exchange as the nation's marketplace." The number of Americans who could "explain the functions of the Exchange" rose nearly 20 percent. The number who knew "that companies must meet certain standards before the Exchange will permit their stocks to be listed for trading" increased 36 percent in the same five-year period.[27]

The growth of numbers of people who knew about or were involved at all in the stock market is important evidence that something other than a reevaluation of optimal forecasts of the long-run path of future

24. New York Stock Exchange, *Share-ownership 1952* through *1970* (NYSE, 1953 through 1971). The rise before 1970 of shareownership involved a trend toward somewhat more egalitarian distribution of stock. In 1958, 83.2 percent of stock value was owned by individuals with the top 10 percent of income. By 1970, this had fallen to 75.4 percent. See Friend, Blume, and Crockett, "Stockownership," p. 27.

25. New York Stock Exchange, *Share-ownership 1975, 1980,* and *1981* (NYSE, 1976, 1981, and 1982).

26. New York Stock Exchange, *The Public Speaks to the Exchange Community* (NYSE, 1955), p. 54.

27. See New York Stock Exchange, *The Investors of Tomorrow,* title page and p. 6 (NYSE, 1960).

dividends was at work in producing the bull market. Any model that attributes the increase in stock prices to a Bayesian learning process will not stand up to the observation that most of the investors at the peak of the bull market were not involved or interested in the market at all at the beginning of the increase.

Evidence about changing relations between individual investors and their agents takes two forms: evidence regarding the rise of stockbrokers and of publicity campaigns from them and evidence regarding the investment club movement.

Between 1954 and 1959 stockbrokers were growing in reputation. In the 1954 New York Stock Exchange survey 30 percent of the adult population said they would turn first to a broker for investment advice; by 1959 this figure had risen to 38 percent. During this five-year period, stockbrokers replaced bankers as the first source of investment advice. An estimated 9 million adults said they were contacted by brokers in 1959, compared with fewer than 5 million in 1954.[28]

The New York Stock Exchange initiated an investors' education program as part of a broader shareownership program. Begun in 1954, the program by 1959 had a list of 2,500 lecturers in 85 cities. Lectures were held in local high schools as part of adult education programs by lecturers "bent on carrying the investing gospel . . . wherever there were ears to hear."[29]

By 1959 the program had conducted 4,500 lecture courses reaching 525,000 persons or about 4 percent of the total number of shareholders in 1959. The investor education program used all the media, including advertisements in newspapers and magazines and on radio. As early as 1954, when the program was only six months old, 5 percent of the adult population in the United States could identify the New York Stock Exchange as the source of the slogan "Own Your Share of American Business."[30]

In contrast the 1970s was a period of low profits for the New York Stock Exchange and advertising in newspapers and magazines was suspended. In 1975 competitive commissions were established and amendments to the Securities Act threatened the viability of the New York Stock Exchange. Prices of seats on the exchange dropped. In response to the problems, the exchange in 1977 severely cut back the

28. New York Stock Exchange, *Investors of Tomorrow*, pp. 9, 14.
29. See *New York Times*, September 20, 1959.
30. New York Stock Exchange, *The Public Speaks*, p. 10.

investors' education program and dropped the adult education program. Lack of public enthusiasm for the program was also offered as a reason for the cutback. The same factors that caused the New York Stock Exchange to suspend its investors' education program may have also had the effect of decreasing the efforts of individual brokers to promote corporate stocks. Such factors as competitive commissions, which reduce the profits in conventional brokerages, have "tended to shrink the numbers of people who are out there trying to encourage individual investors into this market place."[31]

Investment clubs are social clubs in which small groups of people pursue together a hobby of investing. Interest in such clubs might well give some indication of how much stocks were talked about and how much people enjoyed investing. The number of clubs in the National Association of Investment Clubs rose from 923 in 1954 to a peak of 14,102 in 1970 and then fell to 3,642 in 1980.[32] The total number of individuals directly involved in investment clubs and their aggregate wealth is of course small. However, the investment club movement is plausible evidence of a national movement that is not reflected in the membership rolls.

There is in the postwar period evidence of substantial changes in behavior big enough to have a major impact on the market. For example, the percentage of people who said that religion is "very important" in their lives fell from 75 percent in 1952 to 52 percent in 1978.[33] The birth rate hovered around 2.5 percent throughout the 1950s and then began a gradual decline to around 1.5 percent in the 1970s. These changes may reflect changing attitudes toward the importance of family, of heirs, or of individual responsibility for others.

Of all such changes, the one with perhaps the most striking importance for demand for shares in the postwar period is the pervasive decline in confidence in society's institutions after the bull market period. According to poll analyst Daniel Yankelovich:

> We have seen a steady rise of mistrust in our national institutions. . . . Trust in government declined dramatically from almost 80% in the late 1950s to about 33% in 1976. Confidence in business fell from approximately a 70% level in the late 60s to about 15% today. Confidence in other institutions—the press, the

31. Robert M. Gardiner, chairman of Reynolds Securities, Inc., as quoted in New York Stock Exchange, *Share-ownership 1975* (NYSE, 1976), p. 21.

32. Data from the National Association of Investment Clubs.

33. See "Religion in America," *The Gallup Report*, no. 222 (March 1984).

military, the professions—doctors and lawyers—sharply declined from the mid-60s to the mid-70s.[34]

To Yankelovich's list we may add stockbrokers. One of the findings of the New York Stock Exchange 1977–78 survey was that "a negative image of brokers and firms permeates all subgroups and even top quality clients have an unfavorable impression of the industry."[35] By their very pervasiveness, the negative attitudes toward institutions suggest a prejudice rather than an informed judgment.

The Efficient Markets Model

The observation that stock returns are not very forecastable is widely thought to mean that investor psychology could not be an important factor in financial markets. Why is it thought so? If investor fads influenced stock prices, the argument goes, then it would seem that these fads would cause stock price movements to be somewhat predictable. Moreover, because dividends themselves are somewhat forecastable (firms in fact announce changes in their dividends from time to time), and in spite of this we are unable to forecast well any change in returns, it must be true that stock prices in some sense are determined in anticipation of dividends paid. Thus, stock prices should be determined by optimal forecasts of dividends.

The above argument can be formalized by representing the unforecastability of returns by $E_tR_t = \delta$, where E_t denotes mathematical expectation conditional on all publicly available information at time t, R_t is the real (corrected for inflation) rate of return (including both dividends and capital gain) on a stock between time t and time $t + 1$, and δ is a constant. Here, R_t equals $(P_{t+1} - P_t + D_t)/P_t$ where P_t is the real price of the share at time t and D_t any real dividend which might be paid in the time period. This is a first-order rational expectations model of the kind familiar in the literature that can be solved, subject to a stability

34. From a speech, April 1977, quoted in Seymour Martin Lipset and William Schneider, *The Confidence Gap: Business, Labor and Government in the Public Mind* (Free Press, 1983), p. 15. The Gallup Poll also documents a fairly steady decline in confidence in all major institutions over the years 1973–83. See *Gallup Report*, no. 217 (October 1983).

35. See New York Stock Exchange, *Public Attitudes Toward Investing: Marketing Implications* (NYSE, 1979), p. 5.

terminal condition, by recursive substitution.[36] Out of the negative result that we cannot seem to forecast returns we thus get the powerful efficient markets model:[37]

$$P_t = \sum_{k=0}^{\infty} \frac{E_t D_{t+k}}{(1 + \delta)^{k+1}}. \quad (1)$$

Equation 1 asserts that real price is the present discounted value of expected future dividends, and in this sense price anticipates optimally (that is, takes into account all publicly available information) the stream of dividends that the stock will pay in the future.

There is a fundamental error in this argument for the efficient markets model: it overlooks the fact that the statistical tests have not shown that returns are not forecastable; they have shown only that returns are not *very* forecastable. The word *very* is crucial here, since alternative models that have price determined primarily by fads (such as will be discussed below) also imply that returns are not very forecastable.

We can get some idea at this point of the power of the regression tests of the efficient markets model against importantly different alternatives. Consider an alternative model in which the true (theoretical) R^2 in a regression of aggregate returns of corporate stocks on some set of information variables is 0.1. Given that the standard deviation of the real annual returns on the aggregate stock market is about 18 percent, such an R^2 implies that the standard deviation of the predictable component of returns is about 5.7 percent per year. Thus, under this alternative

36. One rearranges the equation to read $P_t = bE_tD_t + bE_tP_{t+1}$, where $b = 1/(1 + \delta)$, and then uses the fact that $E_tE_{t+k} = E_t$ if $k > 0$. One substitutes in the above rational expectations model for P_{t+1}, yielding $P_t = bE_tD_t + b^2E_tD_{t+1} + b^2E_tP_{t+2}$. One repeats this process, successively substituting for the price terms on the right hand side. The terminal condition assumption in the text is that the price term, $b^nE_tP_{t+n}$, goes to zero as n goes to infinity.

37. Paul Samuelson explains the relationship of this model to the random walk model in his "Proof that properly discounted present values of assets vibrate randomly," in Hiroaki Nagatani and Kate Crowley, eds., *The Collected Scientific Papers of Paul A. Samuelson,* vol. 4 (MIT Press, 1977), pp. 465–70. It should be emphasized of course that there is no agreement on the precise definition of the term "efficient markets model" or whether it corresponds to equation 1. For example, in his well-known survey, Eugene Fama says only that "a market in which prices always 'fully reflect' available information is called 'efficient.' " The empirical work he discusses, however, tests the hypothesis that price changes or returns are unforecastable. See Eugene F. Fama, "Efficient Capital Markets: A Review of Theory and Empirical Work," *Journal of Finance*, vol. 25 (May 1970), pp. 383–417.

model we might well predict real returns of 14 percent in one year and 2 percent in another (these are one-standard-deviation departures from mean return). In an unusual year we might predict a real return of 19 percent or −3 percent (these are two-standard-deviation departures from the mean return). Yet if the alternative model is true with thirty observations (thirty years of data) and one forecasting variable, the probability of rejecting market efficiency in a conventional F-test at the 0.05 level is only 0.42. With two forecasting variables, the probability of rejecting is 0.32, and the probability becomes negligible as the number of explanatory variables is increased further.[38] As I have argued in a paper with Pierre Perron, increasing the number of observations by sampling more frequently while leaving the span in years of data unchanged may not increase the power of tests very much and may even reduce it.[39]

Someone may well wonder if there is not also some direct evidence that stock prices really do anticipate future dividends in the manner represented in equation 1. There is anecdotal evidence that the prices of some firms whose dividends can be forecasted to fall to zero (bankruptcy) or soar to new levels (breakthrough) do anticipate these movements. But these anecdotes do not show that there is not another component of the volatility of prices, a component that might dominate price movements in the stocks whose dividends are not so forecastable. For the aggregate stock market, there is no evidence at all that stock price movements have been followed by corresponding dividend movements.[40]

Some may argue that the constancy of discount rates in equation 1 may not be an appropriate feature for a general model of market efficiency. There are, of course, many variations on this model, such as the recent "consumption beta" models.[41] It is not possible to address all

38. These power computations are based on the usual assumption of normal residuals; as a result the conventional F-statistic is, under the alternative hypothesis, distributed as noncentral F, with $k - 1$ and $n - 1$ degrees of freedom and noncentrality parameter $(n/2)R^2/(1 - R^2)$, where R^2 is the theoretical coefficient of determination under the alternative hypothesis.

39. See Robert J. Shiller and Pierre Perron, "Testing the Random Walk Hypothesis: Power vs. Frequency of Observation" (Yale University, 1984).

40. See Robert J. Shiller, "Do Stock Prices Move Too Much to be Justified by Subsequent Changes in Dividends?" *American Economic Review*, vol. 71 (June 1981), pp. 421–36.

41. My own discussion of these and their plausibility in light of data may be found in Robert J. Shiller, "Consumption, Asset Markets and Macroeconomic Fluctuations," in

these alternatives here. Equation 1 is chosen as the most commonplace version of the efficient markets theory and a version that seems to have figured most prominently in the arguments against market psychology. Moreover, arguments about the power of tests of equation 1 may well extend to some of the other variants of the efficient markets hypothesis.

An Alternative Model

Let us postulate the existence of smart-money investors who, subject to their wealth limitations, respond quickly and appropriately to publicly available information. Consider a story that tells how they might alter the response of the market to the behavior of ordinary investors. This story is no doubt oversimplified and restrictive, but then so is the simple efficient markets model, with which it is to be compared.

Smart-money investors in this model respond to rationally expected returns but to an extent limited by their wealth. Suppose that their demand for stock is linear in the expected return on the market (or if the model is applied to an individual firm, the expected return on a share of that firm) over the next time period:

$$Q_t = \frac{(E_t R_t - \rho)}{\varphi}. \tag{2}$$

Here, Q_t is the demand for shares by smart money at time t expressed as a portion of the total shares outstanding, and $E_t R_t$ is the expected return starting at time t, defined as it is above. The symbols ρ and φ represent constants. Thus, ρ is the expected real return such that there is no demand for shares by the smart money. The real return at which $Q_t = 1$ is $\rho + \varphi$; that is, φ is the risk premium that would induce smart money to hold all the shares. The terms ρ and φ reflect the risk aversion of the smart money as well as the total real wealth of those smart-money investors who have evaluated the stock, the riskiness of the stock, and characteristics of alternative investments.

Ordinary investors include everyone who does not respond to expected returns optimally forecasted. Let us suppose that they overreact to news or are vulnerable to fads. We will not make assumptions about

Karl Brunner and Allan H. Meltzer, eds., *Economic Policy in a World of Change*, Carnegie Rochester Conference Series in Public Policy, vol. 17 (Amsterdam: North-Holland, 1982), pp. 203–38.

their behavior at all, but merely define Y_t as the total value of stock demanded per share by these investors.[42] Equilibrium in this market requires that $Q_t + Y_t/P_t = 1$. Solving the resulting rational expectations model just as we did to derive equation 1 gives us the model

$$(3) \qquad P_t = \sum_{k=0}^{\infty} \frac{E_t D_{t+k} + \varphi E_t Y_{t+k}}{(1 + \rho + \varphi)^{k+1}},$$

so that real price is the present value, discounted at rate $\rho + \varphi$, of both the expected future dividend payments and φ times the expected future demand by ordinary investors. The limit of this expression as φ goes to zero (that is, as smart money becomes more and more influential) is the ordinary efficient markets model that makes price the present value of expected dividends. The limit of this expression as φ goes to infinity (as smart money becomes less and less influential) is the model $P_t = Y_t$, so that ordinary investors determine the price.

Equation 3 and the efficient markets model (equation 1) could be equally consistent with the usual finding in the event-studies literature that announcements have their effect on returns as soon as the information becomes public and have little predictable effect thereafter. Equation 3 has, however, a very different interpretation for the jump in price that coincides with the announcement. The jump does not represent only what the smart money thinks the announcement means for future dividends. It also represents what the smart money thinks the announcement means for the demand for stock by ordinary investors. Equation 3 implies that the price effect of changes in the outlook for future dividends will be governed by equation 1 if Y_t is not also affected by these changes. However, if Y_t is always positive, the discount rate $\rho + \varphi$ in equation 3 is necessarily greater than or equal to the expected return on the market, which is the discount factor in equation 1. If $\rho + \varphi$ is high, then factors affecting expectations of distant dividends will have relatively little effect on price today.

The more persistent is the behavior of the variable Y_t through time (that is, the less we can expect changes in Y_t to be offset by subsequent changes in the opposite direction), the less the moving average in expression 3 will reduce its variance and the more, in general, will be its influence on P_t.

42. That is, Y_t is the total shares demanded at current price times current price divided by number of shares outstanding. If we assume that demand elasticity by ordinary investors is unitary, we might regard Y_t as exogenous to this model.

I argued above that models of the diffusion of opinions suggest a number of possible patterns of response, among them a hump-shaped pattern in which Y_t would rise for a while, level off, and then return to its normal level. The implication for real price P_t of such a hump-shaped response of Y_t to a piece of news depends on the time frame of the response relative to the discount rate $\rho + \varphi$. Suppose the hump can be predicted to build up very quickly and dissipate, say, in a matter of weeks. Then equation 3 implies that there will be very little impact on price. The relatively long moving average in equation 3 will smooth over the hump in Y_t so that it is observed, if at all, only in a very attenuated form. The demand for shares by ordinary investors will show the hump-shaped pattern as smart money sells shares to them at virtually unchanged prices only to buy the shares back after the ordinary investors have lost interest.

If the hump-shaped pattern takes longer to evolve, the effect on price will be bigger. Then as soon as the news that gives rise to the hump-shaped pattern becomes known to the smart money, the price of the stock will jump discontinuously. This jump will be instantaneous, taking effect as soon as the smart money realizes that the price will be higher in the future. After the initial jump, the effect of the news will be to cause the price of the stock to rise gradually as Y_t approaches its peak (not so fast as to cause higher than normal returns after the lower dividend-price ratio is taken into account); the price will peak somewhat before Y does and then decline. Returns, however, will tend to be low during the period of price rise.

A more explicit yet simple example along these lines will illustrate why tests of market efficiency may have low power even if the market is driven entirely by fashions or fads. Suppose that the dividend D_t is constant through time, so that by the efficient markets model (equation 1) price would always be constant. Suppose also that $Y_t = U_{t-1} + U_{t-2} + \ldots + U_{t-n}$, where U_t is white noise, that is, U_t is uncorrelated with U_{t-k} for all k not equal to zero. Suppose current and lagged values for U are in the information set of the smart money. Here, Y responds to an observed shock in U with a rising, then falling (or square hump) pattern. Under these assumptions, $Y_{t+1} - Y_t$ is perfectly forecastable based on information at time t. However, $P_{t+1} - P_t$ will be hardly forecastable from information at time t. It follows from equation 3 that P_t will equal a constant plus a moving average of U with substantial weight on U_t. The theoretical R^2 in a regression of $P_{t+1} - P_t$ on P_t is only 0.015 for the case

$n = 20$ years, $\rho = 0$, and $\varphi = 0.2$. If one included all information (the current and twenty lagged U values) in the regression, the theoretical R^2 would rise, but only to 0.151. If the U_t are for each t uniformly distributed from 0 to 1, and if the constant dividend is 0.5 (so that the mean dividend price ratio is 4 percent) then the theoretical R^2 (as estimated in a Monte Carlo experiment) in a regression of the return R_t on D_t/P_t is only 0.079.

Let us now consider three alternative extreme views of the behavior of Y_t: that it responds to exogenous fads whose origin is unrelated to relevant economic data, that it responds to lagged returns, and that it responds to dividends.

The first extreme view is that Y_t is independent of current and lagged dividends; it is exogenous noise caused by capricious fashions or fads. In this view, Y_t may respond systematically to vivid news events (say, the president suffering a heart attack) but not to any time-series data that we observe. It is reasonable also to suppose that Y_t is a stationary stochastic process in that it tends to return to a mean. Thus, if demand by ordinary investors is high relative to the mean of Y_t it can be expected eventually to decline. If dividends vary relatively little through time, an argument can then be made that would suggest that return is positively correlated with the dividend-price ratio D_t/P_t. In the next section this correlation will be examined with data.

The second extreme view is that Y_t responds to past returns, that is, Y_t is a function of R_{t-1}, R_{t-2}, and so on. Together with equation 2 this gives a simple rational expectations model whose only exogenous variable is the dividend D_t. If we were to specify the function relating Y_t to past returns and specify the stochastic properties of D_t, we would be left with a model that makes P_t driven exclusively by D_t. Depending on the nature of the function and the stochastic properties of D_t, price may overreact to dividends relative to equation 1.

The third extreme view is that Y_t responds directly to current and lagged dividends, that is, Y_t is directly a function of D_t, D_{t-1}, D_{t-2}, and so on. For example, dividend growth may engender expectations of future real dividend growth that are unwarranted given the actual stochastic properties of D_t. Such expectations might also cause price to overreact to dividends relative to equation 1. Such an overreaction (to dividends as well as to earnings) will be studied econometrically below.

My suggestions about the possible behavior of Y_t are perhaps too extreme and special to provide the basis for serious econometric modeling now. However, these possibilities and equation 3 provide the motivation for some exploratory data analysis.

An Exploratory Data Analysis

STOCK PRICES APPEAR TO OVERREACT TO DIVIDENDS

Aggregate real stock prices are fairly highly correlated over time with aggregate real dividends. The simple correlation coefficient between the annual (January) real Standard and Poor's composite stock price index *P* and the corresponding annual real dividend series *D* between 1926 and 1983 is 0.91 (figure 1).[43] This correlation is partly due to the common trend between the two series, but the trend is by no means the whole story. The correlation coefficient between the real stock price index *P* and a linear time trend over the same sample is only 0.60.[44] Thus, the price of the aggregate stock market is importantly linked to its dividends, and much of the movements of the stock market that we often regard as inexplicable can be traced to movements in dividends. One reason that most of us are not accustomed to thinking of the stock market in this way is that most of the data series cover a smaller time interval (years rather than the decades shown in the figure) and sample the data more frequently (monthly, say, rather than the annual rate shown in the figure). The correlation coefficient between real price and real dividends might be much lower with data from the smaller, more frequently sampled time interval or might appear to be more dominated by trend.

The correlation between real price *P* and the real earnings series *E* for 1926 to 1983 is 0.75. This number is closer to the correlation of *P* with a linear time trend. Although the correlation coefficient between *P* and *D* is fairly high, the real price is substantially more volatile than the real dividend. If *P* is regressed on *D* with a constant term in the 1926–83 sample period, the coefficient of *D* is 38.0 and the constant term is −0.28. The average price-dividend ratio *P*/*D* in this sample is 22.4. The real

43. The correlation of *P* with *D* for the years 1871–1925 was 0.84. In this paper, dividend and earnings series before 1926 are from the book which originated what is now called the Standard and Poor's composite stock price index: Alfred Cowles and Associates, *Common-Stock Indexes, 1871–1937* (Principia Press, 1938), series Da-1 and Ea-1. All series are deflated by the producer price index (January starting 1900, annual series before 1900), where 1967 = 100.

44. The correlation of *P* with time for 1871 to 1925 was 0.43.

price moves proportionally more than the real dividend, and as a result *P/D* tends to move with real prices. The correlation in this sample of *P/D* with *P* (0.83) and with *D* (0.67) is strong enough that it can be seen in the figure. The volatility of stock prices relative to dividends is another reason why we tend not to view the stock market as driven so closely by dividends.

One would think that if the efficient markets model (equation 1) is true, the price-dividend ratio should be low when real dividends are high (relative to trend or relative to the dividends' average value in recent history) and high when real dividends are low. One would also think that the real price, which represents according to equation 1 the long-run outlook for real dividends, would be sluggish relative to the real dividend. Therefore, short-run movements in the real dividend would correspond to short-run movements in the opposite direction in the price-dividend ratio.

The observed perverse behavior of the price-dividend ratio might be described as an overreaction of stock prices to dividends, if it is correct to suppose that dividends tend to return to trend or return to the average of recent history. This behavior of stock prices may be consistent with some psychological models. Psychologists have shown in experiments that individuals may continually overreact to superficially plausible evidence even when there is no statistical basis for their reaction.[45] Such an overreaction hypothesis does not necessarily imply that the ultimate source of stock price movements should be thought of as dividends or the earnings of firms. Dividends are under the discretion of managers.[46] John Lintner, after a survey of dividend setting behavior of individual firms, concluded that firms have a target payout ratio from earnings but also feel that they should try to keep dividends fairly constant through time.[47] In doing this, managers, like the public, are forecasting earnings and may become overly optimistic or pessimistic. In reality, the divi-

45. See for example Amos Tversky and Daniel Kahneman, "Judgment under Uncertainty: Heuristics and Biases," *Science*, vol. 185 (September 1974), pp. 1124–31.

46. Marsh and Merton claimed that dividends are determined by management's optimal forecast of long-run earnings. See Terry A. Marsh and Robert C. Merton, "Aggregate Dividend Behavior and Its Implications for Tests of Stock Market Rationality," Working Paper 1475–83 (Massachusetts Institute of Technology, Alfred P. Sloan School of Management, September 1983).

47. See John Lintner, "Distribution of Incomes of Corporations among Dividends, Retained Earnings, and Taxes," *American Economic Review*, vol. 46 (May 1956, *Papers and Proceedings, 1955*), pp. 97–113.

dends and stock prices may both be driven by the same social optimism or pessimism, and the "overreaction" may simply reflect a greater response to the fads in price than in dividends. The apparent response of price to earnings could also be attributed to the same sort of effect to the extent that reported earnings themselves are subject to the discretion of accountants. Fisher Black has claimed that the change in accounting practices through time might be described as striving to make earnings an indicator of the value of the firm rather than the cash flow.[48] An individual firm is substantially constrained in its accounting practices, but the accounting profession's concept of conventional accounting methods may be influenced by notions of what is the proper level of aggregate earnings, and these notions may be influenced by social optimism or pessimism.

The relation between real price and real dividend can be described perhaps more satisfactorily from a distributed lag regression of P on D, that is, a regression that predicts P as a weighted moving average of current and lagged D. One sees from rows one and two of table 1 that when the real price is regressed with a thirty-year distributed lag on current and lagged real dividends, the current real dividend has a coefficient greater than the average price-dividend ratio (22.6 for this sample), and the sum of the coefficients of the lagged real dividends is negative. The sum of all coefficients of real dividends, current and lagged, is about the average price-dividend ratio. Thus, this equation implies that the price tends to be unusually high when real dividends are high relative to a weighted average of real dividends over the past thirty years and low when dividends are low relative to this weighted average.

Rows 5 and 6 of table 1 show the same regression but with real earnings as the independent variable. The coefficient of current earnings is less than the average price-earnings ratio (13.0 for this sample). Compared with dividends, earnings show more short-run variability; therefore these results do not contradict a notion that prices overreact to earnings as well as to dividends. The lower $\overline{R}^2$ in this regression might be regarded as a reflection of the fact that dividends are not really well described by the Lintner model, which made dividends a simple distributed lag on earnings.[49] The $\overline{R}^2$ is high enough that some major movements in stock prices are explained by this regression. For example, the decline

48. See Fisher Black, "The Magic in Earnings: Economic Earnings versus Accounting Earnings," *Financial Analysts Journal* (November–December 1980), pp. 19–24.

49. Ibid.

Table 1. Distributed Lag Regressions for Real Stock Prices or Returns on Real Dividends or Earnings, Selected Periods, 1900–83[a]

						Sample statistic				
Sample period	*Dependent variable*[b]	*Constant*	*Coefficient of current independent variable*	*Sum of coefficients of lagged independent variable*[c]	*Coefficient of lagged error*	*F*	*Significance level of F*	$\overline{R}^2$	*Durbin-Watson*	*Standard error*
				Independent variable is real dividends[d]						
1900–83	*P*	−0.08 (−2.95)	34.64 (14.16)	−11.79 (−4.34)	. . .	257.3	0.00	0.90	0.82	0.07
1900–83[e]	*P*	−0.07 (−1.20)	28.25 (9.13)	−5.37 (−1.14)	0.66 (7.89)	44.49	0.00	0.68	1.86	0.06
1900–82	$R(t + 1)$	0.09 (1.21)	−6.57 (−1.03)	9.62 (1.40)	. . .	2.72	0.05	0.06	2.06	0.19
1926–82	$R(t + 1)$	0.17 (1.33)	−7.62 (−0.94)	5.17 (0.57)	. . .	1.52	0.22	0.03	2.05	0.20
				Independent variable is real earnings[f]						
1900–83	*P*	0.10 (2.61)	11.73 (5.61)	−5.83 (−2.29)	. . .	57.59	0.00	0.67	0.27	0.13
1900–83[e]	*P*	0.17 (1.07)	7.98 (6.52)	−2.58 (−0.48)	0.90 (18.35)	10.74	0.00	0.32	1.61	0.06
1900–82	$R(t + 1)$	0.09 (1.51)	−5.77 (−1.90)	7.45 (1.91)	. . .	2.19	0.09	0.04	1.97	0.19

a. Numbers in parentheses are *t*-statistics. Distributed lags based on second-degree thirty-year polynomial with far endpoint tied to zero were used throughout. The regression method is ordinary least squares except where noted otherwise. The stock price index throughout is the Standard and Poor's composite stock price index.

b. Dependent variable *P* is the stock price index for January divided by the January producer price index. Dependent variable $R(t + 1)$ is the real return from January of the following year to January of two years hence (deflated by the producer price index) based on the stock price index and Standard and Poor's composite dividend series.

c. The sums are for the twenty-nine lagged values and do not include the coefficient of the current independent variable, which is shown separately.

d. Standard and Poor's dividends per share adjusted to the stock price index, total for four quarters, divided by the January producer price index.

e. Method is Cochrane-Orcutt serial correlation correction and sample statistics are for transformed regression.

f. Standard and Poor's earnings per share adjusted to the stock price index, total for four quarters, divided by the January producer price index.

in earnings between 1929 and 1933 explains more or less the decline in P over that period (the regression had positive residuals in all these years). While the reasons for the market decline on particular days in 1929 may forever be a mystery, the overall market decline in the depression is explained fairly well as a reaction (or an overreaction) to earnings.

It is important to investigate whether the pattern of coefficients in rows 1 or 2 (or 5 or 6) of table 1 might be optimal given equation 1. The easiest test of equation 1 suggested by the pattern of reaction of real prices to real dividends documented here is to regress future returns on current and lagged dividends. The efficient markets model of equation 1 implies that returns are unforecastable and the overreaction alternative suggests that D can be used to forecast returns. Such a distributed lag appears in row 3 of table 1. The coefficient of the current dividend is negative and the sum of the coefficients of the remaining lagged dividends is positive. Indeed, as our overreaction story would suggest, when dividends are high relative to a weighted average of lagged dividends (so that stocks are by this interpretation overpriced) there is a tendency for low subsequent returns. An F-test on all coefficients but the constant shows significance at the 5 percent level.[50] A similar pattern of coefficients found when E replaced D in the regression (row 7) suggests a similar overreaction for earnings, but the result is significant only at the 9 percent level.

By looking at the time-series properties of real dividends, one can better see why the pattern of reaction of prices to dividends causes returns to be forecastable. The class of models by Box and Jenkins that employ autoregressive integrated moving averages (ARIMA) has been very popular, and it would be instructive to see how the real dividend series could be represented by a model in this class.[51] Unfortunately, time-series modeling methods are partly judgmental and do not lead all researchers to the same model. In applying such methods one must decide whether to detrend the data prior to data analysis. In previous work I estimated a first order autoregressive model for the log of

50. Tests for heteroskedasticity as proposed by Glejser were run using D, time, and a cubic polynomial in time as explanatory variables. Heteroskedasticity appeared remarkably absent in this regression. See H. Glejser, "A New Test for Heteroskedasticity," *Journal of the American Statistical Association*, vol. 64 (March 1969), pp. 316–23.

51. George E. P. Box and Gwylim M. Jenkins, *Time Series Analysis, Forecasting and Control* (Oakland, Calif.: Holden-Day, 1977).

dividends around a deterministic linear trend. In this model, with the same annual real dividend series used here, the coefficient of lagged log dividends for 1872–1978 was 0.807, which implies that dividends always would be predicted to return half the way to the trend in about three years.[52] This result does not appear sensitive to the choice of price deflator used to deflate dividends. Taking account of the downward bias of the least squares estimate of the autoregressive coefficient, one can reject by a Dickey-Fuller test at the 5 percent level the null hypothesis of a random walk for log dividends in favor of the first order autoregressive model around a trend. Some, however, find models with a deterministic trend unappealing and prefer models that make dividends nonstationary. With a model of nonstationary dividends one can handle the apparent trend by first-differencing the data. The following model was estimated with the real annual 1926–83 Standard and Poor's dividend data.

$$\begin{aligned} \Delta D_t &= \underset{(1.498)}{3.285 \times 10^{-3}} + \underset{(11.753)}{0.850}\Delta D_{t-1} + u_t \\ u_t &= a_t \underset{(-69.434)}{-0.981} a_{t-1}, \end{aligned} \tag{4}$$

where a_t is a serially uncorrelated zero mean random variable. This is what Box and Jenkins called an ARIMA (1,1,1) model. It merely asserts that the change in real dividend is a linear function of its lagged value plus an error term, u_t, that is a moving average of a_t. The t-statistics, in parentheses, are misleading in that the likelihood function for this model has other modes with almost the same likelihood but very different parameter estimates. However, this model will suffice to tell how it might be plausible, given the past behavior of dividends, to forecast future dividends. This model cannot be rejected at usual significance levels with the usual Ljung-Box Q-test. It is noteworthy that when the same model was estimated with the sample period 1871–1925, almost the same parameter values emerged: the coefficient of ΔD_{t-1} was 0.840 and the coefficient of a_{t-1} was -0.973.

This estimated model is one that exhibits near parameter redundancy: the coefficient of a_{t-1} is so close to -1 that the moving average on a_t

52. See Robert J. Shiller, "The Use of Volatility Measures in Assessing Market Efficiency," *Journal of Finance*, vol. 36 (May 1981), pp. 291–304.

almost cancels against the first-difference operator. In other words, this model looks almost like a simple first order autoregressive model for dividends with coefficient on the lagged dividend of 0.850. It is more accurate to describe this model as a first order autoregressive model around a moving mean that is itself a moving average of past dividends. One can write the one-step-ahead optimal forecast of D_t implied by equation 4 in the following form:

$$E_tD_{t+1} = 0.869D_t + 0.131M_t + 0.173 \tag{5}$$

$$M_t \equiv (1-0.981)\sum_{k=0}^{\infty}(0.981)^kD_{t-k-1},$$

where M_t is a moving average of dividends with exponentially declining weights that sum to one. Since 0.981 is so close to 1.00, the moving average that defines M_t is extremely long (0.981 even to the twenty-fifth power is 0.619), and thus the term M_t does not vary much over this sample. Thus, for one-step-ahead forecasts this model is very similar to a first order autoregressive model on detrended dividends.

If real dividends are forecasted in accordance with equation 5, then equation 1 (with discount rate $\delta = 0.080$) would imply (using the chain principle of forecasting) that stock prices should be a moving average of dividends given by

$$P_t = 5.380D_t + 7.120M_t + 11.628. \tag{6}$$

Note that the distant past has relatively more weight in determining the price today (a weighted average of expected dividends into the infinite future) than it does in determining the dividend next period. This model thus accords with the intuitive notion that to forecast into the near future one need look only at the recent past, but to forecast into the distant future one need look into the distant past. Equation 6 implies that P_t, just as D_t, is an ARIMA (1,1,1) process.[53] If I had modeled the real dividend series as a first-order autoregressive model around a trend, then P_t would be a weighted average of D_t (with about the same weight as in equation 6) and a trend.

Equation 6 is very different from the estimated relation between P and D. The coefficient of D_t in equation 6 is 5.380, which is far below the

53. For this result in a more general form, see John Y. Campbell, "Asset Duration and Time-Varying Risk Premia" (Ph.D. dissertation, Yale University, 1984).

estimated value in rows 1 or 2 of table 1. The coefficients of the lagged dividends sum to a positive number, not a negative number.

In summary, it appears that stock prices do not act, as they should, like a smoothed transformation of dividends over the past few decades. Instead dividends look like an amplification of the departure of dividends from such a transformation. It is as if the optimism of investors is too volatile, influenced by departures from trends rather than by the trends themselves.

FORECASTING REGRESSIONS THAT EMPLOY DIVIDEND-PRICE AND EARNINGS-PRICE RATIOS

The most natural test of equation 1 is to regress return R_t on information available to the public at time t. Analogous tests of related models might regress excess returns on information at time t, or regress risk-corrected returns on information at time t. If the F-statistic for the regression (that is, for the null hypothesis that all coefficients save the constant term are zero) is significant, then we will have rejected the model. The simplest such tests use only price itself (scaled, say, by dividing it into earnings or dividends) as an explanatory variable and use the conventional t-statistic to test the model. If fads cause stocks to be at times overpriced, at times underpriced, and if these fads come to an end, then we would expect a high dividend-price or earnings-price ratio to predict high returns and a low dividend-price or earnings-price ratio to predict low returns. This would mean that the most naive investment strategy, buy when price is low relative to dividends or earnings and sell when it is high, pays off.

However, it is not easy to carry out such simple tests. One confronts a number of econometric problems: the independent variable is not "nonstochastic," so that ordinary t-statistics are not strictly valid; the error term appears nonnormal or at least conditionally heteroskedastic; and risk correction, if it is employed, is not a simple matter. There is no agreed-upon way to deal with such problems, and I will not attempt here to deal rigorously with them. It is, however, worthwnile to note that high dividend-price or earnings-price ratios do seem to be correlated with high returns.

Whether stocks with a high earnings-price ratio will have a relatively high return has been the subject of much discussion in the literature. It was confirmed that there is a simple correlation across firms between such ratios and returns.[54] The question then arose, Can such a phenomenon be explained within the framework of the capital asset pricing model if there happens to be a positive correlation between the ratio and the beta of the stocks, or does firm size, which correlates with the ratio, affect expected returns? Recently, Sanjoy Basu concluded that risk-adjusted returns are positively correlated with the earnings-price ratio even after controlling for firm size.[55] As Basu notes, however, his tests depend on the risk measurement assumed.

It is apparently accepted today in the finance profession that expected returns fluctuate through time as well as across stocks. These results are interpreted as describing the time variation in the "risk premium."

The dividend/price ratio or earnings/price ratio has not figured prominently in this literature. Instead the variables chosen for forecasting were such things as the inflation rate,[56] the spread between low-grade and high-grade bonds,[57] or the spread between long-term and short-term bonds.[58]

Table 2 shows that a high dividend-price ratio (total Standard and Poor's dividends for the preceding year divided by the Standard and Poor's composite index for July of the preceding year) is indeed an indicator of high subsequent returns.[59] Thus, for example, the equation in row 1 asserts that when the dividend-price ratio (or "current yield") is one percentage point above its mean, the expected return on the stock is 3.588 percentage points above its mean. Thus, the high current yield is augmented by an expected capital gain that is two and a half times as dramatic as the high current yield. In contrast, equation 1 would predict that a high current yield should correspond to an expected capital loss

54. See for example Francis Nicholson, "Price Ratios in Relation to Investment Results," *Financial Analysts Journal*, vol. 24 (January–February 1968), pp. 105–09.

55. See Sanjoy Basu, "The Relationship between Earnings' Yield, Market Value and Return for NYSE Common Stocks: Further Evidence," *Journal of Financial Economics*, vol. 12 (June 1983), pp. 129–56.

56. See Eugene F. Fama and G. William Schwert, "Asset Returns and Inflation," *Journal of Financial Economics*, vol. 5 (November 1977), pp. 115–46.

57. See Donald B. Keim and Robert F. Stambaugh, "Predicting Returns in the Stock and Bond Markets," University of Pennsylvania, 1984.

58. See John Y. Campbell, "Stock Returns and the Term Structure" (Princeton University, 1984).

59. There is evidence that the strategy of holding stocks with high dividend-price ratios has actually paid off for those investors who followed it. See Wilbur G. Lewellen, Ronald C. Lease, and Gary C. Schlarbaum, "Investment Performance and Investor Behavior," *Journal of Financial and Quantitative Analysis*, vol. 14 (March 1979), pp. 29–57.

Table 2. Forecasting Returns Based on the Dividend-Price Ratio, Selected Periods, 1872–1983[a]

Sample period	Constant	Coefficient of dividend-price ratio	Sample statistic $\bar{R}^2$	Durbin-Watson	Standard error
1872–1983[b]	−0.10 (−1.52)	3.59 (2.85)	0.06	1.85	0.17
1872–1908[b]	−0.02 (−0.20)	2.26 (0.96)	0.00	2.05	0.14
1909–45[b]	−0.14 (−0.88)	3.89 (1.42)	0.03	1.46	0.21
1946–83[b]	−0.16 (−1.70)	5.23 (2.62)	0.14	1.80	0.17
1889–1982[c]	−0.13 (−1.94)	4.26 (3.15)	0.09	1.85	0.17
1926–82[d]	−0.17 (−1.73)	5.26 (2.71)	0.10	2.01	0.21

a. Numbers in parentheses are *t*-statistics. The stock price index throughout is the Standard and Poor's composite stock price index. The dependent variable is the real return on the stock price index from January of the year to January of the following year (average for the month) except where otherwise noted. The return is the sum of the change in the stock price index plus Standard and Poor's four-quarter total of the composite dividends per share as adjusted to the stock price index, all divided by the stock price index. The independent variable is total dividends in the preceding year (which is Standard and Poor's four-quarter total of the composite dividends as adjusted to the stock price index) divided by the stock price index for July of the preceding year.

b. Price deflator is the producer price index.

c. Price deflator is the consumption deflator for nondurables and services.

d. Nominal returns were cumulated for the end of January until the end of January of the following year from monthly data in "Common Stocks Total Returns," Roger Ibbotson and Associates; the price deflator is the January producer price index.

to offset the current yield. The efficient markets hypothesis thus appears dramatically wrong from this regression: stock prices move in a direction opposite to that forecasted by the dividend-price ratio. This is true in every subperiod examined.[60]

In table 3, rows 1 through 5 show analogous regressions with the earnings-price ratio (total Standard and Poor's earnings for the preceding year divided by the Standard and Poor's composite index for July of the preceding year) in place of the dividend-price ratio. These forecasting regressions work in the same direction (price low relative to earnings implies high returns) but are less significant.[61]

60. The same regressions were run using a different price deflator (row five of table 2) and a different measure of return (row six of table 2) with little change in results.

61. The lower significance appears to be due to the relatively noisy behavior of the annual earnings series. If the earnings-price ratio is computed as the average annual Standard and Poor's earnings for the preceding thirty years divided by the Standard and

Table 3. Forecasting Returns Based on the Earnings-Price Ratio, Selected Periods, 1872–1983[a]

Sample period	Constant	Coefficient of earnings-price ratio	Sample statistic $\bar{R}^2$	Durbin-Watson	Standard error
1872–1983	0.01 (0.24)	0.85 (1.41)	0.01	1.90	0.18
1872–1908	0.00 (0.02)	1.28 (0.63)	−0.02	2.16	0.15
1909–45	0.08 (0.72)	0.03 (0.02)	−0.03	1.59	0.21
1946–83	−0.09 (−1.09)	1.86 (2.13)	0.09	1.71	0.17
1889–1982	0.01 (0.19)	0.78 (1.24)	0.01	1.96	0.18
1901–83[b]	−0.04 (−0.68)	1.57[c] (2.38)	0.05	1.81	0.19

a. Numbers in parentheses are *t*-statistics. Dependent and independent variables and price deflators are as in table 2, with earnings in place of dividends.

b. Price deflator is the producer price index.

c. Earnings-price ratio is computed by forming the average real earnings for the previous thirty years (not counting the current year) and then dividing by the real stock price index for January of the current year.

EXCESS VOLATILITY OF STOCK PRICES

Regression tests of the efficient markets model may not fully characterize the way in which the model fails. A simpler and perhaps more appealing way to see the failure of the model represented by equation 1 follows by observing that stock prices seem to show far too much volatility to be in accordance with the simple model.[62] The most important criticism of the excess volatility claim centers on the claim's assumption that stock prices are stationary around a trend of the dividend series.[63] Here I discuss the volatility tests in light of this criticism and present

Poor's composite index for January of the current year (row six of table 3), then the relation between returns and the earnings-price ratio looks more impressive.

62. The arguments for excess volatility in financial markets were put forth independently by Stephen F. LeRoy and Richard D. Porter, "The Present-Value Relation: Tests Based on Implied Variance Bounds," *Econometrica*, vol. 49 (March 1981), pp. 555–74, and by me in several papers beginning with "The Volatility of Long-Term Interest Rates and Expectations Models of the Term Structure," *Journal of Political Economy*, vol. 87 (December 1979), pp. 1190–1219, and in "Do Stock Prices Move too Much."

63. In the case of LeRoy and Porter, the earnings series, instead of the dividend series, was assumed to be stationary.

tests in a slightly different form that deals better with the issue of nonstationarity.

I showed that if the dividend D_t is a stationary stochastic process, then the efficient markets model (equation 1) implies the variance inequality

$$\sigma(P - P_{-1}) \leq \frac{\sigma(D)}{(2\delta)^{0.5}}, \qquad (7)$$

that is, that the standard deviation of the change in price $P - P_{-1}$ is less than or equal to the standard deviation of the dividend D divided by the square root of twice the discount factor.[64] If we know the standard deviation of D, then there is a limit to how much $P - P_{-1}$ can vary if equation 1 is to hold at all times. If the market is efficient, then price movements representing changes in forecasts of dividends cannot be very large unless dividends actually do move a lot. The discount factor δ is equal to the expected return $E(R_t)$, which can be estimated by taking the average return. Before we can use this inequality to test the efficient markets model, we must somehow deal with the fact that dividends appear to have a trend; in an earlier paper, I handled the problem by multiplying prices and dividends by an exponential decay factor as a way to detrend them. This method of detrending has become a source of controversy. Indeed, as I noted in the original paper, the trend in dividends may be spurious, and dividends may have another sort of nonstationarity that is not removed by such detrending.[65] Thus, violating inequality 7 in these tests should not be regarded by itself as definitive evidence against equation 1. Most of the criticism of the variance-bounds inequality has centered on this point.[66] On the other hand, the violation of the variance inequality does show that dividend volatility must be potentially much greater than actually observed historically (around a trend or around the historical mean) if the efficient markets model is to

64. Shiller, "Do Stock Prices Move Too Much."

65. Shiller, "The Volatility of Long-Term Interest Rates."

66. For example, see Marjorie A. Flavin, "Excess Volatility in the Financial Markets: A Reassessment of the Empirical Evidence," *Journal of Political Economy*, vol. 91 (December 1983), pp. 929–56; Allan W. Kleidon, "Variance Bounds Tests and Stock Price Valuation Models" (Stanford University, Graduate School of Business, 1983); and Terry A. Marsh and Robert C. Merton, "Dividend Variability and Variance Bounds Tests for the Rationality of Stock Market Prices," Working Paper 1584-84 (Massachusetts Institute of Technology, Alfred P. Sloan School of Management, August 1984).

Table 4. Sample Statistics for Detrended Price and Dividend Series, Selected Periods, 1871–1984[a]

Sample period	Left-hand side of inequality	Right-hand side of inequality
1877–1984	$\sigma(P5 - P5_{-1}) = 2.83$	$\sigma(D5)/(2\delta)^{0.5} = 3.52$
1887–1984	$\sigma(P15 - P15_{-1}) = 2.93$	$\sigma(D15)/(2\delta)^{0.5} = 1.64$
1902–1984	$\sigma(P30 - P30_{-1}) = 3.39$	$\sigma(D30)/(2\delta)^{0.5} = 1.38$

Source: Equations 7–10.

a. The variables *P*5, *P*15, and *P*30 are the real stock price index detrended by dividing by the 5-year, 15-year, and 30-year geometric average of lagged real earnings respectively; σ denotes sample standard deviation. The variables *D*5, *D*15, and *D*30 are the corresponding dividend series as defined in the text. The constant δ equals 0.08, the average real return on the Standard and Poor's composite stock price index over the entire period 1871–1983.

hold; and this fact can be included among other factors in judging the plausibility of the efficient markets model.

Table 4 displays the elements of the above inequality but with the data detrended in a different and perhaps more satisfactory manner that depends only on past information. Let us define detrended price series *P*5, *P*15, and *P*30 and corresponding dividend series *D*5, *D*15, and *D*30 by

$$(8) \qquad Pk_t = \frac{P_t}{Nk_t} \qquad k = 5, 15, 30$$

and

$$(9) \qquad Dk_t = \frac{D_t}{Nk_t} + P_{t-1}\left(\frac{1}{Nk_t} - \frac{1}{Nk_{t+1}}\right) \qquad k = 5, 15, 30,$$

where

$$(10) \qquad Nk_t = \prod_{j=1}^{k} E_{t-j}^{1/k} \qquad k = 5, 15, 30.$$

The detrended price and dividend series have the following property: returns calculated with *Pk* and *Dk* in place of *P* and *D* in the formula for return R_t are the same as if *P* and *D* had been used. Thus, if equation 1 holds for P_t and D_t, then equation 1 holds where Pk_t and Dk_t replace P_t and D_t, and the same variance inequality 7 should hold for *Pk* and *Dk*. One can think of *Pk* and *Dk* as the price and dividend, respectively, of a share in a mutual fund that holds the same fixed portfolio (whose price is P_t and whose dividend is D_t) but buys back or sells its own shares so that it always has Nk_t shares outstanding. The variable Nk_t is a geometric moving average of lagged real earnings. This may cause the dividend of the mutual fund to be stationary even if the dividend D_t is not. A plot of

$D30$, for example, shows no apparent trend and does not look unstationary. If, for example, the natural log of E is a Gaussian random walk and is thus nonstationary, and if $D_t = E_t$, then Pk_t will be a stationary lognormal process, and Dk_t will be the sum of stationary lognormal processes.[67] We see from table 4 that inequality 7 is not violated for $k = 5$ but is violated for $k = 15$ and $k = 30$. The detrending factor Nk_t gets smoother as k increases.

IMPLICATIONS OF THE FORECASTING EQUATIONS IN CONNECTION WITH THE MODEL

If we choose hypothetical values for ρ and φ in equation 2, we can use one of the equations forecasting R_t and produced in tables 1 through 3 to estimate the paths through time of Q_t and Y_t. Such an estimate will be admittedly quite arbitrary, and of course these forecasting regressions are not prima facie evidence that it would be "smart" to behave as will be supposed here. Considering such an estimate may nonetheless give some insights into the plausibility of the alternative model. We learn immediately in doing this that φ must be very large if swings in Q_t, the proportion of shares held by smart-money investors, are not to be extraordinarily large. This problem arises because stock prices are actually quite forecastable: the standard deviation of the expected return implied in many of the forecasting equations is so large that unless φ in equation 2 is large, Q_t will often move far out of the zero-to-one range.

Figure 2 shows a hypothetical example with estimated values of Y_t and Q_t implied by equation 2 and the forecasting equation based on the dividend-price ratio in row 1 of table 2 for $\rho = 0$ and $\varphi = 0.5$. Also shown is the real price P_t. For these values of ρ and φ, Q_t is always positive and thus Y_t is always less than P_t. The demand for shares by ordinary investors, Y_t, looks on the whole fairly similar to the price P_t itself. This arises because the forecasting equation is related to the dividend-price ratio and because dividends are fairly sluggish, so that Q_t itself resembles the reciprocal of P_t. However, Y_t is somewhat more volatile than P_t, showing a tendency to be lower proportionally at lows

67. If $\log D_t - \log D_{t-1} = u_t$, where u is serially uncorrelated and normal with zero mean and variance s^2, then $E_t D_{t+k} = D_t h^k$, where $h = \exp(s^2/2)$. Calling $g = 1/(1+\delta)$, then if $hg < 1$, it follows from equation 1 that $P_t = gD_t/(1 - hg)$. Substituting this into equation 8 and using equation 10 will provide the stationarity result for Pk and Dk noted in the text.

Figure 2. Hypothetical Demand for Shares by Ordinary Investors and Smart-Money Investors

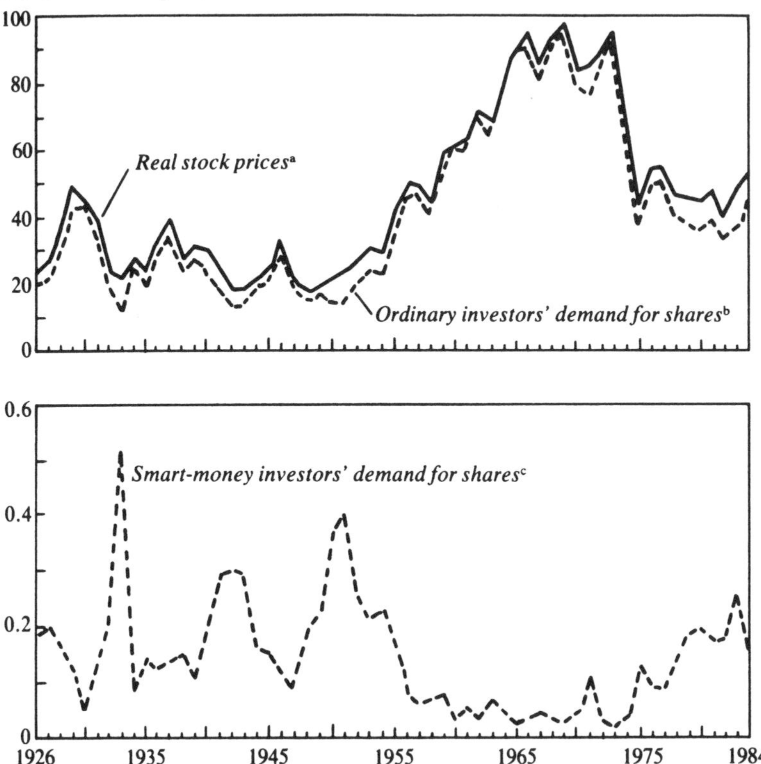

a. Real stock price index (P_t), as described in figure 1, notes a and b.

b. The hypothetical demand for shares by ordinary investors, equal to $P_t(1 - Q_t)$, where Q_t is the hypothetical demand for shares by smart-money investors.

c. The variable Q_t from equation 2 with $\rho = 0$ and $\varphi = 0.5$ and based on the forecasting equation for returns in row 1 of table 2.

and higher proportionally at highs. The overreaction to dividends is more pronounced in Y_t than in P_t. The presence of smart money thus serves to mitigate the overreaction of ordinary investors. The year 1933 stands out for a very large proportion of smart-money investors and a low proportion of ordinary investors. This was the year when the dividend-price ratio reached an extreme high and when the highest returns were forecasted. The late 1950s and early 1960s were times of low demand by smart-money investors: the dividend-price ratio was low then and so they were "smart" ex ante to get out of the market, though of course ex post they would have liked to have stayed in the market. The demand by smart money is currently neither high nor low because the dividend-price ratio is not far from its historical average. The weighted average return ($\Sigma Q_t R_t / \Sigma Q_t$) for 1926 to 1983 was 12.9 percent, in contrast to the average return (mean of R_t) for this period of 8.2 percent.

The volume of trade implied by the movements in and out of shares by smart money between t and $t + 1$ is $| Q_{t+1} - Q_t |$; the average value of this measure for the sample shown in figure 2 is 0.055. In this sample, the New York Stock Exchange turnover rate (reported annual share volume divided by average of shares listed) was between 9 percent (1942) and 42 percent (1982), except for the early depression years, when turnover was extremely high.[68] Thus, the story told in figure 2 is not one of an implausibly high volume of trade. Because corporate stock constitutes less than one-third of all wealth, we are also not talking about implausibly large wealth movements on the part of smart money.[69] Of course, not all household wealth is very liquid. The ratio of the market value of corporate equities to deposits and credit market instruments held by households ranged from 47.7 percent in 1948 to 136.2 percent in 1968.[70]

The results shown in figure 2 are not insensitive to the choice of forecasting equation, though as long as the forecasting equation is a simple regression on the dividend/price ratio (as in table 2), changing the equation has no more effect than changing ρ and φ. If an equation that forecasts with the earnings/price ratio (row six of table 3) is used to compute $E_t R_t$, the pattern through time of Q is somewhat different: Q is still high (though not as high in figure 2) in 1933 and low in the late 1950s and early 1960s. The weighted average return for smart money over this period would be 11.4 percent.

A discount rate $\rho + \varphi$ of 50 percent in equation 3 may or may not

68. New York Stock Exchange, *Fact Book 1983*, p. 68.

69. Between 1945 and 1980 corporate shares held by households and private financial institutions as a proportion of household net worth including tangibles and government debt ranged from 12.6 percent in 1948 to 31.8 percent in 1968. See Board of Governors of the Federal Reserve System, *Balance Sheets for U.S. Economy* (Washington, D.C., April 1981), table 700, "Consolidated Domestic Net Assets with Tangibles at Current Cost, 1945–1980."

70. Ibid.

imply very forecastable returns, depending on the stochastic properties of Y_t. In the hypothetical example, the behavior of Y_t is sufficiently dominated by long (low-frequency) components that returns are not more forecastable than would be implied by the forecasting regression in table 2. A discount rate of 50 percent per year amounts to about 0.1 percent per day (compared to the standard deviation of daily return of about 1 percentage point), so that for event studies involving daily stock price data the discount rate is still very small. If equation 3 were to be applied to individual stocks, we might choose a smaller value of φ and hence a smaller discount rate.

Summary and Conclusion

Much of this paper relies on the reader's good judgment. A great deal of evidence is presented here that suggests that social movements, fashions, or fads are likely to be important or even the dominant cause of speculative asset price movements; but no single piece of evidence is unimpeachable.

The most important reason for expecting that stock prices are heavily influenced by social dynamics comes from observations of participants in the market and of human nature as presented in the literature on social psychology, sociology, and marketing. A study of the history of the U.S. stock market in the postwar period suggests that various social movements were under way during this period that might plausibly have major effects on the aggregate demand for shares. Must we rely on such evidence to make the case against market efficiency? Yes; there is no alternative to human judgment in understanding human behavior.

The reason that the random-walk behavior of stock prices holds up as well as it does may be two-fold. First, the aggregate demand of ordinary investors may itself not be entirely unlike a random walk. Fashions are perhaps inherently rather unpredictable, and ordinary investors may overreact to news of earnings or dividends, which behavior may also make their demand relatively unpredictable.

Second, and on the other hand, as shown by the model in equation 3 the ordinary investors' predictable patterns of behavior are prevented from causing big short-run profit opportunities by the limited amount of smart money in the economy, so that returns may be nearly unpredictable, and tests of market efficiency may have little power. However, in preventing large profit opportunities the smart money may not be preventing the ordinary investors from causing major swings in the market and even being the source of volatility in the market.

Data on stock prices show evidence of overreaction to dividends, and the forecasting equations for returns are consistent with such overreaction. However, an alternative interpretation for the correlation of prices to dividends might be that firms that set dividends are influenced by the same social dynamics that influence the rest of society. There are also other possible interpretations of this correlation; that is why I presented the data analysis as merely confirming that notions of overreaction suggested by qualitative evidence are consistent with the data.

It should also be emphasized that the model in equation 3 involves a present value of expected dividends and that it shares some properties of the efficient markets model. Despite all the inadequacies of the notion of market efficiency, modern theoretical finance does offer many insights into actual market behavior. The robustness of the models to variations like those here is a matter deserving more attention.

[15]

Journal of Economic Perspectives—Volume 4, Number 2—Spring 1990—Pages 19–33

The Noise Trader Approach to Finance

Andrei Shleifer and Lawrence H. Summers

If the efficient markets hypothesis was a publicly traded security, its price would be enormously volatile. Following Samuelson's (1965) proof that stock prices should follow a random walk if rational competitive investors require a fixed rate of return and Fama's (1965) demonstration that stock prices are indeed close to a random walk, stock in the efficient markets hypothesis rallied. Michael Jensen was able to write in 1978 that "the efficient markets hypothesis is the best established fact in all of social sciences."

Such strong statements portend reversals, the efficient markets hypothesis itself notwithstanding. Stock in the efficient markets hypothesis lost ground rapidly following the publication of Shiller's (1981) and Leroy and Porter's (1981) volatility tests, both of which found stock market volatility to be far greater than could be justified by changes in dividends. The stock snapped back following the papers of Kleidon (1986) and Marsh and Merton (1986) which challenged the statistical validity of volatility tests. A choppy period then ensued, where conflicting econometric studies induced few of the changes in opinion that are necessary to move prices. But the stock in the efficient markets hypothesis—at least as it has traditionally been formulated—crashed along with the rest of the market on October 19, 1987. Its recovery has been less dramatic than that of the rest of the market.

This paper reviews an alternative to the efficient markets approach that we and others have recently pursued. Our approach rests on two assumptions. First, some investors are not fully rational and their demand for risky assets is affected by their beliefs or sentiments that are not fully justified by fundamental news. Second,

■ *Andrei Shleifer is Professor of Finance and Business Economics, Graduate School of Business, University of Chicago, Chicago, Illinois. Lawrence H. Summers is Professor of Economics, Harvard University, Cambridge, Massachusetts.*

arbitrage—defined as trading by fully rational investors not subject to such sentiment—is risky and therefore limited. The two assumptions together imply that changes in investor sentiment are not fully countered by arbitrageurs and so affect security returns. We argue that this approach to financial markets is in many ways superior to the efficient markets paradigm.

Our case for the noise trader approach is threefold. First, theoretical models with limited arbitrage are both tractable and more plausible than models with perfect arbitrage. The efficient markets hypothesis obtains only as an extreme case of perfect riskless arbitrage that is unlikely to apply in practice. Second, the investor sentiment/limited arbitrage approach yields a more accurate description of financial markets than the efficient markets paradigm. The approach not only explains the available anomalies, but also readily explains broad features of financial markets such as trading volume and actual investment strategies. Third, and most importantly, this approach yields new and testable implications about asset prices, some of which have been proved to be consistent with the data. It is absolutely *not true* that introducing a degree of irrationality of *some* investors into models of financial markets "eliminates all discipline and can explain anything."

The Limits of Arbitrage

We think of the market as consisting of two types of investors: "arbitrageurs"—also called "smart money" and "rational speculators"—and other investors. Arbitrageurs are defined as investors who form fully rational expectations about security returns. In contrast, the opinions and trading patterns of other investors—also known as "noise traders" and "liquidity traders"—may be subject to systematic biases. In practice, the line between arbitrageurs and other investors may be blurred, but for our argument it helps to draw a sharp distinction between them, since the arbitrageurs do the work of bringing prices toward fundamentals.

Arbitrageurs play a central role in standard finance. They trade to ensure that if a security has a perfect substitute—a portfolio of other securities that yields the same returns—then the price of the security equals the price of that substitute portfolio. If the price of the security falls below that of the substitute portfolio, arbitrageurs sell the portfolio and buy the security until the prices are equalized, and vice versa if the price of a security rises above that of the substitute portfolio. When the substitute is indeed perfect, this arbitrage is riskless. As a result, arbitrageurs have perfectly elastic demand for the security at the price of its substitute portfolio. Arbitrage thus assures that relative prices of securities must be in line for there to be no riskless arbitrage opportunities. Such riskless arbitrage is very effective for derivative securities, such as futures and options, but also for individual stocks and bonds where reasonably close substitutes are usually available.

Although riskless arbitrage ensures that relative prices are in line, it does not help to pin down price levels of, say, stocks or bonds as a whole. These classes of securities do not have close substitute portfolios, and therefore if for some reason they are mispriced, there is no riskless hedge for the arbitrageur. For example, an arbitrageur who thinks that stocks are underpriced cannot buy stocks and sell the substitute portfolio, since such a portfolio does not exist. The arbitrageur can instead simply buy stocks in hopes of an above-normal return, but this arbitrage is no longer riskless. If the arbitrageur is risk-averse, his demand for underpriced stocks will be limited. With a finite number of arbitrageurs, their combined demand curve is no longer perfectly elastic.

Two types of risk limit arbitrage. The first is fundamental risk. Suppose that stocks are selling above the expected value of future dividends and an arbitrageur is selling them short. The arbitrageur then bears the risk that the realization of dividends —or of the news about dividends—is better than expected, in which case he loses on his trade. Selling "overvalued" stocks is risky because there is always a chance that the market will do very well. Fear of such a loss limits the arbitrageur's original position, and keeps his short-selling from driving prices all the way down to fundamentals.

The second source of risk that limits arbitrage comes from unpredictability of the future resale price (De Long, Shleifer, Summers and Waldmann, 1990a). Suppose again that stocks are overpriced and an arbitrageur is selling them short. As long as the arbitrageur is thinking of liquidating his position in the future, he must bear the risk that at that time stocks will be *even more* overpriced than they are today. If future mispricing is more extreme than when the arbitrage trade is put on, the arbitrageur suffers a loss on his position. Again, fear of this loss limits the size of the arbitrageur's initial position, and so keeps him from driving the price all the way down to fundamentals.

Clearly, this resale price risk depends on the arbitrageur having a finite horizon. If the arbitrageur's horizon is infinite, he simply sells the stock short and pays dividends on it in all the future periods, recognizing that the present value of those is lower than his proceeds from the short sale. But there are several reasons that it makes sense to assume that arbitrageurs have short horizons. Most importantly, arbitrageurs have to borrow cash or securities to implement their trades, and as a result must pay the lenders *per period* fees. These fees cumulate over the period that the position remains open, and can add up to large amounts for long term arbitrage. The structure of transaction costs thus induces a strong bias toward short horizons (Shleifer and Vishny, 1990). In addition, the performance of most money managers is evaluated at least once a year and usually once every few months, also limiting the horizon of arbitrage. As a result of these problems, resources dedicated to long-term arbitrage against fundamental mispricing are very scarce.

Japanese equities in the 1980s illustrate the limits of arbitrage. During this period, Japanese equities have sold at the price earning multiples of between 20 and 60 (French and Poterba, 1989), and have continued to climb. Expected growth rates of dividends and risk premia required to justify such multiples seem unrealistic. Nonetheless, an investor who believes that Japanese equities are overvalued and wants to sell them short, must confront two types of risk. First, what if Japan actually does perform so well that these prices are justified? Second, how much more out of line can prices get, and for how long, before Japanese equities return to more realistic prices?

Any investor who sold Japanese stocks short in 1985, when the price earnings multiple was 30, would have lost his shirt as the multiples rose to 60 in 1986.

These arguments that risk makes arbitrage ineffective actually understate the limits of arbitrage. After all, they presume that the arbitrageur knows the fundamental value of the security. In fact, the arbitrageur might not exactly know what this value is, or be able to detect price changes that reflect deviations from fundamentals. In this case, arbitrage is even riskier than before. Summers (1986) shows that a time series of share prices which deviate from fundamentals in a highly persistent way looks a lot like a random walk. Arbitrageurs would have as hard a time as econometricians in detecting such a deviation, even if it were large. An arbitrageur is then handicapped by the difficulty of identifying the mispricing as well as by the risk of betting against it. Are economists certain that Japanese stocks are overpriced at a price earnings ratio of 50?

Substantial evidence shows that, contrary to the efficient markets hypothesis, arbitrage does not completely counter responses of prices to fluctuations in uninformed demand. Of course, identifying such fluctuations in demand is tricky, since price changes may reflect new market information which changes the equilibrium price at which arbitrageurs trade. Several recent studies do, however, avoid this objection by looking at responses of prices to changes in demand that do not plausibly reflect any new fundamental information because they have institutional or tax motives.

For example, Harris and Gurel (1986) and Shleifer (1986) examine stock price reactions to inclusions of new stocks into the Standard & Poor 500 stock index. Being added to the S&P 500 is not a plausible example of new information about the stock, since stocks are picked for their representativeness and not for performance potential. However, a stock added to the S&P 500 is subsequently acquired in large quantities by the so-called "index funds," whose holdings just represent the index. Both Harris and Gurel (1986) and Shleifer (1986) find that announcements of inclusions into the index are accompanied by share price increases of 2 to 3 percent. Moreover, the magnitude of these increases over time has risen, paralleling the growth of assets in index funds. Clearly, the arbitrage trade in which rational speculators sell the new stock and buy back close substitutes is not working here. And simply selling short the newly included stock on the theory that it is now overpriced must be too risky.

Further evidence on price pressure when no news is transmitted comes from Ritter's (1988) work on the January effect. The January effect is the name for the fact that small stocks have outperformed market indices by a significant percentage each January over the last 50 or so years. Ritter finds that small stocks are typically sold by individual investors in December—often to realize capital losses—and then bought back in January. These share shifts explain the January effect as long as arbitrage by institutions and market insiders is ineffective, since aggressive arbitrage should eliminate the price effects of temporary trading patterns by individual investors. Either risk or borrowing constraints keep arbitrageurs from eliminating the price consequences of year-end trading.

Less direct evidence also shows that news is not the only force driving asset prices, suggesting that arbitrage is not successful in eliminating the effects of uninformed trading on prices. For example, French and Roll (1986) look at a period when the U.S. stock market was closed on Wednesdays and find that the market is less volatile on these days than on Wednesdays when it is open. By focusing on Wednesdays, they control for the intensity of release of public information. This result may reflect incorporation of private information into prices during open hours, but it may also reflect the failure of arbitrage to accommodate intraday demand shifts. Roll (1988) demonstrates that most idiosyncratic price moves in individual stocks cannot be accounted for by public news. He finds that individual stocks exhibit significant price movements unrelated to the market on days when there are no public news about these stocks. A similar and more dramatic result is obtained for the aggregate stock market by Cutler, Poterba, and Summers (1989a), who find that the days of the largest aggregate market movements are not the days of most important fundamental news and vice versa. The common conclusion of these studies is that news alone does not move stock prices; uninformed changes in demand move them too.

Investor Sentiment

Some shifts in investor demand for securities are completely rational. Such changes could reflect, for example, reactions to public announcements that affect future growth rate of dividends, risk, or risk aversion. Rational demand changes can also reflect adjustment to news conveyed through the trading process itself. Finally, rational demand changes can reflect tax trading or trading done for institutional reasons of the types discussed above.

But not all demand changes appear to be so rational; some seem to be a response to changes in expectations or sentiment that are not fully justified by information. Such changes can be a response to pseudo-signals that investors believe convey information about future returns but that would not convey such information in a fully rational model (Black, 1986). An example of such pseudo-signals is advice of brokers or financial gurus. We use the term "noise traders" to describe such investors, following Kyle (1985) and Black (1986). Changes in demand can also reflect investors' use of inflexible trading strategies or of "popular models" that Shiller describes in this journal. One such strategy is trend chasing. Although these changes in demand are unwarranted by fundamentals, they can be related to fundamentals, as in the case of overreaction to news.

These demand shifts will only matter if they are correlated across noise traders. If all investors trade randomly, their trades cancel out and there are no aggregate shifts in demand. Undoubtedly, some trading in the market brings together noise traders with different models who cancel each other out. However, many trading strategies based on pseudo-signals, noise, and popular models are correlated, leading to aggregate demand shifts. The reason for this is that judgment biases afflicting investors in processing information tend to be the same. Subjects in psychological experiments tend to make the same mistake; they do not make random mistakes.

Many of these persistent mistakes are relevant for financial markets. For example, experimental subjects tend to be overconfident (Alpert and Raiffa, 1982), which makes them take on more risk. Experimental subjects also tend to extrapolate past time series, which can lead them to chase trends (Andreassen and Kraus, 1988). Finally, in making inferences experimental subjects put too little weight on base rates and too much weight on new information (Tversky and Kahneman, 1982), which might lead them to overreact to news.

The experimental evidence on judgment biases is corroborated by survey and other evidence on how investors behave. For example, extrapolation is a key feature of the popular models discovered by the surveys Shiller describes in this journal. He finds that home buyers as well as investors in the crash of 1987 seem to extrapolate past price trends. Similar results have been found by Frankel and Froot (1986) in their analysis of exchange rate forecasts during the mid-1980s: over the short horizon, professional forecasters expect a price trend to continue even when they expect a long run reversion to fundamentals.

A look at how market participants behave provides perhaps the most convincing evidence that noise rather than information drives many of their decisions. Investors follow market gurus and forecasters, such as Joe Granville and "Wall Street Week." Charging bulls, Jimmy Connors and John Houseman all affect where and how people entrust their money. When Merrill Lynch changed from their charging bulls ad (filmed in Mexico) to a single bull ad ("a breed apart"), many more people chose to take their advice. Financial gurus that attract large followings never claim to have access to inside information. Rather, they insist that they are following reliable models for forecasting future returns. They "make money the old-fashioned way," which is apparently not just by reacting to changes in fundamental economic factors.

So-called "technical analysis" is another example of demand shifts without a fundamental rationalization. Technical analysis typically calls for buying more stocks when stocks have risen (broke through a barrier), and selling stocks when they fall through a floor. "Adam Smith" (1968) refers to the informal theorem of chartism that classifies phases of price movements in terms of categories—accumulation, distribution and liquidation. The suggested trading strategies then respond to the phase of the cycle the security is supposed to be in. These trading strategies are based on noise or "popular models" and not on information.

There can be little doubt that these sorts of factors influence demand for securities, but can they be big enough to make a difference? The standard economist's reason for doubting the size of these effects has been to posit that investors trading on noise might lose their money to arbitrageurs, leading to a diminution of their wealth and effect on demand (Friedman, 1953). Noise traders might also learn the error of their ways and reform into rational arbitrageurs.

However, the argument that noise traders lose money and eventually disappear is not self-evident. First, noise traders might be on average more aggressive than the arbitrageurs—either because they are overoptimistic or because they are overconfident—and so bear more risk. If risk-taking is rewarded in the market, noise traders can earn higher expected returns even despite buying high and selling low on average.

The risk rewarded by the market need not even be fundamental; it can be the resale price risk arising from the unpredictability of future noise traders' opinions. With higher expected returns, noise traders as a group do not disappear from the market rapidly, if at all.

Of course, higher expected returns because of higher risk come together with a greater variance of returns. Noise traders might end up very rich with a trivial probability, and poor almost for sure. Almost for sure, then, they fail to affect demand in the long run. But in principle, either the expected return or the variance effect can dominate.

Learning and imitation may not adversely affect noise traders either. When noise traders earn high average returns, many other investors might imitate them, ignoring the fact that they took more risk and just got lucky. Such imitation brings more money to follow noise trader strategies. Noise traders themselves might become even more cocky, attributing their investment success to skill rather than luck. As noise traders who do well become more aggressive, their effect on demand increases.

The case against the importance of noise traders also ignores the fact that new investors enter the market all the time, and old investors who have lost money come back. These investors are subject to the same judgment biases as the current survivors in the market, and so add to the effect of judgment biases on demand.

These arguments suggest that the case for long run unimportance of noise traders is at best premature. In other words, shifts in the demand for stocks that do not depend on news or fundamental factors are likely to affect prices even in the long run.

Explaining the Puzzles

When arbitrage is limited, and investor demand for securities responds to noise and to predictions of popular models, security prices move in response to these changes in demand as well as to changes in fundamentals. Arbitrageurs counter the shifts in demand prompted by changes in investor sentiment, but do not eliminate the effects of such shifts on the price completely.

In this market, prices vary more than is warranted by changes in fundamentals, since they respond to shifts in investor sentiment as well as to news (Shiller, 1981; 1984). Stock returns are predictably mean-reverting, meaning that high stock returns lead to lower expected stock returns. This prediction has in fact been documented for the United States as well as the foreign stock prices by Fama and French (1988) and Poterba and Summers (1988).

The effects of demand shifts on prices are larger when most investors follow the finance textbooks and passively hold the market portfolio. In this case, a switch in the sentiment of some investors is not countered by a change of position of all the market participants, but only of a few arbitrageurs. The smaller the risk bearing capacity of arbitrageurs, the bigger the effect of a sentiment shift on the price. A simple example highlights this point. Suppose that all investors are sure that the market is efficient and hold the market portfolio. Now suppose that one investor decides to hold additional shares of a particular security. Its price is driven to infinity.

This approach fits very neatly with the conventional nonacademic view of financial markets. On that view, the key to investment success is not just predicting future fundamentals, but also predicting the movement of other active investors. Market professionals spend considerable resources tracking price trends, volume, short interest, odd lot volume, investor sentiment indexes and numerous other gauges of demand for equities. Tracking these possible indicators of demand makes no sense if prices responded only to fundamental news and not to investor demand. They make perfect sense, in contrast, in a world where investor sentiment moves prices and so predicting changes in this sentiment pays. The prevalence of investment strategies based on indicators of demand in financial markets suggests the recognition by arbitrageurs of the role of demand.

Not only do arbitrageurs spend time and money to predict noise trader moves, they also make active attempts to take advantage of these moves. When noise traders are optimistic about particular securities, it pays arbitrageurs to create more of them. These securities might be mutual funds, new share issues, penny oil stocks, or junk bonds: anything that is overpriced at the moment. It also pays to carve up corporate cash flows in ways that make the securities with claims to these flows most attractive to investors. After all, the Modigliani-Miller theorem does not apply in a world where sentiment affects security prices and noise traders themselves do not see through the corporate veil. In such a world, securities that would otherwise be fundamentally perfect substitutes no longer are, and therefore arbitrage that undoes changes in corporate leverage is no longer riskless. Just as entrepreneurs spend resources to build casinos to take advantage of gamblers, arbitrageurs build investment banks and brokerage firms to predict and feed noise trader demand.

When they bet against noise traders, arbitrageurs begin to look like noise traders themselves. They pick stocks instead of diversifying, because that is what betting against noise traders requires. They time the market to take advantage of noise trader mood swings. If these swings are temporary, arbitrageurs who cannot predict noise trader moves simply follow contrarian strategies. It becomes hard to tell the noise traders from the arbitrageurs.

But saying that a market affected by investor sentiment looks realistic is hardly a rigorous test. To pursue this line of thought, we must derive and test implications that are not obvious and perhaps that are new. We consider first the implications of unpredictability or randomness of changes in investor sentiment. Second, we look at implications of strategies followed by investors who buy when prices rise and sell when prices fall, possibly because their expectations are simple extrapolations.

Implications of Unpredictability of Investor Sentiment

Even without taking a position on how investor sentiment moves, we can learn something from the observation that it moves in part unpredictably. Even if arbitrageurs know that noise traders are pessimistic today and hence will on average become less pessimistic in the future, they cannot be sure when this will happen. There is always a chance that noise traders become even more pessimistic first. This unpredictability contributes to resale price risk, since the resale price of an asset depends on the state of noise trader sentiment. If investor sentiment affects a broad range of assets in the same way, this risk from its unpredictability becomes systematic. Systematic risk has a price in equilibrium. Consequently, assets subject to whims of investor sentiment should yield higher average returns than similar assets not subject to such whims. Put differently, assets subject to unpredictable swings in investor sentiment must be underpriced in the market relative to their fundamental values.

De Long, Shleifer, Summers and Waldmann (1990a) describe two applications of this argument. First, stocks are probably subject to larger fluctuations of investor sentiment than bonds. In this case, equilibrium returns on stocks must be higher than warranted by their fundamentals—the latter being given by dividends and by covariation of dividends with consumption. In particular, the difference between average returns on stocks and on bonds—the risk premium—must be higher than is warranted by fundamentals. Such excess returns on stocks are in fact observed in the U.S. economy, and are known as the Mehra-Prescott (1985) puzzle. We can even reverse the argument to say that the high average risk premium is evidence of unpredictability of investor sentiment about stocks.

The second application we examined involves the pricing of closed-end mutual funds. These funds, like open-end funds, hold portfolios of other securities, but unlike open-end funds, have a fixed number of shares outstanding. As a result, an investor who wants to liquidate his holdings of a closed-end fund must sell his shares to other investors; he cannot just redeem his shares as with an open-end fund. Closed-end funds present one of the most interesting puzzles in finance, because their fundamental value—the value of the assets in their portfolios—is observed, and tends to be systematically higher than the price at which these funds trade. The pervasiveness of discounts on closed-end funds is a problem for the efficient markets hypothesis: in the one case where value is observed, it is not equal to the price.

De Long, Shleifer, Summers and Waldmann argue that investor sentiment about closed-end funds changes, and that this sentiment also affects other securities. When investors are bullish about closed-end funds, they drive up their prices relative to fundamental values, and discounts narrow or turn into premiums. When investors in contrast are bearish about closed-end funds, they drive down their prices and discounts widen. Any investor holding a closed-end fund bears two kinds of risk. The first is the risk from holding the fund's portfolio. The second is the resale price risk: at the time the investor needs to sell the fund the discount might widen. If investor sentiment about closed-end funds affects many other securities as well, bearing the resale price risk should be rewarded. That is, closed-end funds should on average sell at a discount. Put differently, the reason there are discounts *on average* is that discounts fluctuate, and investors require an extra return for bearing the risk of fluctuating discounts.

This theory explains why arbitrage does not effectively eliminate discounts on closed-end funds. An arbitrageur who buys a discounted fund and sells short its portfolio runs the risk that at the time he liquidates his position the discount widens and so his arbitrage results in a loss. An arbitrageur with an infinite horizon need not worry about this risk. But if the arbitrageur faces some probability of needing to liquidate his position in finite time, the risk from unpredictability of investor sentiment at the time he liquidates prevents him from aggressive betting that would eliminate discounts.

This theory of closed-end funds has a number of new empirical implications, investigated by Lee, Shleifer and Thaler (1989). First, it predicts that discounts on different closed-end funds fluctuate together, since they reflect changes in investor sentiment. This prediction is confirmed. Second, the theory predicts that new funds get started when investors are optimistic about funds, which is when old funds sell at a small discount or a premium. It is indeed the case that discounts on seasoned funds are much narrower in years when more new funds start. Perhaps most interestingly, the theory predicts that discounts on closed-end funds reflect the investor sentiment factor that also affects prices of other securities, which may have nothing to do with closed-end funds. Consistent with this prediction, Lee, Shleifer and Thaler find that when discounts on closed-end funds narrow, small stock portfolios tend to do well. This suggests that discounts on closed-end funds reflect an individual investor sentiment that also affects returns on small stocks held largely by individuals. These findings bear on previously untested implications of the investor sentiment approach, and so dispel the notion that this approach puts no restrictions on the data.

Implications of Positive Feedback Trading

One of the strongest investor tendencies documented in both experimental and survey evidence is the tendency to extrapolate or to chase the trend. Trend chasers buy stocks after they rise and sell stocks after they fall: they follow positive feedback strategies. Other strategies that depend on extrapolative expectations are "stop loss" orders, which prescribe selling after a certain level of losses, regardless of future prospects, and portfolio insurance, which involves buying more stocks (to raise exposure to risk) when prices rise and selling stocks (to cut exposure to risk) when prices fall.

When some investors follow positive feedback strategies—buy when prices rise and sell when prices fall—it need no longer be optimal for arbitrageurs to counter shifts in the demand of these investors. Instead, it may pay arbitrageurs to jump on the bandwagon themselves. Arbitrageurs then optimally buy the stocks that positive feedback investors get interested in when their prices rise. When price increases feed the buying of other investors, arbitrageurs sell out near the top and take their profits. The effect of arbitrage is to stimulate the interest of other investors and so to contribute to the movement of prices away from fundamentals. Although eventually arbitrageurs sell out and help prices return to fundamentals, in the short run they feed the bubble rather than help it to dissolve (De Long, Shleifer, Summers and Waldmann, 1990b).

Some speculators indeed believe that jumping on the bandwagon with the noise traders is the way to beat them. George Soros, the successful investor and author of *Alchemy of Finance* (1987), describes his strategy during the conglomerate boom in the

1960s and the Real Estate Investment Trust boom in the 1970s precisely in these terms. The key to success, says Soros, was not to counter the irrational wave of enthusiasm about conglomerates, but rather to ride this wave for awhile and sell out much later. Rational buying by speculators of already overvalued conglomerate stocks brought further buying by the noise traders, and enabled the speculators to make more money selling out at the top. Soros is not alone in trading this way; John Train (1987), in his book on successful U.S. investors, calls the strategy of one of his protagonists "Pumping Up the Tulips."

Trading between rational arbitrageurs and positive feedback traders gives rise to bubble-like price patterns. Positive feedback trading reinforced by arbitrageurs' jumping on the bandwagon leads to a positive autocorrelation of returns at short horizons. Eventual return of prices to fundamentals, accelerated as well by arbitrage, entails a negative autocorrelation of returns at longer horizons. Since news results in price changes that are reinforced by positive feedback trading, stock prices overreact to news.

These predictions have been documented in a number of empirical studies. Cutler, Poterba and Summers (1989b) find evidence of a positive correlation of returns at horizons of a few weeks or months and a negative one at horizons of a few years for several stock, bond, foreign exchange, and gold markets. They report the average first order monthly serial correlation of more than .07 for 13 stock markets, and positive in every case. Evidence on overreaction of stock prices to changes in fundamentals is presented for individual securities by DeBondt and Thaler (1985, 1987) and Lehmann (1990), and for the aggregate stock market by Campbell and Kyle (1988). The last paper, for example, decomposes stock returns into the fundamental and noise components and finds that the two are strongly positively correlated, meaning that prices overreact to news.

The finding of a positive serial correlation at short horizons implies that a substantial number of positive feedback traders must be present in the market, and that arbitrage does not eliminate the effects of their trades on prices.

The presence of positive feedback traders in financial markets also makes it easier to interpret historical episodes, such as the sharp market increase and the crash of 1987. According to standard finance, the market crash of October 1987 reflected either a large increase in risk premiums because the economy became a lot riskier, or a large decrease in expected future growth rate of dividends. These theories have the obvious problem that they do not explain what news prompted a 22 percent devaluation of the American corporate sector on October 19. Another problem is that there is no evidence that risk increased tremendously—volatility indeed jumped up but came back rapidly as it usually does—or that expected dividend growth has been revised sharply down. An examination of OECD long-term forecasts shows no downward revision in forecasts of long run growth rates after the crash, even though the crash itself could have adversely affected expectations. Perhaps most strikingly, Seyhun (1989) finds that corporate insiders bought stocks in record numbers during and after the crash, and moreover bought more of the stocks that later had a greater rebound. Insiders did not share the view that growth of dividends will slow or that risk will increase and *they were right*! Fully rational theories have a clear problem with the crash.

The crash is much easier to understand in a market with significant positive feedback trading. Positive feedback trading can rationalize the dramatic price increase during 1987, as more and more investors chase the trend. Positive feedback trading, exacerbated by possible front-running by investment banks, can also explain the depth of the crash once it has started. One still needs a theory of what broke the market on October 19, but the bad news during the previous week might have initiated the process, albeit with some lag. A full theory of the crash remains to be developed: prospects for such a theory look a lot brighter, however, if it incorporates positive feedback trading.

Conclusion

This paper has described an alternative to the efficient markets paradigm that stresses the roles of investor sentiment and limited arbitrage in determining asset prices. We have shown that the assumption of limited arbitrage is more general and plausible as a description of markets for risky assets than the assumption of perfect arbitrage which market efficiency relies on. With limited arbitrage, movements in investor sentiment are an important determinant of prices. We have also shown that this approach yields a large number of implications about the behavior of both investors and speculative prices which are consistent with the evidence. Perhaps most importantly, we have shown that this approach yields some new testable implications about security returns. Some of these implications, such as the ones on closed-end funds, have been tested and confirmed. It is thus not the case that the investor sentiment approach deprives finance of the discipline to which it is accustomed.

Assuming that our approach has some explanatory power and therefore intellectual merit, what are its implications for welfare and for policy? There are two normative issues relevant to the evaluation of noise trading. First, should something be done to prevent noise traders from suffering from their errors? Second, do noise traders impose a cost on the rest of market participants and, if so, how can this cost be reduced? Although answers to these questions ultimately turn on open empirical problems, both theory and empirical work permit some tentative remarks.

Investors who trade on noise or on popular models are worse off than they would be if their expectations were rational (if welfare is computed with respect to the correct distribution of returns). They need not lose money on average, as the simplest logic might suggest. But even if they earn higher average returns, it is because they bear more risk than they think. And even if they get rich over time, it is only because they underestimate the risk and get lucky. If investors had perfect foresight and rationality, they would know that noise trading always hurts them.

Whether the government should do anything to save noise traders from themselves depends on the social welfare function. People are allowed to participate in state lotteries, to lose fortunes in casinos, or to bet on the racetrack even though benevolent observers know that they are being taken to the cleaners. The case for making it costly for investors to bet on the stock market to protect them from their own utility losses is in principle identical to the case for prohibiting casinos, horse races, and state lotteries.

Noise trading, however, can also affect the welfare of the rest of the community. One effect is to benefit arbitrageurs who take advantage of noise traders. These benefits accrue both to those who bet against noise traders and those who feed their demand by providing financial services. Interestingly, the combined receipts of the NYSE member firms amounted to a sixth of the total U.S. corporate income in 1987 (Summers and Summers, 1989). Of course, some of these benefits to arbitrageurs are also a social *opportunity* cost as valuable human and other resources are allocated to separating noise traders from their money.

But noise trading also has a private cost, as it makes returns on assets more risky, and so can reduce physical investment. The overall impact of noise trading on the rest of the market participants and society can be negative (De Long, Shleifer, Summers and Waldmann, 1989). Some have also argued that noise trading in foreign exchange markets distorts the flow of goods between countries and leads to inefficient choice of production. Others have argued that noise trading forces managers to focus on the short term, and to bias the choice of investments against long-term projects. The policy reaction to noise trading can be dangerous as well; for example, sharp contractions of money supply by the Federal Reserve have often been justified as responses to excessive speculation. In this case, the consequences of such policies are more costly than the speculation itself.

Awareness of these costs of noise trading raises the question of what (if anything) should be done about it. Some businessmen and economists have proposed short term capital gains taxes as a way to cripple noise trading, while others, including Summers and Summers (1989) have advocated transaction taxes to the same end. It is not our goal in this paper to evaluate these proposals. We note, however, that one benefit of the research on markets where investor sentiment matters is to allow a more systematic evaluation of these proposals.

■ *This paper draws on our joint work with J. Bradford De Long and Robert J. Waldmann. We are indebted to the Russell Sage and Sloan Foundations for financial support of this research. We are indebted to Carl Shapiro, Joseph Stiglitz and Timothy Taylor for helpful comments.*

THE JOURNAL OF FINANCE • VOL. LII, NO. 1 • MARCH 1997

The Limits of Arbitrage

ANDREI SHLEIFER and ROBERT W. VISHNY*

ABSTRACT

Textbook arbitrage in financial markets requires no capital and entails no risk. In reality, almost all arbitrage requires capital, and is typically risky. Moreover, professional arbitrage is conducted by a relatively small number of highly specialized investors using other people's capital. Such professional arbitrage has a number of interesting implications for security pricing, including the possibility that arbitrage becomes ineffective in extreme circumstances, when prices diverge far from fundamental values. The model also suggests where anomalies in financial markets are likely to appear, and why arbitrage fails to eliminate them.

ONE OF THE FUNDAMENTAL concepts in finance is arbitrage, defined as "the simultaneous purchase and sale of the same, or essentially similar, security in two different markets for advantageously different prices" (Sharpe and Alexander (1990)). Theoretically speaking, such arbitrage requires no capital and entails no risk. When an arbitrageur buys a cheaper security and sells a more expensive one, his net future cash flows are zero for sure, and he gets his profits up front. Arbitrage plays a critical role in the analysis of securities markets, because its effect is to bring prices to fundamental values and to keep markets efficient. For this reason, it is extremely important to understand how well this textbook description of arbitrage approximates reality. This article argues that the textbook description does not describe realistic arbitrage trades, and, moreover, the discrepancies become particularly important when arbitrageurs manage other people's money.

Even the simplest realistic arbitrages are more complex than the textbook definition suggests. Consider the simple case of two Bund futures contracts to deliver DM250,000 in face value of German bonds at time T, one traded in London on LIFFE and the other in Frankfurt on DTB. Suppose for the moment, counter factually, that these contracts are exactly the same. Suppose finally that at some point in time t the first contract sells for DM240,000 and the second for DM245,000. An arbitrageur in this situation would sell a futures contract in Frankfurt and buy one in London, recognizing that at time T he is perfectly hedged. To do so, at time t, he would have to put up some good faith money, namely DM3,000 in London and DM3,500 in Frankfurt, leading to a

* Shleifer is from Harvard University and Vishny is from The University of Chicago. Nancy Zimmerman and Gabe Sunshine have helped us to understand arbitrage. We thank Yacine Aït Sahalia, Douglas Diamond, Oliver Hart, Steve Kaplan, Raghu Rajan, Jésus Saa-Requejo, Luigi Zingales, Jeff Zwiebel, and especially Matthew Ellman, Gustavo Nombela, René Stulz, and an anonymous referee for helpful comments.

net cash outflow of DM6,500. However, he does not get the DM5,000 difference in contract prices at the time he puts on the trade. Suppose that prices of the two contracts both converge to DM242,500 just after t, as the market returns to efficiency. In this case, the arbitrageur would immediately collect DM2,500 from each exchange, which would simultaneously charge the counter parties for their losses. The arbitrageur can then close out his position and get back his good faith money as well. In this near textbook case, the arbitrageur required only DM6,500 of capital and collected his profits at some point in time between t and T.

Even in this simplest example, the arbitrageur need not be so lucky. Suppose that soon after t, the price of the futures contract in Frankfurt rises to DM250,000, thus moving further away from the price in London, which stays at DM240,000. At this point, the Frankfurt exchange must charge the arbitrageur DM5,000 to pay to his counter party. Even if eventually the prices of the two contracts converge and the arbitrageur makes money, in the short run he loses money and needs more capital. The model of capital-free arbitrage simply does not apply. If the arbitrageur has deep enough pockets to always access this capital, he still makes money with probability one. But if he does not, he may run out of money and have to liquidate his position at a loss.

In reality, the situation is more complicated since the two Bund contracts have somewhat different trading hours, settlement dates, and delivery terms. It may easily happen that the arbitrageur has to find the money to buy bonds so that he can deliver them in Frankfurt at time T. Moreover, if prices are moving rapidly, the value of bonds he delivers and the value of bonds delivered to him may differ, exposing the arbitrageur to additional risks of losses. Even this simplest trade then becomes a case of what is known as risk arbitrage. In risk arbitrage, an arbitrageur does not make money with probability one, and may need substantial amounts of capital to both execute his trades and cover his losses. Most real world arbitrage trades in bond and equity markets are examples of risk arbitrage in this sense. Unlike in the textbook model, such arbitrage is risky and requires capital.

One way around these concerns is to imagine a market with a very large number of tiny arbitrageurs, each taking an infinitesimal position against the mispricing in a variety of markets. Because their positions are so small, capital constraints are not binding and arbitrageurs are effectively risk neutral toward each trade. Their collective actions, however, drive prices toward fundamental values. This, essentially, is the model of arbitrage implicit in Fama's (1965) classic analysis of efficient markets and in models such as CAPM (Sharpe (1964)) and APT (Ross (1976)).

The trouble with this approach is that the millions of little traders are typically not the ones who have the knowledge and information to engage in arbitrage. More commonly, arbitrage is conducted by relatively few professional, highly specialized investors who combine their knowledge with resources of outside investors to take large positions. The fundamental feature of such arbitrage is that brains and resources are separated by an agency relationship. The money comes from wealthy individuals, banks, endowments, and other investors with only a limited knowledge of individual markets, and is invested by arbitrageurs with highly specialized knowledge of these markets. In this article, we examine such arbitrage and its effectiveness in achieving market efficiency.

In particular, the implications of the fact that arbitrage—whether it is ultimately risk-free or risky—generally requires capital become extremely important in the agency context. In models without agency problems, arbitrageurs are generally more aggressive when prices move further from fundamental values (see Grossman and Miller (1988), De Long et al. (1990), Campbell and Kyle (1993)). In our Bund example above, an arbitrageur would in general increase his positions if London and Frankfurt contract prices move further out of line, as long as he has the capital. When the arbitrageur manages other people's money, however, and these people do not know or understand exactly what he is doing, they will only observe him losing money when futures prices in London and Frankfurt diverge. They may therefore infer from this loss that the arbitrageur is not as competent as they previously thought, refuse to provide him with more capital, and even withdraw some of the capital—even though the expected return from the trade has increased.

We refer to the phenomenon of responsiveness of funds under management to past returns as performance based arbitrage. Unlike arbitrageurs using their own money, who allocate funds based on expected returns from trades, investors may rationally allocate money based on past returns of arbitrageurs. When arbitrage requires capital, arbitrageurs can become most constrained when they have the best opportunities, i.e., when the mispricing they have bet against gets even worse. Moreover, the fear of this scenario would make them more cautious when they put on their initial trades, and hence less effective in bringing about market efficiency. This article argues that this feature of arbitrage can significantly limit its effectiveness in achieving market efficiency.

We show that performance-based arbitrage is particularly ineffective in extreme circumstances, where prices are significantly out of line and arbitrageurs are fully invested. In these circumstances, arbitrageurs might bail out of the market when their participation is most needed. Performance based arbitrage, then, is even more limited than arbitrage described in earlier models of inefficient markets, such as Grossman and Miller (1988), De Long et al. (1990), and Campbell and Kyle (1993).

Ours is obviously not the first study of the consequences of delegated portfolio management. Early articles in this area include Allen (1990) and Bhattacharya-Pfleiderer (1985). Scharfstein and Stein (1990) model herding by money managers operating on incentive contracts. Lakonishok, Shleifer, Thaler, and Vishny (1991) and Chevalier and Ellison (1995) consider the possibility that money managers "window dress" their portfolios to impress investors. In two interesting recent articles, Allen and Gorton (1993) and Dow and Gorton (1994) show how money managers can churn assets to mislead their investors, and how such churning can sustain inefficient asset prices. Unlike this work, our article does not focus as much on the distortions in the behavior of arbitrageurs, as on their limited effectiveness in bringing prices to fundamental values.

The next section of the article presents a very simple model that illustrates the mechanics of arbitrage. For simplicity, our model focuses on the case where mispricing may deepen in the short run, even though there is no long run fundamental risk in the trade. We thus focus on a case that is closest to pure arbitrage, as opposed to risk arbitrage. Section II establishes the main results of the article, including our results on the effectiveness of arbitrage in extreme circumstances when prices are very far from fundamentals. Section III explores the performance-based arbitrage assumption in more detail. In section IV, we examine some empirical implications of the model. In particular, we extend the logic of the model to the more realistic case of risk arbitrage, rather than the pure arbitrage case modeled in the article. We first ask what are the characteristics of markets in which we expect risk arbitrage resources to be concentrated. We then analyze return predictability and pricing anomalies more generally. Section V concludes.

I. An Agency Model of Limited Arbitrage

The structure of the model follows Shleifer and Vishny (1990). We focus on the market for a specific asset, in which we assume there are three types of participants: noise traders, arbitrageurs, and investors in arbitrage funds who do not trade on their own. Arbitrageurs specialize in trading only in this market, whereas investors allocate funds between arbitrageurs operating in both this and many other markets. The fundamental value of the asset is V, which arbitrageurs, but not their investors, know. There are three time periods: 1, 2, and 3. At time 3, the value V becomes known to arbitrageurs and noise traders, and hence the price is equal to that value. Since the price is equal to V at $t = 3$ for sure, there is no long run fundamental risk in this trade (this is not risk arbitrage). For $t = 1, 2$, the price of the asset at time t is p_t. For concreteness, we only consider pessimistic noise traders. In each of periods 1 and 2, noise traders may experience a pessimism shock S_t, which generates for them, in the aggregate, the demand for the asset given by:

$$\mathrm{QN}(t) = [V - S_t]/p_t. \tag{1}$$

At time $t = 1$, the first period noise trader shock, S_1, is known to arbitrageurs, but the second period noise trader shock is uncertain. In particular, there is some chance that $S_2 > S_1$, i.e., that noise trader misperceptions deepen before they correct at $t = 3$. De Long et al. (1990) stressed the importance of such noise trader risk for the analysis of arbitrage.

Both arbitrageurs and their investors are fully rational. Risk-neutral arbitrageurs take positions against the mispricing generated by the noise traders. Each period, arbitrageurs have cumulative resources under management (including their borrowing capacity) given by F_t. These resources are limited, for reasons we describe below. We assume that F_1 is exogenously given, and specify the determination of F_2 below.

At time $t = 2$, the price of the asset either recovers to V, or it does not. If it recovers, arbitrageurs invest in cash. If noise traders continue to be confused, then arbitrageurs want to invest all of F_2 in the underpriced asset, since its price rises to V at $t = 3$ for sure. In this case, the arbitrageurs' demand for the asset QA(2) = F_2/p_2 and, since the aggregate demand for the asset must equal the unit supply, the price is given by:

$$p_2 = V - S_2 + F_2. \tag{2}$$

We assume that $F_2 < S_2$, so the arbitrage resources are not sufficient to bring the period 2 price to fundamental value, unless of course noise trader misperceptions have corrected anyway.

In period 1, arbitrageurs do not necessarily want to invest all of F_1 in the asset. They might want to keep some of the money in cash in case the asset becomes even more underpriced at $t = 2$, so they could invest more in that asset. Accordingly, denote by D_1 the amount that arbitrageurs invest in the asset at $t = 1$. In this case, QA(1) = D_1/p_1, and

$$p_1 = V - S_1 + D_1. \tag{3}$$

We again assume that, in the range of parameter values we are focusing on, arbitrage resources are not sufficient to bring prices all the way to fundamental values, i.e., $F_1 < S_1$.

To complete the description of the model, we need to specify the organization of the arbitrage industry and the relationship between arbitrageurs and their investors, which determines F_2. Recall that we are focusing on a particular narrow market segment in which a given set of arbitrageurs specialize. A "segment" here should be interpreted as a particular arbitrage strategy. We assume that there are many such segments and that within each segment there are many arbitrageurs, so that no arbitrageur can affect asset prices in a segment. For simplicity, we can think of T investors each with one dollar available for investment with arbitrageurs. We are concerned with the aggregate amount $F_2 \ll T$ that is invested with the arbitrageurs in a particular segment.

Arbitrageurs compete in the price they charge for their services. For simplicity, we assume constant marginal cost per dollar invested, such that all arbitrageurs in all segments have the same marginal cost. We also assume that each arbitrageur has at least one competitor who is viewed as a perfect substitute, so that Bertrand competition drives price to marginal cost. Each of the T risk-neutral investors allocates his \$1 investment to maximize expected consumer surplus, i.e., the difference between the expected return on his dollar and the price charged by the arbitrageur. Investors are Bayesians, who have prior beliefs about the expected return of each arbitrageur. Since prices are equal, an investor gives his dollar to the arbitrageur with the highest expected return according to his beliefs. Different investors hold different beliefs about various arbitrageurs' abilities, so one arbitrageur does not end up with all the funds. The market share of each arbitrageur is just the total fraction of investors who believe that he has the highest expected return. The total share of money allocated to a given segment is just the sum of these market shares across all arbitrageurs in the segment. Importantly, we assume that arbitrageurs across many segments have, on average, earned high enough returns to convince investors to invest with them rather than to index.[1]

The key remaining question is how investors update their beliefs about the future expected returns of an arbitrageur. We assume that investors have no information about the structure of the model-determining asset prices in any segment. In particular, they do not know the trading strategy employed by any arbitrageur. This assumption is meant to capture the idea that arbitrage strategies are difficult to understand, and a lot of specialized knowledge is needed for investors to evaluate them. In part, this is because arbitrageurs do not share all their knowledge with investors, and cultivate secrecy to protect their knowledge from imitation. Even if the investors were told more about what arbitrageurs were doing, they would have a difficult time deciding whether what they heard was true. Implicitly, we are assuming that the underlying structural model is sufficiently nonstationary and high dimensional that investors are unable to infer the underlying structure of the model from past returns data. As a result, they only use simple updating rules based on past performance. In particular, investors are assumed to form posterior beliefs about future returns of the arbitrageur based only on their prior and any observations of his arbitrage returns.

Under these informational assumptions, individual arbitrageurs who experience relatively poor returns in a given period lose market share to those with better returns. Moreover, since all arbitrageurs in a given segment are taking the same positions, they all attract or lose investors simultaneously, depending on the performance of their common arbitrage strategy. Specifically, investors' aggregate supply of funds to the arbitrageurs in a particular segment at time 2 is an increasing function of arbitrageurs' gross return between time 1 and time 2 (call this performance-based-arbitrage or PBA). Denoting this function by G, and recognizing that the return on the asset is given by p_2/p_1, the arbitrageurs' supply of funds at $t = 2$ is given by:

$$F_2 = F_1 * G\{(D_1/F_1) * (p_2/p_1) + (F_1 - D_1)/F_1\},$$
$$\text{with} \quad G(1) = 1, \quad G' \geq 1, \quad \text{and} \quad G'' \leq 0. \qquad (4)$$

If arbitrageurs do as well as some benchmark given by performance of arbitrageurs in other markets, which for simplicity we assume to be zero return, they neither gain nor lose funds under management. However, they gain (lose) funds if they outperform (under perform) that benchmark. Because of the

[1] See Lakonishok, Shleifer, and Vishny (1992) for a description of the agency problems in the money management industry.

extremely poor quality of investors' information, past performance of arbitrageurs completely determines the resources they get to manage, regardless of the actual opportunities available in their market.

The responsiveness of funds under management to past performance (as measured by G′) is the solution to a signal extraction problem in which investors are trying to ascribe an arbitrageur's poor performance to one of three causes: 1) a random error term, 2) a deepening of noise trader sentiment (bad luck), and 3) inferior ability. High cross-sectional variation in ability across arbitrageurs will tend to increase the responsiveness of invested funds to past performance. On the other hand, if the variance of the noise trader sentiment term is high relative to the variation in (unobserved) ability, this will tend to decrease the responsiveness to past performance. In the limit, if ability is known or does not vary across arbitrageurs, poor performance could be ascribed only to a deepening of the noise trader shock (or a pure noise term), which would only increase the investor's estimate of the arbitrageur's future return. The seemingly perverse behavior of taking money away from an arbitrageur after noise trader sentiment deepens, i.e., precisely when his expected return is greatest, is a rational response to the problem of trying to infer the arbitrageur's (unobserved) ability and future opportunities jointly from past returns.

Since our results do not rely on the concavity of the G function, we focus on a linear G, given by

$$G(x) = ax + 1 - a, \qquad \text{with} \quad a \geq 1, \tag{5}$$

where x is arbitrageur's gross return. In this case, equation (4) becomes:

$$F_2 = a\,\{D_1 * (p_2/p_1) + (F_1 - D_1)\} + (1 - a)F_1 = F_1 - aD_1(1 - p_2/p_1). \tag{6}$$

With this functional form, if $p_2 = p_1$, i.e. the arbitrageur earns a zero net return, he neither gains nor loses funds under management. If $p_2 > p_1$, he gains funds and if $p_2 < p_1$, he loses funds. Note also that the higher is a, the more sensitive are the resources under management to past performance. The case of $a = 1$ corresponds to the arbitrageur not getting any more money when he loses some, whereas if $a > 1$, funds are actually withdrawn in response to poor performance.

One could in principle imagine more complicated incentive contracts that would allow arbitrageurs to signal their opportunities or abilities and attract funds based not just on past performance. For example, arbitrageurs who feel that they have superior investment opportunities might try to offer investors contracts that pay arbitrageurs a fixed price below marginal cost and a share of the upside. That is, if, at a particular point of time, arbitrageurs believe that they can earn extremely high returns with a high probability (as happens artificially at $t = 2$ in our model), they can try to attract investors by partially insuring them against further losses. We do not consider such "separating" contracts in our model, since they are unlikely to emerge in equilibrium under plausible circumstances. First, with limited liability or risk aversion, arbitrageurs might be unwilling or unable after mispricing worsens to completely retain (or increase) funds under management by insuring the investor against losses, or pricing below marginal cost. Second, these contracts are less attractive when the risk-averse arbitrageur himself is highly uncertain about his own ability to produce a superior return. We could model this more realistically by adding some noise into the third period return. In sum, under plausible conditions, the use of incentive contracts does not eliminate the effect of past performance on the market shares of arbitrageurs.[2] Empirically, most money managers in the pension and mutual fund industries work for fees proportional to assets under management and rarely get a percentage of the upside.[3] As documented by Ippolito (1992) and Warther (1995), for example, mutual fund managers lose funds under management when they perform poorly. Interestingly, Warther (1995) also shows that fund flows in and out of mutual funds affect contemporaneous returns of securities these funds hold, consistent with the results established below.

PBA is critical to our model. In conventional arbitrage, capital is allocated to arbitrageurs based on expected returns from their trades. Under PBA, in contrast, capital is allocated based on past returns, which, in the model, are low precisely when expected returns are high. At that time, arbitrageurs face fund withdrawals, and are not very effective in betting against the mispricing. Breaking the link between greater mispricing and higher expected returns perceived by those allocating capital drives our main results.

To complete the model, we need to set up an arbitrageur's optimization problem. For simplicity, we assume that the arbitrageur maximizes expected time 3 profits. Since arbitrageurs are price-takers in the market for investment services and marginal cost is constant, maximizing expected time 3 profit is equivalent to maximizing expected time 3 funds under management. For concreteness, we examine a specific form of uncertainty about S_2. We assume that, with probability q, $S_2 = S > S_1$, i.e. noise trader misperceptions deepen. With a complementary probability $1 - q$, noise traders recognize the true value of the asset at $t = 2$, so $S_2 = 0$ and $p_2 = V$.

When $S_2 = 0$, arbitrageurs liquidate their position at a gain at $t = 2$, and hold cash until $t = 3$. In this case, $W = a(D_1 * V/p_1 + F_1 - D_1) + (1 - a)F_1$.

[2] Our research assistant, Matthew Ellman of Harvard University, has solved a model in which allowing arbitrageurs to offer high-powered incentive contracts does not permit the arbitrageurs with better investment opportunities to separate themselves. The result is driven by two factors: first, limited liability precludes contracts from discouraging imitators through large penalties for poor performance, which are more likely to be levied against imitators, and, second, better arbitrageurs have more valuable alternative uses of their time, making it difficult to discourage the imitators by paying only for success since, at the contract necessary to meet the individual rationality constraint of the better arbitrageurs, the imitators still earn enough by sheer luck to cover their lower opportunity costs.

[3] Hedge fund managers typically do get a large incentive component in their compensation, but we are not aware of increases in that component, and cuts in fees, to avert withdrawal of funds.

When $S_2 = S$, in contrast, arbitrageurs third period funds are given by $W = (V/p_2) * [a\{D_1 * p_2/p_1 + F_1 - D_1\} + (1 - a)F_1]$. Arbitrageurs then maximize:

$$EW = (1-q)\left\{a\left(\frac{D_1 * V}{p_1} + F_1 - D_1\right) + (1-a)F_1\right\} + q\left(\frac{V}{p_2}\right) * \left\{a\left(\frac{D_1 * p_2}{p_1} + F_1 - D_1\right) + (1-a)F_1\right\} \tag{7}$$

II. Performance-Based Arbitrage and Market Efficiency

Before analyzing the pattern of prices in our model, we specify what the benchmarks are. The first benchmark is efficient markets, in which arbitrageurs have access to all the capital they want. In this case, since noise trader shocks are immediately counteracted by arbitrageurs, $p_1 = p_2 = V$. An alternative benchmark is one in which arbitrageurs resources are limited, but PBA is inoperative, i.e., arbitrageurs can always raise F_1. Even if they lose money, they can replenish their capital up to F_1. In this case, $p_1 = V - S_1 + F_1$ and $p_2 = V - S + F_1$. Prices fall one for one with noise trader shocks in each period. This case corresponds most closely to the earlier models of limited arbitrage. There is one final interesting benchmark in this model, namely the case of $a = 1$. This is the case in which arbitrageurs cannot replenish the funds they have lost, but do not suffer withdrawals beyond what they have lost. We will return to this special case below.

The first order condition to the arbitrageur's optimization problem is given by:

$$(1-q)\left(\frac{V}{p_1} - 1\right) + q\left(\frac{p_2}{p_1} - 1\right)\frac{V}{p_2} \geq 0 \tag{8}$$

with strict inequality holding if and only if $D_1 = F_1$, and equality holding if $D_1 < F_1$. The first term of equation (8) is an incremental benefit to arbitrageurs from an extra dollar of investment if the market recovers at $t = 2$. The second term is the incremental loss if the price falls at $t = 2$ before recovering at $t = 3$, and so they have foregone the option of being able to invest more in that case. Condition (8) holds with a strict equality if the risk of price deterioration is high enough, and this deterioration is severe enough, that arbitrageurs choose to hold back some funds for the option to invest more at time 2. On the other hand, equation (8) holds with a strict inequality if q is low, if p_1 is low relative to V (S_1 is large), if p_2 is not too low relative to p_1 (S not too large relative to S_1). That is to say, the initial displacement must be very large and prices should be expected to recover with a high probability rather than fall further. If they do fall, it cannot be by too much. Under these circumstances, arbitrageurs choose to be fully invested at $t = 1$ rather than hold spare reserves for $t = 2$. We describe the case in which mispricing is so severe at $t = 1$ that arbitrageurs choose to be fully invested as "extreme circumstances," and discuss it at some length.

This discussion can be summarized more formally in:

PROPOSITION 1: *For a given V, S_1, S, F_1, and a, there is a q^* such that, for $q > q^*$, $D_1 < F_1$, and for $q < q^*$, $D_1 = F_1$.*

If equation (8) holds with equality, the equilibrium is given by equations (2), (3), (6), and (8). If equation (8) holds with inequality, then equilibrium is given by $D_1 = F_1, p_1 = V - S_1 + F_1$, as well as equations (2) and (6). To illustrate the fact that both types of equilibria are quite plausible, consider a numerical example. Let $V = 1$, $F_1 = 0.2$, $a = 1.2$, $S_1 = 0.3$, $S_2 = 0.4$. For this example, $q^* = 0.35$. If $q < 0.35$, then arbitrageurs are fully invested and $D_1 = F_1 = 0.2$, so that the first period price is 0.9. In this case, regardless of the exact value of q, we have $F_2 = 0.1636$ and $p_2 = 0.7636$ if noise trader sentiment deepens, and $F_2 = 0.227$ and $p_2 = V = 1$ if noise trader sentiment recovers. On the other hand, if $q > 0.35$, then arbitrageurs hold back some of the funds at time 1, with the result that p_1 is lower than it would be with full investment. For example, if $q = 0.5$, then $D_1 = 0.1743$ and $p_1 = 0.8743$ (arbitrage is less aggressive at $t = 1$). If noise trader shock deepens, then $F_2 = 0.1766$, and $p_2 = 0.7766$ (arbitrageurs have preserved more funds to invest at $t = 2$), whereas if noise trader sentiment recovers then $F_2 = 0.23$ and price returns to $V = 1$. This example illustrates that both the corner solution and the interior equilibrium are quite plausible in our model. In fact, both occur for most parameters we have tried.

In this simple model, we can show that the larger are the shocks, the further are the prices from fundamental values.[4]

PROPOSITION 2: *At the corner solution ($D_1 = F_1$), $dp_1/dS_1 < 0$, $dp_2/dS < 0$, and $dp_1/dS = 0$. At the interior solution, $dp_1/dS_1 < 0$, $dp_2/dS < 0$, and $dp_1/dS < 0$.*

This proposition captures the simple intuition, common to all noise trader models, that arbitrageurs ability to bear against mispricing is limited, and larger noise trader shocks lead to less efficient pricing. Moreover, at the interior solution, arbitrageurs spread out the effect of a deeper period 2 shock by holding more cash at $t = 1$ and thus allowing prices to fall more at $t = 1$. As a result, they have more funds at $t = 2$ to counter mispricing at that time.

A more interesting question is how prices behave as a function of the parameter a. In particular, we would want to know whether the market becomes less efficient when PBA intensifies (a rises). Unfortunately, we do not believe that general conclusions can be drawn about how ex ante market efficiency (say, as measured by volatility) varies with a. The behavior of time 1 and time 2 prices with respect to a is very sensitive to the distribution of noise trader shocks.

In our current model, prices return to fundamentals at time 3 irrespective of the behavior of arbitrageurs. Also, the noise at time 2 either disappears or gets worse; it does not adjust part of the way toward fundamentals. Under these

[4] The proof of this proposition is straightforward, but requires some tedious calculations, which are omitted.

circumstances, we can show that a higher a makes the market less efficient. As a increases, the equilibrium exhibits the same or lower p_1 (if arbitrageurs hold back at time 1), and a strictly lower p_2 when the noise trader shock intensifies. In particular, arbitrage under PBA ($a > 0$) gives less efficient prices than limited arbitrage without PBA ($a = 0$).

On the other hand, if we modify the model to allow prices to adjust more slowly toward fundamentals, a higher a could actually make prices adjust more quickly by giving arbitrageurs more funds after a partial reversal of the noise trader shock. A partial adjustment toward fundamentals would be self-reinforcing through increased funds allocated to arbitrageurs along the way. Depending on the distribution of shocks over time, this could be the dominant effect. In general, we cannot draw any robust conclusions about ex ante market efficiency and the intensity of PBA.

However, we can say more about the effectiveness of arbitrage under extreme circumstances. In particular, we can analyze whether arbitrageurs become more aggressive when mispricing worsens. There are two ways to measure this. One is to ask whether arbitrageurs invest more total dollars in the asset at $t = 2$ than at $t = 1$, i.e., is $D_1 < F_2$? The second is whether arbitrageurs actually hold proportionally more of the asset at $t = 2$, i.e., is $D_1/p_1 < F_2/p_2$? In principle, it is possible that because $p_2 < p_1$, arbitrageurs hold more of the asset at $t = 2$ even though they spend less on it. Perhaps the clearest evidence of less aggressive arbitrage at $t = 2$ would be to show that arbitrageurs actually hold fewer shares at $t = 2$, and are liquidating their holdings, even though prices have fallen from $t = 1$. In the rest of this section, we focus on these liquidation problems.

We focus on a sufficient condition for liquidation at $t = 2$ when the noise trader shock deepens, namely, that arbitrageurs are fully invested at $t = 1$. Specifically, we have:

PROPOSITION 3: *If arbitrageurs are fully invested at $t = 1$, and noise trader misperceptions deepen at $t = 2$, then, for $a > 1$, $F_2 < D_1$ and $F_2/p_2 < D_1/p_1$.*

Proposition 3 describes the extreme circumstances in our model, in which fully invested arbitrageurs experience an adverse price shock, face equity withdrawals, and therefore liquidate their holdings of the extremely underpriced asset. Arbitrageurs bail out of the market when opportunities are the best.

Before analyzing this case in more detail, we note that full investment at $t = 1$ is a sufficient, but not a necessary condition for liquidation at $t = 2$. In general, for q's in the neighborhood above q^*, where $F_1 - D_1$ is positive but small, investors would still liquidate some of their holdings when $a > 1$. The reason is that their cash holdings are not high enough to maintain their holdings of the asset despite equity withdrawals. The cash holdings ameliorate these withdrawals, but do not eliminate them. For higher q's, however, D_1 is high enough that $F_2/p_2 > D_1/p_1$.

We can illustrate this with our numerical example from Section II, with $V = 1, S_1 = 0.3, S_2 = 0.4, F_1 = 0.2, a = 1.2$. Recall that in this example, we had

$q^* = 0.35$. One can show for this example that asset liquidations occur for $q < 0.39$, i.e., when arbitrageurs are fully invested as well as in a small region where they are not. For $q > 0.39$, arbitrageurs increase their holdings of the asset at $t = 2$.

For concreteness, it is easier to focus on the case of Proposition 3, when arbitrageurs are fully invested. In this case, we have that

$$p_2 = [V - S - aF_1 + F_1]/[1 - aF_1/p_1], \tag{9}$$

as long as $aF_1 < p_1$. The condition that $aF_1 < p_1$ is a simple stability condition in this model, which basically says that arbitrageurs do not lose so much money that in equilibrium they bail out of the market completely. If $aF_1 > p_1$, then at $t = 2$ the only equilibrium price is $p_2 = V - S$, and arbitrageurs bail out of the market completely. In the stable equilibrium, arbitrageurs lose funds under management as prices fall, and hence liquidate some holdings, but they still stay in the market.

For this equilibrium, simple differentiation yields the following result:

PROPOSITION 4: *At the fully invested equilibrium,* $dp_2/dS < -1$ *and* $d^2p_2/dadS < 0$.

This proposition shows that when arbitrageurs are fully invested at time 1, prices fall more than one for one with the noise trader shock at time 2. Precisely when prices are furthest from fundamental values, arbitrageurs take the smallest position. Moreover, as PBA intensifies, i.e., as a rises, the price decline per unit increase in S gets greater. If we think of dp_2/dS as a measure of the resiliency of the market (equal to zero for an efficient market and to -1 when $a = 0$ and there is no PBA), then Proposition 4 says that a market driven by PBA loses its resiliency in extreme circumstances. The analysis thus shows that the arbitrage process can be quite ineffective in bringing prices back to fundamental values in extreme circumstances.

This result contrasts with the more standard models, in which arbitrageurs are most aggressive when prices are furthest away from fundamentals. This point relates to Friedman's (1953) famous observation that "to say that arbitrage is destabilizing is equivalent to saying that arbitrageurs lose money on average," which is implausible. Our model is consistent with Friedman in that, on average, arbitrageurs make money and move prices toward fundamentals. However, the fact that they make money on average does not mean that they make money always. Our model shows that the times when they lose money are precisely the times when prices are far away from fundamentals, and in those times the trading by arbitrageurs has the weakest stabilizing effect.

These results are closely related to the recent studies of market liquidity (Shleifer and Vishny (1992), Stein (1995)). As in these studies, an asset here is liquidated involuntarily at a time when the best potential buyers—other arbitrageurs of this asset—have limited funds and external capital is not easily forthcoming. As a result of such fire sales, the price falls even further below fundamental value (holding the noise trader shock constant). The implication of limited resiliency for arbitrage is that arbitrage does not bring prices close to fundamental values in extreme circumstances.

The problem here may be even more severe than in operating firms. In such firms, the withdrawal/liquidation of assets is limited to the amount of debt that the firm has. In the case of arbitrage funds, unless they have a specific prohibition against withdrawals, even the equity capital can cash out because the assets themselves are liquid, as opposed to the hard assets of an operating firm. This difference in governance structures makes arbitrage funds much more susceptible to costly liquidations. In addition, investors probably understand the structure of industry downturns in operating companies better than they understand why arbitrageurs have lost their money. From this perspective as well, funds are at a greater risk of forced liquidation.

This analysis has one more interesting implication. The sensitivity to past returns of funds under management must be higher for young, unseasoned arbitrage (hedge) funds than for older, more established funds, with a long reputation for performance. As a result, the established funds will be able to earn higher returns in the long run, since they have more funds available when prices have gotten way out of line, which is when the returns to arbitrage are the greatest. In contrast, new arbitrageurs lose their funds precisely when the potential returns are the highest, and hence their average returns are lower than those of the older funds.

III. Discussion of Performance-Based Arbitrage

In our model, performance-based arbitrage, by delinking the expected return on the asset and arbitrageurs' demand for it at $t = 2$, generates the results that arbitrage is very limited. Although it is difficult to deny that PBA plays some role in the world, the question remains whether its consequences are as significant as our model suggests.

For example, one might argue that, even if funds under management decline in response to poor performance, they decline with a lag. For moderate price moves, arbitrageurs may be able to hold out and not liquidate until the price recovers. Moreover, if arbitrageurs are at least somewhat diversified, not all of their holdings lose money at the same time, suggesting again that they might be able to avoid forced liquidations.

Despite these objections, we continue to believe that, especially in extreme circumstances, PBA has significant consequences for prices. In many arbitrage funds, investors have the option to withdraw at least some of their funds at will, and are likely to do so quite rapidly if performance is poor. To some extent, this problem is mitigated by contractual restrictions on withdrawals, which are either temporary (as in the case of hedge funds that do not allow investors to take the money out for one to three years) or permanent (as in the case of closed end funds). However, these restrictions expose investors to being stuck with a bad fund manager for a long time, which explains why they are not common.[5] Moreover, creditors usually demand immediate repayment when the value of the collateral falls below (or even close to) the debt level, especially if they can get their money back before equity investors are able to withdraw their capital. Fund withdrawal by creditors is likely to be as or even more important as that by equity investors in precipitating liquidations (e.g., Orange County, December 1994). Last but not least, there may be an agency problem inside an arbitrage organization. If the boss of the organization is unsure of the ability of the subordinate taking a position, and the position loses money, the boss may force a liquidation of the position before the uncertainty works itself out. All these forces point to the likelihood that liquidations become important in extreme circumstances.

Our model shows how arbitrageurs might be forced to liquidate their positions when prices move against them. One effect that our model does not capture is that risk-averse arbitrageurs might choose to liquidate in this situation even when they don't have to, for fear that a possible further adverse price move will cause a really dramatic outflow of funds later on. Such risk aversion by arbitrageurs, which is not modeled here, would make them likely to liquidate rather than double up when prices are far away from fundamentals, making the problem we are identifying even worse. In this way, the fear of future withdrawals might have a similar effect to withdrawals themselves. We therefore expect that, even when arbitrageurs are not fully invested in a particular arbitrage strategy, significant losses in that strategy will induce voluntary liquidation behavior in extreme circumstances that looks very much like the involuntary liquidation behavior of the model.

The likelihood that risk-averse arbitrageurs voluntarily liquidate their positions in extreme circumstances is even larger if arbitrageurs are Bayesians with an imprecise posterior about the true distribution of returns on the arbitrage strategy. In that case, a sequence of poor returns may cause an arbitrageur to update his posterior and abandon his original strategy. The precision of the arbitrageur's posterior depends on the amount of past data available to estimate the return on the arbitrage strategy and on how much extra weight (if any) is placed on the more recent data. If arbitrageurs (correctly or not) believe that the world is nonstationary, they will use a shorter time series of data. This will cause their beliefs about the profitability of their strategies to be less precise (Heaton (1994)), and to change more in response to the most recent returns. This would further limit the effectiveness of arbitrage in extreme circumstances.

Finally, PBA supposes that all arbitrageurs have the same sensitivity of funds under management to performance, and that all invest in the mispriced

[5] According to the New York Stock Exchange (NYSE) Fact Book for 1993, the total dollar value of U.S. equities held by closed-end funds was only \$20.1 billion compared to \$617 billion for (open-end) mutual funds, \$1,038 billion for private pension funds (who typically have an open-end arrangement with their outside managers), and \$6,006 billion in total U.S. equities.

asset from the beginning. In fact, arbitrageurs differ. Some may have access to resources independent of past performance, and as a result might be able to invest more when prices diverge further from fundamentals. The introduction of a substantial number of such arbitrageurs can undo the effects of performance-based liquidations. If the new arbitrageurs reverse the price decline, the already invested arbitrageurs make money and hence no longer need to liquidate their holdings. However, after a very large noise trader shock that we have in the model, most arbitrageurs operating in a market are likely to find themselves fully committed. Even if some of them have held back initially, at some point most of them entered and even accumulated substantial debts to bet against the mispricing. As the mispricing gets deeper, withdrawals, as well as feared future withdrawals, cause them to liquidate. Admittedly, the total amount of capital available for arbitrage is huge, and perhaps outsiders can come in when insiders liquidate. But in practice, arbitrage markets are specialized, and arbitrageurs typically lack the experience and reputations to engage in arbitrage across multiple markets with other people's money. For this reason, outside capital does not come in to stabilize a market. In extreme circumstances, then, PBA is likely to be important and little fresh capital will be available to stabilize the market.

IV. Empirical Implications

The model presented in this article deals with the case of pure arbitrage, in which arbitrageurs do not need to bear any long run fundamental risk. While even such arbitrage must deal with problems of possible interim liquidations, in most real world situations arbitrageurs also face some long run fundamental risk. In other words, their positions pay off only on average, and not with probability one. Most data that financial economists deal with, such as stock market data, come from markets in which informed investors at best make advantageous bets. In this section, we describe some possible implications of the specialized arbitrage approach for financial markets in which arbitrageurs bear some fundamental risk, including both systematic and idiosyncratic risk. In particular, we show that this approach delivers different implications than those of noise trader models with many well-diversified arbitrageurs, such as DeLong et al (1990).

A. Which Markets Attract Arbitrage Resources?

Casual empiricism suggests that a great deal of professional arbitrage activity, such as that of hedge funds, is concentrated in a few markets, such as the bond market and the foreign exchange market. These also tend to be the markets where extreme leverage, short selling, and performance-based fees are common. In contrast, there is much less evidence of such activity in the stock market, either in the United States or abroad.[6] Why is that so? Which markets attract arbitrage?

Part of the answer is the ability of arbitrageurs to ascertain value with some confidence and to be able to realize it quickly. In the bond market, calculations of relative values of different fixed income instruments are doable, since future cash flows of securities are (almost) certain. As a consequence, there is almost no fundamental risk in arbitrage. In foreign exchange markets, calculations of relative values are more difficult, and arbitrage becomes riskier. However, arbitrageurs put on their largest trades, and appear to make the most money, when central banks attempt to maintain nonmarket exchange rates, so it is possible to tell that prices are not equal to fundamental values and to profit quickly. In stock markets, in contrast, both the absolute and the relative values of different securities are much harder to calculate. As a consequence, arbitrage opportunities are harder to identify in stock markets than in bond and foreign exchange markets.

The discussion in this article suggests a further reason why some markets are more attractive for arbitrage than others. Unlike the well-diversified arbitrageurs of the conventional models, the specialized arbitrageurs of our model might avoid extremely volatile markets if they are risk averse.

At first this claim seems counterintuitive, since high volatility may be associated with more frequent extreme mispricing, and hence more attractive opportunities for arbitrage. Assume that all volatility is due to noise trader sentiment and that the average out-performance of the arbitrageur relative to the benchmark, typically called alpha, is roughly proportional to the standard deviation of the noise trader demand shock. This means that if the arbitrageur switches to a market with twice the noise trader volatility, he also can expect twice the alpha per $1 investment. In such a market, by cutting his investment in half, the arbitrageur gets the same expected alpha and the same volatility as in the first market. He is indifferent to trading in these two markets because alpha per unit of risk is the same and he can always adjust his position to achieve the desired level of risk. This assumes that outside borrowing by the arbitrageur is limited not by the total dollar value of the investment, but by the dollar volatility of investment, which also seems plausible. In this simplified environment, the volatility of the market does not matter for the attractiveness of entry by the marginal arbitrageur.

High volatility *does*, however, make arbitrage less attractive if expected alpha does not increase in proportion to volatility. This would be true in particular when fundamental risk is a substantial part of volatility. For example, increasing one's equity position in an industry that is perceived to be underpriced carries substantial fundamental risk, and hence reduces the attractiveness of the trade. Another important factor determining the attractive-

[6] Some of these activities, such as short-selling and use of leverage, are limited by government regulations or by fund charters. Many institutions such as mutual funds are also restricted in the degree to which their positions can be concentrated in a small number of securities and in their ability to keep their positions confidential.

ness of any arbitrage concerns the horizon over which mispricing is eliminated. While greater volatility of noise trader sentiment may increase long-run returns to arbitrage, over short horizons the ratio of expected alpha to volatility may be low. Once again, this may be true for securities like equities where the resolution of uncertainty is slow and where noise trader sentiment can push prices a long way away from fundamentals before disconfirming evidence becomes available. In this case, the long run ratio of expected alpha to volatility may be high, but the ratio over the horizon of a year may be low. Markets in which fundamental uncertainty is high and slowly resolved are likely to have a high long-run, but a low short-run, ratio of expected alpha to volatility. For arbitrageurs who care about interim consumption and whose reputations are permanently affected by their performance over the next year or two, the ratio of reward to risk over shorter horizons may be more relevant. All else equal, high volatility will deter arbitrage activity.

To specialized arbitrageurs, both systematic and idiosyncratic volatility matters. In fact, idiosyncratic volatility probably matters more, since it cannot be hedged and arbitrageurs are not diversified. Ours is not the first article to emphasize that idiosyncratic risk matters in a world of information costs and specialization.[7] Merton (1987) suggests that idiosyncratic risk raises expected returns when security markets are segmented and investors must incur a fixed cost to become informed and participate in each market. Our view of risky arbitrage activity is easy to distinguish empirically from Merton's view of idiosyncratic risk in segmented markets. In Merton's model, there are no noise traders. As a result, stocks with higher idiosyncratic risk are rationally priced to earn a higher expected return. In our model, in contrast, stocks are not rationally priced, and idiosyncratic risk deters arbitrage. In particular, some stocks with high idiosyncratic variance may be overpriced, and this overpricing is not eliminated by arbitrage because shorting them is risky. These volatile overpriced stocks earn a lower expected return, unlike in Merton's model. A good example is so-called glamour stocks, or stocks of firms with higher market prices relative to various measures of fundamentals, such as earnings or book value of assets (see, for example, Lakonishok, Shleifer, and Vishny (1994)). Since these stocks have a higher than average variance of returns, a rational pricing model with segmented markets would predict higher expected returns for these stocks. In contrast, if we take the view that these stocks are overpriced, then their expected returns are lower despite the higher variance. The evidence supports the latter interpretation.

B. *Anomalies*

Recent research in finance has identified a number of so-called anomalies, in which particular investment strategies have historically earned higher returns than those justified by their systematic risk. One such anomaly, already

[7] The importance of idiosyncratic risk in our framework is a consequence of the assumed specialization, and not of the agency problem per se. The agency problem itself is also a natural consequence of the returns to specialization.

mentioned, is that value stocks have historically earned higher returns than glamour stocks, but there are many others. Our analysis offers a different approach to understanding these anomalies than does the standard efficient markets theory.

The efficient markets approach to these anomalies is to argue that higher returns must be compensation for higher systematic risk, and therefore the model of asset pricing that made the evidence look anomalous must have been misspecified. It must be possible to explain the anomalies away by finding a covariance between the returns on the anomalous portfolio and some fundamental factor from the intertemporal capital asset pricing model or arbitrage pricing theory.

The efficient markets approach is based on the assumption that most investors, like the economists, see the available arbitrage opportunities and take them. Excess returns are eliminated by the action of a large number of such investors, each with only a limited extra exposure to any one set of securities. Excess returns to particular securities persist only if they are negatively correlated with state variables such as the aggregate marginal utility of consumption or wealth.

As we argue in this article, the theoretical underpinnings of the efficient markets approach to arbitrage are based on a highly implausible assumption of many diversified arbitrageurs. In reality, arbitrage resources are heavily concentrated in the hands of a few investors that are highly specialized in trading a few assets, and are far from diversified. As a result, these investors care about total risk, and not just systematic risk. Since the equilibrium excess returns are determined by the trading strategies of these investors, looking for systematic risk as the only potential determinant of pricing is inappropriate. Idiosyncratic risk as well deters arbitrageurs, whether it is fundamental or noise trader idiosyncratic risk.

Our article suggests a different approach to understanding anomalies. The first step is to understand the source of noise trading that might generate the mispricing in the first place. Specifically, it is essential to examine the demand of the potential noise traders, whether such demand is driven by sentiment or institutional restrictions on holdings. The second step is to evaluate the costs of arbitrage in the market, especially the total volatility of arbitrage returns. For a given noise trading process, volatile securities will exhibit greater mispricing and a higher average return to arbitrage in equilibrium. (Other costs of arbitrage, such as transaction costs, are also important (Pontiff (1996)).

We can illustrate the difference between the two approaches using the value/glamour anomaly. To justify an efficient markets approach to explaining this anomaly, Fama and French (1992) argue that the capital asset pricing model is misspecified, and that high (low) book to market stocks earn a high (low) return because the former have a high loading on a different risk factor than the market. Although they don't precisely identify a macroeconomic factor to which the high book to market stocks are particularly exposed, they argue that the portfolio of high book to market stocks is itself a proxy for such a factor, which they call the distress factor.

Our approach instead would be to identify the pattern of investor sentiment responsible for this anomaly, as well as the costs of arbitrage that would keep it from being eliminated. To begin, the glamour-value evidence is consistent with some investors extrapolating past earnings growth of companies and failing to recognize that extreme earnings growth is likely to revert to the mean (Lakonishok, Shleifer, and Vishny (1994), LaPorta (1996)). With respect to risk, the conventional arbitrage of the glamour-value anomaly, i.e., simply taking a long position in a diversified portfolio of value (high book-to-market) stocks, has been roughly a 60–40 proposition over a one year horizon. That is, the odds of outperforming the S&P 500 index over one year have been only 60 percent, although over 5 years the superior performance has been much more likely.[8] Over a short horizon, then, arbitrage returns on the value portfolio are volatile. Even though this risk may be idiosyncratic, it cannot be hedged by arbitrageurs specializing in this segment of the market. Because of the high volatility of the hedge strategy, and the relatively long horizon it relies on to secure positive returns with a high probability, it is likely to be shunned by arbitrageurs, particularly those with a short track record.

Our approach further implies that, in extreme situations, arbitrageurs trying to eliminate the glamour/value mispricing might lose enough money that they have to liquidate their positions. In this case, arbitrageurs may become the least effective in reducing the mispricing precisely when it is the greatest. Something along these lines occurred with the stocks of commercial banks in 1990–1991. As the prices of these stocks fell sharply, many traditional value arbitrageurs invested heavily in these stocks. However, the prices kept falling, and many value arbitrageurs lost most of their funds under management. As a consequence, they had to liquidate their positions, which put further pressure on the prices of banking stocks. After this period, the returns on banking stocks have been very high, but many value funds did not last long enough to profit from this recovery.

The glamour/value anomaly is one of several that our approach might explain. The analysis actually predicts what types of market anomalies can persist over the long term. These anomalies must have a high degree of unpredictability, which makes betting against them risky for specialized arbitrageurs. However, unlike in the efficient markets model, this risk need not be correlated with any macroeconomic factors, and can be purely idiosyncratic fundamental or noise trader risk.

Finally, the specialized arbitrage approach assumes that only a relatively small number of specialists understand the return anomaly well enough to exploit it. This may be questionable in the case of anomalies like the value-glamour anomaly or the small firm anomaly about which there is now much published work. As more investors begin to understand an anomaly, the superior returns to the trading strategy may be diminished by the actions of a larger number of investors who each tilt their portfolios toward the underpriced assets. Alternatively, investors may become more knowledgeable about

[8] The exact odds depend on what sample period and what universe of stocks is used.

the strategies being used and judge arbitrageurs relative to a more accurate benchmark of their peers (e.g., other value managers or a value index), thereby diminishing some of the withdrawals when an entire peer group is performing poorly. The specialized arbitrage approach is clearly more appropriate for difficult-to-understand new arbitrage opportunities than it is for well-understood anomalies (which should presumably not be anomalies for long).

We would nonetheless argue that anomalies become understood very slowly and that investors do not take definitive action on their information until long after a phenomenon has been exposed to public scrutiny. The anomaly is more easily accepted when the pattern of returns is not very noisy and the payoff horizon is short (such as the small firm effect in January). A "noisy" anomaly like the value-glamour anomaly is accepted only slowly, even by relatively sophisticated investors.

V. Conclusion

Our article describes the workings of markets in which specialized arbitrageurs invest the capital of outside investors, and where investors use arbitrageurs' performance to ascertain their ability to invest profitably. We show that such specialized performance-based arbitrage may not be fully effective in bringing security prices to fundamental values, especially in extreme circumstances. More generally, specialized, professional arbitrageurs may avoid extremely volatile "arbitrage" positions. Although such positions offer attractive average returns, the volatility also exposes arbitrageurs to risk of losses and the need to liquidate the portfolio under pressure from the investors in the fund. The avoidance of volatility by arbitrageurs also suggests a different approach to understanding persistent excess returns in security prices. Specifically, we expect anomalies to reflect not some exposure of securities to difficult-to-measure macroeconomic risks, but rather, high idiosyncratic return volatility of arbitrage trades needed to eliminate the anomalies. In sum, this more realistic view of arbitrage can shed light on a variety of observations in securities markets that are difficult to understand in more conventional models.

REFERENCES

Allen, Franklin, 1990, The market for information and the origin of financial intermediation, *Journal of Financial Intermediation* 1, 3–30.

Allen, Franklin, and Gary Gorton, 1993, Churning bubbles, *Review of Economic Studies* 60, 813–836.

Bhattacharya, Sudipto, and Paul Pfleiderer, 1985, Delegated portfolio management, *Journal of Economic Theory* 36, 1–25.

Campbell, John, and Albert Kyle, 1993, Smart money, noise trading, and stock price behavior, *Review of Economic Studies* 60, 1–34.

Chevalier, Judith, and Glenn Ellison, 1995, Risk taking by mutual funds as a response to incentives, manuscript.

DeLong, J. Bradford, Andrei Shleifer, Lawrence Summers, and Robert Waldmann, 1990, Noise trader risk in financial markets, *Journal of Political Economy* 98, 703–738.

Dow, James, and Gary Gorton, 1994, Noise trading, delegated portfolio management, and economic welfare, NBER Working paper 4858.

Fama, Eugene, 1965, The behavior of stock market prices, *Journal of Business* 38, 34–105.

Fama, Eugene, and Kenneth French, 1992, The cross-section of expected stock returns, *Journal of Finance* 46, 427–466.

Friedman, Milton, 1953, The case for flexible exchange rates, in *Essays in Positive Economics* (University of Chicago Press, Chicago).

Grossman, Sanford, and Merton Miller, 1988, Liquidity and market structure, *Journal of Finance* 43, 617–633.

Heaton, John, 1994, Learning and the belief in low-scaled price portfolio strategies, 1940–1993, manuscript, University of Chicago.

Ippolito, Richard, 1992, Consumer reaction to measures of poor quality: evidence from the mutual fund industry, *Journal of Law and Economics* 35, 45–70.

LaPorta, Rafael, 1996, Expectations and the cross-section of stock returns, *Journal of Finance* 51, 1715–1742.

Lakonishok, Josef, Andrei Shleifer, Richard Thaler, and Robert Vishny, 1991, Window dressing by pension fund managers, *American Economic Review Papers and Proceedings* 81, 227–231.

Lakonishok, Josef, Andrei Shleifer, and Robert Vishny, 1992, The structure and performance of the money management industry, *Brookings Papers on Economic Activity: Microeconomics*, 339–391.

Lakonishok, Josef, Andrei Shleifer, and Robert Vishny, 1994, Contrarian investment, extrapolation, and risk, *Journal of Finance* 49, 1541–1578.

Merton, Robert, 1987, A simple model of capital market equilibrium with incomplete information, *Journal of Finance* 42, 483–510.

Pontiff, Jeffrey, 1996, Costly arbitrage: Evidence from closed-end funds. *Quarterly Journal of Economics* 111, 1135–1152.

Ross, Steven, 1976, The arbitrage theory of capital asset pricing, *Journal of Economic Theory* 13, 341–360.

Scharfstein, David, and Jeremy Stein, 1990, Herd behavior and investment, *American Economic Review* 80, 465–489.

Sharpe, William, 1964, Capital asset prices: A theory of market equilibrium under conditions of risk, *Journal of Finance* 19, 425–442.

Sharpe, William, and Gordon Alexander, 1990, Investments, 4th edition, (Prentice Hall, Englewood Cliffs, N.J.).

Shleifer, Andrei, and Robert Vishny, 1990, Equilibrium short horizons of investors and firms, *American Economic Review Papers and Proceedings* 80, 148–153.

Shleifer, Andrei, and Robert Vishny, 1992, Liquidation values and debt capacity: A market equilibrium approach, *Journal of Finance* 47, 1343–1366.

Stein, Jeremy, 1995, Prices and trading volume in the housing market: A model with downpayment effects, *Quarterly Journal of Economics*, 110, 379–406.

Warther, Vincent, 1995, Aggregate mutual fund flows and security returns, *Journal of Financial Economics* 39, 209–236.

Part IV
Bubbles

Explosive Rational Bubbles in Stock Prices?

By BEHZAD T. DIBA AND HERSCHEL I. GROSSMAN*

A number of recent studies address the problem of assessing the contributions of market fundamentals and rational bubbles to stock-price fluctuations—see, for example, Olivier Blanchard and Mark Watson, 1982; Robert Flood, Robert Hodrick, and Paul Kaplan, 1986; and Kenneth West, 1986, 1987. A rational bubble reflects a self-confirming belief that an asset's price depends on a variable (or a combination of variables) that is intrinsically irrelevant—that is, not part of market fundamentals—or on truly relevant variables in a way that involves parameters that are not part of market fundamentals. A basic difficulty involved in testing for the existence of rational bubbles, pointed out by Flood and Peter Garber, 1980, and emphasized by James Hamilton and Charles Whiteman, 1985, is that the contribution of hypothetical rational bubbles to asset prices would not be directly distinguishable from the contribution to market fundamentals of variables that the researcher cannot observe. For example, as Hamilton, 1986, shows, a researcher who is unable to observe or to infer changes in the expectations of market participants, especially if they involve the probable future occurrence of relevant events that are infrequent and discrete, might falsely conclude that rational bubbles exist. In the present context, the probabilities that investors attach to possibilities for future tax treatment of dividend income could act like such an unobservable variable.

*Research Department, Federal Reserve Bank of Philadelphia, Philadelphia, PA 19106, and Department of Economics, Brown University, Providence, RI 02912, respectively. The views expressed are solely those of the authors and do not necessarily represent the views of the Federal Reserve Bank of Philadelphia or of the Federal Reserve System. We thank John Campbell, Robert Shiller, and anonymous referees for helpful comments on earlier versions of this paper.

Diba and Grossman, 1984, and Hamilton and Whiteman, 1985, propose an empirical strategy based on stationarity tests for obtaining evidence against the existence of explosive rational bubbles without precluding the possible effect of unobservable variables on market fundamentals. The present paper implements such tests for explosive rational bubbles in stock prices using a model that assumes a constant discount rate, but that allows unobservable variables to affect market fundamentals and also allows different valuations of expected capital gains and expected dividends. If the first differences of the unobservable variables and the first differences of dividends are stationary (in the mean) and if rational bubbles do not exist, then the model implies that first differences of stock prices are stationary. The model also implies, using an argument adapted from John Campbell and Robert Shiller, 1987, that, if the levels of the unobservable variables and the first differences of dividends are stationary, and if rational bubbles do not exist, then stock prices and dividends are cointegrated of order (1,1).

These theoretical results do not imply that the finding that first differences of stock prices are nonstationary, or that stock prices and dividends are not cointegrated, would establish the existence of rational bubbles. A finding that stock prices and dividends are not cointegrated could result from the nonstationarity of the unobservable variables in market fundamentals, and a finding that stock-price changes are nonstationary could result from the nonstationarity of changes in these unobservable variables. Such findings also could arise from the inappropriateness of the implicit assumption that dividends are generated by an ARIMA process.

The converse inference, however, is possible. That is, evidence that first differences of stock prices have a stationary mean and/or evidence that stock prices are cointegrated with dividends would be evidence against the existence of rational bubbles. Except by extremely unlikely coincidence, misspecification of market fundamentals could not offset the contribution of a nonstationary rational bubble to stock prices. In addition to analyzing the stationarity properties of the observed time-series of real stock prices and dividends, this paper also examines the stationarity properties of simulated time-series of hypothetical rational bubbles to determine whether the stationarity tests can detect the relevant nonstationarity when it is present.

Because it looks for evidence against the existence of rational bubbles, the analysis in the present paper, in contrast to the strategy for finding rational bubbles suggested by West, 1986, 1987, does not require the specification of a true difference equation relating stock prices only to other observable variables. West observes that, if we could find such a true difference equation, and if the data rejected the implied market-fundamentals solution for stock prices, then we could conclude that rational bubbles exist. The problem with this approach is that diagnostic tests—as reported, for example, by Flood et al., 1986—reject the difference equations linking stock prices to dividends implied by a constant discount rate as well as by extended models that relate the discount rate to the intertemporal marginal rate of substitution or that incorporate different valuations for capital gains and dividends. These results underscore the need for an empirical strategy that does not preclude the possibility that market fundamentals for stock prices depend on unobservable variables in addition to dividends.

I. The Model

The theoretical model consists of a single equation that relates the current stock price to the present value of next period's expected stock price and dividend payments and to an unobservable variable—that is,

$$(1)\quad P_t = (1+r)^{-1}E_t(P_{t+1} + \alpha d_{t+1} + u_{t+1}),$$

where

P_t is the stock price at date t relative to a general index of prices of goods and services;

r is a constant real interest rate that is appropriate for discounting expected capital gains;

E_t is the conditional expectations operator;

α is a positive constant that valuates expected dividends relative to expected capital gains;

d_{t+1} is the real before-tax dividend paid to the owner of the stock between dates t and $t+1$; and

u_{t+1} is a variable that market participants either observe or construct, but that the researcher does not observe.

(As suggested above, this unobservable variable could involve the probabilities that investors attach to possibilities for future tax treatment of dividend income.) If α were equal to unity and u_{t+1} were equal to zero for all t, equation (1) would state that the expected real rate of return from holding equity, including expected dividends and expected capital gains, equals the constant r. The information set of market participants at date t on which E_t is based contains at least the current and past realizations of P_t, d_t, and u_t.

Equation (1) is a first-order expectational difference equation. Because the eigenvalue, $1+r$, is greater than unity, the forward-looking solution for the stock price involves a convergent sum, as long as $E_t(\alpha d_{t+j} + u_{t+j})$ does not grow with j at a geometric rate equal to or greater than $1+r$. This forward-looking solution, denoted by F_t and referred to as the market-fundamentals component of the stock price, is

$$(2)\quad F_t = \sum_{j=1}^{\infty} (1+r)^{-j}E_t(\alpha d_{t+j} + u_{t+j}).$$

With α equal to unity and u_t equal to zero for all t, equation (2) would say that the market-fundamentals component of the stock price equals the present value of expected real dividends discounted at the constant rate r.

The general solution to equation (1) is the sum of the market-fundamentals component,

F_t, and the rational bubbles component, B_t —that is,

$$(3) \qquad P_t = B_t + F_t,$$

where B_t is the solution to the homogeneous expectational difference equation

$$(4) \qquad E_t B_{t+1} - (1+r) B_t = 0.$$

A nonzero value of B_t would reflect the existence of a rational bubble—that is, a self-confirming belief that the stock price does not conform to the market-fundamentals component, F_t.

Solutions to equation (4) satisfy the stochastic difference equation

$$(5) \qquad B_{t+1} - (1+r) B_t = z_{t+1},$$

where z_{t+1} is a random variable (or combination of variables) generated by a stochastic process that satisfies

$$(6) \qquad E_{t-j} z_{t+1} = 0 \qquad \text{for all } j \geq 0.$$

The key to the relevance of equation (5) for the general solution of P_t is that equation (4) relates B_t to $E_t B_{t+1}$, rather than to B_{t+1} itself as would be the case in a perfect-foresight model.

The random variable z_{t+1} is an innovation, comprising new information available at date $t+1$. This information can be intrinsically irrelevant—that is, unrelated to F_{t+1} —or it can be related to truly relevant variables, like d_{t+1}, through parameters that are not present in F_{t+1}. The only critical property of z_{t+1}, given by equation (5), is that its expected future values are always zero.

Diba and Grossman, 1988, review and extend theoretical arguments for ruling out rational stock-price bubbles on the basis of the nonnegativity of stock prices and the optimizing decisions of asset holders. George Evans, 1985, develops another theoretical argument for ruling out rational bubbles by requiring that equilibrium rational expectations solutions to the model should be stable in the sense that, given a small disequilibrium deviation from rational expectations, the system should return to rational expectations equilibrium under a natural revision rule. The empirical analysis developed in the present paper complements these theoretical analyses.

II. Stationarity of Stock Prices and Dividends

Consider the market-fundamentals component of the stock price given by equation (2). Assume that the process generating d_t is nonstationary in levels, but that first differences of d_t and u_t are stationary. Then, if rational bubbles do not exist, stock prices are nonstationary in levels but stationary in first differences.

If, however, stock prices contain a rational bubble, then for simple specifications of the process generating z_t, differencing stock prices a finite number of times would not yield a stationary process. Specifically, from equation (5), first differences of a rational bubble would have the generating process

$$(7) \quad [1-(1+r)L](1-L)B_t = (1-L)z_t,$$

where L denotes the lag operator. For example, if z_t is white noise, then an ARMA process that is neither stationary nor invertible generates $(1-L)B_t$. (The only exceptions to nonstationarity discussed in the literature involve rational bubbles that almost surely would burst at a finite future date, as in the specifications of Blanchard, 1979, and Blanchard and Watson, 1982. Such a rational bubble would have innovations with infinite variance, but, as Danny Quah, 1985, demonstrates, it also would have a stationary unconditional mean of zero.)

Allan Kleidon, 1986, analyzes the stationarity properties of stock prices, dividends, and their first differences for Data Set 1 in Robert Shiller, 1981. The work of Blanchard and Watson, 1982; Flood et al., 1986; and West, 1986, 1987, also uses this data set. The price series is Standard & Poor's Composite Stock Price Index for January of each year from 1871 to 1986 divided by the wholesale price index for that month. The dividend series is total dividends accruing to this portfolio of stocks for the calendar year divided by the average whole-

TABLE 1—SAMPLE AUTOCORRELATIONS OF REAL STOCK PRICES, DIVIDENDS, AND THEIR FIRST DIFFERENCES

Number of Lags Series	1	2	3	4	5	6	7	8	9	10
P_t	0.94	0.87	0.84	0.79	0.74	0.68	0.63	0.57	0.51	0.45
d_t	0.95	0.88	0.82	0.78	0.74	0.70	0.65	0.62	0.59	0.56
ΔP_t	0.06	−0.24	0.12	0.17	−0.00	−0.12	0.15	0.00	−0.07	−0.05
Δd_t	0.23	−0.16	−0.07	−0.03	−0.01	−0.01	−0.17	−0.13	0.06	0.14

Note: The price (P_t) and dividend (d_t) series contain 116 observations. Their first differences (ΔP_t and Δd_t) contain 115 observations.

TABLE 2—DICKEY-FULLER TEST RESULTS: NO LAGS

x_t:	P_t	d_t	ΔP_t	Δd_t
$\hat{\mu}$	0.0058	0.0007	0.0002	0.0001
	(0.0166)	(0.0005)	(0.0168)	(0.0004)
$\hat{\gamma}$	0.0006	0.00003	0.0001	0.000001
	(0.0003)	(0.00001)	(0.0003)	(0.000006)
$\hat{\rho}$	0.90	0.87	0.06	0.23
	(0.04)	(0.05)	(0.10)	(0.10)
Standard Error of Estimate	0.071	0.002	0.072	0.002
Φ_3	2.55	3.43	42.38	30.89

Note: Regressions are of the form $x_t = \mu + \gamma t + \rho x_{t-1} +$ residual. "Standard errors" are in parentheses below coefficients. Sample size is 100 in all cases. The statistic Φ_3, calculated like the F-statistic, tests the null hypothesis $(\gamma, \rho) = (0,1)$ against the alternative $(\gamma, \rho) \neq (0,1)$. The rejection region is the set of values of Φ_3 above 5.47 (6.49) for a test of size 0.10 (0.05).

sale price index for the year. Tables 1, 2, and 3 report results similar to Kleidon's results.

Table 1 presents sample autocorrelations of these real stock prices and dividends, and their first differences, for one through ten lags. The autocorrelations of the undifferenced price and dividend series both drop off slowly as lag length increases, suggesting nonstationary means. Their patterns correspond closely to what would be expected for integrated moving average processes according to a formula presented by Dean Wichern, 1973. In contrast, autocorrelations of the differenced series, both for prices and dividends, are consistent with the assumption that these series have stationary means. Thus the autocorrelation patterns suggest that the nonstationarity of real stock prices is attributable to their market-fundamentals component and that explosive rational bubbles do not exist in stock prices.

Tables 2 and 3 report Dickey-Fuller, 1981, tests for unit roots in the autoregressive representations of real stock prices, dividends, and their first differences. For each time-series, the estimated OLS regression is

$$(8) \quad x_t = \mu + \gamma t + \rho x_{t-1} + \sum_{i=1}^{k} \beta_i \Delta x_{t-i} + \text{residual},$$

where Δ is the difference operator. The tables report the statistic Φ_3 of David Dickey and Wayne Fuller, 1981, which is calculated as one would calculate the F-statistic for $(\gamma, \rho) = (0,1)$. The regressions in Table 2 set k equal to zero to test the null hypothesis that x_t follows a random walk with drift against the general alternative $(\gamma, \rho) \neq (0,1)$. The regressions in Table 3 set k equal to four and, thereby, allow Δx_t to follow an AR(4) process. Each regression discards the

TABLE 3—DICKEY-FULLER TEST RESULTS: FOUR LAGS

x_t:	P_t	d_t	ΔP_t	Δd_t
$\hat{\mu}$	0.0046	0.0008	−0.0009	0.0001
	(0.0159)	(0.0005)	(0.0164)	(0.0004)
$\hat{\gamma}$	0.0007	0.00003	0.0001	−0.000001
	(0.0003)	(0.00001)	(0.0002)	(0.000006)
$\hat{\rho}$	0.88	0.83	0.17	0.03
	(0.05)	(0.06)	(0.24)	(0.21)
$\hat{\beta}_1$	0.16	0.35	−0.07	0.25
	(0.10)	(0.10)	(0.22)	(0.19)
$\hat{\beta}_2$	−0.15	−0.14	−0.31	0.01
	(0.10)	(0.11)	(0.19)	(0.16)
$\hat{\beta}_3$	0.21	0.09	−0.14	0.05
	(0.10)	(0.10)	(0.14)	(0.13)
$\hat{\beta}_4$	0.17	0.04	−0.04	−0.01
	(0.10)	(0.10)	(0.11)	(0.10)
Standard Error of Estimate	0.068	0.002	0.070	0.002
Φ_3	3.12	4.42	6.41	10.45

Note: Regressions are of the form $x_t = \mu + \gamma t + \rho x_{t-1} + \Sigma_{i=1}^{4}\beta_i \Delta x_{t-i} +$ residual. "Standard errors" are in parentheses below coefficients. Sample size is 100 in all cases. The statistic Φ_3, calculated like the F-statistic, tests the null hypothesis $(\gamma, \rho) = (0,1)$ against the alternative $(\gamma, \rho) \neq (0,1)$. The rejection region is the set of values of Φ_3 above 5.47 (6.49) for a test of size 0.10 (0.05).

first few observations to adjust sample size to 100. The rejection region, from Dickey and Fuller's Table VI, is the set of values of Φ_3 above 5.47 (6.49) for a test of size 0.10 (0.05).

For the undifferenced time-series of real stock prices and dividends, the statistic Φ_3 does not reject the null hypothesis $(\gamma, \rho) = (0,1)$. For both of the differenced series, the statistic rejects the null hypothesis. The rejections are stronger in Table 2 than in Table 3, probably because the regressions of Table 3 include the regressors Δx_{t-i}, which in most cases do not have significant coefficients and, consequently, reduce the power of the unit root test.

The results reported in Tables 2 and 3 support the impression, based on the sample autocorrelations in Table 1, that both real stock prices and dividends are nonstationary in levels but stationary in first differences. For sample sizes of 100, unit root tests have low power against alternatives slightly less than unity—see, for example, G. B. A. Evans and N. E. Savin, 1984. Accordingly, we cannot have much faith in the result that the undifferenced series are nonstationary and not borderline stationary. The critical finding for our purposes, however, is that, contrary to what the existence of explosive rational bubbles would imply, the data strongly reject the null hypothesis of a nonstationary mean for first differences of real stock prices. In fact, point estimates of ρ for the ΔP_t regressions of Tables 2 and 3 do not differ significantly from zero.

III. Cointegration of Stock Prices and Dividends

Rearranging terms in equation (2) and substituting the resulting expression for F_t into equation (3) yields

$$(9)\quad P_t - \alpha r^{-1} d_t = B_t + \alpha r^{-1}\left[\sum_{j=1}^{\infty}(1+r)^{1-j}E_t \Delta d_{t+j}\right] + \sum_{j=1}^{\infty}(1+r)^{-j}E_t u_{t+j}.$$

If the unobservable variable in market fundamentals, u_t, is stationary in levels, if dividends are first-difference stationary, and if rational bubbles do not exist, then the sum given by the right-hand side of equation (9) is stationary. Thus, although P_t and d_t are nonstationary, their linear combination $P_t - \alpha r^{-1} d_t$, given by the left-hand side of equation (9), is stationary.

Clive Granger and Robert Engle, 1987, define the components of a vector y_t' of time-series to be cointegrated of order (d, b) if all components of y_t are integrated of order d—that is, have a stationary, invertible, nondeterministic ARMA representation after differencing d times—and if there exists a vector δ, other than the null vector, such that $\delta' y_t$ is integrated of order $d - b$ for some $b > 0$. They call δ the cointegrating vector. Using their terminology, equation (9) says that if the processes generating Δd_t and u_t are stationary and if B_t equals zero, then P_t and d_t are cointegrated of order (1,1) with cointegrating vector $(1, -\alpha r^{-1})$.

Drawing on the work of James Stock, 1987, Granger and Engle develop tests for cointegration that involve obtaining an estimate of the cointegrating vector from a cointegrating regression and then applying tests for stationarity to the residuals from this regression. For a test of stationarity of the left-hand side of equation (9), the cointegrating regression would be the OLS regression of P_t on d_t.

One test for stationarity of residuals suggested by Granger and Engle would reject the null hypothesis of no cointegration if the Durbin-Watson statistic of the cointegrating regression exceeds the critical values they tabulate. Another test suggested by Granger and Engle involves estimating Dickey-Fuller regressions of the form

$$(10) \quad \Delta v_t = -\rho v_{t-1} + \sum_{i=1}^{k} \beta_i \Delta v_{t-i} + \text{residual},$$

on the residuals v_t of the cointegrating regression. Granger and Engle tabulate the critical values for statistics denoted ξ_2 and ξ_3, calculated analogously to t-ratios for ρ in equation (10), with k set equal to zero for ξ_2 and to four for ξ_3.

Estimation of the cointegrating regression of P_t on d_t yields a point estimate for αr^{-1} of 30.50 and a Durbin-Watson statistic of 0.61, which is above the 1 percent critical value of 0.51. John Campbell and Shiller, 1987, also estimate such a cointegrating regression and calculate Granger and Engle's ξ_2 and ξ_3 statistics. They find that the statistic ξ_2 rejects the null hypothesis of no cointegration at the 5 percent level, but the statistic ξ_3 (narrowly) fails to reject even at the 10 percent level.

The results of cointegration tests for P_t and d_t, thus, are mixed. The Durbin-Watson statistic rejects the null hypothesis that P_t and d_t are not cointegrated at the 1 percent level, the statistic ξ_2 rejects the null at the 5 percent level, but the statistic ξ_3 fails to reject at the 10 percent level. Moreover, the point estimate for αr^{-1} is somewhat implausible. Specifically, with α set equal to unity, this point estimate would imply a value for r of about 0.033, well below its sample mean of about 0.08. If α is less than unity, then the implied value of r will be even lower than 0.033. (As Terry Marsh and Robert Merton, 1983, emphasize, if the logarithms of stock prices and dividends follow integrated stochastic processes, then a regression of stock prices on dividends, in levels, yields inefficient and possibly biased estimates. This bias could account for the implausibly low values of the required rate of return implied by the cointegrating regression of P_t on d_t.)

IV. Stationarity of the Unobservable Variable

Nonstationarity of the unobservable variable in market fundamentals would be a potential source of lack of cointegration of stock prices and dividends. To explore this possibility, note that equation (1) implies

$$(11) \quad P_{t+1} + \alpha d_{t+1} - (1+r) P_t = e_{t+1} - u_{t+1},$$

where $e_{t+1} = P_{t+1} + \alpha d_{t+1} + u_{t+1} - E_t(P_{t+1} + \alpha d_{t+1} + u_{t+1})$.

TABLE 4—BHARGAVA TESTS OF THE RANDOM-WALK HYPOTHESIS

Statistic	R_1	R_2	N_1	N_2
Null Hypothesis	Random Walk	Random Walk with Drift	Random Walk	Random Walk with Drift
Alternative Hypothesis	Stationary	Stationary	Unstable	Unstable
Rejection Region for test of size 0.05	Above 0.26	Above 0.35	Below 0.006	Below 0.022
$P_t - d_t/0.01$	0.15	0.19	0.05	0.19
$P_t - d_t/0.02$	0.40	0.45	0.12	0.64
$P_t - d_t/0.03$	0.62	0.60	0.31	1.11
$P_t - d_t/0.04$	0.48	0.49	0.44	0.97
$P_t - d_t/0.05$	0.35	0.38	0.35	0.76
$P_t - d_t/0.06$	0.28	0.32	0.26	0.62
$P_t - d_t/0.07$	0.24	0.27	0.21	0.53
$P_t - d_t/0.08$	0.21	0.25	0.18	0.47

Note: The statistics R_1, R_2, N_1, and N_2 are von Neumann-type ratios that yield most powerful invariant tests of the random-walk hypothesis against one-sided stationary and explosive alternatives.

Because the assumption of rational expectations implies that e_{t+1} is not serially correlated, stationarity of the left-hand side of equation (11) is equivalent to stationarity of u_{t+1}. (Of course, in a finite sample, even if u_{t+1} is nonstationary, the left-hand side of equation (11) can appear stationary if most of its variability results from movements in the forecast error e_{t+1}.) Stationarity of the left-hand side of equation (11) implies that the variables $P_{t+1} + \alpha d_{t+1}$ and P_t are cointegrated of order (1,1) with cointegrating vector $[1, -(1+r)]$.

For the present data, the tests suggested by Granger and Engle find cointegration between $P_{t+1} + \alpha d_{t+1}$ and P_t for values of α between 0.5 and 2, which correspond to varying the valuation for dividends from one-half to twice the valuation for capital gains. With α set equal to unity, for example, the Durbin-Watson statistic of the cointegrating regression is 1.82 (well above the 1 percent critical value of 0.51), Granger and Engle's ξ_2 statistic has a value of 8.74 (again above the 1 percent critical value of 4.07), and their statistic ξ_3 has a value of 3.32 (which is below the critical value of 3.77 at the 1 percent level but comfortably rejects the null hypothesis of no cointegration at the 5 percent level).

As Campbell and Shiller, 1987, point out, the difference $P_t - \alpha r^{-1} d_t$ is equivalent to a linear combination of the variables Δd_{t+1}, ΔP_{t+1}, and $P_{t+1} - \alpha d_{t+1} - (1+r)P_t$. Accordingly, the conclusion that Δd_{t+1}, ΔP_{t+1}, and $P_{t+1} + \alpha d_{t+1} - (1+r)P_t$ are all stationary would imply that $P_t - \alpha r^{-1} d_t$ is stationary, independently of the model of stock prices. Thus, the apparently mixed results of Section III on the hypothesis that stock prices and dividends are not cointegrated are puzzling. (Using the same test, Campbell and Shiller, 1986, find that the logarithm of the ratio of dividends to stock prices and the logarithm of dividends are stationary, but, contrary to what an algebraic identity would imply, they fail to reject the hypothesis that the logarithm of stock prices is nonstationary.)

V. Bhargava Tests

Given these problems, alternative tests of the hypothesis that $P_t - \alpha r^{-1} d_t$ is not stationary seem to be in order. To investigate the stationarity properties of $P_t - \alpha r^{-1} d_t$ further, this section reports von Neumann-type ratios, suggested by Alok Bhargava, 1986, that yield most powerful invariant tests of random-walk hypotheses against the one-

TABLE 5—AUTOCORRELATIONS OF FIRST DIFFERENCES OF SIMULATED RATIONAL BUBBLE SERIES

Simulation Number	r_1	r_2	r_3	r_4	r_5	r_6	r_7	r_8	r_9	r_{10}
1	0.94	0.89	0.84	0.80	0.75	0.71	0.67	0.63	0.59	0.56
2	0.93	0.89	0.83	0.79	0.75	0.71	0.67	0.63	0.60	0.57
3	0.92	0.87	0.80	0.77	0.73	0.70	0.65	0.62	0.57	0.55
4	0.93	0.87	0.82	0.79	0.75	0.72	0.67	0.63	0.59	0.56
5	0.91	0.85	0.78	0.74	0.70	0.66	0.63	0.60	0.56	0.53
6	0.95	0.90	0.85	0.80	0.76	0.71	0.67	0.64	0.60	0.56
7	0.94	0.89	0.84	0.80	0.76	0.72	0.68	0.63	0.59	0.56
8	0.93	0.88	0.84	0.79	0.76	0.72	0.68	0.64	0.60	0.57
9	0.90	0.85	0.82	0.77	0.73	0.70	0.64	0.61	0.58	0.55
10	0.65	0.65	0.62	0.56	0.53	0.45	0.51	0.43	0.42	0.36
11	0.94	0.88	0.83	0.78	0.75	0.71	0.67	0.62	0.58	0.55
12	0.91	0.85	0.82	0.76	0.73	0.68	0.64	0.61	0.56	0.53
13	0.92	0.87	0.82	0.78	0.74	0.70	0.67	0.63	0.60	0.56
14	0.62	0.64	0.55	0.60	0.51	0.46	0.44	0.43	0.39	0.40
15	0.80	0.80	0.73	0.71	0.65	0.65	0.58	0.52	0.53	0.48
16	0.94	0.89	0.84	0.80	0.75	0.71	0.67	0.63	0.59	0.56
17	0.90	0.86	0.81	0.76	0.72	0.68	0.65	0.61	0.59	0.55
18	0.93	0.89	0.84	0.79	0.75	0.70	0.66	0.62	0.59	0.56
19	0.94	0.89	0.84	0.80	0.76	0.72	0.68	0.64	0.60	0.56
20	0.94	0.89	0.85	0.80	0.76	0.72	0.67	0.64	0.60	0.57
21	0.46	0.42	0.41	0.29	0.35	0.31	0.27	0.22	0.24	0.29
22	0.93	0.88	0.83	0.78	0.74	0.70	0.66	0.62	0.58	0.54
23	0.93	0.88	0.83	0.79	0.74	0.70	0.66	0.62	0.59	0.56
24	0.94	0.90	0.85	0.80	0.75	0.71	0.67	0.63	0.60	0.56
25	0.94	0.89	0.84	0.80	0.75	0.71	0.67	0.64	0.61	0.57
26	0.93	0.88	0.83	0.78	0.74	0.70	0.66	0.63	0.59	0.55
27	0.83	0.78	0.75	0.70	0.68	0.67	0.62	0.58	0.53	0.49
28	0.94	0.89	0.84	0.80	0.75	0.71	0.67	0.64	0.60	0.56
29	0.56	0.53	0.48	0.51	0.47	0.40	0.41	0.35	0.35	0.35
30	0.94	0.89	0.84	0.80	0.75	0.71	0.68	0.64	0.60	0.56
31	0.89	0.84	0.80	0.75	0.72	0.69	0.65	0.61	0.55	0.53
32	0.93	0.88	0.83	0.79	0.74	0.70	0.66	0.61	0.58	0.55
33	0.11	0.17	0.21	0.17	0.19	0.12	0.23	0.02	0.18	0.06
34	0.94	0.89	0.85	0.80	0.75	0.71	0.67	0.63	0.59	0.56
35	0.40	0.30	0.30	0.25	0.24	0.30	0.31	0.16	0.27	0.20
36	0.93	0.89	0.84	0.79	0.75	0.70	0.66	0.63	0.59	0.56
37	0.94	0.90	0.85	0.80	0.75	0.71	0.67	0.64	0.60	0.56
38	0.94	0.89	0.84	0.80	0.76	0.72	0.68	0.64	0.60	0.56
39	0.95	0.90	0.85	0.81	0.76	0.72	0.68	0.64	0.60	0.57
40	0.94	0.89	0.84	0.80	0.76	0.71	0.68	0.64	0.60	0.56
41	0.95	0.90	0.85	0.80	0.76	0.72	0.68	0.64	0.60	0.57
42	0.94	0.89	0.84	0.80	0.75	0.71	0.67	0.64	0.60	0.57
43	0.90	0.86	0.82	0.77	0.73	0.70	0.67	0.61	0.57	0.54
44	0.95	0.90	0.85	0.81	0.76	0.72	0.68	0.64	0.60	0.56
45	0.84	0.81	0.74	0.71	0.66	0.61	0.58	0.56	0.51	0.49
46	0.94	0.89	0.85	0.81	0.76	0.72	0.68	0.64	0.61	0.57
47	0.94	0.89	0.84	0.80	0.76	0.71	0.67	0.63	0.60	0.57
48	0.93	0.89	0.84	0.79	0.76	0.72	0.68	0.64	0.60	0.57
49	0.93	0.89	0.84	0.79	0.74	0.70	0.66	0.62	0.59	0.56
50	0.90	0.85	0.81	0.76	0.73	0.69	0.64	0.58	0.56	0.53

Note: Table reports the autocorrelations of first differences of simulated rational bubbles series: $B_t = 1.05B_{t-1} + z_t$, where z_t is normally distributed white noise, and B_0 is set equal to zero. For each simulation, r_k, $k = 1,\ldots,10$, is the autocorrelation coefficient at lag k.

sided stationary and explosive alternatives. Tests against one-sided explosive alternatives are relevant because the existence of explosive rational bubbles would imply that $P_t - \alpha r^{-1} d_t$ has an explosive, rather than a unit, root.

Table 4 reports the Bhargava tests for $P_t - \alpha r^{-1} d_t$. The statistic R_1 rejects the null hypothesis of a simple random walk in favor of the stationary alternative for values of $\alpha^{-1} r$ between 0.02 and 0.06, and the statistic R_2 rejects the null hypothesis of a random walk with drift in favor of the stationary alternative for values of $\alpha^{-1} r$ between 0.02 and 0.05. The results of tests based on the statistics R_1 and R_2, concur with the results of two of the Granger and Engle tests reported above and suggest that $P_t - \alpha r^{-1} d_t$ is stationary. (The values of r implied by the tests based on R_1 and R_2, however, still seem somewhat implausibly low.)

The statistics N_1 and N_2 in Table 4 pertain to testing the null hypotheses that $P_t - \alpha r^{-1} d_t$ follows either a simple random walk or a random walk with drift against the one-sided explosive alternative. For all values of $\alpha^{-1} r$, these statistics fail to reject the null hypothesis that $P_t - \alpha r^{-1} d_t$ has a unit root. In sum, the Bhargava tests strongly suggest that stock prices and dividends are cointegrated, and, thus, are consistent with the finding that the first differences of stock prices and dividends and any unobservable variable in market fundamentals are all stationary.

VI. Stationarity Properties of Simulated Rational Bubbles

To verify that our tests would detect explosive rational bubbles if they were present, we applied the same tests to the time-series of simulated rational bubbles with standard normal innovations. The simulations set B_0 equal to zero and r equal to 0.05.

The statistic N_1 of Bhargava rejected at the 5 percent level the null hypothesis of a simple random walk in favor of the unstable alternative in 95 out of 100 simulations. For the same 100 simulations, the statistic N_2 rejected, at the 5 percent level, the null hypothesis of a random walk with drift in favor of the unstable alternative in 94 cases.

First differences of the simulated rational bubbles series also exhibited strong signs of nonstationarity. Table 5 reports the sample autocorrelations of the differenced time-series for the first 50 simulations. The patterns of autocorrelation coefficients in all but six cases (simulations numbered 10, 14, 21, 29, 33, and 35) strongly suggest nonstationarity. The autocorrelation function starts at a value of 0.8 or higher and drops off very slowly. For simulations numbered 10, 14, 21, 29, and 35, the starting values are lower, but the autocorrelations still drop off slowly. (Wichern's results indicate that the latter criterion is a more reliable sign of nonstationarity.) Only for simulation number 33 does the pattern of autocorrelations resemble those of differenced time-series of stock prices and dividends reported in Table 1 above.

The simulation results reported above, of course, do not mean that stationarity tests would detect a rational bubbles component even if its contribution to stock-price fluctuations is quantitatively small. If, however, the excess volatility in stock prices found by West, 1986, were attributable to rational bubbles, then innovations in these rational bubbles would account for 80 to 95 percent of the variance of stock-price innovations. It is likely then that the stationarity properties of stock prices and dividends would reflect the existence of explosive rational bubbles.

VII. Summary

This paper reports empirical tests for the existence of explosive rational bubbles in stock prices. The analysis focuses on a model that defines market fundamentals to be the sum of an unobservable variable and the expected present value of dividends, discounted at a constant rate, and defines a rational bubble to be a self-confirming divergence of stock prices from market fundamentals in response to extraneous variables. The pattern of autocorrelations in the data as well as Dickey-Fuller tests both indicate that stock prices and dividends are nonstationary before differencing, but are stationary in first differences. In contrast, first differences of simulated time-series of rational bubbles exhibit strong signs of nonstationarity.

If the nonstationarity of dividends accounts for the nonstationarity of stock prices, then stock prices and dividends are cointegrated. Although application of the cointegration tests suggested by Granger and Engle produced somewhat mixed results, these mixed results probably reflect low power of the tests rather than either the existence of rational bubbles or the presence of a nonstationary unobservable variable in market fundamentals. Most importantly, alternative tests suggested by Bhargava indicate that the relevant linear combination of stock prices and dividends is neither explosive nor has a unit root. In contrast, time-series of simulated rational bubbles failed the Bhargava tests. In sum, the analysis supports the conclusion that stock prices do not contain explosive rational bubbles.

REFERENCES

Bhargava, Alok, "On the Theory of Testing for Unit Roots in Observed Time Series," *Review of Economic Studies*, July 1986, *53*, 369–84.

Blanchard, Olivier, "Speculative Bubbles, Crashes, and Rational Expectations," *Economic Letters*, 1979, *3*, 387–89.

______ **and Watson, Mark,** "Bubbles, Rational Expectations, and Financial Markets," in *Crises in the Economic and Financial Structure*, P. Wachtel, ed., Lexington: Lexington Books, 1982.

Campbell, John and Shiller, Robert, "Cointegration and Tests of Present Value Models," *Journal of Political Economy*, October 1987, *95*, 1062–88.

______, "The Dividend-Price Ratio and Expectations of Future Dividends and Discount Factors," unpublished paper, October 1986.

Diba, Behzad and Grossman, Herschel, "Rational Bubbles in the Price of Gold," NBER Working Paper No. 1300, March 1984.

______, "The Theory of Rational Bubbles in Stock Prices," NBER Working Paper No. 1990, revised March 1988.

Dickey, David and Fuller, Wayne, "Likelihood Ratio Statistics for Autoregressive Time Series with a Unit Root," *Econometrica*, July 1981, *49*, 1057–72.

Evans, George, "Expectational Stability and the Multiple Equilibria Problem in Linear Rational Expectations Models," *Quarterly Journal of Economics*, November 1985, *100*, 1218–33.

Evans, G. B. A. and Savin, N. E., "Testing for Unit Roots: 2," *Econometrica*, September 1984, *52*, 1241–69.

Flood, Robert and Garber, Peter, "Market Fundamentals Versus Price Level Bubbles: The First Tests," *Journal of Political Economy*, August 1980, *88*, 745–70.

______, **Hodrick, Robert and Kaplan, Paul,** "An Evaluation of Recent Evidence on Stock Market Bubbles," unpublished paper, March 1986.

Fuller, Wayne, *Introduction to Statistical Time Series*, New York: Wiley & Sons, 1976.

Granger, Clive and Engle, Robert, "Dynamic Model Specification with Equilibrium Constraints: Cointegration and Error-Correction," *Econometrica*, March 1987, *55*, 251–76.

Hamilton, James, "On Testing for Self-Fulfilling Speculative Price Bubbles," *International Economic Review*, October 1986, *27*, 545–52.

______ **and Whiteman, Charles,** "The Observable Implications of Self-Fulfilling Expectations," *Journal of Monetary Economics*, November 1985, *16*, 353–73.

Kleidon, Allan, "Variance Bounds Tests and Stock Price Valuation Models," *Journal of Political Economy*, October 1986, *94*, 953–1001.

Marsh, Terry and Merton, Robert, "Aggregate Dividend Behavior and Its Implications for Tests of Stock Market Rationality," Sloan School of Management Working Paper No. 1475-83, September 1983.

Quah, Danny, "Estimation of a Nonfundamentals Model for Stock Price and Dividend Dynamics," unpublished paper, September 1985.

Shiller, Robert, "Do Stock Prices Move Too Much to Be Justified by Subsequent Changes in Dividends?," *American Economic Review*, June 1981, *71*, 421–36.

Stock, James, "Asymptotic Properties of Least Squares Estimators of Cointegrating Vectors," *Econometrica*, September 1987, *55*, 1035–56.

West, Kenneth, "Dividend Innovations and Stock Price Variability," NBER Working Paper No. 1833, February 1986.

______, "A Specification Test for Speculative Bubbles," *Quarterly Journal of Economics*, August 1987, *102*, 553–80.

Wichern, Dean, "The Behavior of the Sample Autocorrelation Function for an Integrated Moving Average Process," *Biometrika*, August 1973, *60*, 235–39.

[18]

Intrinsic Bubbles: The Case of Stock Prices

By KENNETH A. FROOT AND MAURICE OBSTFELD*

Several puzzling aspects of the behavior of United States stock prices may be explained by the presence of a specific type of rational bubble that depends exclusively on aggregate dividends. We call bubbles of this type "intrinsic" bubbles because they derive all of their variability from exogenous economic fundamentals and none from extraneous factors. Intrinsic bubbles provide a more plausible empirical account of deviations from present-value pricing than do the traditional examples of rational bubbles. Their explanatory potential comes partly from their ability to generate persistent deviations that appear to be relatively stable over long periods. (*JEL* G12)

After a decade of research, financial economists remain unsatisfied with simple accounts of stock-price fluctuations. The initial rejections by Stephen LeRoy and Richard Porter (1981) and Robert Shiller (1981) of a simple present-value model based on constant discount rates and rational expectations have not been reversed by subsequent work. Although departures from present-value prices appear to be large and persistent, it has nevertheless proved difficult to find empirical support for parsimonious alternatives to the simple present-value model.[1]

At one time, rational bubbles were viewed as one such alternative. Interest in bubbles has waned, however, in part because econometric tests have not produced persuasive evidence that rational bubbles can help explain stock prices. That is, no one has produced a specific bubble parameterization that is both parsimonious and capable of explaining the data.

In this paper, we propose and test empirically a new rational-bubble specification with both of these properties. Our formulation is parsimonious because it introduces no extraneous sources of variability. Instead, the bubbles we examine are driven exclusively —albeit nonlinearly—by the exogenous fundamental determinants of asset prices. For this reason, we refer to these bubbles as "intrinsic." One striking property of an intrinsic bubble is that, for a given level of

*Graduate School of Business, Harvard University, Boston, MA 02163, and Department of Economics, University of California at Berkeley, Berkeley, CA 94720, respectively. This is a substantially revised version of NBER Working Paper No. 3091. The authors are grateful to John Campbell, John Cochrane, Steve Durlauf, Bob Flood, Jeff Frankel, Greg Mankiw, Jeff Miron, Andy Rose, Julio Rotemberg, Jeremy Stein, and especially Bob Shiller, Jim Stock, and Ken West for helpful comments. Bob Barsky and Brad De Long helped us obtain data. Responsibility for the paper's contents is, however, ours alone. Generous financial support was provided by the John M. Olin, Alfred P. Sloan, and National Science Foundations, and the Division of Research of the Harvard Business School. We also thank the International Monetary Fund's Research Department for its hospitality while an earlier draft was completed.

[1]Marjorie Flavin (1983), N. Gregory Mankiw et al. (1985), Allan Kleidon (1986), Terry Marsh and Robert Merton (1986), John Campbell and Shiller (1987), Kenneth West (1987, 1988a) and Froot (1987) address econometric shortcomings of the original studies. John Cochrane (1989) argues that, in principle, time-varying discount factors could explain failures of the simple present-value model. There is little positive empirical evidence, however, that discount-factor variation alone can explain these failures; see, for example, Shiller (1981), Robert Flood et al. (1986), and Campbell and Shiller (1988a). Robert Pindyck (1984) suggests that low-frequency price fluctuations may be a result of time-varying risk premia driven by changing stock-price volatility. However, James Poterba and Lawrence Summers (1986) argue that volatility is not sufficiently persistent to explain a large portion of low-frequency price movements.

exogenous fundamentals, the bubble will remain constant over time: intrinsic bubbles are deterministic functions of fundamentals alone. Thus, this class of bubbles predicts that stable and highly persistent fundamentals lead to stable and highly persistent over- or undervaluations. In addition, these bubbles can cause asset prices to "overreact" to changes in fundamentals.

Surprisingly, our parametric example of an intrinsic bubble also appears to be capable of explaining long-term movements in stock prices. It turns out that the component of prices not explained by the simple present-value model is highly positively correlated with dividends, as an intrinsic bubble would predict. As a result, an intrinsic bubble fits well both the bull market of the 1960's, a period of high and rising real dividends, and the market decline of the early 1970's. We use our estimated model to separate out the present-value and bubble components of stock prices and find that the former implies a realized annual real return on stocks of about 9.1 percent—very close to the 9.0 percent average for this century.

Of course, there are nonbubble hypotheses that could in principle explain our results. It is often argued that stationary fads or noise trading lie behind departures from present-value prices.[2] Both fads and intrinsic bubbles can generate departures that are highly persistent; but an important theoretical distinction between the two is that the former entail short-term speculative profit opportunities, whereas bubbles alone do not. Because stock-market returns appear to have a predictable component, our empirical tests are designed to separate the bubble from possible sources of predictable returns, such as fads and variable discount rates. While this predictability ultimately should be useful in explaining certain features of the data, our results suggest that it is not the main explanation for the simple present-value model's failure.

A second alternative hypothesis involves possible future changes in regime. It is well known that any bubble path is observationally equivalent to a present-value path for which the process generating fundamentals may change in the future.[3] Our results therefore could be interpreted as evidence of such prospective changes. Indeed, present-value pricing formulas similar in form to the bubble formulas derived below arise in asset-pricing models that assume stochastic regime shifts. In this paper, we posit no specific regime-switch model to explain the apparently nonlinear relationship between stock prices and dividends.[4]

Notwithstanding our empirical results, we find the notion of rational bubbles to be problematic. It is difficult to believe that the market is literally stuck for all time on a path along which price:dividend ratios eventually explode. If the market began on such a path, surely investors would at some point attempt the kind of infinite-horizon arbitrage that rules bubbles out in theoretical models; and since *fully* rational agents would anticipate such attempts, bubbles could never get started. It seems to us an empirical question, however, whether this much foresight should be ascribed to the

[2]For examples of models with fads or noise, see Shiller (1984), Kyle (1985), Fischer Black (1986), Jeffrey Frankel and Froot (1986), Summers (1986), Campbell and Albert Kyle (1988), J. Bradford De Long et al. (1990), and Froot et al. (1990).

[3]Flood and Peter Garber (1980), James Hamilton and Charles Whiteman (1985), and Flood and Robert Hodrick (1986) discuss this observational equivalence.

[4]See Paul Krugman (1987) on regime switches in the stock market; see Krugman (1987) and Froot and Obstfeld (1991) on the foreign-exchange market. Krugman suggests that trigger-price sell strategies can make the price–dividend relation nonlinear. Results like those we report below could be rationalized within a fad model (without bubbles) in which investors perceive "psychological barriers" to upward movements in stock prices. When a price barrier is reached, a group of noise traders might enter the market with some probability, in which case a new barrier is established, or exit ("profit taking"). Speculation by rational investors would, in this environment, create a nonlinear relationship between prices and dividends. An alternative model predicting bubble-like behavior is based on market learning about managerial competence; see Nobuhiro Kiyotaki (1990). Stephen Cecchetti et al. (1990) study the empirical implications of particular nonlinear fundamentals processes.

market. Perhaps agents do not really have as clear a picture of the distant future as the simplest rational-expectations models suggest. Stock prices and dividends might follow a nonlinear relation such as the one we estimate for some time before market participants catch on to the unreasonable implications of very high dividend realizations.

The paper is structured as follows. Section I shows how intrinsic bubbles arise in a standard present-value model. In Section II, we compare some properties of intrinsic bubbles and a more conventional extraneous bubble whose explosive dynamics are driven by calendar time. Section III then turns to the data. We examine the univariate and bivariate time-series properties of United States stock prices and dividends, and we argue that an intrinsic bubble is broadly consistent with the results. In the second part of Section III, we estimate our model directly and test it against several alternatives. Section IV concludes and offers our interpretations of the results.

I. Intrinsic Bubbles in a Present-Value Model

Stochastic linear rational-expectations models can have a multiplicity of solutions that depend on exogenous fundamentals but do not depend on extraneous variables such as time.[5] In this section, we describe how such rational bubbles arise as nonlinear solutions to a linear asset-pricing model. Although our choice of a specific model is guided by the empirical application we have in mind, solutions similar to those derived below arise in a broader class of models.

[5]Included in the category of extraneous variables are irrelevant fundamentals, such as lagged fundamentals that play no economic role apart from their self-fulfilling effect on expectations. The excessive variability of an asset-price solution containing an intrinsic bubble comes entirely from its functional form, not from the introduction of extraneous state variables. An intrinsic-bubble solution is a reduced-form expression that depends only on the exogenous factors objectively affecting the economy, not on extraneous noise. In other words, every intrinsic-bubble solution is a "minimal-state-variable" solution in the sense of Bennett McCallum (1983).

The model is based on a simple condition that links the time-series of real stock prices to the time-series of real dividend payments when the expected rate of return is constant. Let P_t be the real price of a share at the beginning of period t, let D_t be real dividends per share paid out over period t, and let r be the constant, instantaneous real rate of interest. The condition we focus on is

$$P_t = e^{-r}E_t(D_t + P_{t+1}) \tag{1}$$

where $E_t(\cdot)$ is the market's expectation conditional on information known at the start of period t.[6]

The present-value solution for P_t, denoted by P_t^{pv}, is

$$P_t^{\mathrm{pv}} = \sum_{s=t}^{\infty} e_t^{-r(s-t+1)}E_t(D_s). \tag{2}$$

Equation (2) is a particular solution to the stochastic difference equation (1). It equates a stock's price to the present discounted value of expected future dividend payments. We assume that the present value (2) always exists, that is, that the continuously compounded growth rate of expected dividends is less than r.

The present-value formula is the solution to (1) usually singled out by the relevant economic theory as a unique equilibrium price. It can be derived by applying the transversality condition,

$$\lim_{s\to\infty} e^{-rs}E_t(P_s) = 0 \tag{3}$$

and then observing that successive forward substitutions into (1) converge to (2).

Equation (1) has solutions other than (2). By construction, these alternative price paths satisfy the requirement of period-by-period efficiency, but they do not satisfy (3). Let $\{B_t\}_{t=0}^{\infty}$ be any sequence of random vari-

[6]In our empirical implementation of the model below we allow for errors in this equation, which does not hold exactly for United States data (Flood et al., 1986).

ables such that

$$(4) \qquad B_t = e^{-r}E_t(B_{t+1}).$$

Then, $P_t = P_t^{\mathrm{pv}} + B_t$ is a solution to (1), which can be thought of as the sum of the present-value solution and a rational bubble. Clearly, property (4) implies that P_t violates the transversality condition (3) if $B_t \neq 0$.

Rational bubbles are sometimes viewed as being driven by variables extraneous to the valuation problem. However, some bubbles may depend only on the exogenous fundamental determinants of asset value. We call such bubbles "intrinsic" because their dynamics are inherited entirely from those of the fundamentals. An intrinsic bubble is constructed by finding a nonlinear function of fundamentals that satisfies (4). In the above stock-price model with only one stochastic fundamental factor (the dividend process), intrinsic rational bubbles depend on dividends alone.

To see how an intrinsic stock-price bubble might look, suppose that log dividends are generated by the geometric martingale,

$$(5) \qquad d_{t+1} = \mu + d_t + \xi_{t+1}$$

where μ is the trend growth in dividends, d_t is the log of dividends at time t, and ξ_{t+1} is a normal random variable with conditional mean zero and variance σ^2. Using (5) and assuming that period-t dividends are known when P_t is set, we see that the present-value stock price in (2) is directly proportional to dividends:

$$(6) \qquad P_t^{\mathrm{pv}} = \kappa D_t$$

where $\kappa = (e^r - e^{\mu+\sigma^2/2})^{-1}$. Equation (6) is essentially a stochastic version of Myron Gordon's (1962) model of stock prices, which predicts that $P_t^{\mathrm{pv}} = (e^r - e^{\mu})^{-1}D_t$ under certainty. The assumption that the sum in (2) converges implies that $r > \mu + \sigma^2/2$.

Now define the function $B(D_t)$ as

$$(7) \qquad B(D_t) = cD_t^{\lambda}$$

where λ is the positive root of the quadratic equation

$$(8) \qquad \lambda^2\sigma^2/2 + \lambda\mu - r = 0$$

and c is an arbitrary constant. It is easy to verify that (7) satisfies (4):

$$(9) \quad e^{-r}E_t(B(D_{t+1})) = e^{-r}E_t\left(cD_t^{\lambda}e^{\lambda(\mu+\xi_{t+1})}\right) = e^{-r}\left(cD_t^{\lambda}e^{\lambda\mu+\lambda^2\sigma^2/2}\right) = e^{-r}\left(cD_t^{\lambda}e^{r}\right) = B(D_t).$$

By summing the present-value price and the bubble in (7), we get our basic stock-price equation:

$$(10) \quad P(D_t) = P_t^{\mathrm{pv}} + B(D_t) = \kappa D_t + cD_t^{\lambda}.$$

Even though (10) contains a bubble (for $c \neq 0$) and thus violates (3), it is driven exclusively by fundamentals: $P(D_t)$ is a function of dividends only and does not depend on time or any other extraneous variable. $B(D_t)$ is therefore an example of an intrinsic bubble.[7]

The inequality $r > \mu + \sigma^2/2$ can be used to show that λ must always exceed 1. It is this explosive nonlinearity that permits $B(D_t)$ to grow in expectation at rate r. We will assume from now on that $c > 0$, so that stock prices cannot be negative. Negative stock prices would violate free disposability.[8]

[7]Thomas Sargent (1987 pp. 348–9) characterizes a rational bubble as a function $\bar{B}(t, X_t) = e^{rt}X_t$ of time and a variable X_t that obeys $E_t(X_{t+1}) = X_t$. However, his definition does not imply that bubbles have to contain deterministic time components. To write the bubble $B(D_t)$ defined by (7) in Sargent's form, simply let $X_t = e^{-rt}cD_t^{\lambda}$.

[8]Let λ' be the negative root of equation (8). Then the general solution to (1) [within the class of functions $P = P(D_t)$] is

$$P(D_t) = P_t^{\mathrm{pv}} + c_1D_t^{\lambda} + c_2D_t^{\lambda'}.$$

We have imposed $c_2 = 0$ in (10) on the grounds that the stock price P_1 should go to zero (not to infinity) as

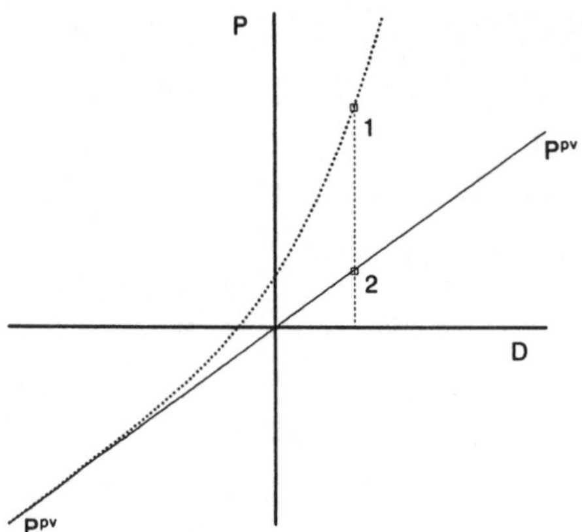

FIGURE 1. INTRINSIC-BUBBLE PRICE PATHS

It might seem paradoxical that movements in a bubble can be completely attributed to movements in fundamentals. Economists are accustomed to an almost instinctive decomposition of asset prices into two components, one dependent on market fundamentals and a second reflecting self-fulfilling beliefs and driven, at least in part, by extraneous factors. In the context of linear models, for example, McCallum (1983) argues that bubble solutions can be avoided by restricting attention to "minimal-state-variable" solutions that depend only on fundamentals. The possibility of intrinsic bubbles reveals that McCallum's approach does not rule out multiple solutions unless some additional requirement (e.g., linearity of the price function) is imposed.

Like all rational bubbles, intrinsic bubbles rely on self-fulfilling expectations. Instead of being driven by extraneous variables, however, these expectations are driven by the nonlinear form of the price solution itself. Figure 1 shows the family of solutions given by (10). The straight line $P^{pv}P^{pv}$ indicates the present-value solution (6); this solution implies that $E_t(P_{t+1}/P_t) = e^{\mu+\sigma^2/2} < e^r$. A point like 1 on the bubble path satisfies rate-of-return condition (1) because of Jensen's inequality. At point 1, the next innovation in log dividends is distributed symmetrically around zero, but the market's belief that the relevant price function has the shape shown means that the expected rise in the stock price and, hence, the current stock price itself are higher at point 1 than at the corresponding point 2 on $P^{pv}P^{pv}$.[9]

dividends D_t go to zero. The argument in the text shows that any variable Y_t whose logarithm follows a martingale with drift μ and variance σ^2 leads to a bubble solution to (1), $P(D_t, Y_t) = P_t^{pv} + B(Y_t)$. Thus, a formula like (7) can be used to construct extraneous as well as intrinsic bubbles.

II. Alternative Bubble Specifications: A Partial Comparison

Why might intrinsic bubbles succeed in characterizing stock prices when other bubble formulations have failed? In this section, we argue that intrinsic bubbles have several empirically appealing properties that the bubble parameterizations used in previous applied studies lack.

To begin, we need to know why bubble explanations of stock prices have fared so poorly. A first reason might be a belief that prices simply do not diverge from their present-value levels.[10] There are strong theoretical arguments behind this view. However, while short-horizon excess-profit opportunities are plausibly quite small, the theoretical conditions required to rule out rational bubbles assume substantial, per-

[9]It is easy to check that various theorems used to identify unique solutions of the form $P(D_t)$ to equations like (1) do not apply under this section's assumptions. For example, (10) is not within any of the classes of solutions considered by Robert Lucas (1978), Rusdu Saracoglu and Sargent (1978), Christian Gourieroux et al. (1982), or Whiteman (1983). The problem is not that the process in (5) is nonstationary. Multiple solutions analogous to (10) exist when (5) is a mean-reverting Ornstein-Uhlenbeck process; see Froot and Obstfeld (1991). Rather, the problem is that standard uniqueness theorems impose additional restrictions, such as linearity of the solution or the assumption that all state variables are restricted to assume values in compact sets. These assumptions rule out solutions such as (10).

[10]Flood and Hodrick (1990) survey the empirical literature on bubbles from this perspective.

haps unrealistic, infinite-horizon foresight on the part of economic agents.

A second reason for the poor empirical track record of bubbles is that the specific parameterizations that have been tested have failed. These parameterizations generally assume that bubbles and, hence, stock prices contain deterministic exponential time trends.[11] However, there is little evidence of such behavior in U.S stock-market data.

Some general specification tests have been employed in the hope that bubbles can be detected without the need to take a stand on a specific bubble form. Even though these tests may have low power, they nevertheless reject the no-bubble null hypothesis frequently. However, they cannot reveal the precise source of rejection, so they yield no hard evidence that bubbles really are the culprits.[12] The tendency to ascribe these rejections to sources other than bubbles has been strengthened both by the theoretical arguments against bubbles and by the failure of the specific parameterizations mentioned above. However, consideration of stochastic bubbles that look quite different from the usual time-driven examples may throw a different light on the specification-test results.

How then do intrinsic bubbles behave, and why might they do a better job of tracking stock prices? First, intrinsic bubbles capture well the idea that stock prices overreact to news about dividends, as argued by Shiller (1984), among others. Equation (10) implies that $dP_t/dD_t = \kappa + \lambda c D_t^{\lambda-1} > \kappa$, so prices move more when dividends change than the present-value formula (6) would predict.

In addition, intrinsic bubbles are not obviously inconsistent with the apparent time-series properties of stock prices. Even though the bubbles are expected to grow at the rate of interest, specific realizations may fluctuate within some limited range for rather long periods. A given dividend realization corresponds to a unique stock price regardless of the date on which the dividend is announced. Because dividends are persistent, deviations from present-value prices may also be persistent. An implication of this property is that, even with a very long data series, the fundamentally explosive nature of an intrinsic bubble might be impossible to detect through diagnostic time-series tests.

Some simulations illustrate these points by comparing the intrinsic bubble in (10) with a particular alternative bubble specification. Each simulation experiment involves three solutions to the difference equation in (1). The first of these is the present-value price P_t^{pv} given by (6); the second is a purely stochastic, nonlinear intrinsic bubble of the form (10), denoted by $\hat{P}_t$; and the third is a bubble that depends on time as well as on dividends:

$$(11) \qquad \tilde{P}_t = P_t^{\mathrm{pv}} + bD_t e^{(r-\mu-\sigma^2/2)t}.$$

The precise formulation in (11) is chosen for two reasons. First, it makes the bubble a function of dividends and thus allows stock prices to overreact to dividend news, just as the bubble in (10) does. Second, (11) follows the majority of parametric bubble tests in adopting a specification in which the extraneous variable t affects prices.

Dividends are assumed to follow (5), and in each experiment successive innovations ξ_t are drawn independently from a normal distribution. P_t^{pv} is calculated using estimates of r, μ, and σ^2 implied by U.S. stock-price and dividend data, and the values of the parameters κ, c, and b are those estimated below in Section III. The simulations are run over 200 years. However, it is important to note that there is little importance to these specific choices of parame-

[11] See Flood and Garber (1980) and Olivier Blanchard and Mark Watson (1982) for specific examples.

[12] The general specification test for bubbles used by West (1987) can alternatively be interpreted as a test of model specification, the purpose for which it was originally proposed by Robert Cumby et al. (1983). A second type of specification test for bubbles compares the time-series properties of prices and dividends, which should differ if condition (1) holds but stock prices contain a rational bubble (see Hamilton and Whiteman, 1985; Behzad Diba and Herschel Grossman, 1988a).

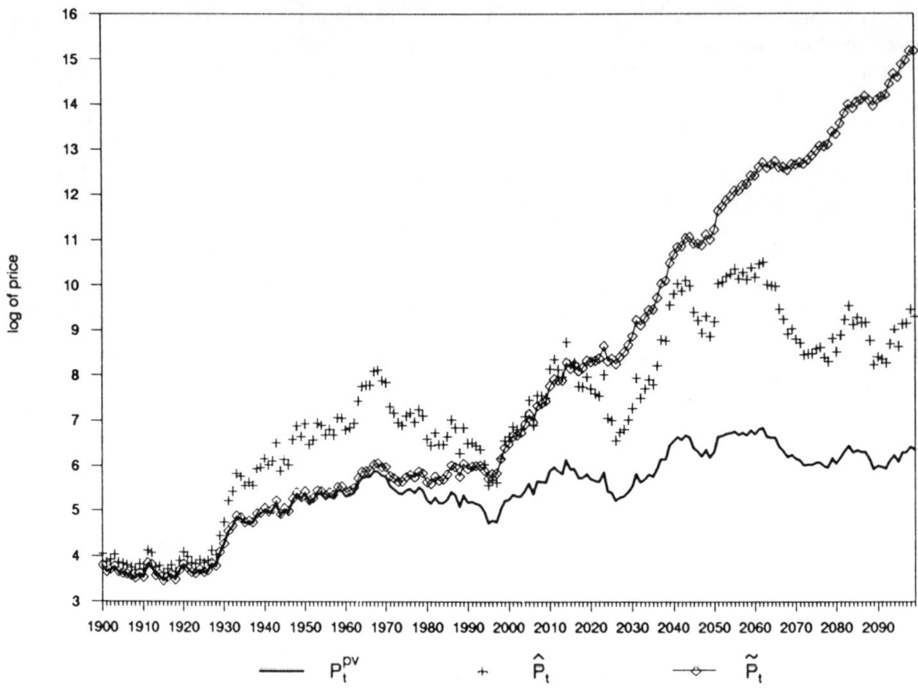

FIGURE 2. SIMULATED STOCK-PRICE PATHS

Notes: P_t^{pv} is the simulated present-value stock-price path assuming that log dividends follow a random walk with trend. $\hat{P}_t$ gives simulated stock prices under the intrinsic bubble in equation (10). $\tilde{P}_t$ gives simulated stock prices under the bubble example in equation (11).

ters and sample size: the qualitative patterns displayed in the following figures are quite general.

Figure 2 shows a first run in which the simulated intrinsic bubble, $\hat{P}_t$, does not produce noticeable explosive behavior within the simulation sample. The percentage overvaluation of stocks is not very different at the end of the sample (the year 2100) than it is around 1970 or 2015. In contrast, the partially deterministic bubble $\tilde{P}_t$ explodes decisively.

The behavior of the time-driven bubble is similar in Figure 3, but the underlying dividend realization makes the explosive expected growth of the intrinsic bubble more apparent. Figures 2 and 3 highlight the sharply different paths for intrinsic bubbles that different paths of fundamentals can produce. (Of course, paths qualitatively similar to the intrinsic-bubble paths could be generated by purely random bubbles that depend on extraneous variables.)

Diba and Grossman (1988b) have argued on theoretical grounds that stochastic rational bubbles cannot "pop" and subsequently start up again. This feature, they assert, makes rational bubbles empirically implausible. Figure 4, however, shows an intrinsic-bubble realization that falls over time to a level quite close to fundamentals. Indeed, if dividends follow a process like (5) but without drift, the logarithm of dividends reaches any given lower bound with probability 1; we can therefore be sure that the bubble term in (10) gets arbitrarily close to zero in finite time. For practical purposes, this is the same as periodically popping and

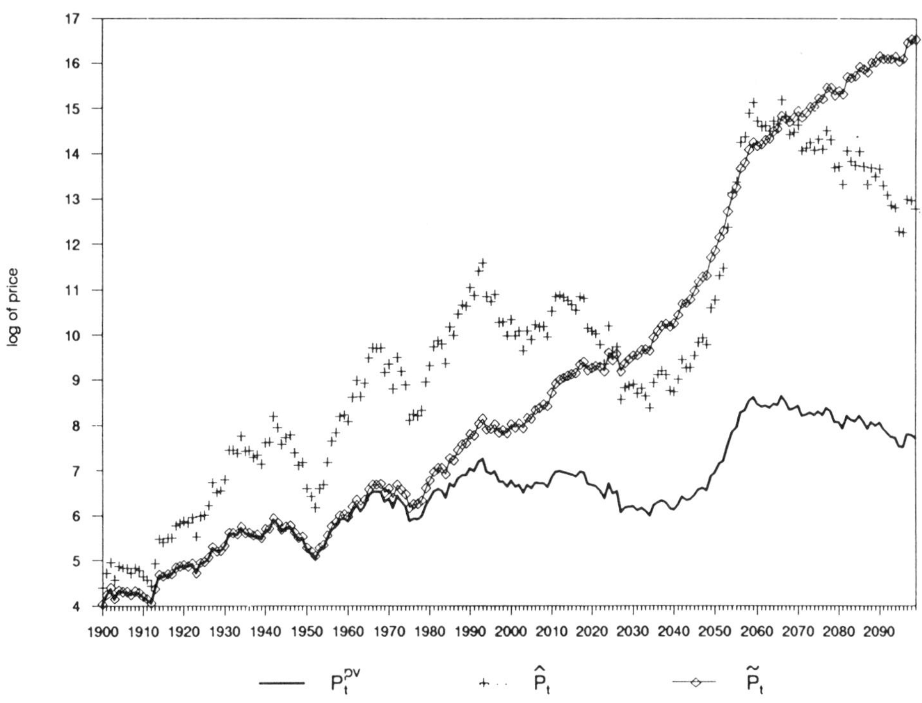

FIGURE 3. SIMULATED STOCK-PRICE PATHS

Notes: P_t^{pv} is the simulated present-value stock-price path assuming that log dividends follow a random walk with trend. $\hat{P}_t$ gives simulated stock prices under the intrinsic bubble in equation (10). $\tilde{P}_t$ gives simulated stock prices under the bubble example in equation (11).

restarting with probability 1. Intrinsic bubbles allow stock prices to get very close to present-value levels and then diverge. (They also, however, allow arbitrarily large divergences.)[13]

Notice that all three simulations share the feature that the intrinsic-bubble path lies above the time-driven bubble in the early part of the sample, but below it by the sample's end. This pattern in the early part of the sample is merely a result of initial conditions and is therefore purely arbitrary.[14] By contrast, the feature that the time bubble eventually exceeds the intrinsic bubble is more general. It is easy to show that, as the sample size T grows, the probability that $\hat{P}_T > \tilde{P}_T$ goes to zero for any set

[13]To gain a sense of the likelihood with which an intrinsic bubble such as the one in (10) is likely to recede dramatically, we ran Monte Carlo experiments on the future evolution of stock prices using stock prices in 1987 as the initial condition. (These experiments use the following parameters, estimated from the data described in the following section: $\sigma = 0.122$, $\mu = 0.011$, $r = 0.086$, $c = 0.34$). We found that the probability that the bubble falls to a level one-half of its size in 1987 in the next 100 years is 81 percent, and the probability that it falls to a level one-quarter of its size in 1987 is 53 percent. These results suggest that, with moderate dividend growth rates, the bubble is likely to appear to shrink substantially over longer time-series samples.

[14]It turns out that, if model (11) is to have any hope of fitting the data, the estimate of b must be very close to zero, implying that $\tilde{P}_t$ is very close to P_t^{pv} for the first part of the sample; see Section III-B and Figure 7.

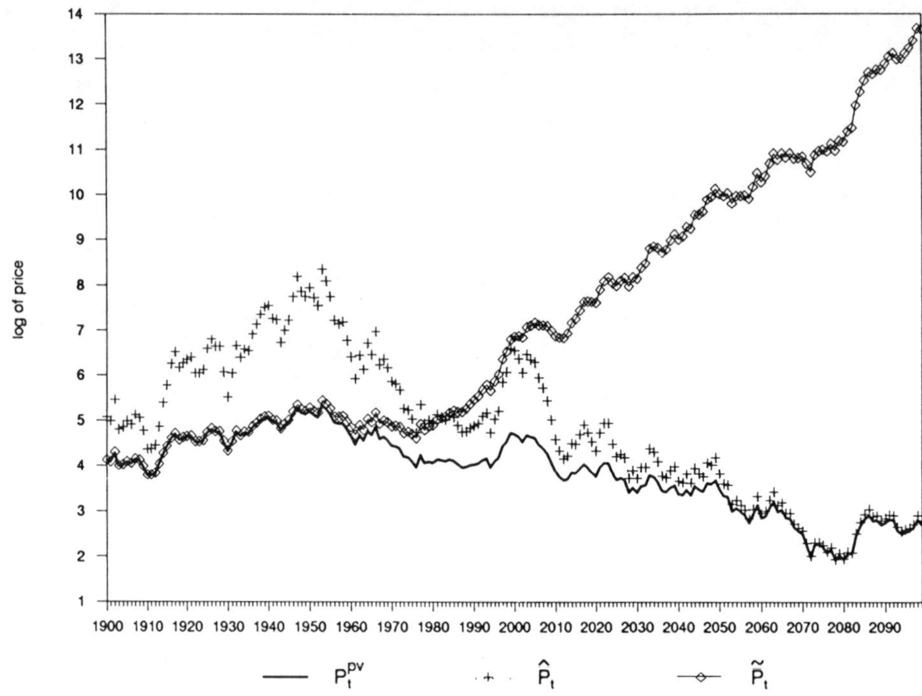

FIGURE 4. SIMULATED STOCK-PRICE PATHS

Notes: P_t^{pv} is the simulated present-value stock-price path assuming that log dividends follow a random walk with trend. $\hat{P}_t$ gives simulated stock prices under the intrinsic bubble in equation (10). $\tilde{P}_t$ gives simulated stock prices under the bubble example in equation (11).

of initial conditions.[15] The intrinsic bubble in $\hat{P}_T$ ultimately exceeds the time-driven bubble in $\tilde{P}_T$ very rarely in large samples, but when it does, it does so by an amount large enough to equalize the two bubbles' expected growth rates.

This latter property is important empirically. It implies that it would be unusual to draw a long dividend series which yields an intrinsic bubble that appears as explosive as a comparable time-driven bubble. Even though intrinsic and time-driven bubbles are expected to grow at the same rate on average, a long intrinsic-bubble sample path is very likely to appear less explosive than the path a time-driven bubble such as (11) generates.

III. Application to the U.S. Stock Market

This section applies the model developed above to U.S. stock-market data. The model's specification is generalized, however, to allow for errors in the difference

[15]PROOF: Define $\psi = r - \mu - \sigma^2/2$ and assume, without loss of generality, that the bubbles are equal at $t = 0$: $bD_0 = cD_0^{\lambda}$. Then,

$$\Pr\left[\tilde{P}_T < \hat{P}_T\right] = \Pr\left[bD_T e^{\psi T} < cD_T^{\lambda}\right]$$

$$= \Pr\left[\psi T < (\lambda - 1)\left(\mu T + \Sigma_{s=1}^{T} \xi_s\right)\right]$$

$$= \Pr\left[r - \lambda\mu - \sigma^2/2 < (\lambda - 1)\left(\Sigma_{s=1}^{T} \xi_s\right)/T\right].$$

Equation (8) implies, however, that $r - \lambda\mu - \sigma^2/2 = \sigma^2(\lambda^2 - 1)/2 > 0$ (recall that $\lambda > 1$). Since $\text{plim}(\Sigma_{s=1}^{T} \xi_s)/T = 0$, the proof is complete.

equation describing stock-price movements, equation (1). Now, time-t prices are given by

$$(1') \quad P_t = e^{-r}E_t(D_t + P_{t+1}) + e^{-r}u_t$$

where u_t is a predictable single-period excess return. Equation (1') implies that (10) is replaced by the statistical model,

$$(12) \quad P_t = c_0 D_t + cD_t^{\lambda} + \varepsilon_t$$

in which $c_0 = \kappa = (e^r - e^{\mu + \sigma^2/2})^{-1}$ and ε_t is the present value of the errors in (1'), $\varepsilon_t \equiv \sum_{s=t}^{\infty} e^{-r(s-t+1)}E_t(u_s)$. Estimation of (12) is complicated by collinearity among the regressors, but dividing by D_t mitigates the problem and leads to

$$(13) \quad \frac{P_t}{D_t} = c_0 + cD_t^{\lambda-1} + \eta_t$$

where $\eta_t \equiv \varepsilon_t / D_t$. The null hypothesis of no bubble implies that $c_0 = \kappa$ and $c = 0$, whereas the bubble alternative in (10) predicts that $c_0 = \kappa$ and $c > 0$.

The new error term,

$$\eta_t = D_t^{-1} \sum_{s=t}^{\infty} e^{-r(s-t+1)}E_t(u_s)$$

is assumed to be statistically independent of dividends at all leads and lags and to have unconditional mean zero. This assumption is critical in the tests below.[16] The error in (13) could be interpreted, for example, as the result of time-varying effective income-tax rates or time-varying discount factors. One could also think of η_t as partly reflecting a fad—a shock to the demand for stocks which is unrelated to efficient forecasts of future dividends. For the latter interpretation, specification (13) allows separate identification of bubble and fad components in stock prices.

Estimation is based on the Standard and Poor's stock price and dividend indexes from the *Securities Price Index Record*, as extended backwards in time by Alfred Cowles and Associates (1939). Following Robert Barsky and De Long (1989), we examine the period 1900–1988, using nominal stock prices recorded in January of each year and deflated by the January producer price index (PPI). Dividends are annual averages of nominal data for the calendar year, deflated by the year-average PPI.[17] We would have preferred data on beginning-of-period-t dividends to match the beginning-of-period-t stock price, P_t. Because these are not available, we use the average of period-t dividends as our measure of D_t.[18,19]

[16]Independence is an unnecessarily strong assumption for some purposes. The tests carried out in the following subsections will produce consistent parameter estimates provided only that $E_t(\eta_t | D_t) = 0$. As a partial check on this weaker assumption, we formed an estimate of u_t / D_t from equation (1'): $\theta_{t+1} \equiv u_t / D_t + \omega_{t+1} = (e^r P_t / D_t) - 1 - (P_{t+1}/D_t)$, where ω_{t+1} is unforecastable given time-t information. We then regressed θ_{t+1} on actual log-dividend changes. The results show that Δd_t has no statistically significant explanatory power for θ_{t+1}.

However, for correct statistical inferences, we must make the stronger assumption that dividends and η_t are independent at all leads and lags. Again, we examined this assumption by regressing θ_{t+1} on changes in log dividends (current, past, and future) and found no significant explanatory power.

[17]Although the price and dividend series extend back to 1871, we chose to begin our sample at 1900 because the composition of the market portfolio becomes increasingly restrictive as one goes back in time. In 1871, the portfolio comprises only 47 stocks, of which 31 are railroads. Because many other authors (e.g., Campbell and Shiller, 1987) have used the longer series, we also ran our statistical tests on the 1871–1986 sample. The results were qualitatively unaffected.

[18]A potential problem with this choice is that D_t may not be completely known at the beginning of period t. Nevertheless, we see two reasons why D_t is likely to be a better measure of the dividend information contained in beginning-of-period-t price, P_t, than is the average period-$(t-1)$ dividend, D_{t-1}. First, P_t is not recorded on January 1, but is itself an average over the period-t month of January. Second, to mitigate the effects of any time lapse between the determination and actual distribution of dividends, it is better to use average period-t dividends than those from period $t-1$. In any case, unless otherwise mentioned, the results below are not importantly different when average period-$(t-1)$ dividends are used to proxy for beginning-of-period-t dividends.

[19]Applying the notion of intrinsic bubbles to aggregate stock price and dividend data raises a question of interpretation. One possibility is that each firm's share price equals the present value of its own dividends, plus an intrinsic bubble on aggregate dividends. Such a

TABLE 1—COINTEGRATING REGRESSIONS OF ANNUAL REAL STOCK PRICES AND DIVIDENDS

Row	Regression equation	Cointegrating coefficient (β)	R^2	DW	$d.f.$
1	$P_t = \alpha + \beta D_t + \nu_t$	36.65	0.85	0.57	87
2	$D_t = \alpha + \beta P_t + \nu_t$	0.023	0.85	0.69	87
3	$p_t = \alpha + \beta d_t + \nu_t$	1.591	0.88	0.69	87
4	$d_t = \alpha + \beta p_t + \nu_t$	0.556	0.88	0.70	87

Notes: Cointegrating regressions are estimated using OLS. The sample period for all regressions was 1900–1988.

A. *The Price–Dividend Relation*

In deriving (13) we assume that the log-dividend process follows a martingale with trend. As an empirical matter, it seems unreasonable to suppose that market participants use only the information in past dividends to forecast future dividends. In Appendix A, we argue, however, that the stochastic process in (5) is a plausible approximation to the mechanism the market uses to forecast aggregate dividends. Appendix A describes several univariate and bivariate tests of the log-dividend specification in (5). We find little evidence against the martingale hypothesis: log-dividend changes are essentially unpredictable when conditioning on the lags of log dividends and/or log price:dividend ratios.[20] The data estimate the parameters in (5) as $\mu = 0.011$ and $\sigma = 0.122$.

A general implication of (13) is that stock prices may appear to overreact to changes in dividends. Also, (13) predicts that price:dividend ratios are nonstationary and positively correlated with dividends. This subsection presents a brief empirical examination of these basic implications of intrinsic bubbles.

First, what does the simple present-value model predict for the sensitivity of prices to changes in dividends? From (6), a one-dollar change in dividends should raise prices by κ dollars. Using the fact that the sample-average gross real return on stocks is $e^r = 1.090$ per annum, we have that $\kappa = (e^r - e^{\mu + \sigma^2/2})^{-1} = (1.090 - e^{0.011 + 0.122^2/2})^{-1} = 14.0$. In general, if P_t and D_t are cointegrated of order (1,1), then under the present-value model the cointegrating coefficient should be approximately κ. Equation (6) also implies that the elasticity of prices with respect to dividends is 1. If log stock price p_t and d_t are cointegrated, it is also with a coefficient of 1.

The first row of Table 1 presents estimates of κ, obtained by regressing prices on dividends. The coefficient is estimated to be 36.7—much larger than the value of 14.0 predicted by the simple present-value model.[21] If P_t and D_t are cointegrated then the ordinary least-squares (OLS) estimate of the cointegrating factor, while consistent, is biased in small samples. In order to bound the cointegrating coefficient, we run the reverse regression (projecting D_t on P_t) in the second row of Table 1. This produces a larger estimate of κ: $1/0.0233 = 42.9$. Even

formulation would remove the incentive for managers to influence the market price of their firms' shares by altering the timing of dividend payments. However, there is a semantic issue of whether the bubble is extraneous to individual companies' share prices.

[20]Some of this evidence may be controversial. We have placed our discussion in Appendix A because the controversial aspects are somewhat tangential to our main argument. Provided one is prepared to accept (5) as a reasonable approximation to the forecasting model investors use, equation (13) will still approximate the relation between the price:dividend ratio and dividends.

[21]Similar estimates of the cointegrating factor are obtained by Campbell and Shiller (1987), Diba and Grossman (1988a), and West (1987), among others.

TABLE 2—UNIT-ROOT TESTS FOR ANNUAL PRICE:DIVIDEND RATIOS

Variable	β_1 With time trend	β_1 Without time trend
Spread, $P_t - 14D_t$	−0.1355 (−2.08)	−0.0702 (−1.14)
Price:dividend ratio, P_t/D_t	−0.2157 (−2.99)	−0.1343 (−2.11)
Log price:dividend ratio, $p_t - d_t$	−0.2122 (−3.55*)	−0.1315 (−2.55)

Notes: Values reported are the coefficients β_1 in the following regressions: with trend, $\Delta x_{t+1} = \beta_0 + \beta_1 x_t + \beta_2 t + \nu_{t+1}$; without trend, $\Delta x_{t+1} = \beta_0 + \beta_1 x_t + \nu_{t+1}$. Standard errors are constructed allowing for an MA(4) process in the residual. The t statistics, reported in parentheses beneath the point estimates, are for the test $\beta_1 = 0$.

*Statistically significant at the 5-percent level, using confidence intervals proposed by Phillips and Perron (1988) and Phillips (1987).

the lower of the two estimates would imply that the required rate of return on stocks less the expected growth rate of dividends is an implausibly low $1/36.7 = 2.7$ percent per annum. (The actual value over our sample period is 7.1 percent.) The third and fourth rows of Table 1 perform analogous regressions in logs instead of levels. Here, the cointegrating coefficient predicted by the present-value model is 1, but the estimates are again much higher—bounded between 1.59 and $1/0.556 = 1.80$. These estimates suggest that simple present-value models cannot explain why price:dividend ratios are so high given historical stock returns or, equivalently, why returns have been so high given price:dividend ratios.

To test whether these estimates are statistically incompatible with the simple present-value model, we examine various measures of the price:dividend ratio, including Campbell and Shiller's (1987) spread, for nonstationarity. Table 2 reports unit-root tests for the theoretically warranted spread ($P_t - 14D_t$) as well as the price:dividend ratio in levels (P_t/D_t) and in logs ($p_t - d_t$) (see Peter Phillips and Pierre Perron, 1988). Results of tests with and without time trends are reported. Under the present-value model, we should reject nonstationarity in each of these regressions; yet in five of six cases we cannot reject the unit-root hypothesis.[22]

We question whether these tests can be decisive, however, because of acknowledged problems with both their size and power.[23] One approach, exemplified by Campbell and Shiller (1987, 1988a, b) and Campbell (1990), is to assume at the outset that the price:dividend ratio is stationary. This assumption is important for their results; for example, Campbell's (1990) attribution of substantial price volatility to predictable excess returns relies crucially on the near-nonstationarity of the price:dividend ratio. Our view is that the ambiguous evidence on stationarity

[22]Some of our results may be sensitive to the timing of dividends. Diba and Grossman (1988a), for example, use lagged dividends and deflate by the wholesale price index (WPI). They find that the log price:dividend ratio, $p_t - d_{t-1}$, is stationary. Using lagged dividends, but deflating by the PPI, Campbell and Shiller (1988a) also reject nonstationarity. Campbell and Shiller (1987) find results similar to those reported above for the spread, $P_t - \kappa D_t$, using data from 1871 to 1986.

[23]For some Monte Carlo evidence on the size of these tests, see G. William Schwert (1988). Tests using lagged dividends (mentioned in footnote 22) may reject too frequently under the assumption that $p_t - d_t$ actually contains a unit root. On the power of unit-root tests applied to price:dividend ratios, see Cochrane (1989).

TABLE 3—ESTIMATES OF EQUATION (13), $P_t/D_t = c_0 + cD_t^{\lambda-1} + \eta_t$

Row	Regression method	c_0	c	$\lambda-1$	F test ($\hat{c}=0$)	R^2	DW	$d.f.$
1	OLS	12.24 (1.14)	0.34** (0.05)			0.57	0.71	87
2	Maximum likelihood	14.18 (1.77)	0.26** (0.06)			0.75	1.91	86
3	OLS	14.63 (2.28)	0.04 (0.12)	2.61* (1.15)	128.0**	0.57	0.71	86
4	Maximum likelihood	16.55 (2.02)	0.01 (0.02)	3.29* (1.45)	9.62**	0.75	1.91	85

Notes: Standard errors are reported in parentheses; OLS regressions report Newey–West standard errors allowing for fourth-order serial correlation and conditional heteroscedasticity. (Higher orders of serial correlation did not yield larger standard errors.) Maximum-likelihood estimates specify the error term as an AR(1) process. The sample period for all regressions was 1900–1988.

* Statistically significant at the 5-percent level; ** statistically significant at the 1-percent level.

makes it worthwhile to move beyond simple time-series diagnostics.

In sum, the evidence presented in this subsection has three important implications for our argument. First, prices are too sensitive to current dividends to be consistent with a simple present-value model. The implication, of course, is that the portion of stock prices unexplained by such a model must be highly correlated with dividends.[24] Second this overreaction apparently cannot be explained by other variables which are incorporated into stock prices and help forecast future dividends. If, for example, when dividends are high investors tend to get other reliable information that dividends will grow more quickly than previously expected, then this information is likely to be incorporated in stock prices, which therefore should Granger-cause dividends. The results in Appendix A suggest, however, that this is not the case. Finally, a specification such as (13) has at least the potential to explain these failures of the present-value model.

B. *A Direct Test for Intrinsic Bubbles*

To see whether this potential is at all realized, we turn in Table 3 to estimates of (13) and several related expressions. Before interpreting the estimates, however, some discussion of econometric issues is in order.

The regressor in (13), $D_t^{\lambda-1}$, presents difficulties because it is explosive. Two assumptions are necessary for valid statistical inferences. If the t statistic from testing $\hat{c}=0$ is to have a known distribution under the null hypothesis, we require that: (i) the residuals, η_t, are distributed normally and identically—but not necessarily independently—with unconditional mean zero; and (ii) the dividend innovations, ξ_t, are distributed independently of the residuals η_t at all leads and lags. Appendix B provides a proof that the standard t statistic does indeed approximate a normal distribution un-

[24]This result is essentially a restatement of Shiller's (1981) volatility findings. West's (1987) general specification test and Campbell and Kyle's (1988) noise-trading model also exploit the excess sensitivity of prices to dividend changes. Stephen Durlauf and Robert Hall (1988) find noise in prices that is more highly correlated with prices themselves than with dividends. Their definition of noise, however, is not the difference between prices and a multiple of current dividends, but the difference between prices and an *ex post* measure of the present value of future dividends.

der these assumptions, despite the presence of the exploding regressor.[25]

A second aspect of estimation requiring discussion is the effect of serial correlation on the estimated standard errors of coefficients. Because theory offers no guide to η_t's serial correlation, the usual standard errors may be incorrect. We try to account for this possibility in two ways. First, we estimate (13) by OLS, but correct the residuals using Whitney Newey and West's (1987) covariance-matrix estimator for serial correlation of unknown form. This estimator allows for conditional heteroscedasticity.[26] Second, since the residuals appear to be well described by a first-order autoregressive process, we compute maximum-likelihood estimates of the parameters under the assumption that the residuals are AR(1).

Finally, there is the issue of how to estimate the exponent, λ, and the present-value multiplier, κ. In some of the regressions below, we do not estimate λ concurrently with the other parameters. Instead, we use the point estimates from the log-dividend process obtained earlier, together with the mean return on stocks over the period, to compute $\lambda = 2.74$.[27] In other regressions, we estimate all parameters simultaneously, without imposing additional restrictions. The restriction that $c_0 = \kappa = 14.0$ is not imposed on the constant term in (13), even though it holds under both the null and alternative hypotheses. Instead, we use the unrestricted estimate of c_0 as a kind of sensibility check on our model.

The first two rows of Table 3 report estimates of (13) using OLS and maximum likelihood. These two regressions constrain λ to equal 2.74. In both cases, $\hat{c}$ is statistically very significant. The estimates are comparable in magnitude and significance for the two estimation methods.[28] In the third and fourth rows, we estimate all of the parameters of the model simultaneously. The point estimates of c_0 are similar to those above, although λ is estimated to be larger and c correspondingly lower.[29] The larger standard error for c is expected here because the derivatives of the likelihood function with respect to the parameters c and λ are highly positively correlated [specifically, these derivatives include the terms $D_t^{\lambda-1}$ and $c_0(\lambda-1)D_t^{\lambda-2}$, with $\lambda > 2$]. Rather than using a t test to judge the importance of the nonlinear term, it is therefore more appropriate to compute an F test of the no-bubble hypothesis, $c = 0$, $\lambda = \hat{\lambda}$, where $\hat{\lambda}$ is the unrestricted estimate of λ. This hypothesis is rejected strongly at any reasonable level of significance.[30,31]

[25]The assumption that η_t in (13) is normal must be approximate because negative values of the price:dividend ratio are excluded. However, the approximation is likely to be accurate because the average value of the price:dividend ratio is equal to more than five times the estimated standard deviation of η_t.

[26]It is plausible to think of the residual in (12), ε_t, as growing at a rate similar to that of dividends. In such a case, we would not expect η_t to exhibit much conditional heteroscedasticity. Indeed, in our estimates the heteroscedasticity-corrected standard errors were similar to the uncorrected standard errors.

[27]We tried a variety of parameter estimates for r, μ, and σ^2. These do have a minor effect on the exponent but are unimportant for the general regression results reported below.

[28]We also tried estimating an extended form of (13):

$$\frac{P_t}{D_t} = c_0 + c_1 D_t^{\lambda-1} + c_2 D_t^{\lambda'-1} + \eta_t$$

where λ' is the negative root from equation (8). Our estimates of r, μ, and σ^2 suggest that $\lambda' = -4.22$. Because $\lambda' < 0$ and dividends have a positive trend, $D_t^{\lambda'-1}$ will be of vanishing importance in explaining prices. Indeed, when we included $D_t^{\lambda'-1}$ in the regression, it had no effect on the estimate of c_1. Furthermore, c_2 was imprecisely estimated and varied widely across different estimation techniques. As we expected, there seemed to be no evidence that the second nonlinear term helped in explaining stock prices. We therefore do not report these results.

[29]Despite these differences in point estimates, there is virtually no improvement in R^2. A likelihood-ratio test cannot reject the hypothesis that row 3 is no improvement over row 1 of Table 3.

[30]We used the Newey-West covariance-matrix estimator for this test. In nonlinear models, t tests and F tests are not equivalent, as the t test is a Wald test (i.e., it is based entirely on the unrestricted model) while the F test is based on the likelihood-ratio principle (i.e., it explicitly compares the unrestricted model with the restricted model in which dividends are unable to explain *any* movements in the price:dividend

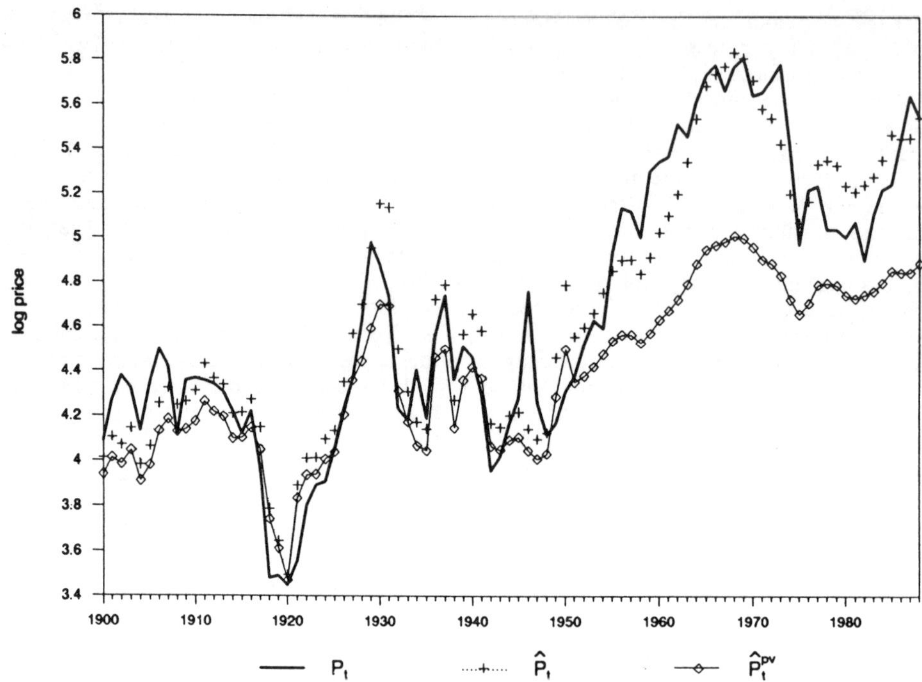

FIGURE 5. ACTUAL AND PREDICTED STOCK PRICES

Notes: P_t is the actual real stock price; $\hat{P}_t = D_t(\hat{c}_0 + \hat{c}D_t^{\lambda-1})$ is the predicted stock price under the intrinsic bubble; and $\hat{P}_t^{pv} = D_t\hat{c}_0$ is the model's predicted present-value stock price.

The finding that c is statistically positive suggests that prices become increasingly overvalued relative to the nonbubble price, P_t^{pv}, as dividends rise. Similarly, when dividends are low, the bubble component of price shrinks: P_t approaches P_t^{pv}. (Recall the dotted curve in Fig. 1, which graphs the relationship between fundamentals and prices implied by $c > 0$.) The size of the bubble (the distance between P_t and P_t^{pv}) explodes as the dividend becomes large. Of course, if realized dividends do not reach a high enough level, the bubble component will remain small.

Note also that the model's estimates of c_0 are sensible. All four estimates from Table 3 imply that P_t^{pv} is measured on average to be close to 14 times current dividends; indeed, each estimate is statistically indistinguishable from $\kappa = 14.0$, the value predicted by the simple present-value model set out above. In our estimates of (13), $\hat{P}_t^{pv} = \hat{c}_0 D_t$ turns out to be consistent with the long-run average return on stocks, because the nonlinear dividend term soaks up a reasonable amount of the excessive sensitivity of actual prices to dividends.

The economic significance of the bubble is, of course, another matter. How large is the bubble component in prices, and how

ratio, $c = 0$). We thank one of the referees for pointing this out.

[31]One way of checking the assumption that ξ_t and η_t are distributed independently is to regress the estimated residuals obtained from (13) directly on current, past, and future changes in the log of dividends. In doing so, we could not reject the hypothesis that leads and lags of Δd_t have no explanatory power for η_t.

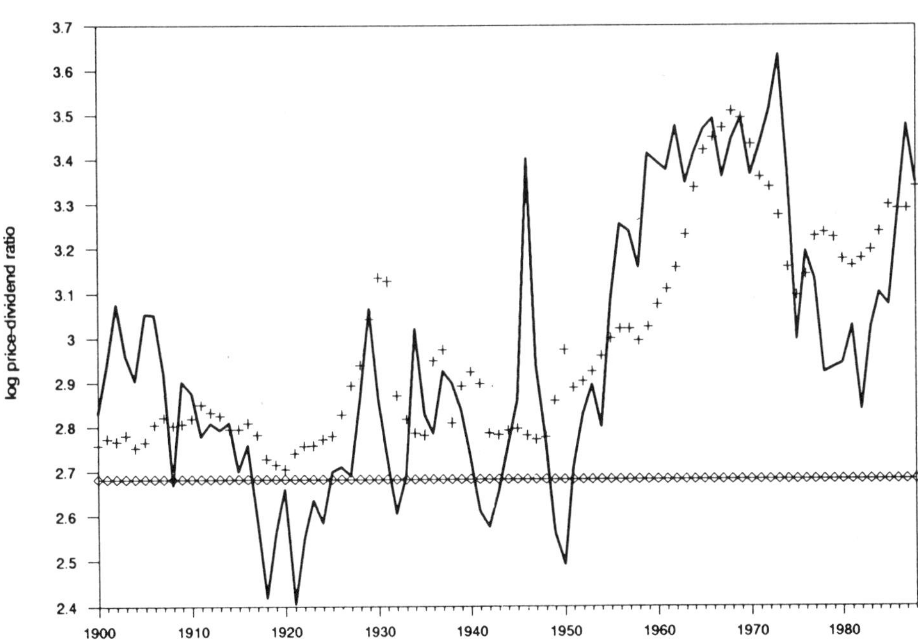

FIGURE 6. ACTUAL AND PREDICTED LOG PRICE:DIVIDEND RATIOS

Notes: $p_t - d_t$ is the actual log price:dividend ratio; $\hat{p}_t - d_t$ is the predicted log price:dividend ratio under the intrinsic bubble; and $\hat{p}_t^{\text{pv}} - d_t$ is the model's predicted present-value price:dividend ratio.

well does the model track actual price movements? Figure 5 helps explore these issues. It compares actual stock prices, P_t, with both $\hat{P}_t^{\text{pv}}$ (the model's estimate of the nonbubble component of prices) and $\hat{P}_t$ (the model's estimated price inclusive of the bubble term). Figure 6 presents comparable graphs of log price:dividend ratios.[32] The figures are striking in two respects.

First there is the sheer size of the bubble itself (the distance between $\hat{P}_t$ and $\hat{P}_t^{\text{pv}}$). It has grown over time and has been particularly large during the post-World War II period. Indeed, the estimates suggest that at this writing the nonbubble level of the S&P 500 is less than 50 percent of its current value! The difference $\hat{P}_t - \hat{P}_t^{\text{pv}}$ is estimated to be this large recently because the levels of both dividends and price:dividend ratios are historically high.

Second, Figures 5 and 6 indicate that $\hat{P}_t$ explains a good deal of actual stock-price movements. The sustained run-up in prices from 1950 to 1968 appears to be captured by the model, as does the post-World War II tendency for stocks to sell at historically large multiples of dividends.[33] The model

[32]Figures 5 and 6 use the estimated coefficients from the third row of Table 3. However, this choice is immaterial to the results: it is almost impossible to distinguish visually among all the models estimated in Table 3.

[33]The model does a better job of explaining movements in the price:dividend ratio in the postwar period than in the earlier part of the century. This is evident in Figures 5 and 6, which show that prices and divi-

also does a plausible job of explaining the year-to-year variability of stock prices. Note from Figure 5 that the variance of dividends appears to have fallen relative to the variance of prices over the sample. Stock-price variability has been puzzling not only because it is so high, but also because it has not declined over time as rapidly as has the variability of dividends. Figure 5 and equation (13) together suggest a possible resolution of this paradox: stock-price volatility has not fallen with that of dividends because the *level* of dividends (and therefore the scope for volatility due to an intrinsic bubble) has been historically high.[34]

Of course, the "fit" of $\hat{P}_t$ in Figures 5 and 6 cannot be judged without a standard of comparison. Because there are infinitely many bubble specifications that depend on time or other extraneous variables, sufficient excavation would allow us in principle to fit perfectly the actual price path.

One way of judging the model's fit is to try alternative specifications. Table 4 helps to compare (13) to specifications in which additional terms are included in the regression, sometimes instead of and sometimes alongside $D_t^{\lambda-1}$. We start by examining the effects of two alternatives, the time-driven bubble term in (11) (divided by D_t) and a linear time trend. In isolation, either of these regressors appears to be a statistically significant determinant of the price:dividend ratio (see rows 1 and 3 of Table 4, either estimation method). However, neither regressor remains statistically significant when the nonlinear term in (13), $D_t^{\lambda-1}$, is added to the regression (rows 2 and 4; as in Table 3, we have set λ at its estimated theoretical value of 2.74). Note that in the OLS estimates, the coefficients on the additional regressors become negative once $D_t^{\lambda-1}$ is added. The coefficients on the nonlinear term, however, remain statistically significant and of the same basic magnitude as in Table 3s.

To see whether the nonlinearity of the dividend term in (13) is important, rows 5 and 6 of Table 4 add a *linear* dividend term, D_t, to the regression. As the earlier results might suggest, D_t is positive and statistically significant on its own. However, once $D_t^{\lambda-1}$ is also included, the estimated coefficient on D_t becomes statistically insignificant, and in the maximum-likelihood estimate its sign is reversed. The signs and magnitudes of the estimates of c appear to be consistent with the results of Table 3, but multicollinearity raises the standard errors of the coefficients.

A second way of judging the model's fit is to compare visually the dividend bubble in (13) with the time-driven bubble $\tilde{P}_t$ defined in (11). Figure 7 graphs the predicted values of the present-value price, $\tilde{P}_t^{pv}$, and the bubble-inclusive price, $\tilde{P}_t$, from OLS estimates (row 1 for OLS estimates in Table 4). In comparing Figures 5 and 7, it is evident that the time-driven bubble, $\tilde{P}_t - \tilde{P}_t^{pv}$, captures little of the post-World War II variability of the stock market. Correlation with dividends, per se, is not enough to enable this bubble to explain stock prices. This result is not surprising: the presence of a deterministic time component forces the time-driven bubble to be essentially zero for most of the sample period.

C. *Tests of an Alternative Hypothesis: Present-Value Prices under Variable Dividend Growth Processes*

In testing our bubble specification, we assumed that ξ_t in (5) and η_t in (13) are independent at all leads and lags. While

dends moved strongly together prior to 1950. Tests for subsample stability tend to reject the hypothesis: the OLS estimate of c in the postwar sample remains statistically significant at about 0.34 but becomes indistinguishable from zero prior to 1951.

[34]To see how much the estimated sensitivity of prices to dividends has changed over time, recall that $dP_t/dD_t = \kappa + c\lambda D^{\lambda-1}$. Using the estimates from Table 3, we can compute rough estimates of dP_t/dD_t, which can be interpreted as the model's prediction of the coefficient in a "cointegrating" regression of prices on dividends. Using average dividends over the period 1951–1988, we find (using row 2 of Table 3) $dP_t/dD_t \approx 14.2 + (0.26)(2.74)(7.86^{1.74}) = 39.9$. Similarly, over the period 1900–1950, $dP_t/dD_t \approx 14.2 + (0.26)(2.74) \times (4.31^{1.74}) = 23.2$. The estimated sensitivity of prices to dividends has therefore nearly doubled over the post-World War II period.

TABLE 4—ESTIMATES OF ALTERNATIVE MODELS, $P_t/D_t = c_0 + cD_t^{\lambda-1} + gX_t + \eta_t$

Row	X_t	c_0	c	g	R^2	DW	$d.f.$
Estimation Method = OLS:							
1	Time bubble, $X_t = e^{(r-\mu-\sigma^2/2)t}$	18.28 (1.47)		0.030* (0.013)	0.21	0.35	87
2	Time bubble, $X_t = e^{(r-\mu-\sigma^2/2)t}$	11.85 (1.09)	0.377** (0.060)	−0.008 (0.010)	0.57	0.75	86
3	Linear trend, $X_t = t$	13.68 (2.22)		0.15** (0.05)	0.35	0.43	87
4	Linear trend, $X_t = t$	12.43 (1.39)	0.364* (0.066)	−0.019 (0.052)	0.57	0.75	86
5	Linear dividends, $X_t = D_t$	6.88 (2.02)		2.273** (0.39)	0.55	0.70	87
6	Linear dividends, $X_t = D_t$	18.09 (8.62)	0.684 (0.448)	2.397 (3.32)	0.57	0.70	86
Estimation Method = Maximum Likelihood:							
1	Time bubble, $X_t = e^{(r-\mu-\sigma^2/2)t}$	18.34 (2.16)		0.027[a] (0.014)	0.75	2.04	86
2	Time bubble, $X_t = e^{(r-\mu-\sigma^2/2)t}$	14.48 (1.86)	0.223** (0.075)	0.008 (0.012)	0.75	1.94	85
3	Linear trend, $X_t = t$	14.02 (2.87)		0.145** (0.055)	0.75	1.99	86
4	Linear trend, $X_t = t$	13.19 (2.16)	0.190* (0.084)	0.060 (0.056)	0.75	1.93	85
5	Linear dividends, $X_t = D_t$	11.39 (2.76)		1.530** (0.420)	0.75	1.93	86
6	Linear dividends, $X_t = D_t$	24.54 (6.64)	0.904* (0.404)	−4.372 (2.710)	0.76	1.91	85

Notes: Standard errors are reported in parentheses; OLS regressions report Newey-West standard errors, allowing for fourth-order serial correlation and heteroscedasticity. (Higher orders of serial correlation did not yield larger standard errors.) Maximum-likelihood estimates specify the error term as an AR(1) process. The sample period for all regressions was 1900–1988. The time-bubble specification (lines 1 and 2) is derived by dividing equation (11) by D_t.

[a]Statistically significant at the 10-percent level; *statistically significant at the 5-percent level; **statistically significant at the 1-percent level.

we have attempted to test this assumption directly, our failure to reject it does not mean that it is true. For example, if dividends follow a more complex stochastic process than (5), persistent variation in the growth rate of dividends could lead to persistent movements in the price:dividend ratio.[35] Such variation in dividend growth rates could invalidate our independence assump-

[35]See Barsky and De Long (1989) for one such model of time-varying dividend growth rates.

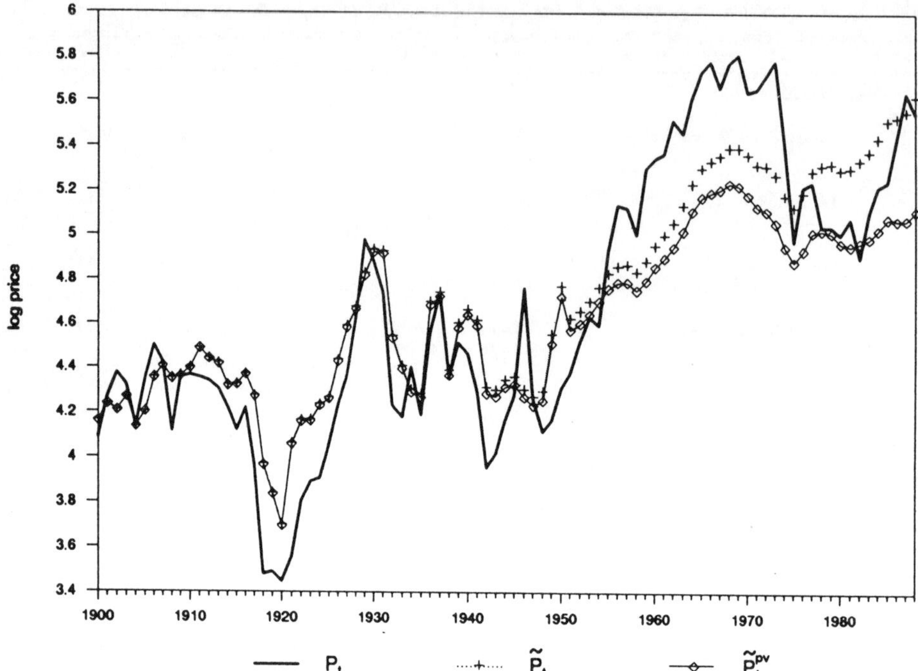

FIGURE 7. ACTUAL AND PREDICTED STOCK PRICES

Note: P_t is the actual real stock price; $\tilde{P}_t$ is the predicted stock price under the time bubble in equation (11); and $\tilde{P}_t^{pv}$ is that model's predicted present-value stock price.

tion by creating a correlation between price:dividend ratios and the level of dividends, even in the absence of a bubble.

In order to explore this possibility in more detail, suppose that the stock price does not contain a bubble but that the growth rate of dividends follows the autoregressive process:

$$(14) \qquad \Delta d_{t+1} = \gamma_1 + \gamma_2 \Delta d_t + \xi_{t+1}.$$

If $\gamma_2 > 0$, a positive shock to the dividend growth rate tends to increase both dividends and the price:dividend ratio, tending to give a positive sample correlation between D_t and η_t in regressions such as (13).

To ascertain the importance of this effect, we ran a set of Monte Carlo experiments. We first estimated equation (14) in the data, finding that $\gamma_1 = 0.008$, $\gamma_2 = 0.1755$, and $\sigma_\xi = 0.122$. Our Monte Carlo procedure was then to draw 88-year paths of dividends, generated randomly according to (14), with ξ_t independently and identically distributed normal. We then estimated P_t^{pv}, the mathematically expected present value of dividends in (2). We then defined $P_t/D_t \equiv P_t^{pv}/D_t + \nu_t$, where ν_t is independently and identically distributed normal and calibrated such that simulated and actual price:dividend ratios have comparable average variability. Finally, we regressed the resulting price:dividend-ratio path on the associated path of $D_t^{\lambda-1}$, as in equation (13), and computed the t statistic for the test of

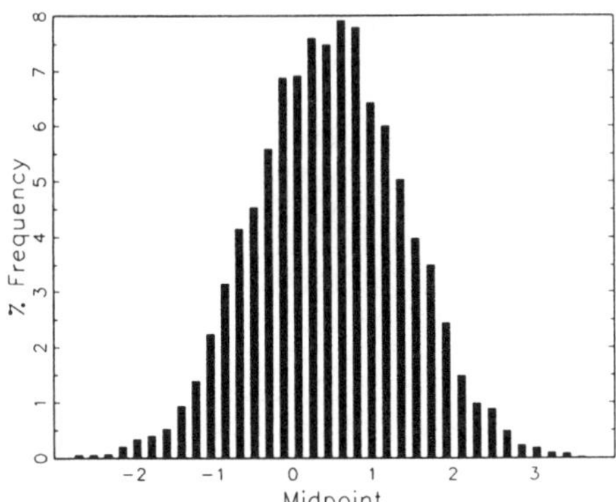

FIGURE 8. MONTE CARLO ESTIMATE OF THE DISTRIBUTION OF THE t STATISTIC FOR $c = 0$ IN EQUATION (10)

Note: The estimates were made under the assumption that dividends follow (14) and that stock prices do not contain a bubble.

$c = 0$.[36] This procedure was repeated 5,000 times.

Figure 8 shows the frequency distribution of the t statistics obtained from this procedure. The distribution is essentially normal, although upward-biased, with a mean of 0.47 and a standard deviation of 0.93. Slightly fewer than 5 percent of the statistics were greater than 2.0, and fewer than 0.3 percent were greater than 3.0. These results suggest that time-varying dividend growth rates could make our test of $c = 0$ in (13) reject too often in favor of $c > 0$, but the bias appears to be too small to explain the large t statistic in the actual data.

IV. Summary and Concluding Remarks

This paper has proposed a class of rational bubbles that depend exclusively on exogenous fundamentals. The resulting class of asset-price solutions has intuitive appeal because it avoids the introduction of extraneous driving variables and captures the idea that prices can overreact to changes in fundamentals.

We applied a version of this model to United States stock-market data. The estimates reveal a strong nonlinear relationship between prices and dividends, which can be interpreted as a rejection of the hypothesis that there is no bubble. The estimates also help to reconcile the historical return on stocks with the level of the price:dividend ratio (and with its correlation with dividends), something that simple present-value models appear to be unable to do. In addition, the estimates imply that the bubble component in today's stock prices is very large. Even if one is reluctant to accept the bubble interpretation, the apparent nonlinearity of the price:dividend relation requires attention.

The hypothesis tests reported above have some desirable statistical properties. Unlike general specification tests, for example, the tests in this paper use estimates that are consistent under both the null and alternative hypotheses (given our identifying assumptions). The tight parametric form of intrinsic bubbles allows us to offer an interpretation of earlier specification-test results, which often did not pinpoint the factors causing model failure.

Our formulation allows variables such as the price:dividend ratio to predict excess returns. To carry out statistical inference, we do require that dividends themselves cannot be used to forecast returns, but in any case there is little direct evidence to the contrary. By relaxing the present-value assumption, the tests allow the data to allocate deviations from the simple present-value model across a bubble term and predictable excess returns. Our interpretation of Section III's results is that, once intrinsic bubbles are admitted as an empirical possibility, the predictability of excess returns no longer appears to be the only cause of the simple present-value model's failure.

It is hard not to be skeptical about the long-run implications of any kind of rational bubble. The fact that our identifying assumptions (that log dividends follow a martingale and that dividend innovations are unrelated to nonbubble components of

[36]As in row 1 of Table 3, we used OLS and set $\lambda = 2.74$.

TABLE A1—UNIT-ROOT TESTS FOR ANNUAL REAL DIVIDENDS

Variable	β_1 With time trend	β_1 Without time trend
Log dividends, d_t	−0.1644 (−2.56)	−0.0545 (−1.40)

Notes: Figures reported are the coefficients β_1 in the following regressions: with trend, $\Delta x_{t+1} = \beta_0 + \beta_1 x_t + \beta_2 t + \nu_{t+1}$; without trend, $\Delta x_{t+1} = \beta_0 + \beta_1 x_t + \nu_{t+1}$. Standard errors are constructed allowing for an MA(4) process in the residuals. The t statistics reported in parentheses beneath the point estimates are for the test $\beta_1 = 0$.

price:dividend ratios) have not been rejected does not mean that they are true. In fact, we suspect that the class of assumptions that cannot be rejected is sufficiently large that, on the basis of currently available data, it may be impossible to determine conclusively whether deviations from present-value prices are nonstationary (i.e., rational bubbles) or stationary (i.e., fads) or even whether such deviations exist at all (i.e., time-varying discount factors or dividend growth rates). Perhaps the results above merely show that there is a coherent case to be made for bubbles alongside these alternative possibilities. If that is so, then we should not feel too comfortable about how well we really understand stock prices.

APPENDIX A

Time-Series Properties of Dividends

In deriving equation (13), we assumed that the log-dividend process follows a martingale with trend. In this appendix we briefly examine the time-series evidence on the dividend-generating process to see whether it is consistent with our assumption.

Table A1 reports tests of the null hypothesis that the log-dividend process, d_t, contains a unit root.[37] We perform the unit-root tests allowing for alternative assumptions about the presence of a time trend. Neither version produces significant evidence against the unit-root hypothesis at the 10-percent level of statistical significance. As noted in the text, the data indicate that $\mu = 0.011$ and $\sigma = 0.122$.[38]

Of course, if the stock price in (10) is to be a correct solution to (1), investors' conditional expectation of d_{t+1} must equal $\mu + d_t$. It follows that the disturbance ξ_{t+1} in (5) must not only be unpredictable given the past history of dividends, it must also be unpredictable given any broader time-t information set that investors use. In particular, because investors' forecasts of future dividends must depend on current dividends only, stock prices (which presumably reflect investor information beyond that in dividends) should not improve the accuracy of dividend forecasts that are based on current dividends alone. This is a strong assumption, so we check to see how well it fares in the data.

Table A2 reports tests for Granger-causality from prices to dividends. In the first row, we regress log-dividend changes on a constant and the lags of both log-dividend changes and log price:dividend ratios. Because the price:dividend ratio should in principle include all information relevant for forecasting future dividends, it should pick up any forecastable nontrend compo-

[37]The tests are those proposed by Phillips (1987) and Phillips and Perron (1988). We allow for fourth-order serial correlation in the residuals, as suggested by those authors. For similar tests, see Kleidon (1986), Campbell and Shiller (1987) (who examine the level, rather than the log, of real dividends), and Campbell and Shiller (1988a).

[38]There is some evidence that the residuals in this regression are not white, indicating that a more complex ARIMA process might perform better. The Durbin-Watson statistic was 1.65, which is inconclusive, but a $Q(27)$ test rejects the hypothesis of no serial correlation in the residuals at a 3.8-percent level of significance. Using the 1871–1986 sample of S&P data, Campbell and Shiller (1988a) reject (at the 5-percent level) the hypothesis that the d_t process contains a unit root. This finding could in principle be due to structural instability over the sample. There is also some evidence of kurtosis in the estimated residuals from equation (5). This could be evidence of time-varying volatility of log-dividend innovations.

TABLE A2—TESTS FOR WHETHER PRICES GRANGER-CAUSE DIVIDENDS

Row	Regression equation	F test (P value)	R^2	DW	$d.f.$	Lag length
1	$\Delta d_{t+1} = \alpha(L)\Delta d_t + \beta(L)(p_t - d_t) + \nu_{t+1}$	0.812 (0.52)	0.13	1.96	75	4
2	$d_{t+1} = \alpha(L)d_t + \beta(L)p_t + \nu_{t+1}$	1.868 (0.12)	0.91	1.98	75	4

Notes: Granger-causality tests are based on OLS estimates and Newey-West standard errors. The sum of the coefficients on the log price:dividend ratio and on the log of price are reported in rows 1 and 2, respectively. The numbers in parentheses are probability values from F tests of the hypothesis that $\beta_i = 0 \; \forall \; i$. Alternative lag lengths were also tried for these regressions, but they did not change the results. The sample period for all regressions is 1900–1988. Constant terms were included in both regressions.

nent of dividend changes. The table reports the sum of the coefficients on $p_t - d_t$ and its lags, as well as an F test of the hypothesis that these coefficients are jointly zero. This test shows that we cannot reject the hypothesis that $p_t - d_t$ has no incremental power for forecasting future dividend changes.[39] The test's formulation is, however, unnecessarily restrictive. If log prices and log dividends are cointegrated of order (1,1) but with a coefficient other than 1, our inferences may not be valid. In the second row of Table A2, we therefore run a less restrictive regression, which asks directly whether log prices Granger-cause log dividends. Once again, the data provide no strong evidence that log prices have incremental predictive power for future log dividends.[40]

In their tests of the present-value model, Campbell and Shiller (1987) report evidence to the contrary: that the spread does Granger-cause future dividend changes. However, these rejections appear to depend on a different convention for dating prices and dividends: Campbell and Shiller use the beginning-of-period price, P_{t+1}, and the average of the previous period's dividend, D_t, to predict average period-$(t+1)$ dividends, D_{t+1} (Campbell and Shiller, 1987 p. 1074).[41] If P_{t+1} contains cleaner, more up-to-the-minute information about the beginning-of-period-$(t+1)$ dividend than does the time-averaged variable D_t, then one would expect to find Granger-causality using the Campbell-Shiller dating convention, even when stock prices contain no information beyond that in the past history of dividends. Furthermore, as we have argued (see footnote 18), substantial information about the current year's dividends could become available during the month of January. We therefore see little basis at present for rejecting the hypothesis that prices do not Granger-cause dividends. While the view that prices contain information beyond that in current dividends is plausible, there just is not much evidence in its favor in these data.[42] We conclude that (5) is a reasonable

[39] We also ran this test in levels rather than logs, using the Campbell-Shiller spread, $P_t - \kappa D_t$, in place of the log price:dividend ratio and using ΔD_t in place of Δd_t. The results, using various measures of κ, are not importantly different from those reported above.

[40] Christopher Sims et al. (1990) and West (1988b) give the asymptotic justification for this procedure. In both regression tests, we used a lag length of 4. Similar tests on alternative lag lengths yielded the same results. We also duplicated these tests on the 1871–1986 data set used by Campbell and Shiller (1987), with no change in the results.

[41] Following the dating convention described at the beginning of Section III, we instead use the beginning-of-period-t price, P_t, along with D_t to predict D_{t+1}. Robert Engle and Watson (1985) also use this convention and obtain Granger-causality results similar to ours.

[42] We ran the regressions in Table A2 using Campbell and Shiller's (1987) dating convention and found results similar to theirs. If there is substantial additional information about future dividends in stock prices, then one might nevertheless expect to find that

empirical approximation to the true process investors use to forecast dividends.

APPENDIX B

Derivation of the Finite-Sample Distribution of the Test for $\hat{c}=0$ in (13)

Consider the model $y_t = cx_t + \eta_t$, where $t = 1,\dots,T$, $y_t = P_t/D_t$, c is a parameter to be estimated, $x_t = D_t^{\lambda-1}$, and the log of D_t evolves according to (5):

$$d_t = \mu t + d_0 + \sum_{s=1}^{t} \xi_s. \tag{B1}$$

For simplicity, we assume that the constant term in (13), c_0, is known and has been removed. Let $\tilde{x}$ represent the random sequence of regressors from time 1 to T, a particular realization of which is given by x. We wish to derive the distribution of the test $\hat{c}=c$, where $\hat{c}$ is the OLS estimate of c. To do this, we require the following assumptions.

ASSUMPTION 1: *The residuals, η_t, are normally and identically, but not necessarily independently, distributed with unconditional mean 0 and autocorrelation function $\delta(k)$.*

ASSUMPTION 2: *The dividend innovations, ξ_t, are independently distributed of the residuals, η_t, at all leads and lags and have mean 0 and variance σ^2.*

To proceed, note that the OLS estimate of c is

$$\hat{c}(\tilde{x}) - c = \frac{\sum_{t=1}^{T} \tilde{x}_t \eta_t}{\sum_{t=1}^{T} \tilde{x}_t^2} = \sum_{t=1}^{T} \left(\frac{\tilde{x}_t}{\sum_{s=1}^{T} \tilde{x}_s^2} \right) \eta_t \equiv \sum_{t=1}^{T} \tilde{w}_t \eta_t \tag{B2}$$

where the $\tilde{w}_t$ are a random set of weights, which by Assumption 2 are independently distributed of the η_t's. By Assumptions 1 and 2, the linear combination in (B2), for a given sample path of the regressors, x, is a weighted average of normals and is therefore normally distributed:

$$\hat{c}(x) - c \sim \mathcal{N}(0, (x'x)^{-1} x' \Omega x (x'x)^{-1}) \tag{B3}$$

where $\Omega_{i,j} = \delta(i-j)$. Notice that since the distribution of $\hat{c}$ depends on the particular realization, x, the unconditional distribution of $\hat{c}$ will be a mixture of normals and will therefore have fat tails. Nevertheless, under both the null and alternative hypotheses, c is estimated consistently.

Even though the unconditional distribution of $\hat{c}$ is not normal, the usual t statistic for $\hat{c}(x) = c$ is distributed $\mathcal{N}(0,1)$, even in finite samples, provided that Ω is known. To see this, note that from (B3) the t statistic is given by

$$\frac{\hat{c}(x) - c}{\sqrt{(x'x)^{-1} x' \Omega x (x'x)^{-1}}} \sim \mathcal{N}(0,1). \tag{B4}$$

Because this distribution does not depend on the sample realization, x, it holds uncon-

prices Granger-cause dividends even when our dating convention is used. The results in Table A2, however, suggest that this is not the case. Campbell and Shiller (1988b) present evidence that a 30-year moving average of past earnings, deflated by the time-t real stock price, helps forecast Δd_t when added to a regression of that variable on its lags and on current and lagged values of $p_t - d_{t-1}$. Shiller (pers. comm.) reports that the explanatory power of this equation declines (but still remains highly significant) when the earnings and spread variables are redefined using the average real stock price for period $t-1$. What is puzzling, if rational expectations are assumed, is that the information content of past earnings apparently is not reflected in past stock prices. If it were, one would expect the lagged stock-price variables in the Table A2 regressions to pick up some of the ability of earnings to forecast future dividends.

We tried regressing the change in log dividends on lagged dividend changes and lagged values of $p_t - d_t$, where p_t is the year average price. We found that lagged log price:dividend ratios had no predictive power for changes in log dividends. However, if the level of log dividends is regressed on lagged log dividends and lagged log average prices, prices have predictive power at the 5-percent (but not the 1-percent) level over 1900–1986.

ditionally. This is true under both the null and alternative hypotheses.

Of course, (B4) assumes that Ω is known. If Ω must be estimated and if η_t is serially uncorrelated, then the expression on the left-hand side of (B4) has an exact t distribution in finite samples. If Ω must be estimated and η_t is serially correlated, then the expression on the left-hand side of (B4) does not have a t distribution in finite samples but will converge to $\mathcal{N}(0,1)$ in distribution as T approaches infinity.

REFERENCES

Barsky, Robert B. and De Long, J. Bradford, "Why Have Stock Prices Fluctuated?" unpublished manuscript, NBER (Cambridge, MA), March 1989.

Black, Fischer, "Noise," *Journal of Finance*, July 1986, *41*, 529–43.

Blanchard, Olivier J. and Watson, Mark W., "Bubbles, Rational Expectations, and Financial Markets," in Paul Wachtel, ed., *Crises in the Economic and Financial Structure*, Lexington, MA: Lexington Books, 1982.

Campbell, John Y., "A Variance Decomposition for Stock Returns," NBER (Cambridge, MA) Working Paper No. 3246, January 1990.

______ **and Kyle, Albert S.,** "Smart Money, Noise Trading and Stock Price Behavior," NBER (Cambridge, MA) Technical Working Paper No. 71, October 1988.

______ **and Shiller, Robert J.,** "Cointegration and Tests of Present Value Models," *Journal of Political Economy*, October 1987, *95*, 1062–88.

______ **and** ______, (1988a) "The Dividend-Price Ratio and Expectations of Future Dividends and Discount Factors," *Review of Financial Studies*, Fall 1988, *1*, 195–228.

______ **and** ______, (1988b) "Stock Prices, Earnings and Expected Dividends," *Journal of Finance*, July 1988, *43*, 661–76.

Cecchetti, Stephen G., Lam, Pok-sang and Mark, Nelson C., "Mean Reversion in Equilibrium Asset Prices," *American Economic Review*, June 1990, *80*, 398–418.

Cochrane, John H., "Explaining the Variance of Price:Dividend Ratios," NBER (Cambridge, MA) Working Paper No. 3157, November 1989.

Cowles, Alfred and Associates, *Common Stock Indexes*, 2nd Ed., Bloomington, IN: Principia Press, 1939.

Cumby, Robert E., Huizinga, John and Obstfeld, Maurice, "Two-Step Two-Stage Least Squares Estimation in Models with Rational Expectations," *Journal of Econometrics*, April 1983, *21*, 333–55.

De Long, J. Bradford, Shleifer, Andrei, Summers, Lawrence H. and Waldmann, Robert J. "The Economic Consequences of Noise Traders," *Journal of Political Economy*, August 1990, *98*, 703–38.

Diba, Behzad T. and Grossman, Herschel I., (1988a) "Explosive Rational Bubbles in Stock Prices?" *American Economic Review*, June 1988, *78*, 520–30.

______ **and** ______, (1988b) "The Theory of Rational Bubbles in Stock Prices," *Economic Journal*, September 1988, *98*, 746–54.

Durlauf, Steven N. and Hall, Robert E., "Determinants of Noise in the Dividend Based Stock Price Model," unpublished manuscript, Stanford University, 1988.

Engle, Robert F. and Watson, Mark W., "Applications of Kalman Filtering in Econometrics," paper presented at World Congress of the Econometric Society, Cambridge, MA, August 1985.

Flavin, Marjorie A., "Excess Volatility in the Financial Markets: A Reassessment of the Empirical Evidence," *Journal of Political Economy*, December 1983, *91*, 929–56.

Flood, Robert P. and Garber, Peter M., "Market Fundamentals versus Price-Level Bubbles: The First Tests," *Journal of Political Economy*, August 1980, *88*, 745–70.

______ **and Hodrick, Robert J.,** "Asset Price Volatility, Bubbles, and Process Switching," *Journal of Finance*, September 1986, *41*, 831–42.

______ **and** ______, "On Testing for Speculative Bubbles," *Journal of Economic Perspectives*, Spring 1990, *4*, 85–101.

______, ______ **and Kaplan, Paul,** "An Evaluation of Recent Evidence on Stock Market Bubbles," NBER (Cambridge, MA)

Working Paper No. 1971, July 1986.

Frankel, Jeffrey A. and Froot, Kenneth A., "The Dollar as an Irrational Speculative Bubble: A Tale of Fundamentalists and Chartists," *Marcus Wallenberg Papers in International Finance*, 1986, *1*, 27–55.

Froot, Kenneth A., "Tests of Excess Forecast Volatility in the Foreign Exchange and Stock Markets," NBER (Cambridge, MA) Working Paper No. 2362, August 1987.

_____ **and Obstfeld, Maurice,** "Stochastic Process Switching: Some Simple Solutions," *Econometrica*, January 1991, *59*, 241–50.

_____, **Scharfstein, David S. and Stein, Jeremy C.,** "Herd on the Street: Informational Inefficiencies in a Market with Short-Term Speculation," NBER (Cambridge, MA) Working Paper No. 3250, February 1990.

Gordon, Myron, *The Investment, Financing, and Valuation of the Corporation*, Homewood, IL: Irwin, 1962.

Gourieroux, Christian, Laffont, Jean-Jacques and Monfort, Alain, "Rational Expectations in Dynamic Linear Models: An Analysis of the Solutions," *Econometrica*, March 1982, *50*, 409–25.

Hamilton, James D. and Whiteman, Charles H., "The Observational Implications of Self-Fulfilling Expectations," *Journal of Monetary Economics*, November 1985, *16*, 353–73.

Kiyotaki, Nobuhiro, "Learning and the Value of the Firm," NBER (Cambridge, MA) Working Paper No. 3480, October 1990.

Kleidon, Allan W., "Variance Bounds Tests and Stock Price Valuation Models," *Journal of Political Economy*, October 1986, *94*, 953–1001.

Krugman, Paul R., "Trigger Strategies and Price Dynamics in Equity and Foreign Exchange Markets," NBER (Cambridge, MA) Working Paper No. 2459, December 1987.

Kyle, Albert S., "Continuous Auctions and Insider Trading," *Econometrica*, November 1985, *53*, 1315–35.

LeRoy, Stephen F. and Porter, Richard D., "The Present-Value Relation: Tests Based on Implied Variance Bounds," *Econometrica*, May 1981, *49*, 555–74.

Lucas, Robert E., Jr., "Asset Prices in an Exchange Economy," *Econometrica*, November 1978, *46*, 1426–46.

Mankiw, N. Gregory, Romer, David and Shapiro, Matthew D., "An Unbiased Reexamination of Stock Market Volatility," *Journal of Finance*, July 1985, *40*, 677–87.

Marsh, Terry A. and Merton, Robert C., "Dividend Variability and Variance Bounds Tests for the Rationality of Stock Market Prices," *American Economic Review*, June 1986, *76*, 483–98.

McCallum, Bennett T., "On Non-uniqueness in Rational Expectations Models: An Attempt at Perspective," *Journal of Monetary Economics*, March 1983, *11*, 139–68.

Newey, Whitney K. and West, Kenneth D., "A Simple, Positive Semi-definite, Heteroskedasticity and Autocorrelation Consistent Covariance Matrix," *Econometrica*, May 1987, *55*, 703–8.

Phillips, Peter C. B., "Time Series Regression with Unit Roots," *Econometrica*, March 1987, *55*, 277–302.

_____ **and Perron, Pierre,** "Testing for a Unit Root in Time Series Regression," *Biometrika*, June 1988, *75*, 335–46.

Pindyck, Robert S., "Risk, Inflation, and the Stock Market," *American Economic Review*, June 1984, *74*, 335–51.

Poterba, James M. and Summers, Lawrence H., "The Persistence and Volatility of Stock Market Fluctuations," *American Economic Review*, December 1986, *76*, 1142–51.

Saracoglu, Rusdu and Sargent, Thomas J., "Seasonality and Portfolio Balance Under Rational Expectations," *Journal of Monetary Economics*, August 1978, *4*, 435–58.

Sargent, Thomas J., *Macroeconomic Theory*, 2nd Ed., Orlando: Academic Press, 1987.

Schwert, G. William, "Tests for Unit Roots: A Monte Carlo Investigation," NBER (Cambridge, MA) Technical Working Paper No. 73, December 1988.

Shiller, Robert J., "Do Stock Prices Move Too Much to be Justified by Subsequent Changes in Dividends?" *American Economic Review*, June 1981, *71*, 421–36.

_____, "Stock Prices and Social Dynamics," *Brookings Papers on Economic Activ-*

ity, 1984, (2), 457–98.

Sims, Christopher A., Stock, James H. and Watson, Mark W., "Inference in Linear Time Series Models with Some Unit Roots," *Econometrica*, January 1990, *58*, 113–44.

Summers, Lawrence H., "Does the Stock Market Rationally Reflect Fundamental Values?" *Journal of Finance*, July 1986, *41*, 591–601.

West, Kenneth D., "A Specification Test for Speculative Bubbles," *Quarterly Journal of Economics*, August 1987, *102*, 553–80.

______, (1988a) "Bubbles, Fads, and Stock Price Volatility Tests: A Partial Evaluation," *Journal of Finance*, July 1988, *43*, 639–55.

______, (1988b) "Asymptotic Normality when Regressors Have a Unit Root," *Econometrica*, November 1988, *56*, 1397–1418.

Whiteman, Charles H., *Linear Rational Expectations Models: A User's Guide*, Minneapolis: University of Minnesota Press, 1983.

[19]

A SPECIFICATION TEST FOR SPECULATIVE BUBBLES*

KENNETH D. WEST

The set of parameters needed to calculate the expected present discounted value of a stream of dividends can be estimated in two ways. One may test for speculative bubbles, or fads, by testing whether the two estimates are the same. When the test is applied to some annual U. S. stock market data, the data usually reject the null hypothesis of no bubbles. The test is of general interest, since it may be applied to a wide class of linear rational expectations models.

I. INTRODUCTION

The seeming tendency for self-fulfilling rumors about potential stock price fluctuations to result in actual stock price movements has long been noted by economists. In a famous passage Keynes, for example, described the stock market as a certain type of beauty contest, in which judges try to guess the winner of the contest: speculators devote their "intelligence to anticipating what average opinion expects average opinion to be" [1964, p. 156]. In recent rational expectations work this possibility has been rigorously formalized, and the self-fulfilling rumors dubbed speculative bubbles [Blanchard and Watson, 1982; Shiller, 1978; Taylor, 1977; Tirole, 1982, 1985]. Recent attempts to detect such bubbles with formal statistical tests have, however, met with mixed success [Blanchard and Watson, 1982; Diba and Grossman, 1984; Flood and Garber 1980; Flood, Garber, and Scott, 1984; Hamilton and Whiteman, 1984].

One possible reason for the inability of the empirical tests to detect the bubbles so often described is that the tests have been few and not very powerful. This paper develops and applies a test for speculative bubbles that (a) allows for a wider class of bubbles than did Flood and Garber [1980] and Flood, Garber, and Scott [1984]; (b) is specifically designed to test against the alternative that bubbles are present, in contrast to the volatility tests of Shiller [1981a, 1981b] and Leroy and Porter [1981]; and (c) may be applied even if prices and dividends are nonstationary, again in contrast to the volatility tests and to the tests in Flood and Garber [1980] and Flood, Garber, and Scott [1984].

*I thank Fischer Black, Whitney Newey, Lawrence Summers, an anonymous referee, and participants in various seminars for helpful comments and discussions, and the National Science Foundation for partial financial support. Responsibility for remaining errors is mine. This paper was revised while I was a National Fellow at the Hoover Institution.

The Quarterly Journal of Economics, August 1987

The basic idea of the present paper's test is very simple and was suggested by the specification test of Hausman [1978]. The test compares two sets of estimates of the parameters needed to calculate the expected present discounted value (PDV) of a given stock's dividend stream, with expectations conditional on current and all past dividends. In a constant discount rate model the two sets are obtained as follows. One set may be obtained simply by regressing the stock price on a suitable set of lagged dividends. The other set may be obtained indirectly from a pair of equations. One of the pair is an arbitrage equation yielding the discount rate, and the other is the ARIMA equation of the dividend process. The Hansen and Sargent [1981] formulas, familiar from rational expectations tests of cross-equation restrictions, may be applied to this pair of equations' coefficients to obtain a second set of estimates of the expected PDV parameters.

Under the null hypothesis that the stock price is set in accord with a standard efficient markets model [Brealey and Myers, 1981, pp. 42–45], the regression coefficients in all equations may be estimated consistently. When the two sets of estimates of the expected PDV parameters are compared, then, they should be the same, apart from sampling error.

But this equality of the two sets will not hold under the alternative hypothesis suggested by, e.g., Blanchard and Watson [1982], that the stock price equals the sum of two components: the price implied by the efficient markets model and a speculative bubble. In this case, the equation that relates price to a suitable set of dividends omits a relevant regressor—the bubble. As long as the bubble is correlated with the included regressors, the coefficients in this equation will be estimated inconsistently. The bubble will not, however, cause estimation of the other two equations to be inconsistent. So the coefficients in this pair of equations, as well as the implied value of the set of expected PDV parameters, will still be estimated consistently. Therefore, when the two estimates of the set of expected PDV parameters are compared, the two will be expected to be different.

Speculative bubbles are tested for, then, by seeing whether the two sets of estimates are the same, apart from sampling error. I check for the equality of the two sets in long-term annual data on the Standard and Poor's 500 index (1871–1980) and the Dow Jones index (1928–1978). The data reject the null hypothesis of no bubbles. The rejection appears to result at least in part because the coefficients in the regression of price on dividends are biased upwards. As is explained in Section II, this is precisely what would be expected if, as is sometimes argued [Shiller, 1984], bubbles reflect an overreaction by the market to news about dividends. A small amount of investigation of a linearized time varying discount rate model suggests that such variation may also help explain the results.

Section II quickly reviews the standard constant discount rate efficient markets model and the definition of a speculative bubble and then explains how the test is performed. Section III presents empirical results from a constant discount rate model and then develops and applies the specification test for a linearized time varying discount rate model. Section IV discusses the empirical results. Some econometric and algebraic details are in an appendix available from the author.

II. The Model and Test

According to a standard efficient markets model, a stock price is determined by the arbitrage relationship (1) [Brealey and Myers, 1981, pp. 42–45]:

$$p_t = bE(p_{t+1} + d_{t+1})|I_t, \tag{1}$$

where p_t is the real stock price in period t, b the constant ex ante real discount rate, $0 < b = 1/(1 + r) < 1$, r the constant expected return, E denotes mathematical expectations, assumed to be equivalent to linear projections, d_{t+1} the real dividend paid to the owner of the stock period $t + 1$, and I_t information common to traders in period t. I_t is assumed to contain, at a minimum, current and past dividends, and, in general, other variables that are useful in forecasting dividends. Time variation in the ex ante discount rate b is briefly considered in subsection III.D.

Equation (1) may be solved recursively forward to get

$$p_t = \sum_{1}^{n} b^i E d_{t+i}|I_t + b^n E p_{t+n}|I_t. \tag{2}$$

If the transversality condition

$$\lim_{n\to\infty} b^n E p_{t+n}|I_t = 0 \tag{3}$$

holds, then $p_t = p_t^*$, where

$$p_t^* = \sum_{1}^{\infty} b^i E d_{t+i}|I_t. \tag{4}$$

Now, the p_t^* defined in (4) is the unique forward solution to (1) as long as the transversality condition (3) holds. But if this condition fails, there is a family of solutions to (1) [Blanchard and Watson, 1982; Shiller, 1978; Taylor, 1977]. Any p_t that satisfies

$$(5) \qquad p_t = p_t^* + c_t, \qquad Ec_t|I_{t-1} = b^{-1}c_{t-1},$$

is also a solution to (1). c_t is by definition a speculative bubble, an otherwise extraneous event that affects stock prices because everyone expects it to do so. An example of a stochastic process for c_t, similar to one described in Blanchard and Watson [1982], is

$$(6) \qquad c_t = \begin{cases} (c_{t-1} - \bar{c})/(\pi_t b) & \text{with probability } \pi_t \\ \bar{c}/[(1 - \pi_t)b] & \text{with probability } 1 - \pi_t \end{cases}$$

$$0 < \pi_t < 1, \qquad \bar{c} > 0.$$

According to (6), strictly positive bubbles grow and pop. In this example, the probability that a bubble grows is π_t, that it collapses is $1 - \pi_t$. The bubble may be intimately connected with fundamentals, with π_t dependent on news about fundamentals. A simple example is $\pi_t = \frac{1}{2}$ for all t, with the bubble popping if and only if the innovation in dividends is negative. If π_t is constant ($\pi_t = \pi$ for all t), each bubble has an expected duration of $(1 - \pi)^{-1}$. (π is not an identifiable parameter.) Combination of several bubbles are possible, each with a different π_t and $\bar{c}$; the growth and collapse of the bubbles may be either tightly or loosely related. See Blanchard and Watson [1982] for further examples and discussion.

Our aim is to test $p_t = p_t^*$ versus $p_t = p_t^* + c_t$, for some nontrivial c_t (possibly one not following the stochastic process (6)). Consider first this wildly implausible case: (a) there is no doubt that p_t and d_t are such that equations (1) and (2) hold. (b) d_t is a zero mean white noise process. Then $Ed_{t+i}|I_t = 0$ for $i > 0$, and $p_t^* = 0$ for all t. It follows from equations (1) to (4), then, that $p_t = 0$ for all t if equation (3) holds: given that the stochastic difference equation (1) is solved in the forward direction (2), the terminal condition (3) insures that (4) is the unique solution to equation (1), for all t. In this blissfully simple environment where (a) there is no doubt about the rational expectations, constant discount rate specification, and (b) no statistical inference is necessary, then (c) the null hypothesis that there are no bubbles should be rejected if $p_t = 0$ for some t.

The basis of the empirical work in this paper is the simple logical proposition illustrated in the previous paragraph: if a univariate stochastic difference equation is solved in the forward direction, a single terminal condition ties down a unique solution. Let us now allow for (a) uncertainty about b and the parameters of the dividend process; (b) the possibility that dividends are an endogenous variable, e.g., because they are smoothed by management; (c) uncertainty about whether the rational expectations, constant discount rate specification (1) really characterizes the data.

(a) Suppose that the actual value of b is not known. In addition, suppose that it is known that dividends follow a zero mean, AR(1) process,

$$d_t = \phi d_{t-1} + v_t. \tag{7}$$

In (7), $|\phi| < 1$, and v_t is a finite variance white noise process. The value of ϕ is not known. It is easy to verify that $\Sigma_1^\infty b^i E d_{t+i}|I_t = \delta_1 d_t$, $\delta_1 = b\phi/(1 - b\phi)$. So if $p_t = p_t^*$,

$$p_t = \delta_1 d_t. \tag{8}$$

The logical proposition described above is applied in this environment by estimating (1), (7), and (8). Equations (7) and (8) may be estimated by OLS, yielding point estimates $\hat{\phi}$ and $\hat{\delta}_1$. Equation (1) may be estimated by rewriting it as

$$\begin{aligned} p_t &= b(p_{t+1} + d_{t+1}) - b[p_{t+1} + d_{t+1} - E(p_{t+1} + d_{t+1}|I_t)] \\ &= b(p_{t+1} + d_{t+1}) + u_{t+1}. \end{aligned} \tag{1'}$$

An instrumental variables estimator, using as instruments variables known at time t—say d_t—will now produce a $\hat{b}$ that is a consistent estimate of b.

To apply the specification test, we compare two estimates of δ_1, the parameter needed to calculate $\Sigma_1^\infty b^i E d_{t+i}|I_t$. That is, we test H_0: $\hat{\delta}_1 = \hat{b}\hat{\phi}/(1 - \hat{b}\hat{\phi})$, and reject the null hypothesis only if the resulting test statistic exceeds an appropriate critical value.

(b) Allowing for endogeneity of dividends [Marsh and Merton, 1984] causes no substantial complications. Let H_t be the set consisting of a constant and current and lagged dividends, $H_t = \{1, d_{t-i}|i \geqq 0\}$. Since H_t is a subset of I_t, equation (4) in conjunction with $p_t = p_t^*$ implies [Hansen and Sargent, 1981] that

$$\begin{aligned} p_t &= \sum_1^\infty b^i E d_{t+i}|H_t + z_t, \\ z_t &= \sum_1^\infty b^i (E d_{t+i}|I_t - E d_{t+i}|H_t), \end{aligned} \tag{9}$$

$$z_t \text{ serially correlated in general,}$$

$$E x_s z_t = 0 \text{ for } x_s \text{ an element of } H_t.$$

To apply the specification test, it is necessary to turn (9) into a regression equation. This can be done conveniently if there is a closed-form expression for $\Sigma_1^\infty b^i Ed_{t+i}|H_t$. Now, $Ed_{t+i}|H_t$ is by definition the forecast of dividends given the past history of dividends. If d_t is stationary, perhaps after differencing, $Ed_{t+i}|H_t$ may be calculated as the usual ARIMA forecast of d_{t+i}. And if d_t is stationary, possibly after differencing, there is a closed-form expression for $\Sigma_1^\infty b^i Ed_{t+i}|H_t$ in the form of a distributed lag on current and past d_t [Hansen and Sargent, 1981]. As in the simple example (7) and (8), the coefficients of the distributed lag are functions of b and the parameters of d_t's univariate ARIMA process. Exact formulas are given in subsection III.A.

When dividends are endogenous and are characterized by an ARIMA process of known order (but unknown parameters), the test can proceed essentially as just described in case (a) above: estimate (1′) by instrumental variables; estimate d_t's univariate ARIMA equation; estimate a distributed lag of p_t on d_t; compare the estimates of the parameters of the distributed lag with those of (1′) and d_t's ARIMA equation. (Actually, if differencing is required to induce stationarity in d_t, it is more convenient to estimate a distributed lag of a difference of p_t on a difference of d_t. See subsection III.A.) So the basic difference from case (a) is that it is acknowledged that d_t's ARIMA equation is simply a convenient way to forecast dividends, and not a statement about the exogeneity of dividends.

It still remains to determine the order of the ARIMA process for d_t. To make the results of as general interest as possible, the empirical work does not assume any particular structural model for dividends. The order of the ARIMA process for d_t is data rather than theoretically determined, in the spirit of the usual Box-Jenkins [1970] analysis. Consistent with such an approach, a variety of ARIMA specifications are tried, to make sure that the results are not sensitive to the exact specification chosen.

It is to be noted that this discussion assumes that arithmetic differencing is sufficient to induce stationarity in d_t. This is because such a condition makes it possible to obtain a closed-form solution to $\Sigma_1^\infty b^i Ed_{t+i}|H_t$. While the usual Box-Jenkins [1970] diagnostics suggest that arithmetic differences suffice to induce stationarity in the data used in this paper (see subsection III.B), much research in finance assumes that log differences are required [Kleidon, 1985]. Since it is also possible to obtain a closed-form expression for $\Sigma_1^\infty b^i Ed_{t+i}|H_t$ when d_t follows a lognormal random walk [Kleidon, 1985], the empirical work (in subsection III.C) briefly considers this specification as well.

(c) Suppose that the specification test described in case (b) indicates that the difference between the two sets of estimates of the parameters needed to calculate $\Sigma_1^\infty b^i Ed_{t+i}|H_t$ is unlikely to result solely from sampling error. Clearly, this can happen for many reasons, in addition to the presence of bubbles.

The possibility that a discrepancy between the two sets of parameter estimates results from certain factors other than bubbles is handled in two ways. In subsection III.D a model with time varying discount rates is linearized as in Shiller [1981a]. It is shown that in such a model one can apply a somewhat more complicated version of the test just described.

The second way that shortcomings of the present value model are considered is by applying diagnostic tests to the estimates of (1′). The diagnostic tests are chosen in light of two alternatives that have figured prominently in related work, that expectations are not rational [Ackley, 1983; Shiller, 1984] and that discount rates are time varying [Leroy, 1984]. The particular tests used are described in Section III. The greater the extent to which these diagnostics suggest that equation (1) is consistent with the data, the more plausible it is to discount expectational irrationality and discount rate variation as significant sources of a discrepancy between the two sets of parameter estimates.

To sum up: the specification test proceeds by estimating (1′), a variety of specifications for the univariate ARIMA process for d_t, and for each such specification, the corresponding distributed lag of p_t on d_t. It applies a battery of diagnostic tests to equation (1′), to see whether equation (1) appears to be consistent with the data. For each specification of the dividend ARIMA process, it applies diagnostics of the sort often used in ARIMA estimation to check whether each specification seems to adequately capture the dynamics of the d_t process. The test then uses each estimate of (1′) and the parameters of the d_t process to calculate an implied value of the parameters that characterize the expected present discounted value of d_t, conditional on current and lagged d_t. It compares these implied values to the estimates directly obtained by a distributed lag regression of p_t on d_t. One possible explanation of any difference between the two sets of estimates is bubbles. This explanation is more compelling, the less likely is the difference to result from sampling error, and the greater the extent to which the diagnostic tests fail to reject (1′) and the specification of the univariate dividend process.

Four final comments are of interest before the empirical work is presented. The first comment concerns how reasonable it is to use the past history of the dividend process to forecast future dividends. It clearly is not reasonable at all in everyone's favorite example of a corporation that has yet to pay out any dividends. It also may not be reasonable if there is a "peso problem" and market participants are rationally considering a small probability event that has not occurred in the sample. There are three points to make. The first is that the best protection against such a problem is to use a long sample period, which is what I did. The second is that certain forms of the peso problem in fact are implicitly allowed under the null, by suitably reinterpreting the parameter b [Shiller, 1981b]. Finally, I tested for the stability of the dividend process; this can detect in-sample switches of the dividend process.

The second concerns the distribution of the estimates of the distributed lag of p_t on d_t when there is a bubble. This is conveniently illustrated when the univariate dividend process is as in (7). Then $p_t = \delta_1 d_t + z_t + c_t$, z_t defined in equation (9). When p_t is regressed on d_t, we have

$$\begin{aligned} \hat{\delta}_1 &= (T^{-1}\Sigma\, d_t^2)^{-1}(T^{-1}\Sigma\, d_t p_t) \\ &= \delta_1 + (T^{-1}\Sigma\, d_t^2)^{-1}(T^{-1}\Sigma\, d_t z_t) + (T^{-1}\Sigma\, d_t^2)^{-1}(T^{-1}\Sigma\, d_t c_t) \\ &\rightarrow p\lim \hat{\delta}_1 = \delta_1 + p\lim\, (T^{-1}\Sigma\, d_t^2)^{-1}(T^{-1}\Sigma\, d_t c_t). \end{aligned} \tag{10}$$

(Recall that $Ed_t z_t = 0$ by construction.) The asymptotic bias in $\hat{\delta}_1$, then, is equal to the asymptotic value of the coefficient of a regression of the bubble on d_t. An additional check on the plausibility of bubbles as the source of any discrepancy of the two estimates of δ_1 comes from looking at the value of the estimate of δ_1 that comes from the regression of p_t on d_t. It is often argued that bubbles result at least in part from an overreaction to news about fundamentals [Shiller, 1984]. If bubbles are present, then, one would expect the point estimate of δ_1 to be biased upwards. More generally, when $\Sigma_1^\infty b^i E d_{t+i}|H_t$ involves more than one lag of d_t, one might expect bubbles to cause the sum of coefficients in the distributed lag projection of p_t onto d_t to be biased upwards.[1]

The third comment is that this test has a substantial advantage over the tests undertaken in Flood and Garber [1980] and Flood,

1. Unfortunately, the discussion in this paragraph cannot, in general, be justified rigorously. In at least certain cases, $T^{-1}\Sigma\, d_t c_t$ will not converge in mean square to a constant. This results from the fact that c_t is growing on average at a rate faster than T^{-1}, i.e., at rate b^{-1}. This is briefly discussed in West [1985], as are the implications of the explosive growth of c_t for the distribution of $\hat{\delta}_1$ under the alternative that bubbles are present.

Garber, and Scott [1984], and that proposed in Sargent and Wallace [1984]. This is that the specification test does not require parametric specification of the bubble process. *Any* bubble that is correlated with dividends can be detected: the bubble described in (6); a bubble as in (6) whose probability of continuing to float π_t depends stochastically on events such as, say, money supply news, or GNP growth, or political events; and combinations of any and all such bubbles.

The fourth comment is that the specification test can be used to test for bubbles in other infinite horizon linear rational expectations models. The idea is to compare two sets of estimates. One set is obtained from the dynamic programming, or equilibrium, solution to the model (i.e., from the model's analogue to equation (12a) or (12b) below). The second set is obtained by applying the relevant Hansen and Sargent [1981] formulas to estimates obtained from two types of equations. The first is the model's Euler equations, or first-order conditions (i.e., the model's analogue to equation (1)). The second is ARIMA equations for the model's forcing variables (i.e., the model's analogue to equation (11a) or (11b) below). The null hypothesis of no bubbles should be rejected only if (a) diagnostic tests on the Euler and ARIMA equations suggest that these equations are acceptably specified, and (b) any difference between the two sets of estimates is unlikely to result from sampling error.

III. Empirical Results

Subsection A describes data and estimation technique. Subsection B presents empirical results. Subsection C extends the specification test to allow for a dividend process that follows a lognormal random walk. Subsection D extends it to test a model that allows discount rates to vary over time.

A. Data and Estimation Technique

The data used were those used by Shiller [1981a] in his study of stock price volatility, and were graciously supplied by him. There were two data sets, both containing annual aggregate price and dividend data. One had the Standard and Poor 500 for 1871–1980 (p_t = price in January divided by producer price index (1979 = 100), d_{t+1} = sum of dividends from that same January to the following December, deflated by the average of that year's producer price index). The other data set was a modified Dow Jones index, 1928–1978 (p_t,d_{t+1}, as above). See Shiller [1981a] for a discussion of the data.

Let me describe the following in turn: (i) identification of the order of d_t's ARIMA process; (ii) estimation of (1′), the d_t process, and the distributed lag of p_t on d_t; (iii) calculation of the variance-covariance matrix of the parameters; (iv) calculation of the basic test statistic; (v) diagnostic tests performed on the equations estimated.

(i) For each data set estimation was done with d_t in levels and with d_t in arithmetic first differences. In each case, only pure autoregressions were estimated, for computational simplicity:

(11a) $$d_{t+1} = \mu + \phi_1 d_t + \ldots + \phi_q d_{t-q+1} + v_{t+1}$$

(11b) $$\Delta d_{t+1} = \mu + \phi_1 \Delta d_t + \ldots + \phi_q \Delta d_{t-q+1} + v_{t+1}.$$

For each data set and for both d_t and Δd_t, two different values of the lag length q were used. One was arbitrarily selected as $q = 4$. The other was selected by the information criterion of Hannan and Quinn [1979]. This criterion chooses the value of q that minimizes a certain function of the estimated parameters, and asymptotically chooses the correct q if the process truly has a finite order autoregressive representation.[2] Thus, for each data set, up to four specifications were estimated: differenced and undifferenced, $q = 4$, and $q =$ lag length selected by the Hannan and Quinn [1979] criterion. In one case (Dow Jones, differenced) the Hannan and Quinn [1979] criterion chose $q = 4$. So for the Dow Jones, only three specifications were estimated.

(ii) If $d_t \sim AR(q)$, as in (11a), then

(12a) $$p_{t+1} = m + \delta_1 d_{t+1} + \ldots \delta_q d_{t-q+2} + w_{t+1}$$

$$m + \delta_1 d_{t+1} + \ldots + \delta_q d_{t-q+2} = \sum_1^\infty b^i E d_{t+i+1} | H_{t+1}$$

$$w_{t+1} = z_{t+1} + c_{t+1}$$

$$z_{t+1} = \sum_1^\infty b^i (E d_{t+i+1} | I_{t+1} - E d_{t+i+1} | H_{t+1}).$$

The formulas linking m and the δ_i, on the one hand, b, μ, and the ϕ_i, on the other, under the null, are given in equation (13a) below.

2. The Hannan and Quinn [1979] procedure selects the q that minimizes

$$\ln \hat{\sigma}_v^2 + T^{-1} 2qk \ln \ln T, \hat{\sigma}_v^2 = T^{-1} \Sigma_{t-1}^T \hat{v}_t^2,$$

for $q < Q$ for some fixed Q, with $k > 1$. I set $Q = 4$, $k = 1.001$.

If $\Delta d_t \sim AR(q)$, as in (11b), then projecting a first difference of $E\Sigma_1^\infty b^i d_{t+i+1}|I_{t+1}$ onto H_t yields

$$\Delta p_{t+1} = m + \delta_1 \Delta d_t + \ldots + \delta_q \Delta d_{t-q+1} + w_{t+1}$$

$$\cdot\ m + \delta_1 \Delta d_t + \ldots + \delta_q \Delta d_{t-q+1}$$

$$= \sum_1^\infty b^i E \Delta d_{t+i+1} | H_t \tag{12b}$$

$$w_{t+1} = z_t + \Delta c_{t+1}$$

$$z_t = \sum_1^\infty b^i (E d_{t+i+1} | I_{t+1} - E d_{t+i} | I_t) - \sum_1^\infty b^i E \Delta d_{t+i+1} | H_t.$$

The z_t variable is dated t rather than $t + 1$ to emphasize that it is orthogonal to H_t but not H_{t+1}. Under the null hypothesis that $c_t = 0$, the disturbances to (12a) and (12b) of course depend only a suitably dated z.

The trivariate system estimated for undifferenced specifications therefore was (1′), (11a), and (12a). For differenced specifications the system estimated was (1′), (11b), and (12b). The discount rate b was estimated from equation (1′) by two-step, two-stage least squares [Hansen, 1982]. The first step was standard two-stage least squares. The second step obtained the optimal, heteroskedasticity consistent estimate. The instruments used were the variables on the right-hand side of the dividend equation (11a) or (11b).

Equations (11a), (11b), (12a), and (12b) were estimated by OLS, with the covariance matrix of the parameters adjusted as described in (iii). Under the null, OLS may be used in (12a) and (12b), since $Ez_{t+1}|H_{t+1} = 0$ in (12a), $Ez_t|H_t = 0$ in (12b).

(iii) For both undifferenced and differenced specifications, the parameter vector estimated was thus $\hat{\theta} = (\hat{b}, \hat{\mu}, \hat{\phi}_1, \ldots, \hat{\phi}_q, \hat{m}, \hat{\delta}_1, \ldots, \hat{\delta}_q)$. $\hat{\theta}$ is asymptotically normal with a $(2q + 3) \times (2q + 3)$ asymptotic variance-covariance matrix V. V was calculated by the methods of Hansen [1982], Newey and West [1986], and West [1986a]. This allows for arbitrary heteroskedasticity conditional on the instruments. It also allows for an *arbitrary* ARMA process for the disturbance to equations (12a) and (12b). An appendix available from the author describes in detail the calculation of V.

(iv) The relationship between the parameters in (12a) and (12b), on the one hand, and b and the parameters of (11a) and (11b), on the other, may be derived in a straightforward fashion from the formulas in Hansen and Sargent [1981]. The corresponding constraints that are implied for stationary specifications are

$$\begin{aligned} 0 &= m - b(1-b)^{-1}\Phi(b)^{-1}\mu \\ 0 &= \delta_1 - [\Phi(b)^{-1} - 1] \\ 0 &= \delta_j - \Phi(b)^{-1}\sum_{k=j}^{q} b^{k-j+1}\Phi_k \qquad j = 2, \ldots, q \\ \Phi(b)^{-1} &= \left[1 - \sum_{i=1}^{q} b^i\phi_i\right]^{-1}. \end{aligned} \tag{13a}$$

The constraints for differenced specifications are

$$\begin{aligned} 0 &= m - [b(1-b)^{-1}\Phi(b)^{-1} + \Phi(b)^{-1} - 1]\mu \\ 0 &= \delta_j - \left\{\Phi(b)^{-1}\sum_{k=j+1}^{q} b^{k-j}\phi_k \right. \\ &\qquad \left. + [\Phi(b)^{-1} - 1]\phi_j\right\} \qquad j = 1, \ldots, q-1 \\ 0 &= \delta_q - [\Phi(b)^{-1} - 1]\phi_q \\ \Phi(b)^{-1} &= \left[1 - \sum_{i=1}^{q} b^i\phi_i\right]^{-1}. \end{aligned} \tag{13b}$$

Let $R(\theta)$ denote either of these $(q + 1) \times 1$ constraints. The null hypothesis is that $R(\theta) = 0$. The test statistic was calculated as

$$R(\hat{\theta})'\left[\left(\frac{\partial R}{\partial \hat{\theta}}\right) V \left(\frac{\partial R}{\partial \hat{\theta}}\right)'\right]^{-1} R(\hat{\theta}). \tag{14}$$

The derivative of $R(\hat{\theta})$ was calculated analytically. Under the null hypothesis, the statistic (14) is asymptotically distributed as a chi-squared random variable with $q + 1$ degrees of freedom.[3]

(v) The final item discussed before results are presented is diagnostic tests on the estimated equations.[4] As explained in the previous section of the paper, a significant value of the test statistic (14) is more compelling as evidence of bubbles the less the extent to which diagnostic tests on (1'), (11a), and (11b) indicate that other source of misspecification are present. Possible sources that have been suggested include failure to allow for expectational irrational-

3. One troublesome aspect of the distribution of the test statistic should be noted. This is that the test may not be consistent: if there are bubbles, the asymptotic probability that the test will reject the null may not be unity, even though the two sets of parameter estimates will be different with probability one in an infinite sized sample. See West [1985] for further discussion.

4. These same diagnostic tests were performed in West [1986c], and the discussion that follows is an abbreviated version of the discussion in section IVA of that paper.

ity [Ackley, 1983] and for time variation in discount rates [Leroy, 1984].

Four diagnostic checks were therefore performed on equations (1′), (11a), and (11b). The first checked for serial correlation in the residuals to the equations, using a pair of tests. Under rational expectations the expectational error u_{t+1} should be serially uncorrelated. If the ARIMA process for d_t is properly specified, so, too, should v_{t+1}, since v_{t+1} is the innovation in the process. The first of the pair of serial correlation tests checked for first-order serial correlation in u_{t+1} and v_{t+1}, using the techniques described in Pagan and Hall [1983, pp. 170, 191]. The second serial correlation test, performed only for v_{t+1}, calculated the Box-Pierce Q statistic for the residuals. This statistic tests for first- and higher order serial correlation [Granger and Newbold, 1977, p. 93].

The second of the four diagnostic checks, performed only on equation (1′), was Hansen's [1982] test of instrument-residual orthogonality. Under the null hypothesis that equation (1) is correctly specified, the test statistic is asymptotically distributed as a chi-squared random variable with q degrees of freedom. This test has the power to detect failures of equation (1) such as expectational irrationality and time variation in discount rates that is correlated with dividends.

The third of the four diagnostic checks tested for the stability of the regression coefficients in (1′), (11a), and (11b). This was done by testing for a midsample shift of the coefficients in these equations. The relevant statistic is asymptotically distributed as a chi-squared random variable, with one degree of freedom for (1′), $q + 1$ degrees of freedom for (11a) and (11b). This test clearly has the power to detect shifts in the discount rate, as well as in the dividend process.

The fourth and final diagnostic check performed is implicit in the estimation procedure described above. Several specifications of the dividend process were used—differenced and undifferenced—with a variety of lag lengths. Since the results did not prove very sensitive to the specification of the dividend process, it appears unlikely that small changes in the specification of the dividend process will affect the results.

B. Empirical Results

Regression results for (1′) are reported in Table IA.[5] The results in Table IA suggest that the basic arbitrage equation (1) is a

5. Tables IA and IB are identical to Tables IA and IB in West [1986c], so the discussion that follows is very similar to the discussion in section IVB of that paper.

TABLE IA
REGRESSION RESULTS: EQUATION (1′)

Data set	(1) Differenced	(2) q	(3) b	(4) ρ	(5) H/sig	(6) Stability/sig
S and P						
1873–1980	no	2[a]	0.9311 (0.0186)	0.0695 (0.0766)	5.50/0.064	4.55/0.033
1874–1980	yes	2[a]	0.9413 (0.0170)	0.0670 (0.0974)	2.87/0.238	0.33/0.566
1875–1980	no	4	0.9315 (0.0158)	0.0661 (0.0754)	6.96/0.138	3.69/0.055
1876–1980	yes	4	0.9449 (0.0136)	0.0671 (0.0984)	3.15/0.533	0.28/0.594
Modified Dow Jones						
1931–1978	no	3[a]	0.9402 (0.0301)	−0.1040 (0.0806)	5.42/0.144	1.56/0.211
1933–1978	yes	4[a]	0.9379 (0.0188)	−0.1182 (0.0752)	5.20/0.267	2.02/0.154
1932–1978	no	4	0.9271 (0.0253)	−0.1112 (0.1493)	6.08/0.108	0.49/0.483

See notes to Table IC.

sensible one. Consider first two diagnostic tests. Column (4) reports the estimates of the first-order serial correlation coefficient of the disturbance to (1′). Since the entries in the column are far from significant at the 0.05 level, there is little evidence of serial correlation in this disturbance. In addition, the entries in column (5), which report the Hansen [1982] test of instrument residual orthogonality, does not reject the null hypothesis of no correlation between the instruments and residuals. The successful results in column (5) are perhaps especially noteworthy, since failures of rational expectations models to pass this test are quite common [Hansen and Singleton, 1982; West, 1986b].

Most important, the discount rate b is estimated plausibly and precisely in all regressions. See column (3) in Table IA. The implied annual real expected returns are a reasonable 6 to 7 percent, and are quite close to the arithmetic means for ex post returns: 8.1 percent for the Standard and Poor's (S and P) index (1872–1981) and 7.4 percent for the Dow Jones index (1929–1979). Moreover, the entries in column (6) give little evidence that the rate was different in the two halves of either sample. The only specification for which the null hypothesis of equality can be rejected at the 5 percent level is Standard and Poor's, undifferenced, $q = 2$. In addition, no evidence

TABLE IB
REGRESSION RESULTS: EQUATIONS (12a) AND (12b)

Data set	(1) Differenced	(2) q	(3) μ	(4) ϕ_1	(5) ϕ_2	(6) ϕ_3	(7) ϕ_4	(8) ρ	(9) Q/sig	(10) Stability/ sig
S and P										
1873–1980	no	2[a]	0.168	1.0196	−0.238			0.045	36.87/0.181	12.93/0.005
			(0.084)	(0.114)	(0.103)			(0.025)		
1874–1980	yes	2[a]	0.034	0.262	−0.214			0.002	22.79/0.824	2.71/0.438
			(0.029)	(0.118)	(0.071)			(0.023)		
1875–1980	no	4	0.150	1.247	−0.480	0.227	−0.029	0.001	21.39/0.875	33.49/0.000
			(0.080)	(0.116)	(0.093)	(0.113)	(0.066)	(0.010)		
1876–1980	yes	4	0.036	0.264	−0.230	0.026	−0.006	0.001	23.98/0.773	4.34/0.501
			(0.031)	(0.115)	(0.094)	(0.080)	(0.153)	(0.011)		
Modified Dow Jones										
1931–1978	no	3[a]	1.945	1.265	−0.664	0.333		0.002	4.05/1.000	7.53/0.111
			(1.037)	(0.112)	(0.108)	(0.098)		(0.054)		
1933–1978	yes	4[a]	0.275	0.302	−0.351	0.051	0.050	−0.024	9.77/0.939	8.06/0.153
			(0.405)	(0.119)	(0.133)	(0.093)	(0.176)	(0.067)		
1932–1978	no	4	1.925	1.263	−0.662	0.330	0.004	0.005	4.06/1.000	10.22/0.069
			(1.900)	(0.111)	(0.203)	(0.209)	(0.134)	(0.022)		

See notes to Table IC.

against the constancy of the discount rate may be found in a comparison of the two halves' mean ex post returns. For the S and P index, these were (in percent) 8.09 (1872–1926) versus 8.12 (1927–1981); for the Dow Jones the figures are 7.87 (1929–1954) versus 6.92 (1955–1979).

The specification of the arbitrage equation (1), then, appears acceptable. Let us now consider the estimates for the dividend process, reported in Table IB. The entries in columns (8) and (9) indicate little evidence of serial correlation in the disturbance to equations (11a) and (11b). Both test statistics in all regressions are far from significant, except for the estimate of the first-order serial correlation coefficient $\hat{\rho}$ for the S and P index, undifferenced, lag length $q = 2$. This regression's Q statistic in column (9) does, however, comfortably accept the null hypothesis of no serial correlation. Overall, then, no serial correlation to the residuals to (11a) and (11b) is apparent. Also, the estimates of most regression coefficients are statistically significant, at least when the lag length q was chosen by the Hannan and Quinn [1979] procedure. Finally, the null hypothesis that the parameters of the dividend process are the same in the two halves of each sample can be rejected at the 5 percent level only for the S and P index, undifferenced. See column (10). In general, then, the specification of the dividend process seems acceptable, with the possible exception of the S and P data set, undifferenced.

Estimates of the third and final equation, (12a) or (12b), are in Table IC. Parameter estimates are fairly precise for undifferenced specifications, less so for differenced specifications.

In contrast to the coefficients of the other two equations, however, the estimates of the coefficients of equations (12a) and (12b) are probably not sensible from the point of view of the simple efficient markets model that says $p_t = \Sigma_1^\infty b^i E d_{t+i} | I_t$. For the estimates of these coefficients are uniformly incompatible with the estimates of the coefficients of the other two equations. The test of whether these estimates are in fact compatible—that is, the test of the null hypothesis that bubbles are absent—may be found in Table II. Equation (14) is calculated in column (4). Every specification but those for the S and P, differenced, rejects the null at any conventional significance level. One of the S and P differenced specifications rejects the null at the 5 percent level, the other at the 10 percent level.

It appears that the reason for the rejection is that the coefficients on dividends in the present value equations (12a) and (12b)

TABLE IC
REGRESSION RESULTS: EQUATIONS (13a) AND (13b)

Data set	(1) Differenced	(2) q	(3) $\hat{m}$	(4) $\hat{\delta}_1$	(5) $\hat{\delta}_2$	(6) $\hat{\delta}_3$	(7) $\hat{\delta}_4$
S and P							
1873–1980	no	2^a	−24.28	31.152	−2.053		
			(11.42)	(6.331)	(4.118)		
1874–1980	yes	2^a	0.79	−4.792	3.632		
			(1.51)	(2.842)	(2.205)		
1875–1980	no	4	−25.52	33.671	−14.257	11.029	−0.910
			(11.78)	(6.967)	(5.684)	(3.971)	(3.423)
1876–1980	yes	4	0.76	−5.099	4.436	−1.850	2.219
			(1.61)	(3.353)	(1.998)	(4.367)	(3.481)
Modified Dow Jones							
1931–1978	no	3^a	−286.78	35.706	−22.869	19.866	
			(99.11)	(8.432)	(8.549)	(3.880)	
1933–1978	yes	4^a	3.93	−10.438	9.213	−1.855	4.846
			(19.06)	(3.531)	(3.345)	(6.241)	(5.280)
1932–1978	no	4	−272.15	35.607	−21.639	20.015	−1.588
			(100.43)	(9.682)	(10.540)	(8.504)	(7.324)

Notes. A superscript a means lag length q chosen by Hannan and Quinn [1979] procedure. Asymptotic standard errors in parentheses. Symbols q, b, μ, ϕ_i, m, δ_i are defined in equations (1), (11a), (11b), (12a) and (12b). ρ = first order serial correlation coefficient of disturbance; H = Hansen's [1982] test of instrument-residual orthogonality, $H \sim \chi^2(q)$; "stability" is test for stability of coefficients, as described in text, distributed as $\chi^2(1)$ in Table IA and $\chi^2(q+1)$ in Table IB; Q is Box-Pierce Q statistic, $Q \sim \chi^2(30)$ for S and P, $Q \sim \chi^2(18)$ for Dow Jones. For the "H," "stability," and "Q" columns, "sig" refers to the probability of seeing the statistic under the null hypothesis.

TABLE II
TEST STATISTICS

Data set	(1) Differenced	(2) q	(3) Degrees of freedom	(4) Equation (14)/sig[b]
S and P				
1873–1980	no	2[a]	3	32.59/0.000
1874–1980	yes	2[a]	3	7.41/0.060
1875–1980	no	4	5	23.92/0.000
1876–1980	yes	4	5	11.40/0.044
Modified Dow Jones				
1931–1978	no	3[a]	4	45.12/0.000
1933–1978	yes	4[a]	5	19.93/0.001
1932–1978	no	4	5	40.22/0.000

a. Lag length q chosen by Hannan and Quinn [1979] procedure.
b. "Sig" refers to the probability of seeing the statistic under the null hypothesis.

are biased upwards. In six of the seven specifications, the sum of the biases in the $\hat{\delta}_i$ (not reported in any table) are positive. (The only exception is the S and P, differenced, $q = 2$.) Now, for undifferenced specifications, if there is a bubble, the bias in the estimate of the vector $(m,\delta_1, \ldots, \delta_q)$ is the probability limit of the vector of estimates of the parameters of a regression of the bubble c_{t+1} on a constant and $d_{t+1}, \ldots, d_{t-q+2}$. (See equation (10).) If bubbles reflect at least in part a tendency of the market to overreact to dividends or to news about future dividends [Shiller, 1984], this upward bias is precisely what would be expected. For differenced specifications the asymptotic bias in the estimate of the vector $(m,\delta_1, \ldots, \delta_q)$ is the probability limit of estimates of the parameters in a regression of the bubble on a constant and $\Delta d_{t+1}, \ldots, \Delta d_{t-q+1}$. If changes in bubbles tend to be associated with changes in lags of dividends, the $\hat{\delta}_i$ will also tend to be biased upward for differenced specifications.[6]

C. Dividends Follow a Lognormal Random Walk

The diagnostic tests discussed in the previous section found little fault with the specifications of the d_t process. Much research in finance, however, assumes that logarithmic and not arithmetic differences are necessary to induce stationarity in dividends [Kleidon, 1985]. As noted in Section II, it is possible to obtain a closed-form solution for $\Sigma_1^\infty b^i E d_{t+i} | H_t$ when $\Delta(\log d_t)$ is an iid

6. As noted in West [1985], the limiting distribution of the regression of c_t on dividends may not in general be a single vector. The statements in this paragraph therefore should be interpreted with caution.

normal random variable. This section applies the specification test, when d_t follows this lognormal random walk.

Suppose that $\Delta(\log d_t) \sim N(\mu,\sigma^2)$. Let $H_t = \{d_{t-i} | i \geq 0\}$. Then $\Sigma_1^\infty b^i E d_{t+i} | H_t = \delta_1 d_t$, $\delta_1 = \exp(\mu + \sigma^2/2)/[b^{-1} - \exp(\mu + \sigma^2/2)]$ [Kleidon, 1985, p. 21]. Our aim is to compare an estimate of δ_1 obtained by regressing p_t on d_t with that obtained from estimates of μ, σ^2, and b. For each of the two data sets, μ and σ^2 were obtained as (a) the sample mean and variance of $\Delta(\log d_t)$, and (b) $\mu = 0$, $\sigma^2 = T^{-1}\Sigma(\Delta \log d_t)^2$. ($T$ = sample size.) Case (b), which imposes $\mu = 0$ and calculates the variance conditional on this, was tried because the point estimate of μ in each data set was insignificantly different from zero. b^{-1} was set equal to the mean ex post return. A convenient way to test the null hypothesis is to note that the formula for δ_1 implies that

$$(15) \qquad \sigma^2 = 2 \log \{(1/b)[\delta_1/(1 + \delta_1)]\} - 2\mu.$$

Since $\Delta(\log d_t) \sim N(\mu,\sigma^2)$, $\hat{\sigma}^2 \sim \chi^2(T)$ when $\mu = 0$ is imposed, $\hat{\sigma}^2 \sim \chi^2(T - 1)$ when μ is estimated. It is straightforward to construct a 99 percent confidence interval around $\hat{\sigma}^2$, as described in Mood et al. [1974, p. 382]. We can then check whether the point estimates of b^{-1}, δ_1, and μ are such that the right-hand side of (15) falls in this confidence interval. Note that such a procedure ignores sampling uncertainty in the estimates of b^{-1}, δ_1, and μ. One reason I am nonetheless applying this procedure is that the usual asymptotic theory does not apply to the regression that produces $\hat{\delta}_1$.

The empirical results are in Table III. The first line for each

TABLE III
EMPIRICAL RESULTS, LOGNORMAL RANDOM WALK

Data set	(2) $\hat{\sigma}^2$	(2) 99% CI	(3) RHS of (15)	(4) $(1/\hat{b})$	(5) $\hat{\delta}_1$	(6) $\hat{\mu}$	(7) $\hat{\rho}$
S and P	0.016	(0.012, 0.026)	0.045	1.081	23.19	0.013	0.176
1872–1980						(0.012)	(0.095)
			0.071			0.0	
Dow Jones	0.024	(0.015, 0.043)	0.043	1.074	23.44	0.008	0.236
1929–1978						(0.021)	(0.137)
			0.059				
						0.0	

Notes. Symbols σ^2, $1/b$, δ_1 defined above equation (15); π defined below equation (15).

The "99% CI" column gives the lower and upper bounds of a 99 percent confidence interval around the entry in column (1). These are calculated for a χ^2 (100) random variable for the S and P (sample size - 109), for a χ^2 (50) random variable for the Dow Jones (sample size - 50), as described in Mood et al. [1974, p. 382].

In column (3), "RHS of (15)" means "right-hand side of equation (15)."

The numbers in parentheses in column 6 are standard errors; in column 7 are asymptotic standard errors.

data set uses the mean of $\Delta(\log d_t)$ for μ, the second imposes $\mu = 0$. Only one point estimate of $\hat{\sigma}^2$ is reported for each data set, since $\hat{\sigma}^2$ was the same to three decimal places whether or not $\mu = 0$ was imposed. The lower and upper bounds for the 99 percent confidence interval are reported in column (2). The mean ex post return for each data set is in column four. The OLS estimate of δ_1 that results from regressing p_t on d_t is in column five. (It may help as a point of reference to state that the mean p_t/d_t ratio for the S and P is 21.05, for the Dow Jones is 22.24.) Column six has the sample mean of $\Delta(\log d_t)$, or zero. Note that for both data sets, the sample mean is insignificantly different from zero, at any conventional significance level. Column (7) has the point estimate of ρ, the first-order serial correlation coefficient of the residual. For both data sets, the estimate is insignificantly different from zero at the 10 percent level, but not at the 5 percent level. Column (3) has the right-hand side of equation (15), calculated from the figures in columns (4) to (6). The numbers in this column are all on or above the upper end of the 99 percent confidence interval for $\hat{\sigma}^2$, reported in column (2).

Apparently, the point estimates of the right-hand side of (15) are too big, or those of the left-hand side of (15) too small, for the data to have been generated by a constant discount rate, lognormal random walk model, without bubbles. This is consistent with the subsection III.B results: one interpretation is that $\hat{\delta}_1$, the coefficient that results when p_t is projected onto d_t, is too big for $p_t = p_t^*$ to be correct. Another interpretation, consistent not only with the earlier results in this paper but of those in a companion paper as well [West, 1986c], is that σ^2, the variance of the innovation in the univariate dividend process, is too small.

It does not, however, seem wise to push either of these arguments too far. One reason is that the simple lognormal random walk specification may not adequately capture the dynamics of the d_t process. The figures in column (7) of Table III suggest some residual serial correlation. A second reason is that the figures in Table III do not really indicate a rejection of the model at the 99 percent level, since sampling uncertainty in the estimates of b^{-1}, δ_1, and μ is ignored. One way to emphasize that this is a practical and not just pedantic point is to consider the effects of column (3) of different values of b^{-1}. Suppose that $b^{-1} = 1.05$, a value within two standard deviations of the point estimates in Table IA. Then all four column (3) estimates would not only fall below the upper end of the 99 percent confidence interval in column (2), but would all be below the point estimate of $\hat{\sigma}^2$ in column (1).

In sum, the, the lognormal specification provides mild evidence against the null that $p_t = p_t^*$, versus $p_t = p_t^* + c_t$.

D. Time Varying Discount Rates

Time variation in discount rates can be allowed under the null, if, as in Shiller [1981a], the model is still linear. Let r_{t+j} be the one-period return expected by the market at period $t + j - 1$. Let $p_t^* = E\{\Sigma_{i=1}^{\infty} [\Pi_{j=1}^{i} (1 + r_{t+j})^{-1}] d_{t+i}\} | I_t$. Under the null hypothesis of no bubbles, $p_t = p_t^*$. Let us linearize p_t^* around $\bar{r}$ and $\bar{d}$; selection of $\bar{r}$ and $\bar{d}$ is discussed below. Define $\bar{b} = (1 + \bar{r})^{-1}$, $\bar{a} = -\bar{d}/\bar{r}$. Then [Shiller, 1981a]

$$p_t^* \approx E\{\Sigma_{i=1}^{\infty} \bar{b}^i [\bar{a}(r_{t+i} - \bar{r}) + d_{t+i}]\} | I_t = \text{(say) } E\{\Sigma_{i=1}^{\infty} \bar{b}^i y_{t+i}\} | I_t.$$

The arbitrage equation corresponding to the null hypothesis that $p_t \approx E\{\Sigma_{i=1}^{\infty} \bar{b}^i [\bar{a}(r_{t+i} - \bar{r}) + d_{t+i}]\} | I_t$ is

$$\text{(16)} \quad p_t \approx \bar{b} E(y_{t+1} + p_{t+1}) | I_t = \bar{b} E[\bar{a}(r_{t+1} - \bar{r}) + d_{t+1} + p_{t+1}] | I_t.$$

As before, solutions to (16) are of the form $p_t = E\{\Sigma_{i=1}^{\infty} \bar{b}^i y_{t+i}\} | I_t + c_t$ for any c_t that satisfies $Ec_t | I_{t-1} = \bar{b}^{-1} c_t$. The null hypothesis we wish to test is that $c_t = 0$.

This can be done by comparing two sets of estimates of expected present discounted values, with expectations conditional on the set of current and past dividends. Now, however, the variable being forecast is not just d_{t+i} but y_{t+i}. This will not involve an arbitrage equation; it will involve dividend and distributed lag equations, as before, and also a new equation, for forecasting expected returns using current and lagged dividends. A brief discussion follows. Algebraic details are available on request.

The linearization parameters, $\bar{r}$, $\bar{b}$, and $\bar{a}$ were chosen as certain simple, plausible functions of the data. For both differenced and undifferenced specifications, the point of linearization for expected returns was the mean ex post return, $\bar{r} = T^{-1}\Sigma [(p_{t+1} + d_{t+1})/p_t] - 1$. Then $\bar{b} = (1 + \bar{r})^{-1}$. When dividends were assumed stationary, the point of linearization for $\bar{d}$ was mean dividends: $\bar{d} = T^{-1}\Sigma\, d_t$. When dividends were assumed to require (arithmetic) differences to induce stationarity, the point was $\bar{d} = (1 - \bar{b})\Sigma_{t=1}^{\infty} \bar{b}^{t-1} E_0 d_t$, $E_0 d_t = E_0 d_0 + tE\Delta d_t$, d_0 a presample value of dividends. Thus, $\bar{d} = d_0 + E\Delta d_t/(1 - \bar{b})$. Note that if dividends are stationary ($E\Delta d_t = 0$) and $d_0 = Ed_t$, this reduces to linearizing around mean dividends. For both differenced and undifferenced specifications, $\bar{a}$ was calculated as $\bar{a} = -\bar{d}/\bar{r}$. See Table IV for the resulting values of $\bar{r}$, $\bar{b}$, $\bar{d}$, and $\bar{a}$.

TABLE IV
LINEARIZATION PARAMETERS

Sample Period	(1) Differenced	(2) $\bar{r}$	(3) $\bar{b}$	(4) $\bar{d}$	(5) $\bar{a}$
1901–1981	no	0.0792	0.9266	4.0054	−50.56
1902–1981	yes	0.0772	0.9283	3.1441	−40.72

The dividend equation is precisely that used in the constant discount rate case, in subsection III.B.

For undifferenced specifications the distributed lag equation was obtained by projecting $E\Sigma\,\bar{b}^i y_{t+i+1}|I_{t+1}$ onto the space of current and lagged dividends H_{t+1}, as in equation (12a). For differenced specifications a difference of $E\Sigma\,\bar{b}^i y_{t+i+1}|I_{t+1}$ was projected onto H_t, as in equation (12b).

The final relationship involved is a regression to forecast expected returns. Let $R_{t+j} = (p_{t+j} + d_{t+j})/p_{t+j-1}$ denote the ex post return. Note that since H_t is a subset of I_t, $R_{t+j} = r_{t+j} + \nu_{t+j}$, with ν_{t+j} orthogonal to H_t. So $ER_{t+j}|H_t = Er_{t+j}|H_t$: a regression to forecast ex post returns also forecasts expected returns. The regressions are

$$(17a) \qquad R_{t+1} = g + \gamma_0 d_t + \ldots \gamma_n d_{t-n} + \eta_t$$

$$(17b) \qquad R_{t+1} = g + \gamma_0 \Delta d_t + \ldots \gamma_n \Delta d_{t-n} + \eta_t$$

η_t serially correlated in general, $Ex_s\eta_t = 0$ for x_s an element of H_t.

One can use (17a) to solve for $E\bar{b}^i[\bar{a}(R_{t+i} - \bar{r})]|H_t$. As before, the dividend equation (11a) yields $E\bar{b}^i d_{t+i}|H_t$. Together these produce the $E\Sigma\,\bar{b}^i y_{t+i+1}|H_{t+1}$. Similarly, (17b) and (11b) yield the distributed lag equation in differenced specifications.

For computational simplicity, the specification test was performed conditional on $\bar{a}$, $\bar{r}$, $\bar{b}$, and the parameters of equations (17a) and (17b). It may be shown that the parameters of the distributed lag equation can be estimated from the regressions

$$(18a) \qquad \tilde{p}_{t+1} = m + \delta_1 d_{t+1} + \ldots + \delta_q d_{t-q+2} + \tilde{w}_{t+1}$$

$$(18b) \qquad \Delta\tilde{p}_{t+1} = m + \delta_1 \Delta d_t + \ldots + \delta_q \Delta d_{t-q+1} + \tilde{w}_{t+1}.$$

The left-hand side variables $\tilde{p}_{t+1}$ and $\Delta\tilde{p}_{t+1}$ are calculated from p_{t+1} and Δp_{t+1}, and lags of d_t and Δd_t, using $\bar{a}$, $\bar{b}$, and the estimates of the parameters of (17a) and (17b). The δ_1 are functions of $\bar{b}$ and the parameters of the dividend process, as written out in equations (13a) and (13b). If the γ_i in equations (17a) and (17b) are identically zero, then $\tilde{p}_{t+1} = p_{t+1}$, $\Delta\tilde{p}_{t+1} = \Delta p_{t+1}$: if the return that is expected conditional on past dividends is constant, the test in this section reduces to that in subsection III.B.

The length of the distributed lag of ex post returns on dividends was set to 30, as in Shiller [1984, Table I]. This was done because OLS standard errors suggested insignificant γ_i for both the Dow Jones and the S and P for a lag length of ten years. Because of degrees of freedom limitations resulting from the thirty-year lag, the test in this section was applied only to the S and P. An unconstrained lag was used, since both γ_0 and the sum of the γ_i were estimated more precisely with this lag than with Shiller's [1984] polynomial distributed lag.

The regression of returns on dividends is reported in Table VA. In contrast to the results of the previous section, some predictability of returns is suggested. γ_0, the coefficient on d_t or Δd_t, was significantly different from zero at the 95 percent level. So, too, was the sum of the other distributed lag coefficients. See columns (3) and (4). The significance of the coefficients is, however, probably somewhat overstated, since, as explained above, some experimentation was done to obtain a specification with significant coefficients.

Table VB has estimates of the dividend equations. These look quite similar to those in Table IB. Table VC has estimates of the distributed lag equations (18a) and (18b). Note that the coefficients are woefully insignificant for differenced specifications.

Results of the test of the null hypothesis of no bubbles are reported in Table VI. The null is strongly rejected for undifferenced specifications, not at all for differenced specifications. The sum of the biases of the $\hat{\delta}_i$ was positive for all specifications except differenced, lag length = 4.

It is rather disturbing that allowing for time varying discount rates yields stronger evidence against the model for undifferenced specifications, weaker evidence for differenced specifications. One possible explanation is that the equation (17) forecasts of future

TABLE VA
REGRESSION RESULTS: EQUATIONS (17a) AND (17b)

Sample period	(2) Differenced	(2) $\hat{g}$	(3) $\hat{\gamma}_0$	(4) $\Sigma_{i=1}^{29} \hat{\gamma}_i$	(5) d.w.
1901–1980	no	0.0623	−0.1560	0.1893	1.93
		(0.0891)	(0.0585)	(0.0693)	
1902–1980	yes	0.1456	−0.1470	−1.2790	1.92
		(0.0349)	(0.0592)	(0.5938)	

TABLE VB
REGRESSION RESULTS: EQUATIONS (12a) AND (12b)

Sample period	(1) Differenced	(2) q	(3) $\hat{\mu}$	(4) $\hat{\phi}_1$	(5) $\hat{\phi}_2$	(6) $\hat{\phi}_3$	(7) $\hat{\phi}_4$
1901–1980	no	2	0.295	1.185	−0.253		
			(0.132)	(0.123)	(0.108)		
1902–1980	yes	2	0.033	0.265	−0.221		
			(0.039)	(0.129)	(0.073)		
1901–1980	no	4	0.266	1.241	−0.500	0.244	−0.046
			(0.124)	(0.124)	(0.099)	(0.116)	(0.070)
1902–1980	yes	4	0.034	0.270	−0.235	0.027	−0.041
			(0.040)	(0.153)	(0.099)	(0.086)	(0.168)

TABLE VC
REGRESSION RESULTS: EQUATIONS (18a) AND (18b)

Sample period	(1) Differenced	(2) q	(3) $\hat{m}$	(4) $\hat{\delta}_1$	(5) $\hat{\delta}_2$	(6) $\hat{\delta}_3$	(7) $\hat{\delta}_4$
1901–1980	no	2	6.39	11.969	4.427		
			(5.63)	(1.418)	(1.778)		
1902–1980	yes	2	0.59	−1.168	0.659		
			(0.58)	(0.844)	(0.713)		
1901–1980	no	4	4.03	13.110	−3.007	1.980	5.047
			(5.27)	(2.086)	(2.356)	(1.423)	(1.932)
1902–1980	yes	4	0.58	−1.129	−0.645	0.147	0.171
			(0.58)	(1.030)	(0.575)	(1.534)	(0.943)

Notes: Asymptotic standard errors in parentheses.
Symbols: q = lag length of dividend autoregression (12a) and (12b); $\bar{r}$, $\bar{b}$, $\bar{d}$, and $\bar{a}$ are defined above equation (16); μ, ϕ_i, g, γ_i, m, and δ_i are defined in equations (12a), (12b), (17a), (17b), (18a), and (18b); *d.w.* is the Durbin-Watson statistic.

TABLE VI
TEST STATISTICS

Sample period	Differenced	q	Degrees of freedom	Equation (14) sig
1901–1980	no	2	3	33.72/0.000
1902–1980	yes	2	3	2.00/0.572
1901–1980	no	4	5	30.86/0.000
1902–1980	yes	4	5	2.67/0.750

See Notes to Table II.

expected returns are quite noisy, and very different from the market's actual expected returns. The fitted values from equation (17a) could then be spuriously leading to a rejection for undifferenced specification, or conversely, those from (17b) could be incorrectly suggesting little evidence against the model for differenced specifications. A priority for future research, then, is performing similar tests with a more tightly constrained parameterization of what determines expected returns. The evidence in this section does little to pin down the extent to which the rejections in the constant discount rate model are due to variations in discount rates.

IV. Discussion and Conclusions

This section contains some concluding comments on the previous section's results. The first comment to make is that any diagnostic tests of (1′) will clearly have arbitrarily small power against "near rational" bubbles that are arbitrarily close to being rational. This is, if $p_t = p_t^* + c_t$, and $Ec_t|I_{t-1} = k^{-1}c_{t-1}$ for some k that is very close to b, diagnostic tests on equation (1′) may well fail to reject equation (1′). Summers [1986] calculated the small sample power of tests similar (though not identical) to those performed in subsection III.B, and, unsurprisingly, found that such tests are unlikely to detect variations in expected returns caused by near rational bubbles.

The presence of near rational bubbles certainly means that equation (1) is, strictly speaking, invalid. This fact does not, however, seem to me to be of great importance for the interpretation or implications of the results of Section III. A near rational bubble that tends to generate nearly constant expected returns will tend to generate nearly the same time series pattern of prices as will a rational bubble. That the tests in subsection III.B have little power to distinguish between such a bubble and a strictly rational one is not, then, very important for the interpretation of the evidence presented in Section III, at least at the level of generality of this paper.

The second comment to make concerns what determines whether a constant expected return specification is a good approximation for the purposes of the specification test. The subsection III.D analysis of a linearized model with time variation in expected returns suggests that the key requirement is not near constancy of returns expected by the market, but near constancy of the return that is expected conditional on the past history of dividends. In the linearized model, $Ep_t^*|H_t = \bar{a}\Sigma_{i=1}^{\infty}\bar{b}^iE(r_{t+i} - \bar{r})|H_t + \Sigma_{i=1}^{\infty}\bar{b}^iEd_{t+1}|H_t$. In that model, then, $Ep_t^*|H_t = \Sigma_{i=1}^{\infty}\bar{b}^iEd_{t+i}|H_t$ not only when $r_{t+i} = \bar{r}$ but also when $Er_{t+i}|H_t = \bar{r}$ for $i > 0$, i.e., when past dividends do not help predict future expected returns. Intuitively, if only past dividends are used to forecast the expected present discounted value of future dividends, and variations in expected returns are independent of past dividends, it is reasonable to forecast expected returns to be at their unconditional mean and to discount future dividends at a constant rate. This statement holds in a strict mathematical sense in a linearized model, and therefore may hold approximately in the underlying nonlinear model.

An implication is that most of the mild evidence against the constant expected return specification in Shiller [1981a, 1984] and all of the somewhat stronger evidence in Flood, Hodrick, and Kaplan [1986] may well not be directly relevant to the interpretation of the results of this paper.[7] It is, of course, of interest to investigate further whether, for the purposes of the specification test, it is adequate as an approximation to consider only variations in expected returns that are predictable from the past history of dividends, and the extent to which such variations explain what seems to be anomalous behavior in the data. This is an important task for future research.

What is required is a reconciliation of what appear to be incompatible price and dividend data. The incompatibility is manifested in an upward bias in the estimates of the coefficients of the projection of prices onto lagged dividends. A reconciliation that involves a parametric model for bubbles, or fads, and which allows for variation in expected returns, is a challenging task for future research.

PRINCETON UNIVERSITY

REFERENCES

Ackley, Gardner, "Commodities and Capital: Prices and Quantities," *American Economic Review,* LXXIII (1983), 1–16.

Blanchard, Olivier, and Mark Watson, "Bubbles, Rational Expectations and Financial Markets," NBER Working Paper No. 945, 1982.

7. Using the same data as in this paper, Shiller [1981a, 1984] and Flood, Hodrick, and Kaplan [1986] obtain coefficients significant at the 5 percent level when the ex post return is regressed on certain sets of lagged prices, dividend-price ratios, and ex post returns. Shiller [1984] also obtains significant coefficients using lagged earnings.

Box, G. E. P., and G. M. Jenkins, *Time Series Analysis: Forecasting and Control* (San Francisco, CA: Holden Day, 1976).

Brealey, Richard, and Stewart Myers, *Principles of Corporate Finance* (New York, NY: McGraw Hill, 1981).

Diba, Behzad T., and Herschel I. Grossman, "Rational Bubbles in the Price of Gold," NBER Working Paper No. 1300, 1984.

Flood, Robert P., and Peter M. Garber, "Market Fundamentals versus Price Level Bubbles: The First Tests," *Journal of Political Economy*, LXXXVIII (1980), 745–70.

——, ——, and Louis O. Scott, "Multi-Country Tests for Price Level Bubbles," *Journal of Economic Dynamics and Control*, VIII (1984), 329–40.

Flood, Robert P., Robert Hodrick, and Paul Kaplan, "An Evaluation of Recent Evidence on Stock Market Bubbles," manuscript, 1986.

Granger, C. W. J., and Paul Newbold, *Forecasting Economic Time Series* (New York, NY: Academic Press, 1977).

Hamilton, James D., and Charles M. Whiteman, "The Observable Implications of Self-Fulfilling Prophecies," manuscript, 1984.

Hannan, E. J., and B. G. Quinn, "The Determination of the Order of an Autoregression, *Journal of the Royal Statistical Society Series B*, XLI (1979), 190–95.

Hansen, Lars Peter, "Large Sample Properties of Generalized Method of Moments Estimators," *Econometrica*, L (1982), 1029–54.

Hansen, Lars Peter, and Thomas J. Sargent, "Formulating and Estimating Dynamic Linear Rational Expectations Models," in Robert E. Lucas, Jr., and Thomas J. Sargent, eds., *Rational Expectations and Econometric Practice* (Minneapolis, MN: University of Minnesota Press, 1981, pp. 91–126.

Hansen, Lars Peter, and Kenneth Singleton, "Generalized Instrumental Variables Estimation of Nonlinear Rational Expectations Models," *Econometrica*, L (1982), 1269–86.

Hausman, Jerry A., "Specification Tests in Econometrics," *Econometrica*, XLVI (1978), 1251–71.

Keynes, John Maynard, *The General Theory of Employment, Interest and Money* (New York NY: Harcourt, Brace and World, 1964).

Kleidon, Allan W., "Variance Bounds Tests and Stock Price Valuation Models," Stanford University Graduate School of Business Research Paper No. 806, 1985.

Leroy, Stephen, "Efficiency and Variability of Asset Prices," *American Economic Review*, LXXIV (1984), 183–87.

——, and Richard Porter, "The Present Value Relation: Tests Based on Implied Variance Bounds," *Econometrica*, LXIX (1981), 555–574.

Marsh, Terry A., and Robert C. Merton, "Dividend Variability and Variance Bounds Tests for the Rationality of Stock Market Prices," Sloan School of Management Working Paper No. 1584–84, 1984.

Mood, Alexander M., Franklin A. Graybill, and Duane C. Boes, *Introduction to the Theory of Statistics* (New York, NY: McGraw Hill, 1974).

Newey, Whitney K., and Kenneth D. West, "A Simple, Positive, Semidefinite, Heteroskedasticity and Autocorrelation Consistent Covariance Matrix," forthcoming, *Econometrica*, 1986.

Pagan, A. R., and A. D. Hall, "Diagnostic Tests as Residual Analysis," *Econometric Reviews*, II (1983), 159–218.

Sargent, Thomas J., and Neil Wallace, "Identification and Estimation of a Model of Hyperinflation with a Continuum of 'Sunspot' Equilibria," manuscript, 1984.

Shiller, Robert J., "Rational Expectations and the Dynamic Structure of Macro Models," *Journal of Monetary Economics*, IV (1978), 1–44.

——, "Do Stock Prices Move Too Much to be Justified by Subsequent Changes in Dividends?" *American Economic Review*, LXXI (1981a), 421–36.

——, "The Use of Volatility Measures in Assessing Market Efficiency," *Journal of Finance*, XXXV (1981b), 291–304.

——, "Stock Prices and Social Dynamics," *Brookings Papers on Economic Activity* (1984), 457–98.

Summers, Lawrence H., "Does the Stock Market Rationally Reflect Fundamental Values," *Journal of Finance*, XXXX (1986), 591–601.

Taylor, John B., "On the Conditions for Uniqueness in the Solution of Rational Expectations Models," *Econometrica*, XLV (1977), 1377–85.

Tirole, Jean, "Asset Bubbles and Overlapping Generations," *Econometrica,* LIII (1985), 1071–1100.

West, Kenneth D., "A Specification Test for Speculative Bubbles," Princeton University Financial Research Memorandum No. 58, 1985.

——, "Asymptotic Normality, When Regressors Have a Unit Root," Princeton University Woodrow Wilson School Discussion Paper No. 110, 1986a.

——, "A Variance Bounds Test of the Linear Quadratic Inventory Model," *Journal of Political Economy,* XCIII (1986b), 374–401.

——, "Dividend Innovations and Stock Price Variability," NBER Working Paper No. 1833, 1986c.

THE JOURNAL OF FINANCE • VOL. XLIII, NO. 3 • JULY 1988

Bubbles, Fads and Stock Price Volatility Tests: A Partial Evaluation

KENNETH D. WEST*

ABSTRACT

This is a summary and interpretation of some of the literature on stock price volatility that was stimulated by Leroy and Porter [28] and Shiller [40]. It appears that neither small-sample bias, rational bubbles nor some standard models for expected returns adequately explain stock price volatility. This suggests a role for some nonstandard models for expected returns. One possibility is a "fads" model in which noise trading by naive investors is important. At present, however, there is little direct evidence that such fads play a significant role in stock price determination.

NEARLY SEVEN YEARS HAVE passed since the publication of the original LeRoy and Porter [28] and Shiller [40] volatility tests. The number of papers analyzing or developing volatility tests on stock prices has now grown to the point that a nonspecialist may have trouble getting even a general sense of the current state of the volatility debate. This paper is intended to help such a nonspecialist, by summarizing and interpreting the literature.

Section I summarizes the techniques and conclusions of some volatility tests that assume constant expected returns. Section II considers whether small-sample bias is likely to explain the excess price volatility found in most of the studies summarized in Section I. The presence of near or actual unit-root nonstationarity in stock prices certainly causes substantial small-sample bias in the test in Shiller [40], and quite possibly in other studies that assume stationarity. Subsequent studies that explicitly allow for unit roots find excess volatility that is typically an order of magnitude smaller than for studies that assume stationarity—but they do still tend to find substantial excess volatility. While not much is known on small-sample bias in tests that allow for unit roots, it does not seem that such bias explains the persistent finding of excess volatility. Indeed, I present a little evidence that certain tests that do *not* find excess volatility have poor small-sample power against interesting alternatives.

The rest of the paper proceeds under the tentative conclusion that stock prices are more volatile than can be explained by a standard constant-expected-return model. Section III considers explaining the excess volatility by adding to the usual constant-expected-return stock price an explosive rational bubble (Blanchard and Watson [3], West [52]). For a variety of theoretical and empirical reasons, this does not seem to produce a satisfactory explanation.

* Princeton University. This paper was prepared for an AEA/AFA meeting on "The Volatility Debate," December 28, 1987. I thank Ben Bernanke and John Campbell for helpful comments and discussions and the National Science Foundation for financial support.

If bubbles are ruled out, so that any deviations from the constant-expected-return stock price are transitory, these deviations will give rise to predictable variations in returns. Section IV considers whether stock price volatility is adequately explained by some standard models for expected returns. The evidence here is somewhat limited, but the answer appears to be no (Campbell and Shiller [7], West [53]). This seems to be true at least in part because such models do not generate sufficient variability in expected returns.

This suggests that it might be useful to consider some nonstandard models for what determines expected returns. Section V interprets "fads" models as arguing that trading by naive investors creates nondiversifiable risk that sophisticated investors must take into account (Campbell and Kyle [5], DeLong et al. [11], Shiller [43]). It follows that an appropriate model for expected returns will reflect such trading. The fads literature is, however, rather new, and has yet to model risk as precisely as have the traditional models discussed in Section IV. There is little direct evidence that trading by naive investors plays a substantial role in stock price determination. Such evidence as there is in favor of fads is largely indirect, and consists of negative verdicts on traditional present-value models. One would prefer a parametric model, so that the model potentially could be rejected because of implausible parameter estimates or painfully large test statistics.

I conclude that the most important direction for future research on stock price volatility is therefore not still more volatility tests, but development of parametric models to explain the excess volatility that some, including me, believe to be reasonably well established. My own sense is that consideration of fads is likely to be productive. But someone skeptical about fads models could reasonably conjecture that any such models will be in as much conflict with the data as are traditional present-value models, and that refinements of these latter models are a more promising avenue for research.

Before turning to a detailed discussion, it is well to remind the reader that this is a partial evaluation of volatility tests, in two senses. First, space constraints preclude detailed discussion of many relevant issues. I give relatively short shrift to some of the topics covered in detail in the survey paper of Gilles and LeRoy [20], which focuses on potential problems with Shiller's [40] test, and of Camerer [4], which discusses in detail how imperfect aggregation of information can lead to seeming excess volatility of stock prices. Second, as a participant in this literature, I am hardly unbiased. While I have attempted to represent all points of view, I have of course emphasized those that I find most compelling.

I. Overview of Empirical Results

Table I summarizes the results of some volatility tests that assume constant ex ante returns. To make this task manageable, I have limited myself to empirical results that in my somewhat arbitrary opinion could be cast in the form V/V^*, where V measures the volatility of the market's forecast of fundamentals, V^* the volatility of the econometrician's measure of fundamentals, and $V/V^* > 1$ indicates excess volatility. This means that while most of the papers cited below

Table I
Volatility Tests, Constant Expected Return

(1) Author	(2) Sample	(3) V/V^*	(4) p-value	(5) unit root?
A. Asymptotically valid under stationarity:				
(1) Blanchard and Watson [3]	annual, 1871–1979	72	.00	no
(2) Kleidon [25]	$T = 100$	25	.05–.50	logarithmic
(3) Leroy and Porter [28]	quarterly, 1955–73	16–148	.01–.50	no
(4) Shiller [40]	annual, 1871–1979, 1928–1979	31–176	n.a.	no
(5) Shiller [45]	$T = 100$	25	.00–.01	logarithmic
B. Asymptotically valid with unit arithmetic roots:				
(6) Campbell and Shiller [6]	annual, 1871–1985	1–67	.00–.50	arithmetic
(7) Mankiw et al. [32]	annual, 1871–1984	0–12	n.a.	arithmetic
(8) West [53]	annual, 1871–1980, 1929–1979	5–10	.00–.01	arithmetic
	$T = 100$	5	.05	arithmetic
	$T = 100$	5	.05	logarithmic
C. Asymptotically valid with unit logarithmic roots:				
(9) Campbell and Shiller [7]	annual, 1871–1986, 1926–1986	2–14	.00	logarithmic
(10) Kleidon [25]	annual, 1926–1979	0–1	.50	logarithmic
(11) Leroy and Parke [27]	annual, 1871–1983	0	n.a.	logarithmic
(12) Shiller [42]	annual, 1871–1979	2	.01	logarithmic

Notes: A column (2) entry of "T = sample size" indicates a Monte Carlo study rather than an empirical point estimate. In column (3), entries were rounded down to zero if $V/V^* < 1$, but otherwise were rounded to the nearest integer. See the text for how V/V^* is calculated for a given entry. Entries in column (4) were rounded as follows: .00 means that the reported p-value is less than .005; .01, between .005 and .01; .05, between .01 and .05; .10, between .05 and .10; .50, greater than .10.

test a number of implications of the model being studied, I will consider only those tests that seem to me to be similar in spirit to the original LeRoy and Porter [28] and Shiller [40] comparison of the variance of a stock price (V) to that of a certain function of dividends (V^*). My sense is that my self-imposed restriction probably selects from the studies cited below the *less* rather than the more striking evidence; the equality tests in LeRoy and Porter [28] and Mankiw et al. [32], for example, yield sharper results than do the inequality tests reported below. Analyses that supply neither new empirical nor Monte Carlo estimates (e.g., Marsh and Merton [33]) are ignored in this section but will be discussed later.

To facilitate the discussion below of whether inappropriate accounting for unit-root nonstationarity explains the results of the volatility tests, the papers in Table I are grouped according to whether the test is asymptotically valid only under stationarity, with a unit arithmetic root (ΔP_t stationary), or with a unit logarithmic root ($\Delta \log(P_t)$ stationary). Listings within each group are alphabetical. In Table I, column (2) gives the sample period. Most of the studies use Shiller's [40] long-term annual data, which splices Cowles Commission data beginning in 1871 to more recent data from the Standard and Poor's Composite

Stock Price Index. For convenience I will refer to this as simply the S&P data. Shiller [40] and West [53] also use the Shiller's modified Dow-Jones. Campbell and Shiller [7] also use the New York Stock Exchange equal- and value-weighted indices. With the exception of LeRoy and Porter, all the studies cited in the Table use annual data, in part to avoid dealing with seasonality in dividends. See the cited papers for additional detail on the data.

Column (3) reports the empirical value of V/V^*, calculated for a given paper as described below. The p-value in column (4) gives the probability of seeing the column (3) value for V/V^*, under the null that the model is equation (4) below and unit roots, if any, take the form indicated in column (5). For Monte Carlo studies, indicated by "T = sample size" in column (2), the V/V^* value is not the median but instead matches an estimated empirical value.

A brief discussion of the models and tests now follows. This may be skipped by readers familiar with this literature. This is intended to suggest the basic ideas involved, but not to spell out the precise details. I will slur over inconsequential differences between the models and tests described below and those in the papers cited (e.g., whether current dividends are known when price is set). Some authors have reported asymptotic p-values for test statistics other than V/V^* (e.g., West [53] reports the p-value for H_0: $V^* - V \geq 0$, for V^* and V defined below). In such cases, I have felt free to associate those p-values with V/V^*, even though the statistic for V/V^* would of course be numerically different. Detailed references to the sources of the entries in Table I may be found in the Appendix.

The constant-expected-return model supposes

$$P_t = b\mathrm{E}(P_{t+1} + D_t \mid I_t), \tag{1}$$

where P_t is a real stock price, b a constant discount rate, $b = 1/(1 + r)$, r is the constant real expected return, $\mathrm{E}(\cdot \mid I_t)$ is mathematical expectation conditional on the market's period-t information set I_t, and D_t is the real dividend on the stock. I_t is assumed to contain, at a minimum, current and past P_t and D_t. Substituting recursively for P_{t+1}, P_{t+2}, etc., and using the law of iterated expectations, gives

$$P_t = \mathrm{E}(\textstyle\sum_0^{n-1} b^{j+1}D_{t+j} + b^n P_{t+n} \mid I_t) \equiv \mathrm{E}(P^*_{t,n} \mid I_t). \tag{2}$$

Suppose that the terminal condition

$$\lim_{n\to\infty}\mathrm{E}(b^n P_{t+n} \mid I_t) = 0 \tag{3}$$

holds (this rules out rational bubbles, as explained below). Then (2) implies

$$P_t = \mathrm{E}(\textstyle\sum_0^{\infty} b^{j+1}D_{t+j} \mid I_t) \equiv \mathrm{E}(P^*_t \mid I_t), \tag{4}$$

where P^*_t is used rather than $P^*_{t,\infty}$ to match Shiller [40]. Since P_t is the conditional expectation of P^*_t,

$$\mathrm{var}(P_t)/\mathrm{var}(P^*_t) \leq 1, \tag{5}$$

if the unconditional variances exist. LeRoy and Porter [28] and Shiller [40] estimate (5), using different techniques to calculate the ratio. Kleidon [25] and

Shiller [45] use Monte Carlo methods to determine the finite-sample behavior of (5) when $\log(D_t)$ follows a random walk and I_t consists solely of lagged dividends. These studies are summarized in lines (2) to (5) of Table I, with V/V^* an estimate of the left-hand side of (5).

The Blanchard and Watson [3] test, in line (1), compares variances of innovations rather than levels. Let $H_t \equiv \{D_t, D_{t-1}, \cdots\}$ be the information set determined by current and lagged dividends; H_t is a subset of I_t. Let $P_{tH} \equiv \mathrm{E}(\sum_0^\infty b^{j+1} D_{t+j} \mid H_t) \equiv \mathrm{E}(P_t^* \mid H_t)$. Then since more information tends to lead to more precise forecasts (West [53]),

$$\{\mathrm{E}[P_t - \mathrm{E}(P_t \mid I_{t-1})]^2 / \mathrm{E}[P_{tH} - \mathrm{E}(P_{tH} \mid H_{t-1})]^2\} \leq 1. \tag{6}$$

The left-hand side of (6), which Blanchard and Watson [3] calculate assuming stationarity of dividends, is reported as V/V^* in line 1.

One of the major problems of the initial volatility tests, emphasized in particular by Kleidon [25] and Marsh and Merton [33], was of course the assumption that variables do not have unit roots. Lines (6) to (8) of Table I summarize some tests that are appropriate if the nonstationarity results from a unit arithmetic root. In such a case, the model (4) implies that P_t and D_t are cointegrated (Engle and Granger [13]), and $P_t - b(1-b)^{-1}D_t$ is stationary (Campbell and Shiller [6]). Basically, a unit arithmetic root causes a linear (but not exponential) stochastic trend in dividends and prices, so subtracting a suitable multiple of D_t from P_t removes this linear trend in P_t and leaves a stationary random variable. Mankiw et al. [32] show that as a result

$$\{\mathrm{E}[P_t - b(1-b)^{-1}D_t]^2 / \mathrm{E}[P_{t,n}^* - b(1-b)^{-1}D_t]^2\} \leq 1 \tag{7}$$

for any finite n, with $P_{t,n}^*$ defined in (2). The V/V^* reported in line (7) results when $n = T - t$, T the last period in the sample.

Campbell and Shiller [6] (line (8)) calculate statistics similar to (6) and (7), expanding H_t to include lagged P_t and D_t. West [53] calculates (6), with H_t defined as in Blanchard and Watson [3] to consist of just lagged dividends, but allows for unit arithmetic roots.

Lines (9) to (12) in Table I report studies that have accounted for nonstationarity by allowing for unit logarithmic roots. Kleidon [25] and Shiller [42] both assume that $\log(D_t)$ follows a random walk, with I_t consisting of only lagged dividends. The model implies that P_t is proportional to D_t, so that

$$\mathrm{var}(P_t/P_{t-1}) / \mathrm{var}(D_t/D_{t-1}) = 1. \tag{8}$$

Kleidon notes that the model (4) also implies that for finite n

$$\{\mathrm{var}(P_{t+n}/P_t) / \mathrm{var}(P_{t+n}^*/P_t)\} \leq 1. \tag{9}$$

Estimates of the ratios in (8) and (9) are reported in lines (12) and (10).

LeRoy and Parke [27] also assume that $\log(D_t)$ follows a random walk. By the logic used to develop (5) above, the model (4) implies

$$\{\mathrm{var}(P_t/D_t) / \mathrm{var}(P_t^*/D_t)\} \leq 1. \tag{10}$$

Line (11) reports this ratio, calculated assuming that P_t/D_t follows an AR(1) process.

Campbell and Shiller [7] work with a linearized logarithmic version of (4), assuming stationarity of the log dividend price ratio and log differences of dividends and prices. Line (9) reports estimates of

$$\text{var}[\log(D_t/P_t)]/\text{var}\{[\log(D_t/P_t)]_H\}, \quad (11)$$

where $\log[(D_t/P_t)]_H$ is the variance of the log dividend price ratio when the ratio is calculated as a forecast from an information set H_t consisting of lagged $\log(D_t/P_t)$ and $\Delta\log(D_t)$.

II. Small-Sample Bias

The initial tests, in lines (1), (3) and (4) of Table I, found extreme excess volatility, with the variance of stock prices or their innovations exceeding a theoretical upper bound by orders of magnitude. The statistical significance of the excess volatility was, however, unclear. For example, LeRoy and Porter [28], using the asymptotic distribution, found a violation significant at the five percent level in only one of their four data sets. As is evident from a glance at the estimates of V/V^* for lines (6) on, allowing for unit roots results in considerably smaller estimates of excess volatility. It seems that these initial tests tend to find spuriously large estimates, at least if unit roots are present.

For the Shiller [40] technique for calculating $V/V^* \equiv \text{var}(P_t)/\text{var}(P_t^*)$, reasons for this are developed in Flavin [16], Kleidon [23, 25] and Mankiw et al. [32]. Assume first that P_t and D_t are stationary, so that the population variances of P_t and P_t^* exist. Even though V/V^* can be estimated consistently, Shiller's [40] procedure tends to produce finite-sample estimates that are spuriously high, with the bias likely to be quite pronounced for the relevant sample sizes. Kleidon [23] (pp. 20–21), for example, reports a simulation with a sample size of 100 in which the population value of V/V^* is .81 but the mean estimated value is 2.2. The Marsh and Merton [33] nonstationary example in which the sample estimate $\text{var}(P_t)/\text{var}(P_t^*)$ is greater than one with probability one, for any size sample, might be interpreted as simply a nonstationary limiting case of the biases noted by Flavin [16] and Kleidon [23] (Mankiw et al. [32]).[1]

While the logic of Flavin [16] and Kleidon [23] does not apply directly to the Blanchard and Watson [3] or LeRoy and Porter [28] tests, the dramatic fall in V/V^* when unit roots are allowed suggests that similar arguments are likely to be relevant for those tests. Indeed, the Monte Carlo simulations in Mattey and Meese [35] indicate that the Blanchard and Watson [3] procedure will tend to spuriously find $V/V^* > 1$ if unit roots are present but, as in Blanchard and Watson [3] (but not West [53]), are not imposed. Similarly, Gilles and LeRoy [20] (p. 64), seem to concede that biases similar to those in Shiller [40] are probably present in LeRoy and Porter [28].

This leaves open the question of whether these biases are so large as to explain the entire excess of V over V^* reported in the various tests in Table I. Whether they even totally explain the Shiller [40] results is debatable. Shiller [45] argues that Kleidon's simulation results (line (2)) are very sensitive to the assumed

[1] See Gilles and LeRoy [20] for an excellent exposition.

dividend/price ratio. Kleidon allows a range for this ratio of about 1.5 percent (p-value of $V/V^* \approx .50$) to about 4 percent (p-value $\approx .05$). If the empirical mean dividend/price ratio of about 5 percent is used, the p-value suggested by Kleidon's simulation falls to .01 (line (5)).

While another iteration of the Kleidon-Shiller debate may well suggest that the p-value of .01 is too low, it seems to me unlikely that small-sample biases will suffice to overturn the conclusion that stock prices move more relative to dividends than is consistent with the model (4). I conclude this for two reasons. First, while there is some conflict among the papers summarized in Table I, there often are differences in assumptions and approach that suggest why some tests find excess volatility while others do not. These differences usually seem to me to argue for the plausibility of the tests that find excess volatility. Specifically, the "1" and "0" entries in rows (6) and (7) tend to result when expected returns of less than 4 percent are assumed. Expected returns closer to the actual sample mean of about 8 percent result in the larger, and statistically more significant, figures in these rows. More importantly, as documented below, the Kleidon (line (10)) and LeRoy and Parke (line (11)) tests, which stand out from the other entries in the Table for finding little or no excess volatility, appear to have poor power against a Shiller [43] "fads" alternative (see Gilles and LeRoy [20] (p. 45)). Since it is just such an alternative that has been proposed as an explanation of the results of other volatility tests (Shiller [43]), the Kleidon (line (10)) and LeRoy and Parke (line (11)) results are not persuasive evidence that the results of other tests are misleading.

The second reason I think it unlikely that small-sample biases will overturn the finding of excess volatility is that the other tests in Table I that allow for unit roots do tend to find violations of the relevant variance bounds. While these violations typically are an order of magnitude smaller than those of the initial tests, they still are numerically large. Since these tests directly allow the (near or actual) nonstationarity that probably is central to the small-sample problems with papers in panel A, there does not seem to me to be a reason to suppose any particular bias. In fact, while there is of course some small-sample bias in these tests (Mattey and Meese [35], West [51, 53]), the evidence on this does not suggest that such bias explains the excess volatility that those tests tend to find. See the entries for West [53] in Table I.

The rest of this section contains a small study of the power of the Kleidon (line (10)) and LeRoy and Parke (line (11)) tests against a Shiller [43] "fads" alternative, or, more generally, any alternative that generates slowly decaying deviations of stock prices from the constant-expected-return price determined by (4). Suppose that

$$\log(D_t) = \mu + \log(D_{t-1}) + \varepsilon_t, \tag{12a}$$

$$\log(P_t) = \tau + \log(D_t) + a_t, \tag{12b}$$

$$a_t = \phi a_{t-1} + v_t, \tag{12c}$$

where

$$|\phi| < 1, \quad \varepsilon_t \sim \mathrm{N}(0, \sigma_\varepsilon^2), \quad v_t \sim \mathrm{N}(0, \sigma_v^2), \quad \mathrm{E}\varepsilon_t v_s = 0 \quad \text{for all } t, s.$$

Equation (12a) says that dividends follow a logarithmic random walk, as in Kleidon [25] and LeRoy and Parke [27]. Equations (12b) and (12c) say that the mean log price/dividend ratio τ is perturbed by the stationary AR(1) random variable a_t. The Kleidon [25] setup is a special case of (12) with $a_t \equiv 0$. In the spirit of O'Brien [37], Shiller [43] and Summers [48], one can interpret a_t as a "fad" that drives the stock price away from the value that would result if the data were generated by a model consisting of (4) and (12a).[2]

The S&P data (1871–1985) were used to calculate point estimates of the parameters in (12). The numbers at the foot of Table II result when μ and σ_ϵ^2 were set to the mean and sample variance of $\Delta \log(D_t)$, τ to the sample mean of $\log(P_t) - \log(D_t)$, $\sigma_a^2 \equiv \text{var}(a_t)$ to the sample variance of $\log(P_t) - \log(D_t)$, ϕ to the sample estimate of $\text{cov}(a_t, a_{t-1})/\sigma_a^2$ and $\sigma_v^2 \equiv (1 - \phi^2)\sigma_a^2$. There are several ways to emphasize that with these parameter estimates, the data generated by (12) are rather different from those generated by a model with constant expected returns and a lognormal random-walk dividend process. First, a shock to a_t that pushes $\log(P_t) - \log(D_t)$ from its mean has a half life of nearly four years ($\phi^4 = .83^4 = .48$). In the sense suggested by Summers [48], this can be argued to be a significant deviation from the constant dividend/price ratio predicted by Kleidon's [25] model. Second, more than half (57 percent, to be exact) of the implied variance of $\Delta \log(P_t)$ is due to shocks to a_t rather than to $\log(D_t)$. Third, the implied standard deviation of the one-period expected return $E[(P_{t+1} + D_t)/P_t \mid I_t]$ is quite substantial, about .05.[3] (The implied unconditional mean return is about 1.08.) For any or all of these reasons, one would hope that a volatility test would distinguish between data generated by (12) on the one hand and (4) and (12a) on the other.

Consider first the LeRoy and Parke test. Computing $\text{var}(P_t/D_t)/\text{var}(P_t^*/D_t)$ requires estimates of just four moments: the mean ex post return, the variance of P_t/D_t and the mean and variance of D_t/D_{t-1} (LeRoy and Parke [27]). But with the parameters listed at the bottom of Table II, data generated by (12) will imply essentially the V/V^* computed by the LeRoy and Parke [27] test, since such data imply essentially these four sample moments. See Table II, panel A. A finding of $V/V^* < 1$ using the LeRoy and Parke [27] test therefore does not in general distinguish the model (4) from the alternative (12).[4]

[2] As emphasized in Section V below, other interpretations are possible. To prevent misunderstanding, I should note that I am not proposing to take (12) as a serious model of stock prices, or even as an adequate characterization of the S&P data: Table 4a in Campbell and Shiller [7] indicates that the assumption that $\Delta \log(D_t)$ and $\log(P_t) - \log(D_t)$ are independent is false. I am merely using (12) to get a quick idea of whether the LeRoy and Parke [27] and Kleidon [25] tests have power against the alternative that there are slow-moving divergences of stock prices from a constant-expected-return fundamental value.

[3] Sketch of algebra: Let I_t consist of past ϵ_t and v_t. Since P_{t+1}/P_t and D_t/P_t are lognormal, and a_t and $\log(P_t) - \log(D_t)$ are independent, it is straightforward to show that $E[(P_{t+1} + D_t)/P_t \mid I_t] = \exp[\mu + (\phi - 1)a_t + .5(\sigma_\epsilon^2 + \sigma_v^2)] + \exp[-\tau - a_t]$. The expected return is thus the sum of two lognormal random variables, and one can grind through standard formulas to compute its variance.

[4] My estimate of V/V^* is considerably higher than that of LeRoy and Parke [27], even though data are quite similar. This is basically because the LeRoy and Parke method of calculating $\text{var}(P_t^*/D_t)$ is very sensitive to the estimated value of the following: [mean expected return]$^{-1}$ × [mean value of D_{t+1}/D_t]. They compute this to be .9548, I get .9427. Were I to use the .9548 figure, V/V^* would fall from .63 to .38, much closer to LeRoy and Parke's estimate of .29.

Table II

Power Against Mean-Reverting Fad

A. Leroy and Parke [27]

	Estimate from S&P	Estimate Implied by Alternative
V/V^*	.63	.63

B. Kleidon [25]

n	Estimate of V/V^* from S&P	Monte Carlo Estimates: Median	Monte Carlo Estimates: Prob $V/V^* > 1$
1	.34	.40	.006
2	.69	.77	.303
5	1.66	1.43	.781
10	4.18	1.90	.920

The alternative data-generating process is (12), with: $\mu = .012$, $\sigma_\epsilon = .1244$, $\tau = 3.0$, $\phi = .83$, $\sigma_v = .1347$. One thousand samples were drawn to generate the Monte Carlo estimates in panel B. Additional details are in the text.

Evaluation of the power of the Kleidon [25] test seems to require a Monte Carlo experiment. The simulation generated 1000 samples of size 115, with the presample values of $\log(P_t)$ and $\log(D_t)$ matched to those of the S&P data in 1871, and the presample value of a_t drawn from its unconditional distribution (with a different draw for each simulation). P_t^* was generated recursively, as in Kleidon [25]. The sample estimates of $\text{var}(P_{t+n}/P_t)$ and $\text{var}(P_{t+n}^*/P_t)$ were calculated in the usual way. As stated in Table I, panel B, the median estimates of $\text{var}(P_{t+n}/P_t)/\text{var}(P_{t+n}^*/P_t) \equiv V/V^*$ were less than 1 for $n = 1, 2$, more for $n = 5, 10$. The question is whether the small values for $n = 1$ and 2 are comforting evidence concerning a model consisting of (4) and (12a). The answer appears to be no. In the Monte Carlo simulations for $n = 1$, for example, only 6 of the 1000 samples produced a V/V^* greater than 1. It appears, then, that Kleidon's [25] test, like LeRoy's and Parke's [27], has poor power against this alternative.[5]

I certainly do not consider this a definitive statement on the power of the various tests in Table I, and fully agree with LeRoy and Parke [27] that additional study of the power of volatility tests is of great interest. Nor do I consider the question of small-sample bias completely resolved. Nonetheless, for the reasons summarized above, it seems unlikely to me that small-sample bias provides the bulk of the explanation for the excess volatility reported in Table I.[6]

[5] My estimates of V/V^* are notably bigger then Kleidon's [25] for $n = 5, 10$. Two minor reasons are choice of discount rate (I use the inverse of the mean ex post return, Kleidon tries various imposed values) and sample period. The major reason is that Kleidon calculates $\text{var}(P_{t+n}/P_t)$ and $\text{var}(P_{t+n}^*/P_t)$ by taking the sum of squared deviations not around the respective sample means but, for both, around an estimate of $E(P_{t+n}/P_t)$. If I had mimicked his procedure, the Table II value of V/V^* for $n = 10$, for example, would be 1.80 rather than 4.18. Because the sample means of P_{t+10}/P_t and P_{t+10}^*/P_t are rather different, Kleidon's technique sharply raises the estimate of $\text{var}(P_{t+10}^*/P_t)$ and thus sharply lowers the estimate of V/V^*. Although Kleidon's technique is appropriate under his null, it clearly results in substantial bias under the present alternative.

[6] I should note that the Marsh and Merton [33] dividend-smoothing argument seems to me to be one of small-sample bias induced by inappropriate treatment of unit roots, as suggested above. Marsh and Merton [33] (p. 485), however, seem to suggest that a desire of managers to smooth dividends by itself invalidates volatility comparisons. This is not correct. A key to the validity of the variance-bounds methodology is a stable set of decision rules by market participants, and a sample large

III. Rational Bubbles

Stochastic difference equations such as (1) have a multiplicity of solutions. The solution (4) is unique provided that the terminal condition (3) holds. But if not, there are an infinity of solutions

$$P_t = \mathrm{E}(\sum b^{j+1} D_{t+j} \mid I_t) + C_t$$
$$\equiv P_t^f + C_t. \tag{13}$$

C_t is any variable that satisfies $\mathrm{E}(C_t \mid I_{t-1}) = b^{-1}C_{t-1} \equiv (1 + r)C_{t-1}$, i.e., $C_t = (1 + r)C_{t-1} + V_t, \mathrm{E}(V_t \mid I_{t-1}) = 0$. C_t is by definition a rational bubble, an otherwise extraneous event that affects stock prices because everyone expects it to do so.[7] Since the solution (13) satisfies the first-order condition (1), expected returns are constant and there are no arbitrage possibilities. (Rational bubbles are possible with time-varying expected returns. See Flood and Hodrick [17]. I use a constant-expected-return model for simplicity.) The "f" superscript on P_t^f is present because P_t^f depends only on fundamentals.

Blanchard and Watson [3] note that it is possible to have bubbles that grow and pop. The following example of a strictly positive bubble is from West [52]:

$$C_t = \begin{matrix} (C_{t-1} - C^*)/\pi b & \text{with probability } \pi \\ C^*/[(1 - \pi)b] & \text{with probability } 1 - \pi \end{matrix} \tag{14}$$

where $0 < \pi < 1$, $C^* > 0$.

The bubble bursts with probability $1 - \pi$, and has an expected duration of $(1 - \pi)^{-1}$. While the bubble floats it grows at rate $(b\pi)^{-1} = (1 + r)/\pi > 1 + r$: investors receive an extraordinary return to compensate them for the capital loss that would have occurred had the bubble burst. Whether or not the bubble bursts can depend on fundamentals (e.g., $\pi = ½$, with the bubble bursting if there is bad news about budget deficits). Alternatively, whether the bubble bursts or not can depend on extraneous "sunspots." It is possible to have a composite bubble, consisting of a linear combination of bubbles like (14), with each (14) bubble having its own π and C^*. Also, π can vary over time (West [52]).

Rational bubbles therefore seem consistent with the recent (1987) pattern of extraordinary stock price increases followed by a dramatic collapse. Rational bubbles also seem a potential rationalization of excess-volatility tests. Even if the bubble is uncorrelated with fundamentals, stock prices move more than the model (4) predicts; if this correlation is positive, so that the market overreacts to news about fundamentals (Shiller [43], DeBondt and Thaler [9]), excessive stock price movements are even easier to rationalize. Moreover, this can be done

enough for the data to accurately reflect the functioning of those rules. See Kleidon [23, 25]. Note that if this key condition is not met, any statistical inference on the joint dynamics of the dividend process, including that in Marsh and Merton [34], is not valid. See Shiller [41] on the related issue of biases that might result when market participants anticipate events that never occurred.

[7] It should be emphasized that, throughout this paper, the term "bubble" refers to the explosive process C_t. By contrast, many authors (e.g., Ackley [2]) use bubbles to refer to any deviation from fundamentals induced by speculation.

with small or even no variations in ex ante returns. The rational-bubble explanation was one that I favored in West [52] and in the initial version of West [53] (which, in fact, was initially titled "Speculative Bubbles and Stock Price Volatility"). I no longer find this interpretation particularly appealing. I will explain this by first reviewing the theoretical literature on bubbles, and then discussing some empirical results.

One immediate theoretical restriction on rational bubbles is that they cannot be negative. If $C_t < 0$ and the stock price is lower than its fundamental, the possibility of an extraordinary capital gain when the bubble bursts must be compensated for by a potential capital loss if the bubble continues to float downward. Since stock prices must be nonnegative, there will be, for any bubble process, a low enough stock price that precludes any further capital loss. Since such a stock price is inconsistent with a bubble, so, too, is any higher stock price that can lead to such a low stock price. By a backwards recursion, there cannot be a negative bubble on a stock, because any such bubble leads to an infeasible price with nonzero probability.

Are positive bubbles similarly inconsistent with rationality? In models where agents have infinite horizons, the answer appears to be yes (Tirole [49]).[8] Any agent who sells a stock at a price higher than its fundamental can exit the market, leaving negative present value for whomever buys it. Bubbles are ruled out when agents have infinite horizons even if traders have differential information and if short sales are prohibited (Tirole [49]).

Positive bubbles are not, however, ruled out in models with finite-horizon agents. Tirole [50] studies this in a nonstochastic, perfect foresight, overlapping-generations model. Each generation will be willing to pay more than fundamental value for an asset, provided the succeeding generation is similarly willing. It is necessary that the bubble not inflate the stock price so fast that stock market wealth ends up exceeding GNP (to take an extreme example). Otherwise, a backwards recursion will rule out bubbles. In Tirole's [50] model, this means that the rate of growth of the economy must be greater than the return on the stock. In such a case, the steady-state per capita bubble may be positive.

While I am not aware of a stochastic version of Tirole's model, intuition suggests (to me, at least) that such a generalization can be accomplished. Some unpleasant issues would, however, have to be handled. Diba and Grossman [12] note that if there ever is a bubble, it would have to be present from the first day of trading: $E(C_t \mid I_{t-1}) = (1 + r)C_{t-1}$ and C_t nonnegative means that if $C_{t-1} = 0$, then $C_t = 0$ with probability one. Merton [36] notes that there must be some mechanism to limit managerial issues of new stock.

More fundamentally, one must ask how reasonable is Tirole's necessary condition that the mean growth rate of the economy be greater than the mean return on the stock price (assuming, again, that this is a necessary condition in a stochastic version of Tirole's model).[9] The mean annual real ex post return on S&P data 1871–1986 is about 8 percent; the mean growth rate of real GNP is

[8] But see Gilles and LeRoy [19], which apparently concludes that bubbles can in principle exist in such models.

[9] See Abel et al. [1] for a discussion of conditions that rule out bubbles in a stochastic environment.

about 3 percent.[10] In the case of a bursting bubble such as in (14), moreover, the relevant comparison is probably between one plus the growth rate and $(1 + r)/\pi > 1 + r$ rather than $1 + r$: one presumably must insure zero probability that the stock price exceeds the value of national output. While taxes and so forth muddy the issue, the excess of the mean ex post return on aggregate stock price indices over the mean growth rate of the U.S. economy does not suggest that Tirole's necessary condition will apply. See Abel et al. [1].

Is the seeming excess volatility of stock prices nonetheless strongly suggestive of rational bubbles? There are several reasons why the answer seems to me to be no. First, Flood and Hodrick [18] argue that at least certain stock market tests, including Mankiw et al. [32], implicitly allow bubbles under the null.[11] Some tests for finite-maturity bonds also find some evidence of excess volatility (e.g., Singleton [46]), which, if true, cannot be due to bubbles; there cannot be a bubble on the final date when the bond matures, and therefore by a backwards recursion there cannot be a bubble at any earlier date. One would like to have a common explanation for the excess volatility that seems to be found in these various tests applied to various assets. Second, as discussed in West [52], while my tests are perfectly capable of finding something that looks roughly like a bubble, they are probably not able to discriminate between a bubble and "noise" that is almost but not quite a bubble: $E(C_t \mid I_{t-1}) = \phi C_{t-1}$, $\phi =$ (say) .99 instead of $\phi = (1 + r) \approx 1.08$. Third, bubbles suggest that stock prices should grow at a rapid rate. If dividends grow more slowly than the rate of return (an assumption implicitly made when $E(\sum b^j D_{t+j} \mid I_t)$ was assumed to be well defined in (13)), the dividend/price ratio should fall and capital gains should take an increasingly large share of ex post returns. But for the S&P data, 1871–1986, this does not seem to be the case. The mean ex post return in the first half of the sample, 1872–1928, is 8.6 percent, with a mean dividend/price ratio of .053; in the second half of the sample the figures are 8.3 percent and .051.[12]

In sum, theory for rational bubbles is still at a preliminary stage. But the theory so far developed suggests conditions for bubbles that are too stringent to make bubbles particularly attractive: the growth rate of the economy must be greater than the return on the stock; any asset with a bubble must have always had a positive bubble; factors other than bubbles must explain any excess volatility on finitely lived assets and perhaps some of the excess volatility on stock prices as well. In addition, the evidence for explosive bubbles in West [52] is at best suggestive and consistent as well with deviations from fundamentals being borderline stationary.

[10] I computed this using the figures for GNP in 1875–1985 in Gordon [21] and for GNP in 1986 in the October 1987 issue of the Federal Reserve Bank of St. Louis's *National Economic Trends*.

[11] The Mankiw et al. [32] test is, however, likely to be unreliable in the presence of bubbles, even though these are allowed under the null. Confidence intervals will be large: in the presence of bubbles, the variance of the Mankiw et al. [32] estimates is blowing up, for exactly the reasons the variance blows up in the presence of a logarithmic random walk (Merton [36]).

[12] As usual, there is also potentially a peso problem, where anticipations of a never-realized shift in the dividend process can look like a bubble that grows and pops. See Flood and Hodrick [17], Obstfeld and Rogoff [38], and Smith [47].

IV. Variations in Expected Returns

A natural candidate to explain any excess price volatility is movements in expected returns. This was of course among the explanations proposed in some of the first published comments on volatility tests (Long [30]), and has been argued more recently by Flood et al. [18]. Indeed, the model (4), and therefore the variance bounds that follow from it, requires only the terminal condition (3) and a constant expected return. So if, in population, there is excess volatility, and bubbles are ruled out, with deviations from the constant-expected-return stock price fundamental being transitory it follows that mathematically expected returns are varying. See Campbell and Shiller [8] and Flood et al. [18] for interpretations of volatility tests as especially powerful tests of the null of constant expected returns.

A general form for a model with time-varying expected returns is

$$P_t = \mathrm{E}[\textstyle\sum_{j=0}^{\infty} (\prod_{i=0}^{j} {}_{t+i}r_{t+i+1}) D_{t+j} \mid I_t], \tag{15}$$

where ${}_{t+i}r_{t+i+1}$ is the one-period return expected by the market in period $t + i$ (e.g., ${}_t r_{t+1} \equiv \mathrm{E}[(P_{t+1} + D_t)/P_t \mid I_t]$). What sorts of movements in expected returns must be occurring to explain the results in Table I?

First of all, these movements apparently must be large. Using a linearized version of (15), but modeling expected returns nonparametrically, Shiller [40] finds that annual real expected returns would have to have a standard deviation of more than 4 percent. West [53] and Poterba and Summers [39], also using linearized models but allowing for unit roots, conclude that even larger movements in expected returns are necessary to rationalize stock price movements.[13] These authors seem to consider this a wider range than is typically considered reasonable.

Second, two volatility tests that allow for time-varying expected returns do not suggest that the excess volatility in Table I is adequately explained by some standard intertemporal models. One study, Campbell and Shiller [7], uses a linearized version of (15) to compute (11), allowing for three different models for expected returns: the return on short debt plus a constant; the consumption-based asset-pricing model (Lucas [31]) with constant relative risk aversion, $U(C_t) = C_t^{-\alpha}$; and the return on short debt plus a term that depends on the conditional variances of stock returns. The information set used to calculate equation (11)'s $\mathrm{var}\{[\log(D_t/P_t)]_H\}$ consists of lagged $\log(D_t/P_t)$, $\Delta \log(D_t)$ and lagged ex post returns.

A second study, West [53], uses (15) with expected returns determined by the consumption-based asset-pricing model, with constant relative risk aversion and a coefficient of relative risk aversion less than two. This model implies a condition like (6), with P_t and D_t replaced by $\tilde{P}_t \equiv P_t C_t^{-\alpha}$ and $\tilde{D}_t \equiv D_t C_t^{-\alpha}$, and $H_t \equiv \{\tilde{D}_t, \tilde{D}_{t-1}, \cdots\}$.

The results of the two studies are reported in Table III. Neither finds that the assumed model of expected returns adequately rationalizes stock price move-

[13] Unlike Shiller [40], however, neither West [53] nor Poterba and Summers [39] give any evidence on the accuracy of their linearizations. West's [53] in particular is unlikely to be very reasonable in the presence of unit roots.

Table III

Volatility Tests, Varying Expected Return

(1) Author	(2) Sample	(3) V/V^*	(4) p-value	(5) return model
(1) Campbell and Shiller [7]	annual, 1889–1986,	2–8	.00	constant premium
	1926–1986	1–8	.00–.50	consumption
		2–12	.00–.50	return volatility
(2) West [52]	annual, 1889–1978	5–30	n.a.	consumption

Notes: See notes to Table I. As explained in the text, in column (5), "constant premium" means expected stock returns have a constant premium over that on short debt; "consumption" means expected stock returns are determined by the consumption-based asset-pricing model; "return volatility" means expected stock returns have a premium over that on short debt, with the premium dependent on the volatility of stock returns.

ments. Campbell and Shiller [8] further find little theoretically plausible connection between stock prices and their measures of expected returns and suggest (p. 35) that the smaller and less significant estimates of V/V^* are found in specifications that seem to pick up certain spurious correlations. It should be noted that both papers allow for unit roots, so that there is no obvious reason to believe that small-sample bias explains the excess volatility.

Now, one could argue about the accuracy of the linearizations used, or about the validity of the models of expected returns assumed in the parametric tests in Table III, or about how well official consumption data capture the utility flows really necessary to test the consumption-based asset-pricing model. There are many nontrivial problems associated with the test just described. But the evidence to date does not suggest that traditional models of return determination successfully explain the seeming excess volatility of stock prices, even in conjunction with small-sample bias.

V. Fads

The tentative conclusion that neither rational bubbles nor traditional models of return determination can explain stock price volatility suggests that a nontraditional model for return determination might be required. In "fads" interpretations of the volatility tests, noise trading by naive investors plays a significant role in stock price determination. Shiller [43] and DeBondt and Thaler [9] argue that psychological and sociological evidence is consistent with individuals following "irrational" trading rules, overreacting to news. Potentially, this both generates wide variations in expected returns and renders inadequate traditional models for return determination.

One simple way to think through the possible effects of fads is to add a factor due to noise trading to the level or log of what would be the fundamental price if expected returns were constant (Campbell and Kyle [5], Poterba and Summers [39], O'Brien [37], Shiller [43]). Equation (12) is a simple example of this (though to capture investor overreaction one might want the innovation in a_t to be positively correlated with the innovation in $\log(D_t)$). Recall that the equation (12) example, with parameters matched to the S&P estimates, does indeed generate wide swings in expected returns, with a standard deviation of about .05. Also, one could of course capture the 1987 runup and then collapse of stock prices by allowing a stationary version of the explosive bubble (14). For example, if $a_t = (\phi/\pi)a_{t-1} + v_t$ with probability π, $a_t = v_t$ with probability $(1 - \pi)$, $0 < \phi$, $\pi < 1$, and $E(v_t \mid I_{t-1}) = 0$, then $E(a_t \mid I_{t-1}) = \phi a_{t-1}$ and a_t is stationary. As in the Blanchard and Watson [3] explosive bubble, investor overreaction is reflected if, say, $\pi = ½$ and the fad "bursts" if there is bad news about fundamentals.

In one interpretation, fads mean that even after risk adjustments there are profitable opportunities, at least for smart investors with long enough horizons. This apparently is the conclusion of some readers of Shiller [40] (e.g., Ackley [2]).

Another interpretation is that while some fraction of trading is done by naive traders, another fraction of trading is done by sophisticated investors who ensure that there are no extraordinary expected returns once risk is properly accounted for (Campbell and Kyle [5], DeLong et al. [11]). This does not mean that stock prices are driven to whatever level they would be in the absence of fads. Risk is created by naive investors, which sophisticated investors must take into account. Such risk might not, however, be captured by traditional models. See especially DeLong et al. [11], which contains a highly stylized model in which nondiversifiable risk created by noise trading causes the prices of two seemingly identical assets to diverge.[14]

There is of course much anecdotal evidence of fads, including the famous beauty-contest passage in Keynes [22]. More formal evidence consistent with stories of investor overreaction may be found in DeBondt and Thaler [9, 10] and Lehmann [26]. These papers find that abnormally high returns can be earned by following a contrarian strategy of buying stocks that recently have had relatively poor returns and shorting stocks that recently have performed well.[15] See DeLong et al. [11] and Camerer [4] for additional examples.

At a more aggregative level, a growing number of studies suggest that there is a significant stationary component to stock prices (Lo and McKinley [29], Fama and French [15], Poterba and Summers [39]). This component (a_t in equation (12)) is associated with econometric predictability of stock returns, using variables such as lagged dividend/price ratios or earnings. The predictability is particularly marked at long horizons, say, over two years (Campbell and Shiller [8], Fama and French [14, 15], Flood et al. [18]).

Poterba and Summers [39] and Shiller [43] interpret this as evidence of slowly mean-reverting fads. But the only unambiguous interpretation of evidence that stock prices do not follow a random walk is that expected returns are time varying. Whether or not the studies just cited imply movements in expected returns that can best be explained by fads is debatable (Fama and French [14]); one can trivially define a_t in equation (12) as simply the log of the ratio of the

[14] It should be noted that in this interpretation of fads, many of the traditional tools of financial analysis are still applicable, with the presence of noise trading an additional constraint facing rational investors. It therefore seems extreme to conclude (Kleidon [24], Merton [36]) that we can allow for fads only by ignoring much of our accumulated knowledge about financial markets. See Shiller [44].

[15] Whether these seeming pricing anomalies reflect not idiosyncratic risk but mismeasured nondiversifiable risk is, however, unclear.

stock price (15), with returns determined by some standard model, to a constant-expected-return price. So evidence of a stationary component is at best suggestive of fads. This applies as well to Campbell and Kyle [5], a fully articulated empirical study that allows for fads. It estimates an explicit model of trading by sophisticated investors, when a residual noise process affects stock prices. It finds that the noise process accounts for over one fourth of stock price movements in the S&P data, 1871–1984, but does not present any evidence that this process results mainly from trading by naive investors.

Traditional present-value models (e.g., those discussed in Section IV) are well enough specified that one can potentially argue that these models cannot adequately explain stock price volatility. I do not believe that the same can be said for fads models that have been developed so far. The quantitative evidence in favor of fads as an explanation of stock price volatility is largely indirect, in the form of negative verdicts on bubbles and on traditional models for returns.

More direct evidence on fads, and tests of restrictions implied by fads, may well be forthcoming shortly. But at present there is little formal positive evidence to sway someone unsympathetic to fads models.

Appendix

This gives detailed sources for Tables I and III. Notation matches that in the cited paper.

Table I: Line (1): Blanchard and Watson [3] (p. 18), V/V^* = ratio of $\hat{V}_c$ to $\hat{V}_c^{\max}$. *Line (2)*: Kleidon [25] (p. 983), Table 2, case (ii); p-value computed from "No. of Gross Violations" column. *Line (3)*: Leroy and Porter [28] (p. 572), Table III, $V/V^* = \gamma_y(0)/\gamma_y^*(0)$; p-value is that associated with f_2^u. *Line (4)*: Shiller [40] (p. 431), Table 2, V/V^* = square of ratio of line (5) to line (6). *Line (5)*: Shiller [45] (p. 7), Table 1, Case C; p-value computed from column (2). *Line (6)*: Campbell and Shiller [6] (p. 1078), Table 3, panel B, $V/V^* = \text{var}(SL)/\text{var}(SL')$ and $\text{var}(\xi)/\text{var}(\xi')$. *Line (7)*: Mankiw et al. [32] (pp. 685, 688), Tables I and II, V/V^* = ratio of $E(P - P^0)^2$ to $E(P^* - P^0)^2$. *Line (8)*: West [53], Table II, $V/V^* = [1 - (.01 \times \text{col}(8))]^{-1}$, for differenced specifications, with p-value in col. (7); Monte Carlo results are from Tables IIIA and IIIB. *Line (9)*: Campbell and Shiller [7] (p. 40), Table 4b, $V/V^* = [\sigma(\delta_t')/\sigma(\delta_t)]^{-2}$, with p-value for H_0: $\sigma(\delta_t')/\sigma(\delta_t) = 1$. *Line (10)*: Kleidon [25] (p. 986), Table 3, V/V^* = square of "Standard and Poor's Ratio" column; p-value computed from "Number of Simulation Violations > 1" column. *Line (11)*: Leroy and Parke [27] (p. 22), V/V^* = square of reported ratio of standard deviations. *Line (12)*: Shiller [42] (p. 237).

Table III: Line (1): Constant premium: Campbell and Shiller [7] (p. 41), Table 5, $V/V^* = [\sigma(\delta_t')/\sigma(\delta_t)]^{-2}$, with p-value for H_0: $\sigma(\delta_t')/\sigma(\delta_t) = 1$. Consumption and return volatility: $V/V^* = [\sigma(\delta_t')/\sigma(\delta_t)]^{-2}$, with p-value for H_0: $\sigma(\delta_t')/\sigma(\delta_t) = 1$; these figures are not reported in the paper but were given to me by John Campbell. *Line (2)*: West [53], Table IVA, $V/V^* = [1 - (.01 \times \text{percentage excess variability})]^{-1}$ for $\alpha \leq 2$.

REFERENCES

1. Andrew Abel, N. Gregory Mankiw, Lawrence H. Summers, and Richard J. Zeckhauser. "Assessing Dynamic Efficiency: Theory and Evidence." NBER Working Paper No. 2097, December 1986.
2. Gardner Ackley. "Commodities and Capital: Prices and Quantities." *American Economic Review* 73 (March 1983), 1–16.
3. Olivier J. Blanchard and Mark Watson. "Bubbles, Rational Expectations and Financial Markets." NBER Working Paper No. 945, 1982.
4. Colin Camerer. "Bubbles and Fads in Asset Prices: A Review of Theory and Evidence." Manuscript, University of Pennsylvania, 1987.
5. John Y. Campbell and Albert S. Kyle. "Smart Money, Noise Trading and Stock Price Behavior." Manuscript, Princeton University, September 1986.
6. John Y. Campbell and Robert J. Shiller. "Cointegration and Tests of Present Value Models." *Journal of Political Economy* 95 (October 1987), 1062–88.
7. ———. "The Dividend-Price Ratio and Expectations of Future Dividends and Discount Factors." Manuscript, Princeton University, October 1987.
8. ———. "Stock Prices, Earnings and Expected Dividends." Manuscript, Princeton University, December 1987.
9. Werner F. M. DeBondt and Richard Thaler. "Does the Stock Market Overreact?" *Journal of Finance* 40 (July 1985), 793–808.
10. ———. "Further Evidence on Investor Overreaction and Stock Market Seasonality." *Journal of Finance* 42 (July 1987), 557–81.
11. J. Bradford DeLong, Andrei Schliefer, Lawrence H. Summers, and Robert J. Waldmann. "The Economic Consequences of Noise Traders." Manuscript, Harvard University, September 1987.
12. Behzad T. Diba and Herschel I. Grossman. "On the Inception of Rational Bubbles." *Quarterly Journal of Economics* (August 1987), 697–700.
13. Robert F. Engle and C. W. J. Granger. "Dynamic Model Specification with Equilibrium Constraints: Co-Integration and Error Correction." *Econometrica* (March 1987), 251–76.
14. Eugene F. Fama and Kenneth R. French. "Dividend Yields and Expected Stock Returns." Manuscript, University of Chicago, November 1987.
15. ———. "Permanent and Transitory Components of Stock Prices." *Journal of Political Economy* (April 1988), forthcoming.
16. Marjorie Flavin. "Excess Volatility in the Financial Markets: A Reassessment of the Empirical Evidence." *Journal of Political Economy* (October 1983), 929–56.
17. Robert P. Flood and Robert J. Hodrick. "Asset Price Volatility, Bubbles and Process Switching." *Journal of Finance* 41 (September 1986), 831–42.
18. ———, and Paul Kaplan. "An Evaluation of Recent Evidence on Stock Market Bubbles." Manuscript, Northwestern University, 1986.
19. Christian Gilles and Stephen F. Leroy. "Bubbles and Charges." Manuscript, University of California at Santa Barbara, November 1987.
20. ———. "The Variance Bounds Tests: A Critical Survey." Manuscript, University of California at Santa Barbara, August 1987.
21. Robert J. Gordon. *Macroeconomics*. Boston: Little, Brown and Company, 1987.
22. John M. Keynes. *The General Theory of Employment, Interest and Money*. New York: Harcourt, Brace and World, 1964.
23. Allan W. Kleidon. "Bias in Small Sample Tests of Stock Price Rationality." Stanford University Graduate School of Business Research Paper 819R, September 1985.
24. ———. "Anomalies in Financial Economics: Blueprint for Change?" *Journal of Business* 59 (October 1986), S469–S499.
25. ———. "Variance Bounds Tests and Stock Price Valuation Models." *Journal of Political Economy* (October 1986), 953–1001.
26. Bruce Lehmann. "Fads, Martingales and Market Efficiency." Manuscript, Columbia University, May 1987.
27. Stephen F. LeRoy and William R. Parke. "Stock Price Volatility: A Test Based on the Geometric Random Walk." Manuscript, University of California at Santa Barbara, August 1987.
28. Stephen F. LeRoy and Richard Porter. "The Present Value Relation: Tests Based on Implied

Variance Bounds." *Econometrica* 49 (May 1981), 555–674.
29. Andrew W. Lo and A. Craig McKinley. "Stock Market Prices Do Not Follow Random Walks: Evidence from a Simple Specification Test." Manuscript, University of Pennsylvania, 1987.
30. John B. Long, Jr. "Discussion." *Journal of Finance* 36 (July 1981), 304–7.
31. Robert E. Lucas, Jr. "Asset Prices in an Exchange Economy." *Econometrica* 46 (November 1978), 1429–45.
32. N. Gregory Mankiw, David Romer, and Matthew D. Shapiro. "An Unbiased Reexamination of Stock Price Volatility." *Journal of Finance* 40 (July 1985), 677–88.
33. Terry A. Marsh and Robert C. Merton. "Dividend Variability and Variance Bounds Tests for the Rationality of Stock Market Prices." *American Economic Review* 76 (June 1986), 1429–45.
34. ———. "Dividend Behavior for the Aggregate Stock Market." *Journal of Business* 60 (January 1987), 1–40.
35. Joe Mattey and Richard Meese. "Empirical Assessment of Present Value Relations." *Econometric Reviews* 5 (1986), 171–234.
36. Robert C. Merton. "On the Current State of the Stock Market Rationality Hypothesis." Sloan School of Management Working Paper No. 1712-85, 1985.
37. James O'Brien. "Speculative Bubbles and the Need for Stock Margin Requirements." Manuscript, Federal Reserve Board of Governors, November 1984.
38. Maurice Obstfeld and Kenneth Rogoff. "Ruling Out Divergent Speculative Bubbles." *Journal of Monetary Economics* 17 (May 1986), 349–62.
39. James M. Poterba and Lawrence H. Summers. "Mean Reversion in Stock Prices: Evidence and Implications." NBER Working Paper No. 2343, August 1987.
40. Robert J. Shiller. "Do Stock Prices Move Too Much to be Justified by Subsequent Changes in Dividends?" *American Economic Review* 71 (June 1981), 421–36.
41. ———. "The Use of Volatility Measures in Assessing Market Efficiency." *Journal of Finance* 35 (May 1981), 421–36.
42. ———. "Reply." *American Economic Review* (March 1983), 236–37.
43. ———. "Stock Prices and Social Dynamics." *Brookings Papers on Economic Activity* (1984), 457–98.
44. ———. "Comments on Miller and Kleidon." *Journal of Business* 59 (October 1986), S501–S505.
45. ———. "The Probability of Gross Violations of a Present Value Variance Inequality." Manuscript, Yale University, July 1986.
46. Kenneth J. Singleton. "Expectations of the Term Structure and Implied Variance Bounds." *Journal of Political Economy* (December 1980), 159–76.
47. Gregor W. Smith. "Apparent Bubbles and Misspecified Fundamentals." Queens University Institute for Economic Research Working Paper No. 692, 1987.
48. Lawrence H. Summers. "Does the Stock Market Rationally Reflect Fundamental Values?" *Journal of Finance* 41 (July 1986), 591–601.
49. Jean Tirole. "On the Possibility of Speculation Under Rational Expectations." *Econometrica* 50 (September 1982), 1163–81.
50. ———. "Asset Bubbles and Overlapping Generations." *Econometrica* 53 (September 1986), 1071–1100.
51. Kenneth D. West. "Comment." *Econometric Reviews* 5 (1986), 273–78.
52. ———. "A Specification Test for Speculative Bubbles." *Quarterly Journal of Economics* (August 1987), 553–80.
53. ———. "Dividend Innovations and Stock Price Volatility." *Econometrica* 56 (January 1988), 37–61.

Name Index

The International Library of Critical Writings in Economics

1. Multinational Corporations
   Mark Casson
2. The Economics of Innovation
   Christopher Freeman
3. Entrepreneurship
   Mark Casson
4. International Investment
   Peter J. Buckley
5. Game Theory in Economics
   Ariel Rubinstein
6. The History of Economic Thought
   Mark Blaug
7. Monetary Theory
   Thomas Mayer
8. Joint Production of Commodities
   Neri Salvadori and Ian Steedman
9. Industrial Organization
   Oliver E. Williamson
10. Growth Theory
    (Volumes I, II and III)
    R. Becker and E. Burmeister
11. Microeconomics: Theoretical and Applied (Volumes I, II and III)
    Robert E. Kuenne
12. The Economics of Health
    (Volumes I and II)
    A.J. Culyer
13. Recent Developments in Macroeconomics
    (Volumes I, II and III)
    Edmund S. Phelps
14. Urban and Regional Economics
    Paul C. Cheshire and Alan W. Evans
15. Modern Public Finance
    (Volumes I and II)
    A.B. Atkinson
16. Exchange Rate Economics
    (Volumes I and II)
    Ronald MacDonald and Mark P. Taylor
17. The Economic Value of Education: Studies in the Economics of Education
    Mark Blaug
18. Development Economics
    (Volumes I, II, III and IV)
    Deepak Lal
19. The New Classical Macroeconomics
    (Volumes I, II and III)
    Kevin D. Hoover
20. The Economics of the Environment
    Wallace E. Oates
21. Post Keynesian Theory of Growth and Distribution
    Carlo Panico and Neri Salvadori
22. Dynamic Labor Demand and Adjustment Costs
    Giorgio Galeazzi and Daniel S. Hamermesh
23. The Philosophy and Methodology of Economics (Volumes I, II and III)
    Bruce J. Caldwell
24. Public Choice Theory
    (Volumes I, II and III)
    Charles K. Rowley
25. Evolutionary Economics
    Ulrich Witt
26. Economics and Psychology
    Shlomo Maital and Sharone L. Maital
27. Social Choice Theory
    (Volumes I, II and III)
    Charles K. Rowley
28. Non-Linear Dynamics in Economic Theory
    Marc Jarsulic
29. Recent Developments in Experimental Economics
    (Volumes I and II)
    John D. Hey and Graham Loomes

30. Monopoly and Competition Policy (Volumes I and II)
    F.M. Scherer
31. The Economics of Technical Change
    Edwin Mansfield and Elizabeth Mansfield
32. The Economics of Exhaustible Resources
    Geoffrey Heal
33. The Economics of Institutions
    Geoffrey M. Hodgson
34. The Economics of Transport (Volumes I and II)
    Herbert Mohring
35. Implicit Contract Theory
    Sherwin Rosen
36. Foundations of Analytical Marxism (Volumes I and II)
    John E. Roemer
37. The Economics of Product Differentiation (Volumes I and II)
    Jacques-François Thisse and George Norman
38. Economic Growth in Theory and Practice: A Kaldorian Perspective
    John E. King
39. Markets and Socialism
    Alec Nove and Ian D. Thatcher
40. Recent Developments in the Economics of Education
    Elchanan Cohn and Geraint Johnes
41. The Theory of Inflation
    Michael Parkin
42. The Economics of Location (Volumes I, II and III)
    Melvin L. Greenhut and George Norman
43. Financial Intermediaries
    Mervyn K. Lewis
44. The Political Economy of Privatization and Deregulation
    Elizabeth E. Bailey and Janet Rothenberg Pack
45. Gender and Economics
    Jane Humphries
46. Macroeconomics and Imperfect Competition
    Jean-Pascal Bénassy
47. Labor Economics (Volumes I, II, III and IV)
    Orley C. Ashenfelter and Kevin F. Hallock
48. The Economics of Altruism
    Stefano Zamagni
49. The Economic Analysis of Rent Seeking
    Robert D. Tollison and Roger D. Congleton
50. Economics and Biology
    Geoffrey M. Hodgson
51. The Economics of Ageing
    John Creedy
52. Fiscal and Monetary Policy (Volumes I and II)
    Thomas Mayer and Steven M. Sheffrin
53. The Economics of Information (Volumes I and II)
    David K. Levine and Steven A. Lippman
54. Transaction Cost Economics (Volumes I and II)
    Oliver E. Williamson and Scott E. Masten
55. Agricultural Economics
    George H. Peters
56. International Debt (Volumes I and II)
    Graham Bird and P. Nicholas Snowden
57. Economics and Discrimination (Volumes I and II)
    William A. Darity, Jr
58. Business Cycle Theory
    Finn E. Kydland
59. International Trade (Volumes I and II)
    J. Peter Neary
60. The Money Supply in the Economic Process
    Marco Musella and Carlo Panico

61. Small Firms and Economic Growth (Volumes I and II)
Zoltan J. Acs
62. Producer Cooperatives and Labor-Managed Systems (Volumes I and II)
David L. Prychitko and Jaroslav Vanek
63. Ethics and Economics (Volumes I and II)
Alan P. Hamlin
64. The Economics of the Family
Nancy Folbre
65. The Economics of Training (Volumes I and II)
Orley C. Ashenfelter and Robert J. LaLonde
66. Chaos Theory in Economics: Methods, Models and Evidence
W. Davis Dechert
67. General Equilibrium Theory (Volumes I, II and III)
Gérard Debreu
68. Economic Growth: Theory and Evidence (Volumes I and II)
Gene M. Grossman
69. Long Wave Theory
Christopher Freeman
70. The Economics of Communication and Information
Donald M. Lamberton
71. The Foundations of Public Finance (Volumes I and II)
Peter Jackson
72. The Theory of the Firm
Mark Casson
73. The Economics of Uncertainty (Volumes I and II)
John D. Hey
74. The Economics of Global Warming
Tom Tietenberg
75. The Development of Ecological Economics
Robert Costanza, Charles Perrings and Cutler Cleveland
76. Economic Growth in the Long Run: A History of Empirical Evidence (Volumes I, II and III)
Bart van Ark
77. The Economics of Productivity (Volumes I and II)
Edward N. Wolff
78. The Economics of Population: Key Modern Writings (Volumes I and II)
Julian L. Simon
79. Political Business Cycles
Bruno S. Frey
80. Cultural Economics: The Arts, the Heritage and the Media Industries (Volumes I and II)
Ruth Towse
81. Law and Economics (Volumes I, II and III)
Richard A. Posner and Francesco Parisi
82. Independent Central Banks and Economic Performance
Sylvester Eijffinger
83. Culture, Social Norms and Economics (Volumes I and II)
Mark Casson
84. Industrial Policy and Competitive Advantage (Volumes I, II and III)
David B. Audretsch
85. The Economics of Housing (Volumes I and II)
John M. Quigley
86. Economic Demography (Volumes I and II)
T. Paul Schultz
87. Trade and the Environment: Economic, Legal and Policy Perspectives
Alan M. Rugman and John J. Kirton with Julie A. Soloway
88. The Economics of Fiscal Federalism and Local Finance
Wallace E. Oates
89. Price Theory and its Applications
Bernard Saffran and F.M. Scherer

90. Women in the Labor Market (Volumes I and II)
Marianne A. Ferber
91. Market Process Theories (Volumes I and II)
Peter Boettke and David Prychitko
92. Input–Output Analysis (Volumes I, II and III)
Heinz Kurz, Erik Dietzenbacher and Christian Lager
93. Mathematical Economics (Volumes I, II and III)
Graciela Chichilnisky
94. The Foundations of Regulatory Economics (Volumes I, II and III)
Robert B. Ekelund, Jr.
95. The Economics of Marketing
Martin Carter, Mark Casson and Vivek Suneja
96. Service Industries in the Global Economy (Volumes I and II)
J.R. Bryson and P.W. Daniels
97. Economic Justice (Volumes I and II)
Giorgio Brosio and Harold M. Hochman
98. Foreign Exchange Intervention: Objectives and Effectiveness
Sylvester C.W. Eijffinger
99. Economic Anthropology
Stephen Gudeman
100. Consumer Theory
Kelvin Lancaster
101. The Economics of Famine
Jean Drèze
102. Microeconomic Theories of Imperfect Competition
Jean J. Gabszewicz and Jacques-François Thisse
103. The Economics of Executive Compensation (Volumes I and II)
Kevin F. Hallock and Kevin J. Murphy
104. The Foundations of Long Wave Theory (Volumes I and II)
Francisco Louçã and Jan Reijnders
105. The Economics of Commodity Markets
David Greenaway and C.W. Morgan
106. Corporate Governance (Volumes I, II, III and IV)
Kevin Keasey, Steve Thompson and Mike Wright
107. Economic Welfare: Concepts and Measurement (Volumes I and II)
John Creedy
108. Economic Forecasting
Terence C. Mills
109. Recent Developments in Game Theory
Eric S. Maskin
110. The Economics of Increasing Returns
Geoffrey Heal
111. The Economics of Corruption and Illegal Markets (Volumes I, II and III)
Gianluca Fiorentini and Stefano Zamagni
112. The Economics of Price Discrimination
George Norman
113. The Economic Theory of Auctions (Volumes I and II)
Paul Klemperer
114. The Economics of Regional Policy
Harvey W. Armstrong and Jim Taylor
115. Economic Integration and International Trade
Carsten Kowalczyk
116. The Political Economy of Science, Technology and Innovation
Ben Martin and Paul Nightingale
117. The Economics of Science and Innovation (Volumes I and II)
Paula E. Stephan and David B. Audretsch
118. Innovation, Evolution of Industry and Economic Growth (Volumes I, II and III)
David B. Audretsch and Steven Klepper

119. The Economics of Energy (Volumes I and II)
Paul Stevens
120. Privatisation in Developing Countries (Volumes I and II)
Paul Cook and Colin Kirkpatrick
121. The Economics of Tourism (Volumes I and II)
Clem Tisdell
122. The Economics of Unemployment (Volumes I, II, III and IV)
P.N. Junankar
123. Privatisation and Corporate Performance
David Parker
124. Income Distribution (Volumes I, II and III)
Michael Sattinger
125. International Finance (Volumes I and II)
Robert Z. Aliber
126. Welfare Economics (Volumes I, II and III)
William J. Baumol and Charles A. Wilson
127. The Theory of Trade Policy Reform
Carsten Kowalczyk
128. The Economics of Defence (Volumes I, II and III)
Keith Hartley and Todd Sandler
129. The Economics of Property Rights (Volumes I and II)
Svetozar Pejovich
130. Gender and Development: Theoretical, Empirical and Practical Approaches (Volumes I and II)
Lourdes Benería with Savitri Bisnath
131. The Economics of Politics (Volumes I and II)
Dennis C. Mueller
132. Economic Theory and the Welfare State (Volumes I, II and III)
Nicholas Barr
133. The Regulation and Supervision of Banks (Volumes I, II, III and IV)
Maximilian J.B. Hall
134. The Political Economy of Monetary Union
Paul De Grauwe
135. The Economics of Sport (Volumes I and II)
Andrew Zimbalist
136. The Economics of Advertising
Kyle Bagwell
137. Regulation, Economics and the Law
Anthony I. Ogus
138. The Economics of Barter and Countertrade
Rolf Mirus and Bernard Yeung
139. The Economics of Technology Transfer
Sanjaya Lall
140. The Political Economy of Development (Volumes I, II and III)
Amitava Krishna Dutt
141. Macroeconomics and the Environment
Mohan Munasinghe
142. Happiness in Economics
Richard A. Easterlin
143. Speculation and Financial Markets (Volumes I and II)
Liam Gallagher and Mark P. Taylor
144. Public Procurement (Volumes I and II)
Sue Arrowsmith and Keith Hartley
145. The Economics of Intellectual Property (Volumes I, II, III and IV)
Ruth Towse and R.W. Holzhauer
146. Forecasting Financial Markets (Volumes I and II)
Terence C. Mills
147. The Economics of Labor Unions (Volumes I and II)
Alison Booth

Future titles will include:

New Developments in Exchange Rate Economics
Lucio Sarno and Mark P. Taylor

Long Term Trends and Business Cycles
Terence C. Mills

The Economics of Migration
Klaus F. Zimmermann and Thomas Bauer

The Economics of Language
Donald M. Lamberton

The Economics of Budget Deficits
Charles Rowley, William F. Shughart and Robert D. Tollison

The Economics of Structural Change
Harald Hagemann, Michael Landesmann and Roberto Scazzieri

Cost-Benefit Analysis
Arnold C. Harberger and Glenn P. Jenkins

Alternative Theories of the Firm
Richard Langlois, Tony F. Yu and Paul Robertson

International Financial Integration
Sylvester C.W. Eijffinger and Jan J.G. Lemmen

The Economics of Poverty and Inequality
Frank A. Cowell

Recent Developments in Labor Economics
Orley C. Ashenfelter and Kevin F. Hallock

Imperfect Competition, Nonclearing Markets and Business Cycles
Jean-Pascal Bénassy

The Economics of Project Appraisal
David L. Bevan

Recent Developments in Transport Economics
Kenneth Button

Recent Developments in Urban and Regional Economics
Paul C. Cheshire and Gilles Duranton

Path Dependence
Paul David

Global Capitalism
John Dunning

The Economics of Transfer Pricing
Lorraine Eden

Cognitive Economics
Massimo Egidi and Salvatore Rizzello

The Economics of Crime
Isaac Ehrlich

The Distribution of Tax Burdens
Don Fullerton and Gilbert E. Metcalf

Comparative Law and Economics
Gerrit de Geest and Roger Van Den Bergh

The International Economic Institutions of the Twentieth Century
David Greenaway and Robert C. Hine

Intra-Industry Trade
Herbert Grubel and Peter Lloyd

The Economics of Schooling
Eric A. Hanushek

The Economics of Conflict
Keith Hartley and Todd Sandler

The Economics of Organisation and Bureaucracy
Peter M. Jackson

The Economics of Networks
Michael Katz and Carl Shapiro

The Economics of Business Strategy
John Kay

The Economics of Natural Hazards
Howard Kunreuther and Adam Rose

Personnel Economics
Edward P. Lazear and Robert McNabb

Economics and Religion
Paul Oslington

Forms of Capitalism: Comparative Institutional Analyses
Ugo Pagano and Ernesto Screpanti

The Economics of Public Utilities
Ray Rees

The Economics of Modern Business Enterprise
Martin Ricketts

Complexity in Economics
J. Barkley Rosser, Jr.

New Developments in Public Choice
Charles Rowley

Recent Developments in International Investment
Alan M. Rugman

Cartels
Stephen Salant and Margaret Levenstein

The Economics of Free Trade
Robert W. Staiger

The Economics of Contracts
Lars A. Stole

The Economics of Leisure and Recreation
Clem Tisdell

The Economics of the Mass Media
Glenn Withers

Recent Developments in Evolutionary Economics
Ulrich Witt

Multinational and Public Policy
Stephen Young

Time in Economic Theory
Stefano Zamagni